east timor

a rough passage to

independence

James Dunn

LONGUEVILLE
BOOKS

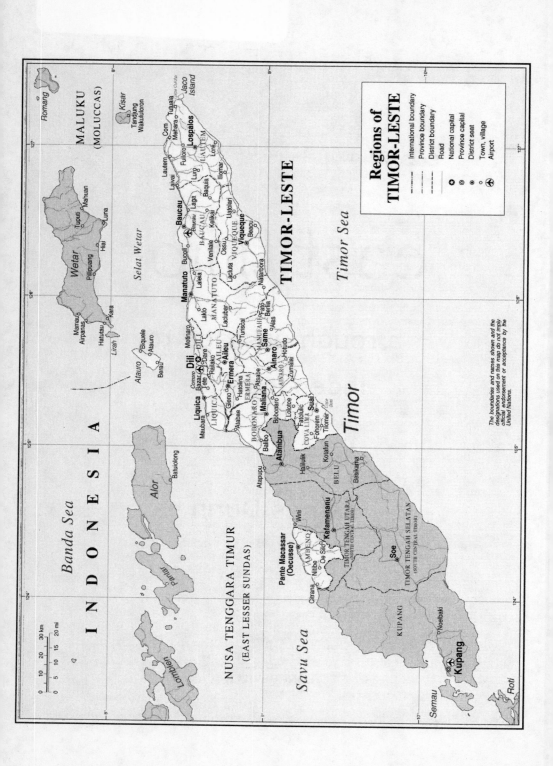

Regions of
TIMOR-LESTE

- – – – International boundary
- – · – Province boundary
- – · · – District boundary
- ——— Road
- ✪ National capital
- ◉ Province capital
- ⊙ District seat
- • Town, village
- ✈ Airport

The boundaries and names shown and the designations used on this map do not imply official endorsement or acceptance by the United Nations.

TIMOR-LESTE

Timor Sea

Banda Sea

MALUKU
(MOLUCCAS)

Romang

Kisar
Tandjung
Wakululoron

Wetar

Selat Wetar

Mamaulo
Airpanas
Hatutau
Kara
Lirah

Pililpuang
Hial
Luna
Mahuan
Tupati

Ataúro
Biquele
Ataúro
Berau

Díli
Comoro
Bazar Tete
Railaku
Metinaro

Com
Tutuala
Mehara
Jaco
Island

Lautém
Lospalos

Baucau
Laga
Baguia

Laivai
Lugo
Luro
Loré

Viqueque
Ossu
Beaçu

Manatuto
Bucoli

Laclo
Laclubar
Natarbora

Laleia
Soibada
Fato
Berlia
Alas

Tunisçai
Barique

Manatuto

VIQUEQUE
Uatolari
Uatu-Carbau
Iliomar

Venilale
Kelikai

IBIQUALI
Baucau

LAUTEM

Same
Holudo
Zumalai

Aileu
Aisake
Atsabe

Ainaro

Ermera
Gleno
Hatolina

Liquiça
Maubara
Mabae

Maliana
Bobonaro
Lolotoe
Fatobuto
Fohorem
Tilomar

Suai

COVALIMA
(SOUTH-WEST TIMOR)

Atsábe
Balibo
Haliulik

Kotafun

BELU

Besikama

BOBONARO

ERMERA

AILEU

AINARO

LIQUIÇA

Timor

Pante Macassar
(Oecusse)

Citrana
Nitibe
Oe Silo
Wini
Kefamenanu

AMBENO

TIMOR TENGAH UTARA
(NORTH-CENTRAL TIMOR)

TIMOR TENGAH SELATAN
(SOUTH-CENTRAL TIMOR)

Soe

KUPANG

Noelbaki

⊕ **Kupang**

Savu Sea

Roti

Semau

NUSA TENGGARA TIMUR
(EAST LESSER SUNDAS)

I N D O N E S I A

Alor
Batuolong

Lomblen

Pantar

Atapupu
Atambua

0 10 20 30 km
0 5 10 15 20 mi

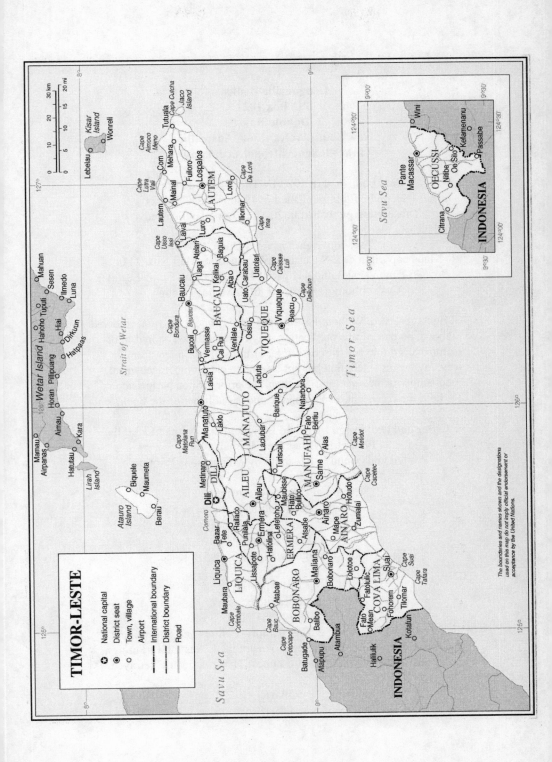

TIMOR-LESTE

✪ National capital
◉ District seat
○ Town, village
✈ Airport
········· International boundary
— — — District boundary
——— Road

The boundaries and names shown and the designations used on this map do not imply official endorsement or acceptance by the United Nations.

INDONESIA

INDONESIA

OECUSSI

Savu Sea

Timor Sea

Strait of Wetar

Wetar Island

Atauro Island

Lirah Island

Kisar Island

Jaco Island

Dili

Baucau

LAUTEM

BAUCAU

VIQUEQUE

MANATUTO

DILI

AILEU

MANUFAHI

AINARO

ERMERA

LIQUICA

BOBONARO

COVA LIMA

30 km
20 mi

Longueville Books
PO Box 102
Double Bay
New South Wales 1360 Australia
info@longuevillebooks.com.au

First published in 1983 by The Jacaranda Press
Second edition published in 1986 by ABC Books
This edition published in 2003 by Longueville Media

Cover and text design by David Longfield and Anouchka Inglis
Typeset in Times New Roman 11/10
Printed and bound in Australia by McPhersons Printing

National Library of Australia
Cataloguing-in-Publication data

Dunn, James.
East Timor : a rough passage to independence.

3rd ed.
Includes index.
ISBN 1 920681 03 5.
1. East Timor - History. 2. East Timor - Politics and government.
3. East Timor - Foreign relations - Australia. 4. Australia - Foreign
relations - East Timor. I. Dunn, James. Timor: a people betrayed.

959.87

James Dunn was a government official specialising in international relations for more than 30 years: first as a defence analyst, specializing on Indonesia, then a diplomat, serving first in Portuguese Timor as consul (1962-1964), then as West European desk officer, followed by postings to Paris and Moscow.

From 1970 to 1986 he was Director of the Foreign Affairs Group of the Parliament's Legislative Research Service, in effect the senior foreign affairs adviser to the Australian federal parliament. Sent on a fact-finding mission to East Timor in 1974, his report recommended self-determination. He was appointed leader of a mission sent to Timor by the Australian Council for Overseas Aid in 1975 with one primary aim being to negotiate the return of the Portuguese provincial government in order to head off the Indonesian invasion.

In 1977 he testified in favour of East Timor's self-determination before a committee of the US Congress and then the Fourth Committee of the UN General Assembly and then in 1999 he was a UN observer at the plebiscite—remaining in Dili until evacuation in September. He returned to Timor shortly after the InterFET intervention and acted as an adviser to the newly established UNTAET mission leaders.

In October 2001 he was commissioned to submit an expert's report on Crimes Against Humanity in East Timor and conducted a diplomacy course in Dili for potential diplomats.

Since resigning from Parliament in 1986 Dunn has dedicated himself to work on international human rights, in particular, a series of human rights congresses. In 1986 he was co-president of the Second World Congress on Human Rights at Dakar. He became a member of the Federation des Droits de l'Homme, and was also founding president of the Human Rights Council of Australia. In 1995 he delivered the Coventry Peace Lecture.

He has been a foreign affairs columnist, first with *The Bulletin*, and more recently as a regular columnist with the Fairfax newspapers.

In 1999 he was awarded the ACFOA human rights award, and in 2001 was invested as a member of the *Order of Australia* (AM). In 2002 he was conferred the honour of *Grande Official* of the Order of Prince Henry by Dr Jorge Sampaio, the President of Portugal.

Contents

Foreword

President of the Democratic Republic of East Timor,
His Excellency Mr. Xanana Gusmão

James Dunn has had an association of more than 40 years with East Timor, and his long concern for the sufferings of my people is well known. This sympathy comes out strongly in his latest book, which deals with the major events in our history from the arrival of the Portuguese in the early 16th century right up to our independence. In it he gives us a picture of life in Timor in the last years of Portuguese rule, unravels the events that led to Indonesian military intervention in October 1975 and reveals how we stood alone in the uncaring international environment of 1975. He recounts with compassion the years of suffering that followed, and the crisis that engulfed the resistance movement. This work traces our recent history from that low point when Nicolau Lobato was captured and killed to the revival of the resistance and the resurgence of the independence movement.

This book takes us through the exciting events that followed the fall of the Suharto regime, leading ultimately to the UNAMET interregnum, and the exciting outcome of the plebiscite. It gives an account of the UNTAET mandate, and of the shaping of our political system.

East Timor: A rough passage to independence is a sensitive tribute to the courage and determination of the East Timorese people. Accumulating the experience of a variety of functions and roles, the author is an acute and sensitive observer and participant of the different phases of our long and complex process. I can hardly think of anyone other than James Dunn in a position to undertake a 'long duration' analysis of our recent history.

James Dunn recognises the difficulties facing our impoverished nation, but shares our confidence in the capacity of our People to overcome them and prosper as a small but distinguished member of the international community.

Xanana Gusmão
February 2003

Do that good mischief, which may make this island
Thine own forever, and I, they Caliban,
For aye they foot-licker.

William Shakespeare, *The Tempest*

Preface

When the second edition of *Timor: A People Betrayed* was prepared in 1996 it was beyond my wildest dreams that in five years an independent Democratic Republic of East Timor would be in existence. There were of course grounds for cautious optimism. East Timor's captive nation status had come to be increasingly recognised in the international community, but the major powers with influence in Jakarta had accepted the annexation as a *fait accompli*. They were obviously disinclined to do other than encourage the Suharto Government to treat the East Timorese better—in particular to end gross human rights abuses by reducing the Indonesian military presence in the province. In reality the Indonesian Government's defiance of international protests had continued without serious challenge, and the change in the territory's prospects came unexpectedly, prompted by developments unrelated to the Timor problem. The change came from within Indonesia, following the collapse of the Suharto regime. Up to this time President Suharto had been resolutely opposed even to the proposal that the East Timorese be granted some form of autonomy.

The outlook back in 1996 was, nevertheless, less gloomy than thirteen years earlier when the first edition was published. The post-Cold War world was a different place, with an international agenda less tolerant of violations of international human rights standards. In 1983 East Timor's situation was not widely understood, and, in any case, it was overshadowed by Cold War related issues, such as the Soviet invasion of Afghanistan and conflicts in Africa and the Middle East. Thirteen years later the Cold War was over, and greater attention was being given to situations involving gross human rights abuses. The awarding of the Nobel Peace Prize to Bishop Carlos Belo and Jose Ramos Horta had the effect of raising East Timor's profile around the world. When President Habibie indicated a readiness to review the territory's status, he was encouraged to do so by the representatives of those Western nations that had hitherto not opposed its annexation.

East Timor's case was also given a boost by other developments. There was the appointment to the position of UN Secretary General of an outstanding and inspirational leader, Kofi Annan, who had long held a special interest in the problems faced by minorities. From the time of his appointment in 1997 the new UN chief made the search for a just settlement of the Timor problem one of his priorities. Kofi Annan's appointment rather conveniently coincided with President Habibie's unexpected rise to power, and the latter's move to open negotiations towards a settlement of a problem once described by Ali Alatas as the pebble in Indonesia's shoe. Another factor was the major shift in Australia's stand on East Timor which, until 1998, was one of solid support for the territory's incorporation into Indonesia. There is a touch of irony about this policy shift. In 1974 the Whitlam government, arguably the most radical and innovative in Australia's history, had shamefully ignored Timorese appeals for support for their self-determination, and had encouraged Indonesian incorporation of the Portuguese colony. Twenty-four years later a radical shift was undertaken by one of this country's most conservative governments, which itself had at first been content to continue Australia's support for East Timor's annexation.

This work incorporates much of the material in *Timor: A People Betrayed*, but it is more than another edition. It is redesigned to meet the country's changed circumstances. However, its aim is still to provide an account of how the Timor tragedy, with its huge humanitarian cost, unfolded, and some answers to the questions past events raised. For example, what was the colony like under Portuguese rule, and why were they there for so long? What was the nature of the resistance, especially the Fretilin movement, and what transpired during the invasion? This work contains a fresh, and more detailed, approach to events from the Santa Cruz massacre in 1991 to independence in May 2002. The book does not, of course, exhaust these subjects. It does, however, provide a general picture of a tragic history spanning almost a generation, which should help promote an understanding of the remarkable East Timorese people to those now dealing with the new nation, as well as readers interested in how the Timorese got to where they are today.

The story is not only about East Timor. It focuses on that other tragedy, the failure of the Australian conscience to respond to an appeal for help from a small and weak neighbour, to whom it was historically in debt. This lapse contributed to the failure of the international conscience, at a time when the protection of the human rights so grossly violated in East Timor had become a central part of the international agenda, a process supported with some vigour by Australia. This saga reveals aspects of Australian politics and values that many would rather not know; in particular those contradictions in our performance as a responsible member of the international community.

This insight into Australia's view of the outside world supports the contention of Alan Renouf, a former head of our foreign affairs department, that Australians have been a frightened and intimidated people. Australia failed to seize a rare opportunity to provide some intellectual and moral inspiration to the affluent developed world of which we are part, and to those millions of Asians in our neighbourhood who continue to strive for more just, humane and democratic forms of government. Until some 30 years ago Australia chose to be an unobtrusive member of the affluent Western club, a follower and not a leader, a role that suited our lack of confidence in our capacity to behave as a truly independent nation. As Australia's political leaders saw it—and continue to do so—to survive we need a powerful protector, and as an insurance policy we should not move too far from an alignment with the foreign-policy priorities and interests of that protector. In relation to our traditional alliance with the United States, such considerations influenced the performance of the Fraser government, of the Labor governments after 1983, and continue to deeply influence the Howard government, as the crisis involving Iraq has amply demonstrated. Until President Suharto was deposed, nearly all Australian governments seemed obsessed with the related concern that to take a moral stand on Timor would have antagonised the Suharto regime, thus endangering this country's security.

The key player in the formulation of the policy that contributed to the Timor tragedy was Mr. Whitlam, who was Prime Minister when the drama began to unfold. Paradoxically, Whitlam was one of Australia's most independent-minded prime ministers, a leader less swayed than his predecessors by the exigencies of Australia's alliance with the United States. At first, that is after the Lisbon coup of 1974, his vision and his support for the principle of self-determination, inspired the Timorese. To me, then a foreign affairs adviser to the Parliament, Whitlam had come into office in 1972, after two decades of conservative governments, like a fresh breeze into a stagnant room. His breadth of vision and his determination to open up new horizons to the Australian people were immensely stimulating to one who had long been dismayed at our traditionally narrow, insular and intimidated view of the world around us. His achievements during his short term in office gave Australians a new confidence and sense of self-reliance, a stronger sense of purpose as independent actors on a rapidly changing international stage. No doubt, one motive for Whitlam's response to events in Timor was his fear that Australia's involvement in the decolonisation process would inhibit his efforts to expand these new horizons. Perhaps he believed that this country would have become bogged down in an acrimonious and confrontational dispute with Indonesia, reviving the 'yellow peril' fears of the past, and forcing us back, as it were, into our isolationist and rather racist shell.

Whatever his motives, Mr. Whitlam misjudged the importance of Australia's international responsibility to assist with the decolonisation of East Timor, its obligation to a small and vulnerable neighbour, whose people had rallied to our support in 1942, the darkest hour in our history. Clearly we had a debt to discharge. Whitlam failed to take account of the predictable humanitarian consequences of Indonesian aggression against the colony. Tragically, Mr. Whitlam chose not to use his considerable influence with President Suharto who for months had opposed the military intervention so vigorously advocated by a small group of hawkish generals. He apparently feared an Australia reaction that would have negatively influenced western members of the important aid consortium, the Inter-Governmental Group on Indonesia. If the Australian Prime Minister had put to use the considerable international influence he had acquired, in the circumstances of the time it would probably have ensured that the military seizure of East Timor did not take place. Such a course of action would undoubtedly have generated some tensions in our relationship with Indonesia. However, the relationship could hardly have deteriorated further than it eventually did because of the refusal of the Australian people to endorse our official policy of accommodation,

Although Prime Minister Whitlam shaped Australia's stand on East Timor, his government was no longer in office when the actual military seizure of the territory took place. It was the government of Malcolm Fraser, a leader with a conscience, which abandoned the Timorese to their cruel fate, ignoring their desperate appeals for help in deference to a narrow perception of where Australia's national self-interest lay. It was the Fraser government—and the Hawke government that succeeded it—that remained unmoved at the brutal suppression of the Timorese independence movement, while loudly assailing the Russians for their intervention in Afghanistan. As this account shows, the Liberal–Country Party Coalition government of the time recognised East Timor's incorporation into Indonesia at a time when bitter fighting was raging throughout the territory with its helpless people being slaughtered indiscriminately.

The Timor story is not only an indictment of Australian foreign policy. It reveals a great deal about the weakness of the current world order in relation to the position of minorities and small states. It exposes the yawning gap between the noble rhetoric of international humanitarian instruments that are supposedly in force, and the reality of international commitment and resolve. The United States, which had the power and influence to prevent the invasion, declined to do so. Although key officials knew about the conspiracy led by Indonesian generals, they took steps to conceal the ugly truth from Congress in order to shield a regime considered to be of strategic importance in the post-Vietnam War period. At one stage, while the United States was denouncing human rights violations by Soviet forces in Afghanistan, it was covering up even more serious violations in East Timor. Until Kofi Annan came to office at the United Nations, the Timor saga highlighted the continuing vulnerability of small nations and communities in a United Nations system dominated by the major powers. The Timor experience underlines the fact that the world body is only as effective at implementing the high standards it has set for the global community as its major member states are prepared to make it, and exposes that even the so-called responsible member states cannot be trusted to behave responsibly, even when gross human rights abuses are at stake.

The long hoped-for change in East Timor's fortunes came in 1999, when a UN-sponsored mission made possible what was to constitute a genuine act of self-determination. Almost twenty-four years after the Indonesian military intervention, the people of East Timor unequivocally voted to go their own way. It was a stunning outcome, a result marred by a terrible TNI-organised punishment. Indonesia's occupation ended as it had begun—in a wave of violence and bloodshed. The devastation of the country presented the UN rescue mission with a difficult challenge, but the outcome clearly demonstrated that if such a mission is fully supported by the international community the UN can fulfil the role set down for it, when the Charter was signed fifty-seven years ago. East Timor's experience provides two contrasting lessons: the grim consequences of dismal failure, and a lesson in effective peace-enforcing and national rehabilitation. In short, if member nations fully support the world body it is truly our best means to secure and maintain world peace.

I have attempted in this work to bring together the various aspects that need to be taken into account if the reader is fully to understand the many dimensions to the Timor affair. These range from the injustices and suffering inflicted on the Timorese people to the dismal failure of the international system, and of Australia and the United States in particular. In this context I have sought to dispel some myths about what transpired in East Timor, some of which have been kept alive for the convenience of those who encouraged the misconceptions that a communist threat existed in the Portuguese colony, that Fretilin was a party under significant communist influence, and that the UDT, the main party opposed to Fretilin, invited Indonesia to intervene and carry out integration. Also, it will be seen that the civil war in August 1975 was the culmination of months of subversive actions by the Indonesian military, operations designed to destabilise the situation in the colony. It was this interference, rather than the weakness of the Portuguese administration, that brought about the collapse of East Timor's decolonisation.

I have also sought to unravel the events of the last four years that led to East Timor's liberation and independence. The causes of the so-called militia violence that gripped East Timor in 1999 are dealt with in some detail, as is the controversy over UNAMET's failure to provide adequate security protection. The InterFET intervention and the UNTAET mandate are also covered. When judged against the scene of destruction in October 1999 the achievements of this UN mission, under the able leadership of Sergio Vieira de Mello, are impressive. For this new but very poor nation the road ahead is a hard one, as post-independence incidents have demonstrated. This time, however, the East Timorese are enjoying the benevolence and commitment of the international community. The new nation's long-term prospects for peace and prosperity continues to depend heavily on three countries—Indonesia, Portugal and Australia—all of whom failed to live up to their responsibilities in 1975. Of special importance to the future well-being and security of the East Timorese is the need for close cooperation between Australian and Portugal.

This book is based on a careful analysis, over a period of twenty-eight years, of a wide variety of source material—including hundreds of interviews with Timorese refugees, interviews with the leaders of Timorese political parties, a critical study of several hundred messages sent via Darwin by Fretilin, information gathered since August 1999, and information from a number of well-placed Indonesian sources and other visitors to East Timor. I have tried to piece together an account of the bitter resistance, the suffering and the brutality that occurred in the years following the invasion, as well as the last bloody year of occupation. Serious crimes against humanity perpetrated during this period are referred to mostly in general terms. They constitute acts of state terrorism, the details of which need to be unraveled and analysed. To hide from them is to hide from the history of East Timor.

Over the years I have been greatly assisted by books, reports and articles by reputable authors, highly respectable agencies like Amnesty International and Human Rights Watch, and, not least, a wide variety of material from the East Timorese themselves.

I have many debts to acknowledge in writing this book. I begin with a tribute to the six newsmen who were killed in East Timor in 1975. It was their courage and commitment, and the refusal at that time of the Australian government to carry out a proper investigation into these tragic incidents, that inspired me to take a stand on this issue, and to write the Timor story. Greg Shackleton, Gary Cunningham, Tony Stewart, Malcolm Rennie and Brian Peters at Balibo, and Roger East at Dili, lost their lives in courageous attempts to bring out the truth of what was happening at that time, in the finest traditions of investigative journalism. Had they not perished, or had their murder been taken seriously at the time, the whole course of events might conceivably have been very different—but that, of course, is precisely why they were not allowed to live.

My gratitude for the publication of the first edition of this book in the first instance goes to the University of Adelaide Foundation, and especially to the then vice-chancellor the late Professor Donald Stranks for his personal interest and encouragement. The fellowship awarded me by the foundation made it possible to get this work well under way, and to carry out valuable fieldwork. I am also indebted to the Politics Department of the University of Adelaide, to the Menzies Library of the Australian National University and to the Parliamentary Library for valuable research assistance. I am especially indebted to the long friendship and encouragement of Lord Avebury of the British Parliament's Human Rights Group, and to concerned Timor-watchers in Australia and abroad.

There are those with whom I have long shared a deep concern about the anguish and aspirations of the Timorese. They include Jill Jolliffe, herself the author of two books on the Timor problem, and of a volume of press articles over the past two decades, and Professor Roger Clark of Rutgers University, New Jersey. I have longstanding debts to Kevin Sherlock and Sue Roff for their tireless work on bibliographies and to Pat Walsh, now a key UN adviser in East Timor, for his past invaluable assistance in the collecting and disseminating of information.

There are many others whose friendship and writings on the Timor problem have been a great help, and their efforts to establish the truth of the matter have been a source of inspiration. They include Arnold Kohen of Washington, Dr Peter Carey of St Anthony's College, Oxford, Dr John Taylor of the University of the South Bank, London, the late Dr Herbert Feith of Monash University, Melbourne, and David Scott. I am also indebted to many journalists who, over the years, have produced valuable material on the subject. Among them are the late Peter Hastings, David Jenkins and Hamish Macdonald of the *Sydney Morning Herald*. In relation to recent events I am particularly indebted to Ian Martin and Major General Mike Smith for access to their comprehensive reports on UNAMET and UNTAET. I am also indebted to many UN officials, Timorese and others in East Timor, who encouraged me to produce an updated version of *Timor: A People Betrayed*, and to David Longfield and Clare Calvet of Longueville Books who made it possible. Not least, I owe more than I can repay to my wife, Wendy, who has endured the demands of East Timor for a large part of our married life.

The most valuable source of inspiration and information has, however, been the East Timorese themselves. Their extraordinary determination, their capacity to suffer, and their tolerance, have deeply impressed those of us who have come to know them. I have been especially inspired by President Xanana Gusmão, Dr Jose Ramos Horta, Bishop Carlos Belo, Mario Carrascalão and his brother João and, in particular Mario and Terezinha da Cruz, with whom I shared nights of militia terror in August 1999. I am also deeply grateful to those Indonesians who encouraged me over the years, and especially during my recent work on crimes against humanity in 1999. This book is in no way intended to arouse anti-Indonesian sentiments. Its accusations are against a section of the military, from whose oppressive behaviour the people of Indonesia have themselves suffered for some three decades. The advancement of Indonesian democracy depends heavily on the courage and the commitment of those Indonesian reformers who also campaigned for East Timor's right to self-determination at considerable risk to their own safety.

The story of East Timor since 1975 is not a pretty tale. It is a shameful story of conspiracies against a small and vulnerable people, an account marked by deceit, hypocrisy, mendacity, and plain irresponsibility. Some might prefer that this sorry tale not be told, but the truth must be brought out. Let me finish with a quote from a work by Noam Chomsky which analyses, among others, the Timor saga:

> If we do not like what we find when we look at the facts—and few will fail to be appalled if they take an honest look—we can work to bring about changes in the practices and structure of institutions that cause terrible suffering and slaughter. To the extent that we see ourselves as citizens in a democratic community, we have a responsibility to devote our energies to these ends.

Noam Chomsky, *Towards a New Cold War:*
Essays on the Current Crisis and How We Got There
(New York, Pantheon Books, 1982, p. 337)

James Dunn
December 2002

East Timor: Select Chronology

1974

25 April	Armed Forces Movement coup deposes Salazarist regime in Lisbon, and subsequently Portugal's colonies are granted right to self-determination.
5 May	In East Timor, Governor grants Timorese the right to set up political parties. Horta meets Adam Malik, Indonesian Foreign Minister, who assures him that Indonesia will support East Timor's independence.
6 September	At meeting with Suharto in Wonosobo Prime Minister Whitlam states his preference for East Timor to be incorporated into Indonesia.
December	TNI generals set up *Operasi Komodo*, a covert operation with aim of Securing incorporation of East Timor.

1975

20 January	UDT and Fretilin form coalition for independence.
26 May	Following pressure from Indonesia UDT withdraws from coalition.
11 August	After meeting with TNI generals UDT leaders seize power in Dili, but retain aim of independence.
18 August	Armed conflict with Fretilin breaks out.
27 August	Portuguese Governor and administration withdraw to Atauro.
16 October	Major TNI military assault on Balibo–Maliana area. Five newsmen for Australia killed by TNI at Balibo.
28 November	Faced with creeping advance of Indonesian troops, Fretilin unilaterally declares independence.
7 December	Major Indonesian assault on Dili.
22 December	UN Security Council calls on Indonesia to withdraw troops from East Timor. Fretilin forces (Falintil) continue to resist in mountainous interior.

1976

17 August | President Suharto signs legislation incorporating East Timor as Indonesia's 27th province.

19 November | Indonesian relief agencies report that 100,000 Timorese have been killed since invasion.

1977

13 March | Author testifies before Congressional committee on atrocities committed by TNI in East Timor following invasion.

1978

20 January | Australia recognizes *de facto* Indonesian occupation of East Timor.

31 December | Nicolau Lobato, Fretilin President, is killed by Kopassus troops led by Major Yunus Yosfiah and Captain Prabowo.

1979

June | Australia recognizes *de jure* Indonesian sovereignty over East Timor.

1981

March | Xanana Gusmão appointed leader of resistance movement.

20 December | ICRC allowed by Indonesia to resume limited role in East Timor. Its officials report on appalling condition of Timorese people.

1982

3 November | UNGA resolution again condemns annexation, and instructs Secretary General to initiate consultations towards achieving comprehensive resolution of Timor problem.

1983

16 May | Monsignor Costa Lopes is replaced by Monsignor Carlos Felipe Ximenes Belo as Apostolic Administrator of East Timor.

August | As many as 1,000 Timorese killed in massacre by Indonesian troops at Creras, near Viqueque.

1985

9 December | Indonesia and Australia announce plans to develop jointly petroleum resources of the Timor Gap.

1989

12 October | Pope John-Paul visits Dili, and consecrates Cathedral.

11 December | Treaty on exploitation of Timor Gap resources is signed by Australian and Indonesian governments.

1991

12 November | TNI troops open fire on unarmed Timorese demonstration. More than 200 persons killed, many after the shooting.

1992

20 November | Xanana Gusmão arrested by Indonesian troops at secret location in Lahane, Dili.

September | Abilio Soares succeeds Mario Carrascalão as Governor of East Timor.

1996

November | Nobel Peace Prize awarded jointly to Bishop Carlos Belo and Jose Ramos Horta.

1998

21 May | President Suharto is forced to resign, and is replaced by Dr. B J Habibie.

15 June | 15,000 students demonstrate in Dili, calling for referendum and release of Xanana.

18 June | Foreign Minister Ali Alatas makes new proposals to Portugal.

July | President Habibie makes autonomy proposal to East Timorese. Major Generals Sjafrei Sjafruddin and Zakky Anwar Makarim plan at ABRI HQ the setting up of militia to counter growing support for independence.

12 August | Major General Adam Damiri and Colonel Tono Suratnam meet with pro-integration leaders and tell them they must organize to protect integration.

29 December | Letter from Prime Minister Howard to President Habibie urged Indonesia to address East Timorese desire for act of self determination.

1999

21 January | President Habibie informs colleagues of plebiscite proposal.

27 January | It is announced in Jakarta that President will ask MPR to grant independence to East Timor if autonomy proposal is rejected.

February | Militia violence erupts in various parts of province.

6 April | About 40 Timorese killed in massacre at Liquiça.

17 April | Massacre at house of Manuel Carrascalão, with 17 killed, including Manuelito, Carrascalão's son.

27 April | At a meeting with Prime Minister Howard, President Habibie proposes to hold self-determination ballot in August.

1 May | Megawati Sukarnoputri announces that referendum will be cancelled if she wins forthcoming election.

5 May	Agreement between Indonesia, Portugal and the UN is signed in New York.
4 June	UNAMET mission, led by Ian Martin, commences work in East Timor.
16 July	Voter registration begins.
4 August	Voter registration ends.
30 August	The self-determination ballot takes place, with over 97% voter participation.
4 September	Election results announced at Mahkota Hotel, with 78.5% voting against Indonesia's autonomy proposal. TNI/militia onslaught begins within an hour, causing most foreigners to flee.
6 September	Massacre at Ave Maria Church, Suai, claiming some 200 lives. Killings and destruction at Bishop Belo's house in Dili.
8 September	Massacre at Maliana police station, claiming over 50 lives. Following urgent action by Kofi Annan, Security Council mission dispatched to Jakarta and East Timor. Secretary General urges Indonesia to accept international intervention.
10 September	Massacre at Passabe, Oecussi, claiming over 70 lives.
12 September	Security Council authorizes InterFET force. TNI and *Polri* begin withdrawal.
19 September	Major General Cosgrove arrives in Dili. InterFET deployment begins next day. Xanana returns to East Timor.
25 September	Killing of nuns, brothers and Indonesian journalist in Luatem.
19 October	Indonesian MPR formally accepts referendum outcome.
25 October	UN Security Council establishes UNTAET (Res. 1272).
1 November	Last Indonesian troops leave East Timor.
17 November	Newly appointed head of UNTAET, Sergio Vieira de Mello, commences duties in Dili.

2000

23 February	InterFET transfers military command to UNTAET, and begins withdrawal.
21 June	33 member, Timorese National Consultative Council established.
12 July	Transitional Cabinet comprising 4 UN representatives and 4 East Timorese is established.
6 September	Six UNHCR officials murdered at Atambua by armed militia.
15 November	National University of East Timor is opened.

2001

16 March	SRSG announces East Timor's first democratic election for 30 August.
9 June	CNRT disbanded to make way for party election campaigns.

3 July	Agreement between East Timor Transitional Administration and Australian Government on revenues from Timor Gap oil/gas exploitation.
30 August	Elections for Constituent Assembly take place peacefully, with Fretilin winning 57.3% of vote.
20 September	New Timorese Council of Ministers, with 24 members, is sworn in.
22 October	Constituent Assembly adopts resolution requesting UNTAET to hand over sovereignty to elected Timorese government on 20 May 2002.
26 October	East Timor Defence Force formally inaugurated.
31 October	UN Security Council supports Kofi Annan's recommendation that the UN continue a supporting role in East Timor after independence.
30 November	Constituent Assembly approves structural outline of Constitution.

2002

31 January	Constituent Assembly votes to transform itself into East Timor's first legislature after proclamation of independence on 20 May.
22 March	East Timor's first constitution signed into force by Constituent Assembly.
14 April	Presidential elections held with Xanana Gusmão and Xavier do Amaral as candidates. Xanana captures 82.7% of vote and is subsequently declared president-elect.
20 May	The new nation, the Democratic Republic of East Timor, is formally born at a ceremony in Dili, attended by Kofi Annan and many foreign dignitaries. UNTAET mission ends.

* * * *

Chapter One
The land and its people

To observers of the dramatic changes in postwar South-East Asia, the Portuguese colony of Timor had, by the mid-1960s, assumed a quaint and somewhat incongruous appearance. This most remote of Portugal's 'overseas provinces' consisted of the eastern half of the easternmost island of the Nusatenggara group, the small enclave of Oecussi on the north coast of the Indonesian sector, the island of Atauro, north of Dili, and to the east the tiny islet of Jaco. Yet in spite of Timor's remoteness from the metropolitan power, Portuguese navigators first set foot on its soil a mere two decades after Christopher Columbus made his epic voyage across the Atlantic.

Although the total area of East Timor is only 18,900 square kilometres the territory presents a picture of great diversity, in terms of both geography and ethnic composition. The island is of recent geological formation, featuring a mountainous interior, with several peaks soaring more than 2500 metres in altitude from the rugged central backbone that arches unevenly for much of the territory's length. Halfway along its length is Tata Mai Lau, the highest peak, rising majestically some 3000 metres above sea level. It was in these rugged highlands that hundreds of tiny villages, interlinked by a maze of mountain trails, were once to be found. It was here that an Australian commando force resisted numerically superior Japanese forces in 1942 and 1943, and here that a Fretilin guerrilla force waged a bitter resistance against the Indonesian invaders after December 1975. Also here are a number of lovely fertile mountain valleys whose permanent springs assure water for agriculture and drinking throughout the long dry season.

On the south coast there is an extensive coastal plain, most of it covered with tropical vegetation, while on the north coast rugged mountain spurs go right down to the sea. But, from the point of view of the livelihood of the Timorese, the most important plains are the highlands at Baucau and Lautem in the east, and the low-lying lands at Maliana near the Indonesian border.

East Timor's diverse landscape is matched by a diversity of climatic conditions. Generally speaking, there are two distinct seasons—a dry season from May to October when very little rainfall occurs in the north and central zones, followed by a monsoon season that settles over most of the island between November and April. Not surprisingly, the sharp geographical variations produce very different temperature and rainfall patterns. The littoral is hot and humid, with average temperatures ranging from 19°C to 31°C, but in the central region of the cordillera it is much cooler, with temperatures at the mountain villages of Maubisse and Hato Builico, for example, falling as low as 4°C in July and August when, in the past, open fireplaces were in frequent use to warm the residences of Portuguese officials, affluent Timorese, and Chinese merchants. Rainfall in Timor is both varied and uneven; it ranges from an annual average of about 560 millimetres at Manatuto, on the north coast, to sometimes in excess of 3000 millimetres at Iliomar in the south-east.

Few of Timor's rivers have permanent courses. Most have their sources in the central cordillera where seasonal conditions make them one of the dramatic variables of the island's environment. The main permanent streams are the Laclo and the Lois on the north coast, and the Tafara, Be-Lulic and Laclo-Sul, which rise on the southern slopes of the central mountain chain and flow into the Timor Sea. Numerous other streams become cascading torrents in the Wet when, in the past, they frequently sever Timor's arterial roads; in the Dry, however, they are little more than hot, stony creek beds. These streams are key elements in the ongoing drama of East Timor's landscape.

The character of Timor's vegetation reflects the island's position at the confluence of tropical Indonesia and the dry north-west of Australia. The jungle of the south coast gives way to bushland on the slopes, a bush dominated by eucalypts and acacias. On the mountain crests and ridges tropical montane rain and cloud forests are to be found, while grass savannas are encountered in the foothills and on the plains. For much of the year the dry north coastal fringes have a depressingly arid appearance, with thickets of gnarled and stunted trees. The rains bring about a pleasing conversion to a soft green cover. The vegetation mosaic for a large part of East Timor is, in the words of one observer, 'a lush green carpet during the rainy season, changing to a scorched brown landscape during the dry season'.

Into this complex and changing geographical setting, successive migrations of various peoples, from Melanesia, from continental Asia and, in the more recent past, from the islands to the west, have woven a surprisingly intricate pattern of cultures. In the words of Professor Forman, a leading authority on the anthropology of East Timor,

> It manifests an ethnic heterogeneity which characterizes the entire region from the Philippines to Australia and from the islands east of Papua New Guinea to the Malagasy Republic.

Timor, noted Professor Forman,

did not come under the aegis of the early Javanese/Islamic principalities and, historical conjecture notwithstanding, Indo-Javanese and Islamic influences barely can be noted, except insofar as Dutch hegemony later effected the spread of some ideas, particularly in the political domain, to western (now Indonesian) Timor. East Timor, under Portuguese rule, was largely exempt from those influences.[1]

Although Malays, Makassarese and Papuan-type people came to Timor and left traces of their presence, neither Hinduism nor Islam reached this remote island when these cultural influences were spreading across the archipelago. In general the Proto-Malay type predominates, with most of the Timorese being dark-skinned and lightly built. But from an ethno-linguistic point of view the situation is even more complicated. There are more than thirty distinct ethno-linguistic groups in East Timor; they can be placed into two dominant language families, the Malayo–Polynesian, or Austronesian, and the Papuan, or non-Austronesian. Although some words have been borrowed, there are surprisingly few links between Bahasa Indonesia and the languages of East Timor.

The most widely spoken languages in the territory were, before the 1975 invasion, Tetum (or Tetung), Mambai, Bunak, Kemac, Tocodede, Galoli, Makassae and Dagada. Of these, Tetum has become a kind of lingua franca and is spoken or understood in most parts of the island. Also of special importance are Mambai, Kemac and Makassae, for these are the native tongues of more than 300,000 people in the east-central zone, in the central mountain districts and in the more populated border areas to the west.

According to official Portuguese estimates the population of East Timor was more than 650,000 in 1974, having increased from the census figure of 609,477 in 1970. However, church officials who kept their own estimates, based on the accounts of the missions scattered across the province, claimed that the population was as much as 5 per cent higher than the official figure, a claim to which many of the Portuguese officials subscribed. The main reason for this discrepancy was that the villagers consistently understated their numbers to provincial officials in an attempt to reduce the burden of the head tax and, in the past, to evade the various forms of conscription for road construction and other extensive repair programs carried out in the dry season. If the church estimate is accepted as the more reliable population count, there were more than 680,000 people in East Timor in 1975, 97 per cent of them Timorese

Before Portuguese colonisation was well established, East Timor was divided up into a number of kingdoms, or *rais*, often called *reinos* by the Portuguese, each of which was under a petty king or *liurai*. The *rais* were made up of a number of *sucos*, or tribal groups, most of which were in turn broken up into clans (*ahi matan*) or village units the Portuguese called *povoações* (literally, 'settlements'). This order the colonial authorities used as a model for the local administrative system of indirect rule, adapting it as their control gradually extended across the territory.

In practice, the Portuguese system of colonial rule meant direct control at the provincial level and the circumscription, or district, level (in the last years called *concelho*), with the administrators' presence having little direct impact on the population at large until the twentieth century. Timor's urban centres have until recently been small. In 1970 there were only 28,000 people in the capital, Dili, and its environs. More than 80 per cent of the population dwelt in the hundreds of small hamlets, or *povoações*, scattered across the territory. Until the 1970s most of these people had only infrequent direct contact with representatives of the metropolitan power. Official dealings, such as they were, amounted to little more than the annual collection of population figures, levying a head tax on the adult males, and collecting levies on livestock. In most cases these onerous and, in hard times, unpleasant tasks were not the lot of Portuguese officials but of the *chefe de suco* (head of the tribe), a Timorese appointed by the government to carry out administrative duties at the tribal level. But his responsibilities were fairly limited, with other aspects of social and political authority remaining in the hands of the traditional local rulers.

For most of the four centuries of the Portuguese presence in Timor, few outside cultural influences trickled down to the roots of Timorese society. Ordinary people lived totally within the confines of the realms of the traditional rulers, in a form common to other parts of South-East Asia. Before 1912 the *liurais* dominated native society absolutely, and even managed to maintain a continuing challenge to Portuguese colonial authority. A series of rebellions between 1894 and 1912 led to several bloody 'pacification' operations by the Portuguese, and to the defeat of the rebel *liurais* whose powers and authority were subsequently diminished. However, the system of indirect rule continued, and as far as the local population was concerned the influence of the traditional rulers remained considerable. Indeed, it was not until the overthrow of the Salazarist regime in 1974 that the rulers began to meet a serious challenge from other indigenous political forces which had emerged from the ranks of the educated elite. By this time many of the *liurais* had become pillars of the Portuguese colonial system. Some of them continued to retain their own armies—though ill-equipped—and to use local military ranks (usually lieutenant colonel or colonel). With their powers bolstered by colonial authority which tended to undermine the few elements of democracy in the traditional electoral process, some local rulers became oppressively authoritarian towards their subjects, and supported the Salazarist regime's uncompromising opposition to decolonisation. Not surprisingly, it was these traditional rulers to whom the Indonesian military turned when, in mid-1976, they sought to construct a facade of legitimacy to conceal the falsity of the formal act of integration. The *liurais* subsequently became prominent in the puppet government of the '27th Province': the *liurai* of Atsabe, Guilherme Goncalves, became the provincial governor, while another prominent ruler, the *liurai* of Maubara, Gaspar Nunes III, became chairman of the local legislative assembly, the DPRD-II (the Dewan Perwakilan Rakyat Daerah, or Regional People's Representative Council, Stage II).

Beneath the *liurais* were the *datos*, or princes, and further down the line a class of village chiefs, known as *tumengengs*, who dealt with most aspects of the day-to-day lives of the ordinary people. The Timorese tended to keep strictly to the confines of their village units, although the village itself might be moved from time to time in the ongoing search for more fertile land and better sources of water. Social and religious life in the Timorese village continued to be strongly influenced by traditional animistic beliefs, which were of a similar pattern throughout the territory. According to these beliefs the spirits of the dead are an essential element in the living environment and their presence as evil or good spirits must always be taken into account. In their traditional lifestyle the Timorese are surrounded by *luliks*, or sacred objects, symbols of good, evil, or of the unknown. Certain trees, crocodiles, snakes, eels, and so on, have magic powers attributed to them, as interpreted by the *nai* or *dato lulik*, a kind of village sorcerer or priest. The penetration of Christianity into the roots of native society weakened, but did not destroy, these beliefs. Indeed, many Christian villagers continue to subscribe to them, and to preserve their *luliks* with pagan reverence. The animists, for their part, often ascribed supernatural powers to mission priests who, invariably dressed in white robes, from time to time made visits even to remote villages. The church in East Timor did not engage in forced conversion, although for more than a century the ruling elite had been pressed to accept Catholicism and to send their children to church schools. In Timorese society Christianity thus tended to become the religion of the elite and the better-educated, many of whom in turn continued to defer to aspects of traditional beliefs. Partly for this reason, Christian and animist prejudices and practices came to coexist with a degree of harmony.

The Portuguese developed the *suco* as the basic administrative unit, but the real basic unit of habitation was the hamlet, the *povoaçõ*. The hamlet consisted of between three and a dozen or so houses, constructed mainly of timber bamboo and *palapa*, or palm leaves. But the style of construction and the design varied remarkably from region to region. In the east, especially in the Lautem–Tutuala area, intricately adorned houses on stilts were to be found, while round houses predominated in the central mountain region, and rectangular abodes were to be found along the north coast. In the mountain regions hamlets often adorned the tops of hills and peaks, a reminder of past needs for defence against surprise attack by traditional enemies. Most settlements were also well away from the roads, but they were invariably interlinked by a maze of tracks, along which the Timorese moved at impressive speed.

The lifestyles of two of the major ethno-linguistic groups were described by two American anthropologists in their testimony before a subcommittee of the Congressional Committee on International Relations in June 1977. Professor Forman observed that the Makassae were:

> a simple people, not terribly sophisticated in the economic and political matters which concern us, but well attuned to social, economic, and political necessities engendered by their own historical reality. They live primarily by the cultivation

of corn and root crops in patrilineally inherited ancestral gardens; grow rice in elaborately sculpted and irrigated mountain terraces; herd water buffalo, goats and pigs; raise chickens and fighting cocks; and weave *ikat* cloths which, along with their crops and livestock, ancient swords, glass beads and a few gold amulets, comprise the totality of their exchangeable wealth.[2]

The Mambai occupy most of the central region to the south and west of Dili. They are essentially a mountain people. Another anthropologist, Elizabeth Traube, told the same congressional subcommittee that most of native social life transpired:

> on the surrounding hills and high valleys of Timor's rugged interior. There the Mambai eke out a subsistence based on the swidden cultivation of rice, corn, and root crops. Gardens are individually held and cooperatively worked by kin groups. Mambai also herd water buffalo, goats, and pigs, which are primarily used in formal ceremonial exchanges. Most families own small coffee holdings which are the major source of cash income.[3]

The Mambai hamlet tended to be small, ranging from three to five houses, forming a part of a loosely organised village community.

Although there were hamlets and villages scattered along East Timor's extensive coastline, with fewer in the south, partly because of the greater incidence of malaria, the Timorese are, on the whole, poor seafarers. Traditional native boats tended to be small and crudely constructed, and to be used strictly for inshore, calm-weather sailing. Thus the abundant supplies of marine life on the many coral reefs offshore were grossly underexploited in a country whose inhabitants suffered from protein deficiency, and often from serious food shortages towards the end of the dry season. A number of reasons have been advanced for this poor level of seafaring skills. It has been attributed to the Proto-Malay background of the Timorese; yet elsewhere such peoples have been able to develop these skills. Also, while it is true that most of the population live in the mountains or away from the coast, this is also the case in other islands in the Indonesian archipelago where seafaring and fishing skills have nonetheless been acquired. One possible explanation is that, in centuries past, the colonial power actively discouraged shipping movement between Timor and other islands in the eastern sector of the Lesser Sundas, particularly when Portuguese authority was being challenged by the *liurais*. Another obvious explanation is that the Portuguese sought to preserve their last foothold in the East Indies from the encroachments of the more powerful and dynamic Dutch by sealing off the territories under their control from outside influences. It is also noteworthy that East Timor does not possess harbours that would give all-weather protection to larger craft.

Whatever the reason, very few Timorese have taken to the sea, which partly explains why northern Australia did not have to contend with an influx of 'boat people' after the Indonesian invasion. The exception to the rule is the Galoli-speaking people of the island of Atauro, who are proficient at sailing and fishing. However, even the Atauroans lack the navigation skills and vessels suitable for other than short inter-island voyages in fair-weather conditions.

Although the pace of East Timor's economic and political development was painfully slow when compared with that of the more vigorous systems under other Western colonial powers, a substantial increase in education in the last decade of Portuguese rule, the growth of small urban centres and the expansion of government had brought significant changes to Timorese society by the mid-1970s. The nature and the effect of these changes has generally been underrated. The most profound of these influences was in education. In 1953 there were only 8000 children in 39 primary schools; by 1964 the figure had risen to 17,000 in 165 schools, and in 1974 it had increased to almost 60,000 students in 456 schools. Although the numbers continuing on to secondary school remained low, thousands of Timorese had gained a modest level of literacy. When I returned to East Timor in mid-1974, after an absence of ten years, the social and political environment of the towns and larger villages was radically different. A Westernised Timorese town-dwelling community was in evidence.

By the late 1960s and early 1970s the newly educated young Timorese were moving into responsible government and service positions in significant numbers, although they were much less in evidence in the growing commercial sector, which remained predominantly in Chinese hands. By 1974 there were many Timorese among the senior officials in the central provincial administration, while in the thirteen districts or *concelhos* 60 per cent of positions at levels below the top regional administrative post, that of *administrador do concelho*, were held by Timorese. There were Timorese journalists, and Timorese technical personnel at the airports and in the meteorological service. In two fields—the church and the military—the significant Timorese presence was to be of crucial importance in the development of the independence movement and in the subsequent long campaign of armed resistance to the Indonesian occupation.

Of a total of 44 priests in East Timor in 1974, 25 were Timorese, most of them having graduated from the Dare seminary in the earlier stages of their clerical education. This Jesuit seminary, the Seminaria da Nossa Senhora de Fatima, which lies in the hills directly behind Dili, had a profound influence on Timorese intellectual development, not merely because it was one of the two leading educational institutions of the territory: it was the only institution in which almost all of the students were full-blooded Timorese. Those students who did not go on to become priests normally ended up in the professional ranks of the civil service, or joined the army where they usually acquired non-commissioned rank. Since the early 1960s more and more Timorese had been recruited into the army where they were to win the respect of the Portuguese military establishment which regarded them as troops that would perform well in guerrilla warfare. Thus, by 1974, most of the ordinary ranks and non-commissioned officers were Timorese. This 'indigenous army' consisted of some 3000 first-line troops and as many as 7000 of the second-line category, enabling the Portuguese army to maintain only a skeleton presence in the territory, and to concentrate its limited resources on the growing challenge to its authority in the African colonies.

Although it might be true to say that the Portuguese presence in East Timor had little direct effect at the lower levels of native society, in many indirect ways influences had been seeping into the cultural and religious life of the village at an increasing rate for some decades, thus sowing the seeds of change. The fact that the Timorese were relatively poor, and that the land was underdeveloped, though no poorer or less developed than the countryside in the neighbouring Indonesian province of East Nusatenggara, led many observers to reach exaggerated conclusions as to East Timor's backwardness.

The Chinese community of East Timor, according to official census statistics compiled in 1970, at that time numbered 6120 persons, but as this figure omitted a large number of *mestiço* Chinese–Timorese who considered themselves Chinese in cultural terms, the real figure was perhaps twice that number. Chinese contacts with East Timor go back to the fourteenth century, to the early development of the sandalwood trade between China and the eastern part of the Indonesian archipelago. In the first centuries of Portuguese settlement and colonisation a brisk trade developed with Macau. A letter written in 1704 by Antonio Coelho Guerreiro, the Portuguese governor of the time, identified five Chinese merchants in the colony in relation to the collection of taxes. It is probable that the community was indeed much larger. At the time it seemed that the Chinese were more readily accepted by the Dutch than by the Portuguese governors who believed that some Chinese merchants were encouraging the Timorese to resist Portuguese authority. It was the opposition of Chinese merchants to an attempt by the Portuguese to levy customs duties that led to the loss of Atapupu in 1818 to the Dutch. In 1893, according to Portuguese sources, the revolt of the important kingdom of Maubara was actually instigated by Chinese traders in that kingdom.

Thus, although the Chinese have had a long relationship with the Portuguese in Timor, in which they were to become one of the pillars of indirect rule, relations with the colonial authorities were never entirely easy, and few had become assimilated into Portuguese culture. Their community had always preserved its pluralist character, and the Portuguese and Timorese tended to regard them as aliens, a relationship reminiscent of their position in other former colonies in South-East Asia before gaining independence. But nowhere was Chinese dominance of commerce greater than in East Timor. In the early 1960s, of the 400 or so wholesale and retail enterprises in the Portuguese colony all but three or four were in Chinese hands. The latter were controlled not by Timorese but by Portuguese. The import-export trade was dominated by the Chinese who also acted as the middlemen in the purchase of grain—and, to a lesser extent, coffee—from the Timorese. And this role the colonial power strongly supported. In 1963 a senior Portuguese army officer, troubled by the low prices the Timorese were being paid for rice, urged the government of the time to buy directly from the Timorese to maximise the benefit accruing to both parties. His proposal was rejected, however, by the senior official responsible, who pointed out that such an arrangement would upset the established order.

The Chinese were caught somewhat uncomfortably in the middle of colonial society from several points of view. They were regarded as opportunistic aliens by both the Portuguese and the Timorese and their loyalties were a constant subject of speculation. Even at the end of the colonial period few Chinese held Portuguese citizenship, most of them holding passports issued by Taiwan, represented in Dili by a consul until shortly after the Indonesian invasion. The consul and the local Chinese Chamber of Commerce were frequently called to account by the provincial government for the behaviour of members of the community, even including those Chinese whose ancestors had come to the island many centuries earlier. Thus, members of the community looked to Taiwan, Hong Kong and, surreptitiously, to China, as their cultural and spiritual homes. Their children attended Chinese schools where they studied Mandarin, Chinese history and Chinese culture, based on the Taiwan syllabus, and where they wore uniforms adorned with nationalist insignia. At home their language was usually Cantonese. Few Chinese spoke Portuguese fluently, although many spoke Tetum, especially those living in the small towns and villages in the interior.

The Chinese minority were mostly concentrated in Dili and in the larger towns, but they were to be found wherever villages were large enough to attract retail outlets. Some of the wealthier Chinese possessed coffee plantations and rice fields, but very few lived outside the precincts of the towns and larger villages. In the capital and larger towns the Chinese communities maintained a closely knit social organisation, stayed clear of sensitive political issues, and rarely mixed with the Portuguese or the Timorese. In the villages their relations with the Timorese were closer, with some intermarriage taking place between Chinese men and Timorese women who, nevertheless, had to endure an inferior status in the eyes of the community at large. The Portuguese were much more tolerant of such mixed marriages.

After the communist victory in Peking, the Portuguese authorities kept a close watch on the activities of the Chinese, but they never had any cause for alarm. In spite of their at times oppressive grip on the economy of the colony, their lack of interest in the politics and objectives of Salazar's *Estado Novo*, or New State, their unintegrated status in local political and cultural life, and their distinct opportunism, the Chinese were law-abiding and displayed little interest in nationalist or communist causes. Many became sceptical about Taiwan's policies and aspirations, but the diplomatic link with Taipei and the traditional role of the consul discouraged any challenge to the established order. In the secondary schools Taiwan's influence was assured through its control over the appointment of key teaching staff. The threatened position of the Chinese communities in Indonesia and certain other South-East Asian countries made East Timor, despite its isolation and low level of development, seem a pleasant haven. Finally, although there may have been a certain glamour about China's burgeoning economic and military power in the 1950s and early 1960s, the upheaval of the Cultural Revolution and its aftermath did nothing for Peking's image in East Timor.

In the weeks following the announcement of the coup in Lisbon in April 1974, the Chinese in Dili and some other towns were to get their first inkling that the tolerant disposition of the Portuguese was not shared by the emerging leaders of the Timorese political associations. To many of the Timorese the Chinese were the very symbols of economic oppression, forcing them to accept rock-bottom prices for their agricultural produce and to pay exorbitant prices for essential goods in the village shops. In the eyes of educated Timorese, the Chinese stranglehold over the economy had to be broken. The Chinese, most of whom were hard-working traders, understandably favoured the continuation of Portuguese colonial rule.

To the west of Dili, between the beach and the airport, was a small 'Arab' community of about 500 persons which was, if anything, more closed than its Chinese counterpart. Its members were Moslems, whose origins were more Arab than Indonesian. According to Portuguese sources the community's founders were merchants who came from Surabaya and Makassar (Ujung Pandang) and who, before World War II, had owned small shops selling mainly fabrics and perfumes, a form of trading later taken over by the Chinese. In 1975 they were in diverse trades or professions, including farming, fishing, mechanical trades, and the public service. Most of the members of this community spoke a form of Bahasa Indonesia, but many also spoke Portuguese and were registered as Portuguese citizens. Some were among the few supporters of integration with Indonesia, but others, such as Mari Alkatiri, East Timor's first prime minister, became strong supporters of the independence option.

It was probably more accurate to describe the Portuguese element in East Timor as 'metropolitan' rather than white, since many of its members were Goan, African, or mixed-caste. Essentially they were the ruling caste of East Timor. They comprised the senior civil servants (with a few exceptions), the military commanders, other officers and some of the NCOs, the executive staff of the province's one financial institution, the Banco Naçional Ultramarino, and the management of the two large Portuguese enterprises in East Timor, SAPT (Sociedade Agricola Patria e Trabalho, also known as the Sociedade) and SOTA (Sociedade Orientale do Transportes e Armazens), which engaged in coffee-growing and export, and in general wholesale and retail activities. There were also a number of prosperous Portuguese coffee planters, but very few who had spent a lifetime on the island. Undoubtedly the most powerful figures in the colony were the governor—who in the last decade of Portuguese rule was usually an army officer of the rank of colonel or brigadier—the senior military officers and the senior administrators, who exercised wide powers in their *concelhos*.

Unlike the other communities, the metropolitans were largely a transient group, with the exception of the district administrators. Most of them came to the province for postings of between three and five years and some developed a deep attachment to the land, its people and their culture. Others regarded their postings to the remoteness and isolation of East Timor, with its relative poverty, poor facilities, bad communications and thin facade of culture, as an ordeal to be coped with. In the oppressive heat and discomfort of Dili their social intercourse was confined to the small ruling elite that met almost daily to yearn for the bright lights, restaurants and *fados* (folk songs) of Lisbon, or the more exciting and comfortable lifestyles of Lourenco Marques and Luanda. But the Portuguese had no monopoly on such subcultures and attitudes; they were present in any remote Western colony in which living conditions were difficult. The main problem to be faced in East Timor, which made it intolerably dull for many officials and their families, was the slow pace of life, the feeling that nothing was changing; then, paradoxically, as Indonesian anti-colonialism reached a frenetic pitch in the days of President Sukarno there loomed the spectre of uncertainty about the future. On the other hand some dedicated officials spent most of their careers in the province where they established a close rapport with the Timorese and took an interest in the island's culture and in its social and economic environment.

One interesting group was the *deportados*, the exiles who, mostly for political reasons, had fallen foul of the Salazar regime and had been deported to Timor. They included a former newspaper editor, army officers, communists, socialists and even liberals. Some married Timorese women and became coffee planters and, after the 1950s, gained a certain respectability in the eyes of the regime. Thus, Manuel Carrascalão, a former Young Communist who had been injured in a bomb-throwing incident in Salazar's first years in office, was rehabilitated following his courageous role during the Japanese occupation, and later became a member of the provincial assembly. His sons (by a Timorese woman) became leaders of the Timorese conservative party, the UDT. The second eldest, Mario, eventually became governor of the province after the annexation. Through intermarriage and their farming activities, most of the *deportados* developed a close affinity with the Timorese. They occasionally took up the latter's grievances with local officials or pressed the government to render assistance to depressed areas suffering from adversity. Their knowledge of the terrain and the Timorese proved invaluable to the Australian commandos in 1942. They also played a role in passing on ideas about democracy to the educated Timorese.

The pattern of cultures, religions, and lifestyles within East Timor was therefore both complex and diverse. Although there were ethnic links across the border with West Timor there was no real historical or ethnic basis for Indonesian claims to the allegiance of the people in the Portuguese colony. The exclusion of Indo–Javanese and Indonesian–Islamic influences from the area, and the effect of the long overlay of Portuguese cultural influence strengthened differences that already had a historic dimension. An early Portuguese source recorded that the two main groups in Timor differed:

> a great deal from each other, making up as it were two provinces and two peoples, the eastern part being inhabited by the Belus...and the western part by the Vaiquenos (the Portuguese name for the Atoni) in the province called Serviao.[4]

Differences were also exacerbated by differences in the character of Dutch and Portuguese colonial rule. The gap between Portuguese and Dutch cultures and intellectual traditions has always been a substantial one and its divisive effect on the Timorese could clearly be seen by visitors to Kupang and Dili at any time during the past 250 years.

Notes

1 Shepard Forman (Testimony before US Congress, 28 June 1977), in Human Rights in East Timor. Hearings before the Subcommittee on International Organizations of the Committee on International Relations of the US House of Representatives, 28 June and 19 July 1977 (Washington: US Government Printing Office, 1977), p.15.
2 Ibid., p. 17.
3 Elizabeth Traube, ibid., p. 21.
4 Quoted in H. G. Schulte Nordholt, *The Political System of the Atoni of Timor*, The Hague: Martinus Nijhoff, 1971, pp. 161-162.

Chapter Two
The historical background

Portuguese navigators ventured to the eastern islands of the Lesser Sundas shortly after their conquest of Malacca in 1511. It has been suggested that the Portuguese may have reached Timor as early as 1512, but probably the earliest reference to the island was contained in a letter, dated 6 January 1514, from the Commander of Malacca, Rui de Brito Patalim, which refers to its plentiful supply of sandalwood. However, the Portuguese were by no means the first outsiders. Decades before their arrival Chinese seamen had reached the island and had concluded that it was their best source for the supply of sandalwood. According to C. R. Boxer, 'A Chinese chronicle of 1436 remarked that "the mountains are covered with sandal-trees and the country produces nothing else"'.[1]

Although the Portuguese at once joined in the sandalwood trade, it was another fifty years before a settlement was established, and it was not on Timor, but on the island of Solor where Antonio Taveira, a Dominican friar, landed and set about converting the local population to Christianity. A mission station was established, and a fort constructed to protect the new converts from the marauding bands of Moslem raiders. The 'Islands of Solor', of which Timor was then considered a part, at once became an outreach of the diocese of Malacca, and its priests, most of them from the five Dominican religious establishments in India, converted thousands of the inhabitants of the islands of Flores, Lombok, Alor, Roti and Timor. Around the Solor fort a settlement of mixed races developed, consisting of 'the offspring of Portuguese soldiers, sailors, and traders from Malacca and Macao, who intermarried with the local women', and who were to become known as 'the Topasses' from the Dravidian word *tupassi*, meaning 'interpreter'.[2] Similar communities were soon established on Flores and Timor—indeed, when the Portuguese moved to Larantuka in Flores, in the face of Dutch pressures, the Topasses for a time became known as 'Larantuqueiros'.

This group of *mestiços*, whose descendants are still to be found in many parts of Timor, soon became the dominant element within the colony. It was the

Topasses who transmitted Portuguese culture and influence to Timor, and who alternated between supporting and challenging Portuguese rule. Two families, the de Hornays (who emerged from a marriage between a Dutch deserter and a Timorese convert) and the da Costas, produced two of the most powerful chieftains in Timor who, when they were not fighting each other, at various times challenged both the Dutch and Portuguese presence.

The first two centuries of Portuguese influence were largely taken up with missionary activities, although the priests eagerly participated in the sandalwood trade. Churches were built on several of the islands, and a seminary was established on Solor. In 1640, for example, there were said to be twenty-two churches and ten missionaries actively engaged in the propagation of the faith. Trade in sandalwood, horses and slaves prospered. However, with the decline of Portuguese power and the growing strength of the Dutch in the East Indies, the mission centres soon came under threat. The first major blow to Portugal was the loss of Malacca to the Dutch in 1641, followed by the seizure of the Dominican settlement at Kupang, Timor's best harbour. A few years later the Portuguese were expelled from Makassar, to which many of the refugees from Malacca had fled. But thanks largely to the loyalty and military prowess of Topasses like Antonio de Hornay the Portuguese were able to counter the Dutch threat to most parts of the Solor Islands colony. On Timor several of the chiefs had accepted Christianity and Portuguese sovereignty and, led by Domingos da Costa and de Hornay, they vigorously attacked the Dutch at Kupang and almost drove them from the island.[3] Earlier the Topasses, with Portuguese help, had overwhelmed the west Timorese kingdom of Wehale and had become the new *liurais* of Serviang, or Servião, on the western sector of the island. In eastern Timor lived the Bello, or Belu, people, who did not accept Portuguese overlordship until later, although in the long run they were to prove the more faithful colonial subjects. De Hornay's successes led to his emergence as the colony's military commander and, from 1673, the virtual ruler of the territory where missionary activities were beginning to decline as military, political and economic considerations came to outweigh the propagating work of the Dominicans.

It was not until early in the eighteenth century that the seat of colonial government was established on the island of Timor. At the time the island was divided into 62 petty kingdoms, 16 in Serviao and 46 in 'the province of the Bellos', many of whose elites had been converted to Catholicism, although somewhat superficially. According to Boxer, 'their attendance at the mission churches alternated with their participation in animistic sacrifices and orgiastic war-dances'.[4] Timor came under the viceroys of Goa, but the latter's authority was never strong, and from time to time the Dominicans combined with the Topasses to reject unpopular appointments of governors. For most of the second half of the seventeenth century the Topasses were the lords of the colony who summarily disposed of their opposition, including the Portuguese.

One of the most oppressive was Domingos da Costa who had installed himself as governor at Larantuka on Flores, having expelled his predecessor from that island. In a move to reassert the viceroy's authority, in 1701 Antonio Coelho Guerreiro was nominated first official governor of Timor and Solor. His arrival was obstructed by da Costa, so he moved the seat of colonial authority to Lifau in what later became the enclave of Oecussi, on Timor, where for most of his short appointment he was under siege from da Costa and his allies.

In his dealings with the *liurais* Coelho established a pattern of colonial administration that his successors were to emulate for more than two centuries. Although he was unable to obtain reinforcements he managed to erode the powers of most of the Timorese rulers one by one, and to make them dependent upon Portuguese authority. He conferred the rank of colonel on loyal *liurais* (with an occasional promotion to brigadier in especially deserving cases), and lower ranks on other leading officials of the kingdoms, a practice that continued to the last years of Portuguese rule. In this way Coelho Guerreiro was able to entice many of the Timorese elite formally to recognise Portuguese sovereignty. Nevertheless, after a brief respite, Portuguese authority was under intermittent challenge from those *liurais* who sought to oust the whites from the island, or as a consequence of Dutch intrigues. In 1769, one year after taking office, Governor Antonio Teles de Meneses took the historic decision to move the capital from Lifau to Dili. This offered better natural protection against surprise attacks, as well as calmer waters for shipping.

In a steady process of attrition the Portuguese lost to the Dutch their other possessions in the eastern part of the Lesser Sundas, and a border agreement concluded in 1859 was the first of a series of settlements that was to culminate in the agreement of 1913 known as the Sentenca Arbitral. After 1769 the Portuguese authorities came into closer contact with the people of eastern Timor, but this did not make their relations any easier or any better. They slowly penetrated the rugged interior of the island but, because of their weak military strength, (Meneses arrived at Dili with fewer than thirty troops at his disposal), and unrelenting opposition from some Timorese kingdoms, it was not until the mid-nineteenth century that the establishment of administrative and military posts in the inland districts began in earnest.

After the move to Lifau the military and economic roles of the colony began to assume greater importance than the missionary activities that had been predominant in the sixteenth century. Indeed, the governors grew increasingly impatient with the missionaries who had frequently become involved in revolts or opposition to Portuguese authority, and for some years after 1834 they were expelled from Timor. But, with the decline of the sandalwood trade and the further weakening of Portugal's position in Europe, so too declined Timor's importance as a part of Lisbon's far-reaching empire. In an atmosphere of deepening isolation, life in the colony lapsed into apathy, corruption, and squalor. For much of the time until the mid-nineteenth century Dili was under siege from the *liurais*, some of whom could put thousands of troops into the field of battle. However, the Portuguese survived and maintained a semblance of control by their command of the seas and by playing off one kingdom against another.

In those circumstances, from all accounts there was little glamour in the life of a colonial official or settler in East Timor. A Dutch visitor early in the nineteenth century was shocked at the squalor and misery of Dili where even the houses of the officials 'were miserable, dirty and poor'. As for the officials, they appeared 'to have given themselves up to an indolent mode of life, all their actions being redolent of laziness and apathy'.[5] Lord Wallace, who spent several months in East Timor between 1857 and 1861, described Dili as 'a most miserable place compared with even the poorest of the Dutch towns'.[6] Of the administration he wrote:

> The Portuguese government in Timor is a most miserable one. Nobody seems to care the least about the improvement of the country...after three hundred years of occupation there has not been a mile of road made beyond the town, and there is not a solitary European resident anywhere in the interior. All the government officials oppress and rob the natives as much as they can, and yet there is no care taken to render the town defensible should the Timorese attempt to attack it.

Wallace concluded:

> Timor will for many years to come remain in its present state of chronic insurrection and mis-government.

However, some other observers, such as H. O. Forbes, were less harsh in their criticisms of the Portuguese.[7] As it happened Forbes was in Timor at a time of relative peace, although the power of the *liurais* was far from broken. Nevertheless, the pattern of indirect rule, according to which local rulers retained autonomous powers in their territories, was already established, and was not so different from the Dutch practice in the neighbouring islands. Indeed, although conditions in Dili would have at the time seemed primitive when compared with those in Batavia or Surabaya, the position of the Dutch administration in the nearby Lesser Sundas was not so different. For example, Cora du Bois, in her work on the island of Alor, observed that the first Dutch administrator did not come to the island until about 1908. As late as 1938 there was only a handful of officials and one doctor.[8] In Dutch Timor there were few white officials outside Kupang until the beginning of the nineteenth century. Although Portuguese colonialism, as practised in Timor, continued to manifest a languid and squalid character throughout the nineteenth century, some important changes were taking place beneath the surface. True, the importance of sandalwood had declined, but such crops as wheat, sugar cane, coffee and potatoes had been introduced and by the 1850s were being exported in modest quantities. By 1881 coffee production had reached more than 2500 tonnes, though most of the profits would have ended up in Portuguese pockets.

A general decline in political and economic conditions at the end of the nineteenth century precipitated a further series of Timorese rebellions, and the

Portuguese were unable to regain complete control of their colony until the outbreak of World War I. An attempt by Governor Antonio Francisco da Costa to assert a tighter military and administrative control, and more effective tax collection, provoked an angry reaction from most of the Timorese rulers, and in 1893 the revolt of Maubara, one of the most important native kingdoms to the west of Dili, was the first of a series of uprisings that devastated much of the central sector of the colony. Thus, when Governor Celestino da Silva arrived to take up his appointment in 1894 his colony was in a sorry state. He was greeted with open revolt, internecine warfare, economic depression, and anarchy. In some areas agriculture had been abandoned, and annual coffee production, always the index of Timor's level of prosperity had declined to 800 tonnes.

In 1895, after two campaigns against rebel forces with only limited success, Celestino da Silva put together a force of some 28 Europeans and more than 12,000 other troops, most of them Timorese warriors supplied by loyal *liurais*, and set out to crush what by this time had become a major uprising led by Dom Boaventura of Same (then called 'Manufahi'). Several months of bitter fighting ensued with massacres being committed by both sides before Governor da Silva claimed victory and set about tightening up his military and civil administration. As a result of his military successes Timor became independent of the authority of the Portuguese colony of Macau and the governor was henceforth to be directly responsible to Lisbon. But the resistance was far from over and Timorese again and again challenged Portuguese authority and took up arms against the colonial forces. Thousands of them perished in battle and from diseases such as cholera, which swept across the land. Early in 1912, in an intense campaign against Boaventura in the Same area, according to Portuguese accounts, 3424 rebels died and 12,567 were wounded, with 289 killed and 600 wounded on the Portuguese side.

In Portuguese eyes Governor da Silva was one of the great governors of East Timor. Certainly he was largely responsible for the 'pacification' of the colony, but the cost in human suffering was enormous. In the periods of peace he also improved the administration, setting up 11 military district commands and 48 posts. He is also credited with having achieved a dramatic improvement in agriculture by introducing new crops and improved farming techniques, changes that were of most benefit to the Portuguese (da Silva founded SAPT, the largest plantation and export/import company in Timor), the *mestiços*, many of whom became prosperous planters, and the Chinese who became established as the merchants and middlemen of the colony.

On the eve of the outbreak of World War I, Portuguese Timor was undoubtedly the most economically backward colony in South-East Asia, its living conditions often a subject of derision to the few who ventured to it. But Portuguese authority had been established throughout the territory and the powers of the *liurais* substantially reduced. The boundary problem, which had frequently led to conflict with the Dutch, was settled in two agreements between Portugal and Holland, the Lisbon Convention of 1893 and the Sentenca Arbitral of April 1913. With a territorial administration now established, with improvements in agriculture, and in conditions of relative peace, East Timor seemed ready to go. In fact changes took place only very slowly, and the colony tended to drift into a torpid state, its remoteness and isolation shielding it from the mounting pressures for change elsewhere in South-East Asia. In the thirty years of peace before World War II the Portuguese returned to the earlier languid and apathetic form of administration. There was, as one observer put it, 'little administration and less development' although the 'officials managed to keep themselves occupied'. Schools had been established as early as 1734 at Oecussi and 1747 at Manatuto, but in 1940 there were only about 1000 children in primary schools in the entire territory.

Although the British, Dutch and French regarded the Portuguese colonial style with a mixture of disdain and amusement, if we take account of Portugal's small size and weakness as a European power after the seventeenth century, it is remarkable that Lisbon was able to maintain an empire, let alone an outpost like East Timor. Portugal emerged from World War I in dire economic straits and in a state of serious political instability. The coming to power of Dr Antonio de Oliveira Salazar in the late 1920s and the establishment a few years later of the *Estado Novo* (a fascist-style corporative state based on Mussolini's Italy) may have brought stability to Portugal, but it did not bring economic prosperity.

The Depression left Portugal on the verge of bankruptcy and by the time a measure of recovery was in sight the disruptive effects of World War II were already being felt. During this period the problems of Timor were disregarded or neglected. In the perspectives of the metropolitan government Timor barely registered its existence and, in any case, there were no funds available for its social or economic development. In Lisbon, Timor was known for its modest production of high-quality coffee and as a safe, distant place of exile for opponents of the Salazar regime. Economically, it was considered as something of an embarrassment, for although the coffee exports enriched a few Portuguese and Chinese, the colony of Timor was a drain, albeit a small one, on Portugal's meagre resources. Portugal's subsidy was so small that, apart from some road construction and other improvements in the administration's infrastructure, very little economic development took place on Timor. On the eve of World War II the capital, Dili, had no electricity and no town water supply; there were no paved roads, no telephone services (other than to the houses and offices of senior officials), and not even a wharf for cargo handling. According to the wife of a Portuguese official, who arrived at Dili in 1941, 'there was little of interest to offer the curiosity of outsiders. Apart from one or two exceptions, the design of buildings was simple, vulgar, and tending to uniformity'.[9]

But in those years if there was unrest among the Timorese, it was not manifested as opposition to Portuguese rule. Although the depressed economic conditions of the times had some effect on local production, their simple economy with its barter system was largely shielded against the worst effects of the Depression. To most Timorese the prevailing peaceful conditions would have been a pleasant alternative to the conditions of insecurity during the bloody wars of the past. There were the obligations of forced labour for the Portuguese, mostly in road work, but these working conditions were rather better than those imposed by the *liurais*. There was no talk of independence or nationalism. East Timor had been virtually sealed off from the neighbouring islands of the Netherlands East Indies and, in any case, the Indonesian nationalist movement showed no interest in the Portuguese colony. Furthermore, in the carefully controlled and censored education system of Salazar's Portugal the very few Timorese or *mestiços* who travelled to the metropolitan power to continue their studies were not exposed to the ideas of liberalism, socialism, nationalism or communism that in Britain, the Netherlands and France had sowed seeds of discontent and revolution among the indigenous elites of their South-East Asian colonies. While the *deportados* talked freely to their Timorese friends, to the *liurais*, *datos*, *chefes de suco*, and the few Timorese who had gained sufficient education to be admitted into government service, Western democratic ideas seemed strangely irrelevant to local conditions.

Timor's sleepy isolation was, however, to be shattered early in 1942 by events of World War II. The initial intrusion was not by the Japanese Imperial Army, but by Allied forces. Only ten days after the Japanese attack on Pearl Harbor a contingent of just above 400 Netherlands Indies and Australian troops disembarked from the transport *Soerabaja* and landed on a beach to the west of Dili, disregarding the protests of Governor Ferreira de Carvalho, who insisted that their 'protection' was unnecessary. It does seem that the Allied decision to intrude into East Timor and thus jeopardise its neutrality was based largely on speculation that the Japanese intended to invade and use the territory as a base for operations against Australia. In fact in several urgent diplomatic cables from Berlin the Germans stressed the paramount importance of respecting the neutrality of Portuguese territories. Evidently the Germans were apprehensive that any Japanese move against a Portuguese territory would provoke Lisbon into offering the Allies base facilities in the Azores, a move that would deal a severe blow to U-boat operations against Allied shipping. Had the Allies not intruded into the territory and transformed it into a war zone the Timorese may have escaped the ordeal they were subsequently to endure.

The Japanese, apparently convinced that the Allies planned to seize East Timor, ultimately committed more than 20,000 troops to what became a virtual occupation of the colony. The Australian 2/2nd Independent Company, later to be joined by the 2/4th, conducted an extraordinarily successful rearguard action against the Japanese for twelve months. This vigorous and enterprising campaign by a force of only about 400 men inflicted about 1500 casualties on their enemy in return for a loss of only about 40 men, and it has come to be acknowledged in Australia as one of the epics of the Pacific War. Much less well acknowledged and recorded are the terrible humanitarian consequences the conflict inflicted on the Timorese people, caught up in what was a struggle between two alien cultures.

The accounts of Australia's Timor campaign do show, however, that the success of this Australian rearguard action was in large measure due to the selfless support given the commandos by the Timorese with whom they developed an easy relationship, and the cooperation and assistance of most of the Portuguese.[10] The whole operation served to pin down a large number of crack Japanese troops at a time when Japan's forces were advancing towards Australia at an alarming pace. Mounting enemy pressure caused the Australians to be evacuated in January 1943. The Japanese then conducted punitive expeditions, sometimes using the notorious Black Column troops, at great cost in lives to the local population. Many fought on against the Japanese long after the Australians had departed, but the risk of savage reprisals was a deterrent to most. In areas where the Australians had been active, villages were razed and families wiped out, especially on the south coast between Uato Lari and Uato Udo, the atrocities being committed by both Japanese and Black Column troops.

These excesses ensured that most of the population remained bitterly hostile to the invaders until the very end. Although the Australians who served in Timor later repeatedly recorded their gratitude for the dedicated and selfless support they received from most of the Timorese, few seemed to fully appreciated the terrible suffering their intervention inflicted on the people of the territory, who may otherwise have escaped the war. The commandos brought the territory into the front line of the war, and then withdrew after only twelve months, in effect abandoning a people who had become partisan to their cause, but who were then left almost defenceless, to the whims of a vengeful and oppressive invader. For Australians in January 1943, the Timor campaign was a closed book; but for the people of Timor the war had only just begun.

The territory was placed under a tough military occupation, its people being regarded by the occupying authorities as hostile. The principal targets for retribution were those who had actively helped the commandos, including the large number of *criados*, the name for personal servants and guides. This forlorn group was virtually abandoned near the mosquito-infested mangrove swamps of Quicras, not far from the evacuation point used by the Australians. Some locals were evacuated during the campaign, but there was a clear preference for Europeans or *mestiços*, when the final evacuation took place on 10 January. Colonel Callinan, the force commander, later wrote:

> I told their leader, Dr Brandao, that I would attempt to evacuate all pure-blooded Portuguese. [As for the others] It was obvious to them that this was the end, and most of them would have to face alone the Japanese and their supporters; so it was a case of every man for himself.[11]

And it indeed became a question of the survival of the fittest. The *criados* were treated as collaborators by the Japanese and were executed or brutally treated if caught. A few became collaborators in a desperate effort to survive, for which they were to face severe punishment at the hands of the Portuguese after the surrender.

In most parts of the colony the war had a devastating effect on the livelihood of the Timorese. Many farms were abandoned, especially in fighting zones, and most of what little food production there was went in forced deliveries to the Japanese. In addition to the destruction caused by the war and by looting the occupiers, the Timorese had to endure devastating bombing raids by Allied aircraft operating out of Darwin. An intelligence report of August 1945 from the Services Reconnaissance Department provides a little insight into these ordeals.[12] In a reference to Allied bombing attacks, the reporting agents noted in passing that 'the only results of air attacks heard was the killing of a large number of Ossu natives in the large Christmas attack'. The report noted that in most areas the hamlets had disappeared, having been burnt to facilitate the search for 'whites', and that 'food is very scarce even in the villages, since the Japs' demands run very close to the supplies available'. It was also recorded that 'there is practically no meat available, the only food being maize, some rice, a few sweet potatoes, and very occasionally dried game meat in minute quantity'. Food demanded by the Japanese was 'never paid for except occasionally by invasion paper, whose value as cigarette papers is appreciated by the natives'.

The agents reported that the Timorese were yearning for a return of the Allies. 'They have pleaded with us to arrange an invasion immediately, since the Japanese are very weak, and an invasion would mean an end to the constant suffering under the Jap regime. The Japs beat the natives if their orders are not carried out to the letter.' The Timorese were 'forced to cooperate with the Jap [sic] in defensive measures since to do otherwise means severe castigation, sometimes death.' The agents' report also noted that the 'penalty for harbouring or assisting us or any other whites was death to the chiefs and all members of the village concerned'.

The Portuguese were not spared the cruel consequences of the war. For some time after the invasion the Portuguese colonial administration continued to function, its officials being instructed by the governor to remain neutral in the fighting raging around them. Most, though not all, of the colonial officials were unsympathetic to the Japanese and surreptitiously supported the Australian commando operation at great personal risk. The Japanese soon came to distrust all Portuguese, who were often humiliated or brutally treated by the invaders or, at the latter's behest, by the Black Column. A number of officials were murdered at their posts; an administrator at Manatuto who, because of his pro-fascist inclinations was not unsympathetic to the invaders, was shot by a Japanese patrol because he refused to supply them with a vehicle. To the *deportados* and the anti-Salazarists the war was a *cause célèbre*; they not only enthusiastically cooperated with the Allies, some continued to resist long after the Australian withdrawal, providing Allied military intelligence officials in Darwin with invaluable information about enemy shipping and aircraft movements, and ground operations. One such group was captured near Lacluta by the Japanese in August 1943 and its members were summarily executed.[13]

The war, the activities of the Black Column and Japanese intrigues which sought—at times with success—to reopen the wounds left by the uprisings earlier in that century and to exploit traditional rivalries between various *sucos* and kingdoms, soon made the position of the Portuguese administration untenable. By the end of 1943 Portuguese sovereignty was reduced to a zone of concentration at Liquiça, west of Dili, the hospital at Lahane, and the nearby residence of the governor. Communications with Macau were completely severed, and the colony's telephone system, linking the central administration with the outlying posts, was taken over by the Japanese. In areas where the Black Column operated freely the lives of the Portuguese district officials were in constant danger, and they eventually chose the comparative safety of the special zone at Liquiça. After a visit by a Portuguese delegate from Macau in March 1944 conditions improved a little and the internees of Liquiça were allowed to go to the nearby mountain village of Basartete where most were located when the war ended. Harsh oppression by the occupying forces continued, and with the deteriorating food situation and the lack of any form of health service many Portuguese were to join the thousands of Timorese who perished from hunger and disease.

Thus, when the Japanese finally surrendered the scene in Timor was one of human misery and devastation. Dili had been badly damaged by Allied bombing, and the other main towns and villages partly destroyed, either by bombing or by the wanton destruction inflicted by the occupying forces. One-quarter of the 400 Europeans had perished, some at the hands of the Japanese, others from starvation or disease. The human cost has never been precisely calculated, but it clearly was enormous. The Portuguese population figures give some indication of the great loss of life. In 1930 Timor's population was estimated at 472,221, while the figures for 1947 show that, despite a pre-war growth rate of just over one per cent, it had fallen to 433,412. Official estimates suggest that 40,000 Timorese died as a result of the war, but the real figure must have been much higher, probably more than half as high again, if the growth rate is taken into account.

As a result of the Allied intrusion in December 1941 and the subsequent military operations in the territory, East Timor was one of the great catastrophes of World War II in terms of relative loss of life. Having in mind the human cost alone, Portuguese Timor suffered far worse than any other South-East Asian country occupied by the Japanese. Yet, in the war histories and other accounts of the Timor campaign, this aspect has never been properly acknowledged. It was as if the people of Timor were such shadowy and anonymous figures that Australians, who bore a heavy responsibility for the catastrophe, simply could not comprehend their suffering and pain. Historians have, by and large, been insensitive to the anguish and injustice that lay behind what most recall merely as an epic military operation that weakened Japan's capacity to threaten Australia in

1942. Even in the press reports of the surrender of the Japanese in the Portuguese colony, the plight of the Timorese was clearly not a matter of great moment. On 27 September 1945 the Melbourne *Herald* reported the handing-over ceremony that had taken place on the waterfront of Dili three days earlier:

> In a moving ceremony attended by Australian Navy and Army officers, Merchant Navy and Portuguese officials, Timor natives, Arabs and Chinese on the banks of Dili Harbour, Portuguese Timor, respects were paid to Australian commandos who lost their lives in defence of the island...Natives freed from Japanese dominance waited patiently on the shore, keenly studying every movement of the six Australian navy ships anchored in the harbour...Brigadier Dyke then laid a wreath of bougainvillea and roses in memory of the victims of Japanese aggression in Portuguese Timor. The Governor laid a similar wreath in memory of the gallant Australians who fell in his territory. After the sounding of the last post by an Australian naval bugler the crowd dispersed, many in tears.[14]

In fact, the formal surrender of the Japanese forces on the island took place not at Dili but at Kupang where the commanding officer was located. The Japanese were soon moved out of East Timor to Atapupu on the Dutch side of the border, and the nightmare was formally over.

Two Portuguese warships arrived at Dili on 27 September, followed two days later by a troopship carrying a military expedition; a simple official communiqué that 'complete order has been established throughout Timor following the restoration of Portuguese sovereignty' marked the resumption, in practice, of Portuguese rule. The newcomers found a desolate and economically devastated colony. Even the governor, who had been a virtual prisoner in his residence, was in a 'threadbare half-starved condition', to use the words of the Australian diplomat, W. D. Forsyth, who was present at the surrender.[15] Most of the population were close to starvation. There was little commercial activity, the plantations of coffee, cocoa and rubber—the colony's most prosperous economic sector—had nearly all been abandoned, and most had degenerated into bushland, while Timor's livestock population had been reduced to less than a third of its pre-war level.

Dili was mostly in ruins, having been bombed almost out of existence by the Allies, and the roads were impassable. The war seemed to have taken the country back to the Stone Age. The task of reconstruction would have presented any colonial power with a challenge. As it turned out, Portugal, weakened as a result of the war in Europe, excluded from Marshall Plan assistance, and shunned by many Western European countries because of the regime's fascist character, was in no position to take up such a challenge. Furthermore, the rising tide of nationalism in South-East Asia and the virulent anti-colonialism of the Sukarno regime were to make the Portuguese position in East Timor seem increasingly insecure and indefensible, and to make the area unattractive for the modest government and private investment available in the postwar years. While Angola and Mozambique were able to tempt investors with the promise of profitable returns, Timor could offer nothing but uncertainty, in a land poor in natural resources.

There was, however, no agitation for change from the territory's indigenous population. The war left the Timorese rural economy, such as it was, devastated, and the savagery of the occupation left the people demoralised. On the other hand, the Japanese had not created the legacy of an indigenous challenge to the colonial order, as they had done in the Netherlands East Indies. They failed to turn the local population against the colonial power. A few Timorese no doubt willingly joined the Japanese, some serving in the notorious Black Column, but the Japanese practice of using the local recruits as cannon fodder in their fight against the Australians soon caused this service to lose its attraction. As the Australian force commander was to report later, the Timorese who were not forced into contact with the Japanese generally remained loyal to the Portuguese. Some even waged hopeless, and costly, guerrilla campaigns against the occupiers long after the Australians had withdrawn from the island. To most Timorese the Black Column was part of yet another *malai* (a Tetum word meaning 'foreigner') intervention which had created conditions infinitely harsher and more oppressive than those prevailing under the Portuguese, and had revived all the horrors associated with the wars earlier in the twentieth century. Indeed, in those circumstances most Timorese yearned for the peace and stability of the colonial rule between the world wars and so, in the postwar years the Portuguese, unlike the Dutch, French and British, did not have to contend with agitation for self-government.

In the postwar years the Portuguese colonial government reasserted its authority vigorously and, at times, ruthlessly, especially in those areas where loyalty to the Portuguese flag had been undermined. Movement from one area to another was more strictly controlled than before, and a closer surveillance of the border with West Timor was implemented, especially after Indonesia became independent in 1949.

In an atmosphere of apathy and uncertainty the rehabilitation and development of Portuguese Timor moved at snail's pace. As few funds were available from Lisbon, and the impoverished Timorese could contribute little to the colony's revenue by way of taxation, much of the extensive road repair work and the reconstruction of damaged buildings was carried out by a form of forced labour, arranged through the *liurais* or the chefes do suco. Following the proclamation of two organic laws, the first in 1951 and the second in 1953, all of Portugal's overseas territories, including Timor, became overseas provinces. Timor's first five-year plan was then launched with almost half of the appropriation being set aside for the reconstruction of the capital and the remainder being evenly divided between reconstructing the interior and the development of agriculture and livestock resources. In fact, little progress was made until the late 1950s. In spite of the sufferings of the people (including the Portuguese) during World War II, the territory's urgent needs were obviously not a matter of priority to the Salazar government. Indeed, between 1945 and 1958 the governors were usually of the modest rank of major or captain. Most of the development was concentrated around the administration, although some attention was at last given to the setting up of a broadly based primary school system.

When I took up the post of Australian consul in Dili in January 1962 the scars of the war that had ended sixteen years earlier were still very much in evidence. The rusty hulks of Japanese vessels still lined the harbour foreshore, while bomb-damaged buildings were to be seen in several parts of the town. There were no sealed streets or roads and it was only later in that year that the citizens of the capital were to enjoy the luxury of a town electricity supply. Some streets were sealed in 1963, and the Baucau airstrip, the province's main link with the outside world, was completed during this period. It was not until 1965 that the wharf at Dili was in use for shipping. Hitherto the port facilities of the capital had been grossly inadequate, the unloading of vessels being carried out by landing barges or, in the case of fuel, by the intriguing technique of rolling drums into the harbour current, which would slowly carry them on to the beach.

The capital had now taken on a new and pleasing appearance with its tree-lined streets screening traditional-style pastel-coloured houses, most of them for officials and the well-to-do. Although it was apparent to the visitor that Timor was a poor, undeveloped country, the general appearance was of a slow-moving, orderly and stable society with little evidence of racial tensions. Travel restrictions for security reasons were at that time unknown, and during my extensive tours of the interior and border areas of the province I was never escorted. The towns and villages all showed evidence of some reconstruction, and several of them, such as Ermera, Baucau and Maubisse, had become neat and attractive. Beyond the towns and administrative villages, more than 80 per cent of the population lived in tiny hamlets, in conditions little unchanged since the beginning of Portuguese colonisation.

The overall economy was, however, picking up from the depths to which it had plunged during World War II. Coffee production had risen from 700 tonnes in 1938, having declined to nothing during the war, to almost 2500 tonnes in 1963. Rubber and copra were also being exported in modest quantities, though production of these commodities had been affected by the unstable world market conditions of the previous five years or so. One important and encouraging development was a sharp increase in grain production. In 1963 production of maize reached 21,000 tonnes, and rice more than 10,000 tonnes. In addition more than 30,000 tonnes of sweet potatoes and manioc were harvested. For most of the Timorese peasants farming techniques had changed little, with slash-and-burn methods still extensively in use, but the agricultural scene in 1963 demonstrated that the province could easily become self-sufficient in food and thus substantially raise the level of nutrition. The livestock population rose impressively in the postwar years. When the Japanese surrendered there were only about 800 head of cattle left in the colony; by 1960 the number had risen to 24,000 and in 1969 to more than 67,000. The goat, pig and horse populations had more than tripled during the same period, while the figure for the water buffalo, the mark of prestige in village society, had doubled.

The postwar growth of education has already been mentioned. Initially, education was largely in the hands of the church missions which, as late as 1964, were responsible for about 60 per cent of primary school children. The pace of development continued during the 1960s and early 1970s. By 1973 the number of primary school pupils had risen to more than 57,000, or some 50 per cent of school-age children, in 456 schools. In 1974 there were about 1200 students in secondary education preparatory schools. There was no university in East Timor, and secondary education facilities remained limited, but by 1974 more than 1000 students were in various secondary institutions, ranging from the Lyceum to technical schools and the Jesuit seminary at Dare. For university education, the Timorese had to go to Portugal, and partly for this reason on the eve of decolonisation Timor had few university graduates. After having completed secondary school most chose to become teachers, enter government service or join the army.

While Portugal's authority was reasserted ruthlessly in the immediate postwar years, the process appears to have been much less harsh and traumatic than in neighbouring Dutch territories where the political order had been disrupted by the Japanese occupation and the subsequent challenge by the Indonesian nationalists. In Sulawesi, for example, according to Indonesian accounts almost 30,000 civilians died in the Dutch 'pacification' campaigns.[16] In Timor most collaborators served jail sentences, most of brief duration. Perhaps the best known was Arnaldo dos Reis Araujo, a leader of Apodeti, the party favouring integration, whom the Indonesians appointed their first governor of the '27th Province' shortly after the 1975 invasion.

By the early 1960s the character of Portuguese rule in Timor was not particularly oppressive, although there were constant reminders that the province was an integral part of Salazar's corporative state. The administration of Colonel Themuda Barata, the governor of the time, was akin to a benign paternalism, and cases of political repression were in reality few. A unit of PIDE (Policia Internacional e de Defesa do Estado—the Portuguese repressive apparatus) had been sent to the province to deal with 'communistic' subversive elements, but its agents were generally ineffective. The governor did his best to restrain its activities, discouraging PIDE agents from harassing *deportados* and other political dissidents. Nevertheless, the authorities maintained a tight censorship of the press and radio, and of material coming into the territory. The Timorese were able to have almost no contact with adjacent Indonesian territories, the exception being with the West Timorese, who were allowed to attend the weekly markets on the Portuguese side of the border, but under the watchful eyes of the frontier security authorities.

The fact that Portuguese rule was never challenged in East Timor while President Sukarno was in power in Indonesia seems remarkable, although it is clear why the Portuguese hold on the territory never became a target for the anti-colonial invective of the volatile Indonesian leader. Although Sukarno aspired to world leadership of the campaign against colonialism and imperialism, until 1962 his main target, to the point of obsession, was West Irian. And when West Irian had been 'regained', he became absorbed with the Konfrontasi campaign against Malaysia. In a sense, during the decade in which aggressive anti-colonialism was the preoccupation of Indonesian foreign policy, Portuguese rule in Timor survived by default. The exclusion of the colony from Jakarta's territorial claims was repeatedly used in both the West Irian and Konfrontasi campaigns to counter growing fears that Indonesia was bent on an expansionist course, and that Jakarta's ultimate goal was to absorb the adjacent territories. In reality, the Portuguese possessions in Asia were so inconsequential, and Portugal was so weak militarily and economically, that its presence was hardly taken seriously by the Indonesian leaders, whose attention was riveted on the Netherlands, the United States, Britain and, to a lesser extent, France. Portuguese Timor posed no strategic threat to Indonesia (the Portuguese took great care to avoid any action that might antagonise their large and often unpredictable neighbour), while the territory held no attraction from an economic point of view.

The Indonesians did let it be known that, although they laid no claim to East Timor, they would be happy to support any Timorese independence movement or other form of opposition to colonial rule. From the late 1950s representatives of a Timorese independence movement were based in Jakarta, but it was a nondescript set-up, with the leaders being almost unknown to the East Timorese, while the Indonesians gave the group little more than token recognition and encouragement.

In 1959 there was one serious incident involving Indonesians. It was the only act of rebellion against Portuguese rule in the postwar period, an uprising in the Viqueque area, and it shook the colony. It is unlikely that the Indonesian government was implicated or was aware of the conspiracy. It began with the unexpected arrival in the province of a boat carrying fourteen Indonesian remnants of the Permesta movement, one of the components of the so-called 'Colonels' Revolt', a rebellion against President Sukarno and the central government, whose leaders were mostly discontented territorial commanders. Perjuangan Semesta (Permesta for short, or Total Struggle) was a movement against the Indonesian central government led by the local military commander Colonel Warouw. Among the remnant were Lubis and Kawilarang from Jakarta, Simbolon and Hussein from Sumatra and Warouw, five colonels, and Major Sumual from East Indonesia. This party apparently fled from South-East Sulawesi in 1958 following the defeat of Permesta by an expedition sent from Jakarta. They asked the Portuguese authorities for political asylum, and were in due course given permission to remain in the Baucau area. Apparently the Indonesians soon found that the Portuguese colonial system was not to their taste, and they began to intrigue with dissident Timorese in the Viqueque–Ossu, Baucau–Uato Lari areas, and in Dili, in an attempt to organise the overthrow of the colonial regime. The exiles also managed to procure the support of the Indonesian consul in Dili, evidently acting without Jakarta's consent or knowledge. As things turned out a rejected lover of one of the leaders divulged the planned coup to the police in Dili and counter-measures were taken just in time. However, bitter fighting took place in the Ossu, Viqueque and Uato Lari districts where the Portuguese military made cynical use of the second-line troops of neighbouring kingdoms traditionally hostile to the Viqueque Timorese. The coup was suppressed swiftly and in bloody fashion. More than 150 were killed and many arrests were made. About 60 Timorese were exiled to Angola and Mozambique, while the Indonesian refugees were later expelled from the colony.

The consul was recalled by his government and reportedly reprimanded for his part in the affair. The Indonesian government disclaimed any complicity in the plot, but this the Portuguese, who were poorly informed about the political upheaval in Sulawesi, were inclined to doubt. There was little evidence that it was anything more than a local initiative by the Indonesian fugitives, able to exploit discontent among the local administration. The plot was rather amateurish and, even had it not been compromised, it probably would not have succeeded in dislodging the Portuguese—at least not without intervention from Indonesia.

The incident was never repeated. Disputes continued to occur at the border from time to time, occasionally leading to casualties or even loss of life. They usually erupted over such matters as cattle stealing or disputes within tribal communities straddling the frontier, and they posed no challenge to Portuguese rule. Such incidents did cause an outbreak of jitters in Dili and speculation about Indonesian intentions. A high point of such nervousness came in 1962 when the Dutch finally conceded West Irian to Indonesia. It was widely feared that East Timor would be the next target for liberation, but the *ganyang Malaysia* ('crush Malaysia') campaign introduced a new dimension, granting, it seemed, a reprieve to the colonial administration. As it turned out, after the Suharto regime came to power, relations between the Portuguese military authorities in East Timor and the Indonesian military on the other side of the island improved markedly. Hostility towards communism provided an element of strong common interest, while the Portuguese were impressed by the *Orde Baru's* efforts to normalise relations with Indonesia's nearest neighbours, and to dispel fears of Indonesian expansionism.

After 1966 arrangements were informally agreed to for the settlement of border problems, and a more relaxed atmosphere settled over the territory. By the early 1970s, Timor and Macau were the only Portuguese territories not under pressure from independence movements. By the time of the April Coup in Lisbon in 1974 a close personal relationship had developed between Colonel Aldeia, the Portuguese governor, and Colonel El Tari, the Indonesian governor of the province of East Nusatenggara, of which West Timor forms the main part.

Notes

1 C. R. Boxer, 'Portuguese Timor, a Rough Island Story: 1515-1970', *History Today* 10, no. 5 (1970), pp. 34-55.
2 C. R. Boxer, *The Topasses of Timor* (Amsterdam: Koninklijke Vereeniging Indisch Institut, 1947), p. 12.
3 Artur Teodoro de Matos, Timor Portugues: 1515-1769 (Lisboa: Instituto Historico Infante Dom Henrique, 1974), ch. 3.
4 Boxer, *The Topasses of Timor*, p. 14.
5 D. H. Kolff, *East Timor: Nationalism and Colonialism* (St Lucia: University of Queensland Press, 1978), quoted in Jill Jolliffe, p. 32.
6 Alfred Russel Wallace, *The Malay Archipelago* (London: Macmillan, 1869), quoted in Jolliffe, East Timor, p. 33.
7 Henry O. Forbes, 'On Some of the Tribes of the Island of Timor', *Journal of the Anthropological Institute* (1883): pp. 402-430.
8 Cora du Bois, *The People of Alor* (Minneapolis: University of Minnesota Press, 1944), p. 16.
9 Cacilda dos Santos Oliveira Liberato, *Quando Timor foi Noticia* (Braga: Editora Pax, 1972), ch. 2.
10 Bernard J. Callinan, *Independent Company* (London: Heinemann, 1953), pp. xxivxxv.
11 Ibid., pp. 216, 222.
12 Intelligence report, Operation SUNLAG, Services Reconnaissance Department, 21 August 1945 (courtesy of the Australian War Memorial Library).
13 Carlos Brandao, *Funo: Guerra em Timor* (Oporto: Ed. AOV, 1946), ch. 11.
14 Melbourne *Herald*, 27 September 1945.
15 W. D. Forsyth, 'Timor II: The World of Dr Evatt', *New Guinea and Australia, the Pacific and South-East Asia*, 10, no. 1 (1975), pp. 31-37.
16 George McTurnan Kahin, *Nationalism and Revolution in Indonesia* (Ithaca: Cornell University Press, 1952), p. 145.

Chapter Three

The last years under
Portuguese rule

Although subtle changes took place in the pattern of Portugal's administration of its most remote territory in the period following World War II, the assumptions underlying Salazarist colonial rule, and the very low position held by East Timor in Lisbon's order of priorities, were hardly conducive to any shifts of a radical nature. First, the economy of the metropolitan power continued to be weak as Portugal did not share in the dramatic resurgence of economic activity in Western European countries in the 1950s. The Portuguese escudo remained stable, but by 1965 the nation had become the poorest in Western Europe. The central government in Lisbon pinned its hopes for recovery on the glittering prospects offered by its African possessions, especially Angola, while far-off Timor was merely a drain on Portugal's diminishing resources, a poor, backward territory with an uncertain future. In 1964 a senior Portuguese official confided that his country would be happy to turn East Timor over to the United Nations, if it were not for the implications such a move would carry for the other overseas provinces. For many civil servants a posting to Dili was a kind of penance, and the Timor province was seldom visited by top-ranking officials.

After 1966 the Suharto regime became firmly entrenched in power in Jakarta and as unrest and insurgency gripped Portugal's African possessions the Timor province became one of the few peaceful and stable segments of the sprawling Portuguese empire, but the demands of the wars in Angola, Mozambique and Guinea–Bissau further eroded the metropolitan power's capacity to invest in Timor's development. As the regime in Lisbon mobilised its full military might in a desperate bid to retain the African provinces of such vital importance to Portugal's economy, Timor remained at the bottom of the priority order. Yet the Portuguese became more relaxed and confident about their South-East Asian colony, reducing their military presence. More than half of the European military force which, at one time, amounted to more than 2000 men, was sent to Africa where the pressure of insecurity was mounting each year. The places of the Portuguese were eagerly taken by Timorese who soon formed the bulk of the regular forces in the province. By 1975 all of the ordinary ranks and most of the NCOs were Timorese, but it was not until the last year of Portuguese rule that a couple of full-blooded Timorese, among them Rogerio Lobato, were promoted to commissioned rank—that of *alferes*, or junior lieutenant.

Although the organic law was introduced in 1953 Timor was only formally declared an overseas province in November 1963. Its legislative council came into existence a year later with eleven elected members. After a few years this became a legislative assembly with its membership expanded to twenty-one, ten of whom were elected by a limited direct suffrage, based on property and literacy qualifications. The remainder were chosen along corporative lines, that is, two members chosen by the administrative corps; two members by businesses, associations and economic interests; two members by unions and professional associations; two members by 'cultural and moral interests'; and two by the governing authorities. The function of the assembly was to 'advise and assist' the governor who presided over its meetings. Real power rested in the hands of the governor, the representative of the 'Government of the Portuguese Nation'. He exercised legislative functions when the assembly was not in session. Consistent with the authoritarian character of the corporative state, the assembly functioned as an arena for the mobilising of public support for policies generated in Lisbon, and as something of a barometer of public opinion. Its composition always assured the governor of a comfortable majority, obviating the need for him to exercise his power of veto. The assembly played little role in preparing the Timorese for self-government, an outcome alien to the Salazar regime. The few Timorese who served on it were mostly *liurais* whose vested interest was that of preserving feudal power and privileges derived from indirect rule. The province also elected a deputy to the national assembly in Lisbon, and as with other provinces it sent 'electors' to cast votes for the president of the republic. However, these functions more closely resembled ceremonial roles than exercises in democracy.

Before the coup of April 1974 the political system in East Timor simply reflected the character of the Portuguese dictatorship, though it was somewhat tempered by the province's remoteness and the limited number of personnel available for control and repression. As in Portugal, a single political party and other functional organisations served to mobilise support for the regime, rather than to act as a check on its actions and policies. No serious opposition was permitted to exist. The power and the authority of the state were reinforced by the political repressive apparatus PIDE (later to become DGS, the Directorate-General of Security) which, in Timor, kept the 'oppositionists' and other malcontents under surveillance and occasionally took repressive action against them. PIDE also kept a careful watch on potential sources of 'harmful' outside influence, including the increasing flow of tourists from Australia and, not least, the occasional visitors from Indonesia.

Security and surveillance outside towns were largely the responsibility of the provincial administration which managed the control of movement from one area to another and other political matters through the *chefe* (later *administrador*) *do posto*, the equivalent of a patrol officer in colonial New Guinea and through the *chefe de suco* and *liurai*. Of even greater significance, however, was the tight censorship of the media which were in government hands. Through the government's control of the one newspaper, *A Voz de Timor*, with a circulation of between 4000 and 7000 copies per week and of the radio station near Dili, in Timor's remote circumstances it was able to ensure that the literate segment of the population heard and read what it wanted them to know. Most of the foreign news came in censored form from Portugal and the other overseas territories (with little about the growing unrest and dissident activity in Guinea–Bissau, Angola and Mozambique), and there was almost no reporting of events in the South-East Asian region. Thus, during the intense stages of the West Irian and Konfrontasi campaigns the Timorese were told little about the turbulent events taking place in neighbouring Indonesia. Radio Australia provided an important alternative source of information to those who had access to short-wave radios but, until the last years of Portuguese rule, only a handful of Timorese spoke English well enough to understand its broadcasts. Better informed were the young Mandarin-speaking Chinese, avid listeners to foreign Chinese-language programs.

The colony's remoteness and its linguistic isolation—Tetum bearing little resemblance to modern Bahasa Indonesia, apart from some word-borrowing from the Malay and Javanese languages—presented natural obstacles to the penetration of outside ideas, including nationalist sentiments and the spirit of anti-colonialism. It should also be noted that the Portuguese were greatly assisted in their control measures by a lack of outside interest in the undermining of the established order, and by the low level of both political awareness and political discontent among the Timorese. It was only in the early 1970s that occasional articles indirectly critical of the system began to appear in the Catholic publication *Seara*, some of whose contributors—who included Nicolau Lobato, Jose Ramos Horta, Francisco Xavier do Amaral, Manuel Carrascalaõ, Domingos de Oliveira, Francisco Borja da Costa and Mari Alkatiri—were later to emerge as leaders of the two main political parties.[1]

It is a curious fact that although the border with Indonesian Timor divided some *sucos*, who maintained contact (usually on market days on the Portuguese side) even during times of tension, these districts were never sources of disaffection, or of opposition to Portuguese rule. One reason is that the border areas of Indonesian Timor were a kind of quiet backwater, compared with the turbulent political currents, the conflict and the intrigue elsewhere in Indonesia, at least until 1966 when the blood-letting that followed the attempted coup of September 1965 also spread to West Timor. However, this event hardly endeared the system under which their neighbours lived to the Timorese on the Portuguese side. True, the border people perceived some obvious benefits of life in Indonesia, but they also became acutely aware of its disadvantages, its unsettled character. There education was more extensive, and thus the level of literacy was higher, and the people in the Indonesian province could move about more freely, but, economically, it was a very poor area that the central government in Jakarta had sadly neglected. For example, the best attended markets were those on the Portuguese side of the border, the markets in Indonesian Timor having little for sale, and then only at exorbitant prices. When I visited Bobonaro, one of the main border towns on the eastern side, in mid-1974, a Timorese who had just returned from a visit to the Indonesian province declared:

> There would be no point in our joining with Indonesia after decolonisation. Their side is poorer than ours, and instead of the Portuguese over us we would have the Javanese. This would be recolonisation, not decolonisation.

Many people in the neighbouring Indonesian province openly resented Java's Moslem and military overlordship and this caused most of the Timorese leaders, after 1974, to regard Javanese rule as essentially a colonial manifestation. Despite Portuguese efforts to discourage any provocative actions or statements that might antagonise the Indonesians, between 1958 and 1966 a steady undercurrent of anti-Indonesian sentiment developed in East Timor.

During the West Irian and Konfrontasi crises the Portuguese became resigned to an inevitable attempt by the Sukarno regime to seize their province at some time and such apprehensions were imparted to the Timorese with whom they came in closest contact. Although it was the policy of the provincial government to avoid provoking Indonesia, this did not prevent individual officials from constantly reminding the Timorese of the disasters that would befall them in the event of the departure of the colonial power.

In its last fifteen years the provincial territorial administration was developed considerably, although the pattern and style of colonial rule changed little. The province was divided into thirteen administrative divisions, called *concelhos* or councils (previously called *circumscriptions*), with populations ranging from 25,000 in Oecussi to 84,000 in Baucau. The administration of the *concelhos* was headed by the *administrador do concelho* whose local powers and discretion were in practice very extensive. Apart from his administrative duties, he exercised the powers of a magistrate, chief of police, commander of second-line troops, coordinator of economic activity and development plans, and so on. He also usually acted as mayor of the town in which his office and residence, invariably a spacious and solid Portuguese-style dwelling, bustling with servants, was located. The *administrador do concelho* was usually Portuguese, although not necessarily white—there were one or two Goans and some *mestiços*. These senior officials tended to be authoritarian, politically conservative, and loyal servants of the old regime, but some were highly trained and, by doing their best with the limited resources available to them, won the respect of the people of their districts. Others sought merely to preserve the status quo and to enjoy the perks of office.

The *concelho* was divided into between four and six *postos* or subdistricts, each administered by an *administrador do posto*. By 1974 there were some 58 *postos*, and the staffing pattern had changed in the previous decade, with 60 per cent of these posts now being filled by Timorese, who were generally less conservative and had closer links with the people than the *concelho* administrators. These officials were among the Timorese to become politically active when, after April 1974, the new regime permitted the formation of political associations. Unlike their Portuguese masters, the young Timorese post administrators as a rule harboured little enthusiasm for the practice of indirect rule. They favoured reducing the powers of local rulers, as a step towards a more democratic system. They also developed a more informal relationship with their communities in their *postos*, sometimes joining with the *chefes de suco* to resist the oppressive demands of the *liurai*.

The Portuguese military occupied a leading role in East Timor, a role it had played since the eighteenth century. In the long history of the Portuguese presence most of the governors had been army officers (all since the end of World War I), and from time to time the colony had been under direct military administration. In times of crisis, the army often had to cope with the consequences of maladministration or missionary intrigues. In the postwar years, especially in the 1960s and 1970s, the army became increasingly critical of the civil administration and of conditions in Timor in general. This was particularly true of the junior officers. Many of them felt that the army would have to suffer the consequences of a system of administration that was outdated, and had achieved little after so long. (This attitude was one of the ingredients of the discontent which eventually erupted into the April Coup in Lisbon in 1974.) Then there was the problem of boredom. A posting to East Timor was a dull prospect after the bright lights of Lisbon and the more developed African colonies. On the other hand, as insecurity resulting from the widening insurrection engulfed Portugal's African empire, the prospect of a two-year sojourn in the peaceful environment of the remotest province became much more enticing.

From 1960 onwards the Timor military command, usually under a colonel, was divided into several military regions, the most important of which was the frontier region with its headquarters at the town of Bobonaro. The number of European troops varied, reaching a high point of only about 2500 in the early 1960s, including infantry, an artillery battery and a cavalry unit equipped with light armoured vehicles. Although for centuries the Portuguese had used Timorese warriors in large numbers to bolster their small garrisons, it was not until the 1960s that they began to train the Timorese for service in the regular army. They were to discover, not surprisingly, that the Timorese, with their long-standing warrior traditions, adapted easily to modern soldiery. Gradually Timorese soldiers took the place of Europeans, and by 1974 there were almost 3000 fully trained Timorese in the regular army (as mentioned earlier, many were noncommissioned officers, but none was an officer), and a second-line force of perhaps 7000 with basic military training. Thus, by August 1975, as Governor

Lemos Pires was to lament when the civil war broke out, there were only about 200 troops from Portugal in the colony, just 70 of them combat troops.

The process of bringing Timorese into the regular army ranks contributed to the growth of political awareness among the educated. A large part of the military training was in the hands of non-commissioned officers and the *alferes*, or junior lieutenants. Many of the *alferes* had been conscripted from the ranks of university students or young graduates in Portugal who tended to be opposed to the Salazar regime. As a group they tended to develop close relations with the Timorese soldiers under them, whose education they sought to advance. But the political consciousness they awakened was not about nationalism, but about opposition to fascism, or specifically to the authoritarian corporative state that Salazar's Portugal resembled. They knew little about politics in the developing world, and even less about the radical changes that were taking place in South-East Asia.

Junior-officer contacts with the Timorese were expanded through the special role played by the army in the last twenty or so years of Portuguese rule when these officers began to supplement the existing primary and secondary educational facilities. (By 1973 there were more than ninety military schools, or *escolas militar*.) Many of these part-time—and voluntary—teachers came from the ranks of the politically unreliable officers whose academic qualifications were not matched by military skills, and those who had developed a caring interest in the Timorese. In this way, the Timorese often got better instruction from the military than was available to them from the ordinary teachers. For example, the Lyceum in Dili had the services of Colonel Pastor Fernandes who was in virtual exile for his part in an abortive coup attempt against Salazar in 1959. Fernandes was a liberal intellectual and physicist, formerly a professor at the military academy in Portugal. A former associate professor of medicine who had been arrested and exiled for being in possession of socialist literature was also working as a part-time teacher. For the troops in the interior of the island, teaching broke down the monotony of their isolation, and forged links with those Timorese with a thirst for education. As early as 1966 these special schools, as they were called, made up more than 15 per cent of the total.

The unrest that spread through the ranks of the armed forces in Africa also infected the attitudes of Portuguese troops in East Timor, especially from the rank of captain downwards. The senior officers generally were loyal to the regime, although even they were privately disparaging about the low level of development, the poverty of the people, and the business monopoly of the Chinese in the colony. But some of the discontent and growing radicalism of the junior officers and the ordinary ranks clearly rubbed off on their Timorese subordinates, especially the non-commissioned officers. The Portuguese army's increasing disenchantment with the established order and the economic system in Portugal of growing affluence at the top and increasing poverty at the bottom, and their bitterness at having been conscripted to serve the hopeless and unreal cause of Portugal's 'civilising mission', ultimately affected the thinking of the educated Timorese. This influence helps to explain why years later, in 1975, the Timorese troops were, by and large, more attracted to the radical Fretilin movement than to the relatively conservative UDT, whose leaders tended to be more concerned to preserve the status quo in the province. Further, the military at all levels were hostile to the political repressive apparatus (PIDE/DGS) and obstructed its attempts at surveillance, thus protecting dissident views and activities from security countermeasures. In Timor where the PIDE delegation was small and where its profile was deliberately kept low so as not to attract the critical attention of the increasing flow of Australian tourists, the army seemed to enjoy a kind of immunity from its activities, an immunity certainly not shared by the civil administration. Portuguese African political values also affected the Timorese or *mestiço* soldiers who had seen service in the African territories. These included Roque Rodrigues, son of a Timorese mother and Goan father, whose political views were profoundly influenced by Frelimo sympathisers he met while serving as an *alferes* in Mozambique. Today Rodrigues is defence minister in the new republic.

The considerable broadening of Portugal's education program in East Timor during the last decade of Portugeuese rule has already been described. In health and social welfare the colonial power's achievements were unimpressive and have been the subject of a good deal of justified criticism. In spite of some improvements in the last fifteen years, on the eve of independence the health of the Timorese population was seriously undermined by diseases such as tuberculosis and malaria which, compounded by continuing malnutrition, kept infant mortality at a staggering level with some observers claiming that, in a few areas, it had reached as high as 50 per cent in the early 1970s. Foreign observers often criticised the Portuguese for their lack of doctors, hospitals and equipment, but East Timor was much better off in this respect than the neighbouring Indonesian province of East Nusatenggara. In 1973 there were more than twenty doctors in East Timor, two regional hospitals and eight district medical centres (which the Portuguese sometimes called hospitals). There were 48 health posts throughout the province, staffed by paramedical personnel.

The hospital in Dili, the main medical centre, was well equipped by contemporary standards in the region. In 1966 Willard Hanna, a visiting US authority on South-East Asian affairs, described it as 'a first-class institution, with a well-equipped operating room and a full staff of doctors, including various specialists, who can and do call upon military doctors for assistance'.[2] The military doctors were considered a part of the general medical service and were usually in the majority (in 1973, fourteen of the medicos were from the military). As in most colonial situations the problem was that the medical services were largely concentrated in the towns and larger villages, barely reaching the *povoaçoes* where some 70 per cent of the population—and the most needy—lived. In the last years of Portuguese rule there were, however, a number of successful vaccination campaigns which appear to have reached most of the population. There were also efforts to reduce the incidence of tuberculosis in some of the worst-affected mountain districts. Malaria and influenza, however, continued to take many lives with more than 60,000 cases of each of these scourges registering for treatment annually.

The most neglected areas were disease-control, nutrition and lack of elementary health services at the village level, accessible to the population at large. In spite of these shortcomings there was evidence that the health and appearance of the population had improved markedly in the decade before mid-1974. In 1974 I visited some of the worst-affected areas and it was clear from the physical condition of the inhabitants of villages like Leti Foho and Atsabe, and from the presence of health posts, that the position was very much better. The rate of population growth was increasing rapidly: in the 1950s the rate was about 1.6 per cent, rising to 1.7 per cent in the 1960s. According to official figures the rate had grown to 2 per cent by the mid-1970s. Whatever the shortcomings of the Portuguese system, health and nutrition conditions appear to have been no worse than in the adjacent Indonesian islands.

By 1974 the economy of the province was improving up, but its character had changed little. Not far from Dili's thin facade of affluence most of the Timorese continued to eke out a bare existence in their form of subsistence agriculture that was often based on the destructive *ladang* or slash-and-burn system, maize being the principal crop. The Chinese merchants' control of retail commerce was firm and they had strengthened their position in the cultivation and export of coffee. The little economic advancement that had taken place benefited mainly the Chinese, the small Portuguese business community, and a number of coffee planters (the most prosperous of whom were Chinese, Portuguese, *mestiços* and some Timorese— often *liurais*). Coffee was the dominant commercial crop. In 1973 coffee accounted for 146,000,000 escudos of the total value of exports of 161 million escudos. Timor's income from non-coffee exports amounted to only about AUD8000—a mere 10 per cent of the total—the latter figure including copra, the only export commodity of which the Timorese were among the main producers.

Of the twenty-five largest enterprises in Timor, all but two Portuguese firms were Chinese. These were SAPT, established by Governor Celestino da Silva at the end of the 1800s, and SOTA, the successor to the pre-war Asia Investment Company that had come under Japanese control. Both of these firms covered the full spectrum of business activity in Timor: they possessed large plantations (mostly coffee) and engaged in import/export, wholesaling and retailing. SAPT was the enterprise more closely linked with the provincial government which held 48 per cent of its shares. The largest Chinese firm, and the most dynamic business in the province, was Sang Tai Hoo, owned by two brothers who dominated the province's commercial contacts with Asia, mainly with Hong Kong, Singapore and Macao. The major Chinese enterprises were also involved in most aspects of economic activity in Timor. All in all there were more than 400 such businesses, which between them controlled about 95 per cent of business activity in the Portuguese territory. Not all Chinese were affluent, a fact that community leaders were quick to point out that some 20 per cent were no better off than the Timorese, although by this they did not mean the hamlet Timorese, but the rather more affluent indigenous component of town populations.

There was very little industry in the province. What there was remained undeveloped and organised on a local artisan basis. There was some wood preparation and furniture manufacturing on a small scale, some textile processing, and alcohol and bread production. Apart from the undersea oil deposits to the south of the island, East Timor is yet to be proven to be rich in minerals, although for years Portuguese administrations placed high hopes on the discovery of oil or copper deposits in commercially exploitable quantities. In the postwar years oil offered a kind of panacea for Timor's future. Because it actually seeped out of the ground at a location near the town of Suai, the Portuguese presumed that a rich discovery was only a matter of time. However, although an Australian-based company, Timor Oil Ltd, carried out exploratory operations in the area from 1956 onwards, sometimes in a desultory fashion, the only real prospect, according to my information, appeared to be in offshore drilling.

In 1972 an Australian company, International Oils Exploration and Amalgamated Petroleum, negotiated a 'farm-in' agreement with Timor Oil which resulted in the drilling of two wells near Betano on the south coast of the province, and after some encouraging reports of oil traces a similar arrangement was entered into with Woodside-Burmah in February 1974, with the search being extended offshore from the south coast. Meanwhile, the Broken Hill Proprietary Company (BHP) obtained a concession early in 1972 for onshore exploration of possible mineral resources. BHP's main interest at the time was said to be in steel-hardening additives. These exploration activities terminated in 1975 when the political situation in the province began to deteriorate, and little is known about what was achieved.

The one industry that had a promising future was tourism. Although there had been a slow trickle of curious visitors in the 1950s, it was not until 1963 that the first contingent of tourists from Darwin arrived in Timor, emerging from a TAA Fokker Friendship that had just touched down on the newly constructed airstrip at Baucau. This excellent strip had been designed to accommodate Boeing 707 and DC8 airliners, and the Portuguese had hoped to siphon off some of the international flights between Australia, New Caledonia and New Zealand on the one hand, and Singapore on the other, in the days when most aircraft refuelled at Darwin. Unfortunately, by the time this fine strip was completed, the era of longer-haul flights had arrived, and even Darwin's importance rapidly diminished.

The role of the church
One very important component of the Portuguese colonial system was the Catholic Church. Yet the Timorese were not predominantly Christians. Although missionary activity was Portugal's main preoccupation in the colony for most of the first two centuries, by 1975 the number of baptised Catholics was only

200,000, or about one-third of the total population. This relatively low level of conversion seems all the more surprising because the church had a free hand in Timor throughout the long period of colonial rule, during which it did not have to compete with Islam or with Protestant missions. Furthermore, for the first two centuries the Dominican friars, many of them Goans, were the predominant power and influence in the colony. The Topasses grew up in the social and political environment created by them.

In this early period the missionaries were closer to the Timorese than were the military and colonial administration establishments. On more than one occasion the missionaries joined with the Topasses or other *liurais* in rebellions against the colonial government. But the clergy in Timor was rather less aggressive than elsewhere in Asia in its crusades to propagate the faith. Also, in the nineteenth century the Portuguese authorities moved to reduce the power of the missionaries who were expelled from the colony for a time. For some years then there were only four or five missionaries in East Timor. In the first phase of its penetration the church did have an effect by indirect means on the Timorese élites, often antagonising the Portuguese colonial authorities.

The modern period of the church's development began after 1912, that is, after the wars of pacification, when conditions for missionary activities were again favourable. Even so the rate of conversions before the outbreak of World War II was not very impressive because of the low level of education and the lack of funds during the depression years, and not least because of a certain apathy and lack of motivation for missionary work on the part of the clergy. The suffering and devastation of the years under Japanese occupation gave some impetus to the work of the missions in the postwar period, especially in the field of education in which the church was to play the major role. For example, of the 39 primary schools in the colony in 1952, 33 were run by the missionaries. In that year there were about 60,000 Timorese Christians, with the figure being augmented by another 10,000 annually.[3] There were 34 missionaries, of whom 28 were secular priests, and only one was not Portuguese.

By 1974 the Catholic establishment had increased to 44 priests (25 of them Timorese), 8 brothers, 49 nuns, 160 teachers and 37 catechists. The number of Catholics had increased dramatically to 196,570 in 1973—out of a population of 659,102 (church estimate). There were more than 80 mission posts in the three parishes of the province, though many did not have priests permanently in residence. By the early 1970s East Timor had virtually become a Catholic state, although baptised Christians were still in the minority. Catholicism was the religion of the elite and of all those with some semblance of education, as well as of thousands of illiterates. The *liurais* and other chiefs had for the most part been converted in the eighteenth and nineteenth centuries. Indeed, one governor had decreed that the children of the chiefs must attend religious schools. As the religion of the leaders and the literate, Christianity soon became a kind of status symbol, although many baptised Christians continued to retain their animist beliefs and superstitions. On the other hand, the educated Timorese were more disciplined in the practice of their faith than were the Portuguese. For example, even some left-wing Fretilin leaders attended mass daily, a degree of devotion observed by very few expatriates.

In the twentieth century the spread of Christianity served two important purposes from the Portuguese state's point of view. It had a unifying effect and, particularly under the Salazar regime, the church was considered an important vehicle for the promotion of patriotism. The Portuguese flag in many *sucos* had become a prized *lulik*, and it was paraded and virtually worshipped in some districts. The flag and the church were presented as symbols of the temporal and spiritual majesty of Portuguese civilisation. The church in Timor was of a secular character and in the *Estado Novo* it functioned in a kind of alliance with the state.

In 1940 Portugal signed a Concordat and Missionary Agreement with the Vatican, under which religious activities in the overseas provinces were regulated. In matters of religion this institutionalised the authority of the church, and in matters mundane it promised the security of an assured income. But in a number of ways the church suffered from this cosy alliance. Not least, it appeared to have become bureaucratic and undynamic, most of its officials accepting uncritically the dubious social and political goals of the Salazar regime. The church did not accept all government policies, but its commitment to the basic objectives of the regime afforded it little scope for independent action. In a sense the state perceived the central role of the church as giving a moral legitimacy to Portugal's revamped colonial order and its historic 'civilising mission'. Within this framework there was little room for the expression of a social conscience.

In spite of the constraints imposed by its role within the corporative state, and of the apathy of some of the clergy, in the postwar years the church became an influential and respected force among the Timorese, including those who had not espoused the faith. The clergy had not resorted to coercion to bring about conversions, and there were no anti-Catholic movements in Timor to generate negative or hostile attitudes. But, more importantly, the priests were respected for their tolerance and their frequent timely intervention with the administration on behalf of Timorese seeking to redress injustices or to obtain assistance of one kind or another. Also, the clergy often visited remote villages that were seldom seen by *concelho* officials. Its representatives regularly collected information and statistics. The villagers were less inhibited in their relations with church officials than with those of the state because the former neither taxed nor punished them. The church officials' demands were few and most priests were prepared to take up grievances against local officials or *liurais*, often providing the most effective channel open to the Timorese. In times of distress and suffering, for instance during the Japanese occupation and after the Indonesian invasion, the people turned to the clergy for succour and comfort, although there was often little the church could do to bring about real relief.

The church in Timor was not without its serious shortcomings, apart from the apathy and conservatism of many of its priests. Its social work tended to be concentrated on the main towns and villages where most of the Catholics were to be found, and the most needy received too little of its attention. The church's capacity to act as a social conscience and to press for reforms, as in Latin America, was seriously weakened by its alliance with the state, and its dependence on the latter for financial support. On the other hand, with more than 80 mission posts the church's information resources were probably the best in the province. Many officials believed that the Catholic Mission's record of the census was more reliable than the figures collected by the government, thus, in 1973, according to the official mid-year estimate, East Timor's population stood at about 649,000, but as the Church Mission assessed it the figure was 659,102 people. As in the early years of Portuguese influence, the clergy, with their mission posts and extensive role in primary education, had a closer and more informal relationship with ordinary Timorese than any of the other arms of the Portuguese colonial establishment in Timor.

No account of the place of the Catholic church in East Timor would be complete without mentioning the role of the Jesuits who ran the Seminary of Nossa Senhora de Fatima at Dare, in the hills behind Dili. The Jesuits had been in Timor for only a century or so, and theirs was a chequered career, reflecting the uneasy relationship between church and state that had persisted until Salazar came to power—and also suspicious attitudes towards the Jesuits from within the hierarchy of the Portuguese branch of the church. As recently as 1910 some Jesuit priests and Canossan sisters were expelled from Soibada and Manatuto.

The importance of the tiny group of Jesuits in recent times was in their role from 1958 as teachers in the seminary which, apart from being the highest institution of learning in the colony, was attended mostly by Timorese, rather than the sons of Portuguese officials. The Jesuits were often critical of the colonial system and social conditions in the province and some of the priests sought to enlighten their charges about the changing scene elsewhere in Asia, about the nationalist movements, and occasionally about more progressive approaches to development. From the Timorese point of view the environment of the seminary was much less conformist and conservative than in other high schools, and an easy informal atmosphere prevailed within its grounds. The seminary tended to make the Timorese more conscious of themselves, their country, its colonial predicament and its future. In other schools there was a much greater emphasis on things Portuguese, in which the small, remote province of East Timor played an insignificant and servile part. The alumni of the seminary were to become an influential part of a new Timorese elite. A few chose to become priests, but many turned to teaching or joined one of the branches of the local civil service or the military. That many of them subsequently joined Fretilin gave the seminary an undeserved reputation for radicalism, especially in Jakarta. Although they were less conservative than the Portuguese secular clergy, the Jesuits were hardly exponents of revolution.

Ironically, Father Rabago, a former rector of the seminary, was among those who were later to see in Fretilin the seeds of a communist movement.

When the Portuguese withdrew from Dili at the end of August 1975, it was just over 200 years since Governor Meneses had moved the seat of government there from Lifau in Oecussi. In that long period of settlement their material achievements were unimpressive, and they left the colony as one of the poorest and least developed countries in the developing world. It has thus become fashionable in some countries to place the blame for the tragic events of later years on the Portuguese. Yet in some ways the Portuguese have been done a serious injustice. Would East Timor have been more developed today if the Portuguese had abandoned the island in the nineteenth century and left it to the Dutch? It would then have become part of Indonesia and would have endured the neglect experienced by the other half of the island and by the nearby islands of Alor and Wetar which are probably less developed than was East Timor on the eve of the Indonesian invasion. Perhaps this territory was doomed to be neglected not just because of Portuguese indolence. It had no fine harbours, no strategic importance, and a geographical setting well away from the main sea-lanes and tourist centres. These disincentives would have kept the interest and investment of any colonial power at a very low level, and by the twentieth century Portugal was by far too poor to do other than preserve the status quo.

As a system of colonial rule the Portuguese practice was probably no worse than other colonial systems. The style of the corporative state gave it an oppressive appearance, but, at least in the last years, despite its paternalistic and somewhat authoritarian character, it was not so oppressive. Its main weakness was that it did not prepare the Timorese for the possibility of a future without Portugal, and it certainly did not encourage the Timorese to identify with Timor's Asian environment. In a sense, the long years of Portuguese influence, the form of education and religious teaching, served to alienate the Timorese from the South-East Asian family of cultures to which they belong. In spite of the relatively low level of literacy—which is not the only measure of cultural influence in a colonial context—the Timorese were to a point 'Latinised', partly through assimilation in the days of the Topasses who became Portuguese and then drifted into the ranks of the elite of Timorese society.

In a sense it was the weakness and smallness of Portugal that moulded the peculiar style of its colonial rule and its relations with the indigenous peoples. From the outset the community of representatives of the colonial power had to bargain, compromise and make deals with the Timorese *liurais* and it was mostly the Timorese warriors, commanded by loyal chiefs, who fought the colonial battles, and not Portuguese soldiers.

In administration localisation was less a matter of principle than a matter of necessity. Even in commerce it was the Chinese that emerged as the medium for indirect commercial exploitation—the wholesalers, the shopkeepers, and the food and grain merchants.

Thus, the pattern of Portuguese colonial rule was determined by this small colonial power's limited human resources. This was particularly true in relation to religious activities. By the time a large section of the population had been converted by Catholic priests, most of the ordinary parish priests were Timorese. It emerged then that, from the Timorese point of view, the Portuguese had a much less visible and oppressive presence than was the case with most other colonial regimes. As a general rule it was Timorese troops or Timorese police that dealt with uprisings or malcontents, even after World War Two. In commerce it was the Chinese that forced the Timorese to sell cheaply and to buy at exorbitant prices. And finally the unpleasant tasks of collecting taxes and conscripting labour for public works (a practice abandoned in the last years of Portuguese rule) were assigned to *chefes de suco* and Timorese officials who had to deal with local objections.

The Portuguese capacity for assimilation, and the almost complete absence of colour prejudice, removed a traditionally important source of discontent from the colonial scene in East Timor. When I was in the colony in the early 1960s, I was struck by the racial mix at every level of government. The chief justice was Goan and his wife Chinese, the leading surgeon African and the director of customs Timorese. Indonesian propaganda since the invasion, which was sometimes been repeated by prominent foreign visitors to the '27th Province', claimed that in Portuguese times the beach near Dili, Aria Branca, was reserved for whites. Whatever the faults of the colonial power, nothing could have been further from the truth than this allegation. That particular beach (which I frequented) was patronised by an extraordinary mixture of races, with Europeans, Africans, Indians, Chinese and Timorese, all seeking relief from Dili's oppressive tropical climate.

Notes

1   Jill Jolliffe, *East Timor: Nationalism and Colonialism* (St Lucia: University of Queensland Press, 1978), pp. 55-56.
2   Willard Hanna, Reanimated Relic, American Universities Field Staff Reports Service, *South-East Asia Series*, vol. 15, no. 9 (Hanover, NH, 1966), p. 6.
3   Helio A. Esteves Felgas, *Timor Portugues* (Lisboa: Agencia Geral do Ultramar, 1956), pp. 381-384.

Chapter Four
The Lisbon coup and the Timorese political awakening

The coup mounted by the Armed Forces Movement in Lisbon on 25 April 1974 took the political and military establishments in Timor completely by surprise. This dramatic development caused immediate embarrassment to the governor, Colonel Aldeia who, only a couple of days before, had publicly denounced the Armed Forces Movement (or MFA—Movimento das Forcas Armadas) for their growing criticism of the regime of Marcelo Caetano who had replaced Dr Salazar in 1968. However, Colonel Aldeia's personal discomfort aside, Timor was very remote from the drama that was being played out in the streets of Lisbon and, apart from the disbanding of the political police apparatus, the Directorate-General of Security, and a few other organisations that were regarded as ideological pillars of the old regime, life was at first little affected by the upheaval in Lisbon. Initially there were few changes in the provincial administration itself; indeed, a number of senior old-guard officials who were hostile towards the new regime and the new spirit in Lisbon, continued in office in Dili, some of them in sensitive political positions. Even among those who welcomed the dismantling of the old order there appeared to be a belief that, as Timor had been outside the mainstream of Salazarist politics, it should not have to undergo the trauma of a purge. In those first few months, with the cautious and rather conservative General Spinola at the helm in Lisbon, there was a strong emphasis on moderation.

In Timor the situation was reasonably calm on the surface, at least during the first few weeks. When action was taken against an official it was mild and restrained. One fairly senior official who had been denounced as a fascist by an influential group in Lisbon, for example, was merely dismissed from one of the two positions that he had managed to occupy (it was not uncommon for officers of the administration to hold more than one post, and to receive remuneration for both). In spite of Timor's surface calm, it soon became apparent that the radical changes in Lisbon had shaken the system to its very foundations, and those in favour of radical political change in the status of the colony presently began to assert themselves. They greeted the news of the coup with great excitement and revelry, and the reports that the new regime would in time allow the overseas provinces to determine their own future gave rise to a fever of anticipation among the Timorese elite. Their mood of expectation and optimism was matched by apprehension and withdrawal on the part of many officials, priests, and planters, and many of the *liurais*, who feared radical solutions or were opposed to any changes that would threaten their privileged existence.

One group that was severely shaken by the events in Lisbon was the Chinese community. In the excitement and uninhibited revelry that followed the news of the coup, strong anti-Chinese sentiments were expressed openly by a number of young Timorese and there were dark hints that the Chinese would at some time be expelled from East Timor or be deprived of their assets. Such sentiments, and the mounting criticism of 'Chinese economic exploitation' that quickly followed the relaxation of controls over political expression and assembly introduced by the new regime, caused an initial reaction which must have been close to panic, especially in the light of the historical experiences of the Chinese elsewhere in South-East Asia. But there were surprisingly few incidents directly related to the radical changes in Lisbon. Governor Alves Aldeia held office for another three months or so, in spite of his untimely attack on the MFA group. The government of General Spinola seemed anxious to restrain the momentum for change, and the authorities decreed that no violence would be tolerated from groups of whatever political persuasion. However, one of the earliest actions of the leaders of the new political movements that had been formed was to seek to ease the tensions in the Chinese community. They recognised that to revive the confidence of the commercial sector it was necessary to allay Chinese apprehensions, and to convince the merchants that their role in the future economic and political life of East Timor was secure. In spite of these efforts, the Chinese community as a whole viewed its future with considerable gloom and misgivings, and fears that its long economic overlordship was inevitably coming to an end were reinforced by a growing conviction that the difficulties ahead made these well-meaning attempts at reassurance worthless.

There was at first some uncertainty about what plans, if any, the Spinola regime had for Timor. The new Portuguese leaders were absorbed with the three crisis areas in Africa—Guinea–Bissau, Angola and Mozambique—and major differences over future relations with the overseas provinces soon began to forge a rift between General Spinola and the MFA officers. Spinola had visions of remodelling the colonial structure into a Portuguese community, which his more radical MFA colleagues perceived as a variant of the system under Salazar. Although for a time the MFA leadership had moved into the background, the conservatism and hesitancy of Spinola and some other members of the Junta of National Salvation (in effect the provisional government) soon caused the younger officers—the architects of the coup—to conclude that the new leaders could not be trusted with the crucial task of dismantling the old regime and its already crippled colonial structure. By July 1974 it had become apparent that the Spinola government was planning to establish a presidential regime that would implement a slow decolonisation process, leading to a Lusitanian federation or commonwealth. From then on, the rift between the president and the MFA leaders began to widen, culminating in the former's resignation in September, following a desperate attempt by the president's supporters (the 'Spinolistas') to dislodge members of the Armed Forces Movement and certain left-wing elements from key positions in the government.

In East Timor, Colonel Aldeia was to remain in office as governor until July 1974, but he was no longer the symbol of Portuguese colonial authority. The most powerful figure in the colony was Major Arnao Metelo, the delegate of the MFA, who was later destined to become a vice-premier of the fifth provisional government. The implications for Timor of the Lisbon coup prompted Australia, in mid-1974, to send a small fact-finding mission to East Timor, of which I was a member. During this visit to the province, it was clear from talks with Metelo and the governor that the new leaders had so far given little thought to the future of their most remote territory. The governor seemed not to take seriously the prospect of an independent East Timor and gave the impression that he was not averse to the idea of integrating the colony with Indonesia. Aldeia perceived only two realistic options for the future of East Timor: a continued association with Portugal, or integration with Indonesia. Metelo, on the other hand, was inclined to brush aside the governor's views and he spoke at length on the need to canvass the wishes of the Timorese. It has been suggested that Metelo favoured handing over the territory to Indonesia and that he favoured the pro-integration party, Apodeti, but I did not gain this impression from talks with him.[1] He did remark that he felt an obligation to be protective of Apodeti, but his reason for this was plausible enough. He acknowledged that the party enjoyed little support, but declared that it was necessary to ensure that this option was clearly presented to the Timorese in order not to provoke Indonesian opposition to the process of decolonisation.

Although Portuguese policy on the future of the Timor colony was relatively unformed at the time, it was the Portuguese who spelt out the three options for the future in June 1974—a continued association with the metropolitan power, independence, or integration with Indonesia—around which political activities were to gravitate until the events of August 1975. The small elite of the territory, which included Timorese, *mestiços*, Chinese and a few Portuguese, had already responded to their new-found political freedom with surprising speed and vigour. Although the regulations prohibiting the formation of political parties were not repealed, within a matter of weeks of the April Coup three political 'associations' were formed—the Timorese Democratic Union (Uniao Democratica Timorense or the UDT), the Association of Timorese Social Democrats (Associacão Social Democrata Timorense or ASDT–the forerunner of Fretilin), and the Timorese Popular Democratic Association (Associacão Popular Democratica Timorense or Apodeti).[2] These three political organisations were formed between 11 and 27 May, that is, within slightly more than a month of the Lisbon coup. In a sense the Portuguese statement about the options for the future constituted an official interpretation of political trends of the time. What in retrospect appears extraordinary is that the colonial power took the unusual step of implicitly suggesting to Indonesia a right it did not possess. In effect, at the very outset of the decolonisation process the Portuguese accorded a legitimacy to the idea of the integration of East Timor into Indonesia, in a move to appease the latter, rather than as a considered reflection of the popular will. Furthermore, by proclaiming specific options the Portuguese tended to predetermine the process of self-determination itself.

From the beginning the bustle of political activity was largely centred on full-blooded Timorese and the *mestiços*, partly because the provincial government sought to prevent officials and the military from becoming embroiled in local politics. However although most expatriates observed this restriction, Timorese officials and some of the soldiers soon began to disregard it. Before the Lisbon coup there had been no organised nationalist movement as such, and no identifiable opposition to the Portuguese presence, although for the previous two or three years a political dialogue had been going on between a dozen or so members of the Timorese elite on the political and economic situation in the province, and on the possibility that it might become independent at some time in the future. The fact that a growing number of small states had already emerged from their colonial bondage clearly gave impetus to these discussions, and a cautious optimism was present when the events of April 1974 injected an unexpected reality and urgency into what had been a relatively casual and speculative debate.[3]

The UDT

The first of the political associations to be formed was the Timorese Democratic Union, which was proclaimed at a public meeting on 11 May 1974, little more than two weeks after the Lisbon coup. Its convenors and original members were mostly officials and smallholders, many of whom were *mestiços*. The founding president was Mario Carrascalão, a 37-year-old forestry engineer whose father had been deported to Timor in the early 1930s because of his activities as a communist youth leader, and whose mother was Timorese. The other leaders of the UDT were Francisco Lopes da Cruz, a 33-year-old customs officer, Domingos de Oliveira, also a customs official, Cesar Augusto da Costa Mousinho, a wealthy senior administration official, and João Carrascalão, Mario's brother. The leadership of the UDT, that is the fourteen members of its Central Committee, were generally conservative, representing as they did the more prosperous citizens, the administration and the wealthier planters. Three of them, Mario Carrascalão, da Cruz and Mousinho, had been representatives of the Accão Nacional Popular, the only political party allowed to exist under the Salazarist regime, in the provincial Legislative Assembly. Although Mario Carrascalão provided the UDT with leadership and organising skills, as a former senior ANP official he was identified with the old regime, and partly for this reason he was later replaced as party leader by Lopes da Cruz. Yet, in spite of the UDT members' anti-communism, on the whole their attitudes were to the left of those of the right-wing parties in Portugal. The views and aspirations of Domingos de Oliveira and the Carrascalão brothers were, in those early days of Timorese political activity, not so very different from those of the moderates of ASDT/Fretilin.

Initially the platform of the UDT seemed in harmony with the cautious and conservative stand of the Spinola administration in Lisbon. Its main objective, according to its manifesto, was 'progressive autonomy' within 'a pluri-continental and multi-racial Portuguese community', which was to be achieved 'by an increasing participation of Timorese in all sectors of public administration at all levels...but always under the Portuguese flag'. But its initial declared aims were not without contradictions. For example, it came out in defence both of the right to self-determination and of the right 'of the integration of Timor into a Portuguese-speaking community'. It spelt out a number of basic democratic principles, including 'freedom of thought and meetings', 'defence of the universal rights of man' and the need for 'a more equitable distribution of income'. From the beginning the party was a mix of conservatives who were opposed to any major changes that would threaten their privileged existence, and idealists whose differences with Fretilin were largely matters of emphasis rather than substance. It started out as a party strongly in favour of a continued association with Portugal and as a champion of Portuguese culture, and inevitably it was to be denounced by its opponents for promoting a continuation of the colonial status of East Timor. In fact, within a matter of a few weeks the attitudes of its leaders to independence shifted perceptibly, and when I questioned Mario Carrascalão at the end of June it was already clear that the UDT leaders were becoming increasingly attracted to the goal of eventual independence, although, in the words of their leader, it might take 'perhaps fifteen or twenty years'. By September, UDT leaders had declared publicly that independence was the party's ultimate goal, and it was describing itself as 'a political party that advocates federation with Portugal as an intermediary stage between the present position and complete independence of Timor'.

From the time of its inception the UDT, although the more conservative of the two main parties, appeared to be somewhat flexible. It was supported by most of the Portuguese and Timorese who were opposed to change, yet the provision in its constitution that office-bearers should be natives of Timor, or must have resided there for at least ten years, tended to keep the conservatives out of executive positions, and to exclude Portuguese expatriates from positions of direct influence. The leaders' decision to declare full independence as the ultimate goal shocked many of the UDT's conservative supporters, but they could be safely ignored because, in terms of political choices, there was nowhere else for them to turn. Their only hope lay in the *mestiço* Timorese-dominated Central Committee with its ingrained hostility to 'communistic' influences and its continuing insistence that, whatever happened, close links must be maintained with Portugal. However, once the objective of independence had been accepted other attitudes began to change. Within three months of the April Coup it was evident that some of the UDT leaders were becoming convinced that East Timor could develop economically much more rapidly if the Portuguese connection were weakened and were eventually severed. They confided to me in mid-1974 their belief that if the relationship with Portugal were placed on a more 'realistic' political and cultural basis East Timor could attract an inflow of capital and economic assistance from other external sources, such as Australia, the United States, Japan, and multilateral aid agencies like the Asian Development Bank. There was already evidence of Japanese and Australian interest in tourism and mineral exploration and, in their view, there was ample scope for an expansion of commercial links with Australia. It was clear that some UDT leaders were hoping that Australia would sometime assume a predominant role in Timor's economy which had, hitherto, been Portugal's jealously guarded preserve.

At the time of its formation the UDT was more apprehensive about the territory's future relations with Indonesia than were the Social Democrats (ASDT). While its leaders proclaimed the need to develop friendly relations with their large neighbour, the party's program, which was proclaimed at the time of its formation, stated that office-bearers 'must not have belonged to a political ideology which supports the alienation of the province to any foreign power'. Since it was already clear that Australia had no intention of assuming any of Portugal's colonial responsibilities, this restraint was evidently incorporated into the basic program with Indonesia alone in mind. But, in spite of its early appearance on East Timor's political stage, the UDT was slow to develop international activities and contacts. In mid-1974 the leaders were still mulling over whether to visit Jakarta or not when one of the ASDT leaders, Jose Ramos Horta, returned from what, at the time, appeared to have been a triumphant visit to the Indonesian capital. And, in spite of the UDTs strong interest in Australia, Horta had made several visits to Australia before the UDT leaders got around to it. Even an offer from the Taiwanese consul of a couple of free visits to Taipeh later in 1974 was taken more seriously by the ASDT leaders than by those of the UDT who declined the offer outright.

The UDT began as the largest of the three political associations in the province, but it soon started to lose ground to ASDT. The links between certain of its leaders and the old order, the concentration of its political activities on the towns and on those members of the elite in the administration or among the affluent, and its initial reluctance to support independence as an ultimate goal, appear to have caused some of its original followers to swing to ASDT. From time to time some UDT leaders were branded as neo-fascists by ASDT propaganda (and later, for quite different reasons, by Indonesian-controlled clandestine broadcasts), but most of them were not far to the right, most favouring the kind of reforms that would have established the basis for a conventional developing world democracy. However, the leaders seemed to lack a coherent plan and as issues arose the initiative was frequently lost to the more dynamic and purposeful ASDT/Fretilin leadership. There seemed to be an ever-changing balance of power between the right, as represented by Mousinho and Lopes da Cruz, and the moderates, Domingos de Oliveira and the Carrascalão brothers, with the leaders' statements on policy at times appearing to be contradictory. By early 1975 the party had clearly come under even more moderate influence. True, Lopes da Cruz had become president, but his influence was slight compared with that of the nationalist de Oliveira and the Carrascalãos. The party began to develop a strong anti-colonialist, nationalist image. As Jill Jolliffe observed at the time, the UDT seemed to be in direct competition with Fretilin when its leaders declared their commitment to 'endeavour to destroy monopolies, capitalism and the class system in Timorese society', although this socialist pronouncement had added to it a rider: 'this should not, however, be a dogmatic principle but will be a permanent guide to action'.[4]

ASDT/Fretilin

The Fretilin Party (Frente Revolutionaria de Timor–Leste Independente— Revolutionary Front for an Independent East Timor) was established a week or so after the UDT, as the Association of Timorese Social Democrats (Associacão Social Democrata Timorense or ASDT). It was formed on 20 May 1974 and its program was published two days later. In its communiqué it described itself as 'being based on the universal doctrines of socialism and democracy' and as being committed to 'the right to independence (progressive autonomy with a view to independence)', and to 'the rejection of colonialism and to counter measures against neo-colonialism'. The communiqué, which was framed in relatively mild language, called for 'the immediate participation of those Timorese elements who are so qualified in the administration and local government as a form of preparation so that in the long run they will be able to carry out functions presently exercised by those recruited from outside'. In what was rather a brief statement, it declared itself against racial discrimination and corruption and in favour of 'a policy of good-neighbourliness and cooperation in all sectors, and at all levels, with the countries in Timor's geographical area, but preserving unconditionally the higher interests of the Timorese people'. The ASDT leaders also spoke of a lengthy time frame for the process of decolonisation, which, they told the Australian fact-finding mission in mid-1974, would probably need to continue for eight to ten years to produce an adequate political and economic infrastructure. The organising committee of ASDT consisted of nine persons, nearly all of them full-blooded Timorese.[5] They included Francisco Xavier do Amaral, Nicolau Lobato, Aleixo Corte Real and Rui Fernandes, as well as Jose Ramos Horta. These were officials from the administration whose backgrounds were not very different from those of the UDT leaders. The first two, Xavier do Amaral and Lobato, were to remain as the two main leaders of ASDT/Fretilin for more than three years.

When the ASDT was formed, Francisco Xavier do Amaral was 37 and with Lopes da Cruz and Domingos de Oliveira of the UDT, he was an official in the customs department of the province. The son of a *liurai* in central East Timor, Xavier went to the Jesuit seminary at Dare from the Catholic preparatory school at Soibada. He once told me that his ideas about nationalism and his opposition to colonialism began in his last years at the seminary. Xavier was at Macau, furthering his studies as a priest, when he heard about the uprising of 1959 from some of his former fellow students who had been in sympathy with the revolt. He did not proceed to ordination, but returned to Timor and worked as a schoolteacher until 1968, when he joined the customs service, and would probably have become its director had he not resigned to become a full-time political leader.

Xavier is a quietly spoken, humble and intellectual figure. He seemed an incongruous and unlikely personality to head what was to become East Timor's most dynamic and radical political organization. A Timorese of diminutive stature, he was invariably dwarfed by his Fretilin colleagues, and he often seemed more like the party's mascot than its leader. But Xavier was an impressive speaker with charismatic appeal, and he soon became a very popular public figure. By the end of 1974, to the ordinary Timorese, Xavier do Amaral was the very symbol of Fretilin. As Jill Jolliffe wrote:

> Xavier is the true populist leader of the East Timorese; wherever he travels he is mobbed by people and is known at the village level through most of the territory. He maintains a constant air of bewilderment at the injustices he feels have been imposed on his people. He is the one nationalist to whom the traditionally stiff Portuguese administration officers afforded a grudging natural respect.[6]

Nicolau Lobato was very different from the gentle and outgoing Xavier. Tall, purposeful, disciplined and proud, he was the very embodiment of a self-reliant nationalist. Although he was almost ten years younger than Xavier, Lobato seemed more mature and self-confident, and he soon became the real leader of Fretilin. Lobato was a full-blooded Timorese from the central region where his family had been part of the traditional ruling elite. He was a devout Catholic and also a product of the Dare seminary where he was a student when I first met him in the early 1960s. At one time Lobato had aspired to become a priest, but like Xavier he had turned first to teaching and then to a career in the government administration, including some years in the army, in which he attained the rank of sergeant. Before the ASDT was formed, Lobato worked in the finance department in Dili. Both Xavier and Lobato were more popularist than socialist in their perceptions of how to work out a model for the future state of East Timor. Both were influenced by the experiences and ideas of Frelimo of Mozambique, but to a lesser extent than has often been contended. Xavier emphasised the need for the Timorese to be self-reliant and for them to be cautious about applying the revolutionary or colonial experience of other countries to the situation in East Timor, while Lobato spoke at length about the need to work out political and economic structures that were neither Marxist nor capitalist, but were best suited to the peculiar conditions prevailing in the colony. But, while Xavier, who speaks English reasonably well, impressed foreign visitors with his moderation, tolerance, and charismatic influence on his audiences, it was Lobato's strong leadership qualities—his determination, self-discipline and military experience—that were to transform Fretilin from a loose political organisation into an armed resistance that was to keep a better-equipped and numerically superior Indonesian force at bay for more than three years.

Within a couple of weeks of its formation ASDT began its international activities by sending Jose Ramos Horta to Jakarta, where he was to meet Foreign Minister Adam Malik, and one of Indonesia's most influential generals, Ali Murtopo. Although Horta was not even a member of the original organising committee of ASDT he was soon to become its spokesman and, in Australia and Indonesia, its best-known leader. He was occasionally referred to in the press as the 'Fretilin leader' when his formal position was Secretary for International Relations. Horta developed his party's foreign links with skill from the outset, but he was never a central figure of influence within the party in East Timor. However, no other Fretilin leader was able to rival Horta's astute and sensitive appreciation of the treacherous external political environment that began to threaten the process of decolonisation by the end of 1974, or his capacity to project a credible and attractive image of Fretilin, as a responsible and progressive nationalist movement, among interested parties in Australia. Inevitably, his attempts to generate the widest possible support and sympathy from all sections of the Australian political spectrum led to accusations that he was a manipulator, and to doubts about his political sincerity in both the right and the left—in Timor as well as in Australia. Thus, in Indonesia he has been described as communist or neo-Marxist, by one Australian author as a power-hungry pragmatist (in a curious account which grossly exaggerated Horta's role in the party)[7] and, by the left, as a right-winger who was ever ready to do a deal with the Indonesian generals.

Jose Manuel Ramos Horta is a *mestiço*, one of a large family whose father, a former petty officer in the Portuguese navy, had been deported to Dili in the mid-1930s. His mother was a Timorese who came from the Same district near the rugged southern slopes of Timor. After studying at the Lyceum in Dili he took up journalism, but a political indiscretion in which he criticised Portuguese colonialism led to his being exiled to Mozambique for a year or so. Although he was able to resume his career with *A Voz de Timor* after his return to Dili, a daring article entitled 'The Myth and the Reality' again brought him to the attention of the political police and he was on the verge of once more being sent into exile when the April Coup occurred. Horta was one of the first wave of Timorese political activists and he played an important role in the launching of ASDT; the fact that he was not among its first office-holders was largely because he deliberately chose to remain in the background. For one thing, being a *mestiço* was something of a disadvantage, the first Timorese appointed to office being full-blooded indigenes. But Horta had always preferred to operate behind the scenes, perhaps because of his reluctance to enter into total commitment to any political party, a trait that caused his detractors to question his loyalty, or to attribute sinister designs to some of his activities.

It was Jose Ramos Horta who carried out ASDT's first major assignment, and the first international contact by any of the Timorese leaders—the Jakarta talks with Adam Malik and General Murtopo. The Australian fact-finding mission was still in Timor when Horta returned, exhilarated by the warm reception he had been given by Malik. He had managed to obtain from Foreign Minister Malik a written statement, the contents of which seem extraordinary in the light of later events. In this letter Malik welcomed the prospect of an independent East Timor, a position from which he was subsequently forced to retreat in deference to the very different views of more influential Indonesians like General Ali Murtopo, who had determined that integration with Indonesia was the only acceptable option from Jakarta's point of view and that the Timorese should be encouraged, or pressed, to accept it. Horta's early visit to Jakarta and the seemingly generous response he was able to elicit from Malik gave a considerable boost to ASDT's fortunes. Moreover, the substance of the discussions was conveyed to the UDT leaders, and the apparent readiness of the Indonesian leaders to accommodate the idea of an independent East Timor was a major factor in swinging the Democratic Union leaders around to a more positive and definitive stand on the question of independence.

The result of Horta's Jakarta visit acted as an endorsement to ASDT's objective of independence, suggesting as it did that one of the major obstacles, the possible opposition of the Suharto regime, had been overcome effortlessly. The ASDT's response appeared to be equally generous. After his return Horta confided to me that, if Indonesia had been prepared to support self-determination for East Timor, he believed that his party, and even the UDT, would consider allowing Indonesia to handle defence and the bulk of foreign affairs matters for the new state, in a gesture he intended to counter the fears some generals apparently entertained that the new state might in some way threaten the security of Indonesia. At the time I felt that this spirit of goodwill offered a superb opportunity for some kind of cooperative arrangement in which Australia, as well as Indonesia, might become involved so as to underwrite the decolonisation process. Unfortunately, the exploitation of this early atmosphere of goodwill was never seriously contemplated in Jakarta or Canberra.

The ASDT leaders decided to follow up their Jakarta initiative with a visit to Australia and, despite an attempt by the department of foreign affairs to stall him, Horta turned up in Canberra in July 1974, within days of the return of the fact-finding mission, somewhat to the annoyance and apprehension of the departmental officers dealing with Indonesia and the question of East Timor's future. It was Horta's expectation that the Whitlam government, which had given strong emphasis to Australia's support for decolonisation and self-determination, would also give strong support to, and perhaps even guarantee, East Timor's right to independence. In fact, the government and its foreign affairs advisers reacted coolly to his presence in Canberra and, in his few contacts with them, guardedly to his attempts to elicit a clear statement that the government's unequivocal support for the granting of self-government to non-self-governing peoples also applied to the people of East Timor. Although Horta had been able to have a relaxed and informal chat with Malik in Jakarta, in Canberra his visit was deliberately played down. Protocol objections as to his official standing were raised somewhat cynically, and he was not able to meet the minister for foreign affairs or the head of that department. At the time some observers described his visit as a washout, but this was not really the case. He met parliamentarians, academics, union leaders, church and foreign-aid representatives and the media, and was thus able to establish the basis for a bipartisan and public interest in the rights of the East Timorese that was thereafter to make the issue a matter of national concern in Australia.

During Horta's absence from Timor, the ASDT began to shift towards a more radical position as the political momentum of decolonisation increased. Although it was soon to become evident that the blessing Adam Malik had given to the Timorese road to independence was not going to be endorsed by the Indonesian military establishment, whose influence with the president was far greater than that of the foreign minister, Timorese enthusiasm and political activism continued to mount in Dili. Press reports surfacing in Jakarta and Canberra that some generals were opposed to independence for the Portuguese colony served only to strengthen the resolve of ASDT and to propel it towards more radical activities and rhetoric. As early as August 1974 certain sections of the Indonesian media, especially the newspaper *Berita Yudha*, which was controlled by Ali Murtopo's faction, began to accuse the Social Democrats of seeking communist backing. In the circumstances, it is hardly surprising that the goodwill towards Indonesia was soon transformed into suspicion and hostility. But the enticing goal of independence had become firmly implanted in the minds of ASDT members, and membership of the party increased rapidly in August and September. This goal became its central focus, an objective that was not negotiable. Party leaders gradually became dissatisfied with the mild 'social democrat' title, which most felt was an inappropriate borrowing from the Western European political context and of little relevance to conditions in East Timor. Thus, on 12 September 1974, ASDT became Fretilin, the Revolutionary Front for an Independent East Timor, and its political program was accordingly adjusted to a more radical mould. Its attitude towards other parties hardened and it declared itself 'the only legitimate representative of the people', demanding an immediate declaration from the Portuguese authorities that they would eventually grant independence to the colony. Fretilin members became increasingly hostile to the pro-integration party, Apodeti, already a mouthpiece for certain Indonesian interests, and impatient with the UDT because of the latter's conservative approach to change and its initial reluctance to come out unequivocally in favour of the goal of independence.

Fretilin's shift to a more radical position also to some extent reflected political change in Lisbon. In August and September relations between President Spinola and his conservative supporters, on the one hand, and Prime Minister Colonel

Vasco dos Santos Goncalves, and his left-wing MFA backers, on the other, further deteriorated, and at the end of September the president resigned, following a desperate attempt by his supporters to dislodge the MFA group. In Portugal, as in Timor, there was little change to affect the lives of the ordinary citizens in the first few months after 25 April—the main change in evidence was the adorning of all wall space with political graffiti and the dazzling folk art of political posters. From September onwards, however, the centre of power was of a much more radical complexion. Spinola was succeeded by Costa Gomes, the former army chief of staff, and the government came under the control of a strange gathering of idealistic army socialists whose leaders included Fabiao, Vasco Goncalves, and Otelo de Carvalho. The Western press began to express fears that Portugal was sliding steadily in the direction of a left-wing military dictatorship.

The fact that these changes in Portugal more or less coincided with Fretilin's shift to a more radical posture was fortuitous, but a left-wing government coming to power, bent on accelerating the process of dismantling the empire, gave a considerable boost to Fretilin's aspiration to become the vanguard of the East Timorese revolution. The expectation that Fretilin's power would be boosted by the shift to the left in Lisbon apparently caused an upsurge of alarm in Jakarta, as well as among conservative groups in Timor, but there were no real grounds for these anxieties. The MFA's socialist objectives were confined to the restructuring of the metropolitan economy and society, and the new regime was little interested in the politics of East Timor. Indeed, some of the new leaders were evidently not averse to the idea of conceding East Timor to Indonesia as a means of quickly disposing of a remote, irrelevant and embarrassingly poor piece of Portuguese territory, and some of them were apparently not greatly concerned about whether the niceties of decolonisation were observed. It was not until after the visit late in 1974 by Minister for Interterritorial Coordination Dr Antonio de Almeida Santos that the Portuguese began to comprehend the strength and extent of nationalist feeling in the province.

In the meantime, press reports in Australia that Prime Minister Whitlam had indicated a preference for East Timor's integration into Indonesia in his talks with President Suharto in September 1974 caused an angry reaction among the Timorese and strengthened support for Fretilin's more radical program. It also led to a more determined stand on self-determination and independence by the UDT. It exposed the attitudes of certain Australian policy makers who apparently felt that if Australia kept subtly suggesting to the Timorese the advantage of integration, and studiously avoided the use of the evocative term 'independence' in the context of East Timor's future, the Timorese might somehow take the hint and abandon their crazy ideas about setting up a state of their own.

Fretilin's membership expanded very quickly in the last four months of 1974 and may have exceeded that of the UDT, although the claims by both as to the extent of their followings were difficult to assess. Late in 1974 Horta claimed that his party had more than 80,000 supporters and a few months later the UDT leaders told me that they had some 100,000 Timorese behind them. The fact that allegiances of entire *sucos* changed from time to time, based on political shifts at the top, made a true assessment very difficult. My impression was that, by the middle of 1975, Fretilin had the edge on its opponent largely because it was seen as the main independence party, and was also giving more attention than the UDT to political work outside the main towns and villages. Fretilin was also more aggressive, disciplined and purposeful in its political activities, and its plans for the creation of cooperatives and for a more equal distribution of land attracted widespread interest among the Timorese. It also called for a more Timor-oriented education system and for the promotion of a better understanding of Timorese culture as an element of nationalism. However, although its political personality changed as it assumed the mantle of a revolutionary front, it remained essentially a popularist, Catholic party whose leaders' attitudes were attuned more to the socialist aims and experiences of similar movements in developing countries, but especially in Africa, than to those of any communist state. There were a number of young radical students who had returned from Lisbon fired with revolutionary fervour and joined Fretilin, whose radical pronouncements caused them to be denounced by conservatives as communists or Marxists, but in reality it is doubtful whether there was a single communist among the thousands of Timorese who threw in their lot with the independence movement.

Apodeti

The political movement advocating the third option, integration with Indonesia, was the Timorese Popular Democratic Association, or Apodeti. Apodeti emerged from a meeting attended by thirty or forty Timorese on 27 May 1974. It was at first called the Association for the Integration of Timor into Indonesia but, in a move to soften public reaction to what the founders realised was a far from popular prescription for their future, the name was changed. However, from the beginning there was never any doubt about what the party stood for, although it did insist that Timor should have an autonomous status. Apodeti's original manifesto, in the first of its thirteen articles, declared itself in favour of

> an autonomous integration into the Republic of Indonesia in accordance with international law.

From my discussions with Apodeti leaders in the following weeks, the rationale behind integration seemed to be of a negative character. They seemed to hold the belief that East Timor was economically unviable and would therefore never be able to stand alone politically. In a roundabout way the leaders also seemed to be saying that if the colony were not handed over to Indonesia the latter would seize it at some future date. This was implicit in the preamble of the manifesto which declared:

> In the present historicopolitical context, abstaining from sentimental wishful thinking and unfounded pride, any precipitate choice could be the ruin of Timor and of the future of its sons

Apodeti leaders also claimed that there were close ethnic and cultural links between the peoples of East and West Timor. They urged in their manifesto:

> the teaching of the Indonesian language as a compulsory subject at all secondary schools, and the opening of elementary schools teaching Indonesian as the first language, without necessarily abolishing the present Portuguese schools

It is interesting to note that, although Apodeti tried to present itself as the most Timorese of parties, it was the one party that did not advocate the teaching of Tetum.

The Apodeti manifesto set out an impressive list of rights it proposed to promote, some of which would have made its basic aim of integration almost unattainable. To begin with, the 'autonomous integration into the Republic of Indonesia', as the Indonesians were themselves soon to point out, was not provided for in the Indonesian constitution. Apodeti leaders declared their commitment to basic human rights and freedom of expression which, if adhered to, would have effectively ruled out any deal with Jakarta. Another curious provision, for a party that favoured the integration of the colony into a predominantly Moslem state, was the mention of the specific rights of the Catholic church whose 'doctrine has consolidated our sociopolitical activities'. Neither Fretilin nor the UDT accorded any special privileges to the church in their declared plans. Another contradiction emerges from the specific reference to the upholding of the Portuguese language and culture in one paragraph, and in another the reference to 'the right of students to study at foreign universities, especially at the universities in Indonesia and Australia'. Curiously, there was no mention of Portugal.

Although thirty Timorese signed Apodeti's manifesto, its following probably never exceeded more than a few hundred. Its early support came from some of those who had been involved in the 1959 insurrection, from the 'Arab' community near Dili, and from a couple of kingdoms, the most important of which was Atsabe, whose *liurai*, Guilherme Goncalves, was to provide the party with its only significant territorial base in East Timor. Goncalves, who was usually referred to as the 'King of Atsabe', was one of Timor's most despotic rulers; it has been alleged that early in 1975 he used force to send many of the young men of his realm to a special Indonesian intelligence base near Kupang where they were to undergo training for guerrilla operations. But Goncalves was not one of the founding leaders of Apodeti. First president of the party was Arnaldo dos Reis Araujo, at 60 one of the oldest of the Timorese leaders. He had been imprisoned in the postwar period for his collaboration with the Japanese occupation forces—an allegation he later admitted to at the United Nations during one of the debates on the Timor question (in which Japan was siding with Indonesia). Araujo, later to become Indonesia's first choice as the governor of the '27th Province', had been the owner of a cattle run near Zumalai on the south coast. In mid-1974, at the behest of Elias Tomodok, the Indonesian consul in Dili, he visited Jakarta where he appears to have spent three aimless months while the Indonesians worked out their Timor strategy. Although Apodeti immediately became a focus of Indonesian interest, not all Indonesians were impressed with the assessment of the situation in the colony by the party's president. Thus, late in 1974, an Indonesian church source who favoured integration informed his bishop:

When Mr Arnaldo dos Reis Araujo visited Indonesia practically all the Indonesian newspapers uncritically echoed his exaggerated description of the colonial misproportions and suppressions in the province...even a supperficial (sic) look into the situation proofs (sic) the inaccuracy and untruth of the assertion which caused unsympathic (sic) reaction'.[8]

The vice-president of Apodeti was Hermenegildo Martins, a coffee plantation owner who claimed to be a descendant of the Topasses, and the secretary was Casimiro dos Reis Araujo, a son of the president. But the man behind Apodeti's early activities and organisation was Jose Osorio Soares, a 37-year-old former schoolteacher and official in the administration. The party's strategist, he at first tended to operate from behind the scenes but was to become the movement's secretary-general. In 1975, Osorio Soares gave an interesting account to Bill Nicol of why he favoured integration. He said:

We are a poor country. We could end up fighting among ourselves. We do not need neocolonialism, just some control from Indonesia; and if we need some things maybe we can get them from Indonesia. Our customs are the same; only our colonialism is different. We are the one country; we are part of all Timor and Timor is in the middle of Indonesia. Even if Indonesia comes you can still have your customs; they will not destroy them. If we are together and you need something you can ask Jakarta for help. And if you want, you can ask Australia for help. But we do not want fighting among the people of one land.[9]

But earlier Osorio Soares also told me of his fears that an independent East Timor would be weak and vulnerable and might provoke military intervention by Jakarta if the political situation became unstable or if there were a political shift to the left.

The political goals proclaimed by Apodeti proved to be no match for the independence programs of Fretilin and UDT, and at the peak of its influence the pro-integration party was never able to muster more than a small fraction of the politically conscious Timorese. In spite of the ideals expressed in its original manifesto, Apodeti soon became the vehicle for overt Indonesian propaganda and a channel for covert subversive operations, presenting a measure of public endorsement of Jakarta's political strategy for East Timor. Without this support Apodeti would probably not have been taken seriously, if it could have survived at all. But after September 1974, when it was already apparent that the most influential military leaders in Indonesia were opposed to the emergence of an independent East Timor, Apodeti became the focal point for pro-Indonesian activities. The party became a kind of appendage to the Indonesian consulate in Dili from which it began to receive financial, as well as moral, support. And support also came from the other side of the border. As early as 12 September 1974 the Jakarta daily *Sinar Harapan* reported that the governor of the neighbouring Indonesian province of East Nusatenggara, Colonel El Tari, had received Apodeti leaders and had declared his provincial government's intention 'to assist the struggle of Apodeti'. According to this report, the party leaders also told the governor that 70 per cent of the people of East Timor supported integration with Indonesia. This extravagant claim was to be used repeatedly by Indonesian leaders, diplomats and the media, as the campaign to bring about the integration of the Portuguese colony got under way.

By 1975 opposition to joining with Indonesia was so strong that Apodeti's goals and associations made it a target for ridicule and anger and forced it into a defensive position. It was rarely visible and its leaders often had to be provided with bodyguards. Bill Nicol observed:

> Increasingly isolated, with less belief in their own aims and resentful of the position in which they found themselves (they seem to have had little resentment towards Indonesia itself), Apodeti's leaders became more negative in their approach: they tended to become obstructionist, aggressive and violent, and thus even more isolated.[10]

Even the presence of Guilherme Goncalves, the *liurai* of Atsabe, did nothing to advance Apodeti's fortunes. Both Fretilin and UDT began to press for the powers and privileges of such traditional rulers to be reduced, moves which were to attract considerable support from the latter's subjects. By 1975 Fretilin was demanding that the appointment of these rulers be the subject of democratic elections, and in at least one area, in the Lautem district, such an election was held, with the traditionalist candidate being defeated by a more progressive contender.

The growing movement for reform of local government did, however, cause a number of *liurais* to throw in their lot with Apodeti. With the democratisation of the Portuguese colonial administration, and the pressure for structural change from both Fretilin and UDT, integration with Indonesia seemed to offer the petty rulers the only hope of preventing the erosion of their traditional powers and privileges. Their apprehensions were not lost on the Indonesian intelligence agents responsible for encouraging the Timorese to accept integration, and by mid-1975 several of the key dissident *liurais* had been contacted by agents who sought to assure them that their status and privileges would be secure in the '27th Province'. One of the Indonesians responsible for such contacts was Louis Taolin, a relative of the traditional rulers of the Atoni, who was recruited by ABRI's influential Intelligence Coordinating Agency, Bakin, precisely because of this blood link with the Belu *liurais*.

One interesting recruit from the ranks of Apodeti was Tomas Goncalves, a son of Guilherme of Atsabe. He secretly went to Indonesian Timor early in 1975 where he was to become the leader of an Indonesian-trained military group that was groomed in a special intelligence operation codenamed Partisan. In all 300 East Timorese were trained, most of whom were taken from the Atsabe region, with the connivance of the *liurai*. One of the commanders of this military operation was Major Yunus Yosfiah, an officer of the Strategic Reserve Command, Kostrad. Some of these recruits were to accompany Indonesian forces on their first major military operation against Fretilin in mid-October 1975 where Yosfiah was to lead the attack on Balibo. Jose Martins later claimed in his statement to the United Nations Secretary-General:

> To begin with, the Indonesian Army gave military training to Tomas, to his brother Lucio, and to half a dozen Timorese. Later, with the despatch of 300 Timorese recruited by a chefe de suco, Feliciano, a training camp was set up in Atambua; which became an Apodeti headquarters. Officers of the Indonesian Commandos were attached to this Centre, all of them under the command of Major Andreas who came to Indonesian Timor under the guise of a member of the Emigration Service.[11]

Within a year of its formation Apodeti had virtually become a front for Bakin operations, but as the independence option gained in popularity the Indonesians became increasingly sceptical about the pro-integration party's usefulness as a political front organisation. Even senior Bakin officials in their talks with Australian or US diplomats in Jakarta began to acknowledge that Apodeti's cause was not a popular one. Repeated statements by Indonesian leaders that the constitution of the republic could not accommodate an autonomous province of East Timor did nothing to help Apodeti's efforts to make integration look attractive. Not all Apodeti members were in favour of the use of force to bring about this objective. In October 1975, in one of the last television interviews conducted by Greg Shackleton, one of the five Australian newsmen killed at Balibo that month, Jose Osorio Soares insisted that he was opposed to any move by Indonesia to annex the territory by means of force. Perhaps this statement needs to be considered against the situation at the time; East Timor was under de facto Fretilin rule, and Osorio's own freedom was subject to the indulgence of the leaders of the independence movement.

Other political groups

Three other very small parties were formed in East Timor between April 1974 and August 1975. None of these had any significant effect on the local political situation, but their existence was later exploited by Indonesian propaganda in an obvious attempt to diminish Fretilin claims to popular support. In fact, these small factions were tolerated rather than officially recognised by the Portuguese authorities. The most important of the three was Kota, formed in mid-1974 as the Associacão Popular Monarquia de Timor or APMT (the Popular Association of Monarchists of Timor). APMT was set up by several *liurais* who claimed to be descendants of the Topasses. It was traditionalist, conservative and anything but popular. In November it was renamed Kota, from the Tetum Klibur Oan Timur Aswain—'Sons of the Mountain Warriors'. (Incidentally, this was the only political group to use Tetum in its title.) Kota eventually came under the leadership of the intriguing Timorese Jose Martins, the son of a *liurai* from the Ermera district, who had originally been a supporter of Apodeti. Martins told me during an interview in 1976 that he had set out to transform the APMT into a 'distinct Timorese-type party' from its earlier monarchist character with the ultimate goal of independence, to be underwritten by a kind of protectorate relationship involving Portugal, Indonesia and Australia. Martins had spent much of his life in Portugal, returning to Timor only in 1975. In spite of his claim that he contrived to get Kota members interested in ultimate independence, Martins was, in 1975, recruited by Bakin, and he was to work closely with their agent Louis Taolin. Bakin for a time trusted Martins more than any of their handful of Timorese recruits and, after the coup, they placed him in charge of propaganda broadcasts from the Kupang area. According to Jill Jolliffe, 'he cultivated a warrior image, preaching racial superiority, tribal mysticism, machismo'.[12] Martins seems to have been one of Indonesia's most effective collaborators until early in 1976 when, disillusioned, he was to abandon the cause of integration in a dramatic move at the United Nations in New York. Kota's membership appears to have increased after May 1975, but it was never other than a minor party in the Timorese political configuration, with only a few hundred members.

Another small group, the Partido Trabalhista (Labour Party), probably did not exceed a dozen or so members, many of whom came from the same family. Finally, there was the Aditla Party, the Associacão Democratica Integracão Timor–Leste Australia (Democratic Association for the Integration of East Timor into Australia), which would no doubt have become one of Timor's major parties had not its central objective been undermined when the Australian government summarily dismissed the feasibility of such a link. Aditla seems to have started in late 1974 and, according to Bill Nicol, it 'was only the outward manifestation of an organisation which was inwardly seeking to make money out of fears held by the territory's Chinese community that the new politics would be a disaster for them'.[13] Its founder was a local businessman, Henrique Pereira, who claimed to have special links with former members of the Australian commando force. Nicol claims that Aditla's membership rose to 10,000, but it collapsed and nearly disappeared after the Australian government's statement in March 1975 which unequivocally ruled out any prospect of such an integration. In the preceding weeks, however, the enticement of joining with Australia had reportedly been accruing considerable personal gain to its enterprising founder, especially from the Chinese community.

Political manoeuvring in the shadow of integration
The polarisation of the three main parties around three distinct goals tended to exaggerate the differences between their young leaders in that early stage of the territory's political development. The basic aims of Fretilin and UDT, and even of Apodeti, were not so very different. All expressed their opposition to racial discrimination, their support for freedom of expression and religious liberty, and their opposition to corruption. Most of the leading political activists knew one another well. Many were from similar backgrounds and had studied or worked together for many years. Close personal relationships and kinships cut across party alliances, sometimes with great complexity. Most of the Timorese leaders

had close relatives among the leading supporters of at least one of the other two parties. Inevitably, during the first six months of the existence of the two main parties, the differences between them began to widen, often fanned by outside influences, with deepening suspicions and occasional public outbursts of antagonism between some of the leaders surfacing as the parties vied to extend the bases of their support in villages or rural areas. Horta, although a self-declared moderate, from time to time referred to UDT as 'neo-fascist', but in private he and other Fretilin leaders conceded that there was a great deal of common ground between them and most of the leaders of the Democratic Union.

In a sense, the Portuguese administration, by declaring three exclusive options for the future of the colony, provided a format for ideological rivalry as well as political competition. In the beginning the differences in outlook between Fretilin and UDT were far from unbridgeable—indeed, in many ways the leaders were closer than the leaderships of the Pangu Pati (Party) and its opposition, on the eve of Papua New Guinea's independence. But unlike Papua New Guinea the emerging political forces in East Timor had to contend with a weakened and demoralised colonial administration, political subversion and, ultimately, military intervention from one neighbour, and cynical lack of interest and complicity from another. As if these obstacles were not enough, the Timorese were without sponsors and friends in the international arena. Their land had neither the strategic nor the economic importance to entice the support of any of the great powers to whom the Timor question was one that could safely be ignored. In mid-1974 it was my belief that, in spite of the backwardness of East Timor, conditions existed for a smooth process of decolonisation and the emergence, in the course of time, of a reasonably viable state with an economy that would be no more dependent upon external support than the average developing nation in, say, the South Pacific. Most of the ingredients for success seemed present. The colonial power had canvassed the views of the different groups sensitively and, although the Portuguese were in a weakened position, they made it clear that they would welcome outside help in organising an appropriate act of self-determination. Timorese society was not beset by serious communal differences. There was, of course, the position of the small Chinese minority, but this was largely an economic question which even Fretilin was prepared to come to terms with.

At the time of the visit of the Australian fact-finding mission in mid-1974, we could not help but be struck by the relaxed and happy atmosphere prevailing in the towns and villages, as well as the spirit of tolerance and the optimism among the politically active Timorese. But there was also an awareness of the problems that lay ahead, even among the not-so-literate Timorese. Some of the illiterate also had well-formed ideas about their preferences for the future, a reminder that political consciousness is not the exclusive preserve of the literate, especially in communities like that in East Timor where complex indigenous political structures have existed for centuries, under which the inhabitants were from time to time able to exercise choices of a political character. Many of the democratic ideals espoused by the political associations were lost on most of the Timorese, but people seemed to know what self-rule meant, to recognise the need for improved agricultural methods and better education, and to understand something about their basic rights. They seemed to harbour a suspicion of Asian outsiders, no doubt in part a legacy of their harsh treatment at the hands of the Japanese occupying forces and the Black Column troops, many of whom had come from West Timor and nearby islands.

The real political contest in East Timor was between UDT and Fretilin. Apodeti developed out of the Portuguese concession to Indonesian sensitivities. It was largely in deference to Indonesian apprehensions and paranoia that integration was deliberately put forward as an option. Had Indonesia given impartial support to the process of decolonisation and publicly declared its unequivocal support for Timor's right to independence, Apodeti membership would have been insignificant. The political choice in terms of the popular will was essentially between the two major parties whose leaders, in spite of their youth and political inexperience, had made realistic appraisals of the political and economic problems facing the colony. From the outset these Timorese leaders were concerned to put to rest any Indonesian fears that an independent East Timor would threaten the security of the republic in some way. They aspired to gain support from ASEAN generally and to develop relations with the other countries in the Asian region, as well as with Australia. They had no illusions about the colony's needs and economic weaknesses, and the need to change the direction of its commercial links. In short, leaving aside divisive external influences and pressures, the two parties were, initially at least, of the disposition to work cooperatively towards broadly compatible goals.

UDT and Fretilin did join in a coalition in January 1975 at a time when a process of decolonisation was starting to take shape and gain momentum with the parties being subjected to conflicting advice and pressures, but it was an arrangement rather hastily agreed to, and was regarded as something of a 'shotgun wedding', leaving the parties unduly vulnerable to outside meddling. After the meeting between Whitlam and Suharto at Wonosobo, Java, in September 1974, it became clear to the Timorese that the goal of independence could not be taken for granted. Even the new Portuguese MFA regime coming to power under President Costa Gomes, in spite of its radical complexion and professed commitment to self-determination, did not lessen the uncertainties. At least some of the new leaders were believed to favour the integration option, if only as a means of resolving the Timor problem quickly. However, the visit to the colony by the Minister for Interterritorial Coordination Dr Almeida Santos, reminded the Portuguese of the extent of their cultural influence in Timor, sparked feelings of obligation, and forced them to the conclusion that there was almost no interest in any solution that would involve transferring the territory to Indonesia. Almeida Santos seemed to be reaffirming Portugal's earlier commitment to move for a proper act of self-determination when he told a crowd in Dili that 'Timor will be what the majority of the people want it to be'. In November 1974 a new governor, Colonel (later Brigadier) Lemos Pires, and a small group of MFA officers arrived in East Timor, their coming marking the beginning of a more vigorous decolonisation policy with the new MFA administration hinting that the Portuguese might be out of the colony in less than four years. Inevitably the tempo of political activity quickened, injecting new tensions into a situation which, to date, had been surprisingly calm, at least on the surface. But the most destabilising outside influence was a hostile propaganda campaign mounted by Indonesia. A strident flow of propaganda broadcasts from Radio Kupang sought to discredit the two main political parties, branding Fretilin as communist and UDT as a neo-fascist organisation. The Indonesian press carried stories of Communist Chinese infiltration into the colony, reports that were without foundation. There were also false press and radio reports of political violence. For example, on 12 September 1974 *Sinar Harapan* carried in bold headlines a report that the *liurai* of Ainaro and five of his family had been murdered. It was without foundation. Later in the year there were other such false reports of East Timorese fleeing to the Indonesian sector in order to escape violence and persecution.

Notes

1   Luis Filipe Thomaz, *Timor: Autopsia de uma Tragedia* (Lisboa, np, 1977), p. 41.
2   Jill Jolliffe, *East Timor: Nationalism and Colonialism* (St Lucia: University of Queensland Press, 1978), pp. 56-57.
3   This account is based on discussions the author had with UDT and Fretilin leaders.
4   Jolliffe, *East Timor*, p. 77.
5   For an interesting description of the Fretilin leaders see Helen Hill, 'Fretilin: The Origins, Ideologies and Strategies of a Nationalist Movement in East Timor' (MA thesis, Monash University, 1978), pp. 72-83.
6   Jolliffe, *East Timor*, p. 70.
7   Bill Nicol, *The Stillborn Nation* (Melbourne: Viza, 1978), chap. 12.
8   Document from the Denpasar Diocese held by the author, dated 30 October 1974.
9   Nicol, *Stillborn Nation*, p. 58.
10 Ibid., p. 63.
11 Affidavit submitted to the UN Secretary-General, March 1976.
12 Jolliffe, *East Timor*, p. 284.
13 Nicol, *Stillborn Nation*, p. 43.

Chapter Five

East Timor's future options and the Portuguese Administration

Administration
After September 1974 the accelerated pace of political activities in East Timor coincided with a significant shift in the Portuguese attitude towards decolonisation, reflecting more or less the views of the new leaders of the Armed Forces Movement. With Portugal's African empire collapsing around them, the morale of troops and officials in the overseas territories (the *ultramar*) was at an all-time low, and the view that Portugal should abandon its overseas role as quickly as possible was gaining in strength. In Timor, although the situation was reasonably settled, the Portuguese would have welcomed some regional support to speed up the process of decolonisation, and in the first instance they turned to Australia which, because of its affluence, its high standing in East Timor, and its successful record in Papua New Guinea, would, in Lisbon's view, seem to be a valuable ally in a time of pressing need. However, Australia's response was cool and distant. The Whitlam government made it clear at the outset that Australia was not prepared to risk being left responsible for the decolonisation of East Timor; more importantly it was not prepared to risk provoking Indonesian suspicions that it might have designs on the Portuguese colony. It was an unexpected rebuff, coming from a government that had had little sympathy for the old regime and whose leaders had welcomed the Lisbon coup and the new regime's decision at last to allow Portugal's colonial subjects to determine their own future.

The Portuguese were soon to resign themselves to the fact that Australian policy towards East Timor would reflect the high priority the Whitlam government accorded to the improving of relations with Jakarta. But they found it difficult to comprehend that a country which had moved so speedily to recognise the nationalist movement in Guinea-Bissau* (even before the

---

* Opposition to Portuguese rule in this small West African colony was spearheaded by the PAIGC, a liberation movement under the leadership of Amilcar Cabral.

Portuguese took this step) could be so uninterested in the decolonisation of a neighbouring territory whose people, in the light of events during World War II, seemed to have a special claim to Australia's sympathy. In fact, Australian officials did give some private encouragement to an 'internationally acceptable act of self-determination', but this careful choice of words implied a deference not to the rights of the people of East Timor, but to Indonesian sensitivities or perceived Indonesian interests. To the Portuguese the Australian position—at least after the Wonosobo meeting between Prime Minister Whitlam and President Suharto in September 1974—was that the outcome of any decolonisation process should be acceptable to Indonesia, to whom Canberra accorded a 'party principal' status, with the integration of the territory into Indonesia being the preferred end. In short Australia was determined to give no encouragement whatever to the movement for independence. The Portuguese were inclined to share the Australian view that East Timor was probably economically unviable, but they did acknowledge that the factor of economic unviability would no more discourage Timorese nationalists than it had nationalist movements elsewhere.

When the Portuguese publicly informed the Timorese in June 1974 that in due course three options would be presented to them for their choice, it was envisaged that a plebiscite would be conducted as an initial act of self-determination. However, the authorities subsequently decided against this method of determining the future status of Timor because of the difficulty in implementing it in a territory with such a low level of literacy and political consciousness. Although the idea of presenting three options was retained, the Portuguese then favoured the processing of self-determination through a constituent assembly which would be elected on the widest possible suffrage. With the assembly established it was envisaged that the future status of the territory would be worked out step by step, in an evolutionary process encompassing a period of several years.

Initially, the Portuguese believed that an overwhelming majority of the Timorese would opt for some form of continuing relationship with the metropolitan power, a view held even by some of the Fretilin leaders for the first six months or so. When Almeida Santos visited East Timor in 1975 as Minister for Interterritorial Coordination, he and his party were impressed by the existence of a kind of mystical veneration of the Portuguese flag, a loyalty manifested in impressive demonstrations in those parts of the territory visited by his mission. Almeida Santos responded to these manifestations of loyalty to Lisbon with the words: 'It is a part of our policy that the wishes of the population will be respected, and if the wish is that of Timor being connected to Portugal, it will be connected...if there is another wish, it will also be respected. But I take from here the conviction that there is not really another wish'.[1]

Minister Santos, however, was not in a position to commit the government to such a continuing role in Timor. Whatever his views, the prevailing disposition of the leadership of the MFA was that Portugal should rid itself of its colonial liabilities as soon as possible. Inevitably, differences between the authorities in Lisbon and those in Dili arose about the form and management of the decolonisation process. From my discussions with the MFA officers implementing the decolonisation arrangements under the Governor, Brigadier Lemos Pires, it seemed that when Brigadier Lemos Pires and his team swung into action they had a concentrated and short-term operation in mind with integration into Indonesia as at least an acceptable outcome if the Timorese were not averse to the idea. They were soon struck by the intense Timorese opposition to joining with Indonesia and by the determination of the overwhelming majority of the elite to press for eventual independence.

Although the Portuguese administration in East Timor has often been the target of strong criticism-in Australia and in the USA, as well as in Portugal—its small team of idealistic, though perhaps inexperienced, officers* were confronted from the outset with very difficult problems, including growing instability, a rapidly deteriorating economy and, most serious of all, externally inspired intrigue and subversion. With the limited information at their disposal and a lack of diplomatic support, Brigadier Lemos Pires and the MFA officers were at a disadvantage in coping with Jakarta's subversive operations and the contradictory position of the Whitlam government. The Australian government was known to favour of the integration option, but from time to time its representatives also indicated a support for a process of self-determination. One underlying problem was the effect on the colonial administration of a mounting political crisis in Portugal, hence the governor was often unable to get his foreign ministry to give sufficient attention to the increasingly urgent diplomatic aspects of the Timor problem. This situation manifested itself very seriously in August and September 1975 as Brigadier Lemos Pires was later to complain.

It was soon clear to Brigadier Lemos Pires and his MFA colleagues that the tide of support for independence was overwhelming, and irreversible. The only alternative likely to attract widespread support was a continuing link with Portugal on a somewhat different basis, but this was a contingency for which the MFA regime had little enthusiasm. It also soon became clear that the option of integration, whatever its merits, could only be imposed on the Timorese. This presented the administration with a dilemma, for late in September 1974 at a brief meeting between Portuguese Foreign Minister Mario Soares and Adam Malik a tacit agreement that Portugal would not discourage support for *integrasi* was reportedly reached. This was briefly referred to by Ali Murtopo, deputy chief of the intelligence agency, Bakin, in a statement to the Jakarta press. He remarked to the daily *Sinar Harapan* that the meeting between the foreign ministers 'represented a move stemming from the recent official statement by the Government of Portugal that it had no objection to the possibility of

---

* Governor Lemos Pires had himself never been to Timor before November 1974, but Major Jonatas, one of his key advisers, had previously served in the colony.

the integration of Portuguese Timor into Indonesian territory'. Of even more significance was General Murtopo's next remark, as quoted by this newspaper. He added: 'The problem of Portuguese Timor is now clear.'

The position of Mario Soares initially seems to have been that Portugal had a moral obligation to ascertain and to abide by the wishes of the Timorese, although the interests of neighbouring states would be taken account of. According to Indonesian sources the new leaders of Portugal went much further than this. In October, General Murtopo made an unpublicised visit to Lisbon where he raised Indonesia's special interest in the future of East Timor with Portuguese leaders, and drew to their attention Australia's accommodating attitude, as earlier expressed by Prime Minister Whitlam at Wonosobo. An Indonesian account stated.

> When Ali Murtopo began to set out the alternatives facing Timor, President Gomez (sic) cut him short. According to President Gomez there were not three options but two: joining Indonesia or independence under the Portuguese umbrella. Full independence was described by Gomez as 'unrealistic'. Even Timor remaining with Portugal did not accord with the policy of his state.[2]

At this particular meeting one source said that Prime Minister Goncalves told the Indonesian general that full independence was 'nonsense'. This account appears to have had its origins in Jakarta and might not be accurate, perhaps having been designed to exculpate Indonesia from responsibility for its subsequent actions. However, a telegram sent to Dr Almeida Santos during his visit to Timor stated that 'the Prime Minister considers it convenient for you to abstain in public statements from giving emphasis to or even referring to the independence solution on a plane with other solutions'.[3]

The two leaders may well have agreed that integration into Indonesia was preferable to a lingering Portuguese role in the colony. From accounts of the report released by the Portuguese government in October 1981,[4] President Gomes might also have hinted to Murtopo that his government would accommodate Indonesia's special interests. Yet, at least some of his later public statements were not consistent with this position. For example, in December 1974 he told the Rumanian press, during a brief visit to that country, that Timor would 'have the government it desired and should it maintain its ties with Portugal, it will be in terms of a total political and economic decolonization'.[5] It soon became clear to the Portuguese that they had no real alternative but to pursue the other options because the Timorese were not open to persuasion on the integration issue.

Within a month of their arrival the governor and his team had begun to appreciate the complexity of the task before them. Apodeti was little more than an isolated group whose principal source of strength and political inspiration was the Indonesian consulate. Since Portugal was anxious to disengage itself from colonial ties with the territory the only other option was independence and, from Lisbon's point of view, this should be achieved as quickly as possible. The administration's decolonisation strategy seems to have been worked out by a hard core of six officers—Brigadier Lemos Pires, his chief of cabinet Major Adelino Coelho, Major Mota, Major Jonatas and Captain Ramos. They established a military council and, some three months later, a Decolonization Commission, which provided the MFA with effective steering control of its decolonisation activities. One of the most important figures within this structure was Major Mota, the official responsible for political affairs.

The Portuguese decision to give encouragement to the independence movement was not a matter of preference. The MFA group has been accused of displaying a preference for Fretilin, but in fact they attempted to maintain an image of impartiality. However, Fretilin had the advantage of appealing to their concept of what a political front should be like. They shared its left-wing bias and they respected its leaders, most of whom had served in the military and had been influenced by the ideas of those junior officers from whose ranks the MFA was formed. If a Timorese nationalist movement existed it had to be that of Fretilin with its more positive platform on the issues facing East Timor. But the MFA officers concluded that if the Timorese in favour of independence were to have some chance of making their way through the minefield ahead they had no alternative but to form a common front. This might persuade the Indonesians to come to terms with the realities of Timorese nationalism and convince countries like Australia that they should take the Timorese independence movement seriously. Thus, members of the MFA team played an important role, but not necessarily the crucial one, in bringing Fretilin and UDT into a coalition with a common program for independence. This development was hardly in line with Apodeti's interests, but the Decolonization Commission, set up after the arrival of Governor Lemos Pires, insisted that the coalition be open to participation by the pro-integration party. In fact, Apodeti became increasingly uncooperative about the Portuguese decolonisation moves, at an early date opposing the plan to establish a constituent assembly at an early date.

Shortly after his arrival Governor Lemos Pires was made aware of Australia's reluctance to become involved in anything to do with the decolonisation of East Timor. In one of the documents attached to the 'Timor Dossier'* the Portuguese president was informed by the director-general of the foreign ministry, Dr Magalhaes Cruz, in a memorandum written only one week after the arrival in Dili of Lemos Pires and his party, that the Portuguese already knew of Mr Whitlam's views on the future of the colony. According to this document:

> When President Suharto and Prime Minister Whitlam met last September, Prime Minister Whitlam had concluded by giving Australia's agreement to the eventual integration of East Timor into Indonesia, feeling it to be the natural and inevitable solution...This fact gave the Jakarta Government optimism in dealing from then on with the Timor affair and contributed, without doubt, to reinforce integrationist tendencies within Indonesian political circles, which were already acting as pressure

---

* The so-called 'Timor Dossier' is a collection of reports on Timor released by the government in Lisbon, 1981.

groups. It was above all from this meeting that the idea that Timor should be integrated into Indonesia arose, always under the cover of 'the will of the population', which was expected to happen without great risks, difficulties, or problems with third parties.

However, according to this memorandum, in the weeks following the Wonosobo meeting the Australian government had become considerably 'better informed' and at a later discussion about the Timor question between officials—a meeting in the regular series of official-level talks between Australia and Indonesia— the Australian delegation played down 'the significance of the conclusions which President Suharto and Prime Minister Whitlam arrived at (the previous) September'.[6] According to the Portuguese foreign ministry's account the Australians were more restrained, pointing out that:

> Although integration was natural and inevitable, it must be based on an expression of the popular will of the Timorese. Dr Magalhaes Cruz also noted that Mr Whitlam had previously warned 'the Indonesian side' against engaging in 'certain practices which were used by the Jakarta Government in the integration of West Irian'.[7]

This must have seemed ambiguous to both the Indonesians and the Portuguese. Perhaps it gave the Portuguese some hope that Australia might quietly begin to involve itself in some positive way. However, Governor Lemos Pires was clearly dismayed that the Whitlam government could not bring itself to agree to the reopening of the consulate in Dili from which vantage point Australia might have been able to exercise a moderating influence on the main Timorese parties and on the Indonesians. As the governor told the visiting ALP Caucus delegation in March 1975:

> We asked for a Consul in November and have asked about 10 times since. Mr Taylor (political counsellor at the Australian embassy in Jakarta) was asked last week. Mr Woolcott (ambassador) was asked this week...At present, Australia cannot compensate for Indonesian propaganda or understand the day to day happenings in the colony'.[8]

He urged that Australia take a 'strong position on self-choice' and press for a genuine act of self-determination. An Australian consul could be, as the governor put it, 'another referee' who 'by his very presence would simply act as a moderating force'. I recommended such a move in my report of August 1974 and it was eventually to gain some lukewarm support in the department of foreign affairs. A recommendation along these lines was sent to the government in due course, but the proposal was rejected, apparently by Mr Whitlam, thereby abnegating a role for Australia which might conceivable have changed the whole course of history in East Timor.

The Portuguese MFA team soon had to cope with the consequences of increased Indonesian pressure on East Timor. In November 1974 the Jakarta press carried stories of Chinese (specified as 'Maoist') involvement in Timorese affairs, of demonstrations being funded by 'left-wing Chinese', and, in one extraordinary article in Berita Yudha, of four Chinese generals clandestinely entering the Portuguese colony via Australia. By February 1975 the propaganda barrage directed against East Timor had reached a crescendo. The reports and allegations were not just inaccurate or exaggerated; most of them were fabricated. This campaign served to antagonise the Portuguese decolonisation team, to strengthen their commitment to self-determination, and to hasten reaching the coalition agreement between Fretilin and UDT. Although the governor and his team were in no doubt as to the aspirations of the Indonesian government about their colonial charge, and regarded the increasing barrage of propaganda as open Indonesian meddling, they appear to have been unaware of the extent to which the campaign of disinformation was deliberately conceived and organised. The Portuguese knew little about *Operasi Komodo*, the brainchild of Ali Murtopo, launched at an Indonesian Security Council meeting in Jakarta in the previous October to coordinate a campaign to bring about the integration of East Timor largely by means of subversive actions. The existence of this operation, however, had become known to Australian officials shortly after its inception.

The international activities of *Operasi Komodo* operatives seemed to be quite successful from the outset. Most of the disinformation handouts from Antara, the official Indonesian state news agency, were obligingly carried by the foreign press. OPSUS* (Special Operations) organised diplomatic missions sent to Western Europe and North America were received sympathetically. In East Timor, on the other hand, the first phase of the operation was a dismal failure. The crude propaganda techniques and the arrogant behaviour of visiting Indonesians and of the consulate, were reminiscent of the style of the Japanese three decades earlier, and merely generated a hostility towards Indonesia that spread to the villages. It strengthened the Portuguese administration's resolve to ultimately extend to the Timorese their right to choose for themselves. It also eliminated the possibility that the Timorese might be persuaded or seduced into an act of union with Indonesia. In keeping with Lisbon's undertaking to Murtopo, the Portuguese tried to keep alive the option, but thanks to Jakarta's crude intrigues it was an impossible commodity to sell.

For the Portuguese the situation became increasingly difficult to manage after January 1975. While the clumsy Indonesian propaganda campaign had impelled the main political parties towards a common front and had created an awareness of the need for national unity, it had also led to an atmosphere charged with tensions and uncertainty. At that critical time Timor's isolation was further increased by an unrelated event: the destruction of Darwin by Cyclone Tracy. This had forced the suspension of the twice-weekly (TAA) air services to Baucau and for several months the colony was compelled to depend on

---

* OPSUS, a special operations high-level group led by General Murtopo, emerged from an intelligence unit of the Strategic Reserve Command (Kostrad). In its original form it played a key role in Indonesia's subversive operation against West Irian (Irian Jaya after formal integration in 1969) in 1961 to 1962; later, again under Murtopo, it was to perform special operations for the Suharto regime.

the goodwill of its potential aggressor in order to maintain contact with the outside world. The work of the Portuguese governor and his team was further undermined by the deteriorating political and economic situation in Portugal. By early 1975, as a result of the loss of overseas revenue and a drastic decline in domestic production, the economy of the metropolitan power was in a parlous state. For some two years after the April Coup Portugal's economy suffered from the consequences of a series of hasty experiments in the hands of differing political forces. As the MFA leaders were to discover, the task of steering the country through a period of transition towards democracy was an extremely difficult one after half a century of dictatorship. Serious divisions emerged within the military and in an atmosphere of indecision, uncertainty and intrigue, the country lurched from crisis to crisis.

The effects of the growing conflict between the forces of left and right in Lisbon inevitably came to be felt in East Timor with UDT looking to the Spinolistas and the Christian Democrats and Fretilin leaders identifying themselves with the Socialists and the new generation of MFA leaders. In the aftermath of the abortive right-wing coup by forces under the leadership of General Spinola, tensions inevitably began to emerge within the UDT–Fretilin coalition, among other things leading to suspicions by UDT leaders that the MFA officers were conspiring to place Fretilin in the leading decolonisation role at the expense, if not exclusion, of UDT. The effect of these suspicions greatly helped the Indonesians in the second phase of *Operasi Komodo*.

In the meantime, East Timor was rocked by reports emanating from Canberra—said to be from a defence department leak—that Indonesia was planning to invade the colony. The report, which seems to have been deliberately leaked in an intriguing attempt to head off a secret move by certain generals, including Yoga Sugama and Moerdani, to mount an operation against the Portuguese colony, was inspired by a 'pre-invasion' exercise at Lampung in southern Sumatra on 18 February 1975. The Portuguese tried to play down the report, as did the Timorese political party leaders, but a ripple of apprehension swept across the country. What was unnerving to the Portuguese was the fact that the report followed a series of perniciously hostile broadcasts from stations in West Timor which claimed, among other things, that a communist plot was being hatched, and that 'left-leaning' MFA officers had been making secret deals with Fretilin and UDT and were planning to hand over the government of the province to these Timorese in the latter part of the year. The Jakarta press also reported that Apodeti was being systematically persecuted, forcing hundreds of its followers to seek refuge in the western sector of the island. In fact, these reports were nothing less than part of the Bakin operation designed to create fear, divisions and suspicions in the Portuguese colony.

Although Indonesia subsequently denied that it had any intention of invading East Timor, the incident did carry a clear message for the MFA group in the colony. Jakarta did not approve of the coalition move, regarding it as an unacceptable departure from the understanding reached during Murtopo's visit to Lisbon. The atmosphere of mounting alarm in Dili led to one of the most important discussions of the Timor problem, a secret meeting at 11 Mulgrave Street, London between high-level Indonesian and Portuguese delegations on 9 March 1975. The Indonesian party was led by Ali Murtopo and included the Indonesian ambassadors from London and Paris, while the Portuguese mission consisted of Dr Almeida Santos, a minister without portfolio Major Vitor Alves, Secretary of State for Foreign Affairs Dr Jorge Campinos, Dr Castilho and Major Mota from Lemos Pires' Timor Command. The Indonesians were later to claim that at this meeting the Portuguese made some major concessions but, based on my research, this interpretation seems far from accurate.[9] The Portuguese appear to have told the Indonesians that integration was an option for which there was little support in the colony and that it was neither possible nor acceptable for them to contemplate handing over the territory to Indonesia in blatant disregard of the wishes of the Timorese. On the other hand, the Portuguese indicated that they would be receptive to a solution that would allay Indonesian fears and at the same time reflect the wishes of the people.

General Murtopo expressed his disquiet at the fact that both UDT and Fretilin had been in contact with Australia and the UN Commission for Decolonization, but that these opportunities had not been extended to Apodeti. The Indonesians apparently proposed that they be allowed to participate directly in the decolonisation process as an 'interested party'. Murtopo told the Portuguese that his government was under strong pressure, not only from the Indonesian parliament and armed forces, but from the people of Indonesian Timor, some of whom were prepared to 'invade' the colony. Dr Almeida Santos rejected the proposal that Indonesia become directly involved in the decolonisation. According to Dr Campinos, it would have been tantamount to establishing a Portuguese–Indonesian condominium in East Timor which would inevitably give rise to dissension. On the other hand, the Portuguese said that they proposed to set up a consultative council in which the three parties would be represented. This would give Indonesia time to demonstrate to the Timorese the advantages of integration, and this might, in time, attract the support of most of the colony's population.

This was anything but enticing to the Indonesians who pressed the Portuguese to drop the idea of a provisional or transitional government and to set up a special consultative body with high-level Indonesian and Portuguese participation, a body that would advise the governor of the province on the best methods of conditioning the Timorese to come around to accepting integration. The Indonesians also proposed that Consul Tomodok, whose behaviour had offended the Portuguese, be withdrawn from Timor, in exchange for the removal by Lisbon of certain unnamed MFA officers. The Portuguese responded negatively to these proposals, pointing out to the Indonesians that such actions would expose the two governments to the charge that they were scheming to impose neo-colonial solutions. Moreover, the Indonesian proposition would undermine the confidence of the political parties in

Portugal's good intentions, and would lead to demands that the Timor problem be internationalised, a prospect that was very unattractive to the Indonesians.

The Indonesians assured the Portuguese that they would not use military force because this would be in violation of the Indonesian constitution, not to speak of the understanding that had been reached between Jakarta and Lisbon in previous talks. The Portuguese, for their part, promised that they would place no obstacles in the way of Apodeti's activities, provided that the pro-Indonesia party agreed to participate in the transitional government. They informed the Indonesians that the best way to improve their image in the territory would be by means of economic cooperation. Mota told them that the Timorese would need time to come to terms with the idea of integration, and reminded the Indonesians that the unrest that had occurred in the territory was largely caused by Apodeti's crude projection of Indonesia as a country prepared to use its armed might. The Indonesians were urged to correct the threatening and unfriendly image created in Timorese minds by their aggressive broadcasts from Kupang and Atambua. The London talks appear to have ended somewhat inconclusively with the Indonesians merely promising to convey to President Suharto a detailed account of the Portuguese position. It seems that the Portuguese delegation in fact sought to drive home to the Indonesians the need to be patient, flexible and moderate in facing up to East Timor's decolonisation. It was apparent to them, however, that getting Indonesia to accept the course of events was not going to be easy. The Indonesians may have read more into the conciliatory attitudes of the Portuguese than was intended. In the event, it is perhaps conceivable that Murtopo returned to Jakarta mistakenly convinced that the officials carrying out Timor's decolonisation would not be averse to the idea of helping Indonesia promote the concept of integration.

One outcome of the London meeting was the arrival in Dili about a month later of an Indonesian delegation, described publicly as a 'commercial' mission. In fact it included some of the principal actors of *Operasi Komodo*, such as Colonel Sugiyanto (an officer of the RPKAD—Resimen Para Komando Angkatan Darat, or the Army Commando Paratroop Regiment—who was listed as a civilian for the occasion) and Louis Taolin who at once sought to allay Timorese apprehensions and to set the stage for the next phase of the secret operation. For example, a senior member of the delegation, Colonel Pitut, told Fretilin leaders that Indonesia had no ambitions in East Timor and, in principle, supported independence. But with the UDT the Indonesians dwelt on the presence of a communist threat and said they feared that East Timor was ripe for penetration. At these meetings they were able to make an assessment of the Timorese leaders, as well as test the overall political atmosphere. It seems that the Indonesians left Timor with the impression that Apodeti was not an adequate channel for the promotion of their objectives. Apodeti lacked popular support, and its leaders had manoeuvred themselves into a position of isolation. The Portuguese MFA representatives went out of their way to reassure the Indonesians that the pro-integration party's interests were being carefully protected, but they also pointed out to their Indonesian guests that there was a limit to what could be done for a party that simply lacked popular appeal.

In the event, the psychological warfare in the form of broadcasts from Kupang was for a time toned down and tensions in the colony eased accordingly. Even when members of the ALP's Caucus, Foreign Affairs and Defence Committee visited Timor in March, many of the Portuguese and the Timorese political leaders already seemed confident that Indonesia would not invade East Timor, optimistically believing that Jakarta could be persuaded to accept the political realities of the situation. However, the media campaign orchestrated by *Operasi Komodo* operatives was not abandoned. Reports surfacing in the Jakarta press suggested that, behind the scenes, the Indonesians were still seeking to discredit the MFA team, or at least sections of it. On 27 March a leading article in the Indonesian Times stated that, according to 'reliable information gleaned by a roving (Antara) correspondent, a planned absolute takeover of the power in the colony by a combination of groups composed mainly of leading members of the Armed Forces and Fretilin party' had been uncovered. The newspaper went on to claim that 'the Portuguese government in Lisbon fully supports the planned formation of the new, sole party, and the take-over of power by the new political front is now a matter of time only'. The report suggested that 'the young officers who were assigned to the colony a few months ago' were all members of a communist movement in Portugal.

In April, however, Timorese fears were somewhat eased by reports that President Suharto had assured Prime Minister Whitlam at the latter's Townsville meeting early that month that Indonesia had no plans to seize East Timor. As *Angkatan Bersenjata* reported it, the president had explained that Indonesia 'does not have territorial ambitions, let alone (plans) to include the territory of Portuguese Timor within the territory of the Republic of Indonesia by force'. In that same month the Timorese parties and the Lemos Pires administration began making real progress towards establishing the institutions for the transfer of powers. But the negotiations soon ran into difficulties. Apodeti was still refusing to participate in the Decolonization Commission, the purpose of which, the party's leaders complained, ran contrary to their objectives. Apodeti favoured a referendum or plebiscite, but this was strongly opposed by Fretilin, whose leaders argued, as Jose Ramos Horta put it, that 'one does not ask a slave whether he wants to be free'.

UDT–Fretilin relations, on the other hand, began to be affected by the growing crisis between left and right in Portugal, and the UDT's mounting suspicions that its coalition partner and the MFA officers were working hand in glove. Certain UDT leaders, among them Lopes da Cruz and Mousinho, appeared convinced of this, but I have not come across any evidence of such a conspiracy. True, some of the MFA officers and the sergeants were clearly more impressed with Fretilin because it was the best organised party and, in broad terms, they were probably more in sympathy with its objectives, but others sought to remain strictly impartial and to keep within the spirit of the talks with Murtopo in London.

Major Mota, perhaps the key member of the MFA group, apparently made a sincere attempt to preserve the neutrality of the Decolonization Commission in its relations with the parties. On leaving Timor in the following August he told Jill Jolliffe in Darwin that in reality there was not much difference between UDT and Fretilin. The UDT, he said, was more 'functional or bureaucratic' while Fretilin was more concerned to relate its programs to the situations in other Portuguese territories. But the efforts of the MFA officers to establish an impartial image were undermined by local fears that they were agents of the movement's left wing in Portugal. They were constantly being branded as 'communistic' by the Portuguese right in the colony, including certain senior military officers, such as Major Cadete and Major Maggioli, who had considerable influence in UDT circles.

If other circumstances had been normal, the situation would have been manageable. After all, the difficulties encountered by the Portuguese were by no means without precedent. Most colonial powers have had to contend with conflicts and tensions fomented by rivalries between right- and left-wing forces in the course of decolonisation and the more serious consequences have usually been averted. The problem in East Timor was that the growing political tensions and suspicions made local conditions extremely vulnerable to externally inspired pressures, namely the subversive activities of agents of *Operasi Komodo*. More precisely, conditions were ripe for a new and more subtle operation by Bakin operatives, an operation designed to destabilise the increasingly troubled political situation in the colony. As a result of the Sugiyanto–Pitut visit, both Fretilin and UDT were invited to send missions to Jakarta, but the missions were treated very differently. For the Fretilin party, which included Horta and Alarico Fernandes, it was a lavish, if not intimidating, show of hospitality, while for the UDT guests, the leading operatives of *Operasi Komodo*, including Murtopo and Sugiyanto, began in earnest a process designed to wean the conservative Timorese away from their commitment to the coalition.

At one of these meetings, the Indonesians detected the weak link in the UDT leadership, its president, Francisco Lopes da Cruz. The object of the exercise was to split the coalition by subtly nurturing UDT's fears of communism and by the leaders' lack of complete confidence in the political impartiality of the MFA leaders. Fortuitously, when the UDT leaders later visited Australia a few right-wing former commandos also contributed to the Indonesian cause by repeatedly stressing the dangers of communism and, in at least one case, it was suggested that UDT withdraw from the coalition and join Apodeti.

The first phase of talks on decolonisation took place on 7 May 1975, when the commission met with a Fretilin–UDT delegation in the presence of Major Vitor Alves. The agenda included a discussion of the UDT–Fretilin demand that the Portuguese government declare its commitment to independence, the setting up of a constituent assembly, and the arrangements for the transfer of powers. Apodeti did not attend the sessions but, in keeping with the spirit of the London meeting, the Portuguese held separate talks with its leaders outside the main conference. The position of Apodeti was that it would not participate in such talks unless the coalition first agreed to an 'a priori acceptance of the principle of integration with Indonesia'.

In their talks with the coalition parties the Portuguese accepted the right of the Timorese to independence, but they stopped short of declaring their commitment to it. They also opposed a move to deny Apodeti's right to exist as a political party, arguing that the pro-integration party should, as Jill Jolliffe reported it, be brought 'out of clandestinity' and encouraged to participate in the next session of negotiations at Macau in June. The MFA also argued that Apodeti should be represented in the transitional administration, but that if this could not be agreed to they should at least participate in the elections proposed for October 1975. However, Fretilin objected to the idea that Apodeti should participate in the Macau talks, arguing that it was unacceptable for a party that advocated 'recolonisation' to be allowed to play a role in decolonisation talks. The May talks did little to help the shaky coalition. The UDT leaders favoured a gradual progress towards self-government and were somewhat distrustful of Fretilin's impatience with the slow pace of change. Other happenings also placed strains on the relationship, including moves by Fretilin to introduce radical programs designed to bring about drastic changes in education and in agriculture. The idea of forming 'revolutionary brigades' (as proposed by Fretilin) had no appeal for the conservatives in UDT.

Meanwhile, in Lisbon on 29 May, the Timor problem was considered by members of the central body concerned with Portugal's decolonisation program, the National Decolonization Commission, which included President Costa Gomes, Major Vitor Alves, Dr Almeida Santos and Minister for Foreign Affairs Major Melo Antunes. The main question was whether or not the summit should be held if Fretilin refused to participate. In the end it was decided to go ahead regardless of Fretilin's position—on the advice of Vitor Alves and Almeida Santos (a position opposed by the foreign minister).

The rupture of the coalition greatly disturbed the moderates of both parties. In June, Horta confided to me that Mario Carrascalão and Domingos de Oliveira shared his view that a common front was essential to the independence movement and that his confidence that it would eventually be re-established. Fretilin leaders acknowledged that a small vocal group of left-wing students had helped undermine the relationship and this led to some discussion with the governor of a plan to expel them from the colony as a means of healing the rift between the parties. In the event, no real progress towards a compromise appears to have been made. Horta had hoped to convince his party that delegates should be sent to the Macau conference, but he did not succeed and the second series of talks went ahead without Fretilin being present. Most of Fretilin's central committee were adamant that it was unthinkable to discuss decolonisation with a party committed merely to changing the form of East Timor's colonial status.

The Macau talks took place from 26 to 28 June, in spite of Fretilin's boycott. UDT and Apodeti were strongly represented, while the Portuguese delegation included Dr Almeida Santos, Major Vitor Alves and Dr Jorge Campinos. It is difficult to know just what was achieved at Macau. On the surface it seemed that there was considerable progress with the plans for decolonisation. However, East Timor's fate rested largely on what was going on beneath the surface. For one thing, separate talks took place between the Portuguese and a special Indonesian delegation, most of whose members were drawn from the operatives of *Operasi Komodo*, and who were in regular contact with Apodeti and Lopes da Cruz throughout the conference. According to the Timor Dossier, Murtopo's agents were there at the invitation of the Portuguese, that is, of the central government in Lisbon (Lemos Pires, it seems, was neither consulted nor informed about this briefing arrangement). Of course, the presence of Indonesian observers would have been consistent with the measure of understanding that had emerged from the London meeting but, according to an account by Jill Jolliffe, the Timor Dossier indicates that:

> the Portuguese told the Indonesian delegation that in Macau they had drafted Timor's decolonisation statute in such a way that it would give them a year and a few months to work through Apodeti to persuade the East Timorese to support integration.[10]

If this failed and Indonesia resorted to force, the Portuguese could simply bail out.

Jolliffe's account suggests that Lisbon had already resolved to abandon East Timor, but that this plan had apparently not been conveyed to Lemos Pires and his MFA officers who were running the Decolonization Commission. The officials in the colony would have been aware that it would have been impossible for Jakarta to have used Apodeti to persuade the Timorese to accept integration. It does reveal, however, the duplicity and naivety of the central government's Timor policy, as well as the fact that, in the face of determined Indonesian opposition to a genuine act of self determination, and Australia's refusal to help, the Portuguese leaders could not muster the resolve to assert the rights of the people whom they had held in colonial bondage for more than four centuries.

In spite of the intrigue that took place behind the scenes, and in spite of the absence of Fretilin, the conference did make some progress. The draft constitutional law had been prepared by Dr Almeida Santos, after some consultation with representatives of the parties concerned. There was a fundamental difference about the word 'independence'. Apodeti strongly opposed its use. Apodeti's representatives also opposed setting up a transitional government because such a move would further weaken the group's position. The pro-integration party demanded that the colonial power continue to rule the colony until a Popular Assembly had been established. The Portuguese gave considerable weight to the position of Apodeti, letting the Indonesian 'observers' know that this indulgence was going on. In the event, the word 'independence' occurred only once in the final text, provoking UDT leaders to accuse the Portuguese of having given in to Apodeti. It is interesting to note that the UDT had demanded that this term appear clearly and unequivocally in the program for the future. The UDT also criticised the Portuguese for not allowing for a longer period for decolonisation. Privately, Dr Almeida Santos and Dr Campinos sought to reassure the UDT delegation that the proposed decolonisation program, although presented as a compromise, would genuinely reflect the popular will.

The final text was eventually agreed to by the two parties and, less than two weeks after the conference ended, the Portuguese Council of the Revolution formally approved the constitutional law. The new law provided for a three-year period in which to bring about the termination of Portuguese sovereignty. It provided for setting up a high commissioner's council, comprising a high commissioner who was to retain a casting vote, and five 'joint secretaries', two of them Portuguese nominees and three Timorese, it being envisaged that one would be selected or elected from each of UDT, Fretilin and Apodeti. There was also to be a consultative Government Council, consisting of two representatives nominated by each of the regional councils. At a lower level there was to be a council formed in each *concelho*, based on an electoral process that was already under way by July. In addition, each of the three political parties was to nominate four members to the Government Council, making a total of thirty-eight in this consultative body. Under the terms of the new law elections were to be held for a Popular Assembly in October 1976 with Portuguese sovereignty coming to an end two or three years later.

The new decolonisation law might eventually have proved acceptable to all three Timorese parties—even to Fretilin. Although it accorded Apodeti a role out of proportion to its level of popular support, the arrangement seemed to be the least the Portuguese could do to honour the concessions allegedly agreed to at the London meeting with Ali Murtopo. On the face of it the law did acknowledge the right of the Timorese to self-determination and in the circumstances Fretilin and UDT would have had little difficulty in keeping the interim administration on course for independence.

Unfortunately, the constitutional law was announced at a time when all of the political forces in the colony were in disarray, including the Portuguese. The political parties were moving in different directions and the Portuguese community appeared to be too divided and demoralised by events both in Timor and in Portugal to exercise effective leadership. The officials had been unable to persuade the largest party, Fretilin, to take part in the Macau talks, and had shocked its leaders by ensuring an equal representation for the smallest party, Apodeti, knowing that it was little more than an Indonesian front. By July, UDT was also a divided political force, with its president, Lopes da Cruz, having already been secretly recruited to the Indonesian cause by the agents of *Operasi Komodo*. While more and more Timorese favoured eventual independence, the prospects of betrayal were mounting daily. This was a matter of growing concern to the Decolonization Commission, probably the only body genuinely committed to helping the Timorese work out something resembling a freely expressed settlement. Although the MFA officers may have come to regard Fretilin as the most effective and dynamic of the political parties they were deeply disappointed at its failure to control the immoderate behaviour of its small, but vocal, left wing and, most of all, at its Central Committee's refusal to participate in the Macau talks. Some observers have claimed that the MFA officers persuaded Fretilin not to go to Macau, but in many interviews with Fretilin leaders and MFA officers I have never found anything to support this contention. On the contrary, as Major Mota put it in an interview in August 1975: 'We tried again and again to bring Fretilin to the Macau conference table.' Even after Macau the Portuguese continued to urge Fretilin leaders to resume talks with UDT, warning them, especially after the latter had launched their 'show of force', that not to negotiate would inevitably lead East Timor into 'a sea of blood'.

Portuguese attempts to reverse the trend in the deteriorating relationship between the two major parties in June and July were constantly being undermined by their own serious internal differences. Some officers, like Major Maggioli and Major Cadete, not members of the MFA, were outspokenly opposed to the ideas and work of Mota and Jonatas and some appear to have intrigued against the decolonisation policies of the MFA team within the civil administration. Relations with the largely conservative territorial administrators, generally resistant to the reformist ideas of this new generation of Portuguese leaders, also appear to have become strained. Finally, the MFA officers may have erred in attempting to expedite a very complex process in a society totally unaccustomed to radical change and with a team of officials most of whom were lacking in experience in such sensitive roles. The haste, however, was a factor not of their choosing, but of the metropolitan government in Lisbon.

It has been common for some, especially politicians, officials and academics in Australia, to lay most of the blame on the Portuguese for what happened after 11 August 1975, but the shortcomings of the decolonisation program and of those responsible for implementing were among the less serious problems facing the colony at that time, and would not have been unresolvable, and certainly would not have led to the political upheaval that was to follow. After all, difficulties in working out a consensus between opposing political forces were common to virtually all similar decolonisation situations. The situation in East Timor in June and July of that year would have been quite manageable, had not the agents of *Operasi Komodo* deliberately and cynically set out to exploit all elements in the crisis. For Portugal July was a month of deep domestic crisis. In the first week the socialist prime minister and majors Melo Antunes and Vitor Alves withdrew from the government, followed by the resignation of the Social Democrat ministers, thus removing the political leaders who had been most closely involved in the Timor problem.

At least some of the members of the National Decolonization Commission were still of the opinion that Portugal should continue to press for a proper consultation of the wishes of the Timorese and in July the authorities in the colony pressed on with elections for local councils at *concelho* level. These elections gave a return of about 55 per cent to Fretilin candidates, a strong but lesser showing to UDT, and negligible support for Apodeti. The Fretilin victory was clearly not welcomed by the right wing in the territory, and it was their fears and suspicions that Indonesian agents set out to manipulate. False rumours were deliberately circulated by Indonesian agents, some of whom had penetrated deep into the territory. One such story was that Fretilin had set up secret military camps at which Vietnamese officers were providing sophisticated military training. The Portuguese military commander told me that he and his colleagues knew these reports to be without any foundation, but they had difficulty in countering them. Then there were reports of a planned Fretilin coup which were also part of the disinformation campaign by Indonesian intelligence. Even the bishop of Timor, Bishop Ribeiro, was taken in by some of these reports. He told UDT and Kota leaders that he had obtained information that Vietnamese troops had been smuggled into the territory, and urged them to prepare themselves.

In these very difficult circumstances the Portuguese were hardly able to turn to Australia for support. While the Australian government was by no means unaware of the debilitating effect of the ongoing crisis in Lisbon on the situation in Timor, it also knew about the clandestine activities of *Operasi Komodo*. It did not, however, respond to calls for help from Timor. Although Australian diplomats made visits to Dili during 1975, as one Portuguese later bitterly put it, 'They came with eyes full of sympathy, said little, and apparently did nothing.' Major Mota remarked that Australia was always 'expressing concern at what was happening' but in reality did nothing to help. Certainly, as will be discussed later, Australia's influence in Jakarta and, more importantly, in the countries with which Indonesia had close economic and defence links, could have headed off the crisis had the Whitlam government acted responsibly, on the basis of information at its disposal.

Notes

1   Bill Nicol, *The Stillborn Nation* (Melbourne: Viza, 1978), p. 175.
2   Soekanto (ed.), *Integrasi* (Jakarta: Yayasan Perikesit, 1976), reportedly a Bakin-inspired publication.
3   'Estado Maior General das Forcas Armadas, Relatorio de Timor' (1977) (Report of Timor from the Staff Major General of the Armed Forces) in the so-called 'Timor Dossier', a collection of reports on Timor released by the government in Lisbon, 1981.
4   Based on material in the Timor Dossier.
5   Luis Barretto, Testimony before the Permanent Peoples' Tribunal, Lisbon, 1981.
6   Jill Jolliffe, *Canberra Times*, 21 October 1981.
7   The Timor Dossier.
8   ALP Caucus delegation report.
9   Soekanto, *Integrasi*.
10 *Canberra Times*, 19 October 1981.

Chapter Six
Indonesia and East Timor's decolonisation

In spite of the Portuguese apprehensions that were rife in the previous thirty years, it was not until after the Lisbon coup of 25 April 1974 that the Indonesians gave other than cursory attention to the insignificant colony adjacent to their province of East Nusatenggara. When the preparatory talks for Indonesian independence were taking place, some Indonesian leaders urged that the North Borneo territories and East Timor be included in a wider Indonesian Republic, as well as the territories 'from Sabang to Merauke', but a firm position along these lines was never developed. In the event, Portuguese colonial rule over the colony was firmly re-established by the time Indonesia had formally attained independent status in 1949. In the 1950s the central government in Jakarta was much too preoccupied with the task of welding its conglomeration of islands and peoples with their great ethnic diversity into a unified state to give any attention to a remote and impoverished territory like Portuguese Timor. Immediately after independence Indonesian leaders faced serious internal challenges to their authority with insurrections launched by separatist movements such as Kartosuwirjo's Darul Islam in Java, the RMS (Republik Maluku Selatan) movement in the South Moluccas, and the TII (Tentara Islam Indonesia) led by Daud Beureuh in Atjeh. In 1957 and 1958 the central government faced its most serious challenge for the 'Colonels' Revolt' which was only crushed after major military operations in Sumatra and Sulawesi.

In the late 1950s Indonesia seemed to go out of its way to disclaim any designs on Portuguese Timor. In 1957, for example, the Indonesian representative told the First Committee of the United Nations General Assembly that:

> the attempt to link West Irian with East New Guinea simply because the two territories happened to form one island would create a very dangerous precedent, for example, in the case of the islands off Borneo and Timor. Indonesia has no claim to any territories which had not been part of the former Netherlands East Indies. No one should suggest otherwise or advance dangerous theories in that respect.

Three years later Dr Subandrio reaffirmed this position, in an address to the General Assembly. He said that:

> Indonesia explicitly does not make any claim at all to territories such as that in Borneo or Timor which lies [sic] within the Indonesian Archipelago, but was not part of the Netherlands East Indies.

On the island incidents did occur from time to time, but these usually erupted because of internecine disputes within *sucos* straddling sections of the border and they were invariably resolved by local officials with minimum intervention on the part of Lisbon and Jakarta. As we have seen, the 1959 revolt was not engineered by Jakarta, but was inspired by Permesta refugees who had been granted political refuge by the Portuguese, and their abortive attempt to bring about the overthrow of the colonial regime both surprised and embarrassed the central government authorities. Although its aim was not clear the Permesta group was probably not planning to make East Timor part of the republic from which they had been fleeing. The Indonesian consul in Dili may have played a part in the affair, but his complicity seems to have been a personal initiative taken without the knowledge of his masters in Jakarta. The incident left the Portuguese in jitters, but the Indonesians glossed over it, and, as the campaign spearheaded by President Sukarno to 'regain' West Irian gained momentum, the president on occasion sought to exploit Portugal's unchallenged position in East Timor as evidence that Indonesia had no territorial ambitions. When Konfrontasi (the Confrontation of Malaya) got under way, Portuguese Timor's unmolested position was again used to demonstrate that Indonesia had no imperialist ambitions.

There is evidence that, in the 1960s, the Indonesian government, at least while Sukarno was in power, became more sensitive to the continued existence of Portuguese colonial rule in the eastern part of Timor. They began to acknowledge it to be a problem ahead for Indonesian foreign policy, particularly as the Salazar regime's colonial intransigence increasingly became the subject of criticism from developing countries. Indonesia had aspired to a leadership role in the non-aligned movement. At an Afro–Asian meeting in Jakarta in 1961, Ruslan Abdulgani, at the time vice-chairman of Sukarno's Supreme Advisory Council, called on his fellow countrymen 'to fill your hearts with hatred not only for Portuguese colonialism, but for all colonialism still existing on Asian and African soil'. He added that Indonesia's 'eyes and heart are directed towards Portuguese Timor and Goa', still 'under the power of colonialism'. In 1962 General Nasution referred to the situation in Timor as one of 'enslavement'.

The Indian seizure of Goa aroused speculation that East Timor was ripe for a similar operation that would attract only feigned disapproval from Western nations and applause from the non-aligned world. But Indonesia soon became absorbed with the confrontation of Malaysia—a much more serious challenge— and the Portuguese in Timor were merely the butt of a few provocative remarks by Indonesian leaders. Dr Subandrio declared that Indonesia was not ignoring the situation in Timor and on one occasion he uttered a vague threat: 'Do not wait until the Indonesian people's anger flares up.' In September 1963 the then Minister for Information Ruslan Abdulgani was reported as saying:

> Although we are not an expansionist nation we cannot allow people of common ancestry to be persecuted and thrown in prison merely because they want to unite with the fatherland of their ancestors.

But this was one of the few statements to imply that the Timorese should at some stage be absorbed into Indonesia. In the same year a prominent army leader, General Mokogina, was reported in the *Washington Post* as saying:

> If the people of Timor today or tomorrow started a revolution we would support them...After independence, if they wanted to stay independent, fine...If they want to join Indonesia, we will talk it over.

It is probable that these statements did not really reflect an upsurge of interest in liberating East Timor from the yoke of colonialism. These occasional remarks by Indonesian leaders need to be considered against the fact that, at the time, some of the non-aligned states began to contrast the Sukarno regime's frenetic efforts to undermine Malaysia with its near silence on the plight of a neighbouring people under the colonial yoke of the arch-enemy of the Third World states. The remarks by Ruslan Abdulgani and Subandrio might therefore have been merely designed to redress the rhetorical imbalance. The most precise statement of policy appears to have been the moderate comments of Mokogina. In the same year General Nasution, in a reference to both East Timor and North Borneo, remarked: 'We support their struggles, but do not claim their territories.' On the ground, relations were distant but cordial. Indonesia maintained a consulate in Dili, and relations between authorities on the border at Oecussi and at the frontier were correct with the occasional incidents being easily contained. A movement for the liberation of East Timor existed in Jakarta, under a Timorese named Mao Klao—virtually unknown in East Timor, even after April 1974—yet although it was accorded a measure of recognition it appears to have been given no real encouragement.

Under both Sukarno and Suharto there was an underlying complacency in Indonesian political attitudes towards the Timor colony. From Jakarta's point of view the West Irian and Konfrontasi questions were much more important and absorbing and in these disputes East Timor had no strategic significance. No outside power, and certainly none of the major powers, showed the slightest interest in the territory. The Portuguese, after 1963, went out of their way to not provoke Jakarta. In the early 1960s, the authorities in Dili did make several attempts to strengthen links with Australia and, especially after Indonesia launched a military operation against West Irian, to elicit some assurance from Canberra that Australia would not stand idly by if Indonesia were to make a move against their vulnerable colony. But in the strategic reappraisals being undertaken in Canberra in the early 1960s the position of East Timor became less important, and as international pressure on the Salazar regime mounted the Portuguese presence was perceived to be more of a liability than an asset.

Portuguese appeals fell on deaf ears, and Australia's envoys to Timor were given strict instructions not to encourage their hosts in the belief that Australia would come to their rescue in the event of an Indonesian move against them. Indeed, the Menzies government reacted coolly to an approach in 1962 by a group of Portuguese dissidents (including an army colonel, a judge and some other senior officials) who sounded out what would be Canberra's reaction if they were to launch a coup against the Salazar regime's representatives in Timor, a move which they hoped would precipitate Salazar's downfall. In no circumstances, the consul was instructed unequivocally, should the would-be rebels be encouraged to believe that Australia would support their insurrection. The negative reaction from Canberra led to the conspiracy being abandoned. Australia not only kept a distance from the Portuguese position in East Timor: in informal ways, Canberra's stand-off policy was conveyed to Indonesian diplomats, so that Jakarta became aware by the mid-1960s that Australia would not stand in the way of any Indonesian move against the colony, by whatever means. Henceforth, there developed an assumption by Indonesians that Australian diplomats had come to accept that the Portuguese colony's future lay as part of Indonesia.

One can only speculate on what might have happened after Konfrontasi lost momentum, had President Sukarno remained in power, for East Timor would certainly have offered a very tempting target to a regime that was seeking to improve its battered image in the non-aligned bloc. But by 1966 power had slipped into the hands of a right-wing military regime. In the aftermath of the bloody events following the abortive coup the new rulers were anxious to establish a reputation for restraint, moderation and reliability that would facilitate an inflow of Western capital and entice Western commitment to the rescue of the country's flagging economy. The poor colony of East Timor held no interest for the new regime, whose leaders were no doubt gratified to have as a neighbour a regime equally vehemently opposed to communism and generally intolerant of radical influences of any kind. No other country had expressed any interest in East Timor and the new regime noted with satisfaction the growing assumption in Canberra that the colony would fall under Indonesian control should the Portuguese decide to pull out. The issue of Timor's future was so inconsequential that the new regime does not appear to have formed any definite policy on it. In general, however, the Suharto regime's position was influenced by its desire to reassure neighbouring states and territories that Konfrontasi was a nightmare of the past. East Timor would probably, sometime, fall into the republic's lap like an overripe piece of fruit.

At the time most outside observers gave little thought to the rights of the Timorese. An article by an American academic, Professor Donald Weatherbee, written in the aftermath of the 1965 coup, expressed such an attitude. He observed that:

> when Indonesian ideology and interests converge in a Timor "liberation" policy, the Portuguese will be faced with the realities of power in the archipelago.

He concluded:

> In a sense Portuguese Timor is a trust territory, the Portuguese *holding it in trust for Indonesia.*[1]

There was no moral justification, even at that time, for this cursory dismissal of East Timor's right to self-determination, but such a view was common among the few Australian and American officials responsible for handling Indonesian affairs and during informal contacts it was inevitably conveyed to Indonesian officials.

Border skirmishes continued to occur after 1966, but these difficulties were usually resolved in the cordial atmosphere which prevailed between the senior army officers on both sides though there were some curious twists in the relationship. As the result of an initiative by the governor, Colonel Aldeia, who had developed an easy informal relationship with Colonel El Tari, the governor of East Nusatenggara, Foreign Minister Adam Malik was to visit Dili in mid-1972 to discuss setting up a joint border commission to facilitate settling disputes. But, in what was later termed an 'April Fool's Day joke', a report was carried by a Jakarta daily of 1 April of an insurrection in East Timor by an independence movement. An attempt was made to pass it off light-heartedly, but it was said to have been deliberately inspired and it had the effect of sabotaging the proposed visit. On 5 April 1972 the Indonesian embassy in Canberra issued a press release which sought 'to clarify a point made by AAP-Reuters News' that:

> Indonesia will finance and support a liberation movement in Portuguese Timor.

Iterating the policy expressed by General Mokoginta some nine years earlier the release quoted Malik as saying that:

> the movement of [sic] independence in Portuguese Timor will be supported by Indonesia only if the indigenous people of that region sincerely wished independence.

The statement went on seemingly to dissociate Indonesia from any complicity in moves to force the issue. It read:

> Indonesia cannot push them towards independence if the people themselves remain passive about it. It is most important that the issue is not to be forced.[2]

It seems that there was something of a shadow play behind this incident. Who aborted the Malik visit to Timor by leaking a false report of a coup in Dili? Certainly Malik's statement did not please some Indonesian leaders, among them Johnny Naro (vice-president of the Indonesian Parliament and a deputy from the Nusatenggara area), who was not at all in favour of any encouraging the Timorese to set up an independent state if the Portuguese were to be forced out of the colony. He expressed the hope that the Indonesian government would take steps to appeal for the eventual return of Portuguese Timor to Indonesia. The Indonesian people, he said, should show concern at the plight of their 'brothers deprived of freedom, and economically destitute'.

In spite of the minor skirmishes and occasional provocative statements, the foreign ministry appears to have given scant attention to Timor until shortly after the Lisbon coup of April 1974. But it seems that another and more influential centre of power began taking a closer interest in the subject. According to an Indonesian source, a Bakin/OPSUS (Special Operations) group took a look at the position in late 1972 or 1973 and came out strongly against the idea of supporting independence for East Timor, should the Portuguese withdraw or be forced out. With the United States withdrawing from Vietnam, the Indonesian military concluded that even the continuation of Portuguese colonial rule was to be preferred to an independent state which could add a new dimension to Indonesia's security problems.

The Lisbon coup took the Indonesians by surprise, as it did most other countries. At first there were mixed reactions in Jakarta to the prospect of East Timor being decolonised and to the sudden emergence of political parties. According to a secondary source, Malik's off-the-cuff reaction was that the new Lisbon regime's policy towards overseas territories was progressive in character because 'there is the intention to give independence'. Naro, on the other hand, urged that Jakarta take 'preliminary steps and work out a special policy on Portuguese Timor so that finally that area will once again return to Indonesian control'. Although Indonesia had operated the largest consulate in East Timor for many years, with a Bakin agent on the staff, its appreciation of the real situation in the colony was anything but soundly based. This may have been in part because of the restrictions placed on the movements of Indonesian consular staff, but a more important reason was the poor calibre of the staff appointed to the post. The consuls seemed to be adept at converting preposterous rumours into reports that were duly transmitted to Jakarta. For example, when a 7000-tonne Portuguese vessel visited Dili in 1963 and disembarked some 500 troop reinforcements, the Indonesian consul of the time confided to me that he had just informed his government that more than 5000 troops had been landed. Yet it should not have taken a skilled observer to comprehend that that vessel could not have accommodated more than a quarter of that number.

In 1974 Indonesia's man in Dili was Elias Tomodok, originally from the island of Roti, to the south-west of western Timor. I spoke at length with Tomodok during the fact-finding visit to the territory in mid-1974. He seemed obsessed with stories of intrigue and with the view that East Timor must become part of Indonesia. He gave a grossly inflated view of the amount of support for Apodeti and of general attitudes towards the option of integration. According to Bill Nicol, who was not particularly sympathetic to Timorese politicians, Tomodok 'was respected by few' and 'was a fool, but a dangerous and powerful one'. Nicol claimed that Australian intelligence sources in Canberra described cables sent by Tomodok to Jakarta as 'inflammatory and provocative'.[3] But the fact remains that Tomodok was Indonesia's senior representative in the colony in the years before and after the April Coup, and during that time he no doubt supplied his masters with a series of very inaccurate accounts of political, social and economic conditions in the territory would have been a strong advocate of *integrasi*, probably lacing his reports with fiction and falsification to strengthen his case.*

Not surprisingly, the authorities in Jakarta appeared to have an unrealistic picture of conditions in East Timor when the Lisbon coup caused the territory to assume a new importance in Indonesia's foreign-policy perspectives. They may have been genuinely unaware of the strength of the feeling for independence. From the outset Tomodok sought to discredit Fretilin and to portray it as a sinister vehicle for a communist conspiracy, rather than an independence movement. But he did most harm by grossly exaggerating the strength of support for integration with Indonesia. There is evidence that the Bakin/OPSUS group finally began to see through the reporting of the consulate, but their own determination to bring about the colony's integration led them to make convenient use of this material to suit their own ends. On the other hand, in the first few weeks after the coup the Indonesians gained the impression that the Portuguese would remain for some time, and this likelihood took much of the heat out of the Timor problem, at least in the foreign ministry.

This attitude appears to have influenced Adam Malik in his response to Horta's visit to Jakarta in June 1974, which itself gave considerable encouragement to the independence movement. In effect, Jose Ramos Horta was able to obtain a written, unequivocal assurance from the Indonesian Foreign Minister Malik that the government did not object to the prospect of an independent East Timor. This document, a remarkable statement in the light of later events, declared:

> In our view, these developments; the coup and the new regime's decision to allow Portugal's overseas territories to determine their own future; offered a good opportunity to the people of Timor to accelerate the process towards independence, as well as to generate overall national development, and to promote the progress of the people of Timor.

Malik placed on this written record certain principles to which his government adhered which were of particular relevance to the changed situation in Timor. These were:

1. The independence of every country is the right of every nation, with no exception for the people in Timor.
2. The government as well as the people of Indonesia have no intention to increase or expand their territory, or to occupy territories other than what is stipulated in their constitution. This reiteration is to give you a clear idea, so that there may be no doubt in the minds of the people of Timor in expressing their own wishes.
3. For this reason, whoever will govern in Timor in the future after independence, can be assured that the government of Indonesia will always strive to maintain good relations, friendship and cooperation for the benefit of both countries.[4]

---

* In mid-1974 our fact-finding mission had a lengthy meeting with Tomodok, yet in his subsequent published account of events of that year he described our encounter as a meeting with two American diplomats.

Many of the Timorese political leaders who, up to that time, had remained apprehensive as to how Indonesia would react to the emergence of a fully independent state adjacent to West Timor, regarded Malik's letter as a green light of unexpected clarity. Why Malik responded in this way has never been satisfactorily explained. Perhaps it was an off-the-cuff gesture, which may have been undertaken without consulting the relevant sections of his own ministry. As it turned out, Malik unwittingly contributed to an upsurge of Timorese nationalism as well as a disposition of goodwill towards Indonesia. Some ASDT leaders were prepared, in the face of such fraternal warmth, to consider conceding the responsibility for East Timor's foreign affairs and defence to Jakarta. In retrospect it is indeed tragic that the basic ingredients of a compromise solution which would have accommodated both Indonesian and Timorese interests, were never seriously explored.

In reality, when it came to decisions on sensitive foreign-policy issues, Malik's influence in Indonesia's military-dominated leadership was weak. It was soon clear that the views he had expressed to Horta were very much at variance with those of a more influential group of generals who exercised greater influence over President Suharto. This group, including Major-General Ali Murtopo, Lieutenant-General Yoga Sugama, Admiral Sudomo, and Major-General Benny Moerdani, had their own views on foreign policy and, as the senior officials of the two powerful intelligence and security agencies, Kopkamtib (the Indonesian Command for the Restoration of Security and Order) and Bakin, they saw themselves as the custodians of the 'New Order', the *Orde Baru*. These generals possessed formidable resources of their own in the foreign policy-making process through their control of the intelligence agencies and their influence in the diplomatic service: a large number of Indonesia's senior diplomats are generals. Murtopo also had at his disposal the Special Operations (OPSUS) apparatus, which had played an important part in the winding-down of Konfrontasi, and the Centre for Strategic and International Studies (CSIS), a kind of academic-front organisation which had worked closely with both Bakin and OPSUS. In their assessments the key officials of this network quickly arrived at a consensus that an independent East Timor was not in Indonesia's best interests. If the Portuguese were to leave, the territory should be absorbed into Indonesia. Foreign Minister Malik had no power base to match the influence of this formidable grouping on the Indonesian president.

To Adam Malik and some of his foreign ministry colleagues, Indonesia's image as a moderate and stable power in an unstable South-East Asia, in the post-Vietnam period, warranted a positive response to the question of Timor's future, but the Murtopo group perceived the problem very differently. East Timor was located on the periphery of a region of the archipelago that had been largely neglected by national development strategies, where most of the local populations were non-Moslem and where separatist sentiments were never far beneath the surface. The emergence of an independent East Timor would only stimulate unrest and provide a base for any externally inspired sabotage or political meddling. Further, if East Timor came under communist or left-wing influence it could pose a threat to Indonesia's 'soft underbelly'. These security considerations would have been influenced by other domestic factors, as well as the prevailing fear that Vietnam, with its large, experienced and sophisticated military machine and enormous resources of captured war material, would henceforth seek to undermine the security of ASEAN countries, of which Indonesia was probably the most vulnerable.

In Indonesia there was growing disenchantment with the performance of the Suharto regime, the mounting large-scale corruption, the increasing oppressiveness of the military dictatorship, and the widening gap between the grinding poverty of the masses and the ostentatious affluence of the privileged few at the top. The most serious manifestation of this widespread discontent was the so-called 'Malari Affair', an acronym for the 'Incident' of 15 January 1974, when mobs ransacked and rioted in Jakarta, and hundreds were later arrested. It is not without significance that two of the senior officers behind the formulation of the policy to integrate East Timor, Admiral Sudomo and General Yoga Sugama (both trusted associates of the president), had been appointed to the top positions of Kopkamtib and Bakin, as a result of the Malari Affair.

By September 1974 the Murtopo group had evidently resolved that steps should be taken to ensure that Timor became part of Indonesia as soon as possible. The shift to the left of the new regime in Lisbon may have convinced them that the previously ideologically reliable Portuguese could no longer be regarded as trusted anti-communist neighbours and that their tenure should be brought to an early end. Two other events in that month spurred them on to action. In Timor the ASDT assumed a more revolutionary mantle, changing its name to Fretilin and at the same time the UDT party declared itself in favour of independence. But of even greater importance was the outcome of the Wonosobo meeting between President Suharto and Prime Minister Whitlam. It was concluded from this meeting that the Australian leader believed that East Timor was not sufficiently economically viable to become independent and that it should become part of Indonesia. Australia had no interest in the colony, and did not regard itself as a 'party principal' in any negotiations about its future. Prime Minister Whitlam's exact words have never been made public, but the press, and the Indonesians, were apparently left in no doubt about his views. As Hamish McDonald recounted:

> On 6 September 1974, Suharto gained a new advantage when Australian Prime Minister Gough Whitlam, met him for informal talks at Wonosobo, Central Java. Whitlam told Suharto he thought the best solution would be for East Timor to join Indonesia, adding with somewhat less emphasis that the wishes of the Timorese should be respected and that public reaction in Australia would be hostile if Indonesia used force.

McDonald also noted:

> An important factor in reassuring Suharto was not so much what Whitlam said, but the degree of tepo seliru (mutual understanding) Suharto believed the two had reached.[5]

The Australian prime minister's stand opened the way for an international acceptance or, at least, understanding of Indonesia's special interests about East Timor's future and ultimately acceptance of the desirability of integration. In the short time that he had been in office Mr Whitlam had internationally become a well-known and widely respected leader and, under his tutelage, Australia had set out to assume a more dynamic and independent role in the changing global power configuration. Australia's proximity to East Timor, its capacity to monitor the situation in the Portuguese colony, and its close relationship with the Suharto regime, meant that its views on East Timor's future would carry considerable weight with the governments of those nations of greatest political and economic importance to Indonesia. In effect, Australia's tacit consent to the absorption of East Timor into Indonesia was crucial to the sensitive task of acquiring the territory without harming the Suharto regime's much-vaunted image as a stable, 'development-oriented' government, a regime without any territorial ambitions.

The Murtopo group's plans to integrate East Timor, by annexation if necessary, existed even before the Wonosobo meeting took place. As early as July, I was informed confidentially by an official source that key Indonesian generals had already resolved that 'independence for East Timor was simply not on'. But the president, concerned for his high standing in North America and Western Europe, was reluctant to agree with anything that might risk his reputation. Mr Whitlam's stand on the question apparently encouraged the cautious Suharto to agree to the Murtopo plan, and in October, at a high-level meeting, *Operasi Komodo* was born. The aim of this operation was to bring about the integration of East Timor as quickly as possible, preferably by non-military means.

The Indonesians had already assessed that the new MFA regime in Lisbon was anxious to disengage Portugal from its colonial role as soon as possible and, based on Ali Murtopo's October meeting with the then Prime Minister Vasco Goncalves, had concluded that at least some of the leaders were not averse to the idea of handing East Timor over to Indonesia, after a certain period of decolonisation. In September and October Murtopo's group had been busy laying the groundwork in key Western capitals for an understanding of Indonesia's security preoccupations and its special interest in Timor's future. Harry Tjan Silalahi and Liem Bian-Kie (now known as Yusuf Wanandi) of the CSIS became key figures in *Operasi Komodo*. They quietly visited Western Europe and North America while Murtopo, as has already been mentioned, visited Lisbon, among other places. Meanwhile President Suharto, after his meeting with Prime Minister Whitlam, had talks with Tun Razak at Kuala Lumpur where it seems that Indonesian concerns about the future position of the Portuguese colony were discussed, with the Malaysians responding sympathetically.

There was nothing novel about the *Operasi Komodo* plan, and the planners had in fact worked together on a similar project some thirteen years earlier, the aim of which had been to bring about the integration of West Irian, at that time with emphasis on armed insurgency. In 1961 one Major Ali Murtopo and a Major

Rudjito were key figures in the planning of *Operasi Tjendrawasih*, a combined operation designed to facilitate the military penetration of West New Guinea behind Dutch lines. The operation was the first major task of the newly formed Strategic Reserve, better known as Kostrad, a special strike under the command of one Brigadier-General Suharto, whose deputy was a naval officer named Sudomo. An amphibious force moved to the Maluku Selatan area near the West Irian coast in late 1961 and, in due course, some paratroop units were dropped behind Dutch lines. One of these units was under the command of Captain Benny Moerdani who, in 1975, now a major general close to Suharto, was to take charge of the overall planning of the invasion of East Timor. Another young officer involved in *Operasi Tjendrawasih* was Lieutenant Dading Kalbuadi, who as Colonel Dading was to head the attack on Balibo and Maliana on 16 October 1975.

Operasi Komodo began as a subversive operation, the early activities of which have already been referred to. Its main propaganda thrust appears to have started in October 1974 but, according to Hamish McDonald, it did not get properly under way until early in 1975.[6] At first *Operasi Komodo* was more of a propaganda and political campaign than a military operation, providing coordination of diplomatic, subversive and propaganda activities. In this campaign, writes Hamish McDonald,

> Opsus took the leading role, with other agencies contributing where necessary. Ali Murtopo's network ran from Jakarta across to and over the border. Advising on diplomatic strategy were his political backroom team in the Jakarta academic-style institution, the Centre for Strategic and International Studies (CSIS), which had become an important point of contact for foreign diplomats, academics and journalists. Two key figures in the CSIS on Timor were its Director, Harry Tjan Silalahi, the self-effacing former Catholic Party figure, who became respectfully dubbed 'The Foreign Minister' by his military counterparts for his effective secret diplomacy with Portugal and Australia, and Yusuf Wanandi (Liem Bian-Kie), the sometimes volatile West Sumatran-born political strategist who paid particular attention to the USA.[7]

The affidavit of the defector, Jose Martins, which was submitted to the UN Secretary-General early in 1976 also listed many of the personnel who were organising *Operasi Komodo*. According to this account, initially the principal officials were generals Yoga Sugama, Ali Murtopo and Benny Moerdani, Colonel Sugiyanto (also an RPKAD officer who had been close to Murtopo), and Louis Taolin, the West Timorese related to the *liurai* of the Atoni people in that part of the island. Martins, a trusted Bakin agent 'recruited' by Sugiyanto, later contended that General Moerdani, Colonel Agus Hernoto (a communication intelligence specialist), Colonel Sinaga (a Sumatran who had worked with OPSUS), Colonel Dading, Colonel Kasenda and Major Andreas were added later. The operational network included the Sarana Carta Company (which provided a cover for agents), the firm PT Arjuna, Pertamina (which supplied helicopters), Antara news agency (which coordinated the fabrication of 'news items' for international consumption) and the army-controlled newspaper *Berita Yudha* (which appears to have been a vehicle for the dissemination of the falsified press reports).

The international aspects of the operation were handled by Murtopo, occasionally with Sugiyanto, later also by Benny Moerdani, and frequently with the CSIS leaders who maintained close informal links with leading Western diplomats. They were soon able to establish that in Western Europe (Portugal aside) and in North America there was little interest in East Timor. The governments in the non-communist world of importance to Indonesia, namely Western Europe, the United States, India, Japan, and the ASEAN states, tended to sympathise with Jakarta's security anxieties in the uncertain aftermath of the withdrawal of the United States from Vietnam. Indians knew little about the situation in Timor and perceived something of a parallel with their own action against Goa.

Japan had earlier occupied the island for three-and-a-half-years and was of the few countries to be familiar with East Timor. But they knew little about Timor of the 1970s. Japanese diplomats displayed a distinct bias towards accommodating Indonesia's special interests. ASEAN governments, with the qualified exception of Singapore, appear to have accepted without question what their Indonesian colleagues told them about the growing influence of communism in Timor, and at an early stage indicated their preference for *integrasi*. In their approach to the Americans and Western Europeans the Indonesians were able to exploit security fears held in the aftermath of Vietnam. Thus, according to a Portuguese official, NATO representatives had made it clear at the outset that their sympathies were inclined towards Indonesia.

To the CSIS and other elements concerned with the handling of the international relations side of *Operasi Komodo*, Australia's position was of crucial importance in the first year. The stand taken by Mr Whitlam, a position shared by most of the Australian diplomats in Jakarta, was gratifying and encouraging, and may have caused Murtopo and his colleagues to overlook support for the Timorese elsewhere in the Australian community. It should be noted, however, that Mr Whitlam warned President Suharto at Wonosobo that the Australian public would not go along with the use of force. On the other hand, as has already been mentioned, the need to promote a climate of sympathy and understanding in Australia was by no means neglected by *Operasi Komodo*. The Indonesian case they impressed most, though not all, of the Australian right, most of whom manifested a tolerance of, if not support for, Jakarta's moves to annex the Portuguese colony.

The Indonesians appear to have left to the Whitlam government the task of getting the left in Australia to come to terms with 'the realities of the Timor situation', but they had little influence with this group. By the end of 1974 the Suharto regime was under increasing criticism from the left and centre of Australian politics for its suppression of democracy and for the corruption and greed of the military elite. Representatives of the Australian Labor Party, left-wing factions and student bodies were among the first to take a close interest in the situation in Timor and to support the Fretilin party, an interest that was to both irritate and embarrass the Whitlam government.

By the end of 1974 the Indonesians' position had hardened. For example, in December Moh Sabir, the deputy head of the Indonesian mission in Canberra, declared to me that if the Timorese leaders became involved in dealings with left-wing states:

> Indonesia would have no hesitation in seizing the territory by military action [he went on to make what turned out to be an optimistic assertion that it would have] no difficulty whatever in annexing the colony by means of armed force.

The propaganda campaign directed at East Timor in late 1974 and in the first quarter of 1975 has already been mentioned. This was a key operation by elements of *Operasi Komodo*, but one of the least successful. Bakin agents were placed in charge of special broadcasts from a transmitter at Atambua, with selected members of Apodeti helping to prepare material. After the London meeting, the outcome of which obviously dissatisfied Murtopo, Bakin officials decided to intensify this aspect of their disinformation activities. The operations of the Atambua and Kupang stations were further stepped up after the Macau conference. This time the disinformation was channelled deep into East Timor, undoubtedly contributing to the increasing tensions between Fretilin and its rivals, as well as creating public apprehension and suspicions.

During this period Indonesian agents were sent to many parts of the colony, sometimes in the guise of businessmen, sometimes as tourists or tourism officials. They included Louis Taolin who later disclosed something about his role to acquaintances on several occasions. Louis Taolin made a number of secret visits to Atsabe, for talks with the *liurai*, Guilherme Goncalves, as well as to Bobonaro and Suai (on the south-west coast). Other agents were disguised as Timorese and sent to remote areas. Many of them were never detected, although in some cases their covers were transparently thin. In 1975, according to a local resident, one intriguing Indonesian visitor, armed with a camera, went on a tour of the main beaches of the territory, claiming that he was looking for places where he could land cattle from barges.

Early in 1975 the Indonesians stepped up the military side of *Operasi Komodo*, perhaps indicating the impatience of certain generals with the subversive operations. Some small exercises were followed by a major combined armed forces exercise, Wibawa VI/Jaya Nusa, near Lampung in South Sumatra on 18 February, under the overall command of Rear-Admiral Syamsul Bachri (Commander of Kostrad, the Strategic Reserve). The exercise, in which naval bombardment was to be followed by a paratroop drop and a landing at Pantai Pasir Putih, perhaps a coincidence, but *pasir putih* means 'white sands', the name of a well-known beach near Dili-Aria Branca in Portuguese. The exercise was a near disaster: the paratroops were dropped in the wrong place, not one shell hit its target, one vessel ran aground and a P51 Mustang crashed, killing its pilot. The exercise was to have been a prelude to a landing at Dili, but the poor performance of the participating units, and its exposure by an Australian Defence Department source, designed, it seems, to warn the

Indonesians that officials in Canberra knew what they were up to, led to a temporary abandonment of the idea of military action, and to the development of a different kind of intelligence operation, directed from West Timor, with greater emphasis on political manipulation and intimidation.

This next phase of *Operasi Komodo* was also rather more subtle—and ultimately more successful. It appears to have been based on a more realistic appreciation of the political mood of the colony, with the conclusion that support for Apodeti alone, far from helping Indonesia, was manifestly diminishing its influence and with it hopes that integration could be brought about by non-military means. After the Suharto and Whitlam meeting in Townsville, the department of foreign affairs was to inform its minister, Senator Willesee, that the Indonesians had assured the Australian government that they were not contemplating military intervention, that Indonesian propaganda directed against Timor had become less strident, and that Australian intelligence reports had disclosed no evidence of preparations for early military action.[8] The propaganda assault was to resume less than two months later, causing journalist Bruce Juddery who was visiting East Timor at the time to report that 'the Damocles sword of Indonesian intervention once again hangs over the territory'.[9]

The shifts in the activities of the *Operasi Komodo* agents seem to have occurred in March 1975, at about the time of the London meeting and shortly after the related visit to Dili of Colonel Sugiyanto and Colonel Pitut, who had held private talks with all Timorese leaders, including those of Fretilin. In March the operation appeared to be in suspension. Their next moves reflected a more sensitive understanding of the political situation in the colony. The Indonesians began to concentrate their attention on the more right-wing parties, that is, Kota and Trabalhista as well as UDT. The right-wing leaders of UDT, especially Mousinho and Lopes da Cruz, became subjects of special interest, and were invited to Jakarta.

At the first meetings their hosts apparently skirted around the advantages of integration and concentrated on the increasing dangers of communist subversion in the region, on Fretilin's alleged flirtation with it, and the dangers for Indonesia. At the time they impressed on UDT leaders the threat the mounting crisis in Portugal posed to developments in East Timor. As it happened at that time reports were rife in the Western press that a communist government could at any time emerge in Lisbon. Both Mousinho and Lopes da Cruz were obviously impressed by this line of reasoning and with suggestions that they should think carefully about whether to remain in coalition with Fretilin. Indeed, these two UDT leaders later told me that the Indonesians had urged them to form an anti-communist front with Apodeti. It was evident that these arguments particularly impressed da Cruz and, according to a Portuguese official, he was won over to the cause of integration some weeks later. After his conversion the Indonesians arranged for him to visit a number of anti-communist Asian countries (including South Korea and Taiwan) at their expense.

Lopes da Cruz, with his strong anti-communist, anti-Portuguese attitudes and his status as the leader of the second-largest party in the territory was, from Murtopo's point of view, a prize catch, but the Indonesians were also aware that his conversion would not find favour with the majority of the UDT Central Committee. He was therefore urged not to reveal his hand. In fact, da Cruz simply could not at that time have persuaded his party to opt for integration; and to have declared his own change of heart would have been to invite the party to dismiss him. But the first major success of *Operasi Komodo* came with the collapse at the end of May of the coalition, following UDT's withdrawal.

After May the emphasis was again to change. The central target of Indonesian propaganda was now Fretilin, so frequently portrayed as a communist front that foreign journalists in Jakarta began to believe it. After July, however, the real aim of the *Operasi Komodo* activists was to prevent the agreement that had emerged from the Macau meeting from getting off the ground. The subsequent constitutional law was hardly in breach of the understanding reached at the London meeting, but it seems that it caused the Murtopo group considerable concern. Although the law gave Apodeti a status equal to that of the other parties, the Indonesians by then had realised that the pro-integration party's support was so thin that, in the three years proposed for decolonisation, the task of deterring the Timorese from the ultimate choice of independence would be completely beyond it. In the weeks before the UDT coup the Indonesians went all out to destabilise the situation in East Timor. Some of these activities have already been discussed. Reports that the Chinese were involved in a plot inspired by Peking, that Vietnamese troops had secretly entered the country, that Soviet submarines were operating near East Timor, and that arms were being smuggled to Fretilin for the training of their 'secret army' were all deliberately fed into the already unsettled situation in the province by the propaganda apparatus of *Operasi Komodo*, or by word of mouth from Indonesian agents. The Indonesian propaganda machine also exploited reports that Fretilin, or a faction within the party, was planning a coup, reports that were at least dubious. In fact, as Xavier do Amaral, Nicolau Lobato and Horta were abroad at the time, it is unlikely that such a move was being seriously contemplated.

Apart from disinformation, *Operasi Komodo* agents sought to get some of the *liurais* to give open support to the idea of integration. This was handled by Colonel Sugiyanto who, by this time, had become Murtopo's right-hand man. It was Sugiyanto who had won over Lopes da Cruz, and who later recruited Jose Martins as a Bakin agent. According to Hamish McDonald, who claims to have acquired this information from other Indonesian officials, 'Sugiyanto also cultivated the *liurais* (chiefs) and was later to claim that as a result of this unprecedented attention about ten of the thirteen districts were leaning towards Apodeti'.[10] In fact, only three or four of these chieftains were won over.

The international presentation of Indonesia's growing concern at the 'deteriorating situation' in East Timor, also stage-managed by Murtopo's *Operasi Komodo* team, made good progress after May 1975. Perhaps the Indonesians felt that the results of the Macau talks were a setback, but the international mood was increasingly favourable. President Suharto is said to have discussed the Timor problem within the context of the 'communist threat' during his visit to the United States in mid-1975, and on his return to Jakarta he was quoted as saying that East Timor could not really become independent because it lacked economic viability. Until that time the president had avoided making any statements on the Timor question, and for this reason his remarks caused considerable disquiet in Dili, coming as they did only a matter of weeks after a reassuring statement by Adam Malik that Indonesia had 'no intention of playing rough'.

The president's statement seemed to reflect a growing confidence in Jakarta that the countries that mattered to Indonesia were onside, or would agree with any move they might make to force the situation. The Australian prime minister was known to be aware of the Indonesian aims and to be sympathetic to them. To quote McDonald again: 'A quiet visit by the Bakin chief, Lieutenant-General Yoga Sugama, in May 1975 had sounded out, among others, Opposition Leader Malcolm Fraser, and found no reason for alarm'.[11] One interesting ally was the British ambassador to Indonesia, Sir John Archibald Ford who, on 21 July 1975, following a visit to Dili by Gordon Duggan, an officer of his embassy, reported to London in a classified cable that it was in British interests that Indonesia should incorporate East Timor as soon as possible and that if such a move were to cause a furore in the United Nations the British should stay clear of the dispute and avoid becoming involved in action against the Indonesians.[12]

The British envoy's views appear to have been shared by other representatives of Western countries well placed to influence the course of events, among them the American, Dutch, Australian and Japanese ambassadors. Thus with India, the Islamic nations and the ASEAN states onside, and having established that the Soviet Union had no desire to become involved in giving active support to a remote and tiny country of no strategic or political interest to it, the Indonesians canvassed the possibility of a military solution. It is clear that until after the Fretilin victory over UDT, President Suharto remained opposed to a military solution, while even Ali Murtopo was at first not enthusiastic for 'a quick surgical operation'. However the hawks, among them generals Yoga Sugama and Benny Moerdani, kept up their pressure and were eventually able to persuade the president to authorise military intervention.

There is little doubt that the subversive and disinformation activities mounted by Murtopo's *Operasi Komodo* command, against the background of Jakarta's looming threat, were indirectly responsible for the sharp deterioration of the political situation in East Timor between May and August, and for UDT's precipitate 'show of force' which led to the civil war. There is no evidence that the Indonesians were directly involved in the planning of the UDT move, but it was clearly the desired outcome of Indonesian meddling and subversion. Had they not meddled, Fretilin and UDT may not have had an easy relationship, but political divisions of this kind are common, if not healthy, in a democratically organised process of decolonisation, and the differences between the major parties could have been contained with little difficulty.

The subversive activities of *Operasi Komodo* sought to exploit and magnify out of all proportion political differences common to most decolonisations, including the experience of Indonesia. But to make matters worse, this subversion was made possible by the compliance or neglect of outside powers, in particular of Australia. Because of its extensive diplomatic and intelligence sources of information about Indonesia the Australian government was well aware of the existence of *Operasi Komodo*, its aims and at least some of its activities within weeks of its inception. Australia did not make responsible use of this information and in so doing inevitably further encouraged the Indonesian generals to proceed with their sinister operation.

Notes

1   Donald Weatherbee, 'Portuguese Timor: An Indonesian Dilemma', *Asian Survey* (December 1966).
2   Bob Reece, 'Portuguese Timor, 1974', *Australia's Neighbours* (April-June 1974).
3   Bill Nicol, *The Stillborn Nation* (Melbourne: Viza, 1978), p. 257.
4   Extract from copy of Malik letter, June 1974.
5   Hamish McDonald, *Suharto's Indonesia* (Melbourne: Fontana/Collins, 1980), p. 195.
6   Ibid., p. 198.
7   Ibid., pp. 198-199.
8   Documents on Australian Defence and Foreign Policy, 19681975 (Sydney: Walsh and Munster, 1980), p. 189.
9   Bruce Juddery, *Canberra Times*, 11 June 1975.
10 McDonald, *Suharto's Indonesia*, p. 203.
11 Ibid., p. 204.
12 Australian Defence and Foreign Policy, pp. 192-193.

Chapter Seven
Australia and the unfolding crisis in East Timor

Contacts between Australia and Portuguese Timor go back for more than a century, but until World War I these were relatively irregular and few, and interest in Timor in Australia was slight. To the few who gave any attention to the subject, Portuguese colonialism was a matter of amusement and disdain, but Portugal was Britain's oldest ally and its presence in the small territory to the north of Darwin, and the much more visible and more extensive Dutch presence, was of some comfort to a people ever apprehensive that land-hungry hordes from overpopulated and impoverished parts of Asia would surge towards the land of milk and honey with its inviting great wide-open spaces and sparse population. If Portuguese Timor aroused any concern in Australians it was because of fears that Portugal might sell or transfer the territory to a potentially hostile power or, because of its military frailty, be forced to abandon the colony. Therefore interest in East Timor was great only when Australians felt under some immediate or potential threat, in particular, at the time of world wars I and II.

As early as 1903 however, the position of the Portuguese attracted the attention of a member of the New South Wales Legislative Assembly, Dr J. M. Creed, who wrote to the state governor, Sir Harry Rawson, pointing out that the 'especial importance which (Timor) has to the British Empire is its proximity to Australia' and its commanding position in relation to the shipping routes between 'Australian ports, the Philippine Islands and China'. Dr Creed argued that if the Timor colony were to fall into the hands 'of another nation such as Germany, France or Russia' it would endanger British and Australian interests, and yet the territory was 'of so little value to Portugal that that country has from time to time seriously thought of abandoning it'.[1] Clearly, Dr Creed thought that Australia, or perhaps Britain, should seek to acquire the colony by some other means. Evidently the governor took the memorandum seriously enough to forward it to the British government which, in due course, advised him that there was no question of the colony being put up for sale or for disposal in any way.

Australians, though, continued to raise the question with the authorities in London. In January 1905 Prime Minister George Reid informed Governor-General Lord Northcote that 'a rumour is current that the German Government is endeavouring to purchase a portion of the island of Timor for the purpose of establishing a naval station', and urged that the report be checked with the Secretary of State for the Colonies. Again the British later replied, stating that the British embassy in Lisbon had been informed emphatically by the Portuguese foreign minister that 'neither he nor any other Portuguese Minister could listen for a moment to an overture from Germany or from any other Power having in view the purchase of the island'.[2]

The collapse of the Portuguese monarchy in 1910 increased fears in Australia that, in the event of the carving up of the Portuguese empire, East Timor might end up in German hands, a fear that was to intensify as World War I approached. The Portuguese repeated the assurances of the previous regime that they had no intention of selling or giving up East Timor or, for that matter, any of their colonies, and it is far from clear to what extent the Germans were ever seriously interested in the Timor colony. For one thing, its poor harbour facilities would have limited its usefulness as a base for merchant shipping or the marauding German raiders. However, the idea of acquiring the territory for Australia was again bandied about at the beginning of the war, perhaps inspired by a letter from Melbourne. The writer suggested that Australia might, after the war, acquire the Portuguese colony, or even all of the island, to create a 'hill station to lessen the strain of the long, humid summer on the settlers of Northern Australia', a move that might facilitate the task of settling sparsely populated areas of northern Australia.[3] Prime Minister Andrew Fisher apparently liked the idea and asked that the matter be considered further, but it was coolly received by his colleagues and was eventually dropped.

After World War I attention shifted to Japan as the target of suspicions and speculation in relation to East Timor with stories circulating as early as 1920 that the Japanese government had territorial designs on the colony. A year or so later the Australian official responsible for Pacific and Far Eastern matters, Major Piesse, informed the secretary of the prime minister's department that 'Portuguese Timor is reported, on what seems to be good authority, to be under offer to Holland.'[4] There was no substance to these reports and that they were taken seriously reveals just how poorly informed were Australian officials concerned with the affairs of the neighbouring region in those days. Australia's relations even with nearby territories were then being handled by the British diplomatic and consular service, most of whose reports did not reach the eyes of the small band of persons dealing with foreign affairs and defence matters in Canberra. The 'need to know' principle was tightly adhered to, and Australia, in British eyes, did not need to know much. It is also clear that the British often placed perceived Australian interests, in the particular circumstances referred to, secondary to their special relationship with their 'oldest ally'.

However, Australia began to develop some commercial links with East Timor, mostly in connection with oil prospecting, although in the period between the world wars the Portuguese administration did not give foreign companies much encouragement. For example, Major V. M. Newland, the manager of the Adelaide-based Timor Development Company, told the British consul-general at Batavia, Sir Josiah Crosby, that the Portuguese governor, Colonel de Almeida Viana, had made the company's work so difficult that it seemed hardly worth continuing its operations in the colony.[5] The company, which had interests in coffee, eventually suspended its operations, although oil exploration interests continued to operate until World War II.

The stories about Japanese moves to acquire East Timor from the Portuguese usually proved to be unfounded. The Japanese had begun to develop a close interest in the colony though, investing in local companies (especially the SOTA enterprise in Dili), expanding trade, and establishing regular shipping and air links—with the crews being provided by the navy and army for specific intelligence purposes. By the late 1930s Australia had become intensely suspicious of Japanese intentions in Portuguese Timor, and began to respond to British suggestions that steps be taken to counter Japanese diplomatic and economic initiatives. There was a growing conviction that the Japanese were out to acquire East Timor and that, if this were to happen, it would pose a serious threat to Australia's security, not to speak of its sea and air communications with the strategically important British base at Singapore.

A first necessary step was to establish an official mission at Dili. However, this proved to be difficult to arrange. In practice it meant appointing an Australian as British consul in Dili and although David Ross, a senior officer of the department of civil aviation with a background knowledge of Timor, was soon chosen for the position, his status as consul was not resolved until some days after the Japanese attack on Pearl Harbor, and only six days before the Australian–Dutch military intervention in the colony. The Portuguese were anxious not to antagonise the Japanese, while the British, ever mindful of the special position of Portugal in the European theatre of war in the desperate years of 1940 and 1941, were not prepared to force the issue with Lisbon. Although the authorities in London were concerned at the growing Japanese threat, Australian anxieties in 1940 and 1941 about what might happen in East Timor must have seemed barely relevant to a Britain under life-and-death siege by the Luftwaffe and U-boats.

The central purpose of David Ross's mission was to monitor Japanese activities in Timor and to attempt to counter their economic penetration. His mission, assisted by a naval intelligence officer working under cover, performed a valuable service in collecting information on Japanese intentions and activities. It received invaluable assistance from a *mestiço* radio operator, Patricio da Luz, who supplied Ross with copies of messages to and from the sizeable Japanese mission in Dili. As Peter Hastings later put it:

Thus Australia's representation in Portuguese Timor—among the first of our foreign missions—initially comprised a political officer acting as a Civil Aviation Department technical representative assisted in turn by a clerk who was, in fact, a spy, a non-uniformed naval intelligence officer working on behalf of a belligerent in a neutral country.[6]

This intelligence operation came to an early end, for within two months of reaching an agreement on his consular status David Ross was a prisoner of the Japanese. Twice he was sent to the hills to carry messages demanding the surrender of the Australian commando force, and on the second occasion he remained with the commandos and was subsequently evacuated to Australia.

I have already discussed the Allied intrusion into East Timor at some length. It was opposed by Governor de Carvalho who, with only one company of poorly equipped troops at his disposal, was not in a position to resist it. An apology was eventually conveyed by the British to the Portuguese in Lisbon for this action of the Allied forces, whose behaviour, as Prime Minister Curtin admitted, had 'proved unwelcome to the Portuguese Government'. The British were asked by the prime minister to inform the Portuguese that:

the occupation was based on military necessity and that Japanese infiltration or invasion could not otherwise be prevented.

In this cable sent about two weeks after the Allied intrusion, Mr Curtin continued:

we still have every desire to be helpful but we must insist that the defence of Portuguese Timor is crucial both to the Netherlands and to the whole British position in the Far East and there should be no retreat! The faith of the Australian public would be shaken if, having regard to what has already happened, a further withdrawal of occupying forces were to take place at the very door of Australia.

The Australians quickly moved to consolidate their position and to mobilise popular support for the forthcoming engagement with the Japanese, but the British were still uneasy about this transgression. In a cable on 27 December to the Australian prime minister the British felt constrained because of the possible consequences for their sensitive relationship with the Salazar regime:

to emphasize the consequences to the general strategy of the war which will follow if an amicable solution of the Portuguese Timor question is not secured. There is a serious danger that unless a bridge is found, Dr Salazar may proceed to the limit of breaking off relations with the United Kingdom. This would not merely mean the end of a long alliance but may precipitate Axis penetration of the Iberian Peninsula.

The British had just concluded 'highly secret conversations with Portugal' which were expected to help safeguard their position in regard to the 'Atlantic islands' and, thanks to the deliberate breaching of Timor's neutral position, 'the results of those conversations are now in jeopardy'.[7] The Portuguese made an attempt to send several hundred of their own troops to East Timor, but before the convoy had reached East Timor's waters the Japanese had already swept down through the East Indies, and it was forced to sail back to Lourenco Marques.

The Australian commando operation in Timor in 1942 was one of the few success stories in a rather bleak year, and the island's obvious strategic importance to Australia provoked some discussion about its future even before the war had ended. In October 1943, in a statement on international affairs, the then Minister for External Affairs Dr Evatt, said that Australia must henceforth show a closer interest in the nearby islands and territories. Regarding Timor, he stated: 'The island in enemy hands is a constant threat to Australia. If properly placed within the zone of Australian security, it would become a bastion of defence.' But the Allied intervention had revived fears in Lisbon that in some way Australia might exploit the circumstances of the war to acquire their South-East Asian colony. The Portuguese therefore made use of the agreement with Britain about access to the Azores bases to obtain an assurance, among other things, that Portugal's sovereignty over its colonies would continue to be respected. South Africa gave a specific assurance about Angola and Mozambique, and on 14 September 1943 the British chargé d'affaires in Lisbon informed the Portuguese government in a letter that 'His Majesty's Government in the Commonwealth of Australia are glad to associate themselves with assurances already furnished', and 'have noted with great satisfaction Portugal's desire to participate with UN forces against the Japanese in Timor', a position assumed by Lisbon following the Japanese occupation of the colony. In this and other memoranda, plans for close economic cooperation and 'common defence against possible future aggression' in the postwar period were touched on.

As the war neared its end, Dr Evatt and other Australian leaders still hoped that some special arrangement with East Timor would be worked out. On 19 July 1944 Dr Evatt, in a reference to Timor, said that Australia contemplated 'very close post-war relationships covering mutual security, close economic ties and improved facilities in connection with aviation and the like'[8]. On the eve of the Japanese surrender, Australia's high commissioner in London, Mr S. M. Bruce, sounded out his Portuguese colleague on the acquisition of East Timor. He reported: 'I took advantage of my close personal relations with him to ask privately how he thought his Government would react to the suggestion for a lease of Portuguese Timor to Australia for a hundred years.' The Portuguese ambassador's response was anything but encouraging; according to Bruce, 'his reply was that such a suggestion would touch Portugal in her most sensitive spot, namely her prestige'.[9]

The belief by some Australians that a special relationship with the colony would spring up at the end of the war was no doubt encouraged by some of the Portuguese, but the negotiations on defence and aviation never got off the ground. This was partly because of Portuguese suspicions that Australia had designs on the colony in which their own position was anything but strong. The fighting skill, spirit, and easy going ways of the commandos had won great prestige for Australia. In the eyes of the Timorese, Australians enjoyed a reverence some Portuguese found a little threatening, but there was also an underlying bitterness that few Australians could comprehend. Australians saw themselves as having liberated the nearby islands from the cruel Japanese yoke. It never seemed to occur to the Australians that, in the case of Timor, for reasons of narrow self-interest-based on little more than speculation that the Japanese would invade East Timor and use it as a base against the Darwin area—they had forced a people who owed them nothing into a devastating war.

Although the commando campaign was undoubtedly a great military achievement, its success was made possible by the Timorese—and many Portuguese—who, having been induced to support the Allied cause which at the time meant little to them, were than abandoned to a harsh occupation. Adding to their terrible ordeal were the constant air attacks by Allied aircraft operating out of Darwin. But Australians did not see it that way. An Australian view contained in a cable to London at the end of the war, was probably not unrepresentative of attitudes of the time. The author of the cable declared:

> The Portuguese failed us completely in the arrangements made for the defence of Timor...and as a result our forces were left to sustain single handed...for a long period an epic guerilla warfare.

But Portugal was neutral and, if the Allies had not intruded, a defensive action might not have been necessary. And certainly the Australians were engaging in forward defence, not defending East Timor.

Recent research on relations between Berlin and Tokyo during World War II suggests that a Japanese invasion of East Timor was unlikely. For one thing, the Japanese were under heavy pressure from the Germans not to violate Portuguese neutrality which, Berlin feared, might provoke the Salazar government into offering base facilities in the Azores to the Allies. The presence of a Japanese consular mission and intelligence agents in East Timor indicated a high level of interest but, as the Allies should have known, the Portuguese half of the island, with its poor port and airfield facilities, was of limited use as a base for an assault against Australia. Had the Allies not intruded, it is likely that the Japanese would have confined their military intervention to a token presence.

Although some individual commandos were to retain a sense of obligation to the Timorese who had assisted them, Australians as a whole did not harbour any lingering sense of debt or responsibility for the terrible sufferings endured by the Timorese people in the interest of protecting Australia from a Japanese invasion. The Australian press gave scant attention to what had happened in the territory after the commando force was withdrawn, and no one seemed interested enough to find out about it in the postwar years. There was no clamour to provide urgently needed relief for sick, hungry, and frail Timorese who had survived more than three years of harsh occupation only to return to the yoke of colonial rule by a power which was scarcely in a position to tend their desperate needs. On the contrary, Australians tended to regard themselves as saviours who had liberated, or helped to liberate, the nearby island peoples from Japanese imperialism, and it was they to whom these peoples should be grateful. Generally speaking, Australians felt no obligation to contribute to the reconstruction of a colony they had helped devastate, although they had no compunction in criticising the Portuguese for their ineptitude in healing the wounds of war. A lingering Portuguese suspicion that a closer relationship with Australia might weaken their hold on the colony was also an obstacle to implementing the understanding informally reached during the war years.

An Australian consular mission was re-established soon after the war, with Group-Captain Charles Eaton being appointed consul. This level of representation continued until 1971 when the mission was closed. In the postwar years Timor's strategic importance to Australia was alluded to from time to time, but its significance began to wane after the mid-1950s. Although President Sukarno's increasing hostility to the West caused growing anxiety in Canberra, the fact that Indonesia controlled the western part of Timor—which was just as close to Australia as the eastern half of the island and which, at that time, possessed better defence facilities—led to East Timor declining in importance in the eyes of defence strategists. The consular mission was largely a monitoring operation, one generally regarded as being outside the mainstream of external diplomatic relations.

One interesting appointment was that of Mr F. J. Whittaker, who had been the naval intelligence agent working with Ross before the coming of the Japanese. Whittaker spent almost seven years as consul in Dili in the 1950s and during his long appointment the department of external affairs, as it then was, almost lost interest in the Portuguese colony, as it became increasingly absorbed with establishing a diplomatic presence in the great centres of the world. Forgotten and isolated, Whittaker's performance deteriorated. Timor was dear to his heart and it was the centre of his world. If he sighted a strange vessel, he would call the governor and urge that the Portuguese naval patrol vessel intercept it. His dispatches to Canberra were rarely taken seriously, and the mission became increasingly neglected. Disillusioned with Canberra's lack of interest, Whittaker himself on a number of occasions did not get around to opening the diplomatic bags consigned to him until weeks after their arrival. Such was the level of interest in his post that these derelictions of duty passed unnoticed by the departmental authorities in Canberra. On one occasion the consul stumbled across an unopened diplomatic bag that had escaped his attention for more than a year. Although it had contained classified material requiring prompt acknowledgment, his colleagues in Canberra had never bothered to check whether this material had arrived. Yet Whittaker loved Timor and its people, and if in his last years as consul he no longer took his work seriously, one can only blame his inattentive masters in Canberra.

Australian representation in East Timor in a way reflected the character of Canberra's interest in the colony. The residence and chancery, which consisted of a group of roughly constructed masonite huts, erected by the Darwin branch of the department of works in the 1940s, and protected from the fierce tropical sun by ungainly *palapa* over-roofs, created an appropriate impression of impermanence and indecision. The government had no interest in the Timorese and their conditions under Portuguese rule. Even after Australia came out in support of the right to self-determination of non-self-governing peoples, for some time it did little to encourage the Portuguese to accord that right to the Timorese people.

From the early 1960s onwards, as the Salazar regime became increasingly isolated from the international community, the Australian government began to distance itself from Portugal. The closure of the consulate in Dili in 1971 was a decision said to have been related to the opening of a diplomatic mission in Lisbon at about the same time. Hitherto Australia's interests in Portugal had been handled by the British embassy. Although this was partly true, another reason was the government's desire, in the light of the mounting international pressure on Portugal, to extricate itself from a situation that could turn out to be embarrassing and compromising.

In the twenty-five years of its postwar existence the Australian consular mission in Dili was of considerable importance and convenience to the Portuguese, for the only regular access and mail service to East Timor was provided by Australian (TAA) aircraft from Darwin, under charter through Qantas to the Air Transport Service of Timor (TAT). Portuguese officials came to, and departed from, East Timor via Darwin, and from the mid-1960s onwards the TAA aircraft carried over a stream of tourists, most of them from the Darwin area. At last the colony was beginning to fulfil its 'hill station' function. But what the consular staff did not do to any great extent was provide Canberra with other than superficial reports on political conditions within the colony. I began to report in some detail on political, social and economic conditions, but was soon told to cut down on this kind of reporting because it was not going to be read. This not only reflected the lack of interest in Canberra in the people of Timor, it also illustrated just how hard-pressed were desk officers at a time when the overseas service was expanding at a great rate. Unfortunately, it meant that, in spite of the generation of representation in the colony, the government was less than well-informed on the changes taking place in Timor.

By the time West Irian was under siege in 1961 and 1962, Portuguese Timor was no longer considered a 'bastion of defence', as Dr Evatt had referred to it eighteen years earlier, and economically it had yet to establish major links with Australia. The bulk of the colony's trade was with Portugal, Mozambique, Singapore and Hong Kong, and shipping contacts with Australia were infrequent and irregular. The Australian company, Timor Oil Ltd. was again conducting desultory exploration operations in the south coast areas, but by 1963 it seemed to be running out of steam, having not made any promising strikes.

In the early 1960s the Australian foreign affairs and defence policy-making establishments undertook some painful reappraisals of the importance to Australia of Dutch New Guinea and Portuguese Timor. In 1961 the joint chiefs of staff decided that Dutch control of West New Guinea and the continuation of the Portuguese presence in East Timor were no longer of vital importance to Australian defence. With Garfield Barwick holding the portfolio of external affairs, a subtle but fundamental shift in Australian foreign policy took place. It followed the intensification of Indonesian moves to 'regain' West Irian, and constituted an agonising reappraisal of whether or not Australia ought to maintain its opposition to Indonesia's claim to the Dutch colony. The US had informed Canberra that it was no longer prepared to support the Dutch position for which Barwick had little sympathy. Although the inclusion of East Timor in the reappraisal was not specifically spelt out, the message was clear. Timor was mentioned in a Melbourne *Herald* editorial that appeared shortly after the editor had received a lengthy briefing from the minister. Among other things, the editorial stated:

> It is conceded, however, that no guarantee can be accepted that a win by Indonesia over West New Guinea would not be followed fairly soon by pressures for sovereignty in Portuguese Timor, and this is accepted as a likely development within a few years.[10]

Although an attempt was later made to qualify this report it had been decided that the position of the Portuguese in East Timor should not be allowed to complicate the handling of the sensitive, and at times precarious, relationship between Australia and Sukarno's Indonesia. During Konfrontasi it was pondered: 'Why couldn't the Indonesians concentrate on the Portuguese, and leave the British and the Malaysians alone?' Thus, had the Sukarno regime moved against the Portuguese in the 1960s, there would probably not have been other than a token protest from Australia, although Prime Minister Menzies had protested vigorously against India's seizure of the enclave of Goa. The impression was that Australians were so preoccupied, even obsessed, with erecting defence barriers that in the half-century of debate about the status of East Timor the rights and aspirations of the people hardly rated a passing comment because Australia never really focused any attention on the rights and plight of the people.

All this was brought home to me before I left Canberra to take up the position of Australian consul in Dili in January 1962. It was widely believed that, once Indonesia had acquired West Irian, East Timor's days would be numbered. I was about to leave the office of the then secretary of the department, Sir Arthur Tange, who had just farewelled me. He gave me a parting glance and said, 'Oh, Dunn, if things go wrong, we won't be able to pull you out!' I recall looking back at him searchingly and apprehensively, but he was already engrossed in another file, another problem. I could not have had any illusions about the risks ahead because for the previous year I had been a monitor of Indonesian moves to acquire West Irian by military means. The tide had now turned in Australia–Portugal relations as far as Timor was concerned.

For most of the postwar years the Portuguese had been unenthusiastic about a closer relationship with Australia. Now, faced with an aggressive anti-colonialist regime in Jakarta, about to acquire West New Guinea, the Portuguese began putting out feelers for closer links and better economic relations with the only country they could turn to if Indonesia moved against their colony. But the Australian government had all but written off East Timor, and the consul had strict instructions not to encourage any Portuguese to believe that Canberra was prepared to provide help in the event of military intervention from the other side of the border. Faced with the uncertainties of the time, the colony was hardly an enticing subject for commercial activities, let alone investment by Australian enterprises.

When Sukarno's attention shifted to Konfrontasi—the Confrontation of Malaysia—the Australian attitude did not change significantly. In Canberra's view the Portuguese had merely gained some breathing space, but for how long was uncertain. It was only after General Suharto had taken control in Jakarta that the Timor colony would be more secure, but then only for a short period. Ultimately, the colony would be affected by the growing international campaign aimed at forcing Portugal to allow its overseas territories to determine their own futures. The new Indonesian regime's efforts to placate the fears of neighbouring states that Indonesia was expansionist took the heat out of the question of the colony's future, but it did not change the attitudes that had been forming in the minds of politicians and officials in Canberra from the early 1960s.

No thought was given to what the Timorese might want to do. Measured against Papua New Guinea and other colonies in the Asian and African regions, Timor was considered extremely politically and economically backward. The Portuguese were regarded as ineffective colonial administrators and, in the event of Indonesian pressure, their position would be quite indefensible. It was unthinkable for Australia to be lined up against Asian and African nations—many of them members of the Commonwealth—on the side of Portugal which had become their common enemy. For East Timor to move towards independence was, even then, regarded as an 'unrealistic' proposition at a time when the idea of decolonisation, even for large colonies, was not without its critics, at least in the Menzies government. For economically unviable and primitive East Timor to be put up for possible independent status was, in the view of many, unthinkable. How could such a politically backward people, in an economically unviable colony, engage in an act of self-determination? (This view still prevailed in the mid-1970s.) Most conservative political leaders of the time had no love for Indonesia, or any feeling for the Timorese, and little respect for the Portuguese who did not come up to their standards of economic diligence, resourcefulness and efficiency. Therefore, those who had come to the conclusion that East Timor no longer possessed any strategic importance for Australia also concluded that the territory was not worth a confrontation with Jakarta. It was an untidy relic, so why not let the Indonesians have it, and concentrate on buttressing Papua New Guinea against possible Indonesian territorial encroachment?

Some of these views were shared by liberal and left-wing opinion leaders in Australia, for in the early 1960s a new pragmatism was surfacing in the perception of what Australia's relations with Asia should be. The idea that Australia's foreign policy should reflect its unique position among Western nations as the only developed neighbour of some of the poorest countries in the world was gaining in popularity. The immediate challenge was to fashion a closer relationship with

Indonesia. In the late 1950s and early 1960s, support for Indonesia's claim to West Irian increased significantly in Australia, even among those Australians who were alarmed at the growth of the influence of the Indonesian Communist Party (PKI), and the Soviet decision to supply Indonesia with a formidable stockpile of sophisticated weaponry. One view gaining support in US circles was that the expanding influence of the PKI might be curbed if West Irian were handed over to Indonesia. If it were accepted that there was legal substance to Indonesia's claim to West Irian it followed that UN Resolution 1514 of 14 December 1960 about granting independence to colonial peoples did not apply to West Irian. This premise, some argued, linked Timor's status to that of West New Guinea. Australia, it was contended, had to get out of the rut of automatically supporting anti-communist and colonial regimes, a stand that would obstruct Australia's efforts to 'get closer to Asians'. These views coloured attitudes of the left towards Timor. It began to see East Timor as a part of Indonesia, whose inhabitants would be better off if they were to join with the republic, rather than as a colonial people.

And Portugal, the leading villain in a dwindling club of colonial powers, should be pressed to go. To the left and centre of Australian politics, more important than pressing for the rights of individual peoples was the notion that Australia should develop an image more acceptable to the growing community of non-aligned nations. In the light of Mr Whitlam's role in the mid-1970s, a reference to the position of East Timor by him, in his Roy Milne lecture in 1963, is of special significance. Its curious mix of two incompatible propositions was representative of attitudes in the centre and to the left of Australian politics at that time:

> Eastern Timor must appear as an anachronism to every country in the world except Portugal. We shall get nowhere by saying that outside pressure on Portugal is just another indication of the expansionist policy of one of our neighbours. We would not have a worthy supporter in the world if we backed the Portuguese. They must be told in no uncertain terms that the standard of living must be rapidly raised and the right of self-determination fully granted. Our allies hesitate to speak because they are also Portugal's allies in NATO; we are not so embarrassed.

> There have been no reports of uprisings and killings in East Timor, but it is such a closed country that reliable information is extremely difficult to obtain. Through the UN we must act quickly to meet this problem on our doorstep. We learned the lessons of West New Guinea the hard way. We must not become bogged down in another futile argument over sovereignty.

Though Mr Whitlam insisted that the East Timorese be granted the right to self-determination, he clearly had the outcome of independence in mind. His reference to 'the lessons of West New Guinea' and his remark that 'we must not become bogged down in another futile argument over sovereignty' suggest that he believed that East Timor should go the way of West Irian. However, Mr Whitlam, and most others holding this view, knew very little about the Portuguese colony. There were no 'uprisings and killings' in the territory at the time, and there was no dispute over its sovereignty, the Indonesians having just reaffirmed that they had no claim to it. But Mr Whitlam's preoccupation seems to have been with Australia's image abroad. His emphasis was not that Australia should not support Portugal because its position was in defiance of UN Resolution 1514, and contrary to the spirit of the UN charter, but that if Australia backed the Salazar regime it 'would not have a worthy supporter in the world'.

The attitude that this ugly relic of old-world colonialism should not be allowed to get in the way of the urgent task of improving Australia–Indonesia relations came to dominate the views of academics and diplomats by the middle of the decade. After 1966, when Indonesia swung to the right, it became an imperative as Australians, having turned a blind eye to the new regime's savage and brutal repression of alleged communists, actively sought to promote international acceptance of the *Orde Baru*, or New Order as it was sometimes called. Australian sympathy for the Indonesian independence struggle—largely expressed by certain unions whose politics would have been anathema to the Menzies or Suharto governments—was exaggerated into mythology. According to Professor J. A. C. Mackie, a leading specialist in South-East Asian affairs, after the new regime came to power in Jakarta, Australian diplomats played a significant part in the early efforts to establish a consortium to provide large-scale financial aid to the new regime.[11] Academics and diplomats glossed over the Indonesian army's ruthless persecution of its opponents and its cynical disregard of its obligation to the UN in relation to West Irian in 1969, and expounded the merits of the regime's 'moderate' character, that is:

> that the new government was clearly anti-communist and committed to a low-key, unassertive foreign policy, with a new stress on regionalism and 'good neighbourly' relations with nearby countries. The stage was set for the working out of 'a new and more constructive, enduring set of links'.[12]

As the Jakarta–Canberra connection took on the character of a special relationship by the early 1970s, reaching its zenith in the first half of the Whitlam government's term of office, the position of the Portuguese colony of East Timor declined into insignificance and irrelevance. That the colony had almost disappeared from Australian foreign-policy priorities was helped by the Suharto regime's repeated emphatic declarations that it had no territorial claims on any of the adjacent territories, a move designed to remove the tensions and uncertainties lingering after the end of Konfrontasi.

Although there was some improvement in the level of economic relations between Australia and Timor, official political relations further weakened after the closure of the consulate in Dili in 1971. This dismayed and irritated the Portuguese, whose links with metropolitan Portugal were thereby considerably inconvenienced. This move was inconsistent with the circumstances. As a general rule a consular presence reflects the existence of a significant level of commercial and tourist activity between states or territories. In the case of East Timor tourism and commerce had increased significantly with Australian aircraft flying to the island two or three times a week in the years before the closure of the mission in Dili. One reason given for the closure was that a diplomatic mission had been opened in Lisbon, but Australia's embassy in Portugal could not have dealt with consular problems in distant East Timor. The real reason was transparently clear. Australia was now anxious to distance itself from Portugal's colonial position in Timor, as Lisbon's colonial policies were under general attack by the international community. Relations between the Indonesian authorities and Timor's colonial administration were relatively relaxed then, but in Australia a consensus had been reached that the colony would inevitably go to Indonesia, and the early withdrawal of the official Australian presence would serve to eliminate a potential source of embarrassment.

In the three decades between the beginning of the Pacific War and the last years of Portuguese rule in Timor, Australian attitudes had changed radically. In 1941 Timor was regarded as being so vital to the country's defence that Australian troops engaged in an act of invasion, at enormous humanitarian cost to the people of the colony. The future acquisition of the territory as a way of serving Australia's narrow security interests was then being canvassed by the government. However, because of British pressures and Portuguese suspicions, ambitious plans for a special postwar relationship never eventuated. New priorities emerged in the South-East Asian foreground of the Australian foreign policy perspective and, as far as Australia was concerned, the East Timor colony drifted back to the obscurity of the nineteenth century.

Thus, when the process of decolonisation began, paradoxically it was not Australian but Indonesian security interests—that is, Jakarta's fears that an independent state of East Timor could prove a threat to that nation's territorial integrity—that influenced the shaping of the Whitlam government's Timor policy. What had been of vital strategic value in 1941 was, in 1974, irrelevant and dispensable. Just as Australia did not hesitate to jeopardise Timorese welfare and lives in 1941, nor was Canberra, some thirty-four years later, inhibited by any pangs of conscience at the looming risk of grave harm to the wellbeing of the inhabitants of this colony.

On the eve of the April Coup in Lisbon, there existed in Australia a broad consensus about East Timor, a convergence of attitudes towards Indonesia. To the conservatives the Suharto regime, with its fervent anti-communism, deserved full support because it represented a kind of barrier between Australia and the dangers seemingly inherent in the post-Vietnam situation. Therefore, the Suharto regime's anxiety about possible threats to its security was understandable, and should be deferred to by Australia. Thus, when the Indonesians began expressing their fears that an independent East Timor could prove a threat to the republic and began expounding the dangers of communist infiltration into the Portuguese colony, the Australian right provided them with a receptive and sympathetic audience.

Political opinion in the centre and on the centre-left of the political spectrum was also influenced by the perceived importance of Indonesia to Australia and of the need to preserve the diplomatic gains in a relationship that had been carefully cultivated since the Suharto regime had come to office. There were also growing concerns about the nature of the regime, but Indonesia represented a kind of bridge between Australia and Asia. According to this thinking it would have been both unrealistic and harmful for Australian interests to have become involved in seeking to influence the outcome in the small, inconsequential Portuguese colony. Few Australians knew anything about the Timorese, or about their past links with Australia, and even fewer seemed to acknowledge that Australia might be indebted to them. Even the former commandos, some of whom had kept up their links with the Timorese, did not feel obliged in the postwar years to campaign for a better deal for the Timorese. Yet they, of all people, had been aware of the oppressive and economically depressed conditions under which the ordinary inhabitants of the colony had lived. Only a handful of former commandos were eventually prepared come out in support of a people that they had claimed as their saviours, but by then the hour was rather late. Many individual Australians—especially from the Darwin area—had developed a sympathy and affection for the Timorese people, but there was no national consensus that Australia had an obligation to press for the rights of the Timorese to be properly observed in accord with international principles that Australians were strongly supporting.

The view that had developed in political, diplomatic, and academic circles since the early 1960s—in particular, since West Irian had been handed over to Indonesia—that Timor's future lay with Indonesia was inevitably conveyed to influential Indonesian circles by various informal means. The aforementioned views of Professor Donald Weatherbee closely reflected the attitudes of many Australian politicians and diplomats.* In his *Asian Survey* article, recall that Weatherbee concluded that the Portuguese were holding East Timor 'in trust'—for Indonesia.[13] Not surprisingly, when the Lisbon coup brought the question of the Portuguese colony's future to the attention of policy makers in Jakarta, Indonesian reactions were influenced by the conclusion that, in the view of a strong body of opinion in Australia, their acquisition of the territory was inevitable and, to some, even desirable from the point of view of Australia's national self-interest.

Although Canberra had set up its diplomatic mission in Lisbon some years earlier, Australia too was taken by surprise when the officers of the Movimento das Forcas Armadas (MFA) engineered the overthrow of the Caetano government in April 1974. The decision of the new regime of General Spinola to allow the overseas provinces to determine their own future suddenly thrust East Timor into the focus of the Australian foreign-policy apparatus, but because of the lack of representation in Dili the foreign affairs department knew little about the political situation in the colony. Largely for this reason it was decided to send a two-man fact-finding mission as unobtrusively as possible to East

---

* In 1980, when the Indonesian establishment was searching for ways to counter the mounting criticism in US political and academic circles, Professor Weatherbee was selected (with the help of the state department) to go to East Timor to conduct a 'fact-finding' tour.

Timor. I was one of the men on that mission. Before we set out we already knew that certain influential Indonesian generals were taking a close interest in the Portuguese colony and that the prime minister and some key advisers had no enthusiasm for an independent East Timor.

When we left Canberra in mid-June 1974 we were under instructions not to convey the impression that Australia favoured the colony's eventual independence. Although senior officers in the department had hoped that we could make an unobtrusive visit to Portuguese Timor, this was not to be the case. Our mission attracted close attention from the Portuguese, from the leaders of the three newly formed Timorese political parties (then called associations), from the Indonesian consul and his staff, and from the various sections of the community, particularly the Chinese. The Portuguese and Timorese clearly hoped that Australia would be playing a very important role, now that the obstacle of Portugal's colonial intransigence had been removed. Australia's experience with decolonisation in Papua New Guinea, its excellent relations with Indonesia, and the Whitlam government's vigorous support for the principle of self-determination in international forums all seemed to our hosts to make Australia an ideal source of moral and material support for a process it had been quietly nudging the Portuguese to agree to for some years.

It was difficult not to be affected by the atmosphere in the colony at that time. While some of the Portuguese, and especially the Chinese merchants, were anxious about the future, the Timorese were excited and optimistic for reasons that have already been discussed. But above all they seemed to take it for granted that Australia would now play a role in supporting whatever they chose to do. Some of the Timorese openly declared that Australia owed it to them because of their sacrifices on Australia's behalf during World War II. The reason for this attitude was clear enough. Many of the emerging leaders were the sons of Portuguese, Timorese or *mestiços* who had assisted the Australian troops in 1942, and the commandos, whose reputations as fighting men had become part of the island's mythology, were their idols. It was a reminder that although the Timor campaign had involved only a few hundred Australian troops during a year of fighting it had affected tens of thousands of Timorese. Although most of the Timorese leaders were in those early days inclined to be naive and politically inexperienced, they soon realised that an Australian commitment to their right to self-determination would act as a counterpoise to any Indonesian intrigues against them.

It was impossible not to conclude that the only course the Timorese were likely to choose of their own volition was ultimate independence and, in view of the growing number of small states emerging from the remnants of colonial empires, why shouldn't the Timorese be given the same chance? They were prepared to accept a long period of preparation (even Fretilin leaders were speaking of a period of between five and ten years), and with a development program designed to fit the circumstances—to which Australia could contribute—and with Indonesia's cooperation, East Timor's prospects were in fact good. This allegedly unviable, underdeveloped colony could eventually be transformed into a small stable nation. When I returned to Canberra, however, I was to learn that the influential General Murtopo had already made it clear privately that he was strongly opposed to such an outcome and that he had the support of some of President Suharto's other close colleagues, among them Lieutenant-General Yoga Sugama, chief of Bakin, which played a crucial, indeed dominant, role in the shaping of foreign policy.

In my report on the Timor situation I took the opportunity to try to present this issue in broad perspective. When this report was completed copies went to, among others, both the prime minister and Richard Woolcott, a senior foreign affairs official who was soon to become ambassador to Indonesia, on the eve of their departure for the key meeting with President Suharto at Wonosobo in Java. The report raised the following points in its concluding paragraphs:

> Although the Portuguese territory is small in size, and of little consequence in terms of its political and economic importance, its proximity to both Indonesia and Australia and its possible effect on the latter's relations with Australia accord it a special significance. The Australian interest in the future of Timor is conditioned by our preoccupation with Indonesia which, as it were, dominates the foreground in the Australian foreign policy perspective. If Indonesia, despite the assurances of Adam Malik, is opposed to Timor's independence, and has designs on incorporating the province into Indonesia, should Australia become involved in Timor to the extent of risking a confrontation with Jakarta?...

> ...It may seem tempting to pander to those influential elements within Indonesia, who may wish to incorporate Portuguese Timor, in order to avoid the risk of endangering our present good relations with Jakarta. In the long term, however, this policy seems unlikely to serve Australian interests in the region. We could well lose respect in other South-East Asian capitals, particularly in Port Moresby, and, further, we might find ourselves encouraging a dangerous trend in Indonesian politics, with implications inimical to regional security. A more positive course, it might be contended, would be for Australia to seek Indonesia's cooperation in helping to bring about the birth of the new state, if it becomes clear that complete independence is what the Timorese want.

> Whatever the direction of future events in Timor, there is a strong case for resuming consular representation in Dili as soon as possible. The consulate would serve to keep the Government informed on political developments, and at the same time, maintain regular consultations with the Indonesian consular representatives in Timor. One initiative, which the Portuguese would probably in these present circumstances welcome, would be to call for the sending of a mission to Timor, to make an overall assessment of the present situation, and make recommendations concerning the territory's future economic and social development, as well as its future political status. Australian and Indonesian involvement in such a mission, perhaps with other countries, would present a unique opportunity to cooperate in helping the Timorese emerge from their long isolation and colonial bondage, and, to our mutual advantage, extend to the Portuguese some positive and timely assistance. A circumspect Australian participation in such a joint venture would also serve

to weaken the influence of those Indonesians who might seek to subvert the independence movement and incorporate Portuguese Timor into Indonesia against the will of the Timorese.[14]

It soon became clear that these recommendations fell on unresponsive ears, as far as the government was concerned. Prime Minister Whitlam was not at all attracted to the idea of an independent state of East Timor for a number of reasons, not least because such a state could easily complicate the already sensitive relationship between Australia and Indonesia. Mr Whitlam's views appeared to have been formed long before April 1974 but, as they were shared at least in broad outline by most of his advisers on this question in the foreign affairs department—from the political officers in Jakarta right down to the desk level in Canberra—he was probably under no pressure from this quarter to change them. One official, occupying a very sensitive and responsible position in relation to the Timor problem, complained to me: 'I don't see what you are getting excited about! The plain fact is that there are only 700,000 Timorese; what we are really concerned about is our relationship with 130,000,000 Indonesians!' Although not all foreign affairs officials shared this view there was a departmental consensus that the wishes of the Timorese were secondary to the aspirations of the Indonesians—in this case a certain group of generals. Mr Whitlam's view of the Timorese political leaders is best revealed by his remarks in a later article. In a brief reference to the political scene in the colony after the Lisbon coup he said:

> Political parties emerged there for the first time in May 1974. The significant ones at the time were UDT, Fretilin and Apodeti. They were led by mestizos who were among the few in the colony who had received an education and who all seemed to be desperate to succeed the Portuguese as rulers of the rest of the population.[15]

In fact, most of the leaders were full-blooded Timorese.

In September Mr Whitlam held a meeting with President Suharto at Wonosobo, a meeting which strengthened Indonesian resolve to acquire the Portuguese colony by subversive means. The prime minister was accompanied by two senior diplomats who appear to have shared his attitude towards Timor's decolonisation: Australia's ambassador to Indonesia, Bob Furlonger, and Richard Woolcott, who was about to succeed him. Before the Wonosobo meeting the prime minister reportedly had a meeting with General Yoga Sugama. From the outset Sugama was from the outset an aggressive advocate of integration, if necessary, by means of force. One Indonesian leader Mr Whitlam did not meet, according to his own account, was Adam Malik. In a press statement on 13 October 1976, Mr Whitlam declared that the Indonesian foreign minister did not attend his discussions with the president at Wonosobo, or those at Townsville in April 1975. It is intriguing, in view of the importance of the talks, that Malik should have been absent on both occasions. Was it because of the foreign minister's earlier 'indiscretion' with Horta, or was he lacking in enthusiasm for what was unfolding? Probably, it was because the foreign minister was deliberately kept out of the plan by that inner group of generals who had, in effect, taken over all aspects of the handling of the Timor problem.

The official record of the meeting is more guarded than press reports suggested, but Mr Whitlam made clear his preference for Indonesian incorporation of the colony in guarded language.[16] Suharto responded by saying that if East Timor became independent it would give rise to problems. However, such records are noted for their lack of frankness, and reports of well-informed journalists suggesting that the prime minister had all but told his Indonesian hosts that the Portuguese colony was theirs for the taking, should not be discounted.

On such account of the Wonosobo meeting came from the pen of Peter Hastings, a journalist with the *Sydney Morning Herald*, who had close links with the Whitlam entourage. On 16 September 1974 Hastings asked 'why the unseemly public haste to hand Portuguese Timor to Indonesia?' He went on to say:

> Mr Whitlam went much further, one suspects, than his Indonesian hosts required in publicly announcing, by means of a Foreign Affairs official press briefing in Jogjakarta, that 'an independent Timor would be an unviable state and a potential threat to the area', even though the AAP report added that the Prime Minister 'is also thought to have made clear that the people of the colony should have the ultimate decision on their future'.[17]

Mr Whitlam has never disputed such accounts and there can be little doubt that the prime minister's views gave an unexpected boost to Ali Murtopo's ideas on integration and set the stage for the later moves against the colony. This was certainly the way the Portuguese saw it. In Document 2.9 of the Timor Dossier, the head of the foreign ministry in Lisbon on 13 November 1974 informed the president that, at his meeting with Suharto, Mr Whitlam 'had concluded by giving Australia's agreement to the eventual integration of East Timor into Indonesia, feeling it to be the natural and inevitable solution'. This, according to the official, had helped 'reinforce integrationist tendencies within Indonesian political circles'.[18]

The prime minister's assessment was evidently not well-thought out and there was little evidence that his foreign-policy advisers were prepared to draw his attention to the complexity of the problem. As has already been stated the department's views evidently did not differ substantially from Whitlam's simplistic assessment. For example, a departmental background paper, published in September 1974 (after the Wonosobo meeting), concluded, among other things:

> At the present stage Australia has doubts whether the territory would in fact achieve real independence if its people chose completely separate status, given the relative weakness of the economy and its inevitably limited defence capability. Accordingly Australia appreciates Indonesia's concern about the future of the territory and shares its belief that the voluntary union of Portuguese Timor with Indonesia, on the basis of an internationally acceptable act of self-determination, would seem to serve the objective of decolonisation, and at the same time the interests of stability in the region.[19]

This kind of assessment seems to have provoked Peter Hastings who, at that time, was apparently troubled by what might be the consequences of this insensitive treatment of the rights of the Timorese, to refer in a later article to advisers in Canberra:

> who furnished the Prime Minister with such an unsophisticated briefing before he left for Central Java to give away, without being asked, what was not his to give away.

Hastings pointed out that, although integration might be 'the neatest solution', it might well not turn out to be the most practical, and could be 'anything but democratic'. He went on to observe:

> Quite apart from the woeful effect on all mini-capitals from Port Moresby to Suva of Mr Whitlam's urge to give away inconvenient islands, Portuguese Timor may not prove easily digestible to Indonesia, thus causing more problems than if it were independent.[20]

Mr Whitlam's Timor policy was to come under scrutiny in the federal parliament as well as in the press. Up to that time the Opposition parties had shown very little interest in the question, some of their leaders apparently sharing what they understood to be Mr Whitlam's 'realistic' conclusions about what Australia's Timor policy should be. However, Shadow Minister for Foreign Affairs Andrew Peacock had already met Jose Ramos Horta, had been quite impressed by him and became troubled at the prospect of Indonesian interference in East Timor's process of decolonisation. In the budget debate on 30 October 1974, Peacock criticised the government's handling of the Timor question. Following an attack on the government's decision to formally recognise the incorporation of the Baltic States into the Soviet Union, Peacock said that Whitlam ought to convey his view that lack of economic self-sufficiency was an impediment to independence 'to the people of Portuguese Timor whose future he has settled by allowing and accepting their incorporation into Indonesia'. He accused the Whitlam government of prejudging the 'free expression of the Timorese', and declared that, from the Opposition's point of view,

> so far as Timor is concerned it is for the Timorese to decide their future. The Labor Government says that the people of Portuguese Timor cannot be self-sufficient. It ought to tell that to the Nauruans, the Tongans, the Samoans or the Papua New Guineans...So far as Portuguese Timor is concerned we would prefer to see Portugal remain in control and assist with a program for self-determination. It would then be up to the Timorese to determine their own future in a program that they can work out.[21]

But the parliamentary group most troubled by the government's Timor policy was the Labor backbench—and some members of the ministry, especially Tom Uren, who had been taken prisoner by the Japanese in West Timor in 1943. (Mr Whitlam's Timor policy also troubled other ministers, including Bill Hayden, Clyde Cameron, Charlie Jones, Kim Beazley and Lionel Bowen.) One of the first Labor backbenchers to speak out was Chris Hurford who pointed out that Australia, as a traditional supporter of the right to self-determination, could not:

> therefore connive at the denial of these rights to the Timorese people...we have a record to uphold, and to ignore the fate of this territory, in spite of its smallness and

strategic unimportance, would be to risk our diplomatic integrity among the small nations of the South Pacific area.[22]

But Mr Whitlam was unmoved by these criticisms, and soon made it clear that he was not going to encourage his Timor policy to become the subject of public debate. He evidently had no intention of being drawn into any clarification of what had transpired at Wonosobo, or into an elaboration of his own perception of the problem. In reply to several parliamentary questions about the substance of the various consultations with the Indonesians, the Portuguese and Jose Ramos Horta, the prime minister (or those of his advisers who drafted the answers) sought refuge behind such statements as 'discussions were confidential and in accordance with the normal diplomatic practice. It would not be appropriate to reveal details'.[23] When the issue came up for debate in parliament it was acting Minister for Foreign Affairs Bill Morrison, and not Mr Whitlam, who put the government's case. In the earliest of such statements, Mr Morrison said that Australia's policy was based 'on the principles of the UN and Australia's support for the right of self-determination for all colonial people' but added that:

> the Government does not seek any special position in Portuguese Timor and it believes that the views and the attitudes of the people of Portuguese Timor...should be decisive. The Government has indicated that if the people of Portuguese Timor wish to associate themselves in some way with Indonesia, Australia would welcome this provided—and I repeat 'provided'—that the decision were based on an internationally accepted act of self-determination. In short, the Government believes that the Timorese people should be allowed to proceed deliberately towards a decision about their own future, and in discussions with the Portuguese Minister for Overseas Territories this viewpoint came through.[24]

Most significant was Mr Morrison's remark that the government would welcome a move by the Timorese to 'associate' with Indonesia. The same form of words was to become familiar in other government statements on the Timor question. It was used by the prime minister, for example, in his written reply to a question about a previous visit by Horta with the additional statement that 'Australia does not seek any special position' in the Portuguese colony.

It is important to consider the context in which these statements were made. The government well knew that an 'association' with Indonesia was far from the wishes of the vast majority of the Timorese people. It seemed that these carefully chosen words were specifically designed to, among other things, put the Timorese and their supporters on notice that Australia wanted them to join with Indonesia, and had no intention of encouraging the independence movement. That it was seeking no special position meant that it had no intention of becoming involved in the situation. Another form of words that deserves comment was the government's stated preference for 'an internationally accepted act of self-determination'. It seemed to be deliberately avoiding the normal expression 'a genuine act of self-determination'.

The prime minister and his advisers knew that a proper act of self-determination would produce a result not in keeping with the Indonesian objective of integration. What the government seemed to have in mind was some canvassing of opinion in East Timor that would promote Indonesia's objectives and yet satisfy the low level of international interest in the rights of the Timorese. The government and its advisers were under no illusions that such an act would constitute an expression of the preference of the majority of the people, who would eventually 'come to terms' with their new situation. If Australia was to play any part in a dispute over the Portuguese colony its logical role was within the framework of promoting an understanding of Jakarta's special interests and encouraging the Indonesians not to play rough.

Although Andrew Peacock and a few other members of parliament raised the issue of the colony's future, interest in the subject in the federal parliament was limited in 1974. The Timorese did not rate anything like the attention given by the Opposition parties to criticism of the Whitlam government's decision to recognise the incorporation of the Baltic States into the Soviet Union. But the new situation in East Timor soon began to attract the interest of a much wider section of the Australian community. From the ranks of journalists, students, unionists, and aid workers, a steady trickle of visitors went to the island from the middle of 1974 onwards. In 1975 two groups of parliamentarians went to Timor, one in March and another in the immediate aftermath of the civil war. Organisations in support of Timorese self-determination or independence were formed in every Australian state. There were support groups like the Campaign for an Independent East Timor (CIET), the Australia–East Timor Association, and the Friends of East Timor. And, as reports came in of Indonesian moves to undermine the independence movement, the basis of support for the Timorese widened. Some former commandos, clergy from both Protestant and Catholic churches, the Victorian Trades Hall Council, the Australian Union of Students and the umbrella NGO aid agency, the Australian Council for Overseas Aid (ACFOA) all began to take a close interest in the unfolding drama, especially in 1975 when press reports disclosed that Indonesia was on the verge of invading the Portuguese colony.

The invasion scare of February 1975 brought a modicum of unity to a disparate grouping of Australians who had spoken out on behalf of the Timorese. They ranged from members of the Communist Party of Australia to leading union officials such as Bob Hawke and Jim Roulston; to Liberal and Country Party politicians; and not least to many of the nation's leading newspaper editors. The parliament reacted with much more vigour than had been the case after the Wonosobo meeting. Spurred on by a telegram from the Fretilin–UDT coalition in Dili, Mr Peacock successfully moved in late February to have the government's East Timor policy debated in the parliament. The following telegram to Peacock from Timor was incorporated into the debate:

Coalition Fretilin UDT holding over 95% Timor's population call your support independence East Timor. Australia has great responsibility maintenance peace this geographical area thus to prevent any conflict; real will Timorese people must be respected. Coalition is prepared start talks Australian, Indonesian Government for co-operation towards peace political stability SEA.[25]

The main thrust of the Opposition's attack was against Mr Whitlam's alleged approval for Indonesia to take over East Timor. Mr Peacock took care to stress the importance of the Australia–Indonesia relationship, and urged that the government take steps to bring together 'the Timorese, the Indonesians and the Portuguese'. But Mr Peacock also declared: 'The Prime Minister should be able to ensure that the Indonesian Government is not in any way, even inadvertently, imposing constraints on the freedom of action of the East Timorese people.' Mr Peacock was joined by a senior Country Party member, Mr Ian Sinclair who also spoke, though with some reserve, in support of East Timor's right to self-determination, but Opposition leader Malcolm Fraser and deputy leader Doug Anthony appeared to distance themselves from the debate.

As has already been mentioned, it was not the prime minister but Mr Morrison who delivered the government's reply to the Opposition attack. Although the minister's statement was lengthy, in essence it did not depart from the strangely ambiguous 'viewpoint' of the government that Australia had no 'special position' in relation to the decolonisation of East Timor, and he repeated that the government would welcome a decision by the Timorese to associate with Indonesia. Considerable emphasis was again placed on Indonesia's special interests with the fascinating comment:

> We believe that there is time and opportunity for a political solution to be found which will meet the proper aspirations of the people of the Territory and also the natural interests of Indonesia.[26]

Mr Morrison also chose to quote a tendentious article from the Indonesian newspaper, the *New Standard*, which normally reflected military views. The main thrust of the article was that:

> although Indonesia makes no legal claim whatsoever to Portuguese Timor, it regards the Territory as geographically a part of the Indonesian world. For cultural, ethnic and historical reasons an integration of the territory into Indonesia would represent valid decolonisation and the most natural source to that end.[27]

In short, Morrison iterated the government's position with all its ambiguity and contradictions, and he merely increased suspicions that the government was acting as an accomplice to Indonesian moves to acquire East Timor. What the minister did not reveal was that his intelligence advisers were already aware of the existence of *Operasi Komodo* and its sinister aims. Not least, they were aware that the Lampung military exercises were intended as a forerunner to a proposed attack on Dili and Baucau. Clearly the Whitlam government had not budged an inch from its conviction that Indonesia should acquire East Timor and that Australia should not question the means used to bring about that end.

Prime Minister Whitlam continued to be tight-lipped on the subject. His answers to parliamentary questions were clipped, uninformative, and consistent in their style. Yet it is difficult to believe that Mr Whitlam was uninformed. To the prime minister the Timor problem was a sensitive issue that had to be resolved and contained to prevent permanent harm to a relationship of fundamental importance to Australia. It was one issue he chose to keep to himself in Caucus, and even in the Cabinet room. Open discussion of this irritant in the party room and in the parliament would obviously create obstacles to the developing of a new vision and a new role for Australia in an increasingly complex regional and world environment. As Dr Nancy Viviani, one of the foreign minister's advisers, put it in a later article, Mr Whitlam:

> had an undoubted capacity for the broad vision, well matched by rhetoric, and a confident grasp of the problems of balance of power relations among the great powers. He conceived a new role for Australia in international relations, and he wanted Australians to emerge from the shackles of past fears and parochialism, and share his vision. He delighted in the untrammelled nature of the power involved in foreign policy making—he would not consult his Cabinet on foreign policy issues generally, and did not on Timor, and he was loath to have such issues raised in Caucus.[28]

As the Timor crisis deepened, the prime minister's control of the handling of this particular issue within the government became tighter. The circulation of classified cables about the question, and in particular, the distribution of certain highly classified and sensitive intelligence reports about *Operasi Komodo* activities, were further restricted. Thus, day-to-day handling of the Timor question became confined to a small coterie of officials in the department of foreign affairs, in the joint intelligence organisation, and in the embassy in Jakarta. Most of the diplomats in this group were at one with the prime minister in their perception of what Australia's policy should be. The recent release of confidential cables has now disclosed how the view of the Australian ambassador to Jakarta, Richard Woolcott, was in harmony with Mr Whitlam's view, but similar attitudes were held by most of the senior officers in that part of the foreign affairs department. Alan Renouf, the department head from 1974 to 1977, has denied that such a consensus existed,[29] but few of these officials expressed any reservations about the Whitlam policy. It is true, however, that early in 1975 a submission from the desk officer urged the government to re-establish a consulate in Dili, but this proposal was rejected, almost certainly by Mr Whitlam.

As Nancy Viviani later put it, 'Timor policy was indeed Whitlam policy', and in a sense it was a logical extension of the views he stated in his Roy Milne lecture in 1963. East Timor was another West Irian, an untidy colonial relic that was part of Indonesia's geography. And Indonesia was a kind of bridge between Australia and Asia, a people Australians had to come to terms with if they were to forge prejudices and inhibitions of their European heritage. Perhaps, as Nancy Viviani suggests, Mr Whitlam may have feared the 'Balkanisation of South-East Asia', and he may have felt that the emergence of a small state might provoke the intrusion of an outside power, thus endangering regional stability. But it was my impression that the prime minister and his advisers were more concerned that an independent state of East Timor, with its Portuguese cultural traditions, might prove to be a constant irritant in the Australia–Indonesia relationship.

Mr Whitlam seemed to have little patience with mini-states, and the thought of East Timor, which he had often treated as a joke, becoming one clearly did not please him. In an article in the Canberra Times, Gregory Clark (a former diplomat) once referred to Whitlam's 'obsession about the stupidity of creating small nation states'. Alan Renouf, too, refers to this view in his version of the events surrounding the Timor affair. He writes: 'Whitlam also felt that stability was more likely in regions where there were bigger countries; he had no time for "mini-states".'[30] According to this former department head, the prime minister came up with a policy of integration through self-determination, a surprisingly naive concept that revealed a lack of understanding not only of the situation in the Portuguese colony, but of the process of decolonisation. However, it is hard to accept Renouf's contention that the foreign affairs department did not favour the policy of the prime minister. It was, in my experience, supported, if not promoted, by the head of the Indonesian branch and by the ambassador in Jakarta, to speak of only two of the key officials in the policy-making process.

Thus, when Whitlam had his second meeting with the Indonesian president in Townsville in the first week of April 1975 his position was unchanged, although he may have been disturbed by reports that the Indonesians had been on the verge of pursuing their objective by military means a few weeks earlier. Also, from diplomatic and intelligence sources at the government's disposal, he must by then have been well aware of the existence of *Operasi Komodo* and the fact that its agents were already at work in East Timor and elsewhere. From this information, the prime minister and his party would have known that the architect of this operation, Ali Murtopo (then deputy head of Bakin), was a prominent member of President Suharto's delegation. Three other generals accompanied the Indonesian leader—Sudharmono, Tjokropranolo, and Widya Latif—although probably all three of them were in civilian posts.

Murtopo had no opposite number on the Australian delegation, which was mostly foreign affairs officers—Richard Woolcott, Graham Feakes (head of the relevant division), Charles Mott, Mike Curtin and Geoff Forester. Apart from the prime minister's own staff, the only other official present was Phillip MacElligot, of the foreign affairs and defence section of the prime minister's department. Although much of the discussion was about the Timor problem, a subject of concern to the defence establishment, no member of that department was on the Australian delegation. Evidently the prime minister did not want defence views to complicate talks on which he placed great importance. Their absence reflected the growing divergence between the prime minister and the foreign affairs department on the one hand, and the defence community (or, at least, the intelligence and strategic assessments components of it), on the other.

The emphasis at the Townsville talks was informality—the so called 'batik shirt' diplomacy—and at some of the sessions the two leaders were alone, apart from their interpreters. The accompanying officials were briefed about the discussions later—in the Australian case, usually by Geoff Forester, who served as Mr Whitlam's interpreter. East Timor was a main subject at the Townsville meeting, with Mr Whitlam reasserting his view that Timor's future lay with Indonesia, a view with which the Indonesians would already have been familiar. He was apologetic for statements by left-wing elements supportive of East Timor's independence and hostile to Indonesia. Mr. Whitlam was rather disparaging about the Timorese, expressing the view that most were politically uneducated and naïve, but felt that 'in time would come to recognise their ethnic kinship with their Indonesian neighbours'*. The problem was the influence of the educated, most of whom 'were the sons and daughters of Portuguese fathers and Timorese mothers'. The prime minister reportedly urged that force not be used and, according to Alan Renouf, 'stressed that there should be no departure from an internationally acceptable act of self-determination'. The best outcome, however, 'would be incorporation into Indonesia'.[31] The record of conversation may not, however, present a complete account as it is not a verbatim record and could easily have been sanitised. Indonesian officials could not have missed the fact that Whitlam government's acceptance of the territory's integration was incompatible with its declared commitment to the principle of self-determination.

It is interesting to note that Michael Richardson, a respected Asian analyst, later reported that: 'A senior Foreign Affairs official wrote later in a confidential summary that Lt General Ali Murtopo...regarded Mr Whitlam's statement to President Suharto as a "green light" for absorption of the territory'. Richardson went on to state that, 'as a result of the Prime Minister's indiscretion, the Foreign Affairs Department attempted to do some fine semantic tuning with the record of conversation' when the official party returned to Canberra, but 'Indonesia ignored the verbal reshuffling'.[32]

Whatever transpired at the meetings, it is hard not to conclude that a kind of unspoken conspiracy existed—a conspiracy aimed at denying the Timorese the right to choose their own future. Undoubtedly the most serious aspect of the understanding was that, although Australia, it may be assumed, was clearly opposed to the use of armed force, it tacitly acknowledged Indonesia's right to employ subversive means to achieve its end. In so doing, the government was virtually condoning an operation aimed at destabilising the situation in the Portuguese colony, thus increasing the risk of violence and insurrection, conditions under which an act of military intervention by Indonesia would probably attract considerable international support. Therefore, although Mr Whitlam may have sought to urge the Indonesian president to exercise restraint on his generals, the overall operation to get East Timor by illegal means would, from Murtopo's point of view, have been given a green light, at least in principle.

---

* Record of conversation between Whitlam and Suharto, Townsville, 4 April 1975, p. 244, Australian and the Indonesian incorporation of Portuguese East Timor.

In fairness the government, or at least its advisers, did explore some options. Early in 1975, for example, a proposal was apparently put to the Indonesians in a letter which, in essence, suggested that Indonesia and Portugal might cooperate to promote an act of self-determination and if the Timorese chose independence the colony would in practice become a client-state of Indonesia. Linked to the arrangement was an aid package designed to benefit both sides of the island. Apparently the Indonesians reacted somewhat angrily and rejected the proposal out of hand. Officials made some attempt to revive the proposal after the Townsville talks but the Indonesians showed no interest in it. The most troubled advisers though, were in the defence department where the belief still persisted that how East Timor was decolonised was strategically irrelevant to Australia. These dissenting views apparently did not impress Mr Whitlam. In the seminar paper delivered at the Australian National University in November 1979 he wrote:

> There was, however, a small faction in the Department of Defence which, having failed to keep Indonesia out of New Guinea, was now intent on establishing an enclave in the midst of the Indonesian archipelago in case of future conflict with Indonesia.

A submission in August 1974 by the then head of the strategic and international policy division of the department, Mr W. B. Pritchett indicates that at least some senior defence officials had reached a more realistic assessment of the implications of the Timor problem for Australia than had the prime minister and his foreign affairs advisers. The defence department was clearly basing its conclusions on good information from sensitive intelligence sources, as well as on the reports emerging from the Australian embassy in Jakarta. Again in February 1975 in a letter to Graham Feakes, Pritchett stated, inter alia, that:

> Indonesian seizure (of East Timor) by force would be most undesirable and that our common interests would best be served by an Indonesian state associated with Indonesia.

Pritchett also drew attention to the basic weakness of the Whitlam policy, the fundamental incompatibility between the aim of supporting integration into Indonesia and the contention that there should be an act of self-determination.

A visit to East Timor by a parliamentary delegation served to kindle public and political interest in the future of East Timor, and also to speculate about the ideological forces at work behind the various movements. It comprised members of the foreign affairs and defence committee of the Australian Labor Party caucus in the federal parliament, including members of parliament John Kerin, Richie Gun, Gareth Clayton and Ken Fry, and senators Arthur Gietzelt and Gordon McIntosh. The parliamentarians travelled widely and held talks with the leaders of the three parties, members of the MFA Decolonisation Commission, the Chinese community, and Governor Colonel Lemos Pires. After their return to Canberra the members of the delegation made a number of recommendations to the government, based on their assessment that independence for East Timor was inevitable if the Timorese were freely to choose their own future. They concluded that Australia could, and should, play a constructive role in supporting the process of decolonisation by Australia becoming involved in Timor as soon as possible.

The members of parliament urged that the consulate be reopened—a request strongly stressed by the Portuguese governor. They also urged that Australia set up an aid program for the Timorese and provide technical training assistance. The report of the parliamentarians had considerable effect in caucus and among some members of the Opposition, but it did not shift Mr Whitlam from his preference for integration, although at his later meeting with the Indonesian president he may have felt constrained to warn the latter of the increasing Australian support for the independence movement.

About two weeks after the Townsville meeting, the prime minister replied to a letter from Senator Gietzelt, who had written to his leader on behalf of other members of the caucus Timor delegation. At the time this letter provided the best available record of Mr Whitlam's view of the problem. His government's policy, he wrote, was to support:

a deliberate and measured process of decolonisation...an approach which has been accepted by all the major parties involved—Portugal and Indonesia as well as the Timorese political parties. In supporting a measured approach, we have been very much alive to the fact that the inhabitants of Portuguese Timor displayed virtually no political interests before April 1974 coup in Portugal.[33]

In his letter Mr Whitlam was clearly unimpressed with the delegation's findings that the result of allowing Timorese self-determination would be an independent nation. This was based on the conclusion 'that the overwhelming majority of Timorese aspire to independence, and that any action by any outside power to frustrate Timorese independence would be totally without justification'. He continued:

I myself hesitate to accept at face value the claims of the political personalities who have emerged in the first year of political activity in Timor. They have sprung from what appears to have been a political vacuum under the Portuguese. Most appear to represent a small elite class—the educated, the government officials and various other Westernised elements. It may be that this group will be able to win the allegiance of the people of the territory, but their claims are as yet untested. There may well be, below the surface, thoroughly indigenous political forces which would carry the inhabitants of Portuguese Timor in directions different from those on which their present leaders are set.

In these few sentences Mr Whitlam dismissed their political relevance to decolonisation. Yet their demands were not unrealistic. It was not as if the Timorese were demanding independence immediately. What the Timorese leaders wanted Portugal to do was to declare their right to independence, and then carry out a decolonisation program in a period of between three and five years.

Even more curious was the prime minister's comment that:

the division of the island of Timor is no more than an accident of Western colonial history [and that]: four hundred years of Portuguese domination may have distorted the picture which the people of Portuguese Timor have of themselves, and perhaps obscured for them their ethnic kinship with the people of Indonesia. Time will be required for them to sort themselves out.

The frontiers of more than half of the nations of the world were established by 'accidents of Western colonial history', and not least those of Indonesia. Thus, it was the pattern of Dutch colonialism that gave Indonesia its present boundaries, and not natural evolution. The ethnic and cultural configuration of the archipelago suggests that in other circumstances several separate states might have emerged, based on the distinctive cultural and linguistic differences. Such is the nature of developing world nationalism.

There was something vaguely intimidating in Mr Whitlam's remark that the Timorese would need time 'to sort themselves out'. Had such a constraint been imposed on the Indonesians in the late 1940s, the republic might never have emerged in its present form. However, the prime minister did seek to assure his parliamentary colleagues that his government supported self-determination for the Timorese, and if they were to choose independence, 'after careful consideration', Australia would support the decision.

The prime minister went on to deal with the proposal that Australia assist the decolonisation process, based on the strong requests conveyed to the Australian Labor Party delegation by the Portuguese and almost all other groups in the colony. Mr Whitlam wrote that it would be:

> presumptuous for Australia to interfere in the process of decolonisation in the territory'. [This was the preserve of the] parties principally involved—the people of Portuguese Timor and the Portuguese government, with Indonesia occupying the next most important place because of its predominant interests.

Australia was not a 'party principal'; it could provide some modest aid perhaps, but re-establishing the consulate would only be 'misinterpreted by political interests' in the colony seeking to 'use our presence to involve us to an extent which I do not feel would be appropriate for Australia'.

The essence of Mr Whitlam's reasoning came in the first sentence of his last paragraph. The Timor problem, he wrote:

> must be seen against the fundamental importance to us of a long-term cooperative relationship with Indonesia.

In pointing out that the Indonesians had stated that they had 'no intention to settle the matter by force', the prime minister must have felt himself to be on uncertain ground because only about two months earlier, based on advice that the Strategic Reserve (Kostrad) was preparing for an invasion of East Timor with its Lampung exercise, he had sent a personal message to President Suharto. Perhaps he had full confidence in the assurances that the president may subsequently have given him at Townsville. However, the fact remains that his government was well aware at that time of the existence of Indonesia's subversive activities and that the goal of incorporation had not been abandoned.

As Senator Willesee was informed in April, the 'green lights' that had been 'flashing in late February' had changed to a 'steady amber—but not red.[34]

The recommendations of the parliamentary delegation were taken rather more seriously by the foreign affairs department advisers, but given the position of Mr Whitlam, and of the Australian ambassador in Jakarta, their room for manoeuvre was limited. As has already been mentioned, the Indonesians reacted with some irritation to the suggestion that Australia provide aid which would interfere with their own plans for the territory. In July an aid program was discussed, and it might well have materialised had not the UDT coup intervened. It is not clear who rejected the recommendation that an Australian consulate be re-established, but it is probable that the decision was made by the prime minister. One reason for the rejection has been put forward by Nancy Viviani. She wrote that both the idea of an aid program and the reopening of the consulate 'would arouse Indonesian suspicions as to Australia's intentions and particularly its support of Indonesian policy, and a reopened consulate could become the focus of pressure by Timorese parties'.[35]

There is, however, a missing element from the documentation recently released in 2000. It is what the government really knew from its extensive intelligence monitoring of Indonesian military communications. Very little of that information has been released. From my information at the time, Australian advisers were well aware that military preparations for the seizure of East Timor got under way early in 1975, so that the assurances from Indonesian diplomats that force would not be used were meaningless. In July a frank briefing from Harry Tjan confirmed that a plan, presumably under *Operasi Komodo*, to integrate East Timor forcibly, had been agreed to the Indonesian military.* The first step, the urging of UDT leaders to act against Fretilin, which led to the coup, took place at the end of that month. Its unexpected outcome—a Fretilin victory—brought forward Indonesia's military intervention. A great deal was known about these moves to the government. In the circumstances, seeking assurances from Indonesian diplomats that force would not be used seemed to be more for the historical record than a way of dealing with the realities of the situation. In these circumstances to reopen the consulate would risk direct Australian involvement in the conspiracy on the ground.

After Townsville the priority was to persuade the Indonesians to refrain from using force, while avoiding provoking or offending Indonesia. The view of the government and its advisers became increasingly less sympathetic to the position of the Timorese. Even the advisers who were troubled by the government's policy occasionally revealed this sort of bias. Dr Viviani, for example, expresses a mild criticism of the parliamentarians and other Australians for having 'urged the Timorese to go for independence, without considering the costs of this sufficiently

---

* The deputy chief of Bakin, Ali Murtopo, was also patron of CSIS. Hamish McDonald describes CSIS as Murtopo's 'political backroom team' (Suharto's Indonesia, p. 198).

and with little prospect of converting their own Government to this view'.[36]

The level of Australian interest in the Timor situation in the months preceding the UDT coup in August 1975 should not be exaggerated. With economic conditions deteriorating as the country began to feel the full effects of the world oil price crisis, and with the Whitlam government under the increasing pressure from a Senate over which it had no control, Australians were hardly in the mood to give much time or thought to the affairs of the Portuguese colony. The devastation of the airport facilities at Darwin from Cyclone Tracy had caused the temporary suspension of the TAA-operated air link with Baucau and affected the flow of news from the territory. As a result some news items carried by the Australian media were to come via Jakarta where they were subjected to subtle distortion by the media agents of *Operasi Komodo*, as illustrated by the false reports early in 1975 of Timorese refugees fleeing to West Timor to escape persecution by the pro-independence parties.

Attitudes in Australia began to form around ideological and other political perceptions of where the country's interests lay in the affair. Most of those Australians who took a close interest in events in Timor were on the left or in the centre of the political spectrum. Thus, the two delegations that visited the island in March were the Australian Labor Party caucus members and a delegation comprising students, unionists, and church representatives, led by Jim Roulston, a leading Victorian union official. Both delegations were quite impressed with Fretilin and saw it as the leading vehicle for independence, although the parliamentarians were careful to maintain a level of impartiality consistent with their position as backbenchers of the party led by the prime minister. The other visitors tended to associate much more closely with Fretilin, partly because of the links they had already established with Jose Ramos Horta during his previous visits to Australia, and partly because they identified more readily with the proposed reforms and the independence goal of the party of the left.

The Australian Opposition parties held more appeal to the right-wing Suharto regime, and in 1975 they shared the Whitlam government's lack of enthusiasm for an independent East Timor. At first, however, Shadow Minister Andrew Peacock gave considerable moral support to the idea of East Timorese self-determination. He met Horta on several occasions, and won the confidence of many of the other Timorese leaders. Thus it was to Mr Peacock that they addressed their appeal when the possibility of an Indonesian military action against the territory was first reported. Few other Liberals spoke out on behalf of the Timorese, but in fairness it should be said that this was more a reflection of their cautious attitudes to a foreign-policy problem that was far from clear, than an indication that they were insensitive to the rights of the Timorese. Some prominent small 'l' Liberals, like Richard Alston of Victoria and John Dowd of New South Wales, did give strong personal support to the Timorese from the outset. The conservatives among the Opposition leaders from the beginning tended to stress the overriding importance of the relationship with Indonesia though, and specifically the need to sustain a vigorous level of support for the Western-oriented anti-communist Suharto regime.

The threat of communist insurgency in the aftermath of the US withdrawal from South-East Asia was perceived to be very real, and their attitude to Timor had to be understood in the light of such fears. Some conservatives considered that what was often referred to as Indonesian paranoia about communism was an understandable attitude that deserved Australia's indulgence. They were also susceptible to Indonesian propaganda reports about alleged communist infiltration and activities in the Portuguese colony. These congenial attitudes did not escape the attention of the Indonesians, including the planners behind the operation to incorporate East Timor. Therefore, a number of visits were made to Australia, including one by Lieutenant-General Yoga Sugama, who quietly arrived in May 1975 and, according to Hamish McDonald, 'sounded out, among others, Opposition Leader Malcolm Fraser'. Yoga Sugama 'found no reason for alarm'.[37]

The views of the Opposition leader, Malcolm Fraser, probably did not differ significantly from those of Mr Whitlam. If Mr Fraser had entertained any interest in the right to self-determination of the Timorese, he did not disclose it—in his public statements, at least. Nor did the Country Party leader, Mr Anthony, publicly indicate any interest in the unfolding crisis.

The conservative response though was based on an uninformed assessment of the Timor problem. Perhaps both Mr Fraser and Mr Anthony were ideologically disposed to accept Jakarta's propaganda that Fretilin was a communist party, and in August 1975 they were to describe Fretilin in these terms in the parliament. Such statements would have pleased to Jakarta, and would no doubt have added to the Indonesian conviction that Australia was sympathetic to their objectives. The fact remains, however, that the Whitlam government's refusal to make a general statement on the issue to the parliament made it possible for such uninformed and prejudiced views to gain currency. Had the government chosen to put to positive use the background information available to it from intelligence and diplomatic sources, a clear consensus would probably have been achieved, discouraging the Indonesian generals from concluding that the use of force to achieve integration would be accepted by Australian political leaders as a necessary, if not desirable, solution to the Timor problem.

One source of great disappointment to the Timorese was the position of the Returned Services League (RSL), an organisation that in the past had celebrated the Timor campaign as one of the epics of World War II and had acknowledged the critical importance of the support the commandos had received from the Timorese. It seemed that many had forgotten their promises that some time in the future the Australians would return and repay their debt, a belief that in East Timor was carried on from father to son. Despite the fact that some of the former commandos took an active interest in the Timor problem, and several visited the territory in 1974 and 1975, few expressed much public support for the principle that the Timorese should be able to exercise their right to self-determination in the face of external interference. I have mentioned before that one former commando officer at a meeting with UDT leaders vigorously counselled the Timorese to forget about independence and to break their coalition with Fretilin, which he described as communist. The best thing for Timor, one former commando told them was incorporation into Indonesia. This said, some ex-commandos gave valuable support to the Timorese from behind the scenes. One former member of the Timor force, a senior intelligence official at the time of the crisis, was deeply troubled at what was transpiring and he contributed a certain objectivity to the thinking of sections of the defence establishment.

In spite of the moral support of individual ex-soldiers, the RSL played a dismal role. The ex-servicemen's organisation, with its traditional hostility to any cause even vaguely associated with the left, was an early and susceptible target for attention by Indonesian officials, who identified it as an important opinion-forming body among Australian conservatives. Thus, as one RSL state secretary informed me, quite early in the crisis, senior executives of the organisation were treated to a specially arranged dinner meeting by the Indonesian ambassador, where they were lectured, among other things, on the danger of a communist threat emerging in East Timor and posing a risk to regional security and stability. The audience, it seems, responded positively to this disturbing scenario and the Timorese, in spite of the great suffering they had endured on behalf of Australian troops during World War II, were to get little support from the RSL as the tragic circumstances of 1975 engulfed the island. Upholding the rights of the Timorese was no match for the containment of the perceived communist threat.

The response of the churches was also uneven. The fact that the Portuguese colony had a fairly large Christian community attracted some interest, but here, too, many individual judgments were swayed by ideological considerations, as well as by the presence of sizeable Christian minorities in Indonesia with whom many of the Australian clergy had established close links. Church politics were further complicated by the fact that some of Indonesia's leading generals, including General Moerdani (a Catholic who enjoyed a personal friendship with the Papal Nuncio in Jakarta), were Christians. One distinguished Indonesian general, Major-General Simatupang, although long retired from military leadership, was a leading figure in the World Council of Churches. Also, church organisations were anxious not to jeopardise their aid projects in various parts of Indonesia. It was therefore not uncommon for church officials to remark that their organisations wanted to help, but for these various reasons were reluctant to become too closely involved.

The Timor crisis produced major rifts in the Catholic Church, whose largely conservative bishops also tended to be influenced by what they regarded as Indonesia's legitimate fears of communism, and by information emanating from the very conservative bishop of Timor, Bishop Ribeiro. The whole Portuguese revolution had troubled Bishop Ribeiro. His instinctive dislike of the Left filled him with fear of the 'communistic character' of Fretilin, a fear he had managed to convey to some of his senior colleagues in Australia. The bishops were also regular recipients of the National Civic Council's (NCC) *Newsweekly*. The NCC had close links with Ali Murtopo's CSIS—in particular with CSIS director Harry Tjan and Liem Bian-Kie, both Catholics, who played key political roles for *Operasi Komodo*—and this journal has seldom deviated from a position of full support or sympathy for the Suharto government's policies in general. No other Australian publication so consistently and so regularly carried articles alleging communist influence in Fretilin, and none pressed more vigorously for a sympathetic understanding of Indonesia's moves to acquire East Timor. Its views may also have unduly influenced the Indonesian assessment of public support in Australia for integration because it was widely read in influential circles in Jakarta. According to a former staff member of the CSIS, *Newsweekly* was highly praised and carefully read by Harry Tjan who knew and admired the NCC president, Mr B. A. Santamaria, and his associates. The activities of the CSIS were inextricably linked with Bakin.

The mounting crisis in East Timor caused a number of Catholic priests of various orders to take an interest in the rights of the Timorese, and some were to become among their most active supporters—to the chagrin of Mr Santamaria who, in a reference to one such priest, alluded to the misguided activities of a certain 'Marxist-Jesuit'. Among the most active at first was Father Mark Raper, a Jesuit executive member of the Asian Bureau Australia, a member of the 1975 ACFOA mission to Timor. Father Pat Walsh, a Sacred Heart priest, became a member of the Action for World Development movement in Melbourne, and became increasingly involved in support for East Timor.

The strengthening interest of individual groups and the steady stream of visitors to East Timor did not succeed in kindling much Australian political interest in the situation in the colony in the months before to the UDT coup. After March, when it seemed that Indonesia would not intervene militarily, the interest of Australian politicians slackened. However, Timorese leaders continued to come to Australia for informal talks. Horta made further visits and proceeded to widen his contacts to gain further support for the independence movement and for Fretilin's program. It was in May that the UDT leaders Lopes da Cruz and Mousinho visited Australia and talked with, among others, government officials, academics, several former commandos, and the media. In keeping with the government's determination to be 'even-handed' a visit was also arranged for Apodeti leaders, but this time the Timorese concerned were very much under the protective tutelage of officials of Indonesia's embassy in Canberra and its consulates in the major cities.

It was hard for the Timorese to gauge what these visits achieved, apart from some useful contacts and media publicity. The visitors invariably saw officials at the foreign affairs department, and attended seminars at the Australian National University in Canberra and Monash University in Melbourne where their audiences listened attentively and made sympathetic but non-committal comments. In discussions department officials studiously avoided the use of the word 'independence', although they regularly recited Australia's support for 'an internationally acceptable act of self-determination', the meaning of which was probably completely lost on the Timorese visitors, except for Horta who, by the middle of the year, began to make sense of the elusive subtleties in Australian diplomatic jargon.

Notes

1 Peter Hastings, 'The Timor Problem, part 2: Some Australian Attitudes, 1903-1941', *Australian Outlook*, 29, no. 2 (1975): pp. 180-196.
2 Ibid.
3 Ibid.
4 Ibid.
5 Ibid.
6 Ibid.
7 Peter Hastings, 'The Timor Problem, part 3: Some Australian Attitudes, 1941-1950', *Australian Outlook*, 29, no. 3 (1975): pp. 323-334.
8 Ibid.
9 Ibid.
10 David Marr, *Barwick* (Sydney: Allen & Unwin, 1980), pp. 169-174.
11 J. A. C. Mackie, 'Australia's Relations with Indonesia: Principles and Policies', part 2, *Australian Outlook*, 28 (1974): p. 175.
12 Ibid.
13 Donald Weatherbee, 'Portuguese Timor: An Indonesian Dilemma', *Asian Survey* (December 1966).
14 J. S. Dunn, 'Portuguese Timor before and after the Coup: Options for the Future' (27 August 1974), Legislative Research Service, Parliament of Australia, Canberra.
15 E. G. Whitlam, 'Indonesia and Australia, Political Aspects', The Indonesian Connection (seminar held at the Australian National University, 30 November 1979), Research School of Pacific Studies, School Seminar Series.
16 Hugh Armfield, Melbourne Age, 13 September 1974.
17 Peter Hastings, *Sydney Morning Herald*, 16 September 1974.
18 'Relatorio do Governo de Timor' (Report of the Government of Timor), part 2, Document 2.9, the Timor Dossier.
19 'The Future of Portuguese Timor' (11 September 1974), BP/60, Department of Foreign Affairs, Canberra.
20 Peter Hastings, *Sydney Morning Herald*, 19 November 1974.
21 *Commonwealth Parliamentary Debates*, 30 October 1974, p. 3044.
22 Press release from Chris Hurford, 30 October 1974.
23 Answer to Question no. 1178, *Commonwealth Parliamentary Debates*, House of Representatives, 30 October 1974, p. 3135.
24 *Commonwealth Parliamentary Debates*, House of Representatives, 25 February 1975, p. 643.

25 Ibid., p. 642.

26 Ibid., p. 644.

27 Ibid.

28 Nancy Viviani, 'Australians and the Timor Issue', *Australian Outlook*, 30, no. 2 (1976): 197-226.

29 Alan Renouf, *The Frightened Country* (Melbourne: MacMillan, 1979), p. 443.

30 Ibid.

31 Ibid., p. 445.

32 *National Times*, 19 July 1976.

33 This and other extracts are taken from a letter to Senator Gietzelt from Prime Minister Whitlam, dated 22 April 1975.

34 Documents on Australian Defence and Foreign Policy, 1968-1975 (Sydney: Walsh and Munster, 1980), p. 189.

35 Viviani, 'Australians and the Timor Issue'.

36 Ibid.

37 McDonald, *Suharto's Indonesia*, p. 204.

Chapter Eight
The UDT coup and the civil war

The civil war that broke out in Timor in mid-August 1975 stood out in sharp contrast to the *modus vivendi* that had been achieved by the leaders of the two main political parties some six months earlier. Although the coalition was based on a rather hurriedly arrived at consensus, it seemed to presage a rational and positive trend that would facilitate working out a popular solution as to the future status of the province. It was, however, an arrangement that was vulnerable to external political interference and manipulation. Indonesia had helped bring the coalition into being with its clumsy campaign of hostile propaganda broadcasts, but the *Operasi Komodo* operatives now perceived a way of weakening the coalition by shifting the direction of their attack. This strategy was greatly assisted by the growing tensions between the political forces of the right and left in Portugal. After March 1975 the Indonesians had sought to dispel fears that they were planning a military invasion of East Timor and, as has already been discussed, their tactics shifted to winning over the UDT leaders to Jakarta's point of view, that is, to an acknowledgment of the threat of communist subversion to the stability of the region, and of the extent of communist influence in Fretilin, a point of view to which most of the right-wing party leaders were by no means unreceptive.

The flimsy coalition had collapsed at the end of May. Fretilin's refusal to participate in the Macau decolonisation talks, plus the effect of the widening political divisions in metropolitan Portugal on the political atmosphere in Timor, created fertile conditions for the intensified destabilisation activities of Ali Murtopo's agents.* Early in June the Indonesian press claimed that 1500 people from Oecussi had sought refuge in Indonesian Timor to escape 'pressures and threats' from Fretilin. The reality was the contrary. Indonesian troops and

---

* In March there had been an attempt by the right, by Spinolistas, to overthrow the government of Costa Gomes and Vasco Goncalves.

officials had illegally entered the enclave, causing near panic before they were withdrawn. By the end of July East Timor was beset by wild rumours. These included the rumours of a planned Fretilin coup, of smuggling Chinese arms to Fretilin, and that North Vietnamese had secretly entered the Portuguese colony. Bishop Ribeiro was apparently taken in by some of these falsified reports which he confided to UDT and Kota leaders.

According to Jose Martins, Bishop Ribeiro informed the UDT and Kota leaders that 26 to 28 North Vietnamese, holding Portuguese passports and posing as Chinese, had come via Macau and had entered Portuguese Timor to train Fretilin supporters. When Martins asked whether he could prove this, the Bishop replied: 'I am your Bishop, you must believe me!'[1] Such reports had a profound effect on the leaders of the parties opposed to Fretilin who were already alarmed that their parties were rapidly losing further ground to the left-wing party in the country areas. These allegations served to persuade the anticommunist political factions that they would need to prepare for an armed confrontation with Fretilin.

Another event had an even more serious effect on the increasingly tense situation in East Timor. Early in July President Suharto was reported in the Jakarta press as having declared that East Timor could not become independent because it lacked the conditions for economic viability. The president was also reported to have expressed some opposition to the continuation of Portuguese rule—interestingly these remarks were made about the time Harry Tjan informed the Australian Embassy in Jakarta that it had been decided to integrate East Timor. These remarks were at once picked up in Dili where they caused more concern to the UDT leaders than to Fretilin because the former believed that they had established something of an understanding with Jakarta, and that the Indonesians had come to terms with the situation in the colony. Although Fretilin had not gone to Macau, the outcome of the conference had greatly strengthened the conviction of most of the UDT leaders that independence was the only acceptable option and they felt that their seemingly friendly relations with the generals close to the president would result in the Indonesians accepting the inevitable outcome of self-determination. The president's remarks seemed to cut across the assurances that they had believed they were receiving. On that basis João Carrascalão and Domingos de Oliveira went to Jakarta on 25 July where they joined up with Lopes da Cruz and sought an urgent meeting with General Murtopo to seek clarification of the Indonesian position and to obtain an assurance from the Indonesians that independence would be accepted by them if the Timorese chose it.

This important meeting took place on 2 August. On the Indonesian side, General Murtopo was accompanied by his right-hand man, Colonel Sugiyanto, an interpreter called Maria Gabriella, and another man who, at the time, was presented to the Timorese as a journalist, but who they were later to see in the uniform of an army major. At this meeting Murtopo claimed that Fretilin was now a communist movement and that the Indonesians had information that it would move to seize power on 15 August. If Fretilin initiated such a move, the

Timorese were told, Indonesia would act. According to João Carrascalão, he and Domingos de Oliveira tried to persuade the Indonesians that Fretilin was not communist and that its radicalism was limited to a small, though vocal, element within the party. Murtopo, apparently unimpressed by this argument, countered with the warning that Indonesia would not stand by and let East Timor fall under communist influence, indicating that Indonesia would close its eyes to any move by the anti-communist parties to correct the situation.

Carrascalão and de Oliveira apparently trusted Murtopo and Sugiyanto, little suspecting that their hosts were key figures in the operation to bring about the incorporation of their country into Indonesia. Nor were they aware that Lopes da Cruz had committed himself to the Indonesian cause by that time. However, both were troubled by da Cruz's close links with the Indonesians and at his increasingly distant attitude. They, and other UDT leaders, were disturbed that he had gone on an extensive tour, paid for by Indonesian officials of Asian countries, including South Korea, Taiwan, the Philippines and Japan. They also noted that da Cruz was non-committal during the long interview with Murtopo and Sugiyanto, and after the meeting Carrascalão and de Oliveira decided not to take him into their confidence. The two men then flew to Bali where they were contacted by a man who claimed to be a minister of the Malaysian government (but whose identity they were unable to establish) who told them that countries in the region would never allow a leftist regime to gain power in East Timor. It was in Bali that Domingos de Oliveira and João Carrascalão decided to mount a 'show of force' in Timor as soon as possible after their return to Dili. They later said that they did not inform Lopes da Cruz because of their suspicions about him and because their aim was to strengthen East Timor's prospects of independence, not to increase the risk of Indonesian intervention.

The UDT leaders returned to Dili on 6 August where tensions among followers of the two main political parties had further heightened. These tensions appear to have arisen not because of an increase in hostility between the party leaders but because the main leaders of the parties—that is, of both UDT and Fretilin—had been out of Timor for lengthy periods and had not been in the territory to moderate the effects of the acrimonious exchanges between lower-level party officials, and the occasional acts of violence. In July Xavier do Amaral, Nicolau Lobato and Jose Ramos Horta were away from Timor, their absences dispelling the rumour that Fretilin leaders were planning an armed coup aimed at seizing power in the colony. Xavier and Lobato subsequently denied this to me. The small radical wing of Fretilin became more vocal during the absence of its leaders but its power was very limited.*

In contrast, the sudden visit of the UDT leaders to Jakarta appears to have

---

* A confidential report from the office of the governor stated later that 'during July tensions between Fretilin and UDT grew worse leading to some acts of violence in some places outside Dili' ('Report of the Government of Timor', in the Timor Dossier).

given rise to speculation that the conservatives of the province were negotiating some kind of deal with the Indonesians. This led to talk about the need to be ready to take up arms if it became necessary for Fretilin to undertake a pre-emptive strike. That is precisely what Carrascalão and de Oliveira had in mind when they returned to Dili on 6 August. Their aim was not to destroy Fretilin, but to force the moderate leaders to take action against the extremists of their left wing, that is, to agree to their expulsion from the island, a move that had been discussed privately with Horta a couple of months earlier. They would then set up an anti-communist front of the kind that would placate the Indonesian hawks.[2] The UDT leaders were also anxious to expel two MFA officers, majors Mota and Jonatas, whom they suspected of having encouraged the radical elements in Fretilin. There appears to have been no foundation to this suspicion. Ironically, Mota was critical of some of the more provocative activities of the left wing of Fretilin and had been urging them to tone down their rather strident propaganda. In an interview with Jill Jolliffe in Darwin in August, Major Mota accused the left of Fretilin of having behaved provocatively and immaturely, but he did assert that there was no 'real communism' in East Timor.

It is difficult to accept that the Indonesians believed that there was much communist influence in East Timor. With their sizeable consulate in Dili and with the *Operasi Komodo* agents probing the political situation in various parts of the colony, they were better placed than anyone, the Portuguese aside, to assess the situation on the ground. The remarks made by Murtopo and Sugiyanto to the UDT leaders and their statements to foreign diplomats in Jakarta all seem to have been part of the strategy of dis-information, designed to prepare the ground for Indonesian intervention. Some of the reported comments of General Yoga Sugama to US Ambassador Newsom could be interpreted as a kind of verbal shadow play. Yoga told Newsom that UDT could be regarded as socialist and Fretilin as communist, but in the view of Yoga's position as head of Bakin and as one of the main generals behind Komodo, his remarks to the US envoy were not a true reflection of what he believed to be the case. In short, Yoga was probably playing his part to promote a sympathetic understanding and acceptance by Indonesia's main Western allies of a future military intervention against Portuguese Timor. The Indonesians were well aware that foreign diplomats in Jakarta regarded them as being paranoid about communist threats, and Yoga and others were able cynically to exploit this to their own advantage as part of their strategy on Timor.

When the UDT leaders returned to Dili from Bali on 6 August the idea of the seizure of control of the main administration centres was already well-formed in their minds. Carrascalão spoke to Major Barrento of the Portuguese administration, and the latter's account of the talk gives some indication of how bleak the UDT leaders felt East Timor's prospects for self-determination were, after their talk with Murtopo. Barrento told Jill Jolliffe that the UDT leaders:

> were convinced there would be no independence for East Timor under Fretilin and they were doubtful there would be independence even under UDT. Perhaps this was

important for the action they took. They were very conscious of...the need not to offend Indonesia.[3]

Dili was rife with rumours in those last few days before UDT moved to seize power. Senior Portuguese officials later said that representatives of both main parties had come to them with allegations that their opponents were planning military actions. Carrascalão and de Oliveira quickly contacted other colleagues and officials who were sympathetic to their party's aims and began to plan the details of their action. On the Saturday and Sunday the UDT organised a series of rallies to launch an anti-communist movement, Movimento Anti-Communist or MAC, and actions to secure control of key installations began at the same time. One of their first moves was to occupy police headquarters where the police chief, Lieutenant Colonel Maggioli Gouveia, obligingly surrendered to the rebels, and informed the governor, whose palace and other strategic points were surrounded by armed UDT supporters. Fretilin leaders had been warned some hours earlier and had informed the governor, whose initial reaction was reportedly one of disbelief.

An interesting account of the events surrounding the 'show of force', and the UDT leaders' motives, came later from João Carrascalão, the 'commander-in-chief', who dictated a message to an Australian who happened to be in Dili at the time. The statement is important in its disclosure that the leaders' aim was still eventual independence, and not a shift towards Indonesia, as it has often incorrectly been deduced. Carrascalão's statement declared:

> We want to be independent but only when we can see that we can support ourselves. We definitely want linkage with Portugal because we need their help, technically and financially plus the fact that the Portuguese language is spoken throughout the island.

The idea of the 'show of force' seems to have come from Carrascalão and this is evident from his statement:

> I decided to organize this movement who's [sic] spirit is unity, independence, and non Communists for Timor...we had no arms and so decided to dominate the police by using strategy: we knew that all the police follow completely their commandante and we invite him to our H.Q. and we put him in prison there. Then we went to the police and told them that their commandante was in prison and if they didn't surrender we will kill [him]...Then the police handed over all of their guns and...10% of them join our cause. After this we went to the Army H.Q. and we asked for the Second in Command of the Military for the Army not to interfere in our problem because all we want was to oblige Fretilin leaders to have talks with us without violence.[4]

This coup leader later insisted to me that his and de Oliveira's aim was just that: to force Fretilin into talks, to expel the more radical elements of that party from East Timor and to then set up an anti-communist coalition that would head off Indonesian moves to intervene. His attitude to, and treatment of, Lopes da Cruz support this contention. Not only did Carrascalão not take da Cruz into his confidence when he was planning the coup, but shortly after it was launched he placed the UDT president under virtual house arrest because of his growing suspicions of da Cruz' collusion with the Indonesians. Carrascalão and de Oliveira believed that the party leader was keeping something from them. In his talk with Jill Jolliffe, the MFA officer, Major Barrento, was equally mystified at the behaviour of the UDT leader. He said, 'With me he kept his mouth shut and maintained the face of an angel. João Carrascalão was open, but with Lopes da Cruz I never knew what was in his mind.'[5]

While his UDT colleagues were striving to control the increasingly tense situation they had created, Lopes da Cruz managed to escape from his detention with help from Apodeti and the Indonesian consulate.* He then succeeded in getting to Indonesian Timor where he was to contact Sugiyanto and other Indonesian officials who concocted a petition to President Suharto in favour of integration. Da Cruz took little active part in the ensuing civil war. Meanwhile, the UDT coup soon began to run into difficulties. The hopes and expectations of Carrascalão and de Oliveira that their action would precipitate a flood of defections from among supporters of Fretilin and the capitulation of at least the moderate leaders of the party were soon to be dashed. So too were their hopes that they would be able to shift the political direction of events in East Timor without bloodshed.

Fretilin leaders, including President Xavier do Amaral, had succeeded in gaining warning of the coup and most had managed to escape from Dili to Fretilin political strongholds in the mountains, such as Aileu and Remexio, where they quickly proceeded to mobilise their supporters to prepare for countermeasures. Surprisingly few Timorese shifted their allegiance from Fretilin to UDT and the latter's attempt to round up left-wing supporters, which led to some excesses, only served to strengthen opposition to the coup and to fuel tensions in the main towns. As for the Portuguese, the governor called an emergency meeting of his Decolonisation Commission, in effect the top military and administration officials in the province, at which it was decided that the army would stand aloof from both the UDT and Fretilin, and concentrate on avoiding bloodshed and on bringing the leaders of the parties together for talks. The commission at once informed Carrascalão of their decisions and that they would not support the UDT action against Fretilin. Although the governor had fewer than a company of paratroops at his disposal, such was the level of Portuguese influence among the coup leaders that neither he nor his officers were seriously molested or severely restricted by them. The policy the Portuguese observed was one of neutrality. Known as *apartidarismo*, or the standing apart from factional or party conflicts, it had been followed in other colonies where conflicts had broken out between parties or factions. They also lacked the military strength to interfere but, as Major Mota put it in an interview recorded by Jill Jolliffe in Darwin in August 1975:

---

* Da Cruz managed to get a message by telephone to the consul, and it was the Indonesians that were largely responsible for whisking the UDT leader to Indonesian Timor.

UDT tried to put the Portuguese government on the side of UDT to fight Fretilin. The Government would never do that, because the new Portugal respects all opinions...we can say that the Administration in Timor has only one point of view; to respect the population with no interference.[6]

Portuguese sympathies were not, however, undivided. Two officers, Lieutenant Colonel Maggioli and Captain Lino (a relative of João Carrascalão), chose to disregard the *apartidarismo*, and they came out openly in support of the UDT. Maggioli assisted the UDT leaders in Dili, while Captain Lino and his troops, in defiance of the governor's instructions to the Portuguese military, marched to Baucau from Lautem and thence to the capital to join up with the main body of UDT soldiers. The two key MFA officers in the decolonisation process, Major Francisco Mota and Major Jonatas had, during the previous three months, incurred the dislike and suspicions of the UDT, and one of the initial demands of the coup leaders was that these two officials be expelled from East Timor with certain left-wing elements of Fretilin. Mota and Jonatas—certainly the latter—were identified with the left wing of the MFA, and the UDT leaders accused them of having secretly encouraged Fretilin. While it is true that these two officers regarded Fretilin as the more effective and dynamic of the two main parties, the governor and other officers vigorously denied that they had behaved in a partisan way. Mota's remarks in Darwin suggest the contrary. There he told the press that there was not much difference between Fretilin and the UDT; the UDT members were more 'functional or bureaucratic', while Fretilin members were more anxious to relate the situation in Timor to conditions elsewhere in Portuguese territories. Documents in the 'Timor Dossier' suggest that the MFA officers had become increasingly impatient with Fretilin's uncooperative attitude to the UDT and to decolonisation in general. Jolliffe has suggested that remarks made in Lisbon by these officers earlier in the year, where, among other things, they had reportedly declared that the UDT was not a progressive party, may have antagonised the coup leaders.[7] However, it is also true that the reputations of the two officers were deliberately undermined by *Operasi Komodo* agents, who regarded their refusal to discourage the independence option as being hostile to Indonesian interests. In the weeks before the coup MFA officers had been the subject of attacks by the Bakin-controlled radio station in West Timor.* On 17 August the governor sent Mota and Jonatas back to Portugal, via Darwin. This move was seen by the UDT as an indication that at least some of their demands were going to be met. Lemos Pires claimed that the move was not intended to appease the UDT, but to get to Lisbon a detailed assessment of the situation in East Timor. He was also understandably concerned for the safety of these two officers as tensions began to mount in Dili, with a steady increase in acts of violence.

Sending home the two key officers on the Decolonisation Commission did

---

* At the London meeting. The Indonesians probably had Mota and Jonatas in mind when they called for the withdrawal of certain unnamed officers.

nothing to ease tensions in the colony. It caused Fretilin leaders to conclude that Carrascalão and his colleagues had won over the governor and that further negotiations would only weaken the position of their party. They therefore speeded preparations for countermeasures. Thus, the continuing efforts of the Portuguese, now supported by Carrascalão and de Oliveira, were soon to come up against a barrier of mounting suspicions on both sides, aggravated by outbursts of violence, and by the weak position of the MFA after its two leading officials had left the colony. In the first few days of uneasy peace the Portuguese tried to establish contact with the Fretilin leaders, now in the mountains, by making use of Nicolau Lobato's brother Rogerio, an army *alferes*, or junior lieutenant, who had chosen to remain in the capital. At the same time they sought to keep out of the conflict the Timorese troops, whom they knew to be predominantly sympathetic to Fretilin. With this in mind the Portuguese officers attempted to confine the Timorese troops to their barracks, and to convince their noncommissioned officers that they should emulate the MFA stand and adhere to *apartidarismo*. One person who could have played a mediating role was Bishop Ribeiro, but he refused to have anything to do with Fretilin leaders, whom he regarded as being 'communistic'. He was respected by both sides. When street fighting was raging in Dili, he chose to ignore it, briskly and fearlessly striding through the firing lines—the combatants would cease fire to let him pass and then resume when he was out of range. Such was the bishop's prestige that, had he been less partisan and offered his services as a mediator, he might well have been able to head off the crisis.

Indonesia's military commanders were not idle during the week of uneasy peace after the UDT show of force. On 13 August, only two days after the coup, the CIA informed US leaders in Washington:

Indonesia apparently will try to take advantage of the situation in Timor to increase its activities on behalf of the pro-Indonesia Apodeti Party.[8]

Two days later, in another intelligence bulletin, CIA analysts reported:

Intelligence officials associated with Indonesia's year-long clandestine operations against the colony see in the confused situation a chance to turn events to the advantage of the pro-Indonesia party. Special forces units located in Indonesian Timor are preparing teams of Timorese refugees to cross the border and establish guerilla bases near Dili and elsewhere.[9]

On the diplomatic front one of Jakarta's first actions was to obstruct an attempt by a Portuguese special envoy to get to East Timor via Indonesia. A small mission led by Major Antonio Soares reached Jakarta only three days after the action by Carrascalão's forces, but Soares' movement beyond Bali was obstructed at Denpasar airport, and he was not permitted by the Indonesian authorities to fly on to Kupang where a Portuguese government aircraft was waiting to take him to Dili. After having been told by an Indonesian colonel that he could not proceed from Bali, Soares returned to Jakarta and flew back to Lisbon the next day. It is difficult not to conclude that the Indonesians deliberately frustrated this attempt by Portugal to mediate, for had peace been restored to the colony the objective of *Operasi Komodo*—to create chaotic conditions conducive to intervention—would thus have been irretrievably set back.

On the day of Soares' arrival in Jakarta, Lieutenant General Yoga Sugama had sounded out Australian, US, and other diplomatic representatives in Indonesia as to how their governments would react if Indonesian forces were to intervene. According to one interesting account, at a series of meetings over the next three days Minister for Defence General Panggabean, the deputy chief of the armed forces Lieutenant General Surono, and the deputy of Bakin (and organiser of the military aspects of *Operasi Komodo*) urged the president and the government to authorise military intervention in East Timor.[10] According to McDonald, on this occasion Major General Murtopo was not enthusiastic for a quick military solution, although Foreign Minister Malik by this time was supporting the hawks. President Suharto's reluctance to agree to military intervention seems to have prevailed then. A classified cable from Australian Ambassador Richard Woolcott on 18 August stated that President Suharto was still opposed to military intervention, partly because of his fear of the consequences for Indonesia in the forthcoming session of the UN General Assembly, the next round of the meeting of Non-Aligned States, and of the reaction it would incite in Australia. The CIA also reported the president's opposition, noting that he feared an adverse reaction from the US. Ambassador Woolcott's cable confirmed that the Indonesians had obstructed Soares' attempt to get to Dili where it was believed that the UDT leaders, faced with increasing uncertainties, were eager to negotiate. Woolcott claimed that, according to the Portuguese chargé d'affaires in Jakarta, both President Gomes and Soares were prepared to come to terms with the UDT coup, and were anxious to withdraw the Portuguese military from the island.[11] This assessment was shared by the CIA.

It is clear that, although the Indonesians had been very largely responsible, if indirectly, for the UDT move, they were displeased with the way it was turning out. This was reflected in their own press reports in the immediate aftermath of the coup. The *Indonesian Times* gave prominence to the fact that the UDT had set its sights on independence. On 14 August it reported that 'a political party in Portuguese Timor, which claimed Monday it had staged a coup, Tuesday demanded immediate independence'. It referred to the UDT as 'known previously as a moderate group favouring ties with Portugal'. A report in the leading daily, *Sinar Harapan*, claimed that the UDT members were combining with Fretilin against the pro-Indonesia party, Apodeti, an account which may have originated in Komodo's disinformation group. In his conversation with US Deputy Chief of Mission Rieves on 20 August, Yoga suggested that the UDT action could lead to a chaotic situation which would offer opportunities for countries like China and the Soviet Union to gain influence. He was clearly disturbed that the UDT had not united with Apodeti to fight Fretilin and, as has already been mentioned, he described the UDT party as a socialist movement which was strongly influenced by the socialists in Portugal. In this particular conversation Yoga seemed to be suggesting that the mission of Major Soares had been deliberately obstructed because this officer was believed by the Indonesians to be a member of the Portuguese socialist pro-Moscow group.[12]

The Bakin chief's assessment of the political character of the parties in East Timor and Portugal was false. In spite of urging from Australia's perceptive ambassador in Lisbon, Mr Frank Cooper, the embassy in Jakarta evidently was not persuaded that Australia had a responsibility to try to correct the Indonesian assessment, which had exaggerated the dangers of communist influence in Timor out of all proportion.[13] For example, Yoga had also suggested to US Ambassador Newsom that in four or five years hence Portuguese Timor could be pro-Moscow or pro-Peking. That Yoga was one of the main generals behind the intelligence operation to acquire the colony must raise doubts as to whether his 'assessment' was sincere. It could easily have been contrived, being designed to deflect the attention of countries like the US and Australia from the real issues at stake in East Timor. General Yoga Sugama also told Newsom on 22 August that Indonesia had no intention of provoking the situation in Timor, and would not launch military operations when he had advocated the use of military force only five or six days earlier.[14] Preparations for a combined assault were already under way. Yoga Sugama was one of the generals who eventually persuaded the Indonesian president to agree to limited military intervention in the Balibo–Maliana area in October 1975.

It is difficult to pinpoint the beginning of the outbreak of violence between the UDT and Fretilin. Two or three days after the proclamation of the coup, the UDT forces began to round up Fretilin supporters and to imprison them. By 15 August, eighty had been arrested in Dili, and there were reports of some arrests in other towns. Meanwhile, in their attempts at negotiation the Portuguese had placed great store in the mission of Rogerio Lobato. Lobato was sent to the mountains to contact Fretilin party leaders shortly after the coup, but a few days later he returned without results. However, while he was in Dili Lobato did valuable work for his party leaders by contacting and organising Fretilin supporters in the army barracks at Taibesse. On 17 August he was again sent to the mountains, this time by helicopter, to contact Xavier do Amaral in the Maubisse area, the Portuguese believing that Xavier's charismatic qualities could be put to good use in restraining Fretilin supporters, especially the troops. Fighting had begun to erupt in the Maubisse–Turiscai–Same area and the Fretilin president had quietly left Maubisse, disguised in a nondescript Timorese *lipa* (traditional dress) to evade capture.

Two days earlier the Central Committee of Fretilin had decided to confront the UDT action: it had proclaimed its countermeasures, alleging that the UDT forces had been not only responsible for arrests of Fretilin supporters, but had also engaged in 'pillaging, assassinations, rape of women, etc'. The leaders therefore declared 'a general armed insurrection against the traitors of the homeland and for the genuine liberation of the Maubere people'.[15] It took several days for Rogerio Lobato to catch up with Xavier do Amaral and his party, and by that time bitter fighting had already broken out between *sucos* of conflicting party allegiances. The Portuguese helicopter that had taken Rogerio Lobato to Maubisse was detained, the two main administrative towns in the central mountain region—Maubisse and Aileu—were taken over by Fretilin, and the troops of the local military district willingly placed themselves at its disposal. Jill Jolliffe reports that the younger Lobato was little interested in the task that the Portuguese had given him of facilitating negotiations. She wrote:

> Because he politically distrusted the Portuguese as well as their capabilities, Rogerio Lobato spent his time in the week following the coup not in attempting to persuade Fretilin to negotiate as requested but in lobbying the army units for their support, in liaison with Fretilin's Central Committee in the mountains.[16]

A cable from the Australian embassy in Jakarta on 18 August suggests that Fretilin suspicions were not ill-founded. Ambassador Woolcott said that he was told by the Portuguese chargé d'affaires that President General Costa Gomes and Major Soares had in mind was to withdraw the army from Timor and to possibly accept a UDT 'government'.[17] This information suggests that the Portuguese did not know just how tenuous was the UDT position in Dili, although Governor Lemos Pires later claimed that he had been keeping an unresponsive government in Lisbon informed on a day-to-day basis. Nor were the Portuguese aware that the leaders of the UDT coup were no more acceptable to those Indonesian generals in charge of Jakarta's Timor policy than were the Fretilin leadership. Carrascalão and de Oliveira also wanted to clear the path towards independence, a course which had never been acceptable to the generals directing *Operasi Komodo*.

Most UDT leaders tried to prevent bloodshed, but their hastily put together army lacked discipline and coordination, and certain excesses contributed to the outbreak of bitter fighting. In the Same area a UDT leader took it upon himself to execute eleven Fretilin radicals, most of whom were aged between 15 and 20. They included Domingos Lobato, a younger brother of the Fretilin vice-president. In the early days after the coup, Fretilin supporters were also killed by undisciplined UDT bands in Hatolia, Baucau, and even in Dili, although these acts were allegedly neither ordered nor approved by the leaders. By 20 August the Portuguese colony was in the throes of civil war, and more than 2000 Timorese soldiers had left their barracks with their weapons, providing Fretilin with military superiority from the outset. Following a skilful manoeuvre by Rogerio Lobato, who had assumed military leadership of the Fretilin force, the Timorese troops at the headquarters of the Timor garrison at Taibesse seized control of the main arsenal of the colony and, joined by their comrades from the mountains, they soon forced the smaller, and less well-armed, UDT forces on to the defensive.

It is difficult to support allegations by, among others, Gough Whitlam, that the Portuguese handed over their armoury to the troops of Fretilin. With only 70 paratroops, another 150 officers and noncommissioned officers, and miscellaneous noncombatant troops at its disposal, the Portuguese military command was in a helpless and demoralised position. Some of the officers and many of the soldiers had been antagonised by the governor's apparent surrender to the UDT's demand that Mota and Jonatas be expelled, and by Fretilin's failure to respond to their attempts to arrange talks between the leaders of the two parties. The governor and his small band of troops moved to Farol, a suburb of Dili not far from the wharf, where most of the senior Portuguese officials lived. The paratroops sealed off the area, recognised by the warring parties as a more-or-less neutral zone. The governor could not have done much more when the fighting had reached the capital. The tiny Portuguese force of fewer than 100 combat troops was wedged between 1500 UDT soldiers and more than 2000 regular troops under Fretilin command and the nature of the Fretilin attack made communication with its leaders extremely difficult and hazardous.

For several days fighting raged in the streets of Dili, provoking a flood of refugees to the wharf area where they anxiously waited evacuation. Two vessels, *Macdili* and *Lloyd Bakke*, took some 2000 Portuguese, Chinese and Timorese (most of the latter being the families of UDT supporters) to Darwin, while an Indonesian frigate, *Monginsidi*, slipped into Dili and evacuated the staff of the Indonesian consulate. The struggle for control of the provincial capital was bitter, but the casualties sustained in it were fewer than in the tribal-based conflicts in the mountains. Just over 400 people died in the streets of the capital, while damage to the buildings and houses from mortar and light artillery fire was surprisingly light. The character of the civil war was the subject of some exaggeration in press reports in Australia. The *Australian*, for example, carried a sensational description of Dili as 'a blazing, shell-pounded ruin', and reported that 'men wielding cutlasses beheaded and dismembered babies'.[18] In reality, the capital was only slightly damaged, and the reports of babies being beheaded or even deliberately killed seem to have emerged from the realms of macabre fantasy. As Gerald Stone, from Channel 9 Television, Sydney, reported when his team arrived at Dili on 29 August:

Our drive through Dili quickly revealed how much distortion and exaggeration surrounds this war. The city has been taking heavy punishment, with many buildings scarred by bullet holes. But all of the main buildings are standing...Even the Portuguese flag still flew over government administration buildings, and that, in fact, could be a symbol of Fretilin's willingness to reopen negotiations with Lisbon.[19]

The civil war was of short duration—despite media reports to the contrary. By the end of August, that is, only a fortnight after the fighting had begun, the main UDT force had been forced out of Dili and had withdrawn to Liquiça, a town some 25 kilometres to the west, towards the Indonesian border. The bulk of the fighting was already over, and the UDT remnants were already heading for the Indonesian border, the only possible sanctuary open to them.

Near the end of August foreign aid missions and media teams began to enter the territory, most of them from Australia. The first visitors were Gerald Stone's Channel 9 television team and an Australian aid group calling itself the

Australian Society for Inter-Country Aid (Timor) or ASIAT, coordinated by Dr John Whitehall, a young Sydney paediatrician who had previously conducted a similar mission in South Vietnam. The arrival of the ASIAT medical team and an International Red Cross (ICRC) mission under André Pasquier a few days later provided timely assistance for the treatment of the mounting casualties of the fighting. It was just before the aid missions began to arrive that Governor Lemos Pires, with the remaining officials of the colonial administration, and his small contingent of troops, had withdrawn from the wharf area to the offshore island of Atauro, 23 kilometres north of Dili. All of the Portuguese medical staff withdrew with the departing Portuguese officials, leaving the war-ravaged population to the limited resources of the Timorese paramedical staff. It is not clear just why the Portuguese withdrew their doctors at a time when their skills were so urgently needed. There is no evidence that the hospital staff were molested in any way by the warring parties. Some Portuguese medical staff had tried to stay, but were ordered to leave by the military. The ICRC later reported that the Dili Hospital and the Health Department buildings 'had been respected by the combatants and there was no evidence of looting. The staff had continued working during the conflict uninterrupted'.[20] Thus, the Portuguese medical staff had nothing to fear. The governor and his party had apparently not been seriously threatened, although mortars were occasionally accidentally lobbed within the perimeter of the neutral zone.

The main reason for the departure of the Portuguese appears to have been their sense of helplessness and frustration. The administration had been demoralised through being humiliated and ignored by Fretilin and the UDT and it had lost credibility with the local population generally. The policy of standing apart from the conflict had backfired. The leaders of both parties suspected the Portuguese of complicity and conniving, and they were virtually pushed aside and ignored as the situation degenerated into a bloody civil war which arose, as it was revealed, not from the policies of the Lisbon government, but from the designs of a group of generals in Jakarta.

The morale of the Portuguese had also been undermined by the deepening crisis in Lisbon and Portugal's ignominious departure from its African colonies. They lacked the resolve to endure a debacle in Timor, the one colony that had appeared to be so tranquil in the aftermath of the April Coup. Late in 1974 the MFA officers had seemed to gain a certain confidence in their task of guiding Portugal's subject peoples towards a destiny of their own choosing in Timor. By the end of August 1975 it had all turned sour and a demoralised provincial government could see no alternative but to abandon ship. And it was not just the behaviour of the Timorese. Indonesia was two-faced. Publicly, the Indonesian government was calling on Portugal to restore order in East Timor, while privately, having encouraged the disorder, they were pressing Lisbon to allow them to intervene. The Indonesians were also quietly obstructing Portuguese attempts to restore the situation through mediation. An example of this is the deliberate undermining of the Soares mission. Australia, too, was being less than helpful about the political issues. Portuguese appeals for help in dealing with the political, as distinct from the humanitarian, situation were generally unanswered. The governor apparently became concerned at the growing restlessness of the paratroops, whom he was anxious to keep out of the conflict. Therefore, 206 years after Dili had been established, and only sixteen months after the April Coup, the Portuguese administration withdrew from the island of East Timor permanently.

The ASIAT and ICRC medical teams, made up mostly of Australian doctors, quickly took over the Dili Hospital and other health establishments and began to treat the hundreds of serious war casualties. Food and medical supplies were ferried into Dili by RAAF Hercules aircraft and, as the fighting subsided, medical teams and supplies of food were taken to all affected parts of East Timor. The city's power supply, suspended during the fighting, was restored, and some of Dili's Chinese shops began cautiously to reopen. Meanwhile, after some further fighting at Liquiça, the UDT remnants continued their retreat to the west, first to Maubara, thence to Maliana, and the border village of Batugade. By this time the force had diminished to some 500 soldiers, accompanied by about 2500 refugees, most of them the families of the UDT leaders and soldiers. Near the border the UDT forces had taken nineteen of a party of twenty-three Portuguese troops prisoner who had left their garrison post at Bobonaro for Batugade where they had hoped to be picked up by ship. By 24 September the UDT force had crossed the frontier into Indonesia, and Fretilin was in control of all of the territory of East Timor, with the exception of the Oecussi enclave and the island of Atauro.

The defeat of the UDT by Fretilin was swift and decisive, and taking the Indonesians, the Australians and the Portuguese by surprise. During the fighting the Indonesians had contemplated intervening, but the president continued to act as a restraining influence. The CIA was clearly privy to Jakarta's plans for this intervention. Thus, on 29 August, in one of its confidential briefing bulletins, the CIA informed the US president that preparations for a three-pronged attack by Indonesian forces were expected to be completed by the end of August.

> Two battalions are to launch a combined assault against Dili. The largest force of some 6,000 infantry will land at Atapupu in Indonesian Timor and then drive north into the Portuguese half of the island. One Battalion will also land to secure the coastal strip extending eastward from Dili to Tutuala, on the eastern tip of the island. The forces then are to link up and secure control of the complete northern coast from Atapupu to Tutuala. The Indonesians expect some stiff resistance, but are confident they will be successful.[21]

Indonesia's military involvement during the civil war period was minimal. According to João Carrascalão, only a few days after the coup in August a party of Indonesian troops had entered the territory near Maliana, but they complied readily enough when he asked them to withdraw. Later in September a party of Indonesian troops penetrated as far as Atsabe, the headquarters of the pro-Apodeti *liurai*, Guilherme Goncalves. Some of these operations were detected by US intelligence agencies which, on 18 September, reported to the US president that Indonesian 'special forces units' were conducting covert operations in East Timor. 'A combined force of at least 200 special forces troops and Indonesian-trained Timorese guerrillas crossed the border in early September and split up into a number of teams,' it was reported. It was also claimed that one such team was sent as far inland as Ermera 'where they are meeting stiff resistance from Fretilin forces'.[22]

Also, as might be expected, agents of *Operasi Komodo* were very active during that period. Again there is a CIA record to confirm this. An intelligence report of 20 August noted that 'Indonesian military contingency preparations are continuing, as are clandestine operations inside Portuguese Timor.'[23] In August Colonel Sugiyanto and Louis Taolin recruited Jose Martins, the Kota leader who, for some months, had been Bakin's most trusted Timorese contact. Lopes da Cruz had been helped to Indonesian Timor where he assisted Sugiyanto in drawing up the petition calling for the integration of East Timor into Indonesia, a petition which the other Timorese leaders were later pressed to endorse as a condition of their being allowed to enter Indonesian Timor. As one Timorese told me: 'It was the last thing we wanted, but with the Fretilin forces closing in on us at Batugade, and with more than 2000 refugees with us and without food, we really had no alternative but to agree.'[24] Another fascinating operation occurred early in September when an Indonesian helicopter slipped across the border to Atsabe and took Guilherme Goncalves to West Timor.

The intrusion of Indonesian forces into West Timor began in August, although the first contingents appear to have been of modest size. They included, however, troops from the crack Strategic Reserve Command (Kostrad), which had been set up in 1960, fifteen years earlier, to coordinate military operations against Dutch forces in West Irian. Among the units involved was one from West Java, 315 Battalion, a unit of the Siliwangi Division. Three platoons of this battalion secretly entered East Timor near Bobonaro in September with the objective of establishing contact with Apodeti activists. Its activities were related to me some weeks later by one of its members, a Corporal Weli, who had become separated from his comrades and ended up a prisoner of Fretilin in Dili.[25]

The civil war created one serious problem for Indonesia. As fighting neared the frontier districts, especially the heavily populated Maliana area, thousands of Timorese crossed the border to escape a repetition of their World War II experiences. Some were UDT supporters fleeing 'the Fretilin terror', but most were simply trying to get away from the fighting zone, and were not fleeing because of their sympathies for one side or another. The Indonesians were partly responsible for the panic, if only because of the alarming broadcasts emanating from the Bakin-controlled Radio Ramelau in West Timor which broadcast exaggerated and distorted descriptions of the fighting, embellished with false accounts of atrocities and brutalities, most of which were attributed to Fretilin. It was in the border areas that these broadcasts were the only source of information during the civil war, and it was here that their effect was greatest.

The Indonesians wasted no time in exploiting the refugee situation, apparently to strengthen their justification for intervention. It was reported in Jakarta in September that the flow of refugees had reached flood proportions, and that the resources of the area were being severely taxed. Later Father Fernandes, a Timorese priest who served for some months on the refugee committee set up in the border area by the Indonesians said that officials deliberately falsified the number of refugees coming in. In Jakarta it was claimed that more than:

> 45 000 Timorese had entered the Indonesian half of the island, a figure that was accepted as being credible by Australian and American officials in Indonesia, and which was faithfully carried by Western media. Fernandes claimed that the true figure never exceeded 20 000, while some UDT leaders later told me that only 10 000 to 15 000 Timorese had crossed the frontier. Also, a UN visitor to Indonesian Timor in October 1975 commented privately that he doubted the Indonesian claim. The East Timorese soon learned that the lot of a refugee in Indonesia was far from appealing. They were herded into about ten camps in the Atambua–Atapupu area, where their confinement was assured by Indonesian army guards. In spite of the fact that relief aid from a number of countries, including Australia, the Netherlands, New Zealand and Canada, poured into Kupang, according to the refugees very little of it actually got to the people for whom it was intended. The Timorese claimed that Indonesian soldiers and officials could be seen in foreign clothing, and the milk powder from Australia was in evidence in army messes and in a nearby Indonesian hospital, but very little of this relief aid filtered through to the refugee camps.[26]

When the UDT remnants crossed into Indonesian Timor late in September they were disarmed and consigned to one of these refugee camps where conditions soon became grim. Little food was provided by their Indonesian hosts, and most of the men were forced to work long hours in the fields or on the roads. For example, refugees at Wedomo camp said that they had received 100 grams of rice per day, but no flour or meat, with a small supplement of rice for the workers, who had to begin working at 6.00 a.m. Father Fernandes said that the men worked under armed guard, and in some cases were used instead of water buffaloes to pull ploughs. To obtain additional food many of the refugees sold the few remaining valuables that they had carried with them, such as rings and watches, to their Indonesian hosts, whom they accused of behaving more like captors than hosts of the 'petitioners for integration'. The refugees said that they also had to trade personal possessions to obtain medicines or injections from the local medical teams. In one camp where several hundred UDT supporters were located, about thirty Timorese had died of disease and illnesses brought on by malnutrition because they had not been able to obtain treatment. After the end of the fighting between Fretilin and the UDT many of the Timorese tried to return to East Timor, but most were prevented from doing so by their Indonesian guards. In at least one camp the Timorese revolted, but order was soon restored by Indonesian troops and only a few managed to escape.[27]

The plight of the refugees in Indonesian Timor is yet another little-known aspect of the Timor tragedy. Few foreigners were allowed to venture to the area, and then their visits were carefully guided. Very temporary arrangements were made to brighten up the scene. In one camp, according to the inmates, a group of Timorese were unexpectedly issued with food, clothing, medicines, and cooking utensils. Several photographers then appeared and recorded their good fortune but, to the great dismay of the Timorese, the visitors had hardly gone before the supplies were recalled by the camp authorities. In the circumstances, it is not surprising that the Timorese considered themselves to be prisoners, rather than refugees. The UDT leaders, other than the few who decided to go along with integration, were subjected to close supervision. When several members of the foreign press corps in Jakarta made a fleeting visit to Indonesian Timor in September 1975, João Carrascalão tried to arrange a private meeting with one of them. He organised a rendezvous with Tony Joyce of the Australian Broadcasting Commission, but when Joyce turned up he was accompanied by an Indonesian in a white medical coat, whom the Australian introduced as a Red Cross doctor who had asked if he could accompany and assist the Australian journalist. However, according to Carrascalão, he knew that the Indonesian was not a doctor, but a Bakin major, and the Timorese leader's plan to provide a true picture of the situation had to be abandoned.[28] A small number of Timorese leaders, including Lopes da Cruz and Jose Martins, dutifully informed the visiting journalists that the Timorese were united in their resolve to integrate with Indonesia.

Many observers were surprised at Jakarta's apparent indecisiveness during the brief civil war period. An Indonesian decision to send in troops as a kind of police action would have been welcomed by the few countries with any interest in the Timor problem with the exception of Portugal which, after some hesitation, made it clear that it did not want the Indonesians to intervene, other than as part of a multinational peacekeeping force. Such a move would also have caught the supporters of independence in some disarray, and the Indonesians would certainly have received a warmer welcome than they did after the invasion of Dili some four months later. And they were not badly placed to play a neutral role because the pro-integration party, Apodeti, had not been a party to the civil war. In spite of reports from Jakarta suggesting that Fretilin's forces were being resisted by members of the pro-integration party, if anything, the UDT, during its brief interregnum, was more suspicious of Apodeti members than was Fretilin, and a number of them fought alongside Fretilin soldiers in the battle for control of Dili.

The main reason for Indonesia's indecision was that, although the leaders in Jakarta were agreed that East Timor should be incorporated into Indonesia in one way or another, a few were still reluctant to agree to an act of military intervention. In the last week of August Richard Woolcott was still reporting to Canberra that the Indonesian president was persisting in his refusal to agree to intervention, but said that Indonesia could not stand by much longer.[29] On 8 September the CIA reported at length on the president's reluctance to give in to his generals. It informed US leaders in Washington.

President Soeharto himself is ambivalent. Personally he would probably prefer military action because he has an overwhelming fear of communist subversion in Indonesia. He is also concerned about his international image, however, and does not want to revive the ghost of adventurist foreign policies practised under former President Sukarno. Soeharto is also concerned about the impact on Indonesia's bilateral relations with Australia and the US. In both cases he is worried about the loss of military assistance, which he badly wants to improve Indonesia's outdated equipment.

Soeharto has apparently relied heavily on this argument in counselling caution to his military commanders and is now showing some concern that if substantial aid is not forthcoming there will be severe political repercussions for himself. In trying to balance off his various advisers, Soeharto has appeared to blow hot and cold on Timor. When meeting with military advisers he has emphasised his willingness to authorise an invasion should Indonesian security require it. In meetings with his political and diplomatic advisers he has stressed the need to get a new agreement with Lisbon that will settle the Timor problem.[30]

On 11 September Suharto was still evidently counselling moderation and restraint. At a palace ceremony to appoint Brigadier-General Rudjito as ambassador to Papua New Guinea (by coincidence Rudjito, then a major, had been one of the planners of *Operasi Tjendrawasih*, the military operation against the Dutch in West Irian) the president, in a reference to the situation in Timor, stated: 'As a nation that wants to be strong in times to come, whose strength grows vigorously on the basis of sound principles, we must be able to restrain ourselves over temptations of a temporary nature!'[31] In what was in retrospect a remarkable statement, he went on to remind his audience that the wishes of the people of Portuguese Timor about their future must be heeded. He stated that an equal, just, and free opportunity must be offered to all parties in the territory to express their choice without intimidation. Suharto reaffirmed that Indonesia had no territorial ambitions and that it would fully support the Portuguese government's decolonisation process. However, behind the scenes pressure on the president was steadily building up, the principal hawks being generals Yoga Sugama, Benny Moerdani and Defence Minister Panggabean. On 24 August Ambassador Woolcott reported to Canberra that Moerdani and another general close to the president had assured him that when Indonesia decided to move Australia would be forewarned. Australia was to get not less than two hours notice.[32]

Ironically, it was not an intensification of the fighting that finally led the Indonesian leader to agree to the beginning of military intervention, but the defeat of the UDT and the emergence of Fretilin as the *de facto* government of East Timor. The one thing Indonesia could not countenance was the prospect of Fretilin consolidating its position, and gaining international recognition and legitimacy. On 11 September an official Antara news agency report suggested that *Operasi Komodo* was shifting towards a military solution. The report accused Fretilin of atrocities, arson, murder and looting, and claimed that Apodeti controlled most of the interior of the island and was on the verge of launching a guerrilla war against the left-wing party. As the Indonesian military command knew, Apodeti was in no position to challenge Fretilin: its main troops were the 300 or so Timorese *Operasi Komodo* and Bakin officers who had been training in Indonesian Timor since the previous December when, with the complicity of Guilherme Goncalves of Atsabe, they had been somewhat less than voluntarily recruited and smuggled across the border. In the civil war, as we have seen, at least some of the Apodeti 'troops' left in East Timor had chosen to fight on the side of Fretilin. The Antara item also reported that President Suharto had rejected alleged moves by Dr Almeida Santos to give Fretilin *de facto* control of East Timor. According to Dr Almeida Santos he had merely pointed out that Fretilin had effectively gained *de facto* control of the colony. In short, the Indonesians were not prepared to allow the Portuguese to come to terms with a Fretilin de facto government. On the ground, as the CIA were to report in Washington, covert military operations were being stepped up.

Although President Suharto may have fully endorsed the original scheme to bring about the integration of the Portuguese colony by stealth, there is some evidence that he was not fully informed of what his generals were up to, including the exact nature of the deliberate moves to destabilise the situation in the months before the coup. From one well-placed source we learn that Suharto was unaware of the Lampung exercises in the previous February having been planned to be a forerunner of the invasion of the colony. Was Suharto aware of the meeting between the UDT leaders and Murtopo on 2 August, and of what was discussed? Was he aware of just how politically insignificant Apodeti was, and of the general lack of support for integration? Did he know that the UDT 'petition for integration' which Sugiyanto had managed to extract from some of the defeated and demoralised Timorese leaders was anything but a free expression of the latter's aspirations? A cable from the Australian embassy in Jakarta reports that, on 23 August Murtopo told Woolcott that at a meeting on that day Suharto had instructed that he be informed of the situation in Timor twice daily, but it is not clear who gave these briefings and whether or not they were tailored to fit in with the designs of the hawkish generals who closely controlled the information sources.[33] What is interesting is that the Indonesian leader vigorously opposed pressure from his generals for military intervention on 17 August at a time when such an action would have been propitious, from the point of view of gaining some goodwill in East Timor, as well as providing justification to Indonesia's Western and developing world friends.[34] It is conceivable that President Suharto had no detailed knowledge of what his generals had been up to under the guise of *Operasi Komodo*, and he might well have chosen to keep a safe distance from what under the Indonesian Constitution was an illegal operation. It was not until the UDT forces had been routed, and were seeking refuge in Indonesian Timor, that the president was persuaded to agree to a limited military operation. It is conceivable that Suharto was less than fully informed about the degree to which Indonesia was already involved and the extent to which it was responsible for the upheaval.

Australia's reaction

The Australian government had no more forewarning of the UDT coup of August 1975 than it had of the Lisbon coup sixteen months earlier. At first its public statements were few, and were couched in bland terms, with clear emphasis that the situation was a problem for Portugal; Australia was not a 'party principal' to the conflict. However, privately the situation puzzled Australian officials, aware that the UDT leaders had met with Murtopo and Sugiyanto at the end of July. Although some suspected that the Indonesians were behind the coup, others felt that Carrascalão's stated objective of independence and his proclaimed fear of Indonesian intervention were hardly consistent with Jakarta's aim to bring about integration as soon as possible. On 12 August, in a briefing to the foreign minister, the Foreign Affairs Department noted that although the Indonesian foreign ministry seemed to have been genuinely taken by surprise, sensitive sources, probably communications intelligence, had suggested that Bakin had prior knowledge of the UDT action.[35] As Carrascalão later insisted that neither he nor de Oliveira told the Indonesians, it is possible that the leak came from Lopes da Cruz.

At least some of the government's advisers were convinced that the UDT coup was a Bakin set-up, designed to provide a convenient pretext for Indonesian military intervention. It was therefore proposed that the prime minister write to President Suharto, conveying Australia's opposition to the use of force to restore the situation in East Timor, and at the same time reminding the president of his verbal undertaking to Mr Whitlam in Townsville at the meeting of the two leaders in the previous April. The reaction to this proposal reveals much about the moulding of Australia's Timor policy. In a cable from Jakarta on 17 August Ambassador Woolcott expressed his doubts about the wisdom of sending such a letter. He reminded the government that it was dealing with a 'settled Indonesian policy to incorporate Timor' and declared that President Suharto would not welcome such a letter at this stage. According to the Ambassador, Suharto would be looking to Australia for an understanding of what the president, after very careful consideration, decided to do 'rather than what he might regard as a lecture or even a friendly caution'.[36]

In this particular cable our ambassador in Jakarta proposed what Australia's policy should be, a proposal which set the pattern for Australia's Timor policy under the Whitlam and Fraser governments. He suggested that:

> our policies should be based on disengaging ourselves as far as possible from the Timor question; getting Australians presently there out of Timor; leave events to take their course and if and when Indonesia does intervene act in a way which would be designed to minimise the public impact in Australia and show privately understanding to Indonesia of their problems.[37]

What the ambassador was recommending was, as he put it, 'a pragmatic rather than a principled stand but', he added, 'that is what national interest and foreign policy is all about'. The plain fact was that Indonesia was 'simply not prepared to accept the risks they see to them in an independent Timor'.[38] and so, as far as the Australian government was concerned, the fate of the people of the Portuguese colony was sealed.

The cables from the ambassador leave little doubt as to where his own sympathies lay. Clearly he knew little about the Timorese or the situation in the territory. He refers to the UDT and Fretilin leaderships as being largely non-indigenous which suggested that the embassy visitors to Timor just before the invasion had made rather superficial assessments. Most of the Fretilin leaders were, as we have seen, full-blooded Timorese, and most of the UDT leaders were at least Timorese half-caste, which is hardly 'non-indigenous'. The ambassador also seemed to perceive no grounds for doubting the credibility of information he was receiving from Yoga Sugama, Murtopo, Moerdani, Liem Bian-Kie and Harry Tjan, all of whom were leading actors in *Operasi Komodo*, a fact which officials at the embassy and in Canberra would have had revealed to them from 'sensitive source material'.

On 24 August Woolcott concluded in a long cabled assessment that the upheaval in Timor was not really Indonesia's fault, although he conceded that there were 'tendencies in some quarters' to blame Jakarta.[39] Yet it was clearly impossible to exculpate Jakarta from blame for the events in August and September, in spite of the fact that the UDT coup may have been a surprise development from an Indonesian point of view. As has already been discussed, Indonesia's opposition to an independent East Timor and its moves to bring about integration by stealth built up enormous pressures on the political forces in the Portuguese colony and were very largely responsible for the tensions and suspicions that grew up between the UDT and Fretilin between May and August. The Australian government's advisers should have been aware of these facts, and of the extent of Indonesian meddling, but to most of them Jakarta's special interests and the importance of avoiding any confrontations that might undermine the carefully nurtured relationship between the Indonesian and Australian governments seemed to make objective analysis near impossible. The easy way out was to blame the Portuguese for being weak, inept and irresolute. But, whatever the weaknesses of the Portuguese position, it is impossible not to conclude that the domestic political problems of the Timorese would have been easily contained had not their leaders been the subject of intimidation, meddling and outright subversion by the Indonesians, and had the relevant Australian government ministers not compliantly concealed what was going on from public disclosure.

There can be little doubt that the accommodating and understanding demeanour of most Australian diplomats in Jakarta had built up certain expectations among key Indonesian officials by August 1975. In his cable of 17 August Woolcott implicitly admitted this in his remark that the Indonesians were aware of Australian attitudes 'at all levels'.[40] This could reasonably be taken to mean that, in their contacts with Indonesian officials and leaders, the Australians concerned—from the prime minister down to junior diplomats—were unreserved in their support for the objective of integration, even if they had paid lip-service to the principle of self-determination. In Indonesian eyes the Australian government had become a dependable accomplice. Indonesians must have been aware that the prime minister and his advisers knew of their efforts to subvert the Timorese independence movement, and by the end of August were not averse to the idea of Indonesian military intervention.

Prime Minister Whitlam's major statements on the Timor situation on 26 and 28 August seemed to reflect the effect of Woolcott's recommendations. Australia would provide humanitarian relief, but little more than that. The government did not regard itself as 'a party principal' in the Timor situation and, although it recognised that some Australians believed that the government should assume some political obligation to the Timorese and, for example, attempt to mediate, this was not, in Mr Whitlam's view, 'the best approach'. Such views 'could lead to a situation where Australia was exercising a quasi-colonial role in Portuguese Timor'. Thus, the fate of these people (as many as 60,000 of whom had perished as a consequence of Australian intervention in World War II) was 'a matter for resolution by Portugal and the Timorese people themselves with Indonesia also occupying an important place because of its predominant interest'.[41] But what exactly was Indonesia's 'predominant interest'—its illegal moves to incorporate the colony? Here was the Australian prime minister suggesting a major role for the nation whose meddling was largely, if indirectly, responsible for the chaotic situation in the colony.

In another statement two days later, the prime minister went further. As the leader of a government which had known about Indonesian subversive actions against East Timor for more than six months, Mr Whitlam, in his second Timor statement concludes: 'The Indonesian Government, which over the past year has expressed repeatedly its intention not to intervene in Timor, may thus be turned to as the only force capable of restoring calm in the territory'.[42] Far from writing to President Suharto and urging him not to use force, Mr Whitlam, on 28 August, was evidently suggesting that Indonesia be given the task of restoring the peace it had been largely responsible for disrupting! According to Hamish McDonald, the prime minister 'also sent Suharto a private message saying that nothing he said earlier should be interpreted as a veto on Indonesian action in the changed circumstances'.[43]

In view of his apparent awareness of the real Indonesian position, it is tempting to conclude that Mr Whitlam was suggesting that the Indonesians carry out their act of incorporation then and there. This would explain the prime minister's lack of enthusiasm for proposals to internationalise the crisis. At the time it seemed surprising that a leader who had in the past expressed a strong commitment to the UN as the central peace-keeping organisation could see little purpose in sending a good offices committee to East Timor, as suggested by, among others, the Portuguese envoy, Dr Almeida Santos. According to Mr Whitlam, it was not easy 'to see how a UN good offices committee, whose role would be essentially political in character, could function on the ground'.[44] It could have functioned very effectively in fact, as the parties to the dispute were calling for

UN intervention. What seemed to matter was that such a committee would have, in the long term, presented an obstacle to Jakarta's plans for integration.

Australia was better placed than any other country to sponsor negotiations towards a settlement of the Timor crisis in August 1975. Because of its proximity to Indonesia and East Timor, a country little known in the world at large, Australia was in a unique position to acquaint Western states of importance to Indonesia with the real situation in the colony and with the conspiracy of certain generals in Jakarta, and thus build up the kind of international support that would have bolstered the Indonesian president's own opposition to the mounting pressures for military intervention. Yet Australia took the opposite stand. Information from such sources as the British Foreign Office, the Dutch foreign ministry, from Jan Pronk, the then chairman of the Inter-Governmental Group on Indonesia (IGGI— the Western aid consortium for Indonesia), from US State Department officials, and from diplomats of certain other Western countries at the UN shows that Australia's representatives were privately suggesting that events be allowed to take their course—in effect, the Woolcott solution. It was a miserable response to what was probably the first occasion in Australia's diplomatic experience that an initiative from Canberra alone might have prevented an act of aggression. But such an initiative was not to be forthcoming.

Prime Minister Whitlam's public statements about Indonesia's position, some of which have already been quoted, are little short of extraordinary, in the light of the advice he was receiving from some of his advisers. Thus, only two days after Mr Whitlam was told (and not for the first time) by Ambassador Woolcott that it was Indonesia's 'settled' policy to incorporate East Timor, the prime minister was to declare in the House of Representatives that:

> Indonesian policy is to respect the right of the people of Portuguese Timor to self-determination and Indonesian leaders have often denied that Indonesia has any territorial ambitions towards Portuguese Timor.[45]

For months before this statement, Australian foreign policy and intelligence analysts had been monitoring the activities of *Operasi Komodo*. Yet Mr Whitlam was evidently going further towards the Indonesian position than had been suggested by Ambassador Woolcott, whose thesis was that Australia 'should let events take their course'. Mr Whitlam, on the contrary, seemed to be suggesting the course events should take.

The prime minister, and those officials whose advice he heeded, seemed to have a kind of hypnotic fascination with the Indonesian connection and a disdain for, and insensitivity towards, East Timor. To them the Timorese were a nondescript, backward people whose claim to self-rule could hardly be taken seriously. To the prime minister the Portuguese colony was an anachronism and, as we have seen, he was later to write, disparagingly, that the political parties were:

> led by mestizos [sic] who were among the few in the colony who had received an education and who all seemed to be desperate to succeed the Portuguese as rulers of the rest of the population.[46]

His comments on the parties were often inaccurate as well as denigrating. For instance, he had claimed that Fretilin had identified itself with Frelimo of Mozambique and had rejected elections on the grounds that Frelimo had come to power without having been elected. This was not Fretilin's position; it had opposed the plebiscite, not elections, and then on the grounds that, as Horta had put it, 'you don't ask a slave whether he would like to be free'. And, of course, as has already been discussed, only two of Fretilin's Central Committee of forty-five or so were not full-blooded Timorese. According to Mr Whitlam the UDT was an anti-Marxist party with close links with Taiwan, a party that had come to prefer integration with Indonesia to rule by Fretilin. On the contrary, the UDT leaders had been more cautious in their response to overtures from Taiwan than Fretilin had been. In 1974, when the latter's representative in Dili had offered the Timorese technical assistance by way of two scholarships, the UDT rejected the proposal out of hand, while Horta told the Chinese that his party would consider taking up their offer. The only UDT leader to visit Taiwan was Lopes da Cruz, and, as we have seen, his tour was organised by the Indonesians. The UDT never came to prefer integration. Only Lopes da Cruz was won over to this option; for the rest of the leaders who signed the petition, it was not a matter of choice but a case of necessity in the face of severe intimidation.

There is an apparent naivety in the thinking behind some of Mr Woolcott's cables. The ambassador seemed to be accepting uncritically much of what his Indonesian contacts told him. Thus he too tended to exaggerate the extent of Apodeti's influence on Timorese politics. For example, in a cable to Canberra on 24 August 1975 he noted that Apodeti had so far attempted to stay out of the conflict while, in reality, the pro-integration party had such a small following that it was hardly in a position to affect the outcome. Also, Apodeti did not have close relations with the UDT and, as we have seen, during the fighting in Dili some of its members chose to support Fretilin. Mr Woolcott's occasional references to the Timorese leaders were about as disparaging as the remarks of Prime Minister Whitlam. While Mr Whitlam often referred to these leaders as 'mixed caste', in at least one cable Woolcott went further, describing them as 'non-indigenous'. In that same cable he declared that there was no inherent reason why integration with Indonesia should not in the long run be less advantageous to the advantage of the Timorese than a very unstable independence or continued fighting between the 'factions'. Would an independent East Timor have been less politically stable than Indonesia?

Australia's most serious dereliction of responsibility was its refusal to offer to mediate between the warring parties. In August and September, Fretilin, the UDT and the Portuguese had looked to Australia for a diplomatic initiative. In his major statement to the Parliament the prime minister declared cautiously that Australia stood 'ready to take part in any humanitarian action that may be practicable'.[47] The most pressing humanitarian action was the negotiation of a cease-fire, and Australia, which enjoyed the respect of all parties concerned, was best placed to negotiate it. However, the government refused to take up this challenge. Was it afraid of provoking Jakarta's suspicions, or worse, was it reluctant to take any action that might cut across the plans of the Indonesian generals to use the upheaval as a pretext for military intervention? The government called on the Portuguese to resolve the conflict but, at that time, as it well knew, the Lisbon government was in disarray and was powerless to deal with the crisis. Mr Whitlam remarked in his statement that the governor had only a tiny staff and had 'no chance of exerting control over more than a small section of Dili. The Governor thus retains no more than the formal trappings of office'.[48]

Mr Whitlam would have known from the reporting of the Australian ambassador in Lisbon, Mr Frank Cooper, that the political crisis in Portugal at that time had all but paralysed the country's overseas administration and armed forces. Portuguese troops, in defiance of their officers, were refusing to serve in the colonies, and some had refused to go to East Timor. Although Mr Whitlam stated that Australia would never send troops abroad again, troops were hardly necessary to bring about negotiations in Timor in those circumstances. Because of Australia's high standing in the eyes of leaders of the warring parties, a peace mission could have arranged a cease-fire within days. By the end of August the UDT leaders were appealing to Australia for help, while both Horta and Xavier do Amaral were also looking to Australia for guidance.

The Whitlam government moved in the opposite direction: it went to surprising lengths to discourage any Australian involvement outside of the immediate ranks of its officials and advisers. For example, when the fighting broke out I was asked to go to East Timor to accompany André Pasquier, the International Red Cross delegate to the South-East Asian region. Because I was in effect a public servant this arrangement had to be cleared with the foreign affairs department. The head of the relevant branch in the department, Geoff Miller, at first welcomed the proposal and indicated that he would recommend it to the minister. But a day or so later I was contacted by a senior officer who apologetically informed me that the proposal had been vetoed 'at the highest level' (which I took to be the prime minister) on the grounds that there was to be no official involvement of any kind by Australia in East Timor. I was given the intriguing message that it was not an appropriate time for 'another actor on the stage'. At the time it seemed incredible that this country was not even prepared to make available a specialist adviser to a politically neutral and highly respected organisation like the International Red Cross. André Pasquier was compelled to fly to East Timor unaccompanied by anyone acquainted with either the territory or the Timorese leaders of the parties in conflict.

The Australian government did play a helpful role by providing humanitarian relief, such as the reception of refugees, some of whom it helped to get to Darwin from East Timor. More importantly, it provided food and medical supplies through the ICRC mission, supplies that were flown to East Timor on RAAF Hercules transports. In August and September 1975 more than 2500 evacuees came to Australia, most by sea. It should also be mentioned that most of the doctors and nurses who staffed the ICRC mission came from Australia. The government made much of its contribution to the humanitarian needs of the beleaguered colony, but its efforts were essentially of a bandaid nature, and it was careful to forestall any official Australian involvement in the central issues at stake in the conflict. The government was also careful not to get too close to the Portuguese, for fear of provoking Indonesian suspicions. Yet it did not hesitate to hold them responsible for the turn of events in Timor; as government officials put it, the problem was not one Portugal could shrug off to Australia. Australian assistance to the Portuguese in their efforts to get a negotiating team into East Timor was not given with any enthusiasm. A cable from Woolcott on 18 August disclosed that the government was well-aware that the Indonesians were obstructing the mission led by Major Soares, which the Portugese government had attempted to send into East Timor via Indonesia, yet Australia did not offer to transport this mission to the territory via Darwin.

The Soares' mission was acceptable to both Fretilin and the UDT, and its presence in Dili might have led to a truce. On 28 August the *Australian* reported that senior Portuguese officials in Darwin were privately accusing the Australian government of 'deliberately frustrating a Portuguese peace mission's attempts to fly to Timor'. According to this report, the senior officials were 'privately bitter at what they described as "continuous procrastination in Canberra"'.[49] It was reported that the foreign affairs department had told the officials that it would not make an aircraft available to members of the peace mission, and that 'all Portuguese attempts to secure an aircraft over the past 10 days have been met with prevarication and excuses about concern for the safety of mission members'. From this account the Australian government's stand had 'angered and confused' Brigadier-General Enrique Oliveira Rodrigues and Major Rui Ravara, who were attempting to get to the island of Atauro, where they hoped to arrange talks between the UDT and Fretilin leaders. Meanwhile, in Jakarta the Australian ambassador had apparently declined to correct a distorted assessment of the Portuguese political scene by Lieutenant General Yoga Sugama who, it will be recalled, had described Fretilin as 'communist', and the Portuguese Socialist Party as 'pro-Moscow'. When the foreign affairs department (at the instigation of Frank Cooper) urged Mr Woolcott to put the Indonesians right about the situation in Lisbon, the latter replied that he thought this was a task for Indonesia's own envoy. Mr Woolcott went on to remark, however, that he considered Lisbon's fears that crucial decisions by Jakarta could be based on such false premises as being 'exaggerated'.

In fairness to the Australian government, its initial reluctance was later to some extent overcome, and considerable assistance was given to the later mission led by Dr Almeida Santos. An RAAF aircraft was made available at Darwin to take the minister and his party to Atauro. The Australians apparently made it clear to the Portuguese that they shared with Indonesia an opposition to any separate dealings with Fretilin which, at the time of Dr Santos' visit, had already gained the upper hand in East Timor. This attitude made it very difficult for the Portuguese negotiator to achieve anything during his visit because he was all but prevented from entering into any form of negotiations with the party in control of most of the colony.

The Indonesians, for their part, obstructed moves for separate talks with the UDT leaders other than on the basis of Portuguese acceptance of the petition for integration. Therefore, the outcome of Australia's Timor policy, from the time of the coup onwards, was to place the Timorese parties to the civil war in bewildering isolation and to encourage the Portuguese to do likewise, though this might not necessarily have been its intention. In effect, when the civil war ended, Australia joined with Indonesia in seeking to isolate Fretilin, and to obstruct the left-wing party's attempts to gain international recognition.

The UDT coup and the civil war had brought a perceptible shift in the Whitlam government's Timor policy. By encouraging the view that Indonesia was an innocent party to the conflict, a party whose legitimate security interests were under threat, and to whom Portugal might consider turning for assistance in restoring order to the colony, Australia became an accomplice to the Indonesian conspiracy to bring about the incorporation of the territory. Internationally Australia also discouraged suggestions that Indonesia had some responsibility for the coup and, in certain cases, its representatives privately urged the Woolcott view, that events be allowed to take their course. During those critical weeks the Whitlam government could have called for the internationalisation of the Timor problem but did not do so.

Australia declined to participate in a peacekeeping operation, when the UDT and Fretilin leaders had indicated that its presence would be welcomed. This proposal hinged on Australia's cooperation. For some time Indonesia had been pressing Portugal to allow it to send in troops—this was the condition under which the president was prepared to agree to Indonesia's military involvement at that stage—but the Portuguese were not ready to consent to this, partly because of their suspicions that Indonesia was responsible to some extent for the coup in the first place, and partly because they were concerned that Indonesia would use its military presence to promote integration.

The peacekeeping force proposal envisaged a four-power operation, involving Indonesia, Portugal, Malaysia and Australia, and for Lisbon, Australia's participation was essential. Dr Santos sought to gain the government's support in three hours of talks with Mr Whitlam and Mr Morrison. The prime minister was reported to have told Dr Santos that he was 'totally opposed' to any Australian military involvement.[50] This had the effect of scuttling the proposal. The Indonesians, for their part, became annoyed at what they claimed was a betrayal by Santos, accusing him of trying to persuade the Australian government to accept the reality of the Fretilin military victory and to negotiate with the Timorese leaders directly. Thus, although Australia declared itself not to be a 'party principal', by declining a role in negotiations, and by pretending not to see the foul play that was going on, the government became an accessory to a sinister scheme to undermine a legitimate, if at times difficult, decolonisation process in a neighbouring territory.

Australia's Timor policy was largely the policy of the prime minister, who apparently took few of his parliamentary colleagues into his confidence about what was going on, and the options were open to the government. Even Foreign Minister Willesee was less than fully informed, while Mr Whitlam's other Cabinet colleagues, probably with the exception of the defence minister, were not consulted. As has already been mentioned, cables and other correspondence on the Timor crisis were subjected to a very restricted and selective distribution, so that only a small inner group of officials was privy to high-grade intelligence information and government responses. Some officials in the foreign affairs department, and many more in the defence department, became troubled at what they perceived to be Mr Whitlam's real objectives, but few had access to enough information to enable them to make considered judgements.

As Richard Hall and Desmond Ball have pointed out, Australia's electronic intelligence agency, the Defence Signals Division, was able to monitor and to follow closely Indonesia's covert moves against East Timor, but 'sensitive source material' of this kind is highly classified and its circulation tightly restricted.[51] Because of the traditional preoccupation with the protection of information about code-breaking activities governments are usually loathe to make use of this kind of intercepted material. In the case of the Timor situation this source revealed a great deal about Indonesian intentions and about Indonesia's military and intelligence activities in, or against, the Portuguese colony. But, by exercising exceptionally tight control over its distribution, the Whitlam government was spared the embarrassment of having to implicate Indonesia in the Timor crisis, other than to an inner-circle of advisers. An indication of the kind of information available to the government of the time may be discerned from later leaks of CIA briefings to US leaders, for the CIA depended heavily upon Australian sources for its information about Timor. The agency's briefs are exceptionally frank, reporting in some detail Indonesian subversive activities and covert military operations.[52]

The UDT coup and the civil war attracted a great deal of attention from the Australian press, but until journalists were finally able to get into the territory most of the reports were exaggerated and sensational. To many Australians the civil war in East Timor quickly slipped into a Cold War mould: it was simply a struggle between the 'communist' Fretilin and the 'moderate' UDT party, a conflict that understandably troubled Indonesia. Many of the media were easy prey to the reports emanating from Jakarta that Fretilin was receiving arms and other support from China and Vietnam, and to lurid accounts that its troops were slaughtering babies in the streets and perpetrating other indescribable atrocities. In the federal parliament the most concerned group were government backbenchers, who had developed a close interest in the Timor situation as a result of the visit to the territory by several Australian Labor Party parliamentarians in March. Here there was increasing dissatisfaction with the stance of Prime Minister Whitlam, and with his insistence that Australia must adopt a low posture towards the conflict.

As the domestic political crisis in Canberra intensified, the Australian Labor Party backbenchers felt compelled to choke back any public criticism of Mr Whitlam's policies in the interest of the Labor government's survival in office. Mr Whitlam was unmoved by criticism, and was unresponsive to alternative proposals, as several of his party colleagues were to discover. From the account of a prominent Labor backbencher, Manfred Cross, the prime minister angrily tore up one written submission conveyed to him by the caucus foreign affairs and defence committee. Whitlam later wrote disparagingly that 'the Australian Government's efforts at this time to bring the parties together were not helped by a visit to Timor by some backbench partisans of Fretilin'.[53] That particular visit was the September mission to the colony by Senator Arthur Gietzelt and Ken Fry of the Australian Labor Party, and Senator Neville Bonner from the Liberal Party. The mission's conclusions did not help Mr Whitlam's stand, but it did more to bring an understanding of what was happening in East Timor to the parliament than all the government's statements during the previous twelve months.

In spite of the constraints of party loyalty at that difficult time many Labor members did voice their concern at events in Timor. They included Tom Uren, Manfred Cross, Chris Hurford, Dr Richard Gun, Kim Beazley (also a minister of the Whitlam government), John Kerin and senators Georges, McIntosh and McLaren. And these were only the most outspoken critics of their leader's Timor policy, for less than a handful of the parliamentary party members supported Mr Whitlam's handling of the matter.

One of the prime minister's few supporters was Dr Klugman who had little enthusiasm for the growing Australian Labor Party view that Australia should actively support Timor's right to self-determination. In a curiously worded question on 27 August, Dr Klugman asked the prime minister whether it would 'help the position in East Timor, and alleviate the fears of Indonesia if Portugal became a democracy', and whether Mr Whitlam would use his 'good influence to encourage the establishment of a representative Government in Portugal' and 'discourage the military dictatorship by high officers'.[54] It was a strange view for the offending party, the Suharto government, a military dictatorship, was a much less democratic style of government.

In other circumstances the Labor caucus would probably have openly challenged the government's Timor policy and forced the prime minister to take a firmer stand against Indonesia, but political conditions in Australia in the second-half of 1975 were not conducive to a backbench revolt. The government was facing a deepening economic crisis, and Australia was on the verge of the greatest constitutional controversy in its history. The Whitlam government was without a majority in the senate; the Coalition leaders were already threatening to use their control of the Upper House to prevent the passage of the Supply Bill, thereby virtually bringing down the Labor government and forcing the country to an election. In those very tense circumstances, for a Labor member to 'rock the boat' would have been tantamount to an act of treason.

The Coalition parties could have brought considerable pressure to bear on the Whitlam government in August and September, but they did not really give much attention to the Timor problem. Shadow Minister for Foreign Affairs Andrew Peacock, had earlier maintained a close and sympathetic interest in the question, but by the time the civil war had broken out in the territory it was apparent that his interest had changed. The new leader of the Coalition, Malcolm Fraser, showed little interest in the issue. It is possible that his view was influenced by subtle approaches from the Indonesians. It has already been mentioned that one of the key figures behind *Operasi Komodo*, General Yoga Sugama, sounded out Mr Fraser during a quiet visit to Australia in May and had reportedly 'found no reason for alarm'. Mr Fraser's view of the Timor problem has never been clear because he rarely mentioned the subject.

With most other Australian conservatives though, Mr Fraser was evidently impressed with the anti-communist disposition of the Suharto regime. He may therefore have been receptive to those Indonesians who sought to convince Australian political leaders that an independent state of East Timor would imperil the security and stability of the republic. When the UDT coup and the later outbreak of fratricidal fighting thrust the Timor problem before the attention of the Australian parliament, Mr Fraser contributed little to the debate. However, he and the National Party leader, Mr Anthony, raised the spectre of communism coming to East Timor on the wave of a Fretilin victory. Mr Fraser's main contribution to the discussions in parliament in August 1975 was a question to the prime minister about whether Mr Whitlam was 'concerned at all at the possible establishment of communist control in Portuguese Timor so close to Australia'. Also, on the same day—28 August, when Fretilin forces had already gained the upper hand in the fighting in the colony—Mr Anthony asked whether the government 'felt concerned in any way that Timor might become communist controlled'.[55]

On the face of it, these were questions from political leaders whose fear of communism dominated all other considerations, and who cared little about the international humanitarian principles at stake in little East Timor. Mr Whitlam was later to refer to the remarks of his political opponents which, he has claimed, had further stimulated Indonesian paranoia. But, to be fair to the conservative leaders, Mr Whitlam had taken care not to provide the parliamentarians with the kind of information that would have made it possible for them to draw other conclusions. When Tony Lamb, a Labor backbencher, sought to prod Mr Whitlam to do so, Whitlam apparently could not bring himself to make an outright denial of the allegation. He merely stated that 'there is incomplete justification for describing any of the parties in Timor as Communist'.[56] In a reply to another Liberal member, Erwin, who referred to 'the Communist Fretilin forces', the prime minister declared somewhat equivocally:

> I suppose there may be pro-communist elements in Fretilin. I do not believe, on the basis of the information available to me, that Fretilin is totally or predominantly

communist. What I do want to bring home to the honourable gentlemen is that the use of terms like 'communist' about Fretilin, the insinuation that Fretilin is totally, predominantly or largely communist, just arouses the suspicions that there are in all the Moslem countries in our area.[57]

Whatever his reasons, Mr Whitlam chose not to put the fears of the conservatives to rest. It is tempting to conclude that he deliberately sought not to allay their apprehensions so as not to provoke the Coalition into a closer questioning and scrutiny of the government's Timor policy. It seemed that Mr Whitlam was following Richard Woolcott's advice that Australia should prepare the ground for an accommodation of Indonesia's inevitable military action against Timor. To give the impression that Fretilin had some communist tendencies was an effective way of deflecting the interest and sympathy of the Coalition parties.

Andrew Peacock continued to maintain a concern for the rights of the Timorese, and to an extent he succeeded in winning the confidence of the Fretilin leaders. But from April 1975 he was much more guarded in his statements on Timor. His statement in Parliament on 26 August suggested that the Coalition's official position was not so different from that of the government. It acknowledged Indonesia's 'legitimate concern' and noted that East Timor 'forms part of the island archipelago of Indonesia'. Peacock castigated the government for its Timor policy, but this time he was defensive of Indonesia and somewhat evasive about the right to self-determination of the East Timorese. He floated the idea that Australia should actively canvass the support of ASEAN states in seeking a solution to the problem.[58] This idea seemed to have some merit at the time, though some diplomats contended that the other ASEAN states had been so carefully indoctrinated by Indonesia that they had no enthusiasm for such an initiative. Some three days later Peacock repeated this proposal, but he seemed again to be leaning further towards the Indonesian position. He declared: 'Indonesia's deep and legitimate concern regarding the possible outcome of the civil war should be understood by all Australians; the turmoil is occurring in its own archipelago and adjoining its own territory'.[59] The statement said nothing about the position of the Timorese, nor did he mention the possibility of Australia playing a peace-keeping role. The Coalition would not be a champion for East Timor's right to self-determination.

Later in September Andrew Peacock was to be treated to a special briefing by two leading members of the *Operasi Komodo* network, Harry Tjan and Liem Bian-Kie of Ali Murtopo's Centre for Strategic and International Studies. When Andrew Peacock visited Bali on 24 September he was unexpectedly met by these two Indonesians who had been assigned the task of handling sensitive diplomatic, academic, and political, contacts on the Timor operation. Some months later alleged details of this meeting was leaked to the Australian press by Indonesian intelligence, as a move designed to embarrass the then foreign minister, whose stand on the invasion of East Timor had irritated the generals in Jakarta. According to what purported to be a record of conversation Andrew Peacock had assured the Indonesians:

his party would not protest against Indonesia if Indonesia was forced to do something about Portuguese Timor, for example to 'go in' to restore peace there. He recommended that such Indonesian action be given 'open support' by the ASEAN nations, in order to provide 'moral cover' for it. If Indonesia were forced to go in, at the maximum he would criticise PM Whitlam and his Government for hesitating to join in solving the Portuguese Timor problem, thereby forcing Indonesia to act unilaterally...Basically he respects Whitlam's policy in this Portuguese Timor problem, and he personally is of the same opinion.[60]

This episode is discussed at some length later. I have established that the substance of this document was contrived by Harry Tjan months after the meeting took place, although Tjan was later to deny its authorship when confronted by Peacock. Written by Harry Tjan, he kept the document in his CSIS safe for some time, before it was leaked through a Bakin contact in Jakarta. It was then carried to Australia by the then wife of a member of the Australian embassy in the Indonesian capital. Peacock's stand on Timor had softened, but he has insisted that at no stage did he make such a devious and accommodating commitment to the Indonesians.

Mr Whitlam's handling of the issue however, provided his political opponents with an excuse to absolve them from a responsibility which most of them may have had little enthusiasm to accept, had they been acquainted with the full circumstances. They tended to regard Fretilin as a left-wing party whose leaders could not be trusted and whose aims could spell trouble for Australia.

The inclination of most of the Coalition front bench was not shared by all Liberal-Country Party backbenchers. The position of the Timorese was accorded considerable public support by a small group of Liberals, including senators Neville Bonner, Alan Missen, Michael Hodgman and Maurice Niell, although it is probably fair to say that most of them were inconspicuous until after the killing of the members of two Australian television teams at Balibo in October 1975, and until the extent of Indonesia's military involvement on the ground in East Timor had become transparently clear. Nor were all members of the Country Party unmoved by these events. One Country Party senator, who was years later to switch to the Liberal Party, Bernie Kilgariff, had been to Timor and enjoyed close links with the Timorese community in Darwin: he became increasingly troubled at the persistent reports of Indonesia's complicity in the upheaval to the north of his electorate.

Some other members of the Coalition privately registered their disquiet about the Whitlam government's policy, no doubt in some cases because of their fear of the strategic advantages Indonesia might gain from its acquisition of an additional slice of territory adjacent to Australia. But in those crucial months of August, September and October, the Australian parliament's Opposition parties were heavily focused on domestic issues, and with the exhilarating scent of victory in the air, few could bring much of their attention to bear on a marginal issue like the Timor problem—as it happened in the circumstances of the time, one of the few issues on which there was a measure of consensus between the government and Coalition leaderships.

The international response

Although the coup and the civil war were fairly widely reported in the international press, the main assistance from outside the region was aid to Indonesia for the relief of refugees in the western sector of the island. The crisis had been brought to the notice of the UN Secretary-General, yet Timor did not attract much international attention until just before the Indonesian invasion in December 1975. Portugal canvassed the idea of internationalising the problem, but it gained little support for the idea. The international response was also clearly affected because the remote Portuguese colony was somehow inconsequential in the international chess play of the time, a distant land of no strategic or economic significance to the major powers, or to any major power other than Indonesia. Most leading international actors were thus attracted to the position advocated by the British and US ambassadors in Jakarta. Weeks before the events of August the British ambassador to Indonesia reached the conclusion, apparently on the basis of the brief visit to Timor by Gordon Duggan, of the High Commission in Canberra, that the Timorese were in no condition to exercise their right to self-determination, that political dissension was likely to continue for some time and that, therefore, the case for integration into Indonesia was a strong one, hence the ambassador reported to the Foreign Office that, in the circumstances, the best course for Britain was not to become involved. He urged that if Indonesia made a move to seize the colony the British government should stand clear and not oppose Jakarta. In Duggan's view it was in Britain's interests that Indonesia should 'absorb the territory as soon as and as unobtrusively as possible'.[61]

The attitude of the US was little different, although the US government was well-informed about Indonesia's designs on the Portuguese colony, the subversive activities of *Operasi Komodo*, and the beginnings of Jakarta's military intervention. Not least, the US leaders were aware that one of the main reasons President Suharto was reluctant to agree to the forced integration of East Timor was his concern at what the US reaction might be. Thus, on 18 August, the CIA advised the president and other leading officials that:

> Soeharto continues to worry about an adverse reaction from the US, particularly since a move against Timor at this time would come only a few weeks after his visit to Washington.[62]

On 8 September CIA analysts again drew attention to the Indonesian leader's reluctant stand. As has already been noted, they reported that the president was worried about the effect such an operation would have on his image internationally. He was also concerned at what might be its effect on Indonesia's relations with the US and Australia. In the case of the US, the president was apprehensive because of the risk of losing badly needed military assistance.[63]

The US never seriously considered exerting its acknowledged influence to dissuade the Indonesians from military intervention in Timor. On the contrary, only a few days after the UDT coup, Ambassador Newsom told his Australian colleague that he was under instructions from Dr Kissinger not to become involved in discussions with the Indonesians about the Timor question because the US was already involved in, as Woolcott put it, 'enough problems of greater importance overseas at present'. As Newsom perceived it, the US 'should keep out of the Portuguese Timor situation and allow events to take their course'.[64] With the crisis involving the colony escalating, the State Department took the extraordinary step of instructing the embassy in Jakarta to reduce its reporting. According to Woolcott, Newsom commented cynically that 'if Indonesia were to intervene the United States would hope they would do so "effectively, quickly and not use our equipment".'[65]

Another cable from the Australian mission in Jakarta suggests that Newsom provided General Yoga Sugama with a much-more cautious statement of his country's policy on Timor. Yoga was apparently told that the US was anxious not to become involved, but he was also informed that, apart from

a normal humanitarian concern for the welfare of the population and the right of self-determination, the main United States interest was in the impact of any change in Portuguese Timor on U.S. relations with Indonesia.

The ambassador made it clear that the US government 'had no objection to the merger of Portuguese Timor with Indonesia, assuming that this was desired by the local population'.[66] The Indonesian intelligence chief was told though that difficulties could arise if force were used to seize East Timor, and especially if US military equipment was used. This could invoke sections of the Foreign Assistance Act, and place in jeopardy US military assistance to Indonesia. There was some guarded warning, or at least some firmness, in this statement which might well have caused Suharto to delay further his decision to allow military intervention.

It is noteworthy, however, that Newsom's reported remarks to Yoga Sugama were at variance with the views he had confided to Woolcott. The statement could conceivably have been watered down with some off-the-record remarks, a practice sometimes resorted to by diplomats anxious to soften the effect of a blunt formal statement on representatives of a host country. There is evidence that the Indonesians were able to establish that their main problem with the US was not opposition from the State Department or from the administration, but the risk that the issue could end up being probed by a congressional committee where there would be much less sympathy for Indonesia's position. It was probably for this reason that the Indonesian generals took great care to conceal their earliest military operations against the Portuguese colony. But these moves were quickly detected and reported by intelligence agencies, although this knowledge was concealed in a deliberate move to protect Indonesia from public criticism.

Notes

1 Jose Martins, interview with J. S. Dunn, 11 May 1976.
2 Based on talks with former UDT leaders, including João Carrascalão, Mousinho and de Oliveira.
3 Jill Jolliffe, *East Timor: Nationalism and Colonialism* (St Lucia: Queensland University Press, 1978), p. 118.
4 João Carrascalão, signed statement, August 1975.
5 Jolliffe, *East Timor*, p. 118.
6 Ibid., p. 126. Also of interest is Jolliffe's detailed account of the Portuguese position in the coup. See ch. 4.
7 Ibid., pp. 126-27
8 Dale van Atta and Brian Toohey, 'The Timor Papers', part 1, *National Times*, 30 May-5 June 1982.
9 Ibid.
10 Hamish McDonald, *Suharto's Indonesia* (Melbourne: Fontana/Collins, 1980), p. 207. See also van Atta and Toohey, 'The Timor Papers', part 1.
11 *Documents on Australian Defence and Foreign Policy*, 1968-1975 (Sydney: Walsh and Munster, 1980), p. 202. See also the relevant documents in the Department of Foreign Affairs and Trade, Australia and the Indonesian Incorporation of Portuguese Timor 1974-76.
12 Ibid., pp. 203-7.
13 Ibid., pp. 207-10.
14 Ibid., pp. 203-4.
15 Jolliffe, *East Timor*, p. 124.
16 Ibid., p. 129.
17 *Australian Defence and Foreign Policy*, p. 202.
18 *Australian*, 26 August 1975.
19 Quoted in Jolliffe, *East Timor*, p. 142.
20 M. F. Willis, Report of activities of ICRC medical team, 30 August-4 September 1975.
21 Van Atta and Toohey, 'The Timor Papers', part 1.
22 Ibid.
23 Ibid.
24 Interview with a former UDT leader in Portugal, January 1977.
25 The author interviewed Weli in Dili in October 1975.
26 Based on information I obtained from refugees in Lisbon in January 1977.
27 Information concerning these attempts to escape came not only from the refugees in Portugal. When I was in East Timor during the Fretilin interregnum some reports came in from escapees. See J. S. Dunn, 'The East Timor Situation' (report on talks with Timorese refugees in Portugal, March 1977); and also van Atta and Toohey, 'The Timor Papers', *National Times*, part 2, 6-12 June 1982.
28 Based on an interview with Carrascalão in Portugal, 1977.
29 *Australian Defence and Foreign Policy*, p. 215; see also van Atta and Toohey, 'The Timor Papers', part 2.
30 Van Atta and Toohey, 'The Timor Papers', part 1.
31 *Kompas*, 11 September 1975.
32 *Australian Defence and Foreign Policy*, p. 216.

33 Ibid., p. 210.
34 Ibid., pp. 201-5.
35 Ibid., pp. 193-96.
36 Ibid., p. 198.
37 Ibid., p. 199; also quoted in *Canberra Times*, 16 January 1976.
38 Ibid., p. 197.
39 Ibid., pp. 215-17.
40 Ibid., p. 197.
41 *Commonwealth Parliamentary Debates*, House of Representatives, 26 August 1975, p. 492.
42 Ibid.
43 McDonald, *Suharto's Indonesia*, p. 207.
44 *Commonwealth Parliamentary Debates*, 26 August 1975, p. 492.
45 Ibid., p. 493.
46 E. G. Whitlam, 'Indonesia and Australia: Political Aspects', The Indonesian Connection (seminar held at the Australian National University, 30 November 1979), Research School of Pacific Studies, School Seminar Series.
47 *Commonwealth Parliamentary Debates*, 26 August 1975, p. 492.
48 Ibid.
49 *Australian*, 28 August 1975.
50 *Adelaide Advertiser*, 2 September 1975.
51 Desmond Ball, *A Suitable Piece of Real Estate* (Sydney: Hale and Iremonger, 1980), p. 48; also see Richard Hall, *The Secret State* (Sydney: Cassell, 1978).
52 Van Atta and Toohey, 'The Timor Papers', parts 1 and 2.
53 Whitlam, 'Indonesia and Australia'.
54 *Commonwealth Parliamentary Debates*, House of Representatives, 27 August 1975, p. 574.
55 Ibid., 28 August 1975, p. 685.
56 *Commonwealth Parliamentary Debates*, 2 September 1975, p. 822.
57 Ibid., 30 September 1975, p. 1387.
58 Media release, 29 August 1975.
59 Media release from Mr Peacock, 29 August 1975.
60 *National Times*, 27 May 1977.
61 *Australian Defence and Foreign Policy*, p. 193.
62 Van Atta and Toohey, 'The Timor Papers', part 1.
63 Ibid.
64 *Australian Defence and Foreign Policy*, p. 199.
65 Ibid., p. 200.
66 Ibid., p. 205.

Chapter Nine
The Fretilin Interregnum

The defeat of the UDT forces by Fretilin in little more than three weeks of fighting not only astonished the Indonesians and foreign observers, it surprised Fretilin leaders. A little more than six weeks after the abortive UDT coup Xavier do Amaral, Nicolau Lobato and their colleagues were faced with the task of setting up an administration in East Timor. In that short time their movement had been transformed from a political front into an army of sorts, but the challenge of organising a de facto government was something for which Fretilin, a fairly loose political organisation, was totally untrained and unprepared. The flight of refugees to Australia, the retreat of the UDT and its supporters into Indonesian Timor, and the withdrawal of the Portuguese provincial government to the island of Atauro had deprived East Timor of something like 80 per cent of its administration officials. Although some of the Fretilin party leaders had previously been in the colonial service, most of them had resigned their posts some months before the coup to engage full-time in work for the party. The district administrative structure was particularly badly affected by the civil war because nearly all of the senior officials in this vitally important sector of government were no longer available. East Timor was almost entirely without professional personnel as there were no doctors, no engineers, and only one economist, Jose Goncalves (son of the Apodeti leader, the *liurai* of Atsabe), who had studied for some years in Europe.

There were also precious few technicians and skilled tradesmen left in East Timor. Most of the few remaining skilled mechanics, electricians and radio technicians were soon to be consigned to urgent military tasks well away from the principal towns where there was a pressing need for their services. The arrival of the ASIAT medical team, the International Red Cross mission and a number of other aid workers led to the restoration of essential services in Dili and Baucau, as well as to the rapid improvement of the health situation in the territory. ASIAT had links with Michael Darby, an activist of the Australian Right. ASIAT's valuable and timely contribution is a reminder that support for the East Timorese was not strictly confined to the Australian left-wing and liberal elements.

Although the civil war had caused considerable disruption, the extent of the loss of life and the material damage was much less than had been widely believed at first. According to André Pasquier, the leader of the ICRC mission whose teams concentrated on all of the areas where the fighting had taken place, and in the last weeks of the conflict supervised the observance of the Geneva Convention in the battle areas, the total loss of life resulting from the civil war was about 1500, most of them the result of the bitter tribal fighting in the triangle between Aileu, Same and Laclubar. In Dili the death toll was estimated at a little below 450. João Carrascalão later claimed that, in the retreat from Dili to the Indonesian border, he lost fewer than 50 men. In spite of the generally sensational reports that were carried by the Australian press, the physical damage to the main towns was slight. As Jill Jolliffe, one of the earliest journalists to get to East Timor—and who had spent several months in Timor earlier in the year, that is, before the coup—later wrote:

> The city showed little evidence of war damage. In typical Dili style a number of unexploded mortar shells poked out of the asphalt around the airport and at various points of the city; one had to remember not to trip over them. Many buildings were pockmarked by bullet and mortar fire and there was a good deal of broken glass, but little structural damage to the city proper. On the outskirts, as in most of the villages, some traditional houses had been burnt to the ground.[1]

The task of setting up a provisional administration for the province, over which they had just gained de facto control, was formidable for Fretilin. In reality it meant the reluctant transformation of a loose political organisation into a de facto government with the task of reviving the country's comatose economic life. In the upheaval of the civil war the fragile economy of East Timor had ground to a halt. Most shops were closed, farms were not tended or were abandoned and most town services were no longer operating. Dili was teeming with refugees, many of them Chinese who had come to the capital from towns and villages where fighting had disrupted their business operations.

Thanks to the work of the ICRC mission and the ASIAT team which took over the Dili Hospital and other medical centres, the overall health situation was more or less in hand by the middle of October. Power and water supplies were soon restored to the capital, the Fretilin administration proving surprisingly effective in re-establishing law and order and restoring essential services. Immediately after the Fretilin victory in Dili, the party's central committee began to take steps towards normalising the situation. Its leaders took steps to gain the confidence of the Chinese for whom the civil war had been a profoundly disrupting experience. Their businesses had been looted in the wake of the coup, often by UDT supporters, while a new hostility had surfaced in the villages, prompting most of the Chinese to flee to the capital. Fretilin leaders sought to reassure Chinese merchants that their property would be protected and their future status assured but, in spite of their efforts to make the best of their situation, the outlook was gloomy. If the Timorese were to attain self-rule their privileged economic position was destined, sooner or later, to come to an end. If, on the other hand, the Indonesians intervened, the consequences could have been worse. Many wealthier Chinese had managed to leave in the earlier days of the coup; some had the foresight to leave Timor before 11 August. The Australian Labor Party parliamentarians who went to Dili on 16 September were told that many Chinese merchants had managed to leave, taking much of their money with them. Because of this, and the fact that the Fretilin authorities were reluctant to break into Timor's only bank, the Banco Nacional Ultramarino, there was an acute currency shortage in the territory.

Despite all these drawbacks, by mid-October Dili was functioning more or less normally, and the Chinese shops were beginning to reopen. In late September, and in the first-half of October, the Fretilin authorities made visits to all parts of the territory (except Oecussi, which soon came under Indonesian control) by the International Red Cross, ASIAT and members of the aid mission sent to Timor by the Australian Council for Overseas Aid easier. By the end of that period it was clear that an overall improvement in the situation had been achieved. The most serious immediate problem facing the country was a growing food shortage, partly because no imports had come into Timor since the coup, and partly because many farming areas had been abandoned during the crucial preparation and planting period. In normal circumstances several thousand tonnes of grain and other foodstuffs had been imported each year, but because of the war and the subsequent impasse between the Fretilin and the Portuguese, no food supplies, apart from limited Red Cross consignments from Australia, had entered the territory since the previous July. Some rice, corn and other foods were available in parts of the province some distance from Dili, but without ships, and with limited transport and fuel supplies, the Fretilin administration encountered serious distribution problems. Apart from the fuel shortage, transport was affected by a severe shortage of technical maintenance personnel for the vehicles, many of which were soon to become unserviceable.

The Fretilin government was designed essentially to be a temporary one. The leaders acknowledged that the movement lacked the personnel and the experience to conduct the affairs of an independent state, and so they called on the Portuguese to return and resume the decolonisation program. Most leaders still felt though that decolonisation would need to be implemented over several years. In the meantime, pending a negotiated settlement with the Portuguese, the Central Committee of Fretilin was to function as the government, through a number of commissions. A kind of 'troika' principle was applied with each commission being administered by a member of the central committee, a member of Falintil (an acronym for the Armed Forces for the National Liberation of East Timor), and a 'technocrat'. Thus, the Commission for the Control and Supervision of the Economy was run by a military leader, Juvenal Inacio from the Central Committee, and Jose Goncalves, the economist son of Guilherme Goncalves. The Commission moved into appropriate government buildings, but the Timorese took care not to occupy the main Portuguese offices. Thus, the Governor's office and his palace remained empty and under guard. The Portuguese flag still flew, a symbol, as the Fretilin president insisted to me, of their desire for the Portuguese to return to resume decolonisation responsibilities.

This administrative structure had obvious shortcomings, but there was evidence it enjoyed widespread support or cooperation from the population, including many former UDT supporters. In October, for example, Australian relief workers visited most parts of the colony and, without exception, they reported that there was no evidence of any insecurity or significant hostility towards Fretilin. The leaders of the victorious party were welcomed warmly and spontaneously in all main centres by crowds of Timorese. In my own long association with the territory I had never before witnessed such demonstrations of spontaneous warmth and support from the ordinary people of Timor. The Fretilin administration was not without its critics and opponents, but opposition appeared to be largely confined to expressions of dissatisfaction, rather than hostility. Such attitudes were common among the Chinese. Apart from the low level of commercial activity, the Chinese had to cope with hundreds of their refugees, adding to their food supply problems. The Fretilin authorities had 'requisitioned' certain goods from Chinese shops, but there was little evidence of looting. The authorities dealt swiftly and often harshly with thieves, hoarders, and those Timorese soldiers who committed offences against the civil population in the first weeks of the Fretilin interregnum. Thanks to the efforts of the strong man of Fretilin, Nicolau Lobato, the Timorese troops and officials soon attained an impressive standard of discipline.

One of the consequences of the Fretilin victory was that the victors had to look after a large number of prisoners, most of them UDT leaders and their followers. Altogether there were some 2000 of these prisoners in several detention centres. They were classified into two categories—leaders of the coup, and their rank-and-file followers—and they were treated rather differently. I visited the main prison camp at Taibesse, near the army headquarters, and concluded, with most other visitors, that they were being reasonably well treated. I was allowed to wander unescorted through the main detention centre, which housed more than 400 prisoners. In the tropical heat most were bare from the waist up, and it was evident that very few of them had been beaten. The camps were under the close supervision of the International Red Cross mission, whose officials had unrestricted access and, as food became scarcer in Dili, the UDT prisoners were, if anything, in much better physical condition than the ordinary population of the capital. A few prisoners in the compound were not UDT members at all, but Fretilin soldiers who had been imprisoned because of crimes against the civilian population. One prisoner, who had evidently been beaten, turned out to be a Fretilin soldier who had raped a Chinese girl. Some of the UDT leaders were subjected to harsher conditions of confinement, and several of them had clearly been badly beaten. One of the sorriest cases was Augusto Mousinho, one of the leading UDT personalities, with whom I had several discussions. Mousinho had been badly beaten after his capture, and was in custody in the hospital, in a ward with several other UDT leaders who had either been wounded or beaten. I also met and talked with Lieutenant Colonel Maggioli, the former Portuguese police commander, who had sided with the UDT after the coup.

Fretilin leaders claimed that they intended to release the prisoners, or at least most of them, 'soon'. A few weeks after the civil war had ended some were released, most of them UDT activists who had not been involved in the fighting. The Fretilin president and his security chief said that some kind of judicial process would need to be carried out by the Portuguese when they returned, before the release of the hard core could be considered. In one or two mountain camps, detention was said to be a protective measure, especially where bitter tribal fighting had left the victors with scores to settle. Apodeti members were not imprisoned at first, in recognition of the fact that they had not sided with the UDT in the civil war. However, when Indonesia further intensified its propaganda campaign, and when its troops began to engage Falintil units at the border, hostility towards Apodeti mounted, and its members were eventually forced to leave the Indonesian consulate area where they had clustered for some weeks; 150 of them were detained in an old military barracks on the foreshore esplanade. According to Fretilin leaders this action was taken for reasons largely to do with their own safety. When I visited them in October 1975 they were evidently in good health, and were regularly receiving visitors, including foreign journalists.

The Fretilin interregnum may be roughly divided into two periods: the first from late August, when victory was already in the air, until the middle of October, when Indonesia's covert military operation began; the second from that time until the invasion in early December. The first period was a time of hope and enthusiasm. In the euphoria of victory the hitherto tense atmosphere of Timor began to relax. The wounds of the war seemed to be healing speedily. The economy appeared to be slowly recovering and the Fretilin administration was being surprisingly effective in distributing food, and in restoring law and order. As early as 20 September visiting Australian parliamentarians, including a small Australian Labor Party delegation and Senator Bonner of the Liberal Party, reported that Fretilin appeared to be in control of the situation. As Mr Fry and Senator Gietzelt reported to the Caucus Foreign Affairs and Defence Committee after their return:

> Our tour around the island confirmed the claims by Fretilin that they are virtually in full control of the situation. As well as the areas which we visited ourselves, we had reports from Aid and Red Cross personnel of a similar situation in the areas which they had visited. Wherever we went, the Fretilin troops appeared to be well disciplined; they were treating their prisoners well and appeared to have the overwhelming support

of the local population. There was evidence too that some people who had supported UDT originally had changed sides when Fretilin took control...We were satisfied that there was no actual fighting taking place while we were in Timor, and that the only position which was not under Fretilin control was Batugade.[2]

The Australian Labor Party mission's visit undoubtedly encouraged the Timorese. It seemed to hold promise that some urgently needed political and economic support would eventually come from the Australian government. And the parliamentarians were not the only visitors. Journalists representing the major Australian media organisations, and some television crews, flew into Timor and invariably left with favourable impressions, which they reported. Talks with the Portuguese were progressing less favourably, the latter remaining reluctant to enter into separate discussions with Fretilin, partly because of opposition to this course from both Indonesia and Australia, and partly because of the incapacity of the new government in Lisbon to come to grips with the realities of the situation in distant Timor. But during this first period time seemed to be on Fretilin's side, as the situation was viewed from Dili, and it was confidently expected that in due course negotiations would take place not only with Portugal, but with Indonesia. Thus, as the fighting with UDT died down, there was ushered in a brief period of expectation and optimism.

The crisis created by the UDT coup and the civil war that followed had a profoundly maturing effect on the Fretilin leadership. As we have seen, although a party of the left, Fretilin was neither particularly radical nor doctrinaire. True, it was influenced by the new left in Portugal, and by the movements in the former African colonies, especially Frelimo, but these organisations were of diverse political orientations. Fretilin was largely a Catholic party with a strong nationalist commitment, that is, a commitment to the development of a peculiarly Timorese political identity. Of the forty-five or so members of the Central Committee, all but a few were practising Catholics, several of the principal leaders attending mass daily. They were mostly socialist-oriented, but in terms of developing world perspectives, rather than doctrinaire Marxism. Such traditional concepts as the development of cooperatives were central to the future economic format of Timor, in commerce and agriculture. The Timorese leaders were committed to improving the living standards and economic role of the indigenous people, but they insisted that free-enterprise conditions would continue for the Chinese and for other foreign business interests. Broadly speaking, Fretilin's aspirations were not so different from those of Michael Somare's Pangu Pati in Papua New Guinea when that country was on the eve of its independence.

One result of the civil war was a perceptible decline in the influence of the radical wing of Fretilin. The extreme left had never been large, and during the fighting some of the more vocal elements had been killed by the UDT. The effect of Fretilin's victory in the civil war was to thrust into positions of leadership and influence a new generation of military commanders from Falintil. Many of these leaders had played little part in Timorese political activities until after the civil war had ended, and most of them were comparatively conservative in outlook. The new breed of field commanders, on whom the very survival of Fretilin now depended, made it clear that they wanted to be consulted in all major areas of government, hence the evolution of the 'troika' principle. Nicolau Lobato, who had already acquired military and administrative experience, emerged as unquestionably the strongest leader of Fretilin. He and his brother Rogerio played the leading roles in the war against the UDT and although Xavier do Amaral continued to be president his real political power declined after September. He remained an important figurehead in terms of his charismatic qualities as a speaker. His involvement in day-to-day affairs declined, but this quietly spoken Timorese leader was evidently widely respected and admired as the father-figure of Fretilin.

Xavier do Amaral was the internationalist but, as Jill Jolliffe put it,

> The ascendancy of the Lobatos, with their limited overseas experience, stress on self-reliance and the prestige of military victory they carried, rendered the leadership in some ways less accessible to negotiation, a characteristic of mixed value in the coming period...the new leaders perhaps more truly expressed the core of Timorese nationalism, in their blend of the ideas of revolutionary African nationalism, pragmatism and conservative self-reliance.[3]

Horta's position was rather precarious for a time, the other Fretilin leaders having been concerned at some of his reported statements in Australia immediately after the coup in which he appeared to have been urging Fretilin to meet at least some of the UDT's demands. Jose Ramos Horta played an important role in talks with the Portuguese at Darwin; not having been involved in the fighting, he was regarded by them as being untainted by the foray which had forced the governor and his officials into a humiliating withdrawal. He was also valued for the contacts and influence he had built up in Australia.

Fretilin's first major public statement reflected the influence of the moderates of the Central Committee. Following a meeting of the committee on 16 September a statement was issued which made the following points:

1. The affairs of East Timor must be decided by the Timorese people within national territory, without external pressures. Fretilin still recognises Portugal's sovereignty over East Timor and seeks talks with the Portuguese Government's representatives on September 20, 1975, in Baucau (East Timor).

2. The Central Committee of Fretilin would welcome a joint peace force by East Timorese troops and Indonesian troops to jointly control the border areas, to avoid any misunderstandings and unnecessary conflicts. The Central Committee believes this peace force must be of equal numbers on both sides. It is imperative that it starts immediately.

3. The Central Committee of Fretilin would welcome a joint conference with representatives from Portugal, Australia and Indonesia, and the leaders of East Timor in order to eliminate rumours and misunderstandings and to promote friendship and co-operation amongst the people of the region.[4]

The statement also declared that the Fretilin leadership would welcome 'fact-finding missions from ASEAN, Australia and New Zealand, as well as observers from other nations and the press, to assess the situation in East Timor, which is now fully controlled by Fretilin'. The Central Committee expressed its belief that

> regional stability is of utmost importance for the development of the South East Asian nations, therefore, now and in the future, we will strive to promote friendship and cooperation between ourselves and the countries of the region...ASEAN is a factor of stability and a driving force of regional cooperation. East Timor would greatly benefit from integration into ASEAN after independence.

The statement noted the intention of the Timorese to seek 'close cooperation with the countries of the Pacific region, Australia, New Zealand, Fiji and Papua New Guinea' as a means to promote the development and political stability of the region.

The Central Committee also expressed its belief that foreign capital would be important to the development of the territory, and foreign investment would therefore be welcomed, 'provided that the superior interests of the people of East Timor are safeguarded'. It declared that Fretilin was 'a front for national liberation that unites all Timorese nationalists without discrimination of race, religion or political belief', and that its foreign policy would be based on non-alignment.

This quite moderate statement emanated from an organisation which the Indonesians and certain groups and individuals in Australia were branding as communist. No link with any communist state was mentioned or was implied in this important statement, nor was 'communism' or 'socialism' mentioned about domestic or foreign-policy objectives. To some extent it reflected the conservative influence of military leaders like Alves and Fernando Carmo, who had demonstrated their military prowess in the field. Carmo played a major role in halting the Indonesian advance in October and had had close links with the UDT. João Carrascalão was later to claim that Carmo's loyalties were divided, but that his strong opposition to the change in the attitude of Lopes da Cruz to Indonesia, and his fervent nationalism, had led him to swing to Fretilin.

The Fretilin statement seemed to offer a basis for a settlement, and a basis for defusing the tensions that the coup and the civil war had created. The Australian government had been calling on the Portuguese to resume their colonial responsibilities, and here was Fretilin asking them to return. There were some problems, however, and although Horta had several talks with the Portuguese representatives in Darwin, no real progress was made during the first period of the interregnum. Fretilin wanted decolonisation to be resumed on certain conditions favourable to it. It wanted to be recognised as the main political organisation, and, at least initially, for UDT and Apodeti to be banned as political parties. In its view, the UDT had discredited itself by launching the coup, while Apodeti was espousing a cause which was anathema to the popular will. As Alarico Fernandes told an Australian Associated Press (AAP) journalist at the end of September: 'Fretilin has never taken up arms against the legitimate colonial government'.[5]

The Fretilin attitude towards the UDT was understandable enough. The UDT had provoked the conflict by attempting to seize power, but it had also become a target for Indonesian disinformation; according to broadcasts from Indonesia early in September it had sent a petition to President Suharto, calling for integration into Indonesia. This was, in Fretilin's view, a blatant act of national betrayal, coming as it did from its former coalition partner in the independence movement. Reported statements by Lopes da Cruz, now in Atambua, in Indonesian Timor, were hardly conducive to reconciliation. What Fretilin leaders did not know was that although da Cruz was now a willing tool of agents of *Operasi Komodo*, his views were not shared by Carrascalão and most other leaders of UDT, who had become virtual prisoners. Outright lies by da Cruz were being churned out by *Operasi Komodo's* propaganda machine. For example, according to an Australian Associated Press report on 17 September, Lopes da Cruz had informed an Indonesian journalist that twenty North Vietnamese 'military trainers' had been instructing Fretilin soldiers. Another UDT leader was reported as having charged that China's ambassador in Canberra had supplied the Fretilin forces with arms, and that the Catholic bishop had confirmed the presence of North Vietnamese in East Timor. These stories were complete fabrications and the UDT leaders I interviewed later said most stories were simply issued by *Operasi Komodo* agents without Timorese leaders knowing to whom they were attributed. But the subtle nature of this dis-information operation was unknown to Fretilin leaders in Dili who assumed that their UDT countrymen had sold out to the Indonesians. These reports from Indonesian Timor caused a sharp decline in support for the UDT in East Timor. Even the UDT prisoners in Dili (with many of whom I privately discussed the post-coup situation) expressed their shock at this 'betrayal' by Lopes da Cruz and his colleagues. Indeed, several leading UDT personalities, even though a couple of them had been badly beaten by their captors, insisted that they would rather languish in a Fretilin prison camp than be in Indonesian Timor as part of the new pro-integration coalition.

Fretilin leaders were also bitter and suspicious towards Governor Lemos Pires who was now located with his troops and officials on the offshore island of Atauro. It is impossible not to have some sympathy for the governor. In September he was caught up in a cross-fire of accusations and recriminations from the warring political parties, the expatriate community, not least from the Indonesians, and he was getting little help from Lisbon. The UDT accused him of having secretly helped Fretilin get control of Dili, while Fretilin leaders alleged that some senior provincial officials, and perhaps even the governor, had assisted the UDT coup. They were still particularly disturbed at the implications of Lemos Pires' acquiescence—as they interpreted it—to the UDT demand that majors Mota and Jonatas be expelled from East Timor. Xavier do Amaral and Nicolau Lobato were thus strongly opposed to holding talks on the island of Atauro where they feared the Portuguese might well doublecross them, and place them under arrest. The Fretilin leaders clearly wanted the talks to get under way, but the main initial obstacles were the venue, and the question of the participation of the leaders of the defeated parties. The Portuguese suggested Macau as a location, while the Fretilin leaders preferred Baucau or a location in Australia, a proposal that, not surprisingly, won little favour with the Australian government.

There is little doubt that talks could have been arranged within a couple of weeks had it not been for the obstructive efforts of Indonesia. The generals at the helm of *Operasi Komodo* were determined to block any move that might lead to Fretilin gaining a measure of recognition as the de facto government of the colony, and they were thus strongly opposed to unilateral talks between the teams led by Dr Almeida Santos and Fretilin. Dr Santos said that when he visited Jakarta the Indonesians urged him to let them send in troops to East Timor, a request he declined. The Indonesians retaliated by spreading the story in Jakarta that Almeida Santos was proposing to hand over control of East Timor to Fretilin. This allegation Dr Santos vigorously denied later to me. Dr Santos did say that he was not averse to talking with Fretilin because by mid-September this party had evidently gained control of all but the Oecussi enclave. Also, with the fighting nearly over he saw no point in pursuing the proposal that a four-nation peace-keeping force be sent to the territory, a proposal which had received little support from Australia.

The Indonesians were able to gain Australia's tacit endorsement of their opposition to holding unilateral talks with Fretilin and, interestingly, officials in Canberra in effect joined with Jakarta in keeping up the fiction that the civil war was still raging long after the UDT resistance had collapsed. It is doubtful whether the Indonesians would have permitted their UDT and Apodeti 'clients' to participate in any such talks, because by mid-September the Indonesians had resolved to bring about integration as soon as possible. If negotiations had been entered into, it would have only complicated and delayed this process.

Indonesia moved swiftly to undermine Fretilin's claim that it was in control of the Portuguese half of the island. There was no time to lose, for if Fretilin were to gain a measure of international recognition, it could present a serious impediment to Indonesia's plans. Ironically it was the CIA that first produced evidence of the beginning of Indonesian military intervention. Based on communications intelligence (presumably acquired by Australian stations), the Agency reported on 4 September that on the previous day 'two Indonesian special forces groups, consisting of about 100 men each, may have entered Portuguese Timor'.[6] Another force of three platoons entered the Bobonaro–Atsabe area in mid-September with the aim of contacting pro-Apodeti elements and of organising uprisings.

The immediate objective of these penetrations, as a CIA report disclosed, was to pave the way for operations by the Atsabe Timorese under Tomas Goncalves, who had been undergoing training by Colonel Sugiyanto's intelligence officers in Indonesian Timor for several months. This operation had not escaped the attention of US intelligence. On 17 September the State Department, quoting 'a clandestine source', reported that 'Indonesian intelligence...has trained, organised and covertly committed 650 Timorese irregular troops into Portuguese Timor to stem the advance of...Fretilin forces'.[7] Two days later another brief elaborated on these activities: 'Jakarta is now sending guerilla units into the Portuguese half of the island in order to engage Fretilin forces, encourage pro-Indonesian elements, and provoke incidents that would provide the Indonesians an excuse to invade should they desire to do so'.[8] In reality these sorties achieved very little. An Indonesian soldier who had been part of these operations later told me that the special forces units often lost their way and they encountered no pro-Indonesian elements. The Timorese villagers were generally hostile and quickly informed Fretilin of the intruders' presence. In the few clashes that occurred the Indonesian troops performed badly. The failure of these covert guerrilla operations was also picked up by the CIA. On 26 September its analysts reported: 'Clandestine intervention by Indonesian troops on behalf of pro-Indonesian forces in the territory has run into serious trouble. Pro-Indonesian Timorese have proved to be too few, too poorly armed, and too badly trained to offer a serious challenge to the Fretilin forces'.[9] At the same time the Agency disclosed that the Indonesians had suffered casualties, and some soldiers had been captured.

The failure of the September incursion did not, however, weaken the resolve of the generals behind *Operasi Komodo*. The situation merely became more urgent. Washington was told that 'vastly increased Indonesian involvement is now proposed; special forces troops armed with weapons that cannot be traced to Jakarta will be used. Malaysia has reportedly agreed in principle to supply such weapons'.[10] Whether Malaysia came to Jakarta's assistance is not clear: the troops involved in the first major assaults appear to have been armed with a mixture of Chinese, Russian and US weapons. In the meantime the propaganda component of *Operasi Komodo* stepped up its activities. Already by mid-September there were several reports, most of them circulated by Antara, that Apodeti and UDT supporters were rising up against Fretilin. One such report stated that 'Apodeti members are now in possession of light arms. They are all over the colony and are at any time ready to launch guerilla warfare against their rival'.[11] A few days later, Brigadier-General Ignatius Pranoto, commander of the Nusatenggara (Udayana) Military District Command (Kodam) and now a key figure in *Operasi Komodo*, was reported as having informed a Jakarta newspaper that Fretilin controlled only the towns of Dili and Baucau, which had been isolated by the opposing troops. Apodeti and the UDT, the general was reported to have declared, had combined their units for military actions. They retained 'strong influence over the population and were in control of the situation' outside the two main towns.[12] On 22 September the leading Jakarta daily, *Sinar Harapan*, joined in the propaganda—or dis-information—campaign. Troops of Apodeti, it reported, had attacked Fretilin at a number of centres, including Atsabe, Ermera,

Bobonaro, Balibo and Maliana. Its correspondent went on to say that 'Balibo and Maliana were fully under Apodeti's control. Both of these places are reported to be quiet and there is no further fighting'.[13]

These reports were sheer fabricated nonsense. For one thing Apodeti possessed no army. Foreign visitors to East Timor, including the Australian Labor Party parliamentarians, aid workers and the journalists, had been able to establish that Fretilin controlled all of the territory apart from a small pocket around the tiny border village of Batugade, and this small UDT remnant was forced to flee into Indonesia later in September. Even US intelligence was to report on 10 September that, 'although some resistance by the Timor Democratic Union continues, serious fighting between the factions has evidently ended'.[14] Nevertheless, the flow of dis-information from Jakarta, much of it inspired by *Operasi Komodo*, was carried by Australian, US, British and some other foreign media and news agencies, generating some sympathy for Indonesia's false dilemma—what should it do to help the strife-torn people of Timor? Many observers were thus asking the obvious question: how much longer could Indonesia stand by and not intervene with this terrible war going on right on its own borders, posing a threat to its security? At this time the spectre of Vietnamese and Chinese involvement was conveniently raised again in Jakarta. A leading Indonesian general, General Widodo, military commander of the region, alluded to foreign intervention in a statement on 28 September, following his return from a visit to the Indonesian side of the island. According to Associated Press in Jakarta, Widodo declared that Fretilin's skill with modern weapons indicated that it had received outside assistance.

Arms assistance was not one of Fretilin's requirements. The independence movement's troops had acquired a substantial armoury when they took over the Portuguese headquarters in August, a fact well-known to Indonesian intelligence from its sources in Dili. For several weeks the Indonesians had been imposing a discreet blockade to deter or to prevent any outside power from sending military supplies to East Timor.

When it came to establishing its identity and credibility in the world at large, Fretilin got little real help from the foreign visitors who went to East Timor after the civil war. Although a number of journalists from leading Australian newspapers, as well as representatives of the Portuguese and Japanese media, visited Timor in September and October and subsequently filed reports sympathetic to the Fretilin administration and the plight of the Timorese people, Indonesian propaganda, with its lies and distortions, drowned their efforts. Despite their efforts the small band of Timorese leaders failed to get their policies and aspirations across to the outside world. But the forces against them were not merely a paranoid group of Indonesian generals. The Timorese were unknowns, innocents, in a cynical world, in which the fortunes of the weak and unimportant mattered little. Fretilin leaders placed great store in the response from Australia where the media were the most outspoken and best informed on the question of East Timor. To some extent they were taken in, at least in the first month after the civil war, by favourable press reporting and by the many expressions of support and sympathy in Australia. Behind the scenes, however, there was ample evidence of Indonesia's persistent influence in political, religious, press, and academic circles. The reporting of right-wing publications like Santamaria's *Newsweekly* was predictable enough, but the Indonesian disinformation campaign had a much wider effect, especially among pragmatic foreign affairs commentators like Denis Warner. For example, on 5 September Warner commended both the Australian and Indonesian governments for having 'conducted themselves with admirable restraint and with a good deal of compassion'. This well-known Australian commentator went on to state: 'The Indonesians believe, whether rightly or wrongly, that some Chinese communists who fled from Indonesia in the bloodbath that followed the September 30 affair in 1965 have established themselves in Portuguese Timor as a springboard for new adventures in the archipelago'.[15] In retrospect, it was a guileless conclusion, based on a false story, but Warner was not the only one to believe it.

In the aftermath of the civil war, the Australian government was once again well-placed to make public an account of what was really happening in East Timor. It could have conveyed its assessment to Indonesia and other countries, and could have initiated moves towards a negotiated settlement which would have made the return of the Portuguese easier. From its own intelligence sources the Whitlam government must have been aware by mid-September that Fretilin had overwhelmed the UDT and that Indonesian military intervention had already begun. The amount of information available to the United States from intelligence agencies has been disclosed through leaked classified briefings[16] what is less well-known is that much of the 'sensitive source material' on which these detailed briefings were based actually came from Australian sources. In short, the Whitlam government, or at least those few ministers with access to this material, would have been well-informed about Indonesia's military preparations, and about the military operations carried out by special forces units across the border dividing Timor.

Thus, in late September when Indonesia was trying to maintain the fiction that the civil war was still raging, the Australian government could have exposed it as a lie. Not only did the Whitlam government not do this; as we have seen, official spokesmen went out of their way not to discredit the accounts from Jakarta which they knew to be fabrications. In a way the Whitlam government joined with Indonesia to prevent Fretilin from gaining international credibility. It all but dismissed the moderate and conciliatory stance assumed by the Fretilin leaders at their meeting in mid-September which contained the ingredients for a negotiated settlement.

Australia chose to support the tactics of Indonesia, calling for the kind of talks that in the circumstances would have been quite impossible to bring about. In so doing it became part of the conspiracy, not only against Fretilin, but against the vast majority of UDT followers, as well, the party, by the end of September, having almost ceased to exist, with most of its members virtual prisoners of the Indonesians. The 'petition' to President Suharto for integration was another farce. As Jose Martins later wrote, when the UDT remnants finally crossed the border into Indonesia, 'because of orders from Jakarta, no one crossed the border without having signed a petition addressed to the Indonesian President, calling for Timor's integration into Indonesia'.[17] Other UDT leaders later gave similar accounts to me.[18] In the circumstances how could Indonesia have allowed the UDT to participate in talks with Fretilin and the Portuguese?

Fretilin's statement of 16 September elicited no positive response from Indonesia. In an effort to clear the way for talks Xavier do Amaral went further. When asked by a journalist about the sortie into East Timor by the platoons of 315 Battalion, Xavier do Amaral suggested that the operation had been carried out without the knowledge of the responsible Indonesian military authorities. But the only response from Indonesia to this conciliatory interpretation was a fresh barrage of hostile propaganda, which soon made it clear to the Timorese leaders that Jakarta was anxious to avoid entering into any kind of negotiation with Fretilin. For a few weeks, however, there was still hope that Jakarta would eventually come to terms with the new situation; in the meantime talks with Portugal, mostly through Horta, were not going at all well. Fretilin's suspicious attitude towards Governor Lemos Pires had not changed with Dr Santos' presence in Darwin and Atauro. On 18 September the Central Committee indicated that it would prefer to bypass the special envoy and send a delegation to Lisbon to hold talks with the prime minister.

Life in Fretilin's Timor in those first few weeks was deceptively quiet. At the end of September John Edwards of the *National Times* wrote:

> It is impossible to resist the indolent charm of Timor...Dili is such a pleasant place that it is difficult to regard the Timorese revolution with proper gravity. Nothing ever happens on time; some incongruously absurd event...always spoils the solemnity of great occasions; the army is the least Prussian of military forces and its troops the most amiable.[19]

But this indolent charm was to be short-lived. At that very time grey clouds were already gathering on the western horizon.

At about the end of September President Suharto was finally persuaded by the Defence Minister General Panggabean, and Generals Yoga Sugama, Ali Murtopo and Benny Moerdani to agree to military intervention against East Timor. A certain amount of intervention had already taken place, perhaps without the knowledge of the Indonesian president. Events moved quickly in September and Indonesian anxieties about the situation in East Timor increased accordingly, but for reasons quite contrary to the press accounts being circulated in Jakarta. In the inner councils of government it was not the ongoing civil war that caused fears to mount, but that East Timor's war had come to an early end, and the detested Fretilin Party was now in de facto control. To make matters worse, members of the Australian press and other visitors were making their way to the territory in growing numbers, and thus *Operasi Komodo's* falsified presentation of the 'desperate' situation in the Portuguese colony and of the 'communist' character of Fretilin was being exposed. It was clear that, unless a challenge to the claim by Fretilin leaders that they were in de facto control of the territory was mounted quickly, international support for the left-wing front and with it a measure of international recognition, would soon follow. This would be a serious setback to the aims of *Operasi Komodo*, if it did not completely frustrate them. President Suharto's opposition to outright military intervention appears to have weakened during September.

In spite of the fact that Australian diplomats frequently asserted that their government was not really in a position to persuade the Indonesians not to intervene in East Timor yet other sources suggest the contrary. One of the most intriguing of these was a series of letters sent to Ken Fry between March and May 1977, the real authorship of which has never been determined. Although Mr Fry referred to these letters in Parliament, they did not attract much attention at the time. However, it is clear that the writer was very well and accurately informed about the Indonesian stand on Timor at that time. For one thing, the first of these letters was received almost two months before a document believed to have been written by Harry Tjan was brought to Australia and reported in the *National Times* (I understand the whole operation may have been organised by Tjan and Bakin in a move to put pressure on Andrew Peacock). The letters to Ken Fry also focused on the Foreign Minister, summarising some of the points raised in the Tjan record, to which they referred, in such a way as to tempt one to conclude that the two episodes were in some way linked. Could the author of the letters to Fry have seen the Tjan record? This would seem unlikely. According to a sensitively placed source who was in Jakarta at the time, there were only three copies of Harry Tjan's supposed record; one was kept in Tjan's own safe, another in the President's palace, and a third at Bakin headquarters. Also, the style and contents of the Fry letters suggest that the writer was an Australian official serving in the foreign affairs department or the defence department.

According to the second letter sent to Ken Fry, which was received on 24 March 1977,

> only one matter prevented President Suharto from intervening in Timor during all those months leading up to early October 1975. He was under enormous pressure from his generals and other advisers to move and settle the issue once and for all. What was this one card he had up his sleeve? It was the firm promise he had given to Mr Whitlam in Wonosobo and Townsville that Indonesia would never intervene using force in Timor. He quoted this ad nauseam to his advisers—to the point where rumours began to circulate that they were moving to force Suharto's hand! The Foreign Affairs files are *full of evidence* to this effect i.e. that it was the promise to Whitlam that prevented Indonesian intervention. If the truth does not come out now it will when future historians have access to the files! [my italics].[20]

From other evidence it is debatable how seriously President Suharto viewed his commitment to Whitlam. The latter's accommodating stand in August and September suggested that it did not present an insuperable obstacle to the interventionists. Mr Whitlam had intimated publicly that Portugal might be advised to turn to Indonesia for help to restore the situation in East Timor. Although the Indonesians were well aware that there was strong opposition within the Australian Labor Party to the prime minister's stand, they may have felt that, in the circumstances of the time, Mr Whitlam would have no difficulty in containing it. What mattered was that the government and Coalition leaders should be prepared to subordinate their qualms about the use of force in East Timor to an understanding of Indonesia's special interests. If either government or Opposition in Australia were to take issue with an Indonesian military intervention, an angry international reaction, which might do irreparable damage to Indonesia's standing in the world community, would be the likely result.

Perhaps it was such an appraisal that caused the political arm of *Operasi Komodo* to turn its attention to the then Shadow Minister for Foreign Affairs Andrew Peacock. As has been noted, late in September Harry Tjan and Liem Bian-Kie saw Peacock in Bali. Both the letters to Ken Fry and the leak to the *National Times* underlined the significance of this meeting to Suharto's decision to allow military intervention. Both suggest that Andrew Peacock had told the two Indonesians that the Coalition would engineer the withdrawal of Whitlam's commission in November, that it would not object if Indonesia used force to 'restore peace' in East Timor, and that the Liberals admired Suharto and would accord top priority to the relationship with Jakarta. According to the first of the letters to Fry, Tjan and Liem Bian-Kie's report to President Suharto (dated 26/27 September 1975) 'above all else—was instrumental in Soeharto's reluctant decision to use force in Timor, and to move when he did. Indonesian forces attacked Timor a few weeks after the Peacock meeting'. In the second of these letters, the writer sought to explain what had prompted President Suharto to hold back for so long. The answer, he wrote, was 'simple':

> Soeharto is basically a constitutional man. He wanted to proceed legally. His generals disagreed. It was only the promise he had given Mr Whitlam that kept the generals at bay. For the Generals, Peacock's amazing Bali performance was a heaven-sent opportunity. Soeharto had nothing to stand on from that point. A fortnight later the intervention began.

The third letter in the series continued along the same lines, describing Mr Peacock's role as 'the most important story'. The writer claimed that,

> before he went overseas in September 1975, Peacock told the then Indonesian ambassador, Her Tasning, that he was going to Bali and would welcome a meeting with some key officials involved in Timor. He told Her Tasning at the time (in Canberra) that the Liberal Party would support Indonesia—or rather not protest—if Indonesia intervened in Timor. Her Tasning, a General and member of BAKIN, as well as a former Ambassador to Australia, immediately alerted Yoga Sugama, Ali

Murtopo and Harry Tjan. This was the chance Indonesian intelligence had been waiting for. For months Suharto had turned down their pleas for direct Indonesian intervention in Timor. Then he was confronted with Tjan's record, which showed not only that the shadow Foreign Minister and his party would cause no problems for Indonesia if she decided to use force, but that Whitlam himself was on the way out. This was pressed home by the Generals, and Suharto had nothing to stand on. He agreed to a limited armed intervention in early October 1975...Peacock and Peacock alone was responsible for the timing of Indonesian intervention. It is also just possible that Suharto would have held his blood-thirsty Generals at bay indefinitely.

There is a contradictory quality about these letters. The timing of the decision certainly tallies with information from other sources. Only three days after the meeting with Peacock, Indonesian Defence Minister General Panggabean, made aggressive public statements about Fretilin: 'We will smash anyone at all who trespasses across Indonesia's borders', he was quoted by *Antara* as having remarked in Jakarta, in connection with a report that Fretilin mortar bombs had landed on the territory of Indonesian Timor.[21] This incident, which occurred in the final days of the civil war with the UDT, was no doubt deliberately exaggerated to provide a further pretext for an armed response from Indonesia. It was a much less serious act of provocation than sending special forces units in to East Timor some ten days earlier. It is true that about three days after the Peacock meeting at Bali a top-level meeting of officials of the defence and security and foreign affairs departments was held for more than three hours in Jakarta, and a detailed report was handed to the President. Later Panggabean announced that reinforcements would be sent to the Udayana Military Command, the military district covering the Nusatenggara islands (Lesser Sundas). As if to give some appearance of legislative endorsement to intervention, the Indonesian parliament, the Dewan Perwakilan Rakyat (DPR), met in plenary session on the following Saturday, issued a statement criticising Fretilin for its cruelties, and obligingly gave the DPR's full support to the Indonesian government's Timor policies and 'to further steps that are yet more concrete'.[22] It was against this background that the Indonesian leader finally agreed to military intervention, a limited military operation against Fretilin, an operation that was to be disguised as a UDT-Apodeti counterattack.

The letters to Ken Fry are, however, much less convincing on the subject of Andrew Peacock's role and influence on the course of events in Jakarta. Here there appears to be a skilful mixture of fact and fabrication, an art of which Harry Tjan had become a master. It is clear that Tjan added to his alleged record of conversation at a later date, in a move designed to embarrass Peacock, and to add fuel to the controversy of the Whitlam sacking, early in 1977 still a raw and divisive issue in Australian politics. The Indonesians were already aware of the sympathetic attitude of the Coalition leadership long before the UDT coup, reportedly from their talks with Mr Fraser. Their assessment would have been strengthened by the Coalition leadership's reaction to the civil war, when its statements were generally sympathetic to Indonesian interests. As for Peacock's role, it is impossible to believe that an experienced and shrewd politician like Andrew Peacock would have confided so indiscreetly his party's plans to remove Mr Whitlam from office to two Indonesians whom he knew not only to have links with Bakin, but also to have had close links with Australian embassy officials. Peacock has subsequently insisted to me that he simply did not have such confidences to pass on.

These intrigues show just how sensitive was Australia's position at the time, from Indonesia's point of view. A measure of Australian connivance was necessary if the limited or covert military intervention were not to be exposed. It is probable that the Indonesian intelligence agencies were under no illusions as to their neighbour's capacity to monitor their military operations, especially when these were to take place less than 800 kilometres from where they knew Australia to have an electronic monitoring station. As early as 1972, thanks to a revealing and, at the time, embarrassing, article in the US magazine *Ramparts*, Australian activities in this field had been a subject of some public knowledge.[23] Many senior Indonesian military officers, who had undergone extensive military training in the US, would have been well-aware of the vulnerability of their military communications to this kind of surveillance and may have gleaned that the Australian operation was a major source of the material used by CIA analysts to brief the US administration. The Australian authorities however, took good care not to expose the activities of *Operasi Komodo*.

Notes

1   Jill Jolliffe, *East Timor: Nationalism and Colonialism* (St Lucia: University of Queensland Press, 1978), p. 158.
2   Senator Gietzelt and Mr K. L. Fry, Report on visit to Portuguese East Timor, September 1975.
3   Jolliffe, *East Timor*, pp. 152-153.
4   Press statement of Revolutionary Front for an Independent East Timor (Fretilin), Dili,
    16 September 1975.
5   Jolliffe, *East Timor*, p. 155.
6   Dale van Atta and Brian Toohey, 'The Timor Papers', part 1, *National Times*, 30 May-5 June 1982.
7   Ibid.
8   Ibid.
9   Ibid.
10 Ibid.
11 AAP report, 11 September 1975.
12 Ibid., 15 September 1975.
13 *Sinar Harapan*, 22 September 1975.
14 Van Atta and Toohey, 'The Timor Papers', part 1.
15 Melbourne *Herald*, 5 August 1975.

16 Van Atta and Toohey, 'The Timor Papers'.
17 Jose Martins, Affidavit submitted to the UN Secretary-General, March 1976.
18 During interviews in Portugal, January and March 1977.
19 John Edwards, *National Times*, September 1975.
20 This and the following extracts are taken from copies of this correspondence, by courtesy of Mr Ken Fry, MP.
21 *Antara*, Jakarta, 27 September 1975.
22 *Berita Yudha*, 29 September 1975.
23 'US Electronic Espionage: A Memoir', *Ramparts*, 11, no. 2 (1972).

Chapter Ten
Indonesian military intervention begins

In spite of the earlier covert operations, Indonesia's first action in the military assault on Fretilin-controlled East Timor, designated '*Operasi Flamboyan*', did not occur until 7 October. Then Sandi Yudha (Indonesian commandos) troops moved in to dislodge Fretilin from the border village of Batugade, which had been in UDT hands until late September. The immediate aim of the attack was transparent—to keep up the fiction that the civil war was continuing to rage, in an effort to undermine Fretilin's claim to be in de facto control of all of East Timor, and thus to head off the risk of the independence movement gaining international recognition. The Batugade operation was small, probably involving no more than 300 Sandi Yudha, but it was only the first action in a wider front involving some 3200 troops under the command of Colonel Dading Kalbuadi. This force included some East Timorese elements, most of them troops that had been secretly undergoing training at a special camp near the border since the end of 1974. This secret training program was an early initiative under *Operasi Komodo*, and was code-named 'Partisan'[1]. (These Timorese accompanied the Tentara Nasional Indonesia (TNI), Indonesian National Army troops, but were not at first permitted to engage in combat). The force was supported by a limited amount of naval gunfire from warships standing off the coast. It was backed up by support elements at Atambua, including a sizeable intelligence group, which also monitored Fretilin's communications. At first Fretilin claimed that the Indonesians had used jet aircraft, but the air support turned out to be limited to a World War II B-26 bomber, a lumbering DC-3 aircraft used as a gunship, and a Pertamina helicopter which was apparently used for artillery spotting. The Batugade attack was a minor assault when compared with what was to follow, but for the Timorese it marked their first major clash with Indonesian troops, and their first experience of artillery bombardment.

The Batugade operation was widely reported in the Australian media, but officials in Canberra refused to admit to inquiring journalists that Indonesian troops were involved. In fact, they were well aware of the character of this operation. The CIA *Weekly Review*, which would have based its assessment on information shared with Australian intelligence authorities, on 10 October reported the attack in some detail:

> Late last week after several border clashes, Indonesian troops launched an attack against Fretilin positions close to the border. On October 7, a force of 100 special forces troops and Indonesian supporters retook Batugade, forcing Fretilin defenders to withdraw toward Balibo. The troops for this attack may have come from an amphibious task force which ferried some 400 marines and other troops and vehicles to Atapupu on 2 October; two companies of the marines were moved immediately to reinforce positions near the border. According to a clandestine source, Malaysia provided Indonesia in early October with a small quantity of arms and ammunition that cannot be traced to any foreign military assistance given to Indonesia.*

Meanwhile, in Jakarta, official Indonesian sources vigorously denied that Indonesian troops were involved, the armed forces newspaper *Angkatan Bersendjata* reporting that 'UDT forces' had recaptured their 'stronghold' of Batugade. On 8 October a defence ministry spokesman declared that stories about Indonesian military involvement were simply 'untrue'. A Colonel Hudiono told journalists: 'The report is not true. Until now the Indonesian Government has not issued any order for an invasion of Portuguese Timor.' Yet the newspaper *Kompas* did report that Indonesian troops had killed seven Fretilin soldiers and had captured eleven in a clash at the border. A few days later Foreign Minister Malik not only vehemently denied that his troops were involved in the border fighting; but he went on to declare that Indonesia would never be provoked into retaliating. It does seem that Adam Malik, who had not been taken into the confidence of the generals behind *Operasi Komodo*, knew little about the covert operations that had been launched from Indonesian Timor. Apparently he had not been present at any of the talks between the president, Murtopo, Moerdani and Yoga Sugama. Thus, a statement he made on 13 October was substantially at variance with the actual direction of events at that time. He told journalists in Jakarta: 'We had never asked the East Timorese to join Indonesia, neither we have any objection to their formation of an independent nation.' At that very time Indonesian forces had already established a foothold at Batugade, and Kopassandha troops (subsequently named Kopassus) were moving into position at the border for the first large-scale assault against Fretilin.

The Batugade attack had a shock effect on Fretilin. Only two days earlier, on 5 October, the leaders had agreed to send a delegation to Portugal for talks with the National Decolonisation Commission. The Indonesian attack served as a grim warning that a threat to Fretilin's very survival was taking shape. Inevitably the war soon took priority over moves to set up negotiations with Portugal. Reinforcements

---

* According to information obtained from Tomas Goncalves, a Timorese who was to be appointed this military group's first commander.

were rushed to the border area, and a few days after the Indonesian attack Fretilin troops made an unsuccessful attempt to retake Batugade and to force the intruders back into West Timor. The Timorese then concentrated on preparing themselves for further attacks, and on seeking to alert the outside world that East Timor was the victim of a blatant act of aggression by Indonesia.

Murder at Balibo

Adam Malik may well have been ignorant of the military operations that were about to be launched against Fretilin, but the same cannot be said of State Department and defence officials in the US government in far-away Washington. A CIA brief on 11 October makes it clear that the US government, and presumably the Australian government as well, had several days warning that the Indonesians were about to launch a major assault against East Timor. The brief reported that the Indonesian president had approved a 'plan of action that will increase military pressure on Fretilin forces operating near the border'. This plan involved setting up enclaves inside East Timor. The brief then predicted the attack that was, among other things, to take the lives of five Australian newsmen at the town of Balibo. It reported:

> The first of the enclaves is to be established on October 14 when Indonesian units are to attack the town of Maliana. The troops participating in the operation will wear uniforms without insignia and are to carry older, Soviet-made weapons so as not to be identified as Indonesian regulars.[2]

The US intelligence analysts were out by two days in their prediction of the timing of the Indonesian attack, but their assessment was otherwise fairly accurate. Although the town of Balibo has usually been linked with the attack on 16 October, the main objective was the more important regional centre of Maliana. Balibo was to become the focus of world attention because of the killing of five foreign newsmen; however, the town was only one objective in a much wider operation.

The mid-October assault against Fretilin came as no surprise to the Timorese military leaders, who had been anticipating further Indonesian military action after an assault on the border post of Batugade on 7 October. It aroused great agitation and concern. On the evening of 16 October a group of Australians in Dili, including me, then leader of the ACFOA team, was urgently requested to go to the central communications office, known as the Marconi Centre; there Vice-President Nicolau Lobato told us that a 'massive attack' had been launched by Indonesian troops on a wide front, extending from Lebos to Balibo. The Balibo post had been under naval and artillery bombardment and, at that time, Lobato could tell us nothing about the fate of the five Australia-based and three Portuguese newsmen who were known to be in the vicinity of the village. The Portuguese party pulled out of Balibo on the eve of the attack after having failed to persuade the Australian teams to withdraw with them. The Portuguese turned up in Dili some days later, after a harrowing trek across mountainous terrain.

The attack of 16 October was hardly a 'massive' assault when compared with, for example, major battles in the Vietnam War, but from the Timorese point of view it was a spectacular and frightening operation. From the middle of September onwards hundreds of troops, many of them from crack regiments, had been moved into West Timor, mostly through the small port of Atapupu. Overall command of this military phase of *Operasi Komodo* was the ultimate responsibility of Major-General Moerdani who had long been agitating for a military solution to the Timor problem. Moerdani, a graduate of a US military training college, was one of the generals closest to President Suharto. A paratroop commando (RPKAD) officer, he was not without experience in operations similar to the one that was to be launched against East Timor. He had commanded a small paratroop unit which was dropped behind Dutch lines in West New Guinea in 1961 when *Operasi Tjendrawasih* was being mounted against Netherlands forces. General Moerdani also played a major part in the military confrontation of Malaysia in the early 1960s. By August 1975 he was Indonesia's leaking hawk, at one stage reportedly causing Suharto to remark: 'If you listen to Benny you'll be in a war every day.'[3] In the early stage of the Timor campaign, Moerdani was assisted by Brigadier-General Pranoto, the commander of the Udayana military regional command (Kodam), Colonel Sugiyanto (who dealt with the Timorese UDT and Apodeti leaders), and four other colonels—Sinaga, from the intelligence staff, Kasenda from the navy, Agus Hernoto, and not least Dading Kalbuadi, who was the field commander of the October assault on Maliana and Balibo. On the eve of the attack, Moerdani had at his disposal some 3500 troops in the border area, 2000 of whom were used by Dading Kalbuadi, and a handful of aircraft and helicopters.

This time, however, the Indonesians dispensed with the UDT elements that had gone into Batugade with them a week earlier. The UDT contingent, with the exception of a handful of members whom the Indonesians trusted, was ordered back into West Timor where they were unceremoniously consigned to a refugee camp. One apparent reason for this action was that some of the UDT leaders, including João Carrascalão, had begun to complain about the savagery of the Indonesian operation, and about the wanton killing of Timorese civilians. But it must have already been clear to the Indonesians that few of the Timorese in the so-called 'Anti-Communist Movement', which had been set up to provide a clear ideological opposition to Fretilin, had any real enthusiasm for integration.

From now the key Timorese leaders in the pro-Indonesian camp were Lopes da Cruz, who handled political matters, Tomas Goncalves, who acquired the title of military commander, Mario Carrascalão (João's brother) and Jose Martins who, until his defection early in 1976, dealt with public relations. It is also interesting to note that, from this time onwards, Indonesian propaganda began to refer to four, not just two, pro-integration parties, elevating Kota and Trabalhista to the status of major political movements. This change in presentation was obviously designed to give the anti-Fretilin parties a kind of numerical advantage. Kota and Trabalhista, like Apodeti, were tiny factions, without any real popular support. The three parties together would have had some difficulty in mustering the support of as much as five per cent of the politically conscious component of the population. For this reason Kota and Trabalhista had not been accorded official recognition by the Portuguese.

Few Timorese participated in the Maliana operation, and those who did were confined to non-combatant, subordinate roles. These were products of the Partisan training operation, most of them coming from the Atsabe district to the military training centre in West Timor earlier in the year, months before UDT's coup. Contrary to the accounts that emanated from Jakarta, depicting the operation as a UDT–Apodeti–Kota–Trabalhista counterattack against Fretilin, the few Timorese involved in it had left the colony for Indonesia as long as six months before the civil war broke out.

In the operation the Indonesian troops were accompanied by some French Panhard armoured vehicles and a few Russian light tanks. In the attack on Balibo their main support was light artillery and rocket fire, and covering bombardment from a frigate, possibly *Monginsidi*. Despite this support, in other sectors the Indonesians soon found the going difficult, especially in the south where the terrain favoured the defenders and where the troops did not have the luxury of covering fire from the navy. Also, the Falintil soon demonstrated its skill as a guerrilla army in the rugged terrain. At Lebos to the south and near Bobonaro Fretilin troops held the Indonesian advance. In one of these engagements the Timorese counterattacked so vigorously that an Indonesian company fled in disorder, leaving much of its weaponry behind. Although Maliana quickly fell to the Indonesians, later Fretilin counterattacks almost forced the invaders to abandon the town. The stiff Timorese resistance was the subject of comments by the CIA in its briefs to the US government, indicating that, from the very outset, Washington was well aware that Jakarta's military moves to bring about integration were going to be bitterly contested. Thus, on 18 October, only two days after the attack on Balibo, a US intelligence bulletin noted that Indonesian forces had become 'bogged down in some areas after three days of fighting'. Fretilin forces, it reported, were 'putting up stiff resistance in places...One Indonesian unit is apparently surrounded and taking casualties.' Two days later another intelligence bulletin reported that, although there had been some gains, the Indonesian drive into East Timor had 'stalled because of Jakarta's failure to secure the border town of Lebos'. On 24 October, more than a week after the assault began, the situation was no better, according to the CIA:

> The Indonesian military operation launched last week in Portuguese Timor has bogged down. Field commanders apparently under-estimated their logistic problems and the strength of Fretilin forces operating near the border.

Fretilin counterattacks, it was noted, had forced some Indonesian units to 'withdraw to their side of the border.[4]

Although it was the attack on Balibo that created a potentially serious problem for Indonesia, especially in its relations with Australia, that particular sector of the front was only lightly defended and briefly contested by Timorese troops. Also, it was the sector most exposed to naval and artillery bombardment, and the Fretilin military commanders quickly resolved not to attempt to hold what they considered an almost indefensible position. But, because of its significance as one of the most controversial events of the Timor affair, a closer look at just what happened at Balibo follows.

The Indonesian assault in that sector involved about 300 troops, under the command of Major Yunus Yosfiah, who had been a senior member of the Partisan training group.[5] The attack began at about 4.00 a.m., and at near 7.00 a.m. the force entered the village square. The Fretilin opposition consisted of about 40 troops equipped with one machine-gun and small arms. Outnumbered and outgunned, they withdraw as the invading troops entered the village, firing as they retreated. Left in Balibo were the five newsmen who had decided to remain in the village, apparently confident that their non-combatant status would be respected by the other party to the conflict. No doubt they realised that they were taking risks, but Indonesia was, after all, Australia's nearest neighbour, and a great deal had been said in the previous two years about the 'close and friendly relations' that had developed between the two countries. The confidence of these newsmen was not, however, shared by their Fretilin escorts, nor by the Portuguese television crew, both of whom had tried to persuade them to withdraw on the previous day. To allay the fears of Fretilin the newsmen prepared and signed a statement releasing the Fretilin officials from any responsibility for the consequences of their decision to remain and witness the action. And it was certainly action they got: probably within an hour of the entry into Balibo of the Indonesian special forces troops, all five were dead, the circumstances of their deaths creating one of the most controversial and episodes in the entire Timor tragedy.

The group have been commonly referred to as the 'Australian newsmen', but this description is only partly correct—only two members were Australian citizens. These were Greg Shackleton, 29, a television reporter from HSV7 in Melbourne, and Tony Stewart, about 21, a sound recordist from HSV7. The other members of the group were Malcolm Rennie, 28, a British citizen who had been working as a reporter with the Nine Network in Sydney; Brian Peters, 29, also British, who was the cameraman accompanying Rennie; and Gary Cunningham, 27, a New Zealander and the cameraman with Shackleton. The party was not one, but two, television teams from rival networks, sent separately to East Timor within a few days of the reported attack on Batugade with the purpose of establishing proof of whether Indonesian forces were involved in the fighting against Fretilin.*

Behind the decision to send the Channel Nine team was one of Australia's leading current-affairs personalities on television, Gerald Stone, the channel's

---

*For a detailed background of the newsmen, and the circumstance surrounding their murder, see Jill Jolliffe, *Cover-up: The inside story of the Balibo Five* (Scribe Publications, Melbourne, 2001)

news director who had led a television crew to the territory late in August, and had maintained a close interest in developments. In the case of the HSV7 team, the initiative appears to have come from Shackleton, reportedly looking for a break from the monotony of routine reporting in Melbourne. Shackleton, Cunningham and Stewart arrived on 10 October, and the others two days later. Both teams spent little time in the capital before heading for the border, and most of the intervening days were spent in the Maliana–Balibo area where they took some film and conducted a number of interviews.

The Indonesian military assault could not have been a surprise to these crews. There was an expectation that an attack was imminent and, from the battlements of the old fort at Balibo, which offer a commanding view of the coastal stretches on both sides of the border, they had been able to observe the bustle of Indonesian naval activities in the waters nearby. Perhaps a kind of naive spirit of high adventure prevailed among the group, but Shackleton's last recorded interviews indicate that there was also a strong sense of commitment to the task of bringing out the truth about the war in Timor. When the newsmen chose to remain behind, they must have expected to be captured, or at least detained by the Indonesians, and to end up behind Indonesian lines. But, given the good relations between Canberra and Jakarta, they no doubt felt assured of an early release.

Since it took place, this tragic affair has been the subject of many articles, three official reports, and two books of substance. The most disappointing of these was a report by three Australian diplomats (tabled in the parliament in 1976) which shed more light on official attitudes of the time than on the affair. Recently released documents have also shed some official light on the subject, but there are some missing pieces to the puzzle. The documents did not include some very sensitive material from communications intelligence agencies. This 'codeword' material contains the communications between the TNI units at the border and their headquarters in Bali and Jakarta. However, from my research and from the more detailed works of Jolliffe, and McDonald and Ball, the pattern of events leading up to the killing of the newsmen and even the killing itself, is quite clear.

The military assault on the village was an entirely Indonesian military operation in that the commanders and the combatants were Indonesian. A few Timorese, mostly products of the Partisan training operation, were taken along, but they occupied a support role, which is discussed in considerable detail in the work by McDonald and Ball. The dominant Indonesian role is made very clear in the US intelligence agency assessments of the time that were brought to my attention. It can be assumed that these assessments were also available to the Australian government, indicating that the government was not telling the truth when it expressed doubts about who was responsible for the attack. On 31 October the CIA described the operation thus:

> Some 2000 Indonesian regular infantry troops, special forces, marines, and Timorese partisans, launched coordinated attacks along the border and captured at least six border towns in Portuguese Timor on October 16.[6]

The 'Timorese partisans' amounted to about 200 men of the Partisan group.

The troops that entered Balibo appear to have been a mixture of Kopassandha (later Kopassus) and KKO (naval commandos), with some troops from the Brawidjaja Division. Hamish McDonald has suggested that the force was entirely Kopassandha, but several Timorese who were in the village on that day spoke of the presence of the KKO. In October 1995 Dading Kalbuadi (then retired, now deceased), confirmed the details of the attack, and boasted how he had outwitted the defending Timorese by attacking from the east and not from the west.[7] The Fretilin garrison, anxious not to be surrounded and cut off from the main body of Timorese forces, hurriedly withdrew, and the Indonesian soldiers streamed into the village.

The newsmen apparently took painstaking steps to advertise their non-combatant and Australian identities to the advance guard of the attacking forces. Greg Shackleton had painted a large 'Australia' sign on the wall of the house where they were staying, and beneath it he sketched a rough, but identifiable, drawing of an Australian flag. As several witnesses have attested, the newsmen also took care to be dressed in unmistakably non-military clothing, and did not possess any arms. The last Fretilin soldier to withdraw from the village (whose interview I attended in Dili in late October 1975) claimed that the newsmen had moved out into the open and that there was some filming when the attack began. The soldier, an orderly named Guido dos Santos, stated that the newsmen had then moved back towards their house and pointed to the signs on the wall, in an obvious attempt to draw the Indonesian soldiers' attention to their identity.

They did not get their message across. According to this Timorese source, the attackers fired in the direction of the newsmen and he saw one of them fall, apparently after having been hit. The other newsmen then began shouting 'Australians!' and feverishly pointed to the signs on the wall. Dos Santos then withdrew. As he ran he claimed that he could still hear the shouting, but then there was some more firing, and the shouting stopped. About ten days later Roger East, another Australian journalist who was later to meet a similar fate after the invasion of Dili, interviewed some other Fretilin soldiers, who claimed that they had watched the Australians while retreating from Balibo. This version is not so different from that of dos Santos, but it is rather more detailed. One of these soldiers, Lucas Jeronimo, told East:

> The Australians ran toward their house about 200 metres away. One kept stopping, looking back and pointing his camera. He was a big man...The Indonesians kept firing. The man with the bald head [Peters] was still filming, then he cried out and fell down. The other Australians were screaming 'Australians, Australians!' with their hands up. The soldiers circled them and made them turn their backs and face the wall of the house. The firing died down and we crawled away through the undergrowth. We heard the Australians screaming and then there was a burst of automatic fire.[8]

It is now beyond doubt that all five of the newsmen were killed, probably within an hour, not by 'UDT–Apodeti forces', as Indonesian officials have consistently tried to make Australians believe, but by regular troops of the Indonesian armed forces. According to the account of Tomas Goncalves, who led the Timorese component, Major Yunus Yosfiah ordered the virtual execution of the newsmen, and participated in the shooting.

The events of that morning are still the subject of some debate, but there is a consensus on certain points. When the attack began the journalists came out into the open, presumably hoping to establish their non-combatant identities. However, one was hit in early firing. When this firing began another member of the group may have tried to make a run for it, but he was shot before he got very far. The troops then closed in on the remaining newsmen who, by shouting 'Australians' and pointing to the markings on the wall, made a desperate bid to save their lives. One of them appears to have been struck with a knife—perhaps this caused the screaming that the Fretilin soldiers claimed to have heard during their retreat from the village. The surviving members of the party were shot after their capture, perhaps within half an hour, and four of the bodies, presumably excluding the body of the journalist who had tried to run away, were taken into the house. It appears that one of the group was still alive. A Timorese who was present later stated that the newsman was badly wounded, but that he was wearing headphones and had something like a radio strapped on his back. He said that the newsman 'appeared to be almost dead—near unconscious' and was talking into the radio. It could have been Tony Stewart, the soundman, vainly attempting to record something about that terrible incident. According to this source a Timorese moved towards the wounded man, but was ordered back by an Indonesian Marine lieutenant, who then shot the newsman.

The killing of the journalists was reported by radio to operational headquarters at Batugade, thence to Kodam headquarters at Denpasar, and to Jakarta, probably to Moerdani, who may have ordered the executions. Colonel Dading Kalbuadi and Louis Taolin then at once flew to Balibo by helicopter. Their visit was followed by a bizarre sequel to this wanton killing. Two or three of the bodies were taken out of the house, dressed in Portuguese uniforms, of the kind used by Fretilin, which had been discovered among the stores in the local barracks, and then the corpses were propped up behind some captured machine-guns in front of the 'Australia' sign. An Indonesian soldier then proceeded to photograph the scene. Accounts of this macabre incident came from a number of sources, and there can be no doubt of its veracity. One Timorese had been ordered to help remove the bodies, and he noticed that, although the corpses had severe wounds, the uniforms in which they were clad were unmarked. Another, who had served in the Portuguese army, had been ordered by the Indonesians to put into working order the weapons that had been placed in front of the bodies, a task he was unable to fulfil. A former senior UDT leader also related this incident to me. He said that although he had not been there at the time, an Indonesian Bakin officer had later shown him the photographs of the journalists seated behind the machine-guns which were intended to be used to show that the newsmen had been combatants for the cause of Fretilin.

For reasons that are not clear, the Indonesians did not go ahead with this sordid act of disinformation. Perhaps it was because the weapons could not be put in working order, or maybe the scheme was rejected at a higher level. Yet there are some grounds for believing that it was more than the whim of a junior intelligence officer. For one thing, the hoax was set up shortly after Colonel Dading Kalbuadi had arrived at the scene, suggesting that the order to arrange the deception may have come from him, or was at least approved by him.

In Balibo, later in the day the bodies were taken to another house where, together with some other bodies, they were burnt after having been immersed in petrol. This provided the setting for a story that was to emerge from sources in Jakarta, that the newsmen had been killed in a rocket attack by the UDT–Apodeti forces. But before the bodies were incinerated some of their possessions were looted. Not all of the looting was carried out by the Indonesians. João Tavares*, a colleague of Tomas Goncalves who in 1999 became the chief militia commander was reported by a witness to have 'souvenired' a watch from one of the dead newsmen and a camera from another.

There is now evidence that the Indonesians knew the journalists were in the area. According to the account by Hamish McDonald, there were two Timorese radio operators in Colonel Hernoto's communications centre, for the specific purpose of monitoring Fretilin broadcasts.[9] The Indonesians were aware that there were a number of foreigners, including journalists and aid workers, in East Timor. Only a week or so before the Balibo attack ABC, Reuters, and other journalists had visited the border area and their extensive reporting on the situation would not have escaped the attention of Murtopo and Moerdani in Jakarta. In the circumstances, it is virtually impossible to avoid the conclusion that these newsmen were not the victims of an accident or misunderstanding. Hamish McDonald later wrote that, although Indonesian special forces troops involved in the operation denied any prior knowledge of the presence of the television crews at Balibo, they did admit that 'the attacking force was under explicit orders to kill all witnesses to their covert intrusion into foreign territory'.[10] To put it simply, the killing at Balibo, of at least three of the men, was nothing less than an act of murder.

The reaction of the Australian government and its diplomats to the wanton killing of five members of the nation's press corps was consistent with other aspects of its dismal record about the rape of East Timor. What is particularly disturbing is that the Whitlam government must have known about the impending attack some days before it took place. I was warned about it by a sensitively placed senior official before he left for Timor with the ACFOA team on 13 October. Five days earlier, US intelligence analysts, using information to which Australia also had access, advised their government that the attack would

---

* Tavares was subsequently appointed *bupati*, or senior district officer, of the Balibo regency.

be launched in a few days. Hamish McDonald wrote:

> According to sources in Jakarta interviewed by this writer, the Australian Embassy
> was told of plans to attack Balibo two or three days before they were carried out.
> Almost certainly this information would have been passed on to Canberra.[11] Thus,
> the government had at its disposal enough information—and enough time—to warn
> Australians in East Timor of the impending risks at the border. More importantly,
> they could have advised the Indonesians of the presence of journalists in the area,
> and stressed that they should be afforded protection as non-combatants.

Perhaps it would have been difficult to convey such a warning to the newsmen.
The crews were probably already on their way to Timor when the government
became aware of Indonesian plans to attack Maliana and Balibo. But Australian
authorities already knew about the Indonesian operation against Batugade, and
they must surely have concluded that further military operations were to come.
Some officials later claimed that they knew nothing of the newsmen's plans
to visit the border area. It is hard to believe such a claim: their arrival in East
Timor was common knowledge to a number of Australian officials, and it should
have been assumed that they would proceed to the border. The main reason for
sending the television crews was to establish whether the Indonesian military
were involved in the fighting at the border, as Fretilin officials had alleged.
Perhaps government officials knew too little about the situation on the ground in
East Timor itself. It was my distinct impression at the time that some of the key
officials in the relevant policy areas of the foreign affairs department felt that
the less they knew about what was happening in the colony, the easier it was for
them to cope with the contradictory aspects of Mr Whitlam's Timor policy.

Some officials later argued that the news teams should not have ventured into
such a dangerous situation. It was also alleged that the newsmen had rushed off
to East Timor without first seeking a brief from the foreign affairs department,
and informing Australian authorities of what they were planning to do. There is
an element of hypocrisy about such criticisms, which come mostly from official
sources. The Whitlam government's devious handling of the Timor problem, the
contradictory reports coming from Jakarta and the territory, and the reported
dangers being faced not just by a small neighbour, but by a people who had
rallied to Australia's cause during World War II, surely presented the media
of this country with an obligation to expose the truth of the situation to the
Australian public. The Timorese had been appealing to Australia for help
for some time; there was widespread public disquiet at what seemed to be
happening in the Portuguese colony, and conjecture on whether the government
was really facing up to its responsibilities in its handling of the crisis.

Perhaps the news teams should have sought a briefing from government
sources, but this begs the question: just what kind of a briefing would they
have been given at that time? It is hard to believe that they would have been
provided with a frank background assessment. If officials had frankly briefed
the newsmen, the frailty of the Whitlam government's Timor policy would

almost certainly have been compromised. Also, Gerald Stone and others feared, from their earlier experiences, that the government would have merely tried to persuade them not to go. To have consulted officials beforehand would have meant providing the latter with an opportunity to obstruct the venture.

Did the Australian embassy in Jakarta seek assurances from the Indonesian military that aid workers and journalists would be accorded protection appropriate to their status? There is little evidence of this. Notwithstanding the public fiction of the 'civil war' in Timor, frank informal exchanges were going on in Jakarta at that time between Australian embassy officials and Harry Tjan and the military. Apparently the foreign affairs department did make an effort to pass on a warning to journalists in Dili, although it came rather late. According to Jill Jolliffe:

> On the Thursday on which the journalists perished, the head of AAP's Darwin bureau telephoned the Dili correspondent with the information that Foreign Affairs had warned that "something big" was to happen in East Timor that day and that the Dili correspondent should be alerted.[12]

As Jolliffe pointed out, the 'something big' had already happened that very morning, and the newsmen had been dead for some four hours.

Although the official reaction in Australia to reports that the newsmen were missing and may have been killed was slow and extremely cautious, it has been credibly reported that within fewer than 24 hours the government knew that the crews had been killed in an Indonesian military operation. This information came from one of Australia's most closely guarded intelligence operations, the Defence Signals Division (DSD). The role of DSD in this incident has been analysed by Richard Hall, Desmond Ball, and Hamish McDonald.[13] McDonald later wrote:

> After monitoring the battle for Balibo as it happened—through a mass of signals that detailed the movements of small units, ships and aircraft—the Shoal Bay DSD station sent recorded data immediately to DSD headquarters in Melbourne, almost next door to the HSV7 studios in St Kilda Road. That afternoon the analysed material went to the Defence Department's Joint Intelligence Organisation in Canberra. Early in the evening a senior Defence Department official took a report over to Parliament House to Defence Minister Bill Morrison. This was only 12 hours after the attack.

Morrison circulated the report to Prime Minister Gough Whitlam and Foreign Minister Don Willesee. But none of the Australian Labor Party ministers were in a mood to look closely at it. That day Coalition Leader Malcolm Fraser had announced that, because of the loans affair, the Opposition would block Supply in the Senate. Perhaps helped by the general crisis, the permanent head of the defence department, Sir Arthur Tange, argued successfully to Morrison against revealing what had been learnt about Balibo.[14]

As McDonald went on to point out, the reasoning behind this decision appears to have been that the use of this information would 'reveal to the Indonesians the level of signals that could be intercepted and invite them to take counter-measures'.[15] The government—or at least those members of it with access to the highly sensitive code word material—seems to have made the extraordinary decision to banish from their minds any knowledge of the intercepted material. In effect this meant that its later approach to the problem of the 'missing' newsmen was utterly contradictory. It continued to be sceptical and questioning towards allegations which it knew to be absolutely true. No amount of corroborative evidence could bring the government officials and ministers to acknowledge publicly that the newsmen had been killed in a largely Indonesian military operation.

The decision to ignore the DSD material to not risk compromising the source of the information is not without precedent. Similar decisions were made during World War II to conceal that important German codes had been broken. In the case of the Balibo tragedy, the implications of the decision were somewhat wider, and the reasoning perhaps naive. That these encoded messages were vulnerable to modern cryptoanalysis methods, with which Australians were familiar, would have come as no surprise to Indonesian communications experts. That the Whitlam government did not use this information would have given the generals in Jakarta considerable encouragement. That the Australian government was not going to be provoked, even by the killing of five of its newsmen, must have seemed incomprehensible to the Indonesians, and in Jakarta it would have been interpreted as a clear indication that the green light for integration by armed force was still on.*

But the few government ministers, possibly only two, and a handful of foreign affairs and defence analysts were not the only persons to discover that the Indonesians had killed the journalists. John Kerin, at the time secretary of the Australian Labor Party's Caucus foreign affairs and defence committee and a critic of Whitlam's Timor policy, was telephoned by an anonymous caller— presumably a troubled intelligence operative—and provided with some details of the killing at Balibo on 17 October. On the same day a similar contact was made with a Channel Nine executive who had been sent to Darwin. According to McDonald, John Foell was called to the Travelodge lobby and told by a nervous stranger that the newsmen had been 'machine-gunned and their bodies burnt'.[16] It was a case, it seemed, of the troubled consciences of a few intelligence officials outweighing the force of their security pledges.

The official Australian response to the killing of the television crews fell not far short of total inaction. In their attitudes to the incident most officials were defensive, and some were even inclined to blame the journalists for having gone to Balibo in the first place. Implicit in this view was the notion that Australians should have stayed away from Timor and let the Indonesians resolve the problem in their own way, letting 'events take their course'. Those who did not comply with this rule of good sense and discretion could not blame the authorities in Australia, and nor could they expect any quarter from the

---

*See Jolliffe, op.cit. and Desmond Ball and Hamish McDonald, *Death in Balibo; Lies in Canberra* (Allen & Unwin, Sydney 2000)

Indonesians, whose disregard of fundamental international rules of behaviour needed to be judged against Jakarta's fears that the nation's legitimate security interests were under threat.

The lack of concern for what was happening to the Timorese was by no means confined to the Prime Minister and his ambassador in Jakarta. Many of the foreign affairs officials involved in the day-to-day conduct of the Timor policy seemed untroubled by the moral implications of the mounting crisis. Indeed, Australian Labor Party parliamentarians like John Kerin referred to officials such as the head of the South-East Asia Division and the head of the branch dealing with Indonesia—and Timor—as a kind of 'Indonesia Lobby'. Some of the reasons behind such attitudes have already been discussed. But they are also rooted to a large extent in the professional moulding of an Australian diplomat. In that socially incestuous élite community, diplomats soon learn that their loyalties and responsibilities are in the first instance to their peers and those above them. Such career perceptions tend also to shape the way they view Australia's role in the world. The most important countries in the focus of foreign policy makers then, are the major powers and those that rival Australia in size, economic strength, or military power. The important countries are the measure of progress in a diplomat's career. For example, postings to Tokyo, Jakarta, New York, London or Paris indicate that the career diplomat is doing well in the struggle to get to the top, while appointments in Colombo, Cyprus or Nauru may suggest that the diplomat is slipping behind, or is even being passed over, in this form of power game, within the wider power play that characterises much of the management, or manipulation, of international relations.

Inevitably when the Timor crisis began to unfold, the officials involved seemed to have great difficulty in comprehending the situation in the Portuguese colony, to which few of them had ever ventured, and in taking the Timorese seriously. Thus, a kind of consensus of sceptical disinterest and detachment prevailed among those actors who shaped Australia's policy on the question. The underlying prejudices enabled the officials concerned, without qualms, to embark on a policy of systematic deception of the Australian public and, to some extent, of the Parliament. Whatever the constraints on the use of intelligence gained from monitoring Indonesia's communications networks, there was sufficient collateral evidence for the government and its officials to come clean about Indonesian subversive activities, about the attack on Balibo, and the truth about the killing of the journalists. Yet, as we shall see, official spokesmen consistently chose to cast doubt on new evidence of Indonesian involvement, although they must have judged it to be accurate, in a vain attempt to protect a 'special' relationship with Jakarta, a relationship already devoid of mutual respect, and of any special attributes.

Australian government officials went through the motions of investigating the deaths of the newsmen, but their investigations were usually marked by frustrations and superficiality, and the results merely cast further doubts on the government's credibility. A Third Secretary of the Australian embassy in Jakarta, Richard Johnson, arrived in Kupang six days after the killing and, although he was to spend almost three weeks in Indonesian Timor, not once was he able to venture near the frontier, let alone to Balibo. The frustration of the young diplomat's mission was said to have been in retaliation for the anti-Indonesian demonstrations that had occurred in Australia in the wake of the Balibo attack. Meanwhile, the pro-integration UDT leader, Lopes da Cruz, was reported in the Jakarta daily *Kompas*, on 17 October, as having claimed to have discovered the bodies of four Europeans at Balibo near a sign marked 'Australia', a report he was later to deny. A week later in Kupang Mr Johnson received some letters from the anti-Fretilin parties. One of these documents was a statement signed by Lopes da Cruz, Guilherme Goncalves and Jose Martins—respectively the leaders of the UDT, Apodeti and Kota—which declared that when the forces of UDT and Apodeti had attacked Balibo heavy fire had been directed at a house from which 'a counter-attack had been launched', and when the forces arrived at the scene fifteen bodies were found there, 'among them some white people'. These could be the journalists, the letter said. This account, which was all but dictated to the Timorese who signed the statement, formed part of the official version of the attack.[17] That is, no Indonesians were involved and the assault was led by Tomas Goncalves (Guilherme's son), João Tavares and Andreas da Costa. The next major development was on 12 November when General Yoga Sugama handed over some charred human remains, some notebooks, papers and camera equipment which had, for miraculous reasons that the general did not bother to explain, escaped being damaged by the fire that had allegedly burnt the newsmen.

Meanwhile, in Australia pressure was mounting on the Whitlam government in what were to be its last weeks in office. A few days after Balibo—and after the sighting of the DSD-intercepted material—Prime Minister Whitlam and Foreign Minister Don Willesee reported to Parliament that the journalists were 'missing' at 'the scene of heavy fighting between rival factions on Thursday and Friday of last week'.[18] On 29 October the foreign minister was still to persist with the line that no 'definitive information' had 'yet come to hand'. He did mention the account of a Fretilin soldier interviewed in Dili who had 'described the entry of the anti-Fretilin forces into Balibo'. The soldier, whose interview I attended, described the entry of Indonesian troops (Javanese, he called them) into the village. However, to be fair to Don Willesee, who had never been at ease with Mr Whitlam's Timor policy, the deepening Indonesian involvement at Balibo and the killing of the journalists was to profoundly disturb him. The senator may have doubted the information in the decoded intercepted telegram, but further information on the extent of Indonesian military involvement, and the risk of serious humanitarian consequences if it were not stopped, was sent to him by the ACFOA mission in Timor. This message was sent in the aftermath of Balibo with a plea to Australia to use its good offices to persuade Indonesia to pursue its objectives by other means. Faced with mounting public anger towards Indonesia, and impatience with the government's apparently weak response, on 30 October Willesee delivered a major statement in the senate in which he declared that his government had 'viewed with concern widespread reports that Indonesia is involved in military intervention in Portuguese Timor', and urged that 'a solution to the problems in Portuguese Timor should be sought through peaceful means and free of external intervention'.[19] This was the Whitlam government's only major statement to cast some doubt on Indonesia's role in the territory. As it was, the statement was toned down in response to an intervention by Mr Woolcott who declared that, in its original form, it would merely serve to 'stimulate hostility to Indonesia within the Australian community, which it has been our policy to minimise'. Significantly, Woolcott went on to say:

> Although we know it is not true, the formal position of the Indonesian government is still that there is no Indonesian military intervention in East Timor. If the Minister said or implied in public the Indonesian Government was lying we would invite a hurt and angry reaction.[20]

Early in November the Indonesian government evidently began to take stock of the effect of the Balibo affair was having on its image in Australia and elsewhere. The existence of tensions was reportedly conveyed to President Suharto himself by Foreign Minister Adam Malik on 5 November. But, in spite of its knowledge, whether or not suppressed for security reasons, that the newsmen had been killed in an Indonesian operation, the Whitlam government apparently could not bring itself to make a formal protest to Indonesia. More than two weeks were to elapse after the killing before Prime Minister Whitlam dispatched a mildly worded letter to the Indonesian president via the retiring Indonesian ambassador in which he expressed his government's anxiety and sought the President's cooperation in determining the fate of the newsmen. However, the letter was delivered two days after Whitlam's commission had been withdrawn by the Governor-General, and, apparently, no reply was ever sent. A few weeks later, on 5 December, a simple funeral service was held for the newsmen in a cemetery at Jakarta, with a wreath from the embassy and a card which read: 'They stayed because they saw the search for truth and the need to report at first hand as a necessary task.'

The Fraser government inherited the problem of the missing newsmen and evidently chose to continue to deal with it in a similar style. However, Andrew Peacock's visit to Jakarta in April 1976 resulted in an agreement for an Australian on-the-spot investigation. A group of three diplomats from the embassy in Jakarta set out for Timor in what turned out to be a rather futile and naive attempt to clear up the matter by conducting an investigation at Balibo. It was an extraordinary venture in the light of the fact that the government shortly after it took office must have been acquainted with the essential facts about Indonesia's involvement in the Balibo operation and the circumstances in which the newsmen had been killed. There was the question of whether anyone believed that the Indonesian military in East Timor would cooperate with the Australian team to the extent of disclosing how the attack was carried out, and of producing genuine witnesses. Obviously they did not. The scenario was carefully stage-managed for the benefit of this investigation, perhaps on the assumption that the members of the team privately shared the Indonesian desire to dispose of this messy incident as quickly as possible and would not probe beyond the 'evidence' arranged for their attention. In this way Australian honour could be satisfied.

There was growing concern, especially in Washington and Canberra, at the state of Australia–Indonesia relations. The reasons for Jakarta's readiness to agree to this kind of inquiry were clear enough, and the later moves to ensure that the mission spoke to the right people and did not stumble across any incriminating evidence were entirely predictable. What is less clear is why the Australian foreign minister agreed to an arrangement the results of which would do nothing to satisfy the Australian public, but would merely aggravate suspicions, and add to criticisms of Australia's accommodating role. It was tempting to conclude that the Fraser government cynically agreed to this futile exercise in a deliberate attempt to dispose of an obstacle to the normalisation of relations between Jakarta and Canberra. The inquiry was one of the earliest steps by the Fraser government to 'put the Timor problem behind us and look to the future' to use the Prime Ministers words.

On 28 April 1976 the Australian embassy team arrived at Kupang, which they used as their base, travelling by helicopter to East Timor. In their report the team stated that it had 'relied on, and received, the cooperation of the authorities in East Timor and in Indonesia for access to East Timor and transport'. The facts are that during its twelve days on the island with this mission, the team made two relatively brief visits to Balibo where the information from which its findings were derived was obtained. The team went through the motions of a thorough investigation, reporting in detail the damage to individual houses, including the house in which the burnt bodies were alleged to have been discovered, according to Timorese leaders they met who claimed to have led the anti-Fretilin forces' attack on the village.

The Australian team's Indonesian hosts were obviously well prepared for their coming. According to an Indonesian official who had been connected with the operation and to Timorese who were in Balibo at that time (I interviewed them eight months later in the refugee camps at Cruz Quebrada on the outskirts of Lisbon), village residents, among them junior officials who had been in Balibo at about the time of the killing, were ordered to move out of the village. From these sources most of the 'Timorese' whom the Australian team saw were Indonesian soldiers, specially selected from among the troops originating from neighbouring islands where the people resemble the Quemac of the Balibo–Maliana area. It is clear from the team's report that the Timorese whom they questioned were carefully selected. Lopes da Cruz, Guilherme Goncalves and his son had long been trusted agents of *Operasi Komodo*, while João Tavares (misspelt in the report) was a more recent recruit to the Indonesian cause—an official who was far from popular even among non-Fretilin Timorese. In practice, these were the leading collaborators, the front men of *Operasi Komodo*, as their later careers were to show. Guilherme Goncalves was later to be appointed governor of the '27th Province', Lopes da Cruz became the Province's vice-governor, while Tavares was appointed *bupati* (senior district administrator) of the Maliana–Balibo area. The manipulation of the investigation was later to attract this comment from Hamish McDonald:

> What the team saw had, of course, been thoroughly filtered, rehearsed and directed by senior Indonesian military officers who stayed just off-stage 18 miles away in Indonesian Timor at Atambua.[21]

A similar account was later provided to me by a senior Indonesian official.

It seems incredible that the members of the Australian team were not aware that their reception and the testimony that they received were being orchestrated by an Indonesian intelligence operation. Presumably at least the leader, the political counsellor, Alan Taylor, had been informed of what had transpired at Balibo through the 'sensitive source material'. If this were the case, the team's report, in due course tabled in the Australian Parliament, is an intriguing document. In effect, the representatives of a government which had long known that the attack on Balibo had been an Indonesian operation, reported that the information supplied by Lopes da Cruz and his colleagues, 'while vague on several important points, had a certain plausibility'. The report states blandly:

> Persons to whom the team spoke had not known that there were Australians in Balibo at the time of the attack and had assumed that all persons in the town at that time were Fretilin supporters.[22]

Surely, the report should have at least read 'claimed not to have known'. There was no suggestion that all was not fair and square. Not surprisingly, the report was greeted with considerable scepticism in the Parliament, though, it may well have been welcomed with pride and satisfaction by the principals of *Operasi Komodo*.

Based on this inconclusive outcome of its investigation, the Fraser government seemed determined to take no further investigative action about the Balibo killings. New information from Timorese who claimed to have been in Balibo on 16 October, made public by me and by John Dowd, at the time president of the Australian Chapter of the International Commission of Jurists, was to be subjected to critical examination by the Department of Foreign Affairs than the testimony provided to the team that went to Balibo. In reporting the interviews I had conducted, I urged the foreign affairs department to investigate these sources. The report stated:

> The refugee accounts of what happened at Balibo suggest that at least some of the journalists may have been killed deliberately by Indonesian soldiers. These accounts, though by no means conclusive, are on the whole consistent and they seem to open up new avenues of inquiry. The refugees' accounts seem conclusive in one respect: it is surely inconceivable that the attack on Balibo was other than an Indonesian military

operation, in which Timorese participation was small and of the non-combatant kind. That the responsibility for the consequences of this operation rests with the Indonesian military command in Timor would thus seem beyond doubt.[23]

Further interviews were later conducted by John Dowd. John Penlington, of the ABC's London Bureau, went to Portugal and recorded accounts which were, generally speaking, corroborative. Later Jill Jolliffe collected accounts from the refugees in even greater detail. But the Australian government seemed resolved not to be lured into reopening a case that it had been at such pains to dispose of, in an obvious attempt to avert further problem relationship with its giant Asian neighbour. In answers to Parliamentary questions ministers declared that they did not feel that the new information opened any further useful avenues for investigation. However, the federal government was also obliged to admit that it had not carried out any investigations among refugees from the Balibo district of East Timor and that it had no intention of doing so. There was a touch of finality in the official response to the inquiries of Hamish McDonald in July 1979. He was told by the foreign affairs department that it believed that its inquiries 'which were vigorously and persistently pursued, have been as thorough as possible in the circumstances'. One subterfuge resorted to by the Fraser government was the claim that some of the families of the newsmen had asked that the matter not be pursued. From my inquiries such a statement had been made by only one of the victims' relatives, while other relatives were still keen to establish the truth of this tragic incident. Finally, McDonald was told that the government believed that 'the point has been reached where little is where little to be gained by attempting to mount further inquiries into the matter'.[24]

No other incident so clearly exposed the Australian government's lack of commitment, conscience and resolve as the fateful incident at Balibo on 16 October 1975. For the government of the time it was the point of no return. After Balibo, first the Whitlam government and then the Fraser government seemed to be conniving with Indonesia in attempts to head off public reaction to the armed aggression against the Timorese. The killing of the newsmen was probably the worst and the most wanton act of its kind in the history of Australian journalism and yet, incredibly, it evoked not a word of formal protest to Indonesia. On the contrary, Australian officials and politicians consistently concealed the facts, and sometimes sought to discredit new sources of information which they must have known to be true. Others, like Sir Keith Shann, appear to have been duped by Indonesian propaganda. In this way an act of courage, determination and commitment has been denied appropriate official and public recognition. The newsmen may have been somewhat imprudent but, from their reports and from the accounts of those who knew them, there can be no doubt as to their sincerity in seeking to bring to the Australian public the truth about a situation in which Australia's role was quite shameful. But there is an even more important consideration. Had the newsmen succeeded in getting out of East Timor with their irrefutable evidence of Indonesia's deepening military intervention against Fretilin, the public exposure of this situation might have changed the whole course of events for the Timorese. Public reaction in this country might conceivably have forced Prime Minister Whitlam to bring some real diplomatic pressure to bear on the Indonesians; this could have persuaded President Suharto to call off the whole military operation. The way this affair was handled by several Australian governments is probably the most disturbing cover-up in Australia's diplomatic history, a deception designed to protect a policy that was to become discredited by events after the fall of the Suharto regime.

The Whitlam government's increasing deference to Indonesia's real objectives in East Timor, and its fatalistic, if not unquestioning, acceptance of the means that the generals were prepared to resort to achieve them, were not without critics among the government's advisers privy to the sensitive information at its disposal. Mr Alan Renouf, a former head of the foreign affairs department, has said that there was strong opposition to the views of the Prime Minister in that department.[25] However, in my experience there was scant evidence of this, at least among the officials handling the Timor problem. The situation in the Portuguese colony was also being closely watched by analysts in the intelligence and strategic-policy sectors of the Defence Department, who became increasingly anxious at the implications of the government's policy. Thus, only one week before the attack on Balibo, that is, a matter of a few days after Indonesia's covert military involvement began, the head of the Department's Strategic and International Policy Division, W. B. Pritchett, submitted a frank report to his minister, Bill Morrison, which seems to have been a last-ditch appeal to the government to reconsider its policy of distancing itself from the problem and accommodating Indonesia's increasing involvement in the territory. The report pointed out that the government had been pursuing incompatible lines of policy by supporting integration and by suggesting that there should be an act of self-determination, and that at that moment there seemed little prospect of this policy preventing the outcome in Timor from harming Australia's defence interest.[26] While this submission noted the disadvantages in the emergence of an independent state of East Timor, whose existence might create instability and frustration for Indonesia, it implied that the defence advisers had long advocated a policy of urging acceptance of eventual independence for the Portuguese colony, and, even at that late hour, were still in favour of such a course of action. It was argued that Australia could still take up this alternative policy which would satisfy the requirement of self-determination and pull Indonesia back from its position of confrontation. It pointed to the good prospects of Indonesia negotiating a relationship with its weak, small neighbour that would allay its fears— perhaps, the authors argued, over a long period of time Indonesia could manage to absorb the territory or at least establish a position of undisputed dominance. Australia and Indonesia could cooperate to keep out external influences.

Australia, then, could play a constructive role by persuading Indonesia to accept the 'unpalatable reality' of Fretilin which, the paper argued, was likely to remain politically dominant in spite of the fact that some advisers regarded it as the group 'with the guns'. Such an initiative, it was contended, might well set the stage for constructive talks, in which Indonesia's position would be strong. Persuading the Indonesians to revert to such a course would not be easy at that late stage, but it could be achieved through a major effort of statesmanship, and it was certainly an alternative to be preferred to the other options facing Australia. The submission acknowledged that the integration of East Timor was the 'best solution', but went on to argue that such an integration on politically acceptable terms was not a realistic option. This left the task of persuading Indonesia to come to terms with Fretilin as the best policy for Australia.

The Defence Department's submission also warned that if Indonesia were to resort to force, the relationship with Australia was bound to be affected and, with some foresight, described as misplaced the expectation that the Indonesians would be able to force a settlement on the Timorese efficiently and speedily. Although, in retrospect, this assessment made good sense, it did not convince Prime Minister Whitlam and his key foreign affairs advisers that they should review their Timor strategy. Nor is there any evidence that the Pritchett submission had any effect on the Fraser government, in office only one month later. In his later references to the contribution of the Defence Department to the Timor debate, Mr Whitlam was disparaging. In his paper delivered to the ANU seminar, Mr Whitlam had this to say about his defence advisers:

> It is often thought that support for Fretilin was confined to the left in Australia. There was, however, a small faction in the Department of Defence which, having failed to keep Indonesia out of New Guinea, was now intent on establishing an enclave in the midst of the Indonesian archipelago in case of future conflict with Indonesia.[27]

It is obvious from Mr Whitlam's lurid and scathing comment that he had missed the point, as he was inclined to do in his quick rejoinders to remarks or statements by his political adversaries. The Defence Department's assessments were, on the whole, reasoned, soundly based and well-researched; and clearly some of them were prophetic. Had the Prime Minister followed the advice that his government received from this quarter, Australia would have acted differently in October 1975, and might well have averted the grim tragedy that was to follow in East Timor.

Indonesia's creeping intervention and Fretilin's response

The attack on Maliana and Balibo marked the beginning of the second phase of the Fretilin interregnum. The euphoria and optimism that had followed the victory over the UDT force soon began to recede as it became clear that Indonesia had no intention of accepting a Fretilin-dominated East Timor. Mobilising all available hands and halting Indonesia's advance into East Timor soon became the dominant concerns of the Fretilin leaders, displacing the previous top priority accorded to reconstructing and rehabilitating the territory's economy and administration. However, after the initial shock of the attack on 16 October, the situation at the border appeared for a time to become more settled. After having been forced out of Batugade, Balibo and Maliana, the Fretilin troops managed to hold their ground and to consolidate their defences. Beyond the range of their naval guns, and beyond the plains and open bushland, the Indonesians soon found that the Timorese troops were more than a match for other than their crack troops. In hand-to-hand fighting the *Operasi Komodo* troops were to discover that the Soviet AK weapons used by most of them were very much inferior to the Mauser rifles and G-3 machine guns with which the Fretilin troops were equipped. The Timorese fought back skilfully and determinedly, and between the time of the Balibo attack and the middle of November key villages changed hands several times. Timorese who had been present in the area in one particularly fierce engagement reported that more than 200 Indonesian troops were killed. These sources informed me that the stiff resistance sustained by Fretilin troops was an early blow to the morale of the Indonesian soldiers, whose commanders had led them to believe that all armed opposition would be over within a couple of weeks. Instead, under the skilful command of such men as Fernando Carmo, formerly of the Portuguese regular army, the Timorese began to inflict heavy casualties on the invaders. Fretilin's casualties do not appear to have been particularly high at that time, but the loss of the Maliana plain was a severe blow to East Timor's diminishing supplies of food. This fertile plain is one of the richest rice-growing areas in the territory, and the grain was about to be harvested when the attack on Balibo and Maliana was launched, perhaps not by coincidence. Several desperate attempts were made by Fretilin troops to regain control of this strip of 'occupied territory' (they also tried to recover Balibo), but in each case the Timorese were forced back by the superior supporting firepower of the Indonesian forces that made extensive use of light artillery and light armoured vehicles.

An interesting assessment of this first major operation by the forces of *Operasi Komodo* was made by US intelligence agencies between 18 and 31 October. These reports exaggerated the Indonesian gains by claiming, for example, that they had managed to occupy five or six towns when they had captured only two, Balibo and Maliana, but in other respects their information was surprisingly accurate and frank. The agencies gave details of the composition of the invading force of 2000 men, and of the difficulties and resistance that they encountered. Fretilin forces, it was noted, were 'putting up stiff resistance' and, in one case, 'one Indonesian unit [was] apparently surrounded and [was] taking casualties'. Other units 'were reporting extreme shortages of ammunition and supplies'.

Four days after the attack on Balibo a US intelligence agency was to report to its clients:

> The Indonesian military operation into Portuguese Timor has been temporarily blunted by surprisingly strong Fretilin resistance, by the poor condition of Indonesian war material, and by the effects of the wet season on Transportation. The drive into Timor by an Indonesian reinforced infantry battalion resulted initially in some territorial gains in the northern part of the island, but it has stalled because of Jakarta's failure to secure the border town of Lebos. Indonesian troops are receiving

heavy mortar attacks, one of which severely damaged their forward command post over the weekend. Indonesian commanders are continuing to complain about the poor quality of their supporting fire. An intercepted message, for example, revealed that 70 percent of the Indonesian mortar rounds were duds. The Indonesian high command has approved the commitment of another infantry battalion, but it will be several days before that battalion, presently on Java, can reach the battle area. The navy can be expected to increase its fire support in an attempt to repel increasingly strong Fretilin counterattacks against Indonesian troops on the northern shore.[28]

Two days later this well-informed band of Americans told their leaders that 'the Indonesian air force has conducted its first confirmed air strike against targets inside Portuguese Timor. On October 20, a light bomber attacked Fretilin positions around Atabai, 10 miles [16 kilometres] inside the border. Another light bomber will arrive in the area in 10 days; a C-47 gunship is already there.'[29] On 24 October, these sources reported that the Indonesians had amassed some 3500 troops along the border, but that 'counterattacking Fretilin forces, however, had forced some Indonesian units to pull back to their side of the border'.[30]

By the end of October it became evident that Colonel Dading Kalbuadi's covert operation, even with the reinforcements at its disposal, had become hopelessly bogged down and that to make any significant progress in the increasingly difficult terrain, a much larger-scale operation would need to be mounted, at the same time inevitably greatly increasing the risk of its exposure to the outside world. As things stood, Indonesian leaders were still persistently denying any military involvement in the 'civil war' in the Portuguese colony. This fiction was kept prominently before the Indonesian public. Thus, on 18 October, the *Indonesian Times* carried the bold headlines, 'Apodeti, UDT Joint Forces Seize Fretilin Strongholds'. A few days later, on 23 October, the same newspaper reported on its front page that 'Apodeti, UDT forces have successfully captured Bobonaro after killing 100 defending Fretilin men' and that these forces had gained total control of the road leading to Atabai, to the north, in the direction of Dili. The report even went on to quote an *Antara* correspondent, M. S. Kamah, who was allegedly accompanying the 'Apodeti–UDT joint operation and sending reports on its progress'. According to this source these forces were nearing Dili, and had reached Maubara, only 25 kilometres from the capital. These reports were complete fabrications, apparently the work of the press section of *Operasi Komodo*. I and the ACFOA aid mission were in the territory at the time and there was evidence that no such operation existed, the towns referred to being far away from the small north-western pocket occupied by Indonesian troops. However false might have been the reports from Jakarta, they were to be accepted as fact by many of the reputable international newspapers. Thus, the authoritative *Far Eastern Economic Review* reported on 31 October:

> In a string of short, sharp assaults, supported by well-placed mortar fire, UDT and Apodeti units not only recaptured Batugade on the northern coast in the past two

weeks, but moved on southeastwards to retake various other towns and villages not far from the frontier...Showing considerable, if not surprising, momentum, the counter-offensive by pro-Indonesia elements marked what one Western specialist described as a 'major comeback'.

A few days later, on 4 November, the *Sydney Morning Herald* showed that it too had fallen for one of *Antara's* 'special' releases. It reported that 'the Fretilin-held Portuguese East Timor capital of Dili is believed to be under heavy attack from pro-Indonesian UDT and Apodeti forces'. Reports from East Timor were available, but they did not always receive the same prominence. Few newspapers took any interest in a release from Dili on 3 November which, as later events showed, was much more accurate about the position of the UDT. It also reported that some refugees had managed to get back to East Timor from the Indonesian half of the island, and that they had stated that the UDT remnants had been disarmed by the 'Javanese' and had been placed in camps that were 'nothing else but concentration camps'.

On 8 November *Indonesian Times* reported that the 'Apodeti, UDT, Kota and Trabalhista movements' had regained control of the town of Atabai, an administrative village between Maliana and Maubara. Fretilin troops were said now to be 'in a very miserable situation' and were short of ammunition and arms, and had 'exhausted their food reserves'. This village did eventually fall, but to Indonesian regulars, not to the UDT or other groups, and it was not until 28 November that it came under Indonesian occupation. The invading forces were effectively contained within a small area, slightly larger than the territory that they had captured in the attack of 16 October. Only four days after Jakarta had claimed that the anti-Fretilin forces had taken Atabai, the defending Timorese had counterattacked and retaken a part of Maliana for a short time.

Pressures and tensions began to build up in other ways although there were no major offensives for several weeks after Balibo. Indonesian military aircraft regularly appeared over East Timor in the border areas, often bombing the Timorese positions, or where these positions were believed to be, and warships began to patrol near the coast. As US intelligence was to report, there was a 'loose blockade' around East Timor by the Indonesian navy. Several times vessels, believed to be Indonesian warships, ventured close to Dili harbour during the night. On one such occasion, when I was in Dili the Fretilin military authorities, perhaps fearing that a landing would be attempted, declared an alert, blacking out the city, and opening fire on the vessel with a whole range of weapons, from machine-guns and mortars to 75 mm artillery. Fortunately for the townspeople, the vessel did not respond, but disappeared into the night. Such incidents had a draining psychological effect on the morale of the Timorese. An atmosphere of gloom and uncertainty began to settle over Timor. The attack on Balibo and Maliana had a shock effect, but perhaps more disturbing to the Timorese was that it evoked no response from the international community. Of particular concern to the Fretilin leadership was the apparent refusal of the

The author, James Dunn, then Australian Consul, speaking to villagers in 1963.

The Santa Cruz massacre, Dili. (November 1991)

'We need a peace not a misery' —a villager from Odamou, high in the mountains, greets Australian troops arriving in Maliana. (October 1999)

© Jason South / The Age

2500 people lived in the grounds of roofless the Catholic church in the village of Suai, a militia stronghold. (August 1999) © Jason South / The Age

Militia leader Eurico Guterres leads a pro-autonomy rally in Dili on the final day of campaigning. (August 1999)
© Jason South / The Age

An East Timorese government official examines corpses recovered from a mass grave near the coffee growing town on Gleno, 60 km south of Dili. (May 1999)
© Jason South / The Age

Bishop Carlos Belo at an early morning mass at his house in Dili. (May 1999)
© Jason South / The Age

Fretilin founding member, Rogerio Lobato, at the village of Dare in the central highlands. (August 2001) © Andrew Meares / The Sydney Morning Herald

Jose Ramos Horta (R) walks arm in arm with Sergio Vieira de Mello, UN High Commissioner for Human Rights, at Dili Airport on Horta's return to East Timor after a 24-year exile following the Indonesian invasion in 1975.
© Andrew Meares / The Sydney Morning Herald

Francisco do Amaral, first president of East Timor in 1975 and leader of the ASDT party, Timorese Association of Social Democrats, who stood against Xanana in the elections. (August 2001) © Andrew Meares / The Sydney Morning Herald

Xanana Gusmão (centre) pleads with demonstrators disrupting a speech by Indonesian President Wahid in Dili. (February 2000) © Andrew Meares / The Sydney Morning Herald

Independence at last: President Xanana Gusmão watching troops march by on East Timor's first day of freedom. (May 2002) © Craig Abraham / The Age

Australian government to be provoked by the killing of five of its newsmen by Indonesian troops. Mounting evidence of Indonesia's military involvement had been sent to Canberra, but apart from Senator Willesee's restrained statement at the end of October there was no sign that the government was prepared to respond in any way to the desperate appeals sent to it by Fretilin leaders. After the beginning of the first phase of the Indonesian offensive the Fretilin leaders sent appeals for help to many nations of the world, and even sent an appeal to President Suharto, urging a negotiated settlement. But almost everywhere these appeals fell on deaf ears. The rest of the world was not interested in the plight of this little-known South-East Asian community.

The lack of an upsurge in official interest after the Balibo killings finally convinced most of the Fretilin leaders that there was no real prospect of any diplomatic intervention from Canberra to deter Indonesia from moves to annex the colony by armed force. Inevitably the effect of the diffident and unhelpful official reaction from Australia began to show in Fretilin attitudes towards the Australian aid workers in the territory. This particularly applied to the ACFOA mission because of its government links and the fact that I, as its leader, had once served as consul in Dili. Some of Fretilin's disappointment, frustration and disillusionment with Australia's unfriendly response now and then surfaced in the attitudes of officials to the team. However, apart from a certain coolness from time to time, neither the work of the mission nor its relationship with the Fretilin leadership as a whole was seriously affected. The Timorese leaders unhesitatingly cooperated with our fact-finding and aid survey projects, providing to the mission free access and transport to all parts of the territory, apart from the battle zone itself. These facilities were also enjoyed by the International Red Cross mission with whose leader I had regular discussions about the humanitarian situation in different parts of the colony. As did the ICRC, the ACFOA team informed Fretilin that it was recognised not as the legal government of East Timor, but as the de facto administering authority, a position which Fretilin leaders readily enough accepted. The Timorese leaders regularly sought advice on such matters as food production and its distribution, and on means to entice Portugal, the acknowledged administering authority, to return. In most cases they were responsive to any suggestions we made. In the circumstances, the Fretilin administration was a sensitive and responsible organisation to work through, a view shared by André Pasquier of the International Red Cross mission. The ICRC gave close attention to treating and feeding the UDT prisoners who, as the colony's food supplies began to diminish, were the best-fed Timorese to be seen in the Dili area.

Later, the Indonesians were to accuse the ICRC of having favoured Fretilin's political position, and even of having supplied arms to the independence movement. These charges were false but, like so many other Indonesian charges about outside interference or involvement in East Timor, they were only weakly refuted by Australia, whose officials could not for a minute have believed such allegations. André Pasquier was an experienced, dedicated Red Cross official who was ever fastidious about the need to protect the neutrality of his organisation. He took care to avoid any statements or activities that might be construed to be of a political nature. On one or two occasions this caution led him to deny requests by the ACFOA mission to relay radio messages to Australia, although we believed that such messages were hardly political in character. In my experience, the discipline of the members of the ICRC mission kept them well apart from the political issues at stake in East Timor, a detachment that at times irritated other aid workers in the territory. But the rules of the ICRC are strict, and are understandably aimed at facilitating their intervention and humanitarian relief work in the most politically sensitive of conflicts. Unfortunately, this constraint often means that the scope of their assistance is severely limited to bandaid-type operations. In Timor it meant that the mission concentrated on dealing with the humanitarian consequences of the civil war, the treatment of the prisoners, and on providing some relief for areas in which there were food shortages.

The ICRC maintained a mission in East Timor from the end of August, after having secured the agreement of all parties to the conflict to proceed with a protection and assistance program. The wide scope of the activities of this mission, which continued until the eve of the Indonesian invasion of Dili, is an indication of the level of cooperation it received from the Fretilin authorities. A support base was set up in Darwin, and the mission was to receive a major part of its financial, material, and personnel support from Australia. The ICRC's conventional activities developed rapidly (as was recorded in its annual report for 1975) 'with visits to prisoners, exchanges of Red Cross messages, listing of missing persons, etc.' The report stated:

> The ICRC obtained the approval of the FRETILIN to visit freely all the places of detention under its control...From September to 15 October, delegates, usually accompanied by a doctor, visited some 15 places of detention with a total of 1500 prisoners. From 15 October to 15 November, 33 visits were made to 18 places of detention with 1546 prisoners. The ICRC arranged for the transfer of badly wounded prisoners to the hospital at Dili...Relief was also given to the civilians most directly affected by the events, but these needs were relatively small.[31]

During its three months in the colony the mission visited all the major towns and villages of East Timor, including the border town of Maliana before that town was captured by the Indonesians in the middle of October.

Because of the flight of refugees to Indonesian Timor, the western half of the island was also the subject of attention from the ICRC, but the situation there was handled very differently, with much of the assistance sent to Indonesian Timor being misappropriated by corrupt officials, or being 'redirected' surreptitiously by the Indonesian National Red Crescent Society. Although the delegate made one brief visit to the other side of the border, via Darwin and Kupang—in response to pressures from Jakarta—'relief for the refugees' was handled by the Indonesian body, coincidentally largely under the control of the Indonesian military. In these circumstances the ICRC was all but forced to depend upon the

Indonesian national body for much of its information about the situation in the western sector of the island. Thus, its 1975 annual report stated that 'one month after the outbreak of hostilities, the number of refugees [in Indonesian Timor] was 40,000'. Based on my interviews with Timorese leaders of the refugee communities, this figure was probably double the number in western Timor.[32] The ICRC estimate was apparently the figure provided by the Indonesian National Committee, information Geneva was in no position to question or to contradict.

The focus of the ACFOA team's interest in the Timor problem was rather different from that of the ICRC delegates. In the first place, apart from looking at East Timor's immediate needs the team had been instructed to make an assessment of longer term aid requirements. The assault on Balibo occurred early in the mission, presenting us with evidence that the Timorese were no longer fighting a civil war, but were being attacked by Indonesia. This event underscored the central problem facing the territory, whether from the short-term or long-term point of view. The danger of a long and bitter conflict was emerging, and it was clear that, unless that danger could be removed, there was little use in planning a long-term aid program, the project that had the enthusiastic support of Mick Sullivan, ACFOA's energetic executive director, and stimulated considerable interest among many of the agencies within ACFOA. The team could see that Fretilin was not only determined to fight to the end, it had the capacity to wage a long campaign against Indonesia. The Fretilin army, Falintil, had several thousand well-trained troops at its disposal, and when it took over the Portuguese armoury at Taibesse it had gained access to a large stock of modern NATO-style weapons and ample supplies of ammunition. The Portuguese military commander, Colonel Maghalaes, who remained with the Governor on Atauro, told me that with care the Timorese could keep their army effectively equipped for a two-year campaign. The leaders had demonstrated their resolve and their skill in the field of battle. Not least, Fretilin enjoyed widespread popular support, even from Timorese who had supported the UDT before the coup. The elections before the coup had revealed that Fretilin's popular support at that time was about 60 per cent of Timorese, but by the end of September it had probably risen to more than 80 per cent. Support for the UDT and the other small factions had dissipated when the news reached East Timor that they had petitioned for integration with Indonesia. An Indonesian move to annex East Timor by force would be bitterly resisted, and even at the time it seemed to us that extensive bloodshed would be inevitable. It followed that, especially from a humanitarian viewpoint, the most important immediate task was to deter Indonesia from such a course of action, and to break down Fretilin's isolation by encouraging setting up channels for negotiations that would lead to the return of the Portuguese and the resumption of decolonisation. To have ignored these crucial political aspects of the problem would have meant ignoring the main issues, confining ourselves to bandaid relief, and thereby abandoning the Timorese to their fate. At no time, however, did the ACFOA mission consider giving assistance to the Fretilin military forces, as the Indonesians were at that time claiming. Military aid was outside our terms of reference and our capability. In fact the Timorese had no need of it.

With these considerations in mind the ACFOA mission sent an urgent appeal to Australian Foreign Minister Senator Willesee, warning the government that bloodshed would result unless the Indonesians could be deterred from their growing military involvement, of which there was conclusive evidence. The proposed talks between Fretilin representatives and the Portuguese still had not taken place, and it looked as if a meeting which was announced to take place in Rome between Indonesia and Portugal would delay, if not postpone indefinitely, this prospect. With the Indonesians attacking at the border, the need for this contact had become more urgent, and therefore the ACFOA team had talks with the Fretilin leadership and the Portuguese Governor and his aides at Atauro, urging both parties to establish a measure of informal on-the-spot contact without delay. It was clear that Fretilin was anxious to open a dialogue and, especially since an assault on Balibo, most of the leaders were prepared to be more flexible than their earlier statements had suggested. It was our belief that such contacts would lead to the early release of most of the prisoners, and would also clear the way for substantial quantities of food to be sent in to supplement the diminishing local supplies. By the end of October it was clear that the food position would soon be grim in a number of areas—especially in Dili and in the central mountain districts where the civil war had seriously disrupted agricultural production. Governor Lemos Pires was in a key position to authorise sending in emergency supplies from Australia.

At first the prospect of arranging these informal contacts appeared good. Fretilin leaders were quite enthusiastic, although they refused to go to Atauro for fear of being arrested by the Portuguese. Alternatives that I suggested were a meeting on one of the Portuguese naval vessels just outside Dili Harbour, or a visit to Dili by one of the lower-level Portuguese officials. Governor Lemos Pires, while not averse to the idea, was less enthusiastic than the Timorese leaders. He was understandably still suffering from hurt pride. He would be glad to help the Timorese people, he told me, but he would have nothing to do with Fretilin or the UDT. I replied that as Fretilin was in effective control of East Timor's mainland, if he wanted to help the Timorese he had no real alternative but to work through the de facto administration. Finally, the governor agreed to consider the proposal. Such was the level of Fretilin's interest in getting talks going that the president, Xavier do Amaral, and some of his colleagues were eagerly waiting for me at Dili airport when the plane returned from Atauro. A tentative agreement was reached for talks to take place near the end of October but, for various reasons, including Fretilin's annoyance and suspicions—not without grounds—at having been excluded from the talks between Portugal and Indonesia at Rome early in November, the meeting did not take place. As President Xavier do Amaral commented to Jill Jolliffe:

The talks suggest to me that Portugal has made some compromise with Indonesia beforehand. If the Portuguese government did not wish to invite representatives from Fretilin it should at least have invited ASEAN nations, the UN Committee of 24, Australia or other South Pacific nations to participate.[33]

By early November Fretilin leaders were becoming reconciled to their deepening isolation. The statement by Senator Willesee had given them a little encouragement, especially the Australian foreign minister's public acknowledgment that Indonesia might be militarily involved in Timor, and his suggestion that Australia might be prepared to host talks on the Timor problem. Some Fretilin leaders optimistically saw the foreign minister's statement as a sign that the Australian Labor government was about to shift its policy at last. In spite of Mr Whitlam's apparent total lack of sympathy for or understanding of the Fretilin position, Labor backbenchers had shown a continuing interest in their problems, and while this interest and sympathy prevailed Fretilin leaders like Horta and Xavier do Amaral did not abandon hope that Australia might suddenly change its stance and come to East Timor's aid with some real diplomatic muscle. In reality such a change of heart was unlikely, as the prime minister had given no sign of budging on this issue. When Senator Willesee delivered his statement on the situation in Timor at the end of October, his government had less than two weeks to remain in office. What the Timorese did not know was that the minister's original draft had been modified in order not to reveal that Australia knew that Indonesian troops were operating in East Timor. This was as the result of pressures from the Ambassador in Jakarta, who had stated in his cable to Canberra that if the minister's statement were to make it plain that the Indonesians had been lying about their military involvement it would provoke a 'hurt and angry reaction'. If such a viewpoint could cause the minister to water down what had been not a particularly strong statement, there was little hope that the government was about to shift its stance on the Timor problem.

After 11 November some of Fretilin's leaders, including Jose Ramos Horta and Xavier do Amaral, hoped that Andrew Peacock and some of his colleagues might rally the new Fraser government to give them some support, but by mid-November it must have become apparent to them that the high level of interest in the Timor problem that had prompted Mr Peacock to move a motion of public importance in the Australian parliament in the previous January was no longer present. That expression of concern had, however, given Mr Peacock special standing among Fretilin leaders. When the news reached Dili on 11 November 1975 that the governor-general had revoked Mr Whitlam's commission it brought a round of cheers from the left-wing Fretilin leadership in Dili and they telephoned their congratulations from Dili. But Fretilin expectations were doomed to disappointment because, although a number of Liberal members may not have been in agreement with the Whitlam government's Timor policy, it was one of the few issues on which there was something of a consensus between Mr Whitlam and the leaders of the Liberal–Country Party Coalition in Opposition. East Timor was considered too unimportant to be allowed to disrupt Australia's sensitive relationship with Jakarta. The way in which the Whitlam government had handled its Timor policy meant that the Liberal–Country Party Coalition in Opposition was poorly informed about the situation. Its leaders though, made no serious attempt to find out the truth. The Australian Labor Party had sent two delegations to the territory in 1975; the Coalition parties had sent none.

The only Liberal parliamentarian to visit the territory was Senator Neville Bonner, a forthright Aboriginal member of the federal Parliament. Although the senator was impressed with what he saw during his brief stay in Dili in September 1975, in the area of foreign policy his influence was negligible within the Coalition. There was also a growing preoccupation with developing closer relations with ASEAN which implicitly called for an easing of criticism of Indonesia, that regional grouping's largest and most populous member. When Mr Fraser took office, in a caretaker capacity, on 11 November, Timor's sympathisers were in the minority on the government benches of the parliament. The conservative politicians were reluctant to become involved in left-wing causes, whatever their legal or moral merits, and Fretilin had effectively been branded as a left-wing, if not communist, party. Mr Whitlam's own equivocal statements had if anything strengthened this image of the pro-independence movement. The tendency of Liberal–Country Party members to regard Fretilin as a Marxist-type organisation received plenty of coaxing from right-wing foreign-affairs commentators like Mr Santamaria of the National Civic Council. The few statements made by Liberal–Country Party leaders stressed their sympathy for Indonesia's perceived security apprehensions and, in the case of Mr Fraser and Mr Anthony drew attention to the implicit communist threat posed by Fretilin. For example, on 30 October, just before the Fraser government came into office, Senator Carrick, who was soon to become leader of the government parties in the Upper House, asked in the Senate whether 'there was an impression amongst the Portuguese as well as the anti-Fretilin forces that Australia is supporting the Fretilin cause', and whether the Whitlam government had 'taken steps to indicate to the Portuguese and Indonesian governments and to the Apodeti and the UDT that the sustained support for Fretilin by communist and other extreme left-wing organisations in Australia in no way reflects the viewpoint of the Australian people'.[34]

In retrospect the question seems a preposterous one to have been put to the government, given the circumstances. It certainly appeared that way to me, then in Timor witnessing the increasing isolation of Fretilin in the face of precious little practical support from any foreign quarter—and the movement was getting no encouragement from the Whitlam government. A thin trickle of help from individuals and groups in Australia was doing nothing to alter the spectacle of the small Timorese army preparing for what was going to be a lone fight to the death. It was a surprising remark to come from Senator Carrick, who had earlier indicated some interest in the problems faced by the Timorese. He had been captured by the Japanese in West Timor early in 1942, and claimed in Parliament to have some understanding of the Timorese.

Such remarks were a sad commentary on the state of the consciences of those who had been associated with the Allied intrusion into Timor in 1941, an action which had plunged the Timorese people into three-and-a-half years of death, destruction and deprivation, all for the sake of Australia's perceived security interests then. It was one thing that the Australian public at large did not feel a compelling sense of responsibility for the suffering that they had caused the Timorese people in the past: it was a much more serious dereliction that the exservicemen did not make a greater effort to establish the facts about the situation in the territory. Such was the level of interest in Timor that, in the election campaign that was to follow Mr Whitlam's sacking, the conservative (Coalition) parties devoted far more attention to criticism of Labor's decision to recognise the Soviet incorporation of the Baltic States—an act committed some thirty-five years earlier—than they did to the Timor question, where the grim process of illegal incorporation was already well under way.

If lack of information might be advanced as an excuse for the Liberal–Country Party's performance on Timor when it was in Opposition, such an excuse should not have existed after 11 November when the considerable body of evidence incriminating Indonesia was presumably brought to the Fraser government's attention—including the submission from the defence department calling for an urgent review of the Timor policy. This submission could hardly have lacked credibility because its author, Mr Bill Pritchett, was to be appointed permanent head of that prestigious department in due course.* The new government had come into office four weeks before the invasion of Dili which informed observers then considered inevitable. The question in official circles was not whether but when would the invasion occur. Perhaps the constraints imposed by Governor-General Sir John Kerr on the government's caretaker role until after the elections may have restricted its scope for such policy innovations, but deterring an act of aggression which Willesee had more or less begun should not have been outside Mr Fraser's caretaker mandate.

Even at that late hour there were a number of things that the Australian government could have done. It was too late to seek to invoke the support of ASEAN—a favourite theme expounded by Mr Peacock in his last three months as Opposition spokesman on foreign affairs—but the new government could have taken up the issue with Jakarta's key Western friends, whose relationships were of much greater economic and defence importance to Indonesia and pressed them to urge Indonesia to cease its military intervention and to pursue its objective by peaceful means. From the outset the Fraser government acted very much like its predecessor. It acknowledged privately that the Timor situation was a 'mess', but placed the blame for the fiasco on Mr Whitlam. The Timor problem seemed to trouble Mr Peacock, who may have preferred to take a sterner line with Jakarta. On 26 November he issued a public statement acknowledging that

---

*The Fraser government also presumably had access to the kind of analyses, through the existing exchange arrangements, that US agencies were reporting to the US administration.

Indonesia was militarily involved in East Timor, but he heavily qualified his comment with the remark that the problems in the territory 'may have forced the Indonesians into reluctant unilateral intervention'. But by then it offered little solace to the Fretilin leaders, now having to cope with a new and more vigorous offensive by Indonesian troops.

As November wore on, Fretilin was obviously facing a losing battle in its efforts to establish international contacts, other than with Mozambique and Angola, which were hardly in a position to offer other than moral support. The character of the Rome meeting and its outcome were a bitter disappointment, and only served to increase East Timor's isolation, as the Indonesian side had hoped. The Indonesian generals were evidently becoming increasingly confident. On 17 October, the day after the attack on Balibo, the *Far Eastern Economic Review* carried a fascinating interview with Ali Murtopo, during which this architect of *Operasi Komodo* said:

> Indonesia has no territorial ambitions or claims with respect to Portuguese Timor. We simply cannot afford to be distracted by any problems that are not central to the needs of our development process...On the basis of these considerations, it is obvious that...Indonesia could not possibly commit itself to direct physical intervention in Portuguese Timor because of any condition of 'stalemate' there.

We might well wonder what thoughts passed through Murtopo's mind when, having given this interview to Dan Coggin, he returned to his desk and scanned the latest telegrams and reports from the frontline within East Timor.

Although the meeting in Rome between Portuguese Foreign Minister Major Melo Antunes, and Indonesian Foreign Minister Adam Malik was widely hailed in Australia as a step in the right direction, from the very beginning Fretilin was unhappy about the arrangements for the meeting. Talks involving Portugal, Indonesia, and the Timorese political parties were proposed by Major Melo Antunes in a speech before the United Nations in October. Indonesia agreed, but only on condition that the United Nations would not intervene and the political parties would not be present. By excluding the parties, and especially Fretilin, from the talks Portugal almost extended to Indonesia the role of a privileged interlocutor, a status obviously unacceptable to Fretilin leaders. An equally serious blow to the Timorese independence movement was the exclusion of the United Nations from the conflict. Therefore, on the eve of the talks, the Fretilin Central Committee had cabled the Portuguese president that it considered the Portuguese state as the only valid interlocutor in the decolonisation process. The message reminded the Portuguese government that Fretilin controlled all of East Timor 'except the border villages of Maliana, Batugade and Balibo, occupied by Indonesian aggression [sic] forces'. Yet the communiqué which was to emerge from the meeting referred to the conflict in East Timor as if the civil war were still raging, and it in no way acknowledged Indonesia's military intervention. Despite this, the Portuguese were well aware of the true position, a fact that I had been able to glean from my discussion of the nature of Indonesian involvement with the Portuguese military commander, Colonel Maghalaes, at Atauro a week or so earlier.

Here was another farcical act in the Timor tragedy: the colonial power was holding discussions about a civil war that had long finished, with the real aggressor whose forces were already well-established within the Portuguese colony, a fact well-known to the Portuguese party to the talks. There was a fascinating touch in the final communiqué which urged, among other things, a meeting to be held as soon as possible.[35] The generals running *Operasi Komodo* had no intention of allowing such a meeting to take place. As for the 'armed strife', it was they who were in a position to turn it on and off at will, and they were shortly to intensify it. The communiqué also conceded to Indonesia a special position by declaring that 'in the implementation of decolonisation of Portuguese Timor it would be essential also to safeguard the legitimate interests of the countries of the region, particularly the interests of Indonesia as the closest neighbouring country'. Needless to say Indonesia had already surreptitiously asserted its 'special interest' in no uncertain way. The Portuguese position in the talks appears to have been vacillating, uninformed and almost naive. But then Lisbon was getting little encouragement from the outside world. One significant result of the Rome meeting was the reaffirmation that Portugal would not seek UN intervention. The chairman of the Committee of Twenty-Four was also reportedly unenthusiastic for UN involvement at that time.

The Portuguese foreign minister was under great domestic pressure to secure the release of the party of twenty-three Portuguese soldiers, then in Indonesian Timor, who were all but being held hostage by the Indonesians. Also, according to a later remark made by Major Melo Antunes during a private conversation in Lisbon, in his approach to the talks he was influenced by a personal assurance from Adam Malik that, if the outcome of the meeting were acceptable to Indonesia, he (Malik) could restrain the generals from an outright invasion of the colony. While it is possible that one of the reasons the military forces now occupying Maliana had not continued their advance was in deference to the holding of the talks at Rome, Malik was without influence in the Timor affair, having rarely been consulted. He was, therefore, in no position to give such an undertaking. The very assumptions of the agreement were false in a number of respects, especially those underlying the declared urgent need for a cease-fire and for a political settlement involving all of the so-called parties to the conflict. The agreement also suggested a Portuguese endorsement of the Indonesian contention that a string of parties—all of them in favour of integration—were lined up against Fretilin.

By always including Kota and Trabalhista and the UDT and Apodeti, the Indonesians sought to make the anti-Fretilin camp look like a formidable political grouping, one that in November barely existed in West Timor and had few followers in East Timor. Even before the coup these parties had fewer supporters than had Fretilin, as the local elections had shown. The Portuguese had refused to recognise the splinter groups Kota and Trabalhista until then because of their diminutive character, endorsing only three political movements—Fretilin, the

UDT and Apodeti. The last-mentioned had such a small number of followers that it might not have been able to gain legal recognition if it had not been for pressures from Indonesia. Australia welcomed the Rome meeting as a step towards peace, an attitude seemingly based on ignorance or plain naivety.

To Fretilin, the twelve-point memorandum that emerged from Rome was little more than a sell-out. If it had been accepted by them it would have meant negotiating not only from a position of weakness, but also on terms that were utterly unacceptable. Fretilin would have been outvoted on the fundamentally important question of opposition to integration into Indonesia, simply because the other parties had already, albeit in a contrived procedure, petitioned the Indonesian president to be integrated into the republic. Whatever the support for Fretilin as a political movement, in its opposition to integration it was clearly and unequivocally supported by the majority of the people of East Timor, whose wishes the Rome communiqué omitted to take into account.

It was, therefore, understandable that Fretilin leaders were opposed to talks on decolonisation on such terms. As Michael Richardson shrewdly assessed it:

> the Rome agreement pushes Fretilin, the pro-independence party which claims majority support, into a blind alley, from which escape appears impossible...The agreement faces Fretilin with two unpalatable choices. It can either participate in a political settlement that is more likely to result in merger with Indonesia than independence. Or, it can boycott talks and fight on in isolation with the bitter knowledge that the forces opposing it are certain to win because they are getting military backing and other support from Indonesia.[36]

What Richardson did not know at the time was that the other Timorese 'forces' no longer existed, having lost the support of most of the refugees whom the UDT had guilelessly led into a kind of trap in Indonesian Timor. From Fretilin's point of view the outcome of the Rome talks had, in practice, cut East Timor's umbilical cord with Lisbon because the agreement virtually ruled out any further moves for separate talks with the Portuguese administration on Atauro. As for the Portuguese, the outcome at Rome was little more than an Indonesian confidence trick. Their capacity to play any further role in Timor was substantially weakened, at the same time giving the aggressors a much freer hand. And, not least, they came away from the talks without any firm arrangements for the release of the twenty-three Portuguese soldiers being held by Indonesian troops. For Fretilin it was a serious setback to their efforts to break down the wall of political isolation that the Indonesians had now succeeded, by various skilful diplomatic manoeuvres, in erecting around East Timor.

By early November the atmosphere in East Timor began to take on a gloomy, fatalistic character, in spite of the fact that the domestic security situation was generally calm and controlled—except in the war zone near the border. Behind the renewed business and reconstruction activities (many of the Chinese shops had reopened and workers were setting about the repair of damaged buildings and the improvement of town services) a pervasive fear and uncertainty was growing, no doubt nourished by the sounds of bombardment from the Maliana area, which could be heard in Dili from time to time. A continuing barrage of strident propaganda broadcasts from *Operasi Komodo's* station in Indonesian Timor added to the tensions of daily life. Some of these broadcasts were directed against the foreign aid workers in an obvious attempt to frighten them into pulling out of the territory. Australian 'communists' supporting Fretilin, stated the broadcasts, would share the fate of the 'communists' killed at Balibo. Such broadcasts and the scare tactics outside Dili Harbour during the night inevitably affected the nerves of the aid workers, many of whom left Timor at the end of October (including the ASIAT team). One significant departure was that of Frank Favaro, an Australian who ran a hotel in Dili, and who operated a light aircraft. Favaro, it turned out, was an occasional informant for the Australian Secret Intelligence Service. He was a rather unlikely recruit for such a role, apart from the fact that his aircraft gave him considerable mobility. Favaro doubted the ability of the Timorese to run their own country and they, in turn, distrusted him. His dealings with all parties were often clumsy and insensitive to say the least, and by the time he left Dili he was suspected by Fretilin of being an Indonesian spy, by the Indonesians of being a Fretilin spy, and by the Portuguese, who refused him permission to land on Atauro, of being an agent provocateur. He suddenly pulled out of Timor, confiding to me that he had been warned by some mystical source that an Indonesian invasion of Dili would come in a few days. His 'source' was out by about a month.

The sudden departure of many of the Australians added to the tensions in Dili—in fact, I stayed on a little longer to make it look a little less like mass desertion. All of these events, however, caused a significant weakening of Fretilin's earlier insistence that the Portuguese should return and resume decolonisation. When I arrived in Dili in the middle of October, the possibility of a unilateral declaration of independence was ruled out by the Fretilin leaders. Again and again Xavier do Amaral, Nicolau Lobato and Jose Ramos Horta assured the ACFOA team that their immediate objective was to get the Portuguese to return. East Timor, they insisted, did not possess the conditions to become independent without a lengthy period of decolonisation. Even at the end of the first week of November President Xavier do Amaral was still talking about 'when the Portuguese return', but his time frame for the completion of decolonisation had been substantially reduced. Early in October it had been about five years (although it tended to differ from leader to leader), but by early November the period had shrunk to eighteen months or two years.

Fretilin's success in setting up an administration had given a boost to the confidence of the leaders, but they also realised that they were in no position to govern an independent state of East Timor and assume responsibility for its economic development. Yet on 28 November Fretilin unilaterally declared an independent East Timor, a move widely criticised in Australia and elsewhere as the event that provoked Indonesia's formal invasion of the territory. Even some of those sympathetic to the independence movement regarded this act of the UDI (Unilateral Declaration of Independence) as foolish and provocative. However, if closely examined, the way events unfolded between mid-August and the end of November makes the Fretilin declaration of independence much more understandable.

It was the inevitable outcome of intense provocation by Indonesia, and by what was perceived as the indifference of Portugal and Australia. The Whitlam Government's weak response to the murder of the newsmen at Balibo and lack of concern at the aggression was anything but encouraging. After 11 November Australia was in the throes of a bitter constitutional crisis. Also, it was proved impossible to arouse the interest of the United Nations, despite this blatant act of aggression—a serious violation of the UN Charter. Portugal's obligations as the legal administering power were clear. The Portuguese were aware of Indonesia's military intervention, from the monitoring of Fretilin radio communications by the troops under the command of Lemos Pires on the island of Atauro. But Lisbon did not respond. After Batugade was seized the Portuguese merely commented that they were not particularly alarmed by the 'incident'. As Fretilin saw it, they not only ignored Fretilin appeals but based on quite false assumptions they chose to enter into separate negotiations with the aggressors. This created an untenable position for Fretilin and nearly encouraged Indonesia to prepare for an open assault on the colony.

These developments forced the Timorese to the realisation that they stood alone in their struggle, and led them to conclude that Portugal was poised to abandon East Timor. Thus, the outcome of the Rome meeting was to have a profound effect on the Fretilin leadership. It clearly weakened the influence of the 'internationalist' group in the Central Committee, that is, Xavier do Amaral, Jose Ramos Horta and Alarico Fernandes, while Nicolau Lobato's concept of nationalist self-reliance became the predominant motivation. The Timorese could and must stand on their own feet. I had a lengthy discussion on this subject early in November with Nicolau Lobato who, by that time, was the undisputed leader of Fretilin. He was openly sceptical of the usefulness of trying to canvass world opinion in support of East Timor's cause, among the countries of the East or West. Neither had responded so far to his people's pleas for help in their fight against outright aggression. The Timorese must trust in themselves. Their struggle was a just one and they would win out. Understandably, the political perceptions of the Fretilin leaders were being shaped by a cynical view of the outside world and by a growing self-confidence stemming from their remarkable achievements in defeating the UDT forces so quickly, in establishing a surprisingly effective administration of the territory under their control and, not least, in holding the Indonesian advance just outside Maliana.

A fundamental shift in attitudes was occurring, but it could hardly have been regarded as a swing to the left. If anything, Lobato's views had more appeal to the conservative 'military men', as they were called, than to the left wing of Fretilin's Central Committee. The military, after all, had won the civil war, had achieved the restoration of security and order in the villages and towns of Timor and now, as the Indonesian military intervention began in earnest, the very survival and movement depended upon them. In a way they were rather overconfident of their capacity to cope with an invasion. Their early successes may have blinded them to the magnitude of the problem of maintaining an effective resistance indefinitely in East Timor's remote circumstances, and certainly to the diplomatic consequences of being manoeuvred by Indonesia into near-isolation. Horta and Xavier do Amaral were more attuned to such hazards and they had not abandoned hope that some help might come from Australia, despite the discouraging responses so far.

After the attack on Balibo, East Timor was increasingly placed on a war footing and a rigorous military training program was introduced. Mr Whitlam and others have suggested that Fretilin was a military regime, but in spite of the mobilisation that took place this was not the case. In the first place a military regime is normally characterised by a professional corps of officers having assumed political power. Only one or two of Fretilin's leaders had been officers, and then only with the rank of *alferes* or junior lieutenant. The most important leaders had formerly been sergeants in the Portuguese army, and most of them had been out of the service for some years before 1975. Fretilin made a serious attempt to develop an independent civilian administration, but Indonesia's attack inevitably forced military priorities on the leaders.

Even during this time the Economic Commission, Fretilin's central management apparatus, was clearly under non-military direction—it was led by Dr Jose Goncalves. Under its management an attempt was made to get the economy of the colony working, including the farm sector and the business communities of the towns. Although the Commission achieved some success, the two months of its existence were too short for a significant recovery to be achieved. It also faced very difficult problems. For one thing, shipping contacts with East Timor were severed at the time of the UDT coup and there was a kind of blockade until the Indonesian invasion. For another, the only bank in East Timor, the Banco Nacional Ultramarino, had been locked up by the departing Portuguese officials, leaving Timor without banking facilities. No doubt Fretilin could have forced open the vault, but as part of their policy of seeking to hand the administration back to the Portuguese intact, the vault was left unmolested and under armed guard.

Another problem facing the Fretilin administration was that of getting the Timorese and Chinese who had been dislocated by the civil war to return to the villages and towns in the interior and to return productive labour. In Dili the presence of thousands of refugees placed a heavy drain on the diminishing supplies of food, and by the end of October rice and meat were in critically short supply. There were ample supplies of food available in districts to the east and south, but the problem was how to transport it to Dili and to the central mountain districts where serious shortages were beginning to be felt. The departure of the Portuguese and the flight of the UDT refugees to Indonesian Timor had left the territory with a critical shortage of mechanics. Faced also with a dearth of spare parts, the heavy transport vehicles which, in Timor's rough road system and difficult terrain, needed regular and careful maintenance, soon began to fall into disrepair. There was little coastal shipping available, Dili's harbour launch having been commandeered by the military—it had been converted into a gunboat by the simple method of lashing a 75 mm gun to large wooden cross-members and loading the vessel with people to give it the necessary stability when the gun was fired!

The arrival of some supplies in the middle of November on a barge chartered by the Australian Council for Overseas Aid offered the first relief for the population at large. This aid was from non-government agencies, the Australian government having only grudgingly allowed the mission to proceed. This was a point not lost on the Fretilin leaders; a government giving military aid to Indonesia was reluctant to allow supplies of petrol and diesel fuel to be included in the consignment for East Timor, contending that it might be used in vehicles supporting Fretilin's armed struggle against the Indonesian invading forces. In the end, the authorities at Darwin allowed only sufficient fuel to facilitate the use of transport to distribute the other supplies contained in the barge. There was a pathetic quality about this irksome obstruction by the government. The Timorese were fighting a campaign in the mountains near the border, involving only limited use of few vehicles which provided ready targets for Indonesian aircraft and artillery. Apart from food, the barge, *Alanna Fay*, brought some items which were to prove of critical importance to Fretilin after the invasion of Dili—medicines and twelve tonnes of assorted grain seeds. The returning barge carried AUD40,000 worth of coffee, payment for which was lodged with a bank in Darwin.

Faced with the inevitable prospect of a long, hard struggle against the Indonesian invaders, Fretilin leaders began to prepare for a guerrilla campaign. From the end of October trucks, heavily laden with supplies of arms, ammunition and food, were continually grinding up the steep roads to the south of the capital, carrying their precious cargoes deep into the central mountain region, to carefully selected hideouts. These activities, the occasional sounds of gunfire from the direction of the border, plus the deepening isolation of East Timor and the indifference of the outside world, all contributed to an atmosphere of growing despondency and tension. Fretilin had won increased support and respect from the people—including the Chinese—since the end of the civil war but, after Balibo, to most people in the major towns a full-scale invasion by Indonesia seemed inevitable and the Fretilin administration, therefore, appeared transitional and impermanent.

The outcome of the Rome talks further increased rumour and speculation, and when the Indonesians launched a major attack against Atabai and began advancing towards the Lois River an assault on the capital was considered imminent. The Timorese troops were fighting determinedly and courageously, but the task of keeping the Indonesian giant at bay seemed an impossible one. Therefore, to the Chinese, and many of the Timorese, rule by Fretilin was essentially a temporary phenomenon. Although its popularity had increased since August, the independence movement was not without its critics. One of the strongest was Bishop Ribeiro of Timor who regarded Fretilin leaders as 'communistic', an aphorism from the days of the Salazar dictatorship for any socialist inclined movement or politician. With this prejudice, the bishop was an easy target for the Indonesian disinformation campaign. For most of the interregnum his relations with Fretilin were bad. On one occasion, in retaliation for his refusal to say mass to the troops, Fretilin authorities disconnected power and water to his house for a day or so. It was also believed by some members of the independence movement that the Bishop was an exponent of integration, and was in regular contact with Indonesian agents through Catholic members of Apodeti. Early in November there was a move by some right-wing members of Fretilin against elements of the left, described by the former as 'communists', and, according to Jill Jolliffe's account, it was rumoured that the Bishop may have been involved.[37] It is now difficult to determine whether there was any substance to such allegations, but Bishop Ribeiro left no doubt about his hostility towards Fretilin to those of us who talked with him in those tense and uncertain times.

It seems that serious discussion of whether Fretilin should unilaterally declare East Timor independent began in the bitter reaction to the implications of the Rome communiqué. The Timorese were further encouraged by the decision of the Angolan independence movement, the MPLA, to declare Angola an independent state on 11 November, an occasion that was celebrated by a demonstration in Dili organised by Fretilin. The Timorese were also impressed by the fact that some thirty countries recognised the new African nation within a matter of days. But even by the middle of November the Fretilin leaders were by no means convinced that such a step was an appropriate one for Fretilin to take. Hence, one leader, Mari Alkatiri, who had just returned to Dili from a visit to Africa, told Jill Jolliffe:

> Our political situation is not the same as Angola, our economic/political situation is different and our military/political situation...Our situation is different because we are faced with resisting an invasion by more powerful forces. We know that if we declare UDI [Unilateral Declaration of Independence] Portugal will not send warships and we cannot take responsibility for an Indonesian invasion. This is a problem which we would prefer to solve diplomatically.[38]

Meanwhile Horta informed me that pressure for a UDI was building up in the party's leadership, but that he and many of his colleagues hoped to persuade the others to resist it, a policy I also strongly urged. The declaration took Horta and Alarico Fernandes, who was with Horta on the visit to Australia, by surprise. Jill Jolliffe has provided evidence that the decision was taken at short notice, if not impulsively. She wrote:

> The unkempt appearance of some of the leaders, the frenetic all-night flag-sewing

of the 27th and the close sequence of Atabae's capture to the actual independence ceremony suggest that the decision was taken hastily. Indeed, Alkatiri...said on the day that it had been taken only hours earlier.[39]

From my later discussions with Fretilin leaders there can be little doubt that the second major Indonesian offensive, that is, the attack on Atabai (to which Jolliffe referred) was the biggest single factor behind the sudden decision of the Fretilin leaders to declare their country an independent state. The attack began on about 20 November, although the village had been under occasional naval bombardment for several days beforehand. For this operation the Indonesian forces used greater firepower, more armoured vehicles (including both French and Russian) and a World War II bomber. This time two Australian journalists, Michael Richardson and Jill Jolliffe, witnessed part of the assault, including the attacks from the air and sea. Unlike the attack at Balibo, this assault was determinedly resisted by Falintil, who were no longer newcomers to artillery bombardment, and it took the Indonesians a whole fortnight to force the Timorese forces to withdraw from the town. On 24 November Fretilin leaders sent another appeal to the United Nations—to the Security Council—and to various governments, including those of Australia and Papua New Guinea. It informed them that Indonesian forces were attacking Atabai and that, although the situation was still under control, it was nearing 'crisis point'. But no response came from an uninterested outside world. As they saw it from Dili, they were quite alone in what was turning out to be a life-and-death struggle with a cynical enemy that had achieved a massive deception of the international community. To the Timorese, the attack on Atabai was an indication that the Indonesians had encountered no real international obstacles to deter them from proceeding with their plan to destroy Fretilin by means of force. Some of the leaders became convinced that a formal declaration of independence would not only precipitate recognition from certain Third World and socialist states: it would serve to provoke a more active international debate on the Timor issue, and might conceivably attract some material support (although Nicolau Lobato was pessimistic about such a prospect).

To sum up, the Fretilin decision to declare independence for East Timor was neither an act of defiance against the colonial power, nor was it a naive expression of overconfidence in the ability of the Timorese independence movement to govern the territory, as it has sometimes been presented. It was in a sense a desperate measure which was almost forced on the Timorese by the domestic and international circumstances arising from Indonesia's covert aggression against them, and by the refusal of the colonial power, Portugal, and Australia, the United Nations and the world community in general, to intervene to dissuade Indonesia from a gross violation of internationally accepted standards of behaviour. As one Fretilin leader put it to me: 'It is not that we want to be independent yet, or that we are ready for it. But if we are going to fight to the end, we can at least die independent.' And so, on the afternoon of 28 November 1975, in what appears to have been a rather restrained ceremony,

President Xavier do Amaral was driven up to the provincial government's Administrative Palace (in the governor's Mercedes which, up to that time, had not been used), and in the presence of other Fretilin leaders, soldiers, citizens of Dili, curious members of the Red Cross team, and journalists like Jill Jolliffe, Roger East and Michael Richardson, who had no forewarning of the event, he signed a declaration, proclaiming,

> unilaterally, the independence of East Timor, from 00.00 hours today, declaring the state of the Democratic Republic of East Timor, anti-colonialist and anti-imperialist.[40]

As Jill Jolliffe described it later:

> It had been a rather grim, brave little ceremony, not attended by the joy which should properly accompany the birth of a new nation, or the expansive finery of neighbouring New Guinea's independence day three months before...The ceremony was conducted in the knowledge that Indonesian forces were daily moving further into the territory and that the real testing time might only now be starting for East Timor.[41]

It was an act of desperation under conditions of severe provocation which deserved some understanding and sympathy from countries like Australia and Papua New Guinea, especially from officials in Canberra who had some insight into the psychological pressures under which the Timorese leaders were labouring. The official reaction in Australia, and in the few other countries that were taking a casual interest in the Timor situation at that time, was nothing less than cynical: Fretilin was behaving provocatively and irresponsibly, and Indonesian reactions now deserved our understanding. True, Fretilin did receive expressions of support from its former colonial stablemates in Africa, and from Communist Bloc countries, but most responses fell short of outright recognition and came from countries remote from the region, in terms of influence and geography, able to offer only moral support. The new governments in Angola and Mozambique, and Guinea–Bissau, were hardly in a position at that time to give much attention to remote East Timor. China and Vietnam sent messages of warm congratulations, and these states were initially to be Fretilin's most important Asian supporters, although their material aid was confined to some financial support for the 'ministers-at-large of Fretilin' after the invasion.

Indonesia's reaction was predictable—one might well suspect that this was the occasion they had been waiting for. Fretilin's proclamation of independence was the excuse Jakarta needed to justify the mounting of a major military operation to dispose of the left-wing Timorese movement. The Rome talks had given a diplomatic boost to Jakarta's position, the sacking of the Whitlam government had diverted Australia's attention to domestic issues and, at the same time, the Fraser government seemed disposed to go along with the compliant stance of its predecessor. Portugal's ongoing domestic crisis had further sapped that government's interest in Timor while, thanks largely to some skilful disinformation work by Ali Murtopo's agents, sympathy for Indonesia's position had also increased in that region. Not least, apart from its contacts with Australia at the non-government level, and its links with Angola and Mozambique, Fretilin had been effectively isolated and diplomatically neutralised. The US had already made its sympathies clear. It had no intention of becoming involved, while the other superpower at that time, the Soviet Union, was maintaining only a passing interest in the Timor crisis. A matter of much greater concern to the Russians was countering any moves that might lead to the normalisation of diplomatic relations between Peking and Jakarta.

After Fretilin unilaterally declared independence, the official Indonesian response was to deplore the action, and Foreign Minister Malik was later reported to have told Western diplomats that they 'should not be surprised at Indonesia's next move'. It is now known that US and Australian diplomats and their governments were given ample warning of the coming invasion. According to one sensitively placed Indonesian official, about a week earlier Australian and US intelligence representatives at the embassies in Jakarta were privately told of the coming attack. On 29 November Harry Tjan all but warned Australian diplomats in oblique terms of the forthcoming action. He urged that all Australians be advised to leave the colony.* In Washington on 1 December CIA analysts reported:

> According to a reliable source, Indonesia will not initiate large-scale military action against Portuguese Timor until after President Ford completes his visit.

Four days later the CIA came up with a more specific briefing:

> President Soeharto has reportedly approved a plan to begin overt Indonesian intervention in Portuguese Timor soon after President Ford leaves Jakarta...A date for the overt intervention has not been set. It could take place as early as tomorrow, but it is more likely to come a few days later.

By 6 December, however, US intelligence analysts had got it right. They reported: 'The Indonesians will launch their invasion of Portuguese Timor on Sunday'.[42] Hamish McDonald records the event much more explicitly. He wrote:

> An attack on Dili was to have been made on 5 December, the day US President Gerald Ford and his Secretary of State, Henry Kissinger, were due to arrive in Jakarta from China. American intelligence learnt of this highly compromising timetable, and successfully demanded that the operation be postponed until after Ford left on 6 December.[43]

Thus, on 2 December the ICRC mission in Dili received a cable from Australian authorities urging that all Australian nationals should be evacuated from East Timor for their own protection. In case they should hesitate to accept this advice, they were subjected coincidentally to intimidating broadcasts from *Operasi Komodo's* special radio station in Indonesian Timor, darkly hinting that any Australians found in Dili by the invading forces of the 'UDT/Apodeti' would be

---

* See Document 346 in Australia and the Indonesian Incorporation of Portuguese Timor 1974-75.

killed. It was clear that on no account did the Indonesians want any witnesses to be in East Timor when their armed forces moved in.

Meanwhile, in Atambua an 'integration declaration', in reality drawn up by Sugiyanto and Taolin, was proclaimed on 29 November by a small and apprehensive band of representatives of the UDT, Apodeti, Kota and Trabalhista. A couple of days later Adam Malik made a quick visit to Atambua where he told the small group of collaborating Timorese leaders that now Indonesia would 'use full force'. For publication, he was reported to have said:

> Now we meet in Atambua, and soon we shall meet again in Dili. I expect you to invite me to come to Dili soon...Diplomacy is finished. The solution to the East Timor problem is now the front line of battle.

However frank the Indonesians might have been with their Western confidants, they continued to maintain the public fiction of a UDT–Apodeti advance against the weakening Fretilin. In the days before the invasion a series of false reports were fed into Reuters and other news agencies in Jakarta to support this fiction. For example, on 4 December a Reuters report from Jakarta stated that:

> Left wing Fretilin troops in Portuguese East Timor were today reported to have abandoned several forward positions to pro-Indonesia forces advancing on the capital. The semi-official *Antara* news agency said the Fretilin had given up their posts in several villages around Dili, while 65 Fretilin soldiers had surrendered at Railaco, some 18 kilometres west of the capital...Yesterday the Government Radio Republic Indonesia (RRI) reported that the pro-Jakarta forces had advanced to within 20 kilometres after besieging the town of Aileu south of Dili.

As Fretilin reported at the time, and as Timorese who accompanied the Indonesian troops revealed later, there was no military activity anywhere near these places, the only military action being just east of Atabai at the Lois River. But these fabrications were clearly concocted to provide a lead-up to Dili's 'liberation by anti-Fretilin forces'.

Meanwhile in Dili the Fretilin leaders were making the best of what was to turn out to be the last phase of their short tenancy of the capital. The day after the proclamation of independence Xavier do Amaral was sworn in as president of the republic, and a draft constitution was proclaimed. Two days later the first government of the Democratic Republic of East Timor (DRET) was sworn in. It comprised eleven ministers assisted by seven vice-ministers. The main appointments were: Prime Minister Nicolau Lobato, Minister of State for Political Affairs Mari Alkatiri; Minister for Economic and Social Affairs Abilio dos Reis Araujo (he was in Portugal at the time, and was never to join his ministerial colleagues in Timor); Minister for Economic Coordination Jose Goncalves; Minister for Defence Rogerio Lobato, Minister for Internal Affairs and Security Alarico Fernandes; and Minister for Foreign Affairs and External Information Jose Ramos Horta. The order of precedence revealed that Horta had slipped down the ladder of seniority in the party, reflecting to a large extent the failure of international aspects of Fretilin's policies, especially his failure to win the support of Australia, something that was outside his control. It is evident that Fretilin's abandonment by the West had shifted its leaders' political attitudes in a more radical direction, though for tactical, rather than ideological, reasons. Confronted with Western indifference, the leaders looked to socialist and Third World states for support. On 4 December President Xavier do Amaral announced that China would be asked to speak up on behalf of East Timor to ensure the survival of the young republic. Furthermore, with the withdrawal of some members of the ICRC, following broadcasts from Indonesia that foreigners would be executed if caught, Xavier do Amaral appealed to Cuba to send four doctors to Timor, a curious choice because Cuba was to become a strong supporter of Suharto's position on Timor.

Following the proclamation of independence, Fretilin leaders appeared to be under no illusions about the future. Shortly after the event Rogerio Lobato told the Australian correspondents in Dili:

> Acting on information from Fretilin intelligence sources we expect a full-scale attack against East Timor, and particularly the capital Dili, tonight.[44]

But the Timorese had a few more days to wait before they were to start a long and bitter guerrilla war. A few days after the DRET government was formed, three Fretilin leaders flew to Darwin en route to Africa and North America to conduct in virtual exile the diplomatic struggle on behalf of their newly proclaimed state. They were Horta and Alkatiri, who had already been performing this mission, and the Minister for Defence and military commander Rogerio Lobato, in the circumstances an odd choice as Fretilin's armed struggle for survival was about to begin in earnest. Perhaps Xavier do Amaral and Prime Minister Lobato hoped that Rogerio would succeed in procuring military aid for the embattled Falintil but, although he travelled to China, the Soviet Union, and Vietnam, presumably with this objective in mind, most of his comrades-in-arms were to fight to the death with no material assistance from these countries.

* * * *

In retrospect the Fretilin interregnum was surprisingly successful. These young Timorese leaders managed, as we have seen, to re-establish law and order, and to set up a temporary administration during the three months in which their party was the undisputed authority in East Timor. The disciplined behaviour of Fretilin officials in the administration, and their respect for the population at large, including those who obviously did not support them politically, established a standard which the Indonesian occupying forces could never attain. True, its political organisation tended to be top-heavy and deliberations were unduly long and rhetorical—and some of the objectives seemed naive—but Fretilin's great achievement was that it was able to restore order and calm to East Timor in the face of the bitterness left by the civil war without resorting to an oppressive administrative control. During this period it received some help, especially in healing the wounds and in restoring the health of the Timorese affected by the war but, beyond this bandaid form of assistance, aid from the outside world was insignificant.

The Fretilin interregnum administration was very obviously short of administrative skills, many of the trained personnel having fled with the UDT, or having been evacuated with the Portuguese to Atauro (when the fighting began, many went as refugees to Australia), and its methods of dealing with problems were often slow and clumsy. In a way, the towns and villages of the country ran themselves for much of the time. But Fretilin's performance during this period needs to be judged against the fact that, after only one month, the leaders were forced to divert much of their limited skilled workforce to military tasks to counter Indonesia's covert attacks on the territory. That Fretilin could at the same time maintain law and order (I felt safer in the streets of Dili at night than in New York or Washington) says something about the measure of support, cooperation and tolerance it received from the people of East Timor. However, the ACFOA team and other visitors to the territory agreed unanimously that, although some groups like the Chinese, the church officials, and some of the town dwellers longed for the return of the Portuguese (a hope shared by Fretilin), even these would have preferred Fretilin to the pro-integration parties (as they believed them to be) had they been able to choose freely. Some were apprehensive of Fretilin's left-wing tendencies, but in reality it was not an ideologically bound party. Many of its attitudes were unformed, and it was clearly more populist than socialist in its political character. Some critics have made much of its close links with Frelimo, but this relationship was certainly more fraternal than ideological.

While it is evident that Fretilin came more to identify itself with left-wing movements in Africa and some of the communist states, this shift was partly motivated by tactical considerations. In a sense, it was a political direction along which the party was impelled by Indonesian aggression, and by the refusal of Western countries like Australia. These two nations that had proclaimed their commitment to self-determination and their opposition to all forms of aggression, to give appropriate support to the Timorese, whose rights were being so blatantly and cynically contravened. There was much nervousness in certain circles in Australia about Fretilin's left-wing tendencies, but the point should be made that most independence movements seeking to prise their peoples free of colonial bondage have been of a radical or left-wing mould. Was Fretilin more radical than Sukarno's Partai Nasional Indonesia, or even the Partai Sosialis Indonesia of the prominent Indonesian socialist, Sutan Sjahrir, in the late 1940s?

Finally, in judging Fretilin's record in office and its political complexion, it is important to remember that its political personality was shaped by Indonesia's aggressive belligerent response and that its leaders had not pressed for a premature granting of independence. They had tried to persuade the colonial authorities to return to resume decolonisation, an outcome that deserved international support. Against this background, and in the light of the way events unfolded in November, Fretilin's unilateral declaration of independence it was clear that it was not a conspiracy to seize political power in the colony, to the exclusion of other political forces. It was more an act of defiance against a devious and determined aggressor, on the one hand, and a weak and irresolute colonial power, on the other—a last, desperate attempt to evoke a response from an apathetic world. Alas, just as the Indonesians had manipulated the civil war for which they were largely responsible, to suit their own devious ends, they were able to manipulate to their own advantage the Fretilin UDI that they had nearly forced on the besieged Timorese to create a congenial climate of 'understanding' in the international community.

To sum up, the UDT and Fretilin were victims of a conspiracy by a group of ruthless Indonesian generals. It was a conspiracy the Australian prime minister and his government had perhaps unwittingly helped to germinate and develop by their dismissive attitude to the rights of the East Timorese and their accommodating response to the intrigues, subversion and, finally, intervention engineered by *Operasi Komodo*, of which he must have been closely advised. No less guilty of complicity was the US Administration of the time, which was fully acquainted with this deadly Indonesian conspiracy, and much better placed than Australia to influence President Suharto to restrain his generals and allow the Timorese to shape their own future and, not least, to prevent the bloodshed and suffering that was to follow.

As Henry Kissinger put it, in his answer to a question at a news conference in July 1995, Timor was 'a little speck in a huge archipelago'. Portugal has been much maligned for its sorry part in this episode of the Timor tragedy but in its defence, the Portuguese government, weakened and demoralised in the turbulent aftermath of the April coup, deserved the support and not the aloof criticism of the establishments in Washington and Canberra.

Notes

1 Van Atta and Toohey, 'The Timor Papers', *National Times*, part 2, 6-12 June 1982.
2 Ibid.
3 David Jenkins, 'A Guard against Change', *Far Eastern Economic Review*, 21 April 1983.
4 Van Atta and Toohey, 'The Timor Papers', part 2. The CIA assessment tallied very closely with my on-the-spot reading of the situation.
5 David Jenkins, 'The Five Ghosts of Balibo Rise Once More to Haunt Indonesia and Us', *Sydney Morning Herald*, 14 October 1994.
6 Van Atta and Toohey, 'The Timor Papers'. For an interesting account of this incident, see Hamish McDonald, 'Death at Balibo', *National Times*, 7 July 1979.
7 David Jenkins, 'Five Ghosts of Balibo', *Sydney Morning Herald*, 14 October 1994.
8 *Australian*, 10 November 1975.
9 McDonald, 'Death at Balibo'. David Jenkins in his article also claims to have been told by a senior Indonesian military officer involved in the operation at that

time that he was aware of the presence of the newsmen. 'Five Ghosts of Balibo', *Sydney Morning Herald*, 14 October 1995.

10 Ibid.

11 Ibid.

12 Jolliffe, *East Timor*, p. 233.

13 See Richard Hall, *The Secret State* (Sydney: Cassell, 1978), pp. 149-150; Desmond Ball, *A Suitable Piece of Real Estate* (Sydney: Hale & Iremonger, 1980); McDonald, 'Death at Balibo'.

14 McDonald, ibid.

15 Ibid.

16 Ibid.

17 Based on interviews with former UDT leaders in Portugal. In October Guilherme Goncalves, one of the signatories, admitted that the document was a fabrication.

18 *Commonwealth Parliamentary Debates*, House of Representatives, 21 October 1975.

19 Ibid., Senate, 30 October 1975.

20 As reported by Bruce Juddery, *Canberra Times*, 31 May 1976.

21 McDonald, 'Death at Balibo'.

22 Report of the visit to East Timor by the investigation team from the Australian embassy in Jakarta, April/May, 1976.

23 J. S. Dunn, 'The East Timor Situation', Report on talks with Timorese refugees in Portugal, February 1977.

24 McDonald, 'Death at Balibo'.

25 Alan Renouf, *The Frightened Country* (Melbourne: Macmillan, 1979), p. 443.

26 *Documents on Australian Defence and Foreign Policy*, 1968-1975 (Sydney: Walsh and Munster, 1980) pp. 218-225.

27 E. G. Whitlam, 'Indonesia and Australia: Political Aspects', The Indonesian Connection (seminar held at the Australian National University, 30 November 1979), Research School of Pacific Studies, School Seminar Series.

28 Van Atta and Toohey, 'The Timor Papers', part 2.

29 Ibid.

30 Ibid.

31 *ICRC*, Annual Report 1975.

32 Dunn, 'The East Timor Situation'.

33 Jolliffe, *East Timor*, p. 180.

34 *Commonwealth Parliamentary Debates*, Senate, 30 October 1975, p. 1598.

35 Adam Malik and Major Melo Antunes, 'Portuguese Timor: Memorandum of Understanding', Rome, 3 November 1975.

36 Melbourne *Age*, 8 November 1975.

37 Jolliffe, *East Timor*, p. 185.

38 Ibid., p. 200.

39 Ibid., p. 217.

40 Ibid., p. 212.

41 Ibid., p. 215.

42 Van Atta and Toohey, 'The Timor Papers', part 2.

43 Hamish McDonald, *Suharto's Indonesia* (Melbourne: Fontana/Collins, 1980), p. 211.

Chapter Eleven
Invasion, occupation and resistance

The Indonesian assault on the Timorese capital, Dili, came on 7 December 1975, on the thirty-fourth anniversary of the Japanese surprise attack on Pearl Harbor. Although it did not come as a surprise, the Indonesians also dispensed with the niceties of a declaration of war. The attack began at about 2.00 a.m., less than twenty-four hours after President Ford and Dr Kissinger had left Jakarta after their brief visit, the delay agreed to by the Indonesians to spare the American leaders the risk of embarrassment. The long-awaited assault began with a naval bombardment of positions east and west of the town where the Indonesians believed Fretilin artillery batteries were located—information no doubt gleaned from their nocturnal sorties into the outer harbour area. The bombardment was also directed at light gun emplacements near the airport. Just before dawn paratroops from Kopassandha were dropped in the waterfront area, near the prestigious Farol residential quarter. From the outset the operation was marred by a number of miscalculations. Some troops found themselves under fire from other Indonesian units. Once ashore the attackers were to encounter fire from Fretilin forces in and near the city, and it was some hours before the main party of troops was landed.

Major-General Moerdani evidently played a key role in planning the assault on the Timorese capital (code-named *Operasi Seroja*), but operational command, it seems, was probably in the hands of Major General Suweno, *Panglima* of Kowilhan II, one of Indonesia's major regional defence commands. From an Indonesian military source it was 'the biggest military operation since independence', and initially 10,000 troops taken variously from Kopassandha, Kopasgat, Korps Marinir (the Marines), and battalions from the Siliwangi (West Java) and Brawijaya divisions were involved. This sizeable force was assembled at various bases in Java and was then moved to Surabaya by troop trains travelling in the night, to maintain maximum secrecy. The units were staged through several different bases or centres, among them Ambon, Kupang and bases set up on the islands of Wetar and Alor especially for this operation. The original plan appears to have been to attack Dili from the west and south with the forces that had mounted the covert operation against Balibo, Maliana and later Atabai, but that particular operation had become bogged down at the Lois River and, therefore, the assault on Dili was to come from the air and sea, an operation which proceeded clumsily from the very beginning. An interesting account of events on that day has come from the pen of David Jenkins, whose research included discussions with Moerdani and Colonel Dading Kalbuadi. To Moerdani's chagrin, the military command decided on an 'ambitious and unwieldy' combined operation, rather than a 'quick airborne attack' which Moerdani would have preferred. According to this account five Hercules, each with eighty paratroops, flew to the drop zone near the Hotel Tourismo. Unfortunately for the troops, one of the aircraft veered off course, after its jumpmaster had been fatally wounded by ground-fire, and thirty men, each weighed down with heavy equipment, fell into Dili Harbour where most drowned. This incident seems to have sent troops on the rampage, especially those of Battalion 502—then under the command of Major Warsito who later retired as a major-general and was governor of Nusatenggara Barat for a time. Enraged by this incident these troops then turned on the population of Dili, slaughtering perhaps hundreds of them in the first couple of days.[1] A similar account was recorded by Hamish McDonald:

> It turned out a clumsy exercise which caused great civilian suffering and vastly worsened already large diplomatic problems for Jakarta. The first operational test of the new integrated armed forces command structure, it was marked by poor co-ordination and showed up serious deficiencies in the discipline, training and equipment of some of Indonesia's best units. Kostrad (Strategic Reserve Command) Eighteenth Brigade paratroops were dropped on top of Fretilin forces withdrawing from the town, instead of behind to block off their retreat. After taking heavy casualties from Fretilin, the paratroops then came under fire from an Indonesian marine force driving inland. The remnants of the paratroops then rampaged through the town, killing and looting at random.[2]

The Kopassandha were not the only troops to go on the rampage. The attack on the Timorese capital, much of which was uncontested, turned out to be one of the most brutal operations of its kind in modern warfare. Hundreds of Timorese and Chinese were gunned down at random in the streets of Dili. In one such incident, a large number of Apodeti supporters, just released from internment by Fretilin, went out to greet their liberators in the street, only to be machine-gunned for their trouble. Indonesian troops carried out a number of public executions. Some of the condemned were selected at random, and others with the help of Apodeti collaborators. One of the most bizarre and gruesome of these atrocities occurred within twenty-four hours of the invasion and involved the killing of about 150 people. This shocking spectacle began with the execution of more than twenty women who, from various accounts, were selected at random. Some had young children who wept in distress as the soldiers tore them from the arms of their terrified mothers. The women included Isobel Lobato, the wife of Nicolau, and leaders of Fretilin's womens organisations. They were led out to the edge of the jetty and shot one at a time with the crowd of shocked onlookers being forced at gunpoint to count aloud as each execution took place. The process continued, many of the victims being Chinese. These killings were witnessed not only by the captive citizens of the city, but also by the distracted Bishop Ribeiro of Timor, who could see it all from the window of his foreshore residence. He was later to remark that the paratroops had drifted down 'like angels from the heavens', and then had behaved like 'devils'.

The gruesome spectacle at the wharf was not the only execution of its kind to take place in Dili during those early nightmarish days following the invasion. Similar killings were carried out in other parts of the capital before the senseless rampage was to subside. Not even Apodeti members were spared. About thirty supporters of the pro-integration party were shot outside the former Portuguese Military Police barracks. This party of Timorese had been sent to the barracks, and had been ordered to remove weapons and ammunition from it. According to a survivor of this killing, the Indonesian soldiers then asked the men to which political party they belonged. They all answered 'Apodeti', but the Indonesians opened fire on them with machine-guns (which the witness believed were M16s). Most of the group died in the first volley of shooting, but the Indonesians then walked around firing at bodies that showed signs of life. Five Timorese are believed to have survived this massacre, one, now a resident of Perth, by placing his injured hand over his head, lying still, and letting the blood from the wound seep over his head.

A group of Chinese community leaders who, it seems, had come out into the street to offer some kind of welcome to the vanguard of the 'new order' were gunned down. The Chinese, who had been studiously neutral in East Timor's political conflicts—especially since the UDT coup—and who were probably more disposed than any other section of the population to come to terms with integration, were to die by the hundreds in the aftermath of the invasion. In some cases the men were separated from their families and then shot. One such incident indicated the prevailing hostility towards Australians. A spacious apartment at the top of the three-storey Toko Lay building was occupied by twenty-two Chinese at the time of the invasion. They had draped from their front windows a large Australian flag which the previous occupants, a group of ASIAT doctors, had given them. The Chinese hoped that the use of the flag might afford some protection to them. According to witnesses, the sight of the flag appeared to provoke the paratroops who raced into the building where they machine-gunned the men in front of screaming, distraught women and children. The Australian flag was clearly no help to the Chinese, no doubt indicating the effect of the anti-Australian propaganda that had been fed to the troops, to the effect that Fretilin supporters were also communists, and that these included the foreigners in the territory, most of whom were from Australia. There were many other random killings of Timorese and Chinese in the streets and in houses. Apparently, faced with the orgy of indiscriminate killing, many of the residents of the capital retreated into their homes, but this was to afford them little protection. Indonesian soldiers broke into houses, especially those displaying Fretilin or even the UDT flags or symbols, and in some cases shot whole families. In the suburbs near the airport soldiers resorted to hurling grenades through the doors or windows of houses crowded with frightened people, causing heavy loss of life.

One example of the many acts of senseless murder occurred near the airport where some Timorese offered coffee to a couple of paratroops who had approached the house. The soldiers accepted the coffee, drank it, handed back the cups and then shot the two men who had provided it. Another victim was a bent eighty-year-old man who was taken outside and shot because someone had placed a small Fretilin flag outside his house. In yet another example of wanton killing, a member of Apodeti was shot while presenting his party identification card to a group of soldiers.

With the battle against Fretilin raging to the south and west of the city, this orgy of killing was reported to have continued for about a week. According to a Catholic priest in Dili after the invasion, as many as 2000 citizens of the capital, some 700 of them Chinese, were killed in the first few days of the Indonesian invasion. In a letter smuggled out of Timor some months after the invasion an elderly Chinese who had been in the territory during World War II wrote that the Indonesian excesses were far worse than anything he had experienced during the Japanese occupation.

And there was more in store for the Timorese when the first spate of killing was over. From refugee accounts most of the residents of the capital were ordered to assemble at the airport, ostensibly for a residence check. This process took one whole day, but when the people returned to their houses they were to discover the real reason for the muster. Their homes had been ransacked by the occupying troops, and all objects of any value had been removed. One Timorese woman told me that, in her case, the looting had not stopped at radios and furniture—even the windows had been removed. All of this loot and any vehicles and motorcycles the troops could lay their hands on were taken to ships in Dili Harbour and shipped to Java. And then, to round off the orgiastic nightmare, the troops demanded women and girls to help them celebrate their victory. The female relatives of Fretilin members, and members of OPMT— Organizacão Popular da Mulheres de Timor (Popular Organisation of Timorese Women) and UNITEM—União Nacional de Estudantes de Timor (National Union of Timorese Women), Timorese women and students' organisations linked with Fretilin, were singled out for particularly harsh treatment. Most were arrested and imprisoned, some of them in a section of the Hotel Tropical in the centre of Dili. According to several Timorese who had managed to visit an OPMT prison, some of them had ugly scars on their breasts from cigarette burns Bakin torturers had inflicted on them. One visitor to the prison who saw some of the women about six months after the invasion was told by inmates that they had been raped repeatedly and that about half of them were pregnant.

The demands made by the troops for young women were said to have been a daily occurrence and such requests were not to be trifled with. Some men were killed because they objected vigorously to such demands, and many others were severely beaten or imprisoned because they refused to surrender their daughters.

Church and community leaders appealed to the senior Indonesian officers to put a stop to the killing, but there was little response. Colonel Dading Kubuadi coldly reminded one of them that this was war and people got killed in war. Some Indonesian officers were troubled at the brutal and undisciplined behaviour of the troops, but told Timorese leaders that they were powerless to put a stop to it. Even officials in Jakarta felt obliged to admit, usually privately, that some excesses had occurred in the course of the invasion, but claimed that the troops concerned were later disciplined and that order was soon restored, a standard explanation later repeated by Australian and US officials when questioned closely about the attack. The rape of Dili was only the beginning. When the towns of Liquiça and Maubara were eventually wrested from Fretilin's control the Indonesians put to death nearly all members of their Chinese communities. When they finally forced Fretilin to withdraw from Aileu, Indonesian troops, in a brutal public spectacle, machine-gunned the remaining population of the town, except for children under the age of four, who were sent back to Dili in trucks. These infant survivors were ultimately to be placed in an orphanage near Jakarta where the 'poor victims of the Fretilin terror' were to become the subject of the charitable indulgence of Tien Harto, the President's wife, and her coterie of bored wives of the affluent and powerful in the Indonesian capital.

One early victim of the Indonesian attack on Dili was another Australian journalist, Roger East. East was a man of long and varied experience in his profession; he was something of an adventurer who had worked in Cyprus, Spain, China and England, as well as in Australia. There he had gone from being publicity officer for the Country Party in a Queensland electorate to the post of press officer for the Darwin Reconstruction Board, an organisation set up in the aftermath of the devastation caused by Cyclone Tracy. It was while he was in Darwin that his interest in Timor first began, but his decision to go there was said to have been motivated by his outrage at the killing of the newsmen at Balibo. Early in November East set off for Dili and, with the encouragement of the Fretilin leaders, he launched an East Timor news agency. Fretilin obviously felt that its message was not getting across to the outside world though this was hardly the fault of the existing AAP–Reuters representation in Dili, which was in the capable hands of the young Australian journalist Jill Jolliffe.

There can be little doubt that Roger East went to Timor with a commitment to Fretilin, as a journalist and not as a soldier of fortune, or mercenary, which some Indonesians were later to suggest. Before leaving Darwin he was reported to have told his sister: 'These people have been betrayed. Someone's got to go and get the truth out.'[3] But he also made it clear that he was not going there to fight for the Timorese. His brother Bill apparently urged him to arm himself in the event of an Indonesian attack, but his reply was that he 'was too old for that, he had lived too long with just a typewriter'.[4]

Roger East developed a deep affection for the Timorese during those weeks leading up to the invasion of Dili, and when Australian authorities advised their nationals to leave the territory he was the only Australian in Dili to ignore the advice. It must have been a decision he made with his eyes open because he had already been named in the strident propaganda from the *Operasi Komodo* station in West Timor as a communist who would share the fate of his colleagues who had been killed at Balibo. He ignored the attempts of his friends and acquaintances to persuade him to return to Darwin and appears to have planned initially to join Fretilin in the mountains where he intended to continue to report the war in Timor to the outside world. He was last seen by Australians on the eve of the invasion, 6 December, by members of the International Red Cross team who were about to leave for the island of Atauro. According to Jill Jolliffe who was one of the last to leave, he was still staying at the Hotel Turismo which faces the beach, and had not taken up an invitation from the Fretilin leaders to move to the south of the town, presumably in readiness for their withdrawal from the capital.[5] Why East did not follow this advice is not clear, but one plausible explanation is that he delayed his own retreat to the end, in order to send some first-hand reports of the initial attack via the Marconi, the city's telecommunications centre, located near the waterfront. Apparently East managed to send a short dispatch about an hour after the Indonesian forces began their landing, but for some reason the Australian AAP–Reuters office never made use of it, and no record was kept. Perhaps the message was garbled, as the Indonesian troops would already have been in the vicinity of the centre, one of their early objectives, at the time that East was trying to file his story. His last recorded dispatch was received only a matter of hours before the invasion, and it described how the capital had become quiet and almost deserted as many of the Timorese streamed out of the town heading for the comparative safety of the mountains.

There have been a number of accounts of just how Roger East died, the first from Fretilin not long after the invasion and the latest in October 1980, from two Chinese who had just managed to get to Portugal from Timor. In spite of a few discrepancies in some of these accounts, it is possible to put together a rough reconstruction of how and when the Australian journalist was killed. It seems probable that, after having handed in his last dispatch, East went to an apartment not far from the Marconi Centre, where he may have intended to prepare a detailed report on the invasion, before moving to the hills. This apartment was located near where the Indonesian attacking force had a brush with Fretilin troops and sustained some casualties. As it turned out the Fretilin patrol involved in this skirmish was one sent by the Timorese leaders in a desperate and ill-fated last-minute bid to rescue East. The Timorese, who were led by Fernando Carmo, one of East Timor's best military commanders, ran into an Indonesian paratroop unit and, after bitter hand-to-hand fighting, was wiped out. It was not long before the Australian journalist was intercepted by Indonesians troops, and from there he was taken to the execution site at the wharf. A Chinese witness later recounted that on the morning of 8 December he saw a European, whose description resembled that of East, being dragged to the wharf by three Indonesian soldiers.[6] The captive's hands were bound with wire, but he continued to struggle while the soldiers kicked him and prodded him with their bayonets. And during this ordeal East apparently hurled a constant stream of abuse at his captors. Another Chinese recorded the Australian's execution at the wharf. He was standing only a few metres away when East was brought before the Indonesian firing squad. According to this account, Roger East was forced to stand on the edge of the wharf, and was ordered to face the sea. He refused to comply with this order, turned around, and, facing the Indonesians, shouted: 'I am not Fretilin, I am an Australian.' However, his protests were ignored and he was then shot down by the squad, who, from their shoulder badges, were members of Battalion 502, a unit of the East Java Brawijaya Division, then under the command of Major Warsito. East's body fell into the sea, and was presumably among the many corpses that were later washed up on the beach.

The case of Roger East's disappearance was treated with a mixture of disdain and arrogance by the Indonesian authorities, who finally agreed to take up the matter with the forces of the 'Provisional Government of East Timor'. It was then claimed that no one had sighted any trace of the journalist. For a time the Indonesians were suggesting that East had gone to the mountains with the Fretilin forces. One curious report came from Jakarta years later—from an Indonesian army officer who claimed to have seen a report on the execution of the Australian journalist, a report that had said that East was a communist and had been carrying a weapon when apprehended. Apart from the execution, the circumstances, as described, seem improbable, and it is possible that this 'leak' was contrived by certain officials with the aim of disposing of one of the several embarrassing incidents which continued to affect the Canberra–Jakarta relationship. The inquiries carried out by the Department of Foreign Affairs have hardly been exhaustive or enthusiastically followed up. Admittedly the circumstances were not conducive to fruitful investigation. However, after the testimony of the Chinese witnesses in 1980 the Department of Foreign Affairs raised the matter with the Indonesian government and, predictably, was told bluntly that there was no truth in the accounts given by the witnesses, Pedro Lay and Chong Keiu Nhan. Indonesian troops had not shot Roger East, Australian officials were told.

The case of Roger East followed a pattern very similar to the Balibo killings. There is a great deal of evidence of a damning though circumstantial kind that most of the six newsmen who died within a period of less than two months, were in fact murdered by Indonesian troops because, had they been allowed to live, they could have exposed the truth about Indonesia's intervention in East Timor. No formal protest appears to have been lodged by the Australian government.

Not all the residents of Dili were treated with such disregard. The Apodeti leader, Arnaldo dos Reis Araujo, was quickly freed and moved to a safe place. Special treatment was also given to DRET's Minister for Economic Coordination Jose Goncalves, who had chosen to remain in Dili for health reasons. Goncalves' protector was his father, Guilherme, the *liurai* of Atsabe and a leader of Apodeti. But this protection did not extend beyond his son's immediate family. Jose Goncalves' sister-in-law Isobel, the wife of Nicolau Lobato, was dragged off by Indonesian troops to the execution site at the wharf, where she, too, was shot. After some hard negotiating her small son, Jose's life was spared. He was later adopted by Jose Goncalves and, after independence, became an official in the government of East Timor.

When the Indonesian attack began the remnants of Portugal's colonial administration, with a small contingent of troops, were still ensconced on the island of Atauro, where two Portuguese corvettes, *João Roby* and *Afonso Cerqueira*, were at anchor. The presence of these warships had caused the Indonesian naval planners some concern. The corvettes were modern, having not long been commissioned by the Portuguese and, according to later remarks by a senior Indonesian naval officer, had they intervened, they would have been more than a match for the ageing Indonesian warships. But the Indonesians need not have worried. The ships' officers and the remaining officials of the administration merely acted as passive witnesses to the attack on Dili, which could be observed clearly from the island. The radar screens of the corvettes picked up the Indonesian aircraft and with the help of powerful binoculars the officers were able to follow the outline of the attack. Eventually, the Portuguese decided to abandon Atauro and sail to Darwin. They were to have left at 6.30 a.m. on 8 December, but the anchor of one of the vessels had become embedded in a coral outcrop and the departure was delayed for some twelve hours. Thus, at 6.30 p.m. on 8 December, Portugal ignominiously withdrew from its most remote colonial outpost to which its daring explorers had first ventured more than 460 years earlier. In some respects the termination of its long colonial tutelage was an extraordinary anticlimax. The Portuguese were forced out of this particular colony not by impatient nationalists—on the contrary, the Timorese leaders had tried to entice them to return—but by the aggression of a neighbouring power which had publicly denied any claim to East Timor. The corvettes and a group of Portuguese officers were to linger in Darwin for several months in the hope that international reaction to Indonesia's assault on their colony might eventually prompt Jakarta to order the withdrawal of its forces. But Indonesia's determination to integrate East Timor remained unshaken; in the face of the weak resolve of the international community, the Portuguese, with few apparent regrets, withdrew for all time their colonial presence in South-East Asia.

The resistance put up by Fretilin in the streets of Dili was little more than a delaying tactic. But on the outskirts of the town the Timorese troops staunchly held their ground, pinning the invasion forces down for several weeks. On 10 December a second invading force was landed at Baucau to secure East Timor's second-largest town and to gain control of the territory's main airfield, whose strip was designed to accommodate modern commercial jet aircraft. For some reason Fretilin had established only a light defence force at Baucau and the Indonesians were able to acquire control of the town and the airport with little fighting and little loss of life. The town is located on the edge of a high plain, and the Timorese forces felt that the defence of Baucau was beyond their means, yet the Falintil soon began to mount guerrilla attacks on Indonesian positions from bases in the nearby mountains and hills.

Meanwhile, in the Dili area, the Indonesians found themselves pinned down on the small coastal plain between Tibar to the west and the rugged hills projecting out to Aria Branca to the east. With field and naval guns they pounded the Falintil positions in the mountains to the south, but the Timorese were continuously on the move, and sustained relatively few casualties during this early period. Within two weeks of the attack on Dili, the Indonesians must have realised that their campaign to integrate the Portuguese colony was going to involve a long and bitter struggle. Fretilin had at its disposal an army of more than 10,000 men—a hard professional core of some 2500 regular troops and another 7000 who had obtained military training under the Portuguese. A further 10,000 or so were given short courses of military instruction. It was a 'people's army'. None of the Fretilin commanders had been tutored on military tactics or strategy at staff colleges, and none had command experience other than in junior posts (mostly noncommissioned) before the civil war. However, several had already emerged as shrewd and inspiring leaders, especially in the prevailing guerrilla warfare conditions. One of the ablest, Fernando Carmo, was killed in the futile attempt to rescue Roger East, but commanders like Alves, Gusmão (Xanana) Soares and Nicolau Lobato were soon to demonstrate impressive leadership calibre. Their operations forced Indonesia to keep sizeable forces in East Timor throughout the twenty-four years of occupation, inflicting heavy casualties on them.

At the outset they were not short of weapons suitable for guerrilla warfare. The Portuguese had recently replenished their arsenal in East Timor with a wide range of modern NATO-type light weaponry. I once reminded Lobato that the ACFOA mission was concerned with humanitarian and not military aid, the Timorese leader retorted impatiently: 'The one thing we don't need is military aid.' The Falintil had benefited enormously from the experience it had gained in countering *Operasi Komodo's* covert operations under Colonel Dading Kalbuadi since the previous October, operations that had really achieved little for Indonesia. The Timorese had become conditioned to artillery and rocket fire, familiar with Indonesian tactics in the field, and had gained vital experience in the kind of guerrilla fighting most suitable to their situation. In practice, the Timorese leaders had already learnt not to become drawn into battles in which they risked being cut off and isolated, or into engagements with Indonesian units whose superior firepower could inflict heavy casualties and material losses on the exposed Timorese forces. Well before the attack on Dili, as has already been described, Fretilin had been preparing itself for the life-and-death guerrilla campaign that was to follow. Stocks of food, arms and ammunition had been transported to hide-outs in the mountain regions, most of them well away from roads that would eventually help the penetration of Indonesian forces with tanks and other armoured vehicles.

It soon became apparent to the Indonesian operational command—which was accorded Kodam* status—that an even larger military operation would have to be mounted if Fretilin were to be overpowered, and if the Angkatan Bersenjata Republik Indonesia—Armed Forces of the Republic of Indonesia (ABRI) were to move beyond the precincts of Dili and Baucau. And so substantial reinforcements—involving 10,000 to 15,000 troops—were ordered into the fray around Christmas Day and Boxing Day 1975, and additional landings were made at Liquiça and Maubara with massacres of the civilian population being later reported in both towns. Thus, by the end of the year more than 20,000 Indonesian troops were in the small territory. According to an Indonesian source, by April the numbers had risen to 35,000 soldiers. The Indonesian wrote:

> A big portion from all the elite/comando [sic] troops have been sent to Timor, like the red berets (RPKAD, later Kopassus), orange berets (Kopasgat), violet berets (Korps Marinir/KKO), plus troops from Java (especially from West Java (Siliwangi) and East Java (Brawijaya))'.[7]

This source made the interesting comment that Diponegoro (Central Java) units had not been sent to Timor because they were 'Suharto's troops'. Was this an indication that the President was resolved to distance himself from the Timor operation— The above description of the Timor force was supported by a statement in April from the Australian member of parliament Ken Fry who quoted intelligence estimates in Australia. He said that there were some 42,000 troops in the whole of Timor, 32,000 in East Timor and another 10,000 in the western half of the island.

In spite of the presence of this formidable force, well supported by aircraft and naval units, the Indonesians made only very slow progress. Two of their most important targets, the towns of Aileu and Ermera, the centre of the coffee industry, did not fall into their hands for three months. Aileu was taken in February, while Ermera was not captured until 9 April 1976. Ainaro, in the south, was abandoned by Fretilin on 21 February, and the Indonesian forces entered Lospalos in the east a few days later. But after four months of heavy fighting the invading forces were still in control of only a few small pockets

---

*Komando Daerah Militar. The Kodam is a regional command, usually covering a province, or in some cases two provinces.

while the Fretilin forces moved freely throughout most of the country. A Timorese who had served as a guide and an interpreter to one of the senior Indonesian military officers later told me that in the early months of the fighting as the Indonesian forces moved into the central regions they killed many of the Timorese they encountered, and many hamlets were burnt to the ground.[8] Fretilin forces continued to attack and ambush the Indonesian infantry and casualties soon began to mount. The main hospital in Dili was taken over by the army, and its wards were full, with many patients being sent back to Gatot Subroto and other military hospitals in Java. This high casualty rate was referred to in the letter from the Indonesian source already cited. He wrote:

> Actually, it is no secret anymore [sic] in Indonesia. Especially in Jakarta, where the Army hospital (RS Gatot Subroto) and the Airforce hospital at Halim airbase is [sic] overflooded with war victims. And what makes it more tragic is that the families-even their wives-are not allowed to visit their husbands in the hospital. At the same time, news that many Indonesian soldiers were killed by the Timorese is just trickling down in Jakarta and the whole of Java. So knowing that your husband, son or father has to go to Timor is nearly as shocking as a death trial/penalty.

For all parties then, the Timor campaign had a bloody beginning. Although few Timorese were in favour of integration, there can be little doubt that the rapacious and brutal behaviour of the occupying forces greatly stiffened the resolve of the resistance and provided Fretilin with a degree of popular support greater than it might otherwise have enjoyed. After the savagery of the first days of the invasion, tens of thousands of Timorese fled from their homes to the relative sanctuary of the mountain regions behind Fretilin lines, including thousands who had been supporters of the UDT and Apodeti until then. A striking example of the extent of this exodus was contained in a letter written at the end of 1976 to the Governor of the Province by a Timorese official in the Baucau area which, before the invasion, had a population of 85,000.[9] He reported that 32,000 people in his district 'had presented themselves' to Indonesian forces between 10 December and the end of the following February, but that, because of the excesses of the occupying troops, only 9646 remained, the rest having fled to the mountains. A visitor to Ainaro a couple of months earlier reported that there were no Timorese left in the town. The atrocities committed in Dili, Maubara and Liquiça caused entire populations of neighbouring towns and villages to abandon their homes to seek refuge behind Fretilin lines. For most people it seems to have been a reluctant and desperate choice, and I have never encountered any evidence to support the later Indonesian contention that Fretilin troops forced the civilian population to flee to the mountains with them, a contention sometimes repeated by US and Australian officials. On the contrary, Fretilin leaders were to become concerned at their inability to cope with the basic needs of more than half a million people, with limited food supplies, few medicines, and without doctors. As the war intensified the Timorese leaders tried to encourage some of this large, displaced civilian population to return to the Indonesian-occupied areas in an attempt to ease the pressure on the dwindling food supplies at their disposal.

It is hard to understand why the Indonesians behaved with such disregard for the rights and welfare of the Timorese when they had so much to gain— internationally, and in Timor—by treating the Timorese with understanding and respect. There are, however, a number of explanations. Generals Moerdani and Suweno are reported to have ordered their troops to crack down on all opposition, in the hope that this would weaken support for the resistance and bring an early end to the fighting. Individual commanders also reportedly incited hatred of the Timorese through the propaganda that they fed to their troops in an effort to strengthen their fighting spirit. Some were told that they were fighting communists, while others were given to understand that they were embarking on a Jihad, or holy war, against Timorese Christians. The language barrier presented a serious problem. The Indonesians spoke neither Portuguese nor Tetum, and the Timorese at that time had no knowledge of Bahasa Indonesian. But the language problem merely masked a deeper-rooted cultural difference. In religion, some ninety per cent of the Timorese with whom the Indonesian soldiers first came into contact were Christians, especially the residents of the towns and larger villages. The vast majority of the Indonesian soldiers were Moslems from Java, and the only Moslems that the Timorese had encountered were the members of the tiny 'Arab' community near Dili. They kept to themselves and were regarded by some as having a lower status in local society. Then there was the traditional fear and dislike of the Javanese, a tradition kept alive not only by the Portuguese, but also by stories from Timorese on the Indonesian side of the island, many of whom bore a deep resentment of their political domination by the Javanese through the Pemerintah Pusat ('central government'). On the Indonesian side, there have been reports that many soldiers viewed their operation as a further phase in the ongoing campaign to suppress communism that had followed the events of September 1965 (Gestapu), and they set about this task with similar brutality and indiscriminate killing. Fear of Indonesia existed before the invasion on 7 December, but after the terrible experiences of the East Timorese at the callous hands of the invading troops it was transformed into a deep-seated hatred which made the 'pacification' of East Timor a particularly unpleasant, and dangerous, ordeal for the Indonesian soldiers. This aspect was alluded to in the letter from Indonesia previously referred to which remarked:

> When I saw troops coming back from Timor last month (red berets) I was not surprised to see them so delighted, released, talkative, because they have escaped from hell.

The presence of such hostility and the lack of any popular support for *integrasi* did not deter the Indonesians from proceeding with what must be one of the most cynical deceptions of its kind, rivalling Nazi Germany's excuse for the seizure of Sudetenland and Czechoslovakia and, more recently, Saddam Hussein's attempted annexation of Kuwait. In the first place, the Indonesians denied that there was any invasion at all: anti-Fretilin forces—who, if we accepted the Indonesian propaganda build-up before the invasion, had been converging on Dili from the west and south—had forced Fretilin out of the city and Indonesian 'volunteers' had been sent to Timor at their request. In reality, the small band of Timorese collaborators played an even less significant role in the invasion of Dili than they had done at Balibo seven weeks earlier. The Kota leader, Jose Martins, told me that he and several of his colleagues were at Atabai, far away from Dili, when the invasion was launched.

After the invasion the Indonesians brought most of the leaders to Dili, where a 'Provisional Government of East Timor' (PGET) was set up, under Arnaldo dos Reis Araujo, with Tomas Goncalves, Mario Carrascalão, Jose Goncalves (formerly of Fretilin) and Lopes da Cruz as its 'ministers'. According to Indonesian propaganda, the PGET had been set up after the 'anti-Fretilin forces' had taken the capital, and its troops were then preoccupied with the task of mopping up Fretilin remnants in the mountains—with a little help from the Indonesian volunteers. In truth, the PGET had no army, no bureaucracy and little political support. After the invasion in which the so-called 'anti-Fretilin forces' played no part, the Indonesians banned the UDT and the splinter groups, and began to construct their pro-integration political facade around Apodeti. For a few months the PGET was given an aura of independence by the Indonesian generals. Any inquiries about the situation in East Timor, such as the whereabouts of Roger East, and the request by the UN secretary-general for a special envoy to be admitted to the territory, were supposedly relayed by Jakarta to the PGET for a decision. I was told by Timorese officials who were in Dili at the time that the PGET had no separate existence or powers at all. It was under the constant direction of officers like Brigadier-General Dading Kalbuadi (promoted some time after the Balibo/Maliana operation), and a tough Sumatran called Colonel Sinaga, with Sugiyanto continuing his 'liaison' activities. One Timorese leader said that not only were some of the PGET's press releases, which surfaced in Jakarta, written by their Indonesian tutors, but most were prepared without even consulting the Timorese collaborators. In a few cases they were not even seen by the PGET ministers until after their release. In those first few months all activities, foreign contacts, demonstrations, and so on, were carefully orchestrated and controlled. To assist the Bakin officers, a special group of Indonesians who closely resembled the Timorese was brought into East Timor, mostly from nearby islands. On the rare occasions when foreign visitors came to the territory, these 'Timorese' were always present to tell the visitors just what the Indonesian military wanted them to know. An operation of this kind was mounted, as we have seen, for the benefit of the Australian diplomats sent to investigate the killing of the newsmen at Balibo.

When international pressure began to mount unexpectedly in the wake of the invasion certain prominent Timorese were sent abroad to international centres considered important by Jakarta. But before they left, their wives and families were placed in special custody 'for Indonesia's security', as the briefing colonel from Bakin told them. Thus, Mario Carrascalão, Jose Martins and Jose Goncalves were sent to the United Nations, João Carrascalão was sent to the Middle East,

Paolo Pires to the Netherlands, and another emissary to Japan; their task was to convince their audiences that integration reflected the wishes of the majority of the Timorese, and that Indonesia had not invaded their territory. The exercise did not work as well as the Indonesians had intended. Most of the Timorese were still in a state of near shock, after having witnessed, or heard about, the rape of Dili (Jose Goncalves was still upset at the execution of his sister-in-law). At least two of the group, Paolo Pires and João Carrascalão, tried to convey something of the real situation in the former Portuguese colony, but the Indonesians found out about their 'perfidy' and reacted with anger. Carrascalão was placed under house arrest at Kupang where he was to remain until shortly before he was repatriated to Portugal in mid-1976. Pires also managed to get to Portugal. In January the Kota leader, Jose Martins, who had been held in high trust by Bakin, began to disengage himself from the Indonesian embrace, and in the following March he formally 'defected' at the United Nations where he submitted a confidential report on the real extent of Indonesian involvement in East Timor.[10] Another Timorese member of the delegation sent to the United Nations became very distressed in New York and was taken to hospital. The Indonesians apparently suspected that he might defect and, in an extraordinary episode, two members of the embassy staff went to the New York hospital and successfully arranged for the Timorese to be handed over to them. He was then quietly and quickly flown back to Jakarta.

Meanwhile, Indonesia continued to report via Jakarta or Kupang new successes of the non-existent PGET armed forces. Thus, on 1 February 1976 the *Indonesian Times* reported that 'PGET forces have liberated the towns of Suai, Zumalai, Ainaro, Betano, Same, Beaco, Uatolari, Lospalos, Tutuala, Lautem, Matudo, Maibesse, Turiscai, Baquai [Baguia, presumably] and Iliomar without any resistance.' The report also carried a bold threat for a government without troops, ships or aircraft, in short, without armed forces. It said: 'The Armed Forces of the PGET have instructed the shooting of any aircraft and warships approaching East Timor in order to maintain security in the newly liberated areas.' On 9 January Adam Malik made a lightning visit to Dili, accompanied by a few Indonesian and selected foreign journalists. The reception was carefully orchestrated by the military occupation authorities: thousands of troops were deployed beyond the outskirts of the town to prevent Fretilin troops from disrupting the occasion. Military vehicles were moved out of sight and a reception was set up with a liberal sprinkling of Indonesian troops in civilian clothes among the crowd. From the few independent accounts it was a spiritless occasion. One of the journalists was the late Tony Joyce of the ABC who later reported: 'It would be hard to call the Dili welcome a spontaneous demonstration of the feelings of the Timorese people. From the start Mr Malik's flying visit was carefully stage-managed. In Dili about 1000 people were assembled outside Government House. On cue about every five minutes the crowd raised their red and white Indonesian flags and shouted pro-Indonesian slogans.'[11] But Mr Malik recounted the occasion so differently it is hard to believe that the two were describing the same function. When he returned to Jakarta he was reported as telling the Indonesian press that 'the enthusiasm of the people of East Timor for integration with Indonesia is overflowing greatly and cannot be held back...Their system of administration is already the same as that of Indonesia. Security is quite certainly assured, because it is indeed peaceful there.'[12]

In February it was announced that on 31 January all of the political parties had 'dissolved themselves' and that a new unified party had been created. In a statement before the UN Security Council, Guilherme Goncalves announced that a 'deliberative council' had also been established 'to help the provisional government in reaching important decisions'. Goncalves reported that this council, to which he had been appointed chairman, would perform the functions of a provisional assembly, pending setting up a 'People's Assembly'. And so a People's Assembly was formed, not as an elected body but, in the words of a PGET statement, in keeping with 'the traditions and identity of the people of East Timor', suggesting a representative process featuring consensus and consent. This assembly was described as being composed of 'prominent citizens of East Timor', complemented by 'representatives from the concelhos', and including *chefes de suco*, *liurais*, and representatives of religious groups. What really happened was that Indonesian intelligence officers, usually accompanied by Apodeti officials, summoned local rulers and, in some cases, simply directed them to become members of the assembly. The 'elections' were openly rigged, with Timorese being rounded up by Indonesian troops and escorted to polling booths where their votes were cast under the careful scrutiny of the occupation forces. On 31 May it was announced that a thirty-seven member 'Popular Representative Assembly' had, at its first meeting, unanimously approved a petition to the Indonesian president for the territory to be integrated into the Republic of Indonesia, after less than two hours discussion of the proposal. This meeting was witnessed by a number of foreign diplomats and some twenty Indonesian and foreign journalists who spent about three hours in Dili in yet another carefully stage-managed visit. This time, apart from temporarily removing all signs of Indonesia's military presence, the occupying forces took away several hundred grave markers from a square near the wharf which had been converted into an Indonesian military cemetery.

The next step in this extraordinary 'act of free choice' was for a 'petition' from the Popular Assembly to be presented to President Suharto. This was done in grand style. A forty-four-man delegation, including the entire Popular Assembly as well as the PGET, was flown to Jakarta and on 7 June 1976 the petition for integration was ceremoniously handed to the Indonesian leader. In accepting it, President Suharto said that before the act of integration was completely formalised Indonesia wished once again 'to ascertain the wishes of the people of East Timor'. He told the deputation that, 'with the consent of our brothers in East Timor', a mission would be sent from Jakarta for the express purpose of making an on-the-spot assessment of the wishes of the Timorese, so that 'a quick and firm decision' could be taken on the question. Therefore, yet another layer was added to the facade of East Timor's act of free choice. This time a government mission, led by Minister for Home Affairs Amir Machmud, went to the territory. But again the visit was very brief, and would hardly have allowed time for its members to probe beneath the surface calm secured by the military occupation—that is, if any delegates had been so disposed. This was clearly not the delegation's role. Amir Machmud admitted as much before the group left Dili: 'My delegation does not come here to investigate, check or test the authority of the petition for integration with Indonesia.' As in the case of the May visit a number of representatives of foreign missions were included in the entourage—but not including officials from Australia or the United States. Once again a reception was carefully stage-managed, a performance at which the occupying authorities were soon to become expert. The Indonesian troops were moved out of the suburb of Farol where they were occupying most of the houses; some went to the hills behind the capital to ensure that Fretilin did not threaten the proceedings, while others donned civilian clothes and helped make up the crowd, ensuring that it behaved in keeping with the contrived spirit of the occasion. These troops were also instructed to see to it that the Timorese, especially the bolder dissidents, did not make contact with foreigners or the press. A number of former UDT leaders who had become very critical of Indonesia's occupation were imprisoned for the duration of the visit. The other townspeople were ordered into the streets to take part in pro-integration demonstrations. Timorese prisoners, incarcerated in at least three places, were moved away from the city.

The sombre welcome of the Timorese does not seem to have made any impression on Amir Machmud, who made the surprising statement that 'the wish for integration with Indonesia was decided by the whole people of this territory'. He then went on to assure his captive audience, as was subsequently reported in the Indonesian Times, that 'the Republic of Indonesia would not disappoint the hopes of the people of East Timor for swift integration with Indonesia on the basis of Pancasila [the five principles on which the Indonesian Republic is based] and the 1945 Constitution'.[13] The Minister promised the confused and bewildered Timorese that his delegation would do everything in its power 'to make the process of integration as smooth and as quick as possible'. The diplomats who elected to join this 'fact-finding mission' were a curious collection. They included the South Korean, Malaysian, Iranian and Syrian ambassadors, the chargés d'affaires of Afghanistan and Iraq, and lower-ranking representatives from Panama, South Yemen, and India. The facts presumably were not hard to ascertain, because the whole visit took little more than one day. The act of free choice was a very thin and transparent exercise. More than two-thirds of the population of the territory were behind Fretilin lines and Timorese who were officials in the PGET at the time stated that only a handful of those in occupied zones had any enthusiasm for the future that was being forcibly imposed on them.

A confidential report written to President Suharto by the pro-Indonesian governor, Arnaldo dos Reis Araujo, provides an interesting insight into the real situation in June 1976, that is, on the eve of the formal act of integration.[14]

Araujo complained that his government was completely subordinate to the Indonesian army leaders who displayed no confidence in integration. He said that although some Timorese had greeted the Indonesian troops as liberators, their support had changed to opposition with the killing of members of the pro-Indonesian Apodeti. The Governor lamented to the Indonesian president:

> We concede that the looting of private businesses, government offices and the state treasury could be due to the emotions of war, but it is difficult to understand why it continues six months after, leaving everybody in a state of cruel insecurity, that they may lose the little of their savings which have escaped from foreign hands... Day and night, at my home and office, widows, orphans, children and cripples come begging for milk and clothing. I can do nothing but join my tears to theirs, because the provisional Government owns nothing.

His comment on the position of businesses is interesting:

> In Dili 130 business houses have already reopened, but none are under the control of their previous owners, or the Timorese people, and are causing inflation of around 500 to 1,000%. The articles displayed raise many doubts about their origins.

The report also made some revealing comments on the housing situation.

> The military continues to use private houses, leaving the former colonial army barracks vacant, and we have to take into consideration that thousands of refugees are still living in schools, government offices and clinics.

This then was a leading collaborator's description of some aspects of life under the *Orde Baru*, at about the time Minister Amir Machmud had proclaimed that the desire for integration was an expression of the will 'of the whole people of this territory'.

It was at first believed that East Timor would be declared Indonesia's 27th Province on the country's national day, 17 August, but the whole process was rushed forward, in an obvious attempt to present the United Nations and the world with a fait accompli, before the following UN General Assembly session. Thus, on 16 July, a month earlier than expected, the Indonesian Parliament dutifully passed a bill incorporating the Portuguese colony into Indonesia, and on the following day the bill was signed into law, completing the legal formalities of what must have been the most cynical and contrived denial of the right of self-determination in the entire postwar process of decolonisation.

Not surprisingly, the spoils of office went to the small band of Timorese who were trusted supporters of Indonesia. On 4 August Arnaldo dos Reis Araujo, the PGET puppet leader, was appointed Governor of the 27th Province, and Lopes da Cruz, Deputy Governor. Guilherme Goncalves became chairman of the local assembly, the Provisional DPRD (the Dewan Perwakilan Rakyat Daerah, or Regional People's Representative Council). Other trusted Timorese, such as João Tavares and Tomas Goncalves were appointed *bupatis* of the district subdivisions. The *concelhos* now became *kebupatan* to conform with the Indonesian equivalent level of territorial administration. This facade of self-rule was as thin as the act of free choice itself. East Timor was all but under military occupation, and the most powerful man in all matters of administration was Brigadier-General Dading Kalbuadi, now the *panglima*, or territorial commander. The local DPR was managed by Colonel Sinaga, called the 'Black God' by the Timorese, who feared and disliked him. It was, therefore, something of an extravagant exaggeration for the Indonesians to announce some months later that, following the unanimous request of the Timorese DPR, Sinaga had been appointed its secretary, known by the acronym, *sekwilda*.

Meanwhile, the Indonesians had kept up a steady flow of propaganda about the rapidly improving situation in the territory, and the steadily weakening position of Fretilin which, according to Jakarta, had been reduced to a number of terrorist bands. The real situation was very different. For example, on 3 May 1976, Jakarta reported that the East Timorese were now clamouring to join Indonesia and, as the *Indonesian Times* put it, 'no power in the world can check the desire of the East Timorese to join the Republic of Indonesia'. Yet at about that time when rumours spread that emigration to Portugal could be arranged through the Dutch embassy and the International Red Cross, some 27,000 Timorese applied within a week or so to leave Timor before the Indonesians put a stop to recording this flood of applications, and demanded that the list be scrapped.

On the eve of the act of integration life in the occupied areas of the territory continued to be grim and insecure. Most of the Timorese in the capital were concentrated in a few centres, their houses having been looted and occupied by Indonesian soldiers. As one priest who visited Dili at the time commented: 'There were no signs of external bombardment; just houses cleaned out from inside.'[15] Most people had just enough food for one small meal, usually of cassava and rice, each day. There was practically no meat available, and the capital's sizeable colony of dogs had all but disappeared, most of them having been eaten by the starving population. The priest noted that people everywhere were suffering from the effects of severe malnutrition (beri-beri, and the like) and that most of the women in the church where he celebrated mass were in mourning. Little medical treatment was available, the army having taken over Dili Hospital for its war-wounded. And the sounds of war were always to be heard. During the day there was the distant sound of heavy guns and rockets, and often at night Fretilin units launched attacks in the vicinity of the capital. For the Timorese citizens the atmosphere was dominated by insecurity, fear and oppression. It was common for Indonesian soldiers to slap or kick any Timorese who failed to stand to attention as they walked by. To the older people it was reminiscent of the behaviour of the occupying Japanese troops during World War II. Timorese suspected of having links with Fretilin or of opposition to integration were constantly being arrested and taken to the dreaded Bakin interrogation rooms in the Hotel Tropical where they were tortured or beaten, sometimes with Colonel Sinaga or Major Papilaya observing the proceedings. Months after the initial rampage in the aftermath of the invasion, women were still being raped, and men beaten for trying to prevent these brutalities. Excesses such as these prompted the Bishop to write to Adam Malik and complain bitterly about the behaviour of the Indonesian soldiers. Some officials complained to Dading Kalbuadi, now comfortably ensconced in the house formerly occupied by the Mayor of Dili, to be told, with a shrug, that such things are inevitable in war, or that there was simply nothing that he could do about it.

Disobedience of the orders of the military command brought severe penalties, sometimes for seemingly minor offences. For example, on 17 August 1976, three or four Timorese were shot for having refused to attend the National Day, or Harian Merdeka, demonstration. There were penalties for listening to the Fretilin radio and, for a time, to Radio Australia. From time to time Governor Araujo tried to intervene, but this served to antagonise the ruling army officers, who were later to have him removed from office. Even Lopes da Cruz was shocked at what was happening in newly occupied districts and on 10 February he told the Indonesian press in Jakarta of excesses by the troops, but was careful to add that these had occurred as revenge for Fretilin's cruelty. Also during that month da Cruz was to declare that more than 50,000 Timorese had died in the war. However, this statement was later 'clarified' in Jakarta, it being asserted that what the Timorese leader meant was that there had been more than 50,000 victims, the figure including those people who had lost their homes and had sought refuge in Indonesia. This correction was used by Indonesians, and apologists for Indonesia, to illustrate just how inaccurate reporting of the Timor situation was at the time. I was able to interview one of da Cruz's UDT colleagues who stated that da Cruz had used the word 'massacred' and had sought to draw world attention to the killing that was going on in East Timor. But immediately after his statement had been released Lopes da Cruz had a hurried visit from Colonel Sugiyanto who insisted that the statement be changed immediately because it was potentially very damaging to Indonesia. Under the Colonel's 'guidance' da Cruz' remarks were modified and the correction was repeated ad nauseam by Indonesia's sympathisers in the United States and Australia. Tomas Goncalves, one of the foremost integrationists, was distressed at the wanton killing of Timorese in Aileu, and for a time even he was placed under certain restrictions.

On the eve of the formal act of integration in Jakarta, there was no slackening of fighting or of the harsh treatment meted out to the population at large. In May, according to reports from several sources, about 26 people were executed in Liquiça and further mass killings occurred at Maubara and Basar Tete. But one of the bloodiest incidents occurred near Lamaknan (also known as 'Lakmaras') which is just over the border in West Timor. There Indonesian troops who had been badly mauled by Fretilin units took their vengeance on a large refugee settlement housing some 5000 to 6000 people in temporary shelters, Timorese who had served as truck drivers for the Indonesian force reported. These drivers were used by the TNI because of their familiarity with the local terrain. The troops set fire to several of the houses, causing the Timorese to protest angrily. Witnesses said that the troops then turned their guns on the refugee community for several hours, shooting men, women and children. Even Timorese with their hands raised or women on their knees, imploring the troops to stop their senseless killing were often shot. One of the truck drivers said that about 2000 people were killed on that day. The incident so appalled him that he immediately began planning his escape. Another witness, however, claimed that only 1200 were killed on that day. This bloodbath occurred in June 1976 when the Indonesian government and press were telling the outside world that the Timorese had become impatient with the lack of international support for their desire to integrate with Indonesia and that the local assembly had voted unanimously in favour of a petition demanding immediate integration.

In 1976 the Indonesians began to form two Timorese battalions—Battalions 744 and 745 (designated territorial battalions) with East Timorese troops serving under Indonesian officers. The first commander was Major Yunus Yosfiah, and many of his troops were drawn from those trained in the Partisan exercise. Timorese were also conscripted into other paramilitary organisations, principally Hansip (Pertahanan Sipil, or civil defence) units, but there was soon little enthusiasm for such military activities. For one thing, the Indonesians ordered the Timorese to precede them on operational missions against Fretilin. For another, the Timorese soldiers were treated as inferior beings by ordinary Javanese troops. And the senseless and endless killing of their own people alienated them. For example, one Timorese had been a member of a support unit during the covert operations against Balibo, Maliana and Atabai, but when he arrived in Dili some days after the invasion he found his mother in mourning because the invading troops had shot his father. His father had been a male nurse with no links with Fretilin supporters. This informant said that his father had been dressed in his Red Cross uniform when the Indonesians had killed him. The man was then to learn that his younger brother had also been shot. This Timorese managed to leave the army, escaping to Portugal.

In June and July 1976, when the integration formalities were being settled, conditions in Dili eased. More food was available and there were signs that the occupying forces were subject to stricter discipline. But even during this period, to end later in the year, the looting continued. From a number of accounts, the Indonesian troops often complained of not being paid, and told the Timorese that they were forced to collect in kind. One macabre practice in the interior was to force labour gangs of Timorese to dig up the graves of Timorese rulers, some of whom had precious objects buried with them. There were also reported cases of bodies being exhumed by collectors of gold teeth. One early target for large-scale ransacking was Dili Hospital. After the invasion, most of the hospital's sophisticated equipment, which had attracted the praise of the International Red Cross doctors, was dismantled and shipped to an undisclosed destination in Java. Ironically, the hospital was then converted to military purposes, and the local population, at least in the first year or so after the invasion, was forced to rely on a handful of Timorese-trained nurses for most medical treatment.

Meanwhile, the Fretilin forces consolidated their position in the mountains. In many respects life appears to have been easier—at least in the first year or so—behind Fretilin lines than it was in the occupied areas, and a priest, Father de Rego, who spent more than three years in the mountains said that the food situation did not become precarious until the Indonesian offensive of 1977. In a number of fertile valleys and on the slopes of mountains farming was intensified, the results providing a modest but adequate diet for the mountain population, inflated as it was by the tens of thousands of refugees from the towns of the north coast and other occupied areas. The political situation was obviously very much easier. The Timorese were united by the common bond of hostility to a brutal invader. Fretilin dealt severely with traitors, but from all reports dissidents were surprisingly few until a serious division developed in the leadership in 1977. Indonesia regularly accused Fretilin of atrocities and terrorism, but in those three years after the invasion most atrocities were carried out by ABRI soldiers. There were, however, exceptions.

The first was the wanton killing of about 150 UDT and Apodeti prisoners, whom I had tried to persuade the Fretilin leaders to release before I left Dili. A number of them were taken to the mountains by the withdrawing Falintil troops after the invasion. These included Major Maggioli Gouveia, the former chief of police, Vitor Santa, a former senior administration official, and Osorio Soares, an Apodeti leader. The prisoners were taken to Aileu and were killed some weeks after the assault on Dili, reportedly on about 25 December. Although feelings of bitterness and anger were running high in the wake of the slaughter of hundreds of Timorese and Chinese in Dili, intensifying the feeling of bitterness towards the UDT for having set in train the events that led to the invasion, and towards Apodeti for its links with Indonesia, the wanton killing of these prisoners was without any justification. It is not known who ordered the killing, except that it appears that neither Xavier do Amaral nor Nicolau Lobato were involved. It has been suggested that the then Minister for Internal Affairs and Security, Alarico Fernandes was behind the killings, but this he has denied. Nicolau Lobato was probably in a state of bitter anguish, having just learnt of his wife Isobel had been taken out and shot by Brawijaya troops, but he was not at the execution site. The killing of these prisoners was a brutal, inexcusable act, but an understandable, though unacceptable, consequence of the rapacious behaviour of the Indonesian forces in the first weeks after the invasion. It would be less than just to excuse the Fretilin leaders, for their action was a wanton and senseless act of reprisal. However deeply provocative were the Indonesian killings in Dili following the invasion, the Fretilin captives were equally shocked at the invaders' behaviour, and most were not in favour of integration, let alone a brutal occupation.

From the day of the invasion East Timor was effectively isolated, but Fretilin succeeded in establishing a radio link with Australia, which was to remain open for more than two years, in spite of some half-hearted attempts by Australian authorities to close down the Darwin end of the link, seemingly to appease the

Indonesian government. During this time a steady flow of reports on the fighting was passed to Timorese representatives at the United Nations and to interested groups and individuals in Australia, who were thus able to piece together a picture of the armed resistance. Although much of the information contained in these messages was emotive in language and difficult to assess, descriptions of some of the battles and other incidents were corroborated later by accounts from sources in the occupied zones.

From the outset it was apparent that Fretilin's guerrilla-type tactics, its surprise attacks and ambushes, sapped the strength and morale of the Indonesian forces, many of whom appear to have had only a confused understanding of what the war was about. When the Joint Command found the going difficult on the north coast early in 1976 where bad weather added to their difficulties, the Indonesians carried out landings at beaches on the south coast. These landings were designed partly to prevent the UN special envoy from gaining access to Fretilin lines from Darwin, and partly to deter any attempts by Australians to send in arms or relief supplies. On 1 February 1976, US intelligence analysts informed their government that the prospect of a visit to Fretilin by the special envoy, Mr Winspeare Guicciardi, was causing alarm among Indonesian leaders who were determined to block such a venture, even to the extent of sinking the Portuguese frigate that he was proposing to use.[16] However, the south coast operation itself soon ran into difficulties. It was carried out in the wet season, in jungle terrain in which armoured vehicles were of little use to the attacking infantry. Near the Quelan River, the Timorese counterattacked and forced the Indonesians back to the coast where they remained until further reinforcements eventually arrived. Bitter fighting took place in the southern strip between Betano and Fato Berliu on several occasions between January and October 1976.

Indonesian forces moving inland from the north coast gradually succeeded in occupying key centres in the interior, including Ainaro, Maubisse, Ermera and Viqueque. These captures were not always lasting, and important towns like Bobonaro, Ermera and Viqueque were taken for only short periods. Lobato's troops did not have the means to consolidate such gains and the main towns were soon retaken by the Indonesians. In some sectors towns changed hands many times. Indonesian efforts to occupy the Laclubar area, not far from Fretilin headquarters, were repulsed again and again in a period of more than two years. The pattern of the armed resistance began to change after the first six months of fighting. The Timorese leaders soon concluded that it would be suicidal to continue trying to engage in frontal combat the numerically superior and much better equipped Indonesian army units which, thanks to a timely input of military aid from the United States and Europe, steadily increased their firepower.* Large-scale operations involved logistical and tactical conditions

---

* This aid included Bronco aircraft designed for anti-insurgency operations. Hawk fighters were also procured from Britain.

which the Fretilin military commanders were not trained to cope with, so the Indonesian forces, whatever their other weaknesses, always held the advantage in such circumstances, their units being able to make extensive use of light armour, artillery, rockets (the ABRI made some use of rocket launchers), air support and, in areas near the coast, naval bombardment. It was clear that, in the more congenial conditions of the dry season, an attempt by Fretilin to engage in frontal warfare would soon erode and weaken the fighting capability of the Falintil troops. Therefore, from the middle of 1976 onwards, the pattern of Timorese resistance shifted even further towards guerrilla warfare. In their messages sent via Darwin the Fretilin leaders (the voice on the radio was usually that of Alarico Fernandes) consistently claimed that they controlled more than eighty per cent of the territory. To many of the recipients of these telegrams the claims seemed exaggerated, given the size and firepower of the large Indonesian military force in East Timor, but in May 1977 a group of foreign diplomats reported on their return to Jakarta that the Indonesian military force in East Timor controlled one-third of the area and Fretilin one-third with the remainder existing as a no-man's land in which Fretilin forces moved freely. Refugees who came out of Timor at about the same time (none of whom had been supporters of Fretilin) insisted that Indonesian control did not extend beyond two or three kilometres outside the limits of the larger towns and villages. It might be supposed, therefore, that the Fretilin forces were able to move freely throughout most of the territory for more than three years after the attack on Dili in December 1975.

For the purposes of military organisation Fretilin divided the territory into a number of military sectors, most of its operations being launched by small units of less than company size. The character and extent of their political organisation and control have never been very clear, but during this early period, when the resistance movement had a communications network at its disposal, it was able to hold a number of 'national' conferences, with representatives from most districts coming to a central location. As Indonesia was able to seal off the area under Fretilin's control from the outside world, only later was it possible to sketch a rough picture of conditions there from interviews with Timorese who endured those conditions. An early source was Father de Rego.[17] This elderly priest was a fairly typical, conservative cleric of the older Portuguese mould. He had not been a supporter of Fretilin, having been all but forced at gunpoint by Falintil soldiers to go to the mountains with them. Yet de Rego developed a deep respect for the Timorese resistance movement and in particular for its leader, Nicolau Lobato. He insisted that conditions in the mountains were almost normal until 1977 when food began to become a problem. It did not become serious until the Indonesians began sending 'search-and-destroy' missions well into the central mountain region with the deliberate aim of destroying food crops there. Up to that time it appears that a relatively intense agricultural program, conducted by the more skilled farmers among the resistance movement and the villagers, had produced quite impressive results. According to the accounts of other sources, the food position in the mountains was at first much easier than in the towns occupied by Indonesian troops. Admittedly, in the Fretilin areas there were other serious problems, such as no doctors, but, as few of the Timorese under Indonesian rule had access to the doctors sent in by the Indonesians (who concentrated on the treatment of their own wounded), in matters of health they were probably not disadvantaged. The custodians of the health of the Fretilin troops and the community were the paramedical staff who, under the Portuguese system, had been well trained.

The first phase of Indonesia's attempts to destroy Fretilin was not a particularly difficult one to cope with from the point of view of the Timorese resistance. In May 1976 war conditions were relaxed enough for Fretilin to hold a congress with representatives coming from all parts of the territory. At this congress, which took place over two days or so, the delegates also had time to enjoy a festival. However, the discussions were obviously of an urgent nature and, at this meeting, the future strategy of guerrilla warfare was worked out. Fretilin's main tactics were to ambush troop movements and to carry out surprise attacks on Indonesian-occupied towns. The congress decided that political organisation should be tightened, but the conduct of the war was the main priority. Nicolau Lobato's position as the operational leader of the resistance was unchallenged with Xavier do Amaral's responsibilities being increasingly confined to political matters. Considerable attention was given to maximising and rationalising food production to meet the basic needs of the swollen mountain population. Although there was opposition at first to the civilian population leaving Fretilin-controlled areas, largely because it clashed with the independence movement's central propaganda theme—'the people are with Fretilin'; the Timorese were not discouraged from moving back to the areas controlled by Indonesia. Father de Rego said that when problems with food supplies began to emerge, Fretilin leaders began to encourage some of the people to move into Indonesian areas.

It seems that because of the Falintil's determined resistance to the invading troops in the first few months Fretilin was able to intimidate the Indonesian units into conducting a very cautious campaign, and to inculcate fear in the minds of the rank and file of the Indonesian ground forces. The morale of the troops was further eroded by serious logistics problems, some of them caused by Fretilin ambushes, but mostly by bad organisation and lack of coordination. Troops were often not paid for months and they were sometimes without food for several days. It was in these circumstances that the Indonesians treated any Timorese they came across very harshly, beating, or even killing, ordinary hamlet dwellers and looting whatever possessions they could get their hands on. The Timorese in the interior were, it appears, assumed to be hostile, and were treated accordingly. But there was also evidence that many of the invading troops became demoralised and simply refused to fight. The situation that they encountered in the territory was very different from what they had been led to expect. Not only were the Timorese opposed to integration; there had emerged a bitter dislike of Indonesians and things Indonesian. In the first two years of the occupation some Indonesian unit commanders resolved not to engage the Falintil. One Indonesian colonel boasted to a Timorese leader who was supporting integration then, that as soon as he and his men had arrived in the Kodam (military subdistrict) allocated to them, he had established a private truce with the local Fretilin commander and little fighting had taken place between them in that area. 'We haven't lost a soldier', he was reported to have said. The Indonesian will to fight was weakened, not only by logistics problems, but also by the very high casualty rate, the fact that the Falintil units seldom took prisoners, and the lack of public recognition by the government in Jakarta and the Indonesian people (from whom the Timor operation was being carefully concealed) that they had been fighting a war for the Republic.

Throughout 1976 and 1977 the Timorese guerrillas kept up a pattern of regular operations against the occupying forces in the mountains and in the Ermera, Basar Tete and Liquiça areas, not far from Dili, and near the Indonesian border. From time to time attacks were even launched on units near Dili. An indication of the extent of Fretilin's control is that it was able to hold the town of Remexio, only 15 kilometres from the capital, almost without interruption for more than three years. Falintil units also kept up pressure on Indonesian forces at Baucau and Lospalos. The first serious attempt to break the resistance in the interior was undertaken by Indonesian troops in the dry season of 1976 with the support of armoured vehicles, aircraft and helicopters, and with naval bombardment from near Liquiça and from the south coast. But this was a very successful year for Fretilin, still able to exploit its advantage of great familiarity with the terrain. Food and arms supplies were adequate and the success of the guerrilla campaign, during which Falintil losses appear to have been light, kept morale high. Father de Rego commented that, during that year, life in the Turiscai–Laclubar area was almost normal. There were some air attacks, but they were generally inaccurate and there were few civilian casualties.

Fretilin messages regularly contained what, at the time, seemed to be exaggerated claims of losses inflicted on Indonesian forces, but later information from Timorese who had accompanied the invading forces confirmed that their losses were high. Claims of more than 100 Indonesian troops killed were fairly common in Fretilin messages, while their own losses were said to have been small. Most of these claims must have been guesswork because usually Falintil attacks were of the 'hit-and-run' kind. Timorese commanders would have been unlikely to have been in a position to assess the extent of the casualties that they had inflicted on the Indonesian forces accurately. Indonesian casualties were heavy: early in 1977 a high-ranking Indonesian officer told a prominent Dutch official that already some 5000 casualties had been inflicted on the invading forces by Fretilin.

At the end of 1976 the first of a series of Catholic Church reports came to Australia, from an Indonesian organisation that had become very troubled at what had been happening in the former Portuguese colony. The report, mainly about humanitarian relief operations, gave a grim picture of the situation in the territory.[18] Its authors stated that, although they had regarded the earlier report that 60,000 Timorese had perished since the fighting had begun as an exaggeration, Portuguese priests in East Timor had told them that the death toll might already have reached 100,000. The report also provided further evidence that many Timorese had gone to the hills to join Fretilin after the arrival of the Indonesian forces. It mentioned that in Ermera, for example, of the 5000 people who had been there when the ABRI arrived only 1000 were left; the others had fled to the mountains. The report noted that '80% of the territory is not under the direct control of the Indonesian military forces', and referred to the decline in support for integration because of such excesses as 'stealing, robbery, burning houses, violating girls, etc.' by the occupying forces. It noted that the administration of Araujo was 'without any authority', being merely a 'puppet government for the military commander', and that 'if there should be held a real referendum the people will choose Fretilin'. The Indonesian church report also mentioned Fretilin's military tactics, saying that the units of the pro-independence movement avoided frontal attacks or engagements, and were conducting a guerrilla war. It mentioned rumours that the resistance was receiving supplies from Australia, rumours that could hardly have had any foundation. Perhaps they were based on news reports of the abortive attempt by four Australians from Darwin to take some medical supplies to the south coast of East Timor, in the hope of getting them to Fretilin. At about that time there were reports that another small vessel from Australia did succeed in reaching Timor where some medical supplies were handed over to a party of Fretilin troops mounted on Timor ponies, but I have been unable to establish that this extraordinary venture took place.

One of the most disturbing parts of the first report from church sources was that Indonesia was about to use napalm 'because they cannot win the war otherwise' and that the indiscriminately destructive Soviet multiple-rocket launcher known as 'Stalin's organ' was already in use. The use of napalm was later confirmed to me by a US Defence Department official in Washington who insisted that this explosive was not of US origin, but had been manufactured by the Indonesians. This source claimed that it was used extensively for about three months. In the dry conditions of the time in East Timor, napalm would have been a devastating weapon against the tinder-dry *palapa* houses in which most Timorese in the mountains live. These structures would have provided no protection for their occupants.

Until September 1977 there does not appear to have been much change in the situation on the ground in military terms. But early in 1977 in the United States and Western Europe growing criticism of Indonesia's seizure of the colony was embarrassing for Jakarta and caused the military command to launch a major offensive designed to crush the resistance. A trickle of disturbing reports from Timor, from the Catholic church in Indonesia itself, and a report on atrocities committed by Indonesian troops brought the Timor problem to international attention at a time when the leadership of one of the Suharto regime's main international supporters, the United States, was being assumed by Jimmy Carter. A man with a declared commitment to human rights Carter promised to make that a central component of US foreign policy. In nearby Australia, in spite of the understanding position of the Fraser government and its proclaimed desire 'to put the Timor problem behind us and look to the future', disquiet at Indonesia's act of aggression was being fanned by a steady flow of messages via the Fretilin link with the Northern Territory, not to speak of the disturbing reports from non-Fretilin sources. No doubt, as Jakarta saw it, it was imperative that attempts be made to head off an international campaign against Indonesia, which could, among other things, obstruct the Suharto government's aim to use a sizeable slice of its financial gains from the oil bonanza to re-equip the armed forces with modern weapons from Western Europe and the United States. The need for this re-equipment program was made more urgent by the poor showing of the army in East Timor. The first step, therefore, was to bring the war to a quick end and to suppress opposition to integration.

The Indonesian military offensive began in September 1977 following a much publicised offer of amnesty to Fretilin troops and their supporters by President Suharto on Indonesia's national day, 17 August but, in contrast to the amnesty 'carrot', the armed force 'stick' was intended to be kept secret. Launching this operation, involving the injection of another 15,000 troops into the campaign was, however, leaked to the Australian press, almost certainly from Defence Department sources. It was also the subject of a number of urgent telegrams from Fretilin. Another account of the intensified military operation came from the pen of a *Paris Match* journalist, Denis Reichle who managed to smuggle himself into Indonesian Timor, and then managed to get over the border into a Fretilin-held area. He later reported that the Indonesian forces had just strengthened their '20,000 strong East Timor army with an extra 10,000 men', and that these troops were, as he put it, 'systematically wiping out' the populations of villages known to be, or suspected of, supporting Fretilin.

Operations by land forces were intensified and were accompanied by air attacks on Timorese positions and villages in the interior and, from time to time, by naval bombardment from warships. Bitter fighting raged in many parts of the territory, with heavy loss of life on both sides. As Father de Rego and Denis Reichle reported that among the main targets were Fretilin food supplies and the hundreds of small farms in the mountains which, thanks to the improved farming techniques, had been keeping supplies to the beleaguered Timorese at an adequate level. 'Search-and-destroy' operations pushed into the interior, greatly assisted by the newly acquired Broncos (the US OV-10, an anti-insurgency aircraft), the delivery of which had been conveniently expedited by US Defence authorities. At about the same time a senior Australian aircraft industry executive confided to me that the Indonesians were also using the Nomad aircraft they had just procured from Australia. The Nomads were apparently fitted out so that they could be adapted to this 'anti-insurgency' role. Fretilin troops still managed to hold their own for almost eighteen months, but their messages no longer exuded confidence. Their contents revealed that the Timorese leaders knew that they were now fighting a desperate life-and-death struggle.

Perhaps the most graphic and poignant description of the tremendous and traumatic upheaval that these military operations created for the Timorese was contained in a letter from a priest in Dili, sent in November 1977 to two Dominican nuns in Portugal. 'The war', it read:

> continues with the same fury as it had started. The invaders have intensified their attacks in the three classic ways-from land, sea and air...From last September [1977] the war was again intensified. The bombers did not stop all day. Hundreds of human beings died every day. The bodies of the victims become food for carnivorous birds (if we don't die of the war, we die of the plague), villages have been completely destroyed, some tribes (sucos) decimated...and the war enters its third year with no promise of an early end in sight. The barbarities (understandable in the Middle Ages, and justifiable in the Stone Age), the cruelties, the pillaging, the unqualified destruction of Timor, the executions without reason, in a word all the 'organized' evil, have spread deep roots in Timor. There is complete insecurity and the terror of arbitrary imprisonment is our daily bread (I am on the 'persona non grata' list and any day I could disappear). Fretilin soldiers who give themselves up are disposed of-for them there is no prison. Genocide will come soon, perhaps by next December. Taking advantage of the courage of the Timorese they are being recruited to fight their brothers in the jungle [interior]. It is they who march in front of the [Indonesian] battalions to intimidate the targets.[19]

The priest's letter also provided a grim picture of other aspects of life in Timor at that time. The political situation, he said, was 'indescribable'.

> Sabotage and lies dominate the information sector. Integration is not the expression of the will of the people. The people are controlled by the Indonesians and given the character of the oppressor and the level of the Indonesian presence, it is a lamb being led to the slaughter. In the presence of such force there is no resistance; liberty is a word without meaning. The proclaimed liberation is synonymous [sic] with slavery.

The Priest ended his letter with a forlorn and desperate plea: 'Please do something positive for the liberty of the Timorese people. The world ignores us and our grief...we are on the road to complete genocide.' And he concluded with words sounding strangely like an absolution: 'We ask all justice-loving people to save Timor and we ask God to forgive the sins of the Timorese people.'

Another bleak glimpse of the suffering, oppression and destruction of that time was contained in a letter sent from Timor a couple of months later:

> An ever-increasing war rages in Timor. The group of villages in which I lived has been completely destroyed. There is not one soul there...One sees no one else but Indonesian soldiers and Chinese on the streets of Dili; there are very few Timorese for the majority is either in the forest, dead or in jail. The luck of Timor is to be born

in tears, to live in tears, and to die in tears.[20]

This operation did not at first critically weaken Fretilin. Its main casualties were the civilian population who were forced into a hopeless choice: to stay in the mountains and starve, or to surrender to the Indonesian forces and be herded into concentration centres—euphemistically called 'resettlement centres'—where their chances of dying of starvation or disease were, it often turned out, just as great. President Suharto's amnesty offer in reality proved to be anything but the gracious act of pardon Indonesian propaganda tried to portray it to be. The Timorese, who had in the first instance fled from the brutalities and rapaciousness of the invaders (and were not, as Jakarta tried to present it, forcibly taken to the mountains by Fretilin) were encouraged by the Falintil after 1977, to present themselves to the Indonesians because of the increasingly difficult food situation in the interior. For many who chose this option the welcome they received was far from an act of grace and mercy. Many with Fretilin links were shot or tortured, especially in sectors where the ABRI had been mauled by Timorese guerrillas, while the rest were forced, sometimes at gunpoint, into the centres, which were a crude version of the strategic hamlets set up by the Americans in Vietnam. For many Timorese in these resettlement centres famine conditions, disease, and a slow death lay ahead. This was partly because few of the military had any humanitarian interest in the welfare of their sullen and miserable charges, and partly because of the appalling incapacity of the Indonesian administration to provide even a modest regular supply of food and medicines to the refugees. Some of these centres were in remote parts of the province where supply lines were vulnerable to ambushes and were at times inaccessible in the wet season other than by helicopter.

For most Timorese by 1978 there was no alternative but to try their luck with the amnesty, and thousands reluctantly 'reported themselves' to the units of the ABRI. In the wet season of 1977 and 1978 this movement from the mountains took some of the pressure off Fretilin forces and, for reasons that are not clear, there appears to have been a lull in the fighting. In May 1978, at the beginning of the dry season, yet another operation, codenamed 'Skylight', was launched by the Indonesian military command, now under the direct, determined and energetic leadership of newly appointed Minister for Defence General Yusuf. Yusuf, a South Sulawesian, had once briefly served under the notorious rebel leader Kahar Muzakkar before the latter turned against Sukarno and led a rebellion in South Sulawesi. That rebellion was to continue for more than a decade, before finally being crushed by a force led by his former second-in-command, Andi Mohammad Yusuf, in the early 1960s. The long-term aim of 'Skylight' was to round up the Fretilin leaders, but its immediate objective was to destroy the Timorese offensive capability and to establish an effective measure of security before the visit of President Suharto to East Timor in July that year. From a reading of Fretilin messages sent to me via Darwin, and from sources in Jakarta, it is clear that this particular offensive led to a continuous weakening of Fretilin's military position during the next six months. It was not until later in the year though that units of the Timorese resistance were forced out of positions quite near Dili, such as Remexio and Railaco. However, its military strength had been whittled away. With the continuing isolation of the forces of DRET and starvation and disease caused by the war and, to a lesser extent, by Indonesian air attacks on villages and the food-producing mountain valleys, the morale of the resistance weakened.

As pressures built up, it was no surprise to learn in 1977 that serious divisions were beginning to appear within the leadership of Fretilin. When the final break did occur it must have had a demoralising effect on the resistance army. In September Xavier do Amaral was deposed as president, charged with treason and placed in custody. He was accused of plotting to seize full power, of creating division between the military and civilian components of the leadership, of not having given sufficient attention to the war, of having behaved like a feudal lord, and of having planned secret negotiations with the Indonesians. A purge took place with a number of Xavier do Amaral's collaborators being expelled from the Central Committee. The presidency was taken over by Nicolau Lobato who had long been Fretilin's main leader. The precise nature of the conflict has never been made clear. Father de Rego knew about it, but not in great detail. It seems that, as the war progressed, Xavier do Amaral's position weakened. Nicolau Lobato was now emerging as the dominant figure in political matters, as well as the overall military commander and leading strategist.

One major difference between the two men had already been demonstrated before the invasion—Xavier do Amaral's interest was in exploring the possibility of a negotiated settlement, while Lobato was determined and emphasised self-reliance. As the war intensified Xavier do Amaral became increasingly pessimistic about Fretilin's prospects of winning in the face of what must have seemed diminishing hopes for the kind of international intervention that might have brought a chance of victory to East Timor's struggle. Whatever hopes had lingered about a change of heart in Canberra would have been dashed when Australia all but abandoned any further interest in East Timor's right to self-determination in January 1978. It was when the territory was recognised as a de facto part of Indonesia. The new Carter administration in the United States, with its emphasis on human rights, had raised expectation, but Indonesia's paramount strategic importance to Washington prevailed. Further, Fretilin's main supporters, several African states, China, and international and human rights groups, had been unable to break down East Timor's isolation. No supplies were getting to Fretilin, and none of its leaders could get to the outside world to give an account of the situation in the territory. To some of them, therefore, the struggle must have appeared futile and their cause hopeless. It is not surprising that Xavier and some of his Central Committee colleagues should have begun to attempt to negotiate some kind of deal with the Indonesians. They began to wonder whether the war was worth the heavy loss of life that had already been inflicted on their people, and which was bound to reach colossal proportions as Indonesia intensified its attacks on the Fretilin-held areas. Whatever the circumstances, Xavier do Amaral was not a convert to *integrasi*, as suggested. Had this been so, he would have been used extensively by his Indonesian captors after his surrender. Yet this has not been the case. The Indonesians did remove him from Timor and for some years he was a virtual prisoner in the house of Dading Kalbuadi, first in Bali and later in Jakarta, where his role was that of a servant.

The second fracture within the Fretilin leadership manifested itself a little more than a year later when Minister for Information and Internal Security Alarico Fernandes announced over the Fretilin radio that he and some of his comrades had broken away from the Central Committee. Fernandes, whose mother was in Sydney, was well-known as the voice at the other end of the radio link with Darwin. It was claimed by some Fretilin leaders abroad that he had sold out to the Indonesians. This may be true, but the circumstances under which he was captured by, or defected to, the occupying forces are still far from clear. Sources within Indonesia report that Fernandes became separated from the main body of Fretilin and was captured not far from Dili. With the capture of Alarico Fernandes, Fretilin's direct radio link with the outside world was cut and never restored. This division led to fighting between the opposing factions, with a considerable amount of killing in the central Fretilin-controlled areas.

However, the intensified operations launched in the previous year under the command of Benny Moerdani had not succeeded in destroying the resistance, and in May 1978 a new operation was launched, this time under the command of General Yusuf, Commander-in-Chief of ABRI. With freshly equipped troops, supported by aircraft obtained from the United States, the Indonesian forces pounded Falintil positions in several encirclement operations. One report from East Timor tells of sixteen battalions being employed on the ground while the Timorese population behind Fretilin lines was bombed intensely, causing heavy casualties.[21]

No longer were the mountain retreats secure havens. As Father de Rego has graphically described it, much of the population within Fretilin's lines was constantly on the move, fleeing Indonesian 'search-and-destroy' operations or air attacks. Towards the end of 1978 communications began to break down between the guerrilla units. But the worst disaster struck on 31 December when Indonesian forces in a special operation located the bivouac of the Timorese president, Nicolau Lobato. He was killed in the ensuing engagement. Press reports from Jakarta talk of about twenty Fretilin leaders and troops were killed with him and another twelve or more captured. The attack was the culmination of an operation that had begin more than two weeks earlier, and involved 2500 troops, whisked from place to place by helicopters. The force was apparently under Yusuf's direct command, but it also included Major Yunus Yosfiah (of Balibo notoriety) and Lieutenant Prabowo, Suharto's son-in-law, later to rise to the rank of lieutenant-General and Kopassus commander. They played key roles in the killing of Lobato and his men. Apparently, the Timorese leader fought to the end with the same determination and courage that had enabled him to direct one of the most successful guerrilla campaigns of its kind for more than three years.

For more than a year though, the Indonesians had been claiming that Fretilin was finished and that all that remained were 'some roving bands'. Lobato's killing was heralded in Jakarta as a great victory, accompanied by much rejoicing. General Yusuf at once flew to Dili to inspect the body of the fallen Timorese leader. It was photographed against the background of a group of triumphant Indonesian officers, including Brigadier-General Dading Kalbuadi. Timorese in Dili at the time then said that the local reaction was anything but one of rejoicing. A wave of deep sorrow and hopelessness swept across the territory. Even high-ranking Timorese in the Indonesian administration were visibly affected by the news of Lobato's death. In the previous three years Nicolau Lobato had become a legendary figure to Timorese and Indonesians, but to the former he was a symbol of the slender hope that some day the occupying forces would be driven out of East Timor. He and his Falintil soldiers had seemed indestructible, having survived hundreds of air raids, naval bombardments, and the assaults of tens of thousands of Indonesian troops, with their rockets and armoured support. Lobato had become a folk hero, and the symbol of resistance to most Timorese, including those whose political loyalties in 1975 had been to the UDT or Apodeti. For the first time many Timorese felt that theirs was a defeated nation.

After the loss of the radio link with Darwin and Lobato's death, the activities of the armed resistance became very difficult to follow. It was reported that Carvarinho (also known as 'Mau Lear'), the vice-president, took over from Nicolau Lobato, but he too was killed, reportedly on 2 February 1979. In the first few months of 1979 it appears that the Fretilin remnants were in rather poor shape. There were more captures and killings, and groups of demoralised Fretilin troops were reported to have surrendered. However, as at least several hundred of these were shot after they had been taken into captivity, most of the remainder chose to fight on in the mountains with the guerrilla campaign shifting towards the eastern part of the island. Sometime during 1979, probably towards the end of the year when the wet season set in, the remaining units of the armed resistance regrouped and resumed their attacks, usually in the form of ambushes. Refugees who left the territory for Portugal or for Australia at the end of 1979 and early in 1980 reported guerrilla activity in the Ermera–Liquiça–Aileu–Dili area with major operations in the eastern section, where a new Falintil commander, Kay-Rala Xanana—or to use his Portuguese name, Jose Alexandro Gusmão—was emerging. Xanana's position as leader was confirmed in 1981 and for almost a decade Xanana was to lead the resistance, and to establish a reputation, internationally as well as in Timor, as a visionary leader and an extraordinarily effective guerrilla commander. Towards the end of 1979 the organisation CNRM (Concelho Nacional da Resistancia Maubere—National Council of Maubere Resistance) was established with a view to widening the image of the resistance to include all Timorese opposed to integration. The resumption of the armed struggle was disclosed in a letter sent by a Timorese to a relative in a refugee camp near Lisbon. Among other things, the letter stated:

> The armed struggle continues to be intense, particularly in the eastern part of the island...despite the capture of thousands of rebel weapons, G3's and Mausers, in the monsoon season of 1979...I don't know how it's possible for them to do it, but those in the bush are giving strong resistance to tens [sic] of Indonesian battalions which are fighting and pursuing them. The Indonesians are taking casualties. Helicopters arrive daily at Dili Hospital carrying soldiers wounded on various fronts.[22]

This particular letter also referred to Timorese conscripts in Indonesian battalions deserting with their rifles and joining their compatriots in the mountains. Several refugees whom I interviewed in Lisbon in October 1980 also talked about these desertions. For example, there were several accounts of more than 100 Timorese deserting from regular units (Battalions 744 and 745) and from Hansip (civil defence) establishments. Another letter, also written in March 1980, stated that 'the war continues to be hot along guerrilla lines, strongest in the eastern area round Lospalos'.[23] According to this source, discontent had caused no fewer than 500 Timorese to desert. They were said to include 'civil servants and well-respected people, including second line troops of Hansip, who carried their weapons with them'. This injection of fresh recruits evidently boosted the capability of Fretilin, and in 1980 it launched two daring attacks, one in January, not far from Dili, and an even more daring assault on the capital on 10 June in which a number of Indonesian troops were killed, provoking the occupying authorities to carry out reprisals. Four Timorese, whose loyalties were probably under suspicion, were taken to a location south of the capital and summarily executed, in spite of the protests of Timorese church and government officials. Their bodies were reportedly left there for some time, apparently as a warning to the citizens of the capital.

Did the gloating Indonesian generals who gathered triumphantly around the corpse of Nicolau Lobato early in 1979 believe that the guerrilla war was over? If they did, they were to be proved wrong. The mass movement of refugees in 1979 would have hampered the security forces in their attempt to isolate the components of Fretilin after Nicolau Lobato's death. But the brutal treatment of those members of the resistance who surrendered provided the independence movement with a good reason for fighting on. Some were shot shortly after capture, more than 100 members of Fretilin with their families being disposed of in this way at Quelicai in the central eastern sector. Others were tortured, and a handful of captive Fretilin leaders were reported to have been hurled to their deaths from a helicopter somewhere between Dili and Aileu. From information from Timor late in 1980 a number of captured Fretilin supporters were allowed to move freely around Dili for more than a month and then were again taken into custody and are believed to have been executed. In 1981 several hundred Timorese who surrendered to the troops of yet another operation, this time designated *Operasi Keamanan* (security), were reported to have been killed.

Thousands of former members of the independence movement, or their relatives, were imprisoned or were exiled to the offshore island of Atauro, and to certain other Indonesian islands to the north, among them Alor and Wetar. Yet another group of Timorese were imprisoned in East Timor. The harsh treatment of those who surrendered, or who were captured, did nothing to lessen the hostility of the local population towards their Indonesian masters. Over the years many who collaborated with the Indonesians, or supported the idea of integration in the beginning, turned against the occupying forces. The arrogant and rapacious behaviour of the troops converted even many former Apodeti supporters into secret admirers of Fretilin in whose ranks some of them had relatives.

When *Operasi Keamanan* was launched in 1981, it again aimed to overpower Fretilin and to 'restor[e] security', a condition which had not existed since East Timor had been invaded by the ABRI forces. Clearly Fretilin adapted yet again to changed circumstances. Based on refugee accounts, it seems that after 1979 the guerrilla movement fragmented into small groups whose operations proved to be even more difficult for the Indonesian forces to detect. Despite a series of mopping-up operations by the Indonesian army, resistance proved impossible to stamp out. Under the leadership of Xanana, a force of more than 1000 continued, as late as March 1983, to harass Indonesian forces in several parts of the province.

Armed resistance had regrouped surprisingly quickly. As early as March 1979 ten surviving Fretilin leaders managed to have a meeting at Titilara–Laivai where a new strategy—and a new name—was worked out. By the middle of 1980 a revived resistance was able to launch a number of attacks against Indonesian forces, including a daring assault on the Dare military barracks and Dili's television station.[24] However, the killing of Nicolau Lobato ended the first phase of the resistance. For most of the first three years after the invasion Fretilin had a definable territorial base and could act as the protector of a sizeable proportion of the Timorese population. However, the bitter struggle against strengthening odds exacted its toll on the Fretilin leadership. While there were some ideological considerations the main cleft seems to have been between Lobato, and his military men, and political leaders like Xavier do Amaral.

The consolidation of Indonesian rule and the new face of resistance—1979 to 1983

The annihilation of the Lobato leadership, and changing conditions in East Timor, gradually transformed the character of Fretilin/CNRM after 1979. The change was not always reflected in the statements and claims of Fretilin's leaders abroad, but then from the capture of Alarico Fernandes—and his radio—until late 1982 when a new communications channel was established, there was very little contact between the guerrillas and the expatriate leaders. In 1979, in particular, the main aim of the Timorese resistance leaders was to survive, regroup, and establish the necessary support networks with the Timorese community at large. Fretilin remained the violent expression of the attitudes of hatred, frustration and discontent harboured by the majority of the indigenous population, regardless of their past political preferences. It represented a flicker of hope that the *malai*, the foreigner, would eventually be forced to go away and leave the Timorese to work out their own future.

The year 1978 was not only a bad year for Fretilin; it was a grim year for the population at large, as reports from the few aid workers at last given access to parts of the province in 1979, were to reveal. The first frank report on the humanitarian situation at the time came from an Indonesian church organisation, whose representatives had just returned to Jakarta after having spent several weeks in the '27th Province'. It was the first report to provide an assessment of the demographic consequences of the seizure of East Timor, and it at once became the subject of concern and controversy. Referring to the fact that a population of 688,771 had been recorded by the diocese in 1974, it quoted a current estimate supplied by the assistant, Hankam (Defence and Security), which indicated that the population may have declined to 329,271 in the intervening five years, suggesting a catastrophic loss of life since the invasion. It was insisted at the time that the Indonesians were effectively in full administrative control of the territory and, therefore, it seemed plausible that the authorities had been in a position to compile a reasonably accurate estimate of the population. In a statement made by General Yusuf on 2 January 1979 during a talk with Indonesian journalists a few days after Nicolau Lobato was killed, there was no 'rebel strength' left in East Timor. If this had been true, the task of assessing the population in the territory would not have been a particularly difficult one. The figures were immediately disputed with Indonesian military sources contending that there were still many Timorese 'in the mountains' unaccounted for.

The number of casualties from the war, that is those killed in the conflict as opposed to the deaths from related causes such as starvation and disease or illnesses which, in normal circumstances would have been overcome by medical treatment, has been the subject of some controversy. The debate produced something of a statistical tug of war with official Indonesian sources and apologists for Indonesia's seizure of the colony, arguing that between 15,000 and 50,000 people died as a result of the war, many of whom were described as having been 'victims of the Fretilin terror'. At the other extreme, some Fretilin supporters have declared that about half of East Timor's population were wiped out by the Indonesian invading forces. Clearly one extreme sought to minimise the loss of life to diminish the magnitude of the tragedy and the culpability of the Indonesian military occupation, while the other may have contrived to magnify the humanitarian consequences of Indonesia's invasion to attract more international attention to the plight of the Timorese.

Having denied the International Committee of the Red Cross' (ICRC) access to East Timor during the years when it was a killing field the true figure will never be known. It is possible, however, to estimate what the population of East Timor was in 1975, on the eve of the civil war, and to assess the number of people killed in the civil war between Fretilin and the UDT, which cost between 1500 and 2000 lives. From there on a major problem in research is the credibility of the accounts from Indonesian official sources which were often inconsistent. Only Indonesian authorities were in a position to conduct a census. Such a count was conducted in 1980 for the national census. According to this assessment the population of East Timor in that year stood at just above 550,000, representing a decline of at least 130,000. Today the population is given as 770,000. On the basis of the growth rate of between 1.8 and 2.1 per cent per annum today it should be more than 1,200,000. The assessment of the Catholic Church that more than 200,000 East Timorese died as the direct or indirect result of the ABRI invasion is, therefore, plausible. Most may have died of disease or starvation, but this massive loss of population is clearly attributable to the conditions created by the Indonesian invasion.

The exodus of Timorese in the second half of 1975 had little to do with the population decline. It has been claimed that 40,000 to 50,000 Timorese fled into Indonesian Timor during the civil war and that many of them did not return to the eastern part of the island. From refugee accounts only some 20,000 Timorese moved into West Timor and most of them were soon to return to their homelands in East Timor, at that time with strong encouragement from the West Timorese, whose lands are both poor and heavily populated. It is not true that 10,000 Timorese fled to nearby Indonesian islands, or that another 10,000 managed to get to Australia or Portugal.[25] When the invasion was launched there were simply no boats available even for short journeys. As for the exodus to Australia and Portugal, in the eight years following the invasion only about 4000 Timorese managed to get to those countries.

Indonesian officials and apologists for annexation of East Timor claimed that a large proportion of the loss of life occurred in the civil war. The death toll of the civil war being between 1500 and 2000, the needs of the wounded and other victims of that brief campaign were quickly and effectively dealt with by the ICRC and other aid teams in the province with some strength between August and December 1975. The fighting between the UDT and Fretilin would have had little effect on the pattern of population growth. Adding to the death toll the exodus to Darwin in August 1975 of fewer than 3000 people, the figure amounts to less than one-half of the normal growth for that year.

In the early 1980s there were conflicting reports on the state of East Timor's population. In 1982 one senior Indonesian official who had made several visits to the territory told me that there were only about 400,000 people left in East Timor. At the time this raised the question: were Indonesian authorities deliberately inflating the population figure to shield the government from further international scrutiny, especially at the United Nations? Nothing, however, can hide the ugly truth. The official figure used by Professor Mubyarto in his authoritative report was 657,411 people in East Timor in 1987, including at least 40,000 Indonesians. The 1999 population estimate of near 800,000 suggests that figure may have been on the high side. It provides a disturbing indicator of the colossal humanitarian consequences of crushing resistance to integration.

In spite of appeals from the International Red Cross and from organisations like the Australian Council for Overseas Aid, it was not until the second-half of 1979, almost four years after the invasion, that the ICRC and the American Catholic Relief Services (CRS) were allowed to establish a limited presence in the territory. In 1976 and 1977 Indonesian authorities claimed that their Red Cross could handle any humanitarian problems in their new province. They rejected requests by the ICRC to be allowed to resume its activities in the territory after the invasion, at times insinuating that it was not acceptable because ICRC officials had supported Fretilin in 1975. It was alleged on at least one occasion that Red Cross workers had smuggled arms and other supplies to the resistance. Such accusations were groundless. The ICRC mission had behaved with exemplary detachment and impartiality in the Fretilin-administered territory. It is unlikely that Indonesian military authorities believed such a charge, if they did not concoct it. The accusation was probably nothing more than a device designed to keep foreign observers out of East Timor while opposition to independence was being eliminated, and while it was clear that Jakarta's claims to be in full control of the territory were so patently false. It was some time after President Carter came to power that the United States began to put private diplomatic pressure on the Indonesians to allow some international aid workers to set up a relief mission in the territory. Then the Indonesians became anxious to head off Congressional interest in the Timor question. The agreement to readmit the ICRC and CRS missions was largely brought about by a quiet US warning to the Suharto administration that unless some concession was made on humanitarian grounds, public antipathy towards Indonesia in the United States might lead to Congressional obstruction of the military aid and sales program.

Before Indonesia embarked on its military operations in 1977 general living conditions appear to have been worse in the 'occupied areas', as Fretilin called them, than in the areas behind Fretilin lines. It was not just a matter of the oppressive behaviour of the occupying forces. It seems that food production declined sharply and very little food was sent into the province, other than to meet the Indonesian troops' needs. Even the food supplies for the troops were in a parlous state at times. Fretilin sources and information from refugees in 1976 and 1977 told of the ABRI's food position being so bad in the mountain areas that the soldiers were constantly looting crops, stealing cattle and buffalo, ransacking Timorese houses in search of food, and even searching for edible native plants. In these circumstances the lot of the ordinary Timorese within occupied lines was at times desperate. Away from the coast were the best farming areas and some intensive and innovative agricultural methods there had enabled the Fretilin leaders to keep the food situation more or less under control. The food-producing areas under Indonesian control suffered not only because harsh occupation policies had demoralised or decimated the population, but because the best farming lands were subject to guerrilla attacks. Indonesian forces confiscating food crops antagonised and discouraged farmers, many of whom took their skills and whatever belongings had not been looted to the hills where they probably added to the effectiveness of the resistance's agricultural labour force. The flight of population from Baucau and Ermera offers good examples of this shift of population from crop-growing areas. In other places, such as the valley of the Gleno River, the Timorese reportedly preferred to give their surpluses to Fretilin, rather than have them confiscated by the ABRI.

Despite heavy censorship imposed on media by authorities, war in Timor started to cause some public disquiet in Indonesia, especially when casualties began to mount. General Moerdani told one Western official that most units were rotated quickly, spending only two or four months in East Timor because of the unpopularity of the campaign. This quick turnover of troops meant that it became increasingly difficult to prevent information about the Timor war from leaking to the public. It was not that the ordinary Indonesians were opposed to the idea of integration. It all made sense, at least the way in which the proposition had been presented to them. They were told that integration with Indonesia was the wish of most of the people of East Timor, and that the pro-independence forces were largely communists who planned to invite China or Vietnam to set up a base in the territory. What inevitably did cause discontent was that thousands of Indonesian soldiers had been killed or wounded without, seemingly, any formal official or public recognition of their sacrifices. There was the question of compensation, and the need to obtain funds for this purpose was one of the excuses given to me for the military's confiscation of the coffee-trading companies and other businesses in East Timor. Initially, some of the profits of companies such as PT Denok (a firm set up key TNI figures, Moerdani, Dading Kalbuadi and Rajagukuk) were said to have been earmarked for compensation payments to the families of Indonesian soldiers killed in Timor.

Before the end of 1979 few foreigners were allowed into East Timor. The visits that did take place were very short, their programs were carefully planned, and the receptions neatly orchestrated. Usually special security operations were carried out to keep resistance activities away from foreign prying eyes, thus creating the impression that resistance was minimal and that the Indonesian forces were in control of the situation on the ground. However, it is not clear why, in 1976 and 1977, when they appeared to have sufficient strength to do so, Fretilin guerrillas did not make their military presence felt during visits by foreign delegations. Such actions would probably have been costly in men and equipment. Another possibility is that the Timorese may have concluded that, as most of the visitors were sympathetic to Indonesia's position in Timor, such an exercise would have been pointless and costly. For special visits, such as the visit of foreign diplomats and press representatives just before the formalising *integrasi*, the visit of the Congressional representatives William Goodling and Helen Meyner, and President Suharto's brief tour of the province in 1978, security measures were so tight that any challenge by Fretilin would have been very difficult to sustain. On these occasions the Indonesian forces were deployed some kilometres from the towns concerned, preventing the guerrillas from getting close enough to have any effect.

Most of these visits were so skilfully organised that the visitors appear to have concluded that the security situation was less serious than they had until then been led to believe. I have already pointed out that the Timorese were coached on how to participate in welcoming demonstrations, their cooperation being assured by the presence in their midst of significant numbers of Indonesian troops in civilian clothing. Numerous other special effects were implemented. For example, on the day before Mrs Meyner's visit to Dili Indonesian troops and officials moved large amounts of Red Cross clothing, bedding and furniture into a women's refugee establishment which she was to inspect. One of the refugees I later interviewed said that Indonesian officials reclaimed all of these comforts shortly after the visit was over. Another Timorese, working with the Indonesian military since the invasion, described how ABRI aircraft had shot up Fretilin positions and suspected pro-Fretilin villages before an aerial inspection by two Australian diplomats in May 1977.

A leading Timorese politician, who spent some four years in East Timor under Indonesian rule before leaving for Portugal, later said that two weeks or so before any major visit Indonesian intelligence officers prepared the speeches to be delivered to the visitors by the Governor and other officials. Selected groups of Timorese were also instructed by intelligence officers on how to answer any questions that the visitors might put to them. According to this source who himself had been involved in such preparations, graphs and maps, sometimes with false information on Indonesian expenditures and on population, were also prepared by these officials. Through the years the occupation authorities evidently became expert at such dis-information arrangements aided, no doubt, by the ignorance of Timor held by most visitors, or their declared sympathy for the territory's incorporation.

Even the visit of a group of ambassadors from Jakarta to the province at the end of 1978 was not unstructured. At Remexio these diplomats were shocked at the physical condition of the refugees, yet their later public comments suggested that they were taken in by the explanation provided by their Indonesian hosts. Some of the visitors thus guilelessly repeated the story that the Timorese had been forced to go to the hills by Fretilin, and had been held there against their will. Others seemed to accept the explanation that the poor physical condition of the Timorese merely reflected their cultural backwardness and the centuries of Portuguese colonial neglect. This was untrue. Such famine conditions had not existed since the Japanese occupation.

With notable exceptions, the Indonesians had little to fear from such visits. The visitors were either chosen because of their record of support for Indonesia's Timor policy, or they were officials or diplomats from those countries that 'understood' Indonesia's position. As one prominent Timorese later told me that these visitors were seldom interested in probing beneath the surface, even when dubious or transparently false accounts were given them by the Indonesians. A former Timorese guide said that such visitors were often reluctant to follow up suggestions surreptitiously passed to them by Timorese officials on how they might probe behind the orderly facade their Indonesian hosts had arranged for them. One problem was that few visitors were familiar with what Timor was like under Portuguese colonial rule so there was a tendency to accept as credible most of what their hosts told them. For example, the Foreign Minister of Papua New Guinea, who made a brief visit to East Timor, later told journalists that he had been taken to the 'White Sands' (Aria Branca) beach near Dili where, he said, during Portuguese rule, only whites had been allowed to bathe. This was nonsense. More than twenty years before *integrasi*, when Portuguese colonial rule had been authoritarian Timorese frequently used that beach. If there was any discrimination, it was on the grounds of 'civilised' status, a demarcation not unknown in Indonesia. Whatever their shortcomings in other areas, the record of the Portuguese in race relations was probably the best of the colonial powers.

Although reports from church sources, smuggled out in 1976 and 1977, indicated the need for an emergency humanitarian relief program, it was not until well into 1979 that foreign organisations were able to gain limited access to the territory. Before that time aid from foreign countries designated for use in Timor was handed over to the Indonesian authorities, who undertook to channel it through the Indonesian Red Cross, but much of this assistance never got to the people for whom it was intended. In June 1977, the Australian Minister for Administrative Services, in a written reply to a parliamentary question, stated that Australian diplomats who had just visited the province had 'gained the impression that humanitarian assistance was getting through to the people' (letter of 1 June 1977). However, according to information from a Timorese official involved in the organisation of this visit states that the evidence of foreign assistance was set up specially for the occasion. It was persistently reported by church sources within Indonesia that a great deal of foreign aid was being lost through corruption and pilfering by the military. One problem was that the Indonesian Red Cross (the Palang Merah Indonesia), an army-dominated organisation, declined to report on the distribution of goods earmarked for Timor. From refugee and church sources, although a lot of this assistance reached Timor, reports are that a significant amount of it was intercepted by the army and sold through Chinese shops at prices that the ordinary Timorese could not afford. For example, in 1979 a visiting church official noted that bags of maize and rice, humanitarian assistance marked for 'free distribution', were being sold to the population at high prices. In the same year an Indonesian priest noted that medicines were for sale in Chinese shops in a certain village while the health centre responsible for several thousand Timorese in a resettlement camp had at its disposal only 300 chloroquine tablets and five metres of bandages. He also reported that food aid was being sold to the people—rice at 25,000 rupiah a sack, rather higher than the going rate in Dili. A modest, but effective, aid program was being channelled through the church in East Timor from Australian, the United States and Western European church organisations. Military authorities did not encourage this channel, making it clear that they wanted the Indonesian military, and not the church, to be identified in Timorese minds as the main providers of relief and charity. Thus, a consignment by World Vision Australia of 10 tonnes of high-protein biscuit and twenty tonnes of vitamin A-enriched milk was shipped to Dili for distribution by the Indonesian Red Cross only after considerable obstacles had been placed in its path. When consent was finally given, no officers of World Vision were allowed to accompany the supplies to observe their distribution. Despite repeated requests by officials of that organisation, no report on how these relief supplies were handled was obtained from the Indonesian Red Cross. In an assessment of the position the Australian Council for Overseas Aid made the following points:

> All aid has gone to areas under Indonesian control only. Indonesia is very reluctant to admit foreigners. When they have been, their visit has been brief and restricted. All the aid has been sought and given for emergency relief not for production and reconstruction.
>
> ...no thorough independent assessment of the needs, no supervision of distribution, no implementation of an autonomous programme, and no evaluation of the Indonesian Government's aid programme, have taken place.
>
> All the grants have been made to the Indonesian Red Cross for its programme.[26]

In Timor, the military character of the Indonesian Red Cross served to weaken its medical functions. Information from Timor in mid-1978 said all of its doctors were from the military, and at that time their first obligation when fighting was intense was to treat their own casualties.

In 1979 the Indonesian authorities were persuaded to allow a limited international relief operation to be set up in the province and in April the ICRC and the US Catholic Relief Services were invited to conduct surveys of East Timor's urgent humanitarian needs. The first-aid workers were shocked at the human misery they encountered. They estimated that between one-tenth and one-third of the population had perished because of the war, and more than 200,000 of the remainder were languishing in resettlement camps which one relief worker described as being as horrible as any he had seen anywhere, including the Thai–Cambodian border. All of these inmates were in poor physical condition; about one-third of them would die of starvation unless they were treated within the next two months, while the condition of another 20,000 was believed to be so poor that it was probably too late to save their lives. Confronted with the results of these preliminary surveys the Indonesian government agreed to allow relief programs by the ICRC and the CRS which began in about August of the same year, almost four years after the invasion of Dili. These programs were still to be conducted through an Indonesian infrastructure in which the foreign presence was minimal.

For example, the ICRC operation was to be, in the terms of the agreement with Palang Merah Indonesia, 'carried out in the field under the auspices of the Indonesian Red Cross with ICRC material and technical support'. Under this arrangement, the Indonesian Red Cross, whose representative was Brigadier General Dr Moh Saronto, appointed a member of its Central Committee as project officer, to be 'responsible for the implementation of the operation'. An Indonesian doctor stationed in Dili was to be responsible for the missions in the field. The foreign component of the ICRC presence in East Timor seldom exceeded three persons. Still, it was a start, and the teams immediately concentrated their relief work on eight severely affected and isolated areas, covering about 60,000 people. With a staff of more than 190 (only three of them non-Indonesian), and a budget of just below AUD7 million, the mission acted swiftly. Initially the Indonesians evidently insisted that the ICRC pay its way. Thus, the original estimate of a total expenditure of AUD6,966,030 included an appropriation of AUD3,383,400 for the hire of helicopters for transport purposes—as against AUD2,823,910 for food, blankets, and the like. The Indonesian government also insisted that all food aid go first to Jakarta, rather than direct to East Timor, a practice which caused some lengthy delays, and led to protests from Australia, by far the biggest contributor, having made available aid valued at more than AUD3 million. The operation appears to have gone smoothly and efficiently and by the end of 1979 the crisis was reported to be easing.

The CRS operation was of a different character. At that time it seemed that CRS acted as an instrument of US foreign policy in that almost all of its considerable funding for this particular exercise came from the US government's Agency for International Development (AID), which provided the equivalent of almost AUD10 million for the exercise. On paper its objectives were rather broader than those of the ICRC. Its efforts focused on a 'target group of some 200,000 Timorese to whom it supplied such items as non-fat dry milk, rice, cornsoya blend, and soya milk, and its program also included the provision of seeds to villagers so that they might establish their own crops as soon as possible.

From the testimony of US Ambassador to Indonesia Edward E. Masters, to the House Subcommittee on Asian and Pacific Affairs on 4 December 1979, the CRS program looked impressive. Ambassador Masters testified that the head of CRS in Indonesia had just informed him that the distribution of their commodities in East Timor was ahead of schedule, and that 'its program' had already reached more than '75% of the resettlement areas', and was expected to cover them all although the rainy season had begun. Masters was greatly impressed with their work, but then he was also quite impressed with the performance of the Indonesian government. For example, in the same testimony, he said: 'It should be emphasised, however, that this emergency relief is only part of a larger effort in which the Indonesian Government is playing a significant role.' By helping out with communications with the 150 resettlement sites, the Indonesian authorities were greatly assisting the ICRC and CRS efforts. The emphasis of the Indonesian government program, he pointed out, was to regroup the neediest of the population 'into resettlement centers which are located where the land is relatively good and near such communications routes as exist. Under these circumstances, it will be much easier to provide the people with the necessities of life.'[27] And, it seemed, the CRS would give its support to this interesting social reorganisation, which was designed primarily for security reasons. The Americans could hardly have been unaware of this because the 'resettlement centres' were based on the 'strategic hamlet' concept that they had introduced into Vietnam, for precisely the same reasons. It seems that the Ambassador's account of the situation, and of the role of the CRS, was less than candid. He mentioned that CRS 'had people working in Timor' to monitor their programs, but what he did not mention was that these people were Indonesians, many of them selected by the army, not Americans, and they could hardly have been expected to carry out an impartial monitoring of its activities. Late in 1981 a CRS official admitted that the organisation had 'no American personnel stationed in East Timor, because it was CRS policy to leave the administration of its programs to the local people'.[28] In a discussion about the human rights situation in East Timor, a CRS official reportedly declared that the CRS was 'going where the Government of Indonesian wants it to go and doing what the Government of Indonesia wants it to do'. It asked no political questions. 'East Timor relies on the Russians, it's been said around here and it's enough to influence judgements round here' was one revealing remark.[29] It was later disclosed by a senior CRS official that no more than twenty per cent of the organisation's aid was distributed by the church, the rest being channelled through the Indonesian military infrastructure.

This does not mean that CRS aid has been totally ineffective in East Timor. It would only be fair to credit it with having contributed to the substantial improvement that had been achieved in nutrition and health by mid-1980. The ICRC program was very carefully non-political, as it had been under Pasquier in 1975 during Fretilin's short interregnum in the territory, but the same cannot be said about the CRS program. It was blatantly political, in spite of the protests of officials in New York. The CRS steered clear of the underlying human rights issues in the territory, taking care not to suggest that any blame for what had transpired could be placed on Indonesia. Worse, it became a vehicle for the official US policy with the effect of deflecting attention from Indonesia's contravention of the UN Charter by treating the wounds of the victims and by putting some food into their stomachs. As one CRS official seemed to be suggesting, the program was designed as much to help the Indonesians out as to provide humanitarian relief for the Timorese. There can be little doubt that the Indonesian authorities warmed more to the CRS assistance than to the ICRC operation which involved closer monitoring and perhaps opened up the possibility of information leaking to the outside world. The ICRC could not but appreciate the contrast between the complete freedom its mission had enjoyed during the Fretilin interregnum, and the very limited operation it was grudgingly allowed to undertake in 1979. For example, the Indonesians at first contrived to keep the ICRC away from sensitive, though traditional, functions like tracing missing people and family reunification. In 1976 rumours that the ICRC might be permitted to play a role in helping Timorese leave the territory led to thousands of names being recorded on lists, to the anger and embarrassment of the Indonesian military.

From all accounts the Timorese greatly valued the ICRC presence. Its Indonesian and Swiss members alike appear to have carried out their work conscientiously, and their presence evidently exercised a moderating influence on the military in those centres where they were located. Twice the agreement was renewed for a further six months, but early in 1981 it was terminated. Letters from Timor at the time of the mission's departure showed that the Timorese became apprehensive that the occupation authorities would return to the more oppressive policies. The writer of one of these letters pleaded for outside organisations to press for the ICRC's return as soon as possible. Reports from East Timor between July and October 1981 give some inkling as to the real reason the Indonesian military was anxious for the mission to leave the territory. Within weeks of its departure yet another major military operation, *Operasi Keamanan*, was launched against Fretilin remnants, and from the many later reports it is clear that some of the techniques involved would have disturbed the convention-conscious officials of the ICRC.

Although the efforts of concerned Indonesians should not be discounted it was largely through the work of the ICRC and CRS teams that living conditions in East Timor improved significantly in 1980 and 1981. Reports from the province during this time indicate that famine was arrested in the affected areas, and that the physical condition of the Timorese in the resettlement centres visibly improved. In mid-1980 a CRS official, John Donnelly, told the Congressional Committee on Appropriations that 'there was dramatic visible evidence that the program to date has been a success in a life and death situation. Available statistics all showed major drops in death rates'.[32]

These views were more or less endorsed by ICRC officials with whom I had discussions in New York in the following October. The mission in East Timor, they reported, had informed the international headquarters of the organisation that the worst of the food crisis in the territory was under control. It was also claimed that, in spite of continued armed resistance to Indonesian occupation in central and eastern districts, by September 1981 the occupying authorities in East Timor were more securely in control than ever. One foreign visitor who went to the territory in September 1981 had been able to visit several main administrative centres, including Ainaro, Suai and Baucau, in what appeared to be relaxed security conditions. The position in 1982 was a matter of some debate in Australia, especially after a three-day visit to the '27th Province' by former Prime Minister Gough Whitlam, who contended that there were no signs of famine and that conditions were better than ever before. A somewhat less rosy picture was painted by the Australian journalist Peter Hastings, who accompanied Whitlam, but both discredited an earlier report from Apostolic Administrator of East Timor Monsignor Martinho da Costa Lopes, that famine, or the risk of famine, was still present.

The comments of da Costa Lopes, then designated the Acting Bishop, were made in a letter to an Australian bishop. The point of this letter was not that famine continued in East Timor, but that it would recur at some time if food stocks were not sent to the territory. Although he made few public statements, da Costa Lopes was to become a fearless critic of Indonesian policies in East Timor. Direct responsibility to the Vatican, a position announced by the Pope in May 1982, accorded Timorese bishops a special status unrivalled by other Timorese, including the provincial Governor. Bishops da Costa Lopes and his better-known and longer-serving successor, Carlos Belo, were to become outstanding champions of human rights in the province. They intervened to prevent killings, drawing the attention of high-ranking Indonesian officials to major atrocities and allowing some information to get to the world community.

Once the ICRC presence was established in East Timor, Acting Bishop da Costa Lopes began speaking out, to the chagrin of the Indonesian authorities. In 1981 he protested at a number of wanton killings, especially at the Lacluta massacre where several hundred Timorese, including women and children, were killed by Indonesian troops. This particular protest by the Bishop led to a concerted effort by Jakarta to have him discredited and removed. Not long after the release of details about the massacre the visit of former Prime Minister Mr Whitlam was arranged. The visit was organised by the Indonesian Centre for Strategic and International Studies (CSIS) which, since 1975, had played a major international public relations role in relation to the Timor problem. From all accounts Mr Whitlam's reception was carefully orchestrated so that, for example, he did not visit areas experiencing food shortages. But they need not have bothered, for Mr Whitlam was not one for probing the dark side of the Timor affair. His conclusions must have exceeded the expectations of his hosts. Having not visited Timor before the invasion Mr Whitlam returned full of praise for integration, reaching the 'clear verdict' that 'the conditions in East Timor are much better than before the civil war of 1975 and the famine of 1978'. He reported: 'The Indonesian authorities, with the advice of international bodies, have committed themselves to thorough development programs for the province.' Mr Whitlam did not stop there, attributing the misrepresentation of the situation to the 'mendacious' comments of da Costa Lopes.[31] It was not long after these comments that the courageous Bishop was relieved of his post by the Vatican. A similarly glowing account of the 'Indonesianisation' of East Timor came from the pen of Australian journalist, John Hamilton, who spent six days in the territory in 1983, also at the invitation of the CSIS, and later heaped lavish praise on the Indonesian authorities for their development program.[32]

These bold conclusions have not been supported by more detailed information from several other sources whose stays in East Timor were longer, and some of whom are much more familiar with the territory. For example, one person with more than ten years experience in Timor said in August 1982 that there was a critical shortage of food in a number of areas, including Baguia, Luro, Laga, Quelicai and Iliomar. The reasons for the continuing shortage were said to be the effects of resettlement, which had meant moving the people too far away from their fields, the effect of malnutrition, which rendered the people too weak to work, and the lack of water buffalo to plough the fields. The modest supplies of grain that had been available earlier in the year had been exhausted by May. Another visitor to East Timor there several months after the Whitlam visit, spoke of a serious food shortage in the eastern districts of the province.[33] From these accounts, the root problems were the people's debilitated and demoralised state, corruption and food distribution difficulties. In August one observer contrasted famine conditions in these districts with the fact that warehouses in Dili were filled with corn, some of which was rotting. Against these reports the glowing account given by Mr Whitlam sounded quite incredible. It was further discredited by the American journalist Rod Nordland who spent eleven days in Timor in May 1982. He described the province as 'a land beset by widespread malnutrition and hunger', attributing the failure of the grain harvest to *Operasi Keamanan*. The corn had not been planted on time, he said, because the men had been forced to participate in the operations in the mountains.[34]

After his return to Australia, Mr Whitlam became an activist in support of integration for a time. He testified at length to the Australian Senate inquiry into the human rights situation in the province and later, as a private petitioner, to the Fourth Committee of the UN General Assembly. Clearly his view of the problem was shaped by his role in 1974 and 1975 but, in fairness, it is necessary to mention another aspect. Not only was the Whitlam visit of very short; it took place during the last months of the wet season when the presence of a large amount of food from the natural environment would have minimised food problems—at least for several weeks. Whitlam and Hastings were accompanied by ICRC officials, who apparently briefed them about the situation as they saw it. Mr Whitlam later exploited this association in an attempt to reinforce the credibility of his own assessment, but the views of the ICRC were much more guarded. First, the mission had been anxious not to antagonise the Indonesians so that it could continue its work and its officials seemed determined to keep out of the debate begun by the publication of the da Costa Lopes' letter. The ICRC was clearly embarrassed at the way that a former Australian Prime Minister had exploited their brief association. Shortly after the visit one official was reported as saying that a serious shortage of food all over East Timor should not be spoken of, which seemed to imply that it existed in a number of places. He also admitted that in the next few months serious problems were expected to develop in a number of areas, which indeed did occur, as reports from other sources attest.

The war, the ensuing famine, and the social upheaval after 1975 had a devastating effect on East Timor's rural economy, demoralizing the population at large. In October 1981 a seminar in Dili on the development of the province was told by an Indonesian agricultural specialist that the water buffalo (*Kerbau*) population of East Timor had declined from more than 150,000 in the mid-1970s to fewer than 25,000 in 1981. The Indonesian military administration, having done little to resuscitate Timor's food production for some five years after the invasion, began to introduce some farming improvements at Maliana, Manatuto, Baucau, Liquiça, and certain other fertile areas. In the past these areas were usually farmed by the planters, rather than the ordinary people. According to one expert opinion expressed at the Dili seminar, the province's rich valleys, fertile plains and permanent sources of water could become economically self-sufficient in about five years. There was more than a touch of irony about such an assessment, recalling that in 1975, the Indonesians persistently sought to justify the case for integration by arguing that the Portuguese colony lacked the economic viability to contemplate independence. The industry that did attract the attention of the new rulers was Timor's small but profitable coffee industry, the income from which was to become an important source of private gain for a group of senior military officers.

Predictably, the half-hearted early efforts to resuscitate East Timor's shattered economy were concentrated on those sectors from which the new rulers could derive most benefit. Most of the worthwhile enterprises were taken over directly or indirectly by army officers, with little benefit being passed on to the Timorese employees. In some cases the owners had already fled the country, while in others it was necessary to depose the existing management. In the early phase of what was all but the economic rape of East Timor one company was to emerge as the province's dominant enterprise, and that was PT Denok Hernandes International. Ironically it was based on the formally dominant Portuguese enterprise, SAPT, which had the largest coffee holdings in East Timor and was also a leading wholesaler and retailer. Denok was established very early to transfer the assets of the old colonial power to the new colonial rulers, in practice to enrich the generals in charge of the Timor campaign. Denok, it has been said, was 'the only company that landed with the marines'.[35] Behind PT Denok Hernandes International were Generals Moerdani, Dading Kalbuadi (promoted Brigadier-General after the invasion) and Colonel (later general) Rajagukuk, while two Indonesian–Chinese directors, Hendro (Robby) Sumampow and Hartantosutejo, were to provide the business facade for a venture set up to transfer colonial assets to Indonesian generals. Apart from seizing SAPT and other plantations, Denok assumed effective control of the marketing of East Timor's valuable high-grade coffee crop, exporting to Singapore. In this way the men behind Denok made millions of dollars profit in the first five years after the invasion. In effect, while the Indonesian authorities were boasting of how much they were investing in the reconstruction of the province, the military commanders were enriching themselves. Having established a strong capital base with its coffee ventures,

Denok then began to diversify its operations. It sought to monopolise the sandalwood industry, and moved into East Timor's copra industry. It established subsidiaries, one of which, PT Batara Indra, was later to become the major investor in the subsequently discredited casino set up on Christmas Island, a remote Australian island territory several hundred kilometres south of Java. The casino was to become a gambling playground for Indonesian playboys, including Tommy Suharto and his brother-in-law, Lieutenant General Prabowo.

Denok's monopoly was later to be challenged with the setting up of other companies with strong links to the *Orde Baru* establishment. These included PT Nusa Bhakti, owned by Madame Tien Suharto, the wife of the President, and PT Lianbau, which was set up by Prabowo. These enterprises not only acquired their assets on the cheap; they were able to use the power of the military to establish their dominance, imposing rock-bottom prices on Timorese growers.

Another enterprising source of income was emigration. When at last a trickle of Timorese was allowed to leave the province, they first had to part with their assets and then to pay outrageous prices of up to AUD5000 for emigration papers. As few Timorese could meet such costs much of the money was often raised by relatives abroad, that is, by the Timorese communities in Australia and Portugal.

Not surprisingly, dissatisfaction with the handling of East Timor's economy increased as the development of the province got under way. This was strongly expressed in a report to President Suharto by the local assembly in June 1981, suggesting that economic conditions had not improved in the five-and-a-half years of Indonesian rule. In the words of its authors, 'the economic situation of the people of East Timor is now passing through the most tragic phase since the beginning of the civil war in this region'. While it was admitted that:

> quite a lot of financial assistance for the purposes of building up the economy has been received' the report declared that 'the people of East Timor have not yet felt any real benefits from their own efforts in the production of various agricultural products such as coffee, sandalwood, kaset [sic, meaning not clear], candlenut, timber, copper and other produce...

> In East Timor, there is only one enterprise that may purchase coffee in the regions through its representatives at a very low price per kilo. This enterprise is PT Denok. PT Denok is able to monopolise coffee, sandalwood and other produce...PT Denok is a special enterprise located in East Timor in order to absorb all the main economic products of the province for its services to the Government of the Republic of Indonesia.[36]

Coffee planters were forced to accept very low prices for their produce. The report referred specifically to the rapacious exploitation of sandalwood.

> In all the places throughout the region of East Timor where sandalwood has been growing, certain individuals have arrived, bringing people and forcing them to cut down the timber; dead sandalwood trees as well as young sandalwood trees have been cut down and even their roots pulled out. The timber has then been sold in Dili to PT Denok at a very low price even though it should fetch a high price.

The same kind of exploitation was said to be going on for other such resources upon which the Timorese traditionally depended for their livelihood. And so it was that the authors of this document lamented that after five years of integration most of the population was 'not yet able to enjoy stable living conditions'.

Another subject raised by the Assembly report was the misuse of development funds by certain Indonesian officials, including Colonel Kalangi, the *Sekwilda*, or secretary of the region, a position making him one of the most powerful officials in the military-dominated administration of East Timor. Kalangi and his deputy, Captain A. Azis Hasyam, were alleged to have conspired to squander project funds provided by the central government. Assembly members were said to have made on-the-spot investigations into a number of projects involving expenditure of hundreds of millions of rupiahs, and were 'extremely disappointed to discover that they were totally fictitious'. One of those involved in this corruption was a Kalangi relative.

In this appeal to President Suharto the authors told of the misuse of medical supplies, some of which had gone to East Timor as part of foreign-aid consignments. The report asked:

> Where are all those medicines that have been sent here for the people of East Timor by the central government and from abroad in such large quantities? There is a severe shortage of medicines in the hospitals of East Timor whose needs are being neglected although in the shops of Chinese merchants medicines identical to those provided with government assistance are available in huge quantities, in chemist shops as well as in general stores. Where have these medicines come from?[37]

Although economic activity was stimulated by the new development activities, the Timorese had difficulty in obtaining other than low-paid menial work. A condition for an established position in the government sector was the formal acceptance of Indonesian citizenship, a step many Timorese were reluctant to take for fear of closing off the option of leaving their homeland for Australia or Portugal. All in all, with the new configuration of political and economic power in the province the Timorese were to find themselves in a considerably weaker position than had been the case in the colonial days before the Lisbon coup of April 1974. The local Assembly had no real power. This was exposed by the later arrest of those deputies who had dared to complain to President Suharto about the plight of his newly acquired subjects. At every level of government real power was exercised by the Indonesian military. That the report of June 1981 could not dislodge corrupt officers like Colonel Kalangi and Captain Azis Hasyam from their powerful positions in the provincial administration, underlined the powerlessness of those Timorese officials and politicians who accepted positions in the new political and administrative infrastructures set up after *integrasi*.

The 1981 Assembly report did not confine itself to economic issues. It stated that in the districts of Lospalos, Viqueque, Liquiça and Covalima Timorese had been tortured and had been executed for patently trivial reasons. The authors of this report stated that: 'these murders and acts of torture committed by these irresponsible persons or groups have resulted in a situation of instability throughout the region of East Timor'. Among the victims of these atrocities were a number of women prisoners who had been 'tortured with electricity and burnt with cigarettes by some elements of the armed forces who also inflicted immoral sexual acts upon them'. Such allegations had been coming out of Timor for five years, and many were made to me when I interviewed newly arrived refugees in Lisbon in 1977. According to a Timorese women's movement with whom the subject was discussed in 2000, tens of thousands of women were sexually assaulted by soldiers during these twenty-four years of occupation, and not one of the culprits was ever brought to justice.

The reference in the DPRD report to atrocities barely skimmed the surface, revealing little about those four years after the invasion when, as a killing field, East Timor compared with the worst cases in the contemporary world, much worse than Bosnia, for example. It was not until November 1991 that the world at large was given a visible glimpse of the East Timorese ordeal, yet the Santa Cruz massacre was relatively minor when compared with the massacres that occurred between the invasion and the Creras massacre of 1983. Starting with the killing of as many as 2000 in the Dili area in the first week or so after the invasion, known mass killings occurred in 1976 at Suai, near Bobonaro, and at Aileu; in 1977 in the Bobonaro area and at Quelicai; in 1978 in the Matabian area (thousands were killed by indiscriminate air attacks on the civilian population); and executions after the June 1980 attack on Dili by Fretilin. Two other atrocities during this period warrant special attention, the Lacluta massacre of 1981 and the Creras massacre of August 1983. The Lacluta incident occurred in September 1981 while the major Indonesian operation, designated *Operasi Keamanan*, was in progress. Apparently a party of Fretilin guerrillas surrendered with their women and children. According to eyewitness accounts some of the women were taken away by the troops, but the rest, along with the men and children, were shot, their bodies covered with dry grass and leaves and then set alight. Four hundred were said to have been killed.[38] The Creras massacre was one of the worst of its kind. It occurred after yet another 'clean-up' operation by ABRI. It was carried out as a reprisal for the killing of fifteen or seventeen Indonesian troops by Fretilin in a surprise night raid, a raid which itself was launched following a spate of raping and killing of young Timorese girls, including the young wife of a Timorese official. The massacre apparently took place on 21 and 22 August 1983. First some 200 Timorese were burnt alive in their homes, while another 500 hundred were killed at the Be Tuku River. Investigations after October 1999 indicate that one of Indonesia's most notorious commanders, then Major Prabowo, may have played the leading role in carrying out this massacre. According to Mario Carrascalão, provincial governor of the time who personally investigated the atrocity, more than 1000 Timorese of all ages were massacred. Yet there was no international response, let alone pressure on the Suharto government to stop the killing. A statement by an Australian cabinet minister to the effect that the Falintil should stop provoking the Indonesian military was the best that Canberra could come up with!

After the orgy of killing at Lacluta, a Timorese asked an Indonesian soldier why he had killed the wife and child of a Fretilin guerrilla, and the reply was: 'When you clean the field, don't you kill all the snakes, the small and large alike?'[39] Later atrocities suggest that this crude philosophy continued to prevail until the Suharto regime was put on the spot by international outrage at the killings in Santa Cruz cemetery in November 1991. The slaughter that decimated East Timor's population was of a genocidal character. Each of the above incidents, making up only a selective list, provided grounds for an international investigation of some kind into crimes against humanity in East Timor, and the identification of the war criminals responsible. That such an inquiry has never even been canvassed is testimony to the determination of the US and Australian governments of the time to shield the Suharto regime from international human rights criticism, and to the disinterest of the international community at large. Even after the Indonesian withdrawal when UN officials had free access to all parts of the territory there was a reluctance to probe into the nightmares of the past, not least because of the magnitude of the task.

ABRI's military victories over Fretilin, and the presence of the ICRC mission, did not end human rights abuses in the towns of East Timor. Amnesty International continued to amass evidence of the continuing use of torture and of the rape of women. The many accounts of such abuses were a serious indictment of the lack of discipline and the inhumanity of the Indonesian military. To be fair, some officials tried to prevent abuses and injustices, but they were apparently powerless to bring officers like Colonel Sinaga (known as the 'Black God') and Colonel Kalangi to justice. More than a year after the DPRD report to President Suharto, officials implicated in brutality and corruption were still securely in office. The arrest of two of the report's signatories, Leandro Isaac and Sousa Soares, was the only response, a move to silence the petitioners. As it turned out, these two deputies were released following the intervention of the Speaker of the Indonesian Parliament.

Eight years after the assault on Dili the people of East Timor were in a sorry state. They had suffered a severe loss of population, and were, in effect, subject to a far more oppressive political and economic exploitation than they had been forced to endure during the last generation of Portuguese colonial rule. The nightmarish experiences of the late 1970s, which had exacted great suffering and loss of life, may have ended, but the people were still in a depressed state. Their views were very different from the optimistic assessments of visitors like Mr Whitlam, and some Western diplomats, who were evidently persuaded that all the ugliness, backwardness and discontent in East Timor was rooted in the much vilified legacy of Portuguese colonialism.

The internal situation from after 1983
Less than a year after the killing of Nicolau Lobato and other Timorese leaders,

the beleaguered Timorese resistance was able to resume armed opposition, Falintil ranks were replenished by new recruits, many of them deserters from the Timorese battalions, 744 and 745, and from the Hansip paramilitary units, and the resistance was able to carry out some daring hit-and-run attacks on ABRI forces. But the resistance was largely fragmented and uncoordinated until March 1981 when Xanana Gusmão was formally chosen as leader of CNRM forces at a meeting in the Lacluta area. Falantil's revival led the Indonesian military to launch *Operasi Keamanan* which, despite the use of the notorious 'fence of legs'* technique, failed to crush the guerrilla force. The brutal methods used against the guerrillas merely served to intensify hostility towards the military, especially among the young Timorese who provided eager recruits to replace the losses in the Lacluta area.

While the Timorese were soon able to establish a military presence in many parts of the territory, a significant change in political direction and in tactics began to unfold. The political radicalism of the past, especially that espoused by expatriate leaders like Abilio Araujo, perhaps the most Marxist of Fretilin leaders, was abandoned in favour of non-ideological policies designed to appeal to all Timorese, including the UDT and Apodeti supporters. By 1981 even many of the latter had become deeply disenchanted with integration. The changes reflected the realities of the international and internal situation. By the early 1980s there were signs that international political support for the Timorese struggle for independence was declining. With no material support getting to Fretilin from the outside world, the Timorese were forced, as ever, to rely on their own resources. Much of the equipment left by the Portuguese in 1975 had gone, and to replenish their weapons and ammunition Xanana's forces had to depend on captured material, or on black-market purchases. From 1982 onwards Xanana was able to establish communications with Fretilin and CNRM abroad.

Fretilin forces emerged from the Lacluta massacre in good shape. Early in 1983 there were moves initiated by certain Indonesian military commanders for local cease-fires. These led to moves for a wider truce, an idea which reportedly had the support of the ABRI commander of the time, General Yusuf. That the Indonesian military would agree to such a compromising arrangement came as a surprise, but it seems to have reflected a mixture of war-weariness and, for some officers, a distaste for morally offensive operations. Thus on 21 March 1983 Fretilin leaders, including Xanana, met with some Indonesian officers at the small village of Bubu Rate in what was later described as a friendly atmosphere. The Timorese asked that the Indonesians open up East Timor to outside contacts, especially with UN officials, and that Jakarta announce that cease-fire talks were under way. According to later accounts from Xanana the Indonesian response was positive and conciliatory. It was then agreed that they

---

* Timorese were forced to march ahead of the Indonesian troops in their advance into Falintil areas.

should meet three days later. This time the meeting, near the village of Ossu (not far from Viqueque), was attended by Colonel Poerwanto, the East Timor military commander, and by Governor Carrascalão. A cease-fire agreement was signed, and it was agreed to pass on certain proposals from Xanana to the Suharto government. These included the withdrawal of Indonesian troops from East Timor, the admission of a UN peacekeeping force, and free consultations about Timor's future. The accord seems to have gained a measure of acceptance, at least in East Timor.

This was not the case in Jakarta where the prospect of the situation in Indonesia's newest province being internationalised caused alarm bells to ring. It was not a cease-fire, according to officials in Jakarta, but an amnesty offer to Fretilin guerrillas. General Moerdani, who had become Armed Forces Commander, strongly opposed it, and the unfortunate Colonel Poerwanto was relieved of his command. The idea of negotiations would greatly elevate the independence movement's international status, and place integration gravely at risk.

It is clear that the Indonesian military were able to profit from a visit to East Timor by an Australian Parliamentary delegation, led by Mr Bill Morrison, who had been Defence Minister in the Whitlam government. From the outset it seemed that Morrison had little interest in uncovering human rights abuses or in probing Timorese attitudes to integration. His main aim, it appeared, was to use the visit to help remove a troublesome issue from the Australia–Indonesia relationship which, at that time, was in a state of uncertainty. Hence when Fretilin representatives tried to make contact with Morrison on the road between Lospalos and Baucau, and to get him to meet with some of their leaders, their overtures were rebuffed by an Australian politician who apparently had sympathy for their cause. Thus an important opportunity to encourage a process of negotiation was squandered. The outcome served to encourage General Moerdani, who had viewed the negotiations with alarm, in particular, to brush aside his military colleagues in favour of negotiations, and to press for a quick military solution. The mission almost failed in its responsibility to probe behind the thin facade of stability constructed for its convenience. The one exception was Chairman of the Senate Foreign Affairs Committee Senator Gordon McIntosh who did take the trouble to probe beneath the surface and his dissenting report was a refreshing departure from the distorted account put together by Morrison.

Before Morrison left Jakarta to return to Australia Moerdani was able to have a lengthy private meeting with him. They had developed a friendship some years earlier when both were serving at an Asian post. Within days of this meeting Indonesian forces began to move into East Timor. At the end of August the Creras massacre took place, while the Timorese guerrillas who had tried to make contact with the Morrison mission were captured and executed. In September President Suharto declared a state of emergency in East Timor and ordered a 'clean sweep' of the armed resistance.

The mission's report, largely the work of Morrison, aided by an obliging parliamentary research officer, was less than an exercise in impartiality. It ignored or glossed over the human rights dimension of the problem, even misrepresenting the historical background to integration, it seemed, to exculpate Indonesia. The general thrust of the report was that there was no insecurity in East Timor and no evidence of human rights abuses. There was no evidence of insecurity because a cease-fire was in place; as for human rights violations, the hosts took good care that the mission did not stumble across any such evidence. They need not have bothered for only one of the visitors, Senator McIntosh, was apparently interested in the humanitarian situation of the Timorese. The report provided timely help to Prime Minister Hawke and those of his colleagues who were anxious to get Timor off the agenda so that relations with Indonesia could be advanced, especially on negotiations about the oil-rich Timor Sea boundary.[40]

Not only did the cease-fire end; yet another major operation, codenamed *Operasi Persatuan*, was launched. By early 1984 East Timor was swarming with troops—about 20,000 of them, according to Timorese sources—with some interesting personalities among the commanders, reminders that service in East Timor was a major factor in promotion in a military without combat experience outside Indonesia's borders. One security force commander was Brigadier General Yunus Yosfiah, the officer in charge of the troops who had killed the newsmen from Australia in 1975. Another commander was Major General Mantiri, who had commanded a Sulawesi battalion in Timor in 1976, and who was later to become *panglima* of the Nusatenggara regional command. With ICR activities severely curtailed there were no outside witnesses to yet another 'fence of legs' campaign, under which Timorese, young and old, were forced to walk ahead of Indonesian units in their search-and-destroy operations. In 1985 thousands of Timorese chose to go to the hills to avoid this conscription. These operations led to famine conditions, and to widespread reports of summary executions and torture.

The operations continued through the 1980s and into the 1990s, becoming more of an annual military training exercise than a military necessity. Although on each occasion thousands of troops were involved somehow the CNRM forces managed to survive. Xanana did change the style of their operations, for political and tactical reasons. The guerrillas avoided direct confrontations with the Indonesian military where they would be outgunned and outnumbered. With the cruel lessons of Creras in mind Xanana began to avoid any military operation that would risk provoking reprisals against the local population as a successful ambush of Indonesian forces invariably provoked a major counterattack by ABRI forces sporting new equipment. The resistance sought to encourage and to organise passive resistance in the towns and villages.

Xanana was also keen to keep open the option of some kind of negotiations, despite the experience of 1983. He became a towering figure among Timorese because of his prowess as a guerrilla leader and his intellect. CNRM's military wing, Falintil, began to decline in numbers and in its military capability, but an extensive network of non-military support in the towns and villages of East Timor was developed, a network on which its survival depended. As well as the activists, the young Timorese who were prepared to engage in public protest, there were the thousands of Timorese, probably most of the adult population, who provided information and other subtle forms of assistance. To a Timorese population stifled by an oppressive colonial order, Xanana and his Falintil troops remained as a kind of symbol that Indonesian occupation is neither total nor forever. The Timorese leader's arrest on 20 November 1992 came as a crushing blow to the Timorese. However with Xanana's defiant performance before his accusers his leadership stature increased, rather than diminished, despite his imprisonment in Java's Cipenang Prison. He was the symbol of an uncrushable Timorese spirit, inspiring the population at large not to bend before the Indonesian will.

Xanana's successor, Ma' Huno, did not last long; he was captured by Indonesian troops near Ainaro early in April 1993. But the Falintil guerrillas, though perhaps much diminished in number, continued to be active under Konis Santana and other leaders, as a defiant symbol of the determination of the people at large to resist integration until the end. The Falintil exhibited extraordinary discipline during the last period of the occupation—from the fall of Suharto to the InterFET intervention. Faced with enormous provocation as the militia violence mounted in 1999, the guerrillas maintained great discipline, heeding Xanana's commands from prison to maintain a cease-fire. For most of the time they confined themselves to the agreed cantonments, emerging as unbeaten heroes when the Government of President Habibie finally bowed to international pressure, and surrendered East Timor to a UN mandate.

Armed resistance was only a small part of the story of East Timor in the 1980s and 1990s. Indeed, by the late 1980s the main opposition to Indonesian policies came not from the Falintil but from the population at large, with a strong activist element emerging among the young Timorese. These were products of a greatly expanded education system, a central aim of which was to 'Indonesianise' a new generation of Timorese, to educate them to abandon the lost cause of independence, in favour of Indonesian nationhood. Yet the program simply did not work in an environment of oppression and in a community where nearly every family had suffered human rights abuses at the hands of ABRI troops. By the 1990s thousands of young Timorese, many of whom spoke only Indonesian, were to form a common front of opposition to *integrasi*, and were ready to risk the wrath of a ruthless military in occasional demonstrations.

Ever since the invasion the church had assumed an increasingly central role in East Timor. It could not be destroyed like the civil administration. The church did not, however, come to the forefront until some time after the resignation of Bishop Joaquim Ribeiro who, though shocked at the behaviour of the invaders, maintained a low profile until he retired in 1977, exhausted and demoralised. His successor eventually became much more assertive, his criticisms causing the military to press for his replacement—ABRI was not without influence in this regard, thanks to a close relationship between Moerdani and the Papal Nuncio. Reportedly after the latter's intervention in 1983 a new bishop came on the scene, and Costa Lopes retired to Portugal. The new Bishop, Carlos Belo, was much younger than Costa Lopes and, he was Timorese. The Indonesian military at first believed that he would be much easier to deal with. But Bishop Belo was to prove to be anything but amenable. His moral authority and his personal stature were substantially increased by the enormous growth in membership of the church—which increased from below fifty per cent of the population before the invasion to more than eighty per cent in 1996. In the years following the invasion thousands of Timorese embraced the church, not least because it offered the only protection against the excesses of the invaders, and then often it could do little.

Within months of his appointment Bishop Belo courageously assumed the mantle of his courageous predecessor. He protested at the excesses of *Operasi Persatuan*. Less than two years later he published a list of the names of victims of the Creras massacre, and attacked the Indonesian birth control program. He soon became anathema to sections of ABRI, and there were attempts to bring the East Timorese under the authority of the Indonesian church hierarchy. As such a move would have prejudiced East Timor's position at the United Nations, so the Vatican did not go along with it. Yet the Vatican's support was not unqualified. When the Pope visited East Timor in October 1989, where 100,000 Timorese were to attend an open-air mass, the visit was not to the liking of some of the priests, who felt that it would endorse integration. In a pastoral letter Bishop Belo told his congregation: 'The Pope does not come to defend integration, nor does he come to defend independence, nor to indicate political solutions to the problem of East Timor...' At the end of the visit there was some violence, as military personnel, under the command of Colonel Luhud Panjaitan, cracked down on a fringe demonstration in favour of independence.

Despite the weak encouragement he received from the Vatican, Bishop Belo continued to stand up for the rights of his people, winning him the respect of the international community and the devotion of his flock. In a daring move, in February 1989 he wrote to the UN Secretary-General, calling for a referendum on East Timor's future. He played a key role in exposing the true extent of killings in the Dili massacre of November 1991, and maintained pressure on the Indonesian authorities to end human rights abuses. The Bishop's stand was not without cost. There have been a number of attempts to have him removed, and there have been at least two attempts on his life. His position became central in this regard. Whenever young Timorese were arrested or were tortured, it was to the Bishop that the people turned. The Indonesian authorities, fearful of his growing authority outside and inside East Timor, could not ignore him.

While Bishop Belo became the main centre of opposition to human rights abuses in East Timor, the less well-known efforts of other Timorese should not be ignored. They included the previous Governor, Mario Carrascalão, who took office in October 1982. Carrascalão was not an enthusiast for integration, and the excesses of ABRI forces so shocked him that early in the 1980s that he contemplated abandoning a senior diplomatic post the Indonesians gave him in New York. He was reluctant to accept the post of Governor of the province, but was apparently swayed by the pleas of East Timorese who hoped that he could curb the excesses of the military. Once in office he was never to become an eager tool of the military. However, while Carrascalão did succeed on occasion in curbing some of their excesses, his authority was no match for that of the military commanders who opposed his reappointment. A much more amenable Timorese was the last Governor under Indonesian rule. Abilio Soares, who took office in 1992, was the preferred choice of then General Prabowo and was to become a passionate opponent of the independence option in 1999 and a strong supporter of setting up the militia, and of its violent agenda.

Until the end the Indonesian military, or more precisely Kopassus, the Special Forces command, were overwhelmingly the dominant force in East Timor. After the invasion Kopassus officers virtually ran the government of the province, assisted by its intelligence network. Most of the *panglimas* were from Kopassus. Kopassus officers occupied key roles in the provincial government and military officers occupied many of the district administrator positions. East Timor was, therefore, special to the military. Thus the provincial secretary, the *sekwilda*, was usually an officer of the rank of colonel, as was one of the assistant governors. ABRI officers, usually of the rank of major, enjoyed a more-than-equal share of power in each *kabupaten*. In the Indonesian system of the time the military also directly controlled East Timor's police.

East Timor, it seemed, was their special property. They had plotted and organised its seizure, engaged in a long and bloody war with the determined defenders, at the cost of more than 5000 TNI lives. They sought to purge Timorese culture of the desire for independence, in the process resorting to what they knew best—terror and intimidation. There was the dark side. During the occupation military units committed many atrocities. The only one to be investigated was the Dili massacre of 1991, which was by no means the worst. The outcome was less than just. Several soldiers received only short terms of imprisonment, while their commanders escaping with soft reprimands. Therefore when in 1998 Dr Habibie talked of engaging the Timorese in a dialogue about their future, a wave of alarm swept through senior officer ranks and led ultimately to a conspiracy to sabotage the self-determination process and thus prevent the loss of Indonesia's 27th province. It was not just a matter of losing the territory; gravely at risk was the exposure of an appalling record of crimes against humanity and corruption, responsibility for which, at the command level, would implicate a significant proportion of the Indonesian Army's general staff.

The one aspect of integration that Indonesian officials generally boasted about was the economy, which had developed significantly, especially since the early 1980s. On the surface improvements to the infrastructure were impressive. Roads had been upgraded and in many cases sealed between the major population centres. Dili, which once housed a little more than 20,000 had become a city of more than 120,000 by the end of the eighties. The rough grass airstrip near the capital had been replaced by a new airport to the west, towards Tibar. Rural development projects were established in the premium pasture lands around Maliana and in the Lautem district to the east. East Timor, once a world of tiny hamlets, was being restructured into larger village centres. And there was a great expansion in the education system, with East Timor at last having its own university.

The appearance of development, however, is no substitute for self-government. Most of the infrastructural development was designed to meet the military needs of ABRI, and to facilitate developing that sector of the economy from which the generals were able to reap handsome profits. Within two years of the invasion PT Denok was exporting East Timor's coffee to Singapore, much of it from the Ermera district. It is no coincidence that the Dili–Ermera road was one of the first to be upgraded and sealed. By 1983 the pace of East Timor's economic development was accelerated, but at least some of the aid for this development was being supplied by friendly Western governments. Considerable attention was however given to urban development with the construction of better housing, and road, electricity and water supply improvements, especially in Dili. The main beneficiaries of better roads, housing and services were the more than 60,000 Indonesians from elsewhere in the republic who began moving into the province after the invasion.

Those opposed to integration often criticised Indonesia's unpopular transmigration program as a major irritant to the Timorese. However, it seems that East Timor was not really a major recipient of transmigrants, most of the outsiders having travelled independently to the island where they came to dominate the small business sector. The *transmigrasi* (migration) projects at Maliana, Gleno and other locations did create resentment, for it meant confiscating good-quality Timorese farming lands in the first instance and providing the newcomers with housing and other facilities vastly superior to those enjoyed by the local population. The outcome of these development policies, to use the words of the Mubyarto team's report, was to 'marginalise the Timorese' in the economy of the province. It seemed that in every aspect of political and economic life, the Timorese were forced into a marginal status in their own land. The survivors of the holocaust of the late 1970s gained only marginally from this development process. The end result was to consolidate the economic and political power of the new colonial rulers to a degree that the Portuguese never contemplated. Their past sufferings, the politically oppressive form of rule to which they were subjected, and this feeling of being marginalised has resulted in a pervasive community feeling of trauma, identified by Professor Mubyarto's team in 1990. He was to report:

The East Timor problem can only be solved and the development process in this province speeded up, if everyone involved thinks positively and gets rid of the trauma which still dominates their feelings and thoughts.

Notes

1 David Jenkins, 'Day of Fear and Fury', *Sydney Morning Herald*, 2 December 1995. As the Jenkins later reported, Battalion 502 attended the joint exercises, Kangaroo '95 with Australian troops in the Northern Territory.
2 Hamish McDonald, Suharto's Indonesia (Melbourne: Fontana/Collins, 1980), p. 212.
3 Sheryle Bagwell and Everard Himmelreich, 'The Roger East Story', *New Journalist*, May 1979.
4 Ibid.
5 Jill Jolliffe, *East Timor: Nationalism and Colonialism* (St Lucia: University of Queensland Press, 1978), pp. 270-271.
6 Jill Jolliffe, *Canberra Times*, 28 October 1980.
7 Copy of letter received in April 1976.
8 Based on a confidential interview in a Timorese refugee camp in Portugal early in 1977.
9 Copy received from a Timorese source.
10 I hold a copy of this report. I also interviewed Martins.
11 Transcript of an 'AM' broadcast for the ABC, 12 January 1976.
12 *Pelita*, Jakarta, 12 January 1976.
13 *Indonesian Times*, 26 June 1976.
14 For a published account of this report, see Jill Jolliffe's article in the *Canberra Times*, 27 November 1979.
15 Based on an interview conducted in January 1977.
16 Dale van Atta and Brian Toohey, 'The Timor Papers', *National Times*, part 2, 6-12 June 1982.
17 I had several talks with Father de Rego in Lisbon in June 1981.
18 Copy of this report, 'Notes on East Timor', is held by the author.
19 Copy held by the author.
20 Ibid.
21 For details of the military situation see Carmel Budiardjo and Liem Soei Liong, *The War Against East Timor* (London: Zed Books, 1984), pp. 27-36.
22 Copy held by author.
23 Ibid.
24 Budiardjo and Liem, 'The War Against East Timor', pp. 37-39; and Paulino Gama 'A Fretilin Commander Remembers', in Peter Carey and G Cartley Bentley, *Timor at the Crossroads* (London: Cassells, 1995), pp. 10-12.
25 *Sydney Morning Herald*, 9 March 1983.
26 Australian Council for Overseas Aid, *Aid and East Timor*, July 1979.
27 Testimony in 'Famine Relief for East Timor'. Hearing before the Subcommittee on Asian and Pacific Affairs of the Committee on Foreign Affairs, House of Representatives, 96th Congress, 4 December 1979.

28 Father George Cotter and Sue Nichterlein, *Roaming Catholics in East Timor-For Christ's Sake*, September 1980 (copy of article supplied by the authors).

29 Ibid.

30 Testimony in *Famine Relief for East Timor*.

31 E. G. Whitlam, 'The Truth about Timor', *Bulletin*, 30 March 1982.

32 Brisbane *Courier-Mail*, 27 April 1983.

33 I hold a confidential report.

34 Rod Nordland, *Philadelphia Enquirer*, 28 May 1982. As reported in Sinar Harapan in October 1981.

35 John Taylor, *Indonesia's Forgotten War* (London: Zed Books, 1991), pp. 125-127.

36 Laporan Dewan Perwakilan Rakyat Daerah Tingkat 1, Timor Timur, Kepada Bapak President Republik Indonesia Tentang Masalah Dalam Penyelenggaraan di Timor (Report of the first level Regional Peoples' Representative Assembly to the President of the Republic of Indonesia on the subject of organizing the administration of East Timor), 3 June 1981.

37 Ibid.

38 Gama, 'A Fretilin Commander Remembers', in Carey and Carter Bentley, *East Timor at the Crossroads*, p. 102; and Michele Turner, Telling. *East Timor: Personal Testimonies 1942-1992* (Sydney: University of NSW Press, 1992), pp. 185-186.

39 *Official Report of the Australian Parliamentary Delegation to East Timor* (Canberra: AGPS, 1983).

40 Extracts from interview notes help by the author.

Chapter Twelve

International reaction and challenge to integration

When the fighting broke out between the UDT and Fretilin in August 1975 only three countries, Portugal, Indonesia and Australia, had developed other than a cursory interest in the territory. And, as we have seen, the Australian interest was presented as a cautious and distant one, with the Whitlam government asserting that Australia was 'not a party principal to the dispute'. Portugal's interest had also diminished in the face of widespread internal disillusionment with its colonial role, and of the Europe-oriented policies of the central government in Lisbon. The development of Indonesia's designs on the territory was undoubtedly encouraged by the fact that it was the only country in the world with a close and calculated interest in the future of East Timor.

Of the Western nations with a traditionally high level of interest in South-East Asian affairs, only the United States, Britain and the Netherlands took the trouble to ascertain anything about what was happening in the Portuguese colony. But their responses to the unfolding tragedy were shaped by their overriding interest in Indonesia, and not by a concern for the rights of the Timorese to a genuine act of self-determination. The British view of the situation in East Timor in 1975 has already been referred to. In the present context it warrants further examination. In July 1975 Sir John Archibald Ford, the British ambassador to Jakarta, informed the Foreign Office in a cable that, even if the Soviet Union and China did not intervene-and there was no evidence to suggest that they were about to-East Timor was likely to become an increasingly serious 'problem child', strengthening the arguments in favour of its incorporation into Indonesia. Although it was in Britain's interest to avoid 'becoming involved in its future', the recent political developments in Portugal seemed 'now to argue in favour of greater sympathy toward Indonesia should the Indonesian Government feel forced to take strong action by the deteriorating situation in Portuguese Timor'. The Ambassador advised his government that it was 'in Britain's interest that Indonesia should absorb the territory as soon as and as unobtrusively as possible; and that if it came to the crunch and there [was] a row in the United Nations we should keep our heads down and avoid siding against the Indonesian Government'.[1] The Ambassador's view was apparently not shared by all of his colleagues at the Foreign Office but, at least at that time, it seems to have carried the most weight.

Aftermath of the invasion

The coming to power of the Thatcher and Reagan administrations served to consolidate the compliant policies of the previous governments of those countries, and to influence the Western response in general. In that last, but testy, phase of the Cold War the anti-Communist Suharto regime became even more important to right-wing Western governments. The special treatment of Indonesia was soon to be tested. When Argentina seized the Falkland Islands in 1982, the British were confronted with some uncomfortable and embarrassing similarities to the position of East Timor, and Mrs Thatcher's pronouncements on the rights of small territories to determine their own future could just as easily be applied to the Timorese. Portugal was one of the few Latin states to support Britain, but attempts to persuade the latter to vote for the Portuguese initiative in the United Nations in 1982 failed. In fact, the British continued to supply arms to Indonesia, some of which, including jet ground-attack aircraft, appear to have been used in ABRI operations against the Falintil. Thanks, however, to the location in London of leading international human rights NGOs (non-government organisations) the British people could not be kept in the dark about events in East Timor. Amnesty International, which had its international headquarters in London, CIIR, the Catholic Institute for International Relations, and Tapol, an agency focusing on human rights abuses in Indonesia, kept up a steady flow of information about the situation in Timor, and pressures on the Government. The British conscience was stirred by the Santa Cruz massacre and again in 1995 by new revelations concerning the murder of the two Britons among the five newsmen killed at Balibo twenty years earlier.

One country that watched events in East Timor more closely than most in the months prior to the invasion was Japan, but once the invasion took place Tokyo reacted to the unfolding tragedy with cynical indifference. However, although Japan had been regarded by some as having a vital interest in the Portuguese colony, its interest was expressed within the context of the high priority accorded to Japanese relations with Indonesia. Thus, in Tokyo the East Timor problem was perceived in terms of its possible impact on the stability of the region, and of Indonesia in particular, and not in relation to the broader questions of decolonisation or human rights from which Tokyo's foreign policy makers traditionally shied away. Yet Japan was one of the few countries to have any intimate knowledge of the territory and, prior to August 1975, Japanese diplomats, businessmen and journalists had made several visits there. Indeed, three Japanese, including a perceptive journalist from Kyodo News Agency, spent some weeks in the colony during the Fretilin interregnum, and after the mid-October attack on Balibo. It is probable, therefore, that the Japanese were far from ignorant of the real situation on the ground in East Timor, but Tokyo's firm diplomatic support for Indonesia's act of aggression never wavered. When the question of East Timor first came before the UN General Assembly following Indonesia's invasion on 7 December 1975, Japan was among the group of fewer than a dozen states who voted against the resolution calling on Indonesia to withdraw its armed forces and allow for a genuine act of self-determination. The Australian government, whose forces had so blatantly disregarded the welfare of the Timorese people in the 1942-45 period, entertained no qualms of conscience about the rights of the East Timorese when the territory was once again invaded some three decades later. The issue was, however, to attract a surprising amount of attention from parliamentarians and non-government human rights groups. Two decades after the invasion Japan had about fifty Timor support groups, who added weight to the international debate.

Likewise, the ASEAN (Association of South-East Asian Nations) states which cluster around the sprawling Indonesian archipelago all accepted as inevitable, if not desirable, the incorporation of East Timor into Indonesia, regardless of the wishes of its people. Probably none of the other ASEAN states knew much about the issue, most apparently accepting uncritically the version of events provided by Indonesian sources. In the aftermath of the abrupt US withdrawal from Vietnam which sent a shock wave through non-communist South-East Asia, Indonesian paranoia about a possible communist threat from East Timor was, to a greater or lesser extent, shared by other members of the regional grouping.

Nor were the Timorese to get any support from India, Asia's largest non-communist state, in spite of that country's traditional readiness to champion self-determination and independence movements in colonial contexts. India's leaders knew little about East Timor and evidently cared less about its future. In the postwar years there had been almost no contact between India and Timor, and Indian diplomats readily drew a simplistic parallel between Indonesia's position vis-a-vis the Portuguese colony and the earlier position of India in relation to the former Portuguese territory of Goa which its forces invaded and seized in December 1961. Thus, in Indian eyes, the Portuguese presence in East Timor was a colonial anomaly, and Indonesia had an obvious prior claim to the territory. Therefore, from the very outset right up until 1999, India, too, opposed UN efforts to persuade Indonesia to withdraw its forces from the colony. India's action against Goa was of a very different nature: it was the culmination of a vigorously asserted territorial claim and a series of stiff demands that Portugal cede the territory. Indonesia, on the other hand, had consistently denied any territorial claim to East Timor. In 1961 the Salazar regime was obstinately refusing to declare its overseas territories, including Goa, non-self-governing, but in 1975 the new Portuguese rulers were implementing a decolonisation program in which, in deference to Indonesia, the idea of integration was being canvassed-in effect, promoting an option that was without any real basis of support in the colony

Although Australia played a much more active role than the United States in terms of real influence over the Suharto regime, Canberra could not match the powerful leverage at Washington's disposal. The Suharto government's proud boast was that it was non-aligned, but the political character of the regime, with its uncompromising hostility to communism and its opposition to left-wing views generally, propelled Indonesia into the orbit of US influence. After the mid-1960s, when the '30th September' or Gestapu incident precipitated the fall of the Sukarno regime, the Indonesian armed forces became increasingly dependent upon US military assistance. In the mid-1970s the Suharto government's plan to refurbish its armed forces depended heavily upon American technology, indulgence, and political support. The Suharto regime still sought to protect Indonesia's reputation as a moderate, development-oriented nation, which was a bulwark of stability in the South-East Asian region. Jakarta tried by subtle diplomatic means to project two incompatible images-that of a non-aligned regime, respected by the Third World, and at the same time, from the point of view of Washington and its allies, that of a vitally important, stable anti-communist element in overall Western defence strategy. No treaty arrangements existed. But then they hardly needed to be negotiated, because Indonesia's essential strategic importance and political disposition assured it a natural protection.

The coming to power of the Suharto regime had been welcomed by the United States and its allies as a major setback to communist influence in South-East Asia. By the mid-1970s, with the growing uncertainty and instability in relation to the supply to the industrial West of vital energy resources, of which Indonesia was a major provider, and with the uncertain situation in South-East Asia following the American withdrawal from Vietnam, Indonesia's strategic and economic importance in Washington's global perspective was substantially enhanced. Indonesia was not only a major oil producer; the archipelago straddled the seas between mainland South-East Asia and Australia, commanding, as it were, the strategically important seaways between the western Pacific and the Indian Ocean. By the mid-1970s, these had assumed a new importance in the eyes of US strategists, as the expanding Soviet strategic forces began to present new challenges in seas hitherto regarded as secure to Western defence.

In a way, Indonesia's steadfast refusal to enter into any formal security relationship with the United States fitted well into the Nixon-doctrine strategies, including the Reagan administration's view of the world. Outwardly Indonesia was free and independent, unfettered by any formal alliance. In reality, the regime's anti-communism and its dependence upon Western economic and defence support rendered it as much a part of the Asia–Pacific strategic defence complex as countries like South Korea and Japan. On the other hand, the absence of a formal alliance offered the Americans a kind of flexible detachment in relation to their responsibilities and obligations. It was in this broad strategic and, from the Timorese point of view, rather unreceptive context that the crisis involving the Portuguese colony began to unfold.

Few territories or colonies in the non-communist world are without US consular representation, but in 1975 one such exception was East Timor. This did not mean that the United States embassy in Jakarta was ignorant of what had been taking place in the territory following the Lisbon coup of April 1974. A few weeks after the coup, in June 1974, an American embassy official visited Dili and subsequently reported that UDT and ASDT (Fretilin) enjoyed by far the greatest popular support, and described Apodeti as 'a splinter group without serious potential'. Although the Americans maintained only a casual interest in the subsequent political developments in the territory, they were nevertheless privy to the results of the more extensive Australian intelligence monitoring. The Americans distanced themselves from developments in Timor, while indicating to the Indonesians their readiness to accept integration. As Ambassador Woolcott reported to Alan Renouf on 17 August 1975:

> The United States might have some influence on Indonesia at present as Indonesia really wants and needs United States assistance in its military re-equipment program. But Ambassador Newsom told me last night that he is under instructions from Kissinger personally not to involve himself in discussions on Timor with the Indonesians on the grounds that the United States is involved in enough problems of greater importance overseas at present. The State Department has, we understand, instructed the Embassy to cut down the reporting on East Timor.*

As mentioned in an earlier chapter, Woolcott also reported Ambassador Newsom's apparent low level of interest in the Timor problem. 'His somewhat cynical comment to me was that if Indonesia were to intervene the United States would hope they would do so "effectively, quickly and not use our equipment".'2

Some three days later the US ambassador gave a more detailed statement of his government's position on Timor to Lieutenant General Yoga Sugama, one of the leading Indonesian hawks. As subsequently reported by Mr Woolcott he told the Indonesian general that the United States did not want to become involved in the Timor problem, although it had a 'normal humanitarian concern for the welfare of the population and the right of self-determination'. He stressed that the main US interest was the effect any change in the situation might have on US relations with Indonesia. The Americans had no objection to integration and a 'peaceful merger would cause no problems in the United States'. On the other hand, difficulties could arise if the Indonesians chose to use force, and particularly if American military equipment were employed. The general tenor of the Ambassador's statement was that, while his government was not opposed to what the Indonesians were planning to do, if they were to resort to force it might provoke a Congressional reaction which could place the military

---

* See Document 169, *Australia and the Indonesian Incorporation of Portuguese Timor*, DFAT, Melbourne: Melbourne University Press, 2000.

assistance to Indonesia in jeopardy.

As the leaked extracts from the *National Intelligence Daily* later showed, the US administration was provided with a detailed and surprisingly accurate assessment of the unfolding crisis in Timor. The intelligence analysts detected the subversive activities of *Operasi Komodo* and knew about Indonesia's covert military intervention at Balibo before it was launched, as US defence officials told the writer in 1973. Just as Harry Tjan and Jusuf Wanandi were briefing Australian diplomats in Jakarta, Indonesian intelligence officials were also providing their American counterparts with at least equally frank briefings. Certainly, the invasion of Dili came as no surprise, American intelligence officials in Jakarta having been informed by Indonesian officials that it was about to take place more than a week before the event. The attack was conveniently delayed a day, to enable President Ford and Dr Kissinger to get well clear of Jakarta before the beginning of the attack, which the Americans knew would involve the extensive use of their equipment. The American role was thus compliant and accommodating. As a former CIA officer later put it 'we had lots of time to move the Indonesians in a different direction. Instead we got right onto the Indonesian band-wagon'.[3]

General Scowcroft, at the time President Ford's National Security Adviser was subsequently reported as saying that the President and his Secretary of State did not encourage the invasion, but nor did they oppose it. As he recalled: 'It made no sense to antagonise the Indonesians...East Timor was not a viable entity.' According to the source of this remark, a State Department official contended that Dr Kissinger had adopted a policy supportive of Indonesia on the East Timor question partly because of the uncertainties created in South-East Asia by the fall of Saigon. Indonesia was perceived as 'a staunch and powerful friend in a sea of turmoil'.[4] As a State Department briefing put it, in the wake of the assault on Dili:

> U.S. interests at this time would appear to be best served by following Indonesia's lead on the issue while remaining responsive and receptive to Australian and Portuguese views if pressed on us. Our efforts should be devoted to getting the three together to work out what is essentially their problem.[5]

By contrast, Adlai Stevenson, then US permanent representative to the UN, had vigorously denounced India's seizure of Goa in the early 1960s. In East Timor's case Washington monitored Indonesia's meddling and subsequent invasion in studied detachment, and all but condoned the infinitely bloodier and more brutal

---

* The US representative to the United Nations, Daniel P Moynihan, later made the following revealing comment: 'The United States wished things to turn out as they did, and worked to bring this about. The Department of State desired that the UN prove utterly ineffective in whatever measures it undertook. The task was given to me, and I carried it forward with no inconsiderable success. Daniel P Moynihan, *A Dangerous Place, Boston*: Little, Brown and Company, 1978, p. 247

seizure of East Timor by armed force. With its great influence over the Suharto government, the US could at any time have restrained Indonesia. When the first resolution came before the UN General Assembly in the aftermath of the invasion, the United States abstained in the vote, adopting a similar stance on the subsequent Security Council resolution. In the circumstances of the time there can be little doubt that Washington's posture, together with the similarly accommodating attitudes of Japan and India, reinforced Jakarta's determination to defy the demands of the world body, confident that there was no risk of a real challenge to its act of aggression emerging from the UN.*

One particularly murky aspect of United States policy on East Timor was the way in which the administration dealt with the sensitive question of the extensive use by Indonesia of US military assistance which, in other circumstances, might have provoked an uproar in Congress. The illegal use of this equipment—Hercules aircraft were used to ferry in troops, many of whom had not long before acquired American small arms—was essential to the success of the operation. On 10 December 1975, the Sate Department reported: 'There is no doubt U.S. Military Assistance Program equipment was used, and we could be in for part of the blame if the operation is not a quick success.'[6] In order to cope with this problem a modified suspension of military aid was quietly introduced, acknowledging that the military assistance agreement between the two countries had been violated.* According to the terms of this program, 'Such military assistance will be provided for activities helpful to the economic and social development of Indonesia.'[7] Clearly it was a serious violation of the kind that usually provokes angry reactions in Congress.

Administration officials took care to avoid giving publicity to this serious violation of the agreement at the time, in spite of the knowledge that it had taken place. One senior official, Robert B Oakley, Deputy Assistant Secretary for East Asian and Pacific Affairs later told a congressional subcommittee:

> Both in Washington and Jakarta we counselled caution to the Indonesians. We indicated our concern over the possible use of US supplied military equipment, and we assured ourselves that the Indonesian authorities were aware of the appropriate provisions of US law. When Indonesia intervened militarily in December 1975...some US supplied weapons were used. This raised questions for the United States concerning the continuation of our military assistance program.[8]

There is scant evidence that the State Department 'counselled caution'. True, it imposed a modified suspension for about six months, taking no new orders during that period, but the United States proceeded with the supply of existing orders. Under these arrangements, the United States not only continued supplying military assistance, it knowingly provided war materials of the kind urgently needed by the Indonesian military forces to crush armed resistance to the

---

* This was not the first use of such equipment. On a much more limited scale it was used in the attack on Balibo on 16 October and in the assault on Atabai a few weeks later.

invasion. According to an analysis by Professor Noam Chomsky even the modified suspension was not properly observed. He later told the UN General Assembly:

> Contrary to false testimony by government witnesses at congressional hearings, new offers of arms were immediately accepted after the invasion. Then, and since, the flow of arms has been uninterrupted, including attack helicopters and other equipment required to wipe hundreds of villages off the face of the earth, destroy crops, and herd the remnants of the population into internment centres, where they subsist under the conditions already noted.[9]

According to Chomsky between the time of the invasion and 1979, Indonesia received over USD178 million in military aid alone from the United States.

Early in 1976 US officials became alarmed at the Australian government's initial negative reaction to the invasion of Timor. They sought to persuade Australia to back away from its opposition to the Indonesians and urged the new government in Canberra to come to terms with the 'realities', the *fait accompli* of integration. In circumstances vaguely reminiscent of US pressures fourteen years earlier, which were designed to remove an obstacle to Indonesia's acquisition of West Irian, in 1976 the United States sought to persuade Australia to stop publicly criticising Indonesia over the invasion of East Timor and to accept an irreversible situation. A passing crisis involving strategically and economically unimportant East Timor could not be allowed to disturb the vitally important complex of strategic relationships in the western Pacific.

The United States watched impassively as the Indonesians moved to frustrate the efforts of the UN special envoy, Mr Winspeare Guicciardi, to gain free access to all parties in East Timor early in 1976. On 13 January the *National Intelligence Daily* informed US leaders that the Indonesian authorities were carefully stage-managing his reception. On 1 February the State Department reported that Jakarta was determined to block his efforts to get to Fretilin lines and that some Indonesian officials were debating whether to sink the vessel he was proposing to use in order to get from Darwin to the Fretilin-controlled south coast of Timor. The American intelligence agencies faithfully reported other obstacles placed in the way of the visit, including the air attacks on the airfields behind Fretilin lines. However, none of this detailed knowledge of Indonesia's deception and arrogant disregard of the world body caused Washington to shift from its support for Jakarta. As the US ambassador to Jakarta put it earlier, on 10 December: 'Our best course is to take at face value Indonesia's professed desire for orderly self-determination.'[10]

Because of US influence in Jakarta, when President Carter took office in 1977 with his promise to make human rights a central component of US foreign policy, there was evidently an opportunity to press the Suharto regime to reconsider its annexation of East Timor. Military assistance aside, at the time Indonesia was heavily dependent on aid from the IGGI (Inter-Governmental Group on Indonesia) consortium, of which the US was a major provider. However, Indonesia was neatly excluded from the Carter Administration's focus on human rights. Congressional interest in such a remote territory was hard to arouse, and there was no significant shift in America's Timor policy. Of course, as Richard Holbrooke, Assistant Secretary of State for East Asian and Pacific Affairs told the writer in March 1977, the new administration was presented with something of a *fait accompli*. Months before Carter took office East Timor had virtually been recognised as a de facto part of Indonesia. State Department officials also managed to persuade the new administration that Indonesia was in full control of the territory and that the situation was irreversible. Furthermore, a stable Indonesia was of fundamental importance to Western defence. In many cases the Carter administration shared with its predecessor the assessment that the Suharto regime was, from the American point of view—as Holbrooke put it to the writer—'the best of possible alternatives'. With presidential elections coming up in Indonesia in the following year, in the face of some internal unrest, it was believed that American criticism of the Suharto regime might well help precipitate President Suharto's defeat or withdrawal.

Therefore, attempts by liberal Democrats in Congress and by human rights pressure groups to get the Carter regime to take up the Timor question fell on deaf ears. Also, the new political leaders seem to have been persuaded by the State Department's entrenched 'Indonesian lobby' that the Suharto regime's behaviour had not been so bad and that integration would in the long term be the best solution to East Timor's future, virtually mirroring the position of the Whitlam Government. Thus, when the question came up in the first months of the Carter administration, official statements about the situation in Timor suggested either ignorance or disinformation. Early in 1977, one senior official told Congressmen that only about 2000 Timorese had been killed in the war when East Timor church sources were claiming more than 100 000 deaths. A few weeks later the figure was increased to 10 000, but Robert Oakley, the author of this revision, in an obvious attempt to deflect criticism from Indonesia, suggested that much of the killing had taken place in the fighting between Fretilin and UDT. Mr Oakley's statement read:

> We would judge that the number of total casualties, civilian, military, everything else, is probably under 10,000. But this is a very rough guess because no one has any hard figures and most of this took place over a year ago. Most of the violence in which there were major losses of life or wounded, took place during the period between August 1975 and March 1976. That is about the extent of it as best we can judge.[11]

Clearly, the State Department chose to ignore the church report from East Timor. In a letter to a prominent Australian non-government aid official in May 1977 Edward G Ingraham, the Director of the Office of Indonesia, Malaysia and Singapore Affairs in the State Department echoed Oakley's statement:

> Our estimate was that total fatalities in East Timor had been fewer than 10,000, many of them occurring in the internecine fighting that preceded Indonesian intervention. We also noted that there was no evidence the Indonesian Government had condoned atrocities or wanton killings by its forces. To the contrary, steps appear to have been taken to rectify misconduct by individual units and to punish them.[12]

Privately, at least some State Department officials admitted the situation was much less rosy, but it was clear that the administration was not going to say anything in public that would reflect unfavourably upon the reputation or performance of the Suharto regime.

For most of the Carter and Reagan administrations US officials continued with a defensive posture. For example, early in 1977 Oakley suggested that the fighting was almost over: 'There is some resistance left in the countryside. There is no resistance left in the cities. There is a low level of insurgency, but as best we can determine, there are few civilian casualties.'[13] Three years later, in his testimony before the House Subcommittee on Foreign Operations in June 1980, Richard Holbrooke admitted that:

> it was not until late 1978 and early 1979 that centrally directed Fretilin armed activity was fully contained by Indonesian military activity and ceased to pose a significant problem. Some limited guerrilla activities still exist in remote parts of the eastern sector, but the small groups are not in a position to pose a threat to the Indonesian administration of the province or the general population.[14]

However, officials became increasingly uncomfortable with these lines of argument. Great emphasis was placed on the backwardness of East Timor before the invasion, and on Indonesia's development of the territory's infrastructure. Admissions started to be made that an act of self-determination had not really taken place. According to the testimony of Mr Aldrich, the State Department's legal adviser, the United States recognised that the Timorese 'still have a right of self-determination which they have not been able to exercise'. Aldrich made an interesting point in relation to US policy. He declared:

> We recognise the validity of the sovereign authority of Indonesia in East Timor, as we recognised the validity prior to 1975 of the Portuguese sovereignty in East Timor. What I am adding to that is simply that I think, as a matter of legal theory, when a people has a right of self-determination which is generally acknowledged and which we have acknowledged, that right cannot be extinguished except through an act of exercise of that right of self-determination, which I think has not occurred in this case. Therefore, what I am saying is that, as a legal matter, the right of self-determination continues to exist.[15]

In spite of the clear implications of this legal interpretation, the administration's support for Indonesia was not adjusted accordingly. Official interest in Timor declined further under the Reagan administration. America's right-wing friends were not to be subjected to scrutiny and criticism for their shortcomings in the area of human rights. Thus, just as the Carter government adopted the Timor policy of its predecessor, modifying it slightly to accord with the President's proclaimed concern for human rights, the Reagan administration adopted the policy of its predecessor with a shift in the opposite direction. The official position was put into a broad strategic perspective by Assistant Secretary Holbrooke when he told a senate subcommittee in June 1980 that:

the situation in East Timor is one of the number of very important concerns of the United States in Indonesia. Indonesia, with a population of 150 million people, is the fifth-largest nation in the world. It has the largest Muslim population in the world, is a moderate member of the Non-Aligned Movement, is an important oil producer—which plays a moderate role within OPEC [Organisation of Petroleum Exporting Countries]—and occupies a strategic position astride the sea lanes between the Pacific and Indian Oceans. President Suharto and other prominent Indonesian leaders have publicly called for the release of our hostages in Iran. Indonesia's position within the Association of South-East Asian Nations—ASEAN—is also important and it has played a central role in supporting Thailand and maintaining the security of Thailand in the face of Vietnam's destabilizing actions in Indo-China. Finally, Indonesia has provided humane treatment for over 50 000 Indo-Chinese refugees and taken the initiative in offering an island site as an ASEAN refugee processing centre. Indonesia is, of course, important to key US allies in the region, especially Japan and Australia. We highly value our cooperative relationship with Indonesia.[16]

On 14 September 1982, the then Assistant Secretary of State for East Asian and Pacific Affairs John Holdridge spoke approvingly of Indonesia's record in East Timor to a congressional subcommittee, stating that the Reagan administration had accepted the incorporation of the territory, but did recognise that 'a valid act' of self-determination had not taken place.[17]

Criticism of the administration's policy towards East Timor continued within Congress, although Congressional views initially suffered from ignorance of the territory, and the paucity of information about the situation on the ground. The issue nevertheless continued to surface in Congress, thanks to the efforts of representatives like Congressmen Hall and Harkin, and Senators Tsongas and Clairborne Pell from the Democrats, and Durenberger from the Republican side. Behind the congressmen had been committed human rights lobbyists like Arnold Kohen, as well as the increasingly influential Human Rights Watch monitors. On a number of occasions groups of congressmen wrote to the President requesting that more attention be given to the Timor question. In one of these moves, on the eve of a visit by President Suharto in 1982, 102 members of Congress called on the Reagan administration to take a closer look at its Timor policy. In the following October, seventy-five members of Congress, including Senator Edward Kennedy as well as a number of prominent Republicans, signed a letter to President Reagan expressing their concern over the Timor tragedy.

The Reagan administration's inaction did not deter Congress from persisting with its concerns. For example, in October 1988 a bipartisan group of 182 House members, including 29 Republicans, sent a letter to George Schultz, then Secretary of State, urging the administration to address the human rights situation in East Timor. A letter in a similar vein was sent by a sizeable group of senators, including Daniel Moynihan, Clairborne Pell, Richard Lugar and Al Gore. Following Bishop Belo's appeal to the UN Secretary-General in February 1989, an even stronger letter, signed by 118 congressmen, was sent to George Bush.

The Santa Cruz massacre of November 1991 led to a new wave of activity in the US legislature. One letter to President Bush, endorsed by leading senators, including Al Gore, who was soon to become Vice-President, called for support for more vigorous UN action on the Timor Question. The growing concern in Washington was fuelled by increasing NGO interest in the Timor question. Apart from the Timor support groups who had formed active lobbies in Washington and New York, the East Timor question began to attract the close interest of general human rights agencies, like the influential Asia Human Rights Watch organisation. There was not much response to these appeals during the Reagan administration which proved to be even more reluctant than was its predecessor to probe allegations of human rights violations by the Suharto regime. In fact, military assistance to Indonesia steadily increased, with military sales in the 1982-84 period exceeding USD1000 million, including the sale of A-4 Skyhawks, F-5 fighters, additional OV-10s, Hercules C-130s, helicopters, and so on. Within the framework of the Reagan regime's campaign to highlight and to exploit the perceived 'Soviet threat' Indonesia became one of the bulwarks of US Pacific strategy.

The Indonesian generals must have been gratified at the policies of three otherwise very different American administrations. For more than a decade the United States gave Indonesia extensive diplomatic support, its officials, as indicated by their statements before congressional hearings and to the press, having deliberately sought to trivialise the essentially illegal aspects of Indonesia's seizure of East Timor and to cast doubts on the credibility of the persistent reports that Indonesian forces had behaved with callous disregard for the welfare and rights of the Timorese people. In what appeared to have been a matter of deliberate policy, the United States obligingly supplied the kind of military assistance needed by the Indonesians to crush the determined Fretilin armed resistance to their invasion and occupation of the territory.

A subtle change crept into US policy on East Timor in the nineties, especially after the Santa Cruz incident of November 1991. Within days of that incident Congress adopted a resolution calling for the suspension of military training support for Indonesia. A noticeable shift in official policy occurred when President Clinton took office, with encouragement from Vice President Al Gore. In November 1994, for example, the human rights situation in Timor was said to have been raised forcibly by both Clinton and Warren Christopher during APEC meetings in Jakarta. The Timor issue received widespread international media coverage when twenty-nine Timorese entered the grounds of the US Embassy compound in Jakarta, a high-level response that caused dismay in Canberra.

The United Nations
Prior to the overthrow of the Caetano regime in 1974 the situation in East Timor was the subject of only infrequent and cursory interest in the UN. The Portuguese were never really under any great pressure to provide information about their South-East Asian colony, which, they continued to insist, was an

overseas province of metropolitan Portugal. During this time Indonesia's official position, as has already been discussed, was to place on record its support for the right of the Timorese to self-determination, at the same time emphasizing that it had no territorial claims to the colony. In particular, no claim was advanced on the grounds that Indonesia occupied the western half of the island. Indeed, in 1957 the Indonesian representative told the First Committee of the UN General Assembly that 'the attempt to link West Irian with East New Guinea simply because the two territories happen to form one island would create a very dangerous precedent, for example, in the case of the islands of Borneo and Timor. Indonesia has no claims to any territories which had not been part of the former Netherlands East Indies. No one should suggest otherwise or advance dangerous theories in that respect'. [18]

Three years later, Dr Subandrio, the then Indonesian Foreign Minister, told the General Assembly that 'Indonesia explicitly does not make any claim at all to territories such as that in Borneo or Timor which lies within the Indonesian archipelago but was not part of the Netherlands East Indies'. [19]

This position was reaffirmed two years later when the representative said that Indonesia was not 'laying claim to the other part of the island of Timor, which is now under Portuguese rule, despite the fact that the people of that territory belong to the same racial stock as we do'. [20]

If representatives of the Sukarno regime had little to say about Portuguese Timor in the UN, the Suharto government said even less. Indeed, Timor attracted only slight interest until the 29th Session of the General Assembly in 1974, when the question of the colony's future was considered, and then only briefly, as part of the Assembly's overall examination of the status and position of the territories under Portuguese domination. In August of that year the new regime in Lisbon informed the Secretary-General that it intended to meet its obligations with regard to chapter 11 of the UN Charter, in effect announcing that its colonies would now be allowed to choose their own destiny. Two months later the Portuguese Foreign Minister Dr Mario Soares told the UN General Assembly that his government recognised the right of the East Timorese to self-determination and independence. In December 1974, Dr Almeida Santos, in a statement to the General Assembly following his visit to East Timor, said that it was apparent that the majority of the Timorese wished the Portuguese presence in the colony to continue, but that his government would as soon as possible hold a referendum to determine the freely expressed wishes of the people, and would scrupulously abide by the outcome.

The Special Committee on Decolonisation first began to take a serious look at the East Timor problem in June 1975 when it met in Lisbon. However, the Committee confined itself to little more than a statement urging that the necessary steps be taken 'to enable the people of that territory to attain the goals set forth in the Charter of the UN and the Declaration on the Granting of Independence to Colonial Countries and Peoples'. In the critical months that followed, in spite of the apparent inability of the Portuguese to 'normalise' the situation, the UN did not intervene. The sending of a good offices committee to the territory would have been a timely and useful initiative, but for reasons that have already been discussed no such step was taken. It will be recalled that in September 1975, Prime Minister Whitlam, speaking in the Australian Parliament, had expressed scepticism at the prospects of UN intervention when he declared that it was 'not easy to see how a UN Good Offices Committee, whose role would be essentially political in character, could function on the ground'.[21] The subsequent talks between Indonesia and Portugal at Rome also served to keep the UN at a distance from the Timor problem. On the face of it, the world body's exclusion was a deliberate measure based on cynical motives, for here was an international dispute that the UN might have been able to resolve. No conflicting superpower interests were at stake in the crisis and there were no deep-seated ideological cleavages. Indonesia was militarily weak and its leaders were divided on the wisdom of invoking the military dimension of *Operasi Komodo*, and may have responded to international pressures.

When the United Nations finally began to move, it was the eve of Indonesia's invasion, and the hour was already late. On 3 December 1975 a draft resolution was sponsored by Indonesia, and co-sponsored by Australia, Fiji, Japan, Malaysia, New Zealand, Papua New Guinea, the Philippines, and Thailand. The original draft, which drew attention to Portugal's continuing responsibility for the administration of the territory was subsequently to be a subject of some embarrassment to the Indonesian delegation because, as its diplomats in New York were preparing their draft, the sizeable invasion force put together by Major General Benny Moerdani and Major General Suweno was already moving into the staging bases, in preparation for the assault on Dili. The draft, in its revised form, called on all states 'to respect the inalienable right of the people of Portuguese Timor to self-determination, freedom and independence', rights the drafting delegation's military establishment were about to extinguish.[22] It also requested Portugal to continue its efforts by peaceful means to find a solution, by holding talks with the political parties of East Timor, negotiations the Indonesians had of course no intention of permitting to take place.

After the news came of the armed attack on Dili by Indonesia, the nine-power draft resolution was immediately withdrawn, and two others were introduced- one sponsored by Algeria, Cuba, Guyana, Senegal, Sierra Leone, and Trinidad and Tobago, the other by India, Iran, Japan, Malaysia, the Philippines, Saudi Arabia, and Thailand. The first, known as the Algerian draft, expressed 'deep concern at the critical situation resulting from the military intervention of the armed forces of Indonesia in Portuguese Timor', and called on all states to respect the rights of the East Timorese to self-determination, freedom and independence, requesting Portugal to continue every effort to arrange a peaceful solution. It 'strongly deplored' Indonesia's military intervention and called on the latter 'to desist from further violations of the territorial integrity of

Portuguese Timor and to withdraw without delay its armed forces from the territory, in order to enable the people of the territory freely to exercise their right to self-determination and independence'. The Security Council was asked to take urgent action 'to protect the territorial integrity of Portuguese Timor and the inalienable right of its peoples to self-determination', and to send a fact-finding mission to the territory as soon as possible, in consultation with the parties concerned.[23] The Algerian draft was subsequently adopted, the alternative resolution having been withdrawn. It was adopted on 12 December by a vote of 67 for, 12 against, with 53 abstentions. Meanwhile, Portugal severed diplomatic relations with Jakarta and sought the intervention of the Security Council to force Indonesia to withdraw its troops from the territory.

The Security Council met in the week before Christmas 1975 and adopted a resolution which recognised 'the inalienable right of the people of East Timor to self-determination and independence'. It deplored the intervention by Indonesia's armed forces and 'regretted' that the government of Portugal had not fully discharged its responsibilities as the administering power of the territory, under chapter 11 of the Charter. The resolution, in its operative section, called upon all states 'to respect the territorial integrity of East Timor as well as the inalienable right of its people to self-determination' in accordance with the previous General Assembly resolution. It also asked Indonesia 'to withdraw without delay all its forces from the territory' and requested Portugal to cooperate with the UN 'so as to enable the people of East Timor to exercise freely their right to self-determination'. The Secretary-General was requested 'to send urgently a special representative to East Timor for the purpose of making an on-the-spot assessment of the existing situation and of establishing contact with all the parties in the territory and all States concerned in order to ensure the implementation of the present resolution'.[24]

Although Indonesia had obviously anticipated some hostile reaction from the United Nations, where the General Assembly was in session, the extent of opposition to its military assault on East Timor was evidently greater than had been expected, and Jakarta's representatives found themselves very much on the defensive in the world body. The newly independent former Portuguese colonies in Africa, Mozambique, Angola, Guinea–Bissau, and Cape Verde, immediately rallied to the support of the 'Democratic Republic of East Timor', and they succeeded in winning over the majority of African states. Predictably, communist states came out against Indonesia, with the notable exception of Yugoslavia, which abstained. Tito's Yugoslavia had traditionally been reluctant to take a stand against the other founder-members of the non-aligned movement, and Indonesia had hosted the first major conference of this grouping at Bandung in 1955. East Timor was also strongly supported by small states and by most Latin American countries, including Brazil, though certain of the more right-wing regimes, such as those of Chile and Argentina, did not rally to the cause. The voting pattern at the United Nations disclosed a widespread acknowledgment that an act of aggression had taken place, and spontaneous opposition to it. Only eleven other states voted with Indonesia, and they included ASEAN members—except Singapore which, to Indonesia's annoyance, abstained—India, Japan, and Saudi Arabia. The vote against Indonesia would probably have been even stronger had the full facts of the situation been known, and had East Timor itself enjoyed a more important international status. Most representatives simply knew nothing about East Timor.

Indonesia reacted angrily and defiantly to the General Assembly and Security Council resolutions, Foreign Minister Adam Malik insisting that there were no Indonesian troops to withdraw and that support for anti-Fretilin forces was being carried out by 'volunteers'. Portugal was blamed for having been responsible for the chaotic situation in East Timor through its 'agent' Fretilin. Therefore, the Indonesians argued, Portugal no longer had any right to carry out its decolonisation program and, with the setting up of a 'provisional government', the people of East Timor were at last expressing their own wishes about the future. Thus, demands for the withdrawal of the 'volunteers' should be put to the provisional government (the PGET) which, Indonesian officials alleged, had originally requested Indonesia's assistance.

In accordance with the terms of the UN Security Council resolution, the Secretary-General in due course dispatched Mr Winspeare Guicciardi as his special envoy, to make an on-the-spot assessment of the situation in the territory.* Although the 'provisional government' finally agreed that he might visit East Timor, the envoy was permitted to spend only two days in the territory with very brief stays at Dili and three other towns. The severe restrictions placed on his visit were, as we have seen, the subject of comment from US intelligence agencies. On 13 January Washington was told:

> Efforts are reportedly under way to conceal the presence of Indonesian troops and heavy equipment and to repair war damage to Dili. Reports say that the U.N. will be allowed to visit only Dili and other towns securely under Indonesian control, and formal contact will be allowed only with the carefully coached pro-Indonesian regime in Dili.[25]

The special envoy then sought to gain access to Fretilin-held areas from Darwin but, on the eve of his intended visit, Indonesian aircraft attacked the four airfields which had been designated in a radio message from Fretilin as appropriate points of entry. At the same time Indonesian forces launched a major amphibious landing operation on the south coast.

This action caused the Timorese negotiator, Jose Ramos Horta, who was also in Darwin at that time, to inform Guicciardi that the Democratic Republic of East Timor could not guarantee the safety of the UN delegation while Indonesian forces continued to mount their offensive. Although the special envoy's mission

---

* Winspeare Guicciardi had been involved in one of the UN Security Council's few successes, having acted as special envoy in an earlier dispute between Iran and Bahrain.

was given some encouragement by the newly elected Fraser government in Australia, Canberra was not prepared to go out of its way to prevent the Indonesians from thwarting his visit to Fretilin-held areas, a function it could easily have performed. US intelligence reported that some of the Indonesian military leaders were prepared to sink the Portuguese corvette Guicciardi at one point had considered using, but if it had been escorted by an Australian vessel this move would never have been carried out. In due course Guicciardi abandoned his efforts to get to Fretilin, and returned to New York. Not surprisingly, therefore, his report to the Secretary-General concluded that 'any accurate assessment of the situation in East Timor remained elusive'. During his brief visit to the territory his reception was carefully orchestrated and his contacts were, as US intelligence had predicted, carefully coached. As for the views of the East Timorese, he merely noted that there was 'a slender common assumption' that the people of the territory should be consulted, but that such a 'consultation' was very differently interpreted both as to its scope and procedure.[26]

While Fretilin suggested a referendum on the basis of one man one vote with a choice between integration with Indonesia and independence under Fretilin, the puppet provisional government was claiming that the people had already exercised their right of self-determination.

The entire exercise turned out a farce. Secretary-General Kurt Waldheim seemed to act overcautiously. Perhaps, with the United States taking a pro-Indonesian stand, Waldheim was inhibited by the fact that he was soon to come up for re-election. Whatever the Secretary General's motives, some delegates were convinced that he was not pursuing the issue with much vigour or enthusiasm. The UN mission was almost manoeuvred into accepting the 'provisional government' which, in reality, thinly disguised an occupation by the Indonesian armed forces as the de facto government of the territory. A visit to the Fretilin-held areas was essential if the mission were to have any chance of success and that it did not eventuate rendered useless much of the work of the UN special envoy. Australia could have increased the mission's prospects of success by assisting the special envoy to get to the Fretilin headquarters, but the Fraser government was not prepared to risk a confrontation with Indonesia.

When Giucciardi did get to Dili his contacts were very carefully screened and prepared by the Indonesian military before he arrived. At that time most UDT leaders were still hoping that the Indonesians would agree to some act of self-determination, but they were prevented from making contact with the UN representative. In the circumstances, the special envoy's report was largely superficial and unsubstantial. It was presented on 12 March 1976 and, not surprisingly, it did nothing to clarify the situation, it merely summed up Winspeare Guicciardi's frustrations.

The report was discussed by the Security Council in April, and led to the adoption of Resolution 389, which reaffirmed the rights of the people of East Timor to self-determination and independence, and called upon all states to respect the territorial integrity of East Timor. Again, the government of Indonesia was specifically urged to withdraw without further delay all its forces from the territory. The Secretary-General was requested to arrange for his special envoy to continue the assignment entrusted to him by the Security Council at its previous meeting, and to submit a report to it 'as soon as possible'. The resolution, which was sponsored by Guyana and Tanzania, was approved by twelve votes to none, but with two significant abstentions, Japan and the United States.

The resolution was to wither on the vine, until its spirit was revived in 1999. Indonesia continued its open defiance of the Security Council, and in the political circumstances of the time-with the United States urging other powers to come to terms with Indonesia's 'irreversible' action-the Security Council's role in East Timor was virtually suspended for more than twenty-three years. Indonesia was able to exploit not only the widespread ignorance of the situation in East Timor, but also the lack of a substantive commitment among most members of the Security Council to an issue that was well down the priority order of the peace keeping questions demanding their attention. The refusal of the United States to support the Security Council resolution obviously hardened Indonesia's resolve, as did ASEAN states, India and Japan. Also, the fact that the UN Security Council sessions at that time were presided over by China which at that time openly supported Fretilin, had the effect of making Soviet support at best lukewarm. Although the Russians voted for the Security Council resolution, and the earlier resolution in the UN General Assembly, their opposition to Indonesia's seizure of East Timor was quite passive. Moscow appeared to believe that by adopting a somewhat subdued posture it could retain a measure of Indonesian goodwill, and make some gains at China's expense in the South-East Asian region. The Soviet Union did nothing to exploit Indonesia's discomfort and the complicity of the United States.

China, on the other hand, at first gave considerable active diplomatic encouragement to Fretilin, as well as some financial support to the 'ministers-in-exile' of the Democratic Republic of East Timor, in order to help them meet travel and accommodation expenses. However, neither China nor Vietnam—nor any other country, for that matter—was disposed or was able to provide military or other material assistance to the embattled Fretilin forces in East Timor. Their support eventually weakened. By the end of the 1980s, Beijing and Hanoi were both moving to upgrade their relations with the Suharto regime. These diplomatic shifts virtually ensured that Indonesia's act of annexation would not be seriously challenged.

Australia moved promptly to resume its accommodating stance towards Indonesia. Although not then a member of the Security Council, Australia was acknowledged as the only state not a party to the dispute that was reasonably well-informed about the situation in East Timor. By April 1976, however, Australia's earlier opposition to Indonesia had already slackened. Australian Labor parliamentarian Ken Fry, who attended the April session of the Security

Council, later reported:

> It was apparent from our discussions that most European and non-aligned countries were looking to Australia both for information and leadership. On these counts they were disappointed and did not hesitate to express their disappointment. The Australian mission adopted a low-key profile throughout and did not appear to take an active part in the lobbying to strengthen the resolution against Indonesia. They did not appear to be up-to-date or well informed...On the floor of the Council, the Australian mission was seen to be in frequent consultation with the Indonesian mission.[27]

The staunch diplomatic and moral support accorded to Indonesia by Japan and India at the UN evidently encouraged Indonesia's open defiance of the world body. Ken Fry, who testified on behalf of East Timor, recounted that the Japanese ambassador, Mr Kanazawa, who was 'rather rude and aggressive'. Japan turned out to be one of Indonesia's most ardent supporters in the months following the invasion. Tokyo's sympathetic stand clearly prompted one of the pro-integration Timorese leaders, Arnaldo dos Reis Araujo, whom the Indonesians sent to the General Assembly debate to voice support for their case, to proclaim proudly to the United Nations that during World War II he had been one of those who had assisted the Japanese occupying forces. What Araujo did not mention was that for a time he had also rendered valuable assistance to the Australian commando force in Timor.

It was in an obvious attempt to head off further discussion of East Timor at the United Nations that the integration process in the colony was speeded up. Thus, after a series of hasty and contrived meetings of the 'Popular Assembly', on 17 July 1976 the territory was formally incorporated into Indonesia. In the meantime, only two months after the Security Council debate in April, the United States quietly recognised East Timor, *de facto*, as a part of Indonesia. After the formality of integration had been concluded, Indonesia claimed in international forums that the situation in East Timor was henceforth a domestic matter and that further discussion of the subject constituted an act of interference in its internal affairs.

The East Timor question nevertheless continued on the agenda of General Assembly sessions, and in certain other international forums, sometimes to Indonesia's considerable embarrassment and discomfort. From 1976 to 1982 at the UN General Assembly annually adopted resolutions, invariably reaffirming the rights of the Timorese to self-determination and independence. The voting pattern reflected a weakening of international support, with an increasing number of countries concluding that integration was an irreversible *fait accompli*. However, despite an aggressive Indonesian diplomatic campaign, the resurgence of armed resistance and the persistent trickle of reports about oppressive political and social conditions in the territory, ensured the passage of the 1982 resolution (UNGA Resolution 37/30 of 23 November 1983), a narrow victory with fifty votes for, forty-six against, and fifty abstentions. This resolution, which called on the Secretary-General to arrange negotiations between Portugal and Indonesia with a view to achieving a comprehensive settlement, set the pattern for the UN response that endured until President Habibie finally agreed to a UN-sponsored plebiscite in August 1999. The issue also continued to come up annually before the Decolonization Committee, with the East Timor problem eventually becoming the biggest issue before the Committee.

In the mid-1980s the situation was quite different. It seemed that the East Timor question was at risk of drifting off the international agenda. During that time Indonesia made some gains in the diplomatic manoeuvring behind the diplomatic debate. Its hard-core support came, predictably, from ASEAN states, Latin American nations under right-wing regimes with poor records in the field of human rights, most Islamic states, Japan, India, and of course the governments of Australia and the United States. However, the opening up of the territory to limited access, which reflected growing confidence in Jakarta, eventually backfired. Improved access to selected foreigners merely exposed the fact that the people of East Timor still resented their forced integration into Indonesia and continued to hope for eventual independence. The response to the Pope's visit in 1988 and the Santa Cruz massacre in 1991, led to a new wave of international concern. The human rights situation in East Timor also became the subject of regular scrutiny and debate at sessions of the UN Commission on Human Rights, thanks largely to the efforts of NGO's, especially Amnesty International, Asia Watch, Corpus Christi, the International Commission of Jurists, and the growing number of East Timor support groups around the world. The reports of UN special rapporteurs—namely Amos Waco in 1993 and Bacri N'diaye early in 1995—were limited in scope, but they were generally critical of the Indonesian military. The Waco report declared, among other things, 'East Timor continued to be particularly affected by violations of the right to life perpetrated by the Indonesian security forces...' N'diaye's report, which dealt with the Santa Cruz incident, was even more critical.

While Resolution 37/30 offered a glimmer of hope to the Timorese, little progress was made towards its objectives. A number of high-level meetings were arranged between Portugal and Indonesia, but the result was invariably an impasse, essentially because of Jakarta's refusal to discuss the status of the territory. For a decade these contacts were little more than procedural exchanges, or 'talks about talks'. One positive step was a dialogue, held in Europe between the East Timorese parties.

A number of events which flowed from the collapse and the end of the Cold War gave East Timor's fortunes an unexpected boost. The liberation of the Baltic States and the US-led reaction to Iraq's seizure of Kuwait highlighted the fact that East Timor was another small nation in virtual captivity. This did not change things much in terms of the response of the major players in the UN system. In contrast, the activities of non-government human rights and aid organisations greatly increased, encouraged by the pledge of UN leaders to make the 1990s a decade of significant change in relation to the observance of international human rights. In this context East Timor came to be recognised as an outstanding victim of a prevailing cynical disregard for the rights of the small and weak nations. Australia had long been the scene of non-government organisation activities on behalf of East Timor; now more than eighty groups were formed in North America and forty-eight in Japan. Similarly motivated groups were also formed in Eastern Europe, Latin America, and Africa.

To most Western European governments Indonesia's growing economic importance overshadowed the Timor issue, but most at least declined to accord formal recognition of East Timor as part of Indonesia, and abstained in the UN votes in the early 1980s. Later events began to push the East Timor question back into the limelight. Firstly, Portugal became a member of the increasingly influential European Community, and began pursuing a more active policy on East Timor. A second factor was Bishop Belo's letter to the UN Secretary-General in February 1989, in which he called for an act of self-determination.*

These developments served to counter the diplomatic campaigns Indonesia had been conducting since the middle of 1976 to promote support for integration or, where this proved to be difficult, to get governments to come to terms with the 'realities' of the situation. The question was raised during President Suharto's several visits abroad and in talks in Jakarta between Indonesian leaders and distinguished foreign visitors. Non-diplomatic 'envoys' visited key countries such as the United States, the Netherlands, West Germany, Britain, Japan, and countries in Africa and the Middle East to promote Indonesia's point of view. One of the most intriguing of these visits took place early in 1977 when General Moerdani made a secret one-day trip to Lisbon, despite diplomatic relations having been suspended since the time of the invasion. This visit may have been inspired by an Indonesian assessment that the Portuguese might be enticed to accept the status quo. Some Indonesian officials even canvassed the possibility of a modest financial settlement and the repatriation to Portugal of several thousand Timorese, most of them former officials in the Portuguese colonial administration who were stubbornly refusing to come to terms with integration. Moerdani's contact appears to have been limited to one official, a Portuguese general, Morais e Silva, with whom he was already well-acquainted. In the event, nothing concrete emerged from this visit, apart from a report that Moerdani had offered to send several thousand Timorese to Lisbon by ship in return for assurances that they would remain silent about conditions in the territory after the invasion.

These diplomatic sorties gained little for Jakarta but, at the time, they were not without success in those Western countries where there had been a readiness to acknowledge a strategic justification behind Indonesian opposition to the emergence of an independent state of East Timor. This inclination was apparently strong among NATO officials and Indonesia's diplomatic campaigns

---

* For a full text of Bishop Belo's letter see 'I am Timorese' Testimonies from East Timor (CIIR, London, 1990).

coincided, as no doubt was the intention, with a growing conviction in most countries that the situation in the former Portuguese colony was irreversible. The Indonesians were at first greatly assisted in these initiatives by a continuing lack of hard information about the situation in Timor. Once the territory was effectively sealed off from the outside world by Indonesia's armed forces, the only information readily available to the Western press was accounts supplied by the Indonesians themselves. For various reasons, including the negative attitudes of the media and governments, and their reluctance to accord them any credibility, the trickle of reports from Fretilin via the Darwin radio link between 1975 and 1978 received limited and sceptical attention from the press, even in Australia where they were regularly passed on to the main news agencies and newspapers. Of more concern to the Indonesians were other accounts, that is, letters and detailed church reports smuggled out of East Timor and eyewitness accounts from the few refugees who managed to get to Portugal or Australia.

Despite the declining interest of governments there was a steady increase in non-government activities, especially at UN forums. During the UN General Assembly debates in 1980, for example, more than a dozen private petitioners spoke on behalf of the East Timorese. They included representatives of Amnesty International, the Minority Rights Group, the New York-based International League of Human Rights, academics like Professor Ben Anderson of Cornell University, international law specialists, and defence commentators like Admiral La Roque, a former Sixth Fleet commander.* Such an array of petitioners five years after the attack on Dili was a warning to the Indonesians that the Timorese were gaining a strong international following. Along with a law professor from the Sorbonne and a Japanese Catholic Bishop, there were Australians like Labor Senator Gordon McIntosh who had actively supported the East Timorese since his visit to the colony in 1975. The last, and most important, resolution (30/37) just managed to survive against intense Indonesian lobbying, supported by, among others, the Australian mission to the United Nations then led by Richard Woolcott. To complete the cast, Mr Whitlam himself turned up at the United Nations where he made an impassioned appeal to the members to vote with Indonesia and have this troublesome item removed from the agenda of the world body. The spectacle of Mr Whitlam appealing to UN members to abandon East Timor was matched in its cynicism by the efforts of members of the Australian delegation to solicit votes for Indonesia. Certainly Indonesia narrowed the lead, but, given the circumstances, the outcome was not a bad one from East Timor's point of view, although it indicated that a growing number of nations regarded the right to self-determination of the East Timorese as a lost cause. Two-thirds of them, however, were still not prepared, after seven years, to concede to

---

* Several other Australians have addressed the Fourth Committee during UN General Assembly sessions. They include Mr John Dowd, then president of the Australian Chapter of the International Commission of Jurists, the Rev. David Scott, of Community Aid Abroad and me. We participated in the Fourth Committee debate on East Timor in 1980.

Indonesia the legal right to declare that the former Portuguese colony was part of its territory.

The annual Fourth Committee deliberations of the United Nations were the main focal point for the international activities of Fretilin's government for years. Fretilin's 'Minister for Foreign Affairs' for much of this time was Mari Alkitiri, while the movement's president was its most left-wing figure, Abilio Araujo. The best-known activist, however, and certainly the most experienced, was Jose Ramos Horta. Gradually Horta shifted to the centre ground of Timorese politics, especially after the formation of the CNRM, an organisation designed to represent all Timorese, including members of the UDT and Apodeti parties. After the Santa Cruz massacre Araujo was deposed as leader, while Horta resigned from Fretilin and became CNRM's main international negotiator. In a surprising turn, after his sacking, Araujo established contact with Indonesian officials and gained a special status with them, a relationship he used to develop profitable commercial links.

In the 1980s the Timorese independence movement began to give close attention to the UN Commission on Human Rights. In 1983 the Commission condemned human rights abuses in East Timor and called for an act of self-determination. The question has made a regular appearance on the agenda of UNCHR annual sessions right up until 1999. The Timorese were also able to engage the interest of the European Parliament which, in 1988, called for the withdrawal of Indonesian troops, by a vote of 164 to 12, with only 15 abstentions. In June 1991, that is, several months before the Santa Cruz massacre, the Parliamentary Assembly of the Council of Europe called for an arms embargo against Indonesia because of its occupation of East Timor. Timorese representatives have also been given support by the Inter-Parliamentary Union where, in the late 1970s Charles Jones, a Labor parliamentarian who had served as a minister in the Whitlam government, played a leading role in keeping the issue before this international gathering of legislators. Another useful forum was the annual Non-Aligned Movement conference, that is, until Indonesia moved to assume its presidency, and lobbied for the Timor issue to be dropped from its agenda.

In Western Europe, Portugal aside, the Timor case at first attracted most attention in the Netherlands. The Dutch were torn between two conflicting interests. They have long maintained a strong interest in the deteriorating human rights situation in Indonesian, and they also have close economic and defence ties with their former colony. Until the international aid consortium IGGI was disbanded at Jakarta's insistence, the Dutch minister for overseas development traditionally was IGGI's chairman. It was largely because of Jan Pronk's persistent criticism of human rights abuses by the Suharto regime that IGGI was disbanded in favour of donor consortium more amenable to Jakarta.

When Timor was invaded many Dutch leaders immediately perceived something of a parallel with West Irian, which they had been forced to concede in 1962. Moreover, there had been a steady flow of information about moves to annex East Timor from Indonesian church sources, both Catholic and Protestant, especially those in West Timor (where more than 80 per cent of the population is Christian), who retained close links with church organisations in the Netherlands. Furthermore, the Netherlands embassy in Jakarta acted on behalf of Portugal after the latter severed diplomatic relations with Indonesia, causing Dutch diplomats to become closely involved in the many attempts by Timorese to escape via Jakarta. The annexation of East Timor happened at a time when there was mounting concern in Dutch political and academic circles at the increasing corruption and oppression of the military regime in Indonesia, a concern kindled by the vocal opposition to the Suharto regime of many of the thousands of Indonesians living in the Netherlands.

In 1977 a report by the author on atrocities committed against the Timorese by the Indonesian invasion forces was widely reported by the Dutch media, and the reaction to it revealed sharp differences in attitudes towards the Suharto regime with the Minister for Overseas Development Jan Pronk, calling on his government to suspend military sales to Indonesia. Pronk's advice caused immediate concern to the generals in Jakarta because the Netherlands has been a major source of military procurement, and important orders were then being processed. But Pronk's views did not impress his colleagues in the cabinet. Dutch commercial interests were considered of overriding importance and the Dutch authorities were at the time preoccupied with the activities of the Moluccan 'liberation movement', the handling of which depended to some extent upon Indonesia's cooperation.

In the last six years of Indonesian occupation of East Timor other European countries, notably Ireland, Sweden and Norway took an active and sympathetic interest in the plight of the Timorese.

Portugal and Timor after 1975
Although Portugal immediately severed diplomatic relations with Indonesia after the invasion of Dili, and since then consistently voted for the Timor resolution in the United Nations, until 1980 its role as a party principal was rather passive, in part reflecting Lisbon's frustration at the lack of international backing. For the first year or so after the invasion the Portuguese were engrossed in one aspect of the Timor problem-securing the release of the party of Portuguese soldiers who had been detained by Colonel Dading Kalbuadi's forces before the Dili invasion. Although the Portuguese repeatedly insisted that they had no intention of negotiating formal recognition of Indonesia's takeover of their former colony, beyond that point their diplomatic activities on behalf of their East Timorese subjects were uninspiring, at least at first.

They obviously had mixed feelings about the East Timor problem. Many of their politicians, from both right and left of the political spectrum, associated Fretilin's political and military activities with the uncooperative stands of

Frelimo and MPLA, following the April Coup, which had forced on the Portuguese a hasty and humiliating withdrawal from Africa. The new generation of leaders in Lisbon seemed bent on turning their backs on the inglorious past, and there was no enthusiasm for the prospect, however remote its likelihood, of their returning to distant East Timor to resume a decolonisation role and the MFA and left-wing leaders were very sensitive to the weak role Portugal had played when the Timor crisis began to unfold in 1975.

There was some evidence that Costa Gomes and Vasco Goncalves initially gave some encouragement to integration as an acceptable option. Therefore, after the invasion Portuguese government actions created the impression that the new leadership intended to confine itself to a series of formal protests, meanwhile hoping that the problem would somehow resolve itself and go away. A further complication was the differences among the Timorese communities in Portugal, reflecting the civil war divisions. Fretilin supporters tended to associate themselves with left-wing groups and the nationalist movements of the former colonies who were regarded with hostility, disdain or suspicion in metropolitan Portugal which, at the time, was teeming with disgruntled retournados (mostly Portuguese who had been forced to leave the former colonies). And even the left in Portugal was divided over Timor. At the UN Fretilin's champion was China, but the Beijing regime was anathema to the conservative Portuguese Communist Party whose leader, Alvaro Cunhal, maintained an unswerving loyalty to Moscow. Thus, in 1977, when the author visited the Sao Bento, the Portuguese National Assembly, the communist delegates knew little about what had been transpiring in Timor, and seemed to care less about it than any other political group. The other parties were not engrossed with the problem, only one or two deputies ever having visited the Timorese refugee centre at Cruz Quebrada.

By the late 1970s Fretilin's determined resistance and the persistent reports of the harsh treatment being meted out to the Timorese population by the Indonesian invaders began to stir the consciences of the Portuguese politicians. Even so, most were disinclined to become involved in a cause with its roots in the humiliating immediate colonial past at a time when the new generation of leaders was absorbed with domestic issues and the alluring prospect of becoming part of the exciting EC. Interest in the East Timor problem was also undermined by the seemingly irreconcilable divisions among the East Timorese and their support groups, making the negotiation of a common agenda a frustrating task.

In 1980, however, the Portuguese position on East Timor changed significantly. In September, when the conservatives were firmly ensconced in power, the Portuguese government began seriously to study the possibility of coming up with a formal initiative for diplomatic action, an initiative designed to work towards a solution of the Timor problem. The issue simply could not be ignored because an unequivocal obligation had been inscribed into the Constitution. In the words of Article 307 which, in 1982, was in essence incorporated into the revised Constitution:

> Portugal shall remain bound by its responsibility, in accordance with international law, to promote and safeguard the right to independence of Timor Leste.
>
> The President of the Republic, assisted by the Council of the Revolution, and the Government shall be competent to perform all acts necessary to the achievement of the aims set forth in the foregoing paragraph.

Thus, the Constitution committed Portugal to promote the right to independence, not merely the principle of self-determination. The wording of this obligation may seem straightforward, but its implementation was challenging. The main obstacle at first was the difficult relationship between President Eanes and the series of centre coalition governments. The President and his military colleagues of the Revolutionary Council were angered by accusations from the right that they were largely responsible for the breakdown of Portuguese authority in East Timor in 1975. In the event, it was the government of Prime Minister Sa Carneiro that began to press for a solution to the East Timor problem in 1980.

Although many East Timorese suspected that Lisbon's main objective was to overcome an untidy problem, rather than achieve a just settlement for the people of the colony, the 1980 initiative provided a focus as well as a basis for concerted diplomatic action. The government proposed talks with Indonesia, insisting, however, that these should proceed without prejudice to Portugal's position as the acknowledged administering authority in East Timor. It proposed meetings with East Timorese political groups, and representatives of all the parties in the Portuguese National Assembly. In a move to internationalise the issue as much as possible, the government proposed that consultations be held with a number of designated interested countries, such as Australia, Japan, China, the Netherlands, and the United States. The international reaction to this initiative was less than encouraging. Indonesia responded coldly. Jakarta would talk to Portugal only on the basis of acceptance of the status quo, that is, integration. Nor, it seems, did Australia or the United States respond with any enthusiasm. The initiative attracted some interest in Washington during the last months of the Carter administration, but it was clearly outside the radically different agenda produced by President Reagan and his team. The Portuguese received some encouragement from the Dutch and, in 1981, from the new French government under François Mitterand, but there was no hint of any real breakthrough.

Lisbon's problems in mustering international support for its initiative apparently prompted Indonesia to engage in some intriguing informal contacts with certain Portuguese and Timorese contacts in Lisbon. A central figure behind these contacts was the air force officer, General Morais e Silva. He had played a key role in securing the release of the captured Portuguese troops in 1976. Morais e Silva had met with General Benny Moerdani privately in Lisbon in January 1977 when the latter made a one-day visit. It was an audacious venture, by any measure-illegally entering a country which had severed diplomatic relations with Indonesia because of a military annexation the Indonesian general himself had masterminded. Towards the end of 1980 Moerdani arranged an equally intriguing private visit to Indonesia by Morais e Silva who spent several days in Bali in the house of Brigadier General Dading Kalbuadi, before making a quick visit to East Timor where he inspected, among other things, agricultural development at Maliana. On his return to Lisbon, Morais e Silva is understood to have recommended to President Eanes that Portugal come to terms with integration. However, reports of the visit and the recommendations that followed aroused the anger of the East Timorese community leaders in Lisbon who declared that the air force officer was in no position to make an impartial assessment of the situation in East Timor. Morais e Silva may also have been involved in the arranging of a surreptitious and irregular visit to Portugal by an Indonesian delegation in December 1981. The visit was another rather audacious venture, in the light of the Portuguese prohibition on such visits by Indonesians which had been in force since early 1976. What was more extraordinary was the composition of the delegation, which included three important former *Operasi Komodo* personalities, Colonel Agus Hernoto, Major Jusman, and Louis Taolin. All of them had been involved, in one way or another, in the *Operasi Flamboyant* assault in October 1975. The Governor of East Timor Guilherme Goncalves was also reported to have been present. Somehow this party managed to stay at the Estoril-Sol Hotel without the knowledge of the Portuguese foreign ministry. There they interviewed a number of prominent East Timorese and Portuguese, including some officials. The aim of the visit and of the interviews was evidently to build up domestic pressure on the Portuguese government to recognise Indonesian sovereignty over East Timor. The Indonesians' main line of persuasion was that, with the armed resistance having ended, and with support for East Timor flagging in the UN, it was time for Portugal to come to terms with the reality of integration. This daring venture was an audacious move to exploit the sense of frustration and futility that had for some time prevailed in Portuguese political and diplomatic circles.

Portugal's response to Indonesia's vigorous campaign to win international support for integration was not long in coming. The Portugal of the 1980s was no longer a tired, right-wing colonial power, or a nation suffering post-revolution trauma. It had become a democratic country in which had been implanted a strong commitment to international human rights standards. Doing something about the Timor tragedy became not a matter of restoring a colonial link, but of taking steps to right a terrible wrong inflicted on a nation, whose claim to a separate identity had been the outcome of the Portuguese colonial experience. The new response was a joint effort, one shared by Prime Minister Balsemao and President Eanes. A just settlement of the Timor question was to be vigorously pursued by challenging Indonesia to allow for a UN presence and for an act of self-determination. In 1982 Lisbon entered into close consultation with their former African colonies which had hitherto been East Timor's principal supporters in the United Nations, on the strategy to be followed. Envoys were sent to Western European and other countries to promote a better understanding of the problem, and to canvass support for the 1982 UN resolution (30/37). Though countries like Britain, France and Germany, with extensive commercial interests in Indonesia, responded indifferently; others, including Ireland and some Scandinavian states were to become actively supportive, arresting the international drift towards acceptance of integration. When, in 1986, Portugal became a member of the EC, the government found new and influential forums in which to press home its campaign. They were, for example, able to make use of Portugal's presidency of the EC in 1992 to raise East Timor's profile in Europe. For Mario Soares, the country's first civilian president, justice for East Timor became a personal commitment, a commitment enthusiastically accepted by his successor, Dr Jorge Sampaio, a former mayor of Lisbon. These sentiments attracted the dedication of the prime ministers with whom they shared responsibility for handling the Timor problem, including Covaco Silva, whose Social Democrat party held office from the mid-1980s until late 1995 and Prime Minister Guterras, the Socialist leader who succeeded him.

In 1991 pressures on Jakarta, from within and outside the United Nations, led to an agreement for a Portuguese parliamentary delegation to visit East Timor. The visit aroused great excitement among the Timorese, to the concern of the Indonesian authorities. In the end, Jakarta's refusal to allow Jill Jolliffe (then president of the International Press Club in Lisbon) to be included in the press team prompted the Portuguese to cancel the visit. The frustration the cancellation aroused contributed to the Timorese decision to organise what turned out to be the fatal demonstration in Dili on 11 November, an event that shocked the international community into a significant increase in awareness that something needed to be done about East Timor.

The UN-sponsored negotiations proved a frustrating experience for the Portuguese. The only breakthrough was an Indonesian agreement to allow a series of meetings, mostly in Austria, between representatives of all Timorese parties, including supporters of integration as well as its opponents. The meeting, at Burg Schlaining in June 1995, turned into an embarrassment for Indonesian officials, whose attempts to 'coach' the Timorese sent from Indonesia were thwarted when local officials disconnected the telephones. The meeting achieved a surprising level of consensus among the participants who included Governor Abilio Soares, Bishop Belo, Amindo Maio, the Rector of Timor's University, Jose Ramos Horta and other supporters of independence. To Indonesia's irritation, its final statement expressed support for the UN resolution, which endorsed East Timor's right to self-determination.

It was this new commitment that led the Portuguese government in February 1991 to take Australia to the International Commission of Jurists (ICJ) over its conclusion of the so-called Timor Gap Treaty with Indonesia, an arrangement that had the effect of giving full legal entitlement to the parties to exploit seabed resources rightfully belonging to the East Timorese. While Portugal did not win the case, the ICJ's endorsement of the right of self-determination was a not insignificant gesture to the East Timorese. The exercise inevitably did further damage to relations between Canberra and Lisbon with the Australian government angrily claiming that the wrong party had been taken to court. In the light of their performance since 1974, they had little to complain about.*

While international interest in Timor was stimulated by events in the early 1990s, bringing more pressure to bear on Indonesia, the change in the international mood was not enough to weaken President Suharto's determination to reject out of hand demands for an act of self-determination. It was Suharto's fall, brought about by other considerations, that was to start the process of consultation with the people of East Timor. Until that time for the Portuguese the issue continued to be a difficult one. Among her European Union partners, Portugal continued to encounter resistance and apathy. The Gulf War, the liberation of the Baltic States, and the Santa Cruz massacre of 1981, gave the East Timor question an international prominence for the first time. But the territory's remoteness from Europe and North America, its strategic and economic insignificance in sharp contrast to Indonesia's size and economic power, presented formidable obstacles to progress. The Portuguese persisted, however, and the resolution of this problem was one of the two matters described as urgent when the new foreign minister, Dr Jaime Gama, was sworn into office at the end of 1995. They were, therefore, poised to accept the new challenge of encouraging the change of attitude that evolved in Jakarta after Dr Habibie took office in 1998.

The Portuguese have been an easy target for their handling of East Timor's decolonisation in 1975, and their slow response to the territory's annexation. Generally speaking, however, they have been seriously misjudged. They were not a party to the virtual conspiracy to deny the East Timorese their right to self-determination. The guilty parties in that regard were, firstly Indonesia and, secondly, her virtual accomplices Australia and the United States who could have changed the course of history had they acted responsibly. From 1977 onwards the Portuguese also deserve respect for focusing not on the conspiracies and humiliation of the past, but on their persistent efforts to achieve a settlement, based on international human rights standards. Their diplomatic response to appeals to Portugal as the only country with a legal right to challenge Indonesia's illegal seizure of the colony, succeeded in keeping the East Timor question on the international agenda.

---

* For a study of this question, see Roger Clark, 'Timor Gap' in *East Timor at the Crossroads* (Cassell, London 1995), Chapter 4.; and International Law and the Question of East Timor (CIIR/IPJET, London 1995), Section V.

Notes

1 Documents on Australian Defence and Foreign Policy, 1968-1975 (Sydney: Walsh and Munster, 1980), pp. 192-193.
2 Ibid., pp. 199-200.
3 Daniel Sutherland, Christian Science Monitor, 17 December 1980.
4 Ibid., 6 March 1980.
5 Van Atta and Toohey, 'The Timor Papers', part 2.
6 Ibid.
7 Military assistance for a civic action program agreement between the United States of America and Indonesia, 14 April 1967.
8 Robert Oakley, Testimony in 'Human Rights in East Timor and the Question of the Use of US Equipment by the Indonesian Armed Forces', before the Subcommittees on International Organisations and on Asian and Pacific Affairs, of the Committee on International Relations, House of Representatives, 95th Congress, 28 March 1977.
9 Noam Chomsky, Statement delivered to the Fourth Committee of the United Nations General Assembly, October 1979.
10 Van Atta and Toohey, 'The Timor Papers', part 2.
11 Oakley, 'Human Rights in East Timor'.
12 Letter from Edward C Ingraham, US Department of State, 13 May 1977.
13 Oakley, 'Human Rights in East Timor'.
14 'Foreign Assistance and Related Programs: Appropriations for 1981', Hearings before a Subcommittee of the Committee on Appropriations, House of Representatives, 96th Congress, June 1980.
15 'Human Rights in East Timor', 28 June and 19 July 1977.
16 'Foreign Assistance and Related Programs'.
17 Melbourne Age, 16 September 1982.
18 Official records of the United Nations General Assembly, 9th Session, First Committee, 912th Meeting.
19 Ibid., 15th Session, Plenary Meetings, 888th Meeting.
20 Ibid., 17th Session, Plenary Meetings, 1155th Meeting.
21 Commonwealth Parliamentary Debates, House of Representatives, 26 August 1975, p. 492.
22 'Decolonization No. 7: Issue on East Timor', United Nations Department of Political Affairs, Trusteeship and Decolonization, August 1976.
23 Ibid.
24 United Nations Security Council Resolution 384, 22 December 1975.
25 Van Atta and Toohey, 'The Timor Papers', part 2.
26 United Nations Security Council, document S/12011.
27 Report on visit by Ken Fry to United Nations Security Council, debate on East Timor, 10 May 1976.

Chapter Thirteen
Towards the end of the occupation

Australia, Indonesia, Portugal and the United Nations continued to be the key players in the East Timor issue in the 1990s, but international interest in the question widened considerably in the aftermath of the Santa Cruz massacre in November 1991. An issue widely regarded as a lost cause in the 1980s became a burning question as the reality of East Timor's captive-nation status came to be fully acknowledged. The plight of the people was highlighted by unrelated events elsewhere, in particular the liberation of the small Baltic states, the US-led international rescue of Kuwait and the break-up of Yugoslavia, all of which stressed the right to self-determination of small states. The massacre at the Santa Cruz cemetery exposed the fact that ABRI's brutal methods were still being employed after fifteen years of Indonesian occupation, and that opposition to rule from Jakarta was as strong as ever. The early 1990s was also a time of a new emphasis on the implementation of the human rights instruments that had come into force in the previous two decades. International human rights were no longer an expression of idealism, a matter of guiding principles or standards. It had become part of international law, and the extent to which states abided by these standards had become a substantive test of a functioning democracy. Perhaps most important of all, with the ending of the Cold War oppressive regimes could no longer justify their behaviour on the grounds that they were facing communist subversion.

The Santa Cruz massacre and the Indonesian government's weak response to it attracted widespread criticism. It was clearly a response designed to placate international criticism, especially from the United States, the European Union (EU) and Australia. The outcome of the trials of both the demonstrators and the killers turned out to be a farce. The unarmed Timorese demonstrators were meted out harsh prison sentences (ranging from six to twenty years), while the action against the relatively low-ranking troops who did the shooting, was confined to token sentences (six months to eighteen months). As for the commanders, the District Military commander and two other officers were merely removed from their posts. One of them later turned up at Harvard as a MBA student.

Only the Suharto regime's closest Western friends, in particular Australia, the United States and Japan, applauded these outcomes; for most of the rest of the concerned international community the human rights situation in East Timor henceforth attracted more serious attention. In 1994 a five-member parliamentary delegation from Japan, one of Indonesia's strongest supporters since 1975, visited East Timor. The delegation leader expressed strong misgivings about the military presence in the province, which she described as oppressive.

Reports of summary executions and torture, mostly from Amnesty International or Human Rights Watch were accorded more credibility than before, and there were increasing calls for an international inquiry into the humanitarian situation in East Timor. The UN Committee on Human Rights began to take a closer interest in the situation there not long after the Santa Cruz incident. The Committee arrived at a mild consensus of criticism at its 1992 session, a statement that would have been stronger, had it not been for the opposition of representatives of Australia, Japan, and the UK, who argued that the massacre was a low-level initiative and should be regarded as an isolated incident. According to this view the Suharto government should have been praised for its prompt action in investigating the killings.

In the immediate aftermath of the Santa Cruz massacre, international concern began to increase. Immediately after the incident, in November 1991, Amos Wako, the UN Special Rapporteur on torture visited Indonesia and East Timor. His report, published in early 1992, concluded that torture was commonplace and he made eleven recommendations to help address the problem.

Later, in 1995, a more critical and comprehensive report by Bacre Waly N'diaye, a respected Senegalese jurist who was the UN Special Rappporteur on Extra judicial, Summary or Arbitrary Executions, was released. It concluded that the Santa Cruz massacre was a premeditated action based on orders delivered from a higher military level. N'diaye called on the Indonesian authorities to conduct a new and thorough investigation. The report implicitly called into question the credibility of statements by Ali Alatas, and the conciliatory Timor policies of the major powers, in particular Australia and the United States.

While these reports had some impact in the wider international community, in the case of Wako's proposals about three years elapsed before the Indonesian authorities made moves to implement just one of his recommendations—the establishment of the National Human Rights Commission. However, this agency was no match for ABRI which continued to be unresponsive to international appeals. The practice of torture continued in one form or another until the final withdrawal of Indonesian forces in September 1999.

One positive response to the growing international pressures was a move by Indonesian authorities to open up the province a little more. Although visitors continued to be screened and their movements monitored, more foreigners were able to get to East Timor, and in some cases managed to arrange meetings with resistance leaders in the mountains, and pro-independence groups in the major towns. There was also some easing of repression of the local population, although public manifestations of support for independence were not tolerated. The reports that emerged from the outside contacts, which these changes made possible, had an effect opposite to those no doubt intended: instead of easing international concern and criticism, it increased, strongly encouraged by leading human rights non-government organisations. Human rights investigators rejected the claims of the Suharto government that the humanitarian situation had improved and the military presence was therefore being downgraded. According to the annual reports of Amnesty International and the New York-based Human Rights Watch the military remained as ubiquitous as ever, and human rights violations continued to occur. In July 1994 Amnesty International presented the following disturbing assessment to the UN Committee on Decolonisation:

> In the 12 months since Amnesty International last addressed this Committee the organization has received reports of scores of East Timorese tortured or ill-treated by Indonesian security forces. As in previous years, the forms of torture described include electrocution, beating, death threats, faked executions, rape and other kinds of sexual abuse. Taken together, this information confirms Amnesty International's assessment, expressed consistently before this Committee since 1990, that short-term detention, ill-treatment and torture are used systematically in East Timor to intimidate even peaceful opponents of Indonesian rule, and to obtain political and military intelligence. More worrying still, many of those detained and subjected to torture or ill-treatment in the past year have been people trying peacefully to gather or to disseminate human rights information.[1]

From 1995 onwards the agitation of the younger generation of Timorese continued to increase. A number of them sought refuge in foreign embassies in Jakarta, most eventually succeeding in reaching Portugal. The University of East Timor became a centre of protest and also a target for the activities of the *ninja*, a group of Timorese hoodlums recruited and trained by the intelligence component of Kopassus. These young men, often dressed in black, sometimes with balaclavas, assaulted student and other young Timorese who were known to be activists for independence. However, as happened with so many of these operations, in the end they merely served to make the Timorese more determined to keep up their struggle for an end to integration, especially military rule. In the end the relationship between the Indonesian military and the Timorese population did not improve as a result of the easing of restraints, killings, including summary executions. Early in 1995 six Timorese were killed by the military at a village near Liquiça. In this case, in response to Western pressures the incident was investigated. However, many other reported killings attracted little outside interest. In 1997, according to East

Timorese sources, more than 120 young men, most of them students, were arrested and detained.

After Santa Cruz there was a perceptible shift in the direction of Western diplomacy, often resulting from the visits foreign diplomats in Jakarta were now regularly making to East Timor. These visits did not lead to calls for Indonesia to withdraw from East Timor, most of the international diplomatic community regarding integration as an irreversible fait accompli. However there was a growing recognition of the need for a change of direction in Indonesian policy towards East Timor. Some diplomatic visitors became uncomfortable with their governments' accommodating policies, concluding that the abuses of power by the military had created unrelenting hostility among the local population. Even some of the Suharto regime's friends started urging Jakarta to look for a compromise that might satisfy Timorese aspirations. What was happening, they had apparently concluded, was not good for Indonesia.

As for the resistance, Xanana's capture in Dili in November 1992 was an outcome with mixed fortunes for Indonesia. The armed resistance was weakened by his loss, and the subsequent arrest of other independence supporters. His successor, Ma'Huno, was soon to be captured, with Falintil continuing to operate under the command of Konis Santana. The Indonesian military celebrated Xanana's capture as a significant victory, and a show trial in Dili followed from February to May 1993, but these events were soon to backfire on them. Xanana's courageous stand during his trial won him wide respect within as well as outside Indonesia. He was prevented from making his final address to the court, but somehow his statement was smuggled out of East Timor, and won him further respect. His subsequent statements and writings from prison, which, after 1994, were smuggled out by Kirsty Sword* in a clandestine arrangement, served only to confirm his stature as a beloved and respected leader of the East Timorese.[1] He was to become one of the world's most admired political prisoner, an international celebrity, all of this made possible by his own determination, his intellectual development, and an easing of his prison conditions. He continued to command Falintil from Cipinang Prison, and offer the Timorese population at large inspired leadership. He also became one of East Timor's key negotiators, who needed to be consulted by other independence leaders before final decisions were made. He was securely incarcerated in Cipinang Prison, but was never incommunicado. In January 1994 Xanana was visited by Tamrat Samuel, UN Special Rapporteur on East Timor, who sought his advice about the talks between Portugal and Indonesia that had just been resumed. Later in the year he met legal aid and military officials, and in December met with Francesc Vendrell, the UN Secretary-General's special envoy on East Timor, a central figure in the UN's long search

---

* Now Kirsty Gusmão, Kirsty married Xanana Gusmão in 2000.

for a resolution to the Timor problem. He also had a call from Jamsheed Marker, a special UN envoy appointed by Kofi Annan. In April 1997 Xanana called for a referendum. In July of that year he was able to meet with Nelson Mandela who was impressed with the Timorese leader and a month later called on Suharto to release him. Meanwhile a series of dialogues, the annual All-Inclusive Intra-East Timorese Dialogue (AIETD), got under way in 1995. Participants came from Indonesian-controlled East Timor and from the Diasporas in Portugal and Australia. These dialogues were sponsored by the United Nations, but in accordance with conditions imposed by Indonesia. In effect these meetings were precluded from discussing what was uppermost on the minds of most participants, the pursuit of ultimate independence, or at least a formal act of self-determination. However the Timorese delegates did find ways of addressing these issues without any formal statements being made.

Not everything moved forward in the 1990s. Governor Mario Carrascalão, a reluctant representative of Jakarta's authority who sought to defend Timorese interests, was replaced in 1992 by Abilio Soares. Soares was the brother of an earlier Apodeti leader, Osorio Soares, who had been killed by Falintil troops in the aftermath of ABRI's bloody assault on Dili. He was a Timorese with a strong commitment to integration, and a readiness to defer to the wishes of the military, the real rulers of the 27th province. He was the clear choice of the Kopassus commanders who, even in the last year of Indonesian rule, found him a willing tool in their continuing efforts to end opposition to integration.

The capture of Xanana was in a military sense a setback to the armed resistance, but Falintil's tactics had shifted away from military operations, which invariably provoked reprisals against the civilian population. The independence movement had moved to broaden its base to become a popular movement with a new focus on passive resistance. The National Council of Maubere Resistance, CNRM, was given a new image, emphasising its non-partisan character, and bringing a stronger focus on negotiations as a means to achieve the ultimate aim of independence. It was now joined by members of the Apodeti party, who now favoured a referendum. In April 1998, on the eve of Suharto's fall from office, CNRM was renamed CNRT (the National Council of Timorese Resistance), and the imprisoned Xanana was appointed its president.

Even before this change the Timorese leaders of CNRM began a new approach, declaring their movement to be the supreme organisation representing East Timorese nationalists. They urged that Bishop Belo be allowed to take part in the consultations. The bishop was already a spiritual ally. He had publicly denounced the 'deplorable and worsening human rights situation in the territory', and had called for the Indonesian military presence to be substantially reduced, and for the eventual holding of a referendum on self-determination. In his letter Bishop Belo called for an end to Indonesian military occupation and its practices of terror, injustice, and murder.

In that year, 1994 CNRM proposed to the United Nations a Three Phase

Peace Plan. Phase One called for UN-supervised talks between Indonesia and Portugal, aimed at achieving an end to armed conflict in East Timor, the release of political prisoners, reduction of the Indonesian military presence, and the expansion of International Red Cross activities. Phase Two would be a transition stage of autonomy in which East Timorese would govern themselves democratically through their own institutions. Phase Three envisaged preparation for a referendum on self-determination, which would be held within one year of the commencement of this phase. The choice would be between free association or integration with Indonesia, and independence.

These approaches—by CNRT and the Bishop—provided an agenda for negotiations that was to persist until President Habibie began to take the problem seriously in 1998. It was never, however, taken seriously by the Indonesian authorities until Suharto fell from office. In the mid-nineties there were some encouraging responses from within the Indonesian government, especially in relation to a proposal that East Timor be given autonomous status. Indonesia's diplomats were particularly concerned at mounting international pressures, which frequently caused embarrassment. The autonomy option attracted some support from Foreign Minister Alatas who reportedly put it to his president in mid-1994, following a censure from the UN Human Rights Commission, but it was rejected.[2] While it aroused the interest of Australian and US governments, by the mid-nineties the Timorese, buoyed by increased international support, wanted more than autonomy, which would probably not have freed them from the intimidating presence of the Indonesian military. The awarding of the Nobel Peace Prize jointly to Jose Ramos Horta and Bishop Belo in 1996 gave the Timorese fresh encouragement. The people of the territory now had three leaders of considerable international stature, two of whom were now able to present East Timor's case in high-level meetings, including with governments of considerable importance to the Suharto regime. Suharto himself remained obstinately opposed to any concessions until the end which, as it happened, had little to do with Indonesia's illegal occupation of East Timor.

The Indonesian military (known as ABRI until 1999) also remained little changed after the Santa Cruz incident. For most of the twenty-four years of Indonesian occupation the army, or the Special Forces Command, Kopassus, continued to be the real power in East Timor. Under Suharto Kopassus had become a kind of KGB, special sources with special powers and privileges. The Dili commanders received only mild rebukes for the Santa Cruz massacre, and were not deterred from continuing their policies of oppression and ruthless persecution of Timorese pro-independence supporters. Indeed, in March 1992 Major General Theo Sjafei, the new Kopassus commander of the region in which East Timor was located, declared to the Indonesian press: '…if something similar to the 12 November event were to happen under my leadership, the numbers of victims would probably be higher'. However, the military did need to be more careful for there were more inquisitive foreigners in East Timor, some of whom helped expose human rights violations. And these violations continued, although there was no repeat of Santa Cruz until the events of 1999. The commanding role played by Kopassus officers in East Timor was reinforced by the appointment of Lieutenant General Prabowo as commander of this powerful military organisation, in fact the Kopassus role provided an element of continuity in the Indonesian seizure and occupation of East Timor. Officers of Kopassus (or RPKAD, the Army Commando Paratroop Regiment as it then was) planned and led the covert military intervention in October 1975, and thereafter assumed a leading role in the administration of the province. With their prowess as an elite force, and their authority to engage in dirty tricks, special forces officers led military operations, commanded the intelligence network, and resorted to brutal methods to crush opposition to integration. Their intelligence officers tortured prisoners and suspects and carried out summary executions.

In October 1975 the attack on Balibo was led by a Kopassus officer, Captain Yunus Yosfiah. In December 1978 Major Yosfiah and Captain Prabowo conducted a special operation to capture and kill the Falintil leader, Nicolau Lobato. One of East Timor's worst atrocities, the Creras massacre, which is said to have cost the lives of over 1000 Timorese was, according to witnesses, also probably led by Prabowo, by then a lieutenant colonel. Lastly, Kopassus officers played a key role in the setting up of notorious paramilitary units, such as Gada Paksi, of which the militia units formed in 1998 were an extension. Prabowo's promotion to lieutenant general, well ahead of his class, and appointment to command of Kopassus, confirmed both the authority of the special forces command and the rapidly rising power of the president's son-in-law. In practice East Timor was Kopassus territory. The command that had been largely responsible for the colony's annexation would not contemplate the loss of the province to the Republic. Its commanders were, therefore, not disposed to make significant concessions to the Timorese nationalist movement.

* * * *

The fall of President Suharto in May 1998 ushered in a change in attitude to East Timor, but this issue was not a major factor in the collapse of the dictatorship. The end of the *Orde Baru* dictatorship was largely the result of the near-collapse of the Republic's economy coupled with growing disillusionment at the nepotism and corruption that surrounded the president and much of his government. Growing public demand for democratic reform was also a major factor, and this was a challenge to which President Habibie responded early in his presidency. The new thrust of his policies took many by surprise. The new leader had been close to Suharto, having been his protégé at an earlier time, giving rise to an expectation that his presidential style would not bring fundamental changes.

Dr Habibie had no apparent power base of his own, had little influence with either the military or the main Islamic movements and it was at first widely expected that he would be out of the palace in a few months.[3] In fact the volatile Habibie was able to gain wide support, at least at first, by responding to pressures from the impatient Indonesian reform movement which was demanding fundamental changes, mostly to do with the web of nepotism and corruption that Suharto had woven around his presidency. The East Timor problem was not entirely irrelevant to these internal demands, for among the Indonesian reformists there was strong support for a radical change of policy on Timor. It had become increasingly widely acknowledged that the colony had been forcibly and illegally seized, and that the population has suffered harshly under military rule. Justice for the East Timorese became part of a national campaign to reform a military whose brutal methods had also be used against dissident Indonesians.

When the new president came into office he soon found that his government was confronting formidable East Timorese pro-independence leaders, not rebel leaders inexperienced in negotiation. The statures of the imprisoned Xanana Gusmão and the two Nobel Peace Prize laureates, Bishop Belo and Jose Ramos Horta, had grown considerably in the previous five years. These three leaders complimented each other in their approaches to the issue of self-determination. Xanana had emerged as a visionary leader with a strong commitment to ending violence and achieving a reconciliation, not only between the supporters of autonomy and independence in Timor, but also between his people and Indonesian democrats, whom he had come to know through shared experiences in Cipinang Prison. Horta, after two decades of experience as a diplomat at the United Nations, and equipped with appropriate tertiary qualifications, had become a sophisticated and skilful negotiator, ever ready to seize the opportunity of the moment. Bishop Belo had won the respect and admiration of national leaders and of leaders of the Christian churches, for his fearless defence of the rights of his people, and for his religious tolerance. As Nobel Peace Prize winners Belo and Horta were now able to present East Timor's case to government, community and church leaders around the world, and especially in those countries on which Indonesian was dependent for substantial economic assistance if its crippled economy were to recover.

The pro-integration Timorese, on the other hand, were a minority, although there were some prominent figures among them. After the former governor and UDT leader, Mario Carrascalão, withdrew his support for the *status quo*, these Timorese were unimpressive when it came to leadership qualities. They became cast as collaborators, most of whom wanted to remain with Indonesian rule because they had profited from it, financially and in terms of political power. But even among those who had become part of the Indonesian state bureaucracy, there were many who opted for independence now that there was a real prospect for such an outcome.

President Habibie had no shortage of advisers on what he should do about East Timor. He received an early approach from the new UN Secretary-General Kofi Annan who had made a commitment to find a solution to the Timor problem when he took office a year earlier. Kofi Annan had long held a special interest in matters involving minorities, and brought a much-needed energetic approach to the problem. He urged a return to tripartite talks. Thus high-level talks involving Portugal and Indonesia were given a new life with Jamsheed Marker being appointed Annan's special envoy. The autonomy proposal was revived, and Australia's Howard government began to support moves towards a settlement.

Although there was nothing new about the autonomy proposal, the political context in which it was now being raised was profoundly different. While Suharto had repeatedly dismissed the idea, Habibie saw it as a way of negotiating the removal of an irritant in Indonesia's foreign relations at a time when Indonesia was vulnerable to external pressures. His shift towards a more democratic format also had implications for Indonesia's stand on East Timor.

President Habibie's advisers apparently saw their offer of some form of autonomy as an appeasement to the East Timorese that would settle the matter, with most coming out in favour of remaining with Indonesia. They were, however, to be proved very wrong. The offer they came up with merely served to strengthen the determination of the Timorese leaders to press for ultimate independence. The popular view was expressed by Jose Ramos Horta and Bishop Belo on 7 January 1999 when they declared that East Timor should become independent after a period of autonomy. This statement, along with other developments, seemed to trigger militia acts of violence, on the one hand, and public expressions of support for the independence option on the other. Already the Timorese had exploited the new openness by engaging in demonstrations, the first only three weeks after Habibie took office when 15,000 students demonstrated in Dili, demanding Xanana's release and that a referendum be held.*

To the ABRI commanders these developments posed a worrying challenge They were staunchly opposed to making any concessions that would risk encouraging the desire for independence which most understood, from their intelligence monitoring, remained strong in East Timor. As it happened the shift towards democracy that Habibie was promising was encouraging active opposition to Indonesian rule in East Timor and as well as vigorous pro-democracy activities in Jakarta with the two becoming linked. The early

---

* See Lansell Taudevin - *East Timor, Too Little Too Late* (Duffy and Snellgrove, Sydney 1999), especially Chapters 15 to 18, for a perceptive eye-witness account of the political situation in 1998 and early 1999.

demonstrations and other manifestations of agitation by the East Timorese must have been an early warning to the Udayana military command that they were faced with an upsurge of protest. To the Kopassus commanders it was clear that Indonesia was at risk of losing its 27th province. President Habibie may have had no strong feelings about East Timor, but to his military commanders, especially Kopassus officers, it was hallowed ground. Thousands of Indonesian lives had been lost in the twenty-four year campaign to crush the Falintil resistance.

The militia conspiracy—ABRI's response.

On 27 June 1999 there was a clash in Dili between pro-independence and integration supporters that may well have triggered ABRI's response. In the event, according to information from intelligence sources and militia leaders the plan to set up a militia was put together not in East Timor, but at Army Headquarters in Jakarta. It was largely the work of Major General Syafrei Syamsuddin, a senior Kopassus officer whose first military engagement in East Timor was as a junior officer in *Operasi Flamboyan*, and Major General Zakky Anwar Makarim, at the time his Kopassus senior, who was an intelligence specialist. The plan involved the setting up of an extensive paramilitary force with units of roughly battalion strength in each district (*kabupaten*).

The use of the term 'militia' may have sounded new, but the training and use of Timorese in paramilitary units went back to Indonesia's military intervention in East Timor in 1975. In that year the oldest of the paramilitary units, Halilintar, was established following a covert military training program conducted in Indonesian Timor by a special TNI military force, commanded by Colonel Dading Kalbuadi.[4] This operation is discussed in an earlier chapter. Halilintar troops, then led by Tomas Goncalves and João Tavares, accompanied the TNI military force in a support capacity in *Operasi Flamboyan*, the covert military action against Fretilin forces in Indonesian Timor in mid-October 1975 in the aftermath of the latter's victory over UDT. That particular operation was planned by Kopassus commanders in their earlier guise, RPKAD (the Army Commando Paratroop Regiment). It marked the beginning of a TNI policy of using willing Timorese in operations conceived and planned by military commanders in which the former provided a political front designed to mask the leading role of the Indonesian military.

In 1976, some months after the invasion of Dili, most of the Halilintar troops were redeployed to form the beginnings of Battalion 744,[5] a regular territorial unit that was later to be joined by Battalion 745. These units were largely made up of Timorese soldiers, but were staffed by Indonesian officers. Halilintar itself was disbanded in 1982, but continued a shadowy existence as João Tavares' private army, and was reformed in 1998 as one of the most important units in the militia. In the late seventies Timorese were recruited into paramilitary formations, such as the Hansip, or civil defence units, which existed elsewhere in Indonesia. The development of these bodies formed part of the repressive, and at times brutal, campaign against the population of East Timor by the occupying military forces.

It is against this background that the setting up of the militia in late 1998, and the tactics it resorted to, need to be considered. The militia as it existed in 1999 was a kind of extension of the paramilitary force Halilintar and the other paramilitary units formed in the eighties to involve the local population in operations not only against Falintil, the armed resistance, but against the growing phenomenon of passive resistance. The best-known of these early units was Team Alpha (Tim Alfa) which, with Team Saka (Tim Saka), was formed in 1986 in the eastern sector of East Timor by a Kopassus officer, Captain Luhud Pandjaitan, reportedly acting on orders from his commander, then Colonel Prabowo Subianto. Team Alpha's members were trained and paid, and their operations against pro-independence elements organised by Indonesian military officers. Another significant move was the setting up of the Gada Paksi (Gadu Penegak Integrasi—Guards to Uphold Integration) in 1994, also reportedly a Prabowo initiative, aimed at mobilising young pro-integration activists.

The common strand linking earlier paramilitary units and the militia set up in 1998 was the hand of Kopassus. It had become a self-contained military command within Indonesia's military force structure. Its members were specially chosen, received special training and equipment, enjoyed privileges, and were generally regarded as the TNI's elite corps with, in the time of President Suharto, the special mission of protecting the integrity of the Indonesian state. While elements of Kopassus (Group 1 and Group 2) made up a special combat force, other parts of the force from time to time engaged in operations of a covert kind, hence Group 3 dealt with terrorism, while group 4 and Group 5 engaged in intelligence operations against political opposition and other dissident groups. These were the dirty-tricks groups, their actions included kidnapping and 'disappearances'. Financing the covert operations of this Indonesian version of a KGB was facilitated in part through profits from the extensive business operations of Kopassus.[6]

The involvement of Kopassus in East Timor was a central element in the history of the colony's illegal seizure and its occupation. Many of its unit commanders were eventually to become generals. Throughout the twenty-four years of Indonesian rule in East Timor, Kopassus officers played key roles in the administration of the 27th province. Through its own intelligence service, recently known as the SGI, Kopassus had a pervasive presence in the wider community, monitoring, and acting against, the growing ranks of Timorese pro-independence activists. To create a facade of legitimacy the province always had Timorese governors, but senior military officers (usually Kopassus) immediately below the governor were the real centre of power in East Timor.

It appears that even Timorese pro-integration leaders were only consulted about the setting up of the militia after the plan had been drawn up at ABRI headquarters in Jakarta. This conspiracy to frustrate the referendum clearly enjoyed the support of some leading Timorese opposed to change—among them Governor Abilio Soares, Francisco Lopes da Cruz and João Tavares (the Halilintar commander)—but it was essentially a Kopassus initiative, a plan hatched by Generals Syafrei Syamsuddin and Zakky Anwar Makarim between July and September 1998.[7] According to the testimony of Julio Fernandes, the official launch of the militia occurred on 10 or 12 August 1998 at a secret meeting attended by Major General Damiri and Colonel Tono Suratnam, as well as João Tavares, Eurico Guterres, and Cancio de Carvalho. Damiri and Suratnam told those present that they must organise to protect integration. Thus the militia came into being not as a spontaneous response by integration supporters—or even their leaders—but as a Kopassus initiative aimed at sabotaging Timorese moves to seize the opportunity of the moment to achieve independent status. Had the military commanders not come up with this plan, the militia very likely would not have existed, for few of its leading members were either skilled or sufficiently motivated to resort to armed assault and intimidation against the popular will of East Timorese society.

The TNI hostility to the independence movement was apparently welcomed by the hard core of Timorese opposed to change, such as Governor Abilio Soares, Lopes da Cruz, Basilio Araujo, Eurico Guterres, and other Timorese supporters of integration from whose ranks leaders of the militia groups were chosen. As militia violence began to develop, some members became disillusioned and withdrew, and it became increasingly difficult to recruit replacements. In the months leading up to the violence in September 1999, in some areas militia leaders (aided by Indonesian soldiers) resorted to forms of conscription of new members with violence being used on occasion against those who resisted.[8]

The organization of the militia was virtually integrated into the TNI structure in East Timor with the aim of having roughly a battalion of militia in each of the thirteen *kabupaten* (districts). The militia members were paid from a variety of official sources, they were trained by ABRI personnel and arms were provided to them. These included crude homemade weapons which were put on show to give international observers the impression that the militia was a spontaneous and popular phenomenon.[9] In fact all units were provided with automatic weapons. The commanders of these units were chosen or confirmed by local commanders who also had a say in selecting targets. In most cases the militia bases were located next to, or at, ABRI establishments. The following were the main units, the locations, and their leaders:*

---

* Based on an examination of extensive documentary evidence obtained by UNTAET investigations.

Militia designations	Location	Leader
Tim Alfa	Lautem	Joni Marques
Saka/Sera	Baucau	Serka Kopassus Joanico da Costa[10]
	Pedjuang (1959-1975)*	
Makikit	Viqueque	Martinho Fernandes
Ablai	Manufahi	Nazario Corterel
AHI	Aileu	Horacio
Mahidi	Ainaro	Cancio de Carvalho
Laksaur	Covalima	Olivio Mendonça Moruk
Aitarak	Dili	Eurico Guterres
Sakunar	Oecussi	Simao Lopes
BMP (Besi Merah Putih)	Liquiça	Manuel de Sousa
Halilintar	Bobonaro–Maliana	João de Tavares
Dadurus	Bobonaro	Natalino Monteiro
Jati Merah Putih	Lospalos	Edmundo de Conceicao Silva
Darah Merah Integrasi	Ermera	Lafaek Saburai

The above list is not exhaustive. In the Bobonaro–Maliana area, which occupied a special strategic importance because of its border location, there were at least six groups, with Halilintar forming the headquarters. Most units were not fully operational until April 1999. They varied in size, the most prominent being Halilintar and Aitarak. Halilintar's commander, João Tavares, the *bupati* of Bobonaro district, was appointed *panglima* (overall commander) of militia units in East Timor, an appointment said to have been made by TNI officers. TNI's first choice, however, was Tomas Goncalves, whom Kopassus had identified as an effective commander twenty-four years earlier, but Goncalves had become disenchanted with integration and declined the offer. Later in 1999, following the brutal rape of his wife by a senior Indonesian Kopassus officer, Goncalves fled East Timor and defected to the independence movement. The commitment of João Tavares to integration, on the other hand, had not wavered since early 1975 when he had been a founder of the Halilintar force and took part in its first operations in *Operasi Flamboyan*.[11]

Aitarak received most international attention because of its size, its distinctive fascist black-shirt garb, its location in the capital and not least because of the flamboyant style of its commander, Eurico Guterres. Much younger than Tavares, Eurico Guterres' earlier links had been with Fretilin. His parents had been killed by Indonesian troops, while he, then a teenager, had worked as a courier for Falintil before being captured by a Kopassus unit which then

---

* This militia unit title refers to the rebellion against the Portuguese in Viqueque area in 1959 as well as to the few Timorese who supported Indonesian intervention in 1975. The Viqueque rebellion was inspired by Indonesians, though not by the Sukarno government.

managed to reshape his loyalties. He became an active supporter of the military and, through various shady dealings, he also managed to acquire considerable wealth. He was to gain the reputation of being East Timor's leading playboy.

While the first atrocities to attract international attention did not begin until April 1999, militia violence started much earlier. The TNI command became increasingly alarmed at public support for independence which manifested itself in a series of demonstrations and street protests, culminating in the holding of a large rally, of some 30,000 people, in Dili on 11 October 1998, at which there were angry calls for the resignation of Abilio Soares. The next day there was a large protest in Baucau against the Indonesian military presence. Within two weeks TNI troops raided several villages to the south of Baucau, and hundreds of Kopassus troops who had earlier been moved from Java to West Timor, were deployed in the province.

The first report of a militia-type attack was on 27 December 1998 when Gada Paksi members and TNI troops arrested and tortured several men near Maubara. The first killings were reported at Ainaro on 3 January when Mahidi troops attacked independence supporters and killed and injured a number of them. In mid-February Lieutenant Colonel Yayat Sudradjat, head of the Kopassus intelligence unit (SGI) in East Timor and the key link between the East Timorese pro-autonomy leaders and the regional ABRI commanders in Dili and Denpasar, convened a meeting of the militia unit commanders and exhorted them to engage in more violent action, including killing independence leaders and their families.[12] At about the same time Tavares told a large rally in Balibo that war would break out in East Timor if the people rejected the autonomy proposal. The Kopassus plan was under way.

In March the militia units began to operate in earnest. There were a number of reported killings and cases of hundreds of Timorese fleeing to the relative safety of the mountains. In mid-March a Besi Merah Putih (BMP) militia unit surrounded the Carmelite convent in Maubara and threatened to kill those who were aiding the independence movement. Some days later (26 March) Governor Abilio Soares was reported to have told a meeting of militia leaders that the Church had become the enemy of integration, and that the militia must be ready to kill nuns and priests. This was an extraordinary departure from past ABRI policy to respect the Church and, for the most part, its officers. The new approach became an ugly reality during the brutal killings at Suai and in Lautem, and the assault on church institutions in Dili. Reports from Indonesian official sources presented the violence as clashes between pro-autonomy and Falintil troops, but nothing could have been further from the truth. Falintil units, numbering about 2000 men, had moved into agreed cantonments and were, in general, following Xanana's orders not to engage ABRI units, a restraint that caused considerable agitation as militia violence became more systematic and widespread. The *Polri* (Police) units were under orders from the TNI command not to interfere with militia operations, and the latter were, therefore, unrestrained.[13]

The militia operations were stepped up as the movement towards a supervised referendum gathered pace in response to rapidly changing policies in Jakarta. This change in policy direction was under way before John Howard, the Australian Prime Minister, sent his letter to the Indonesian President in December 1998. The letter marked a significant shift in the Australian Government's Timor policy which had previously been accommodating to Jakarta.[14] In cautious language the Australian Prime Minister urged Habibie to consider an act of self-determination, but with a long gestation period that would give the autonomy offer a chance to be accepted by the Timorese. The letter apparently irritated the President, but it still captured his fancy, maybe because of his preference for quick fixes. He was not attracted to long drawn out processes, and in a surprisingly short time came up with a proposal at variance with the conventional belief that the self-determination process should take place over a period of several years. Having mulled over the Howard letter the Indonesian leader came out in favour of a plebiscite which his advisers evidently assured him would result in Timorese support for remaining with Indonesia. At the same time tripartite consultations between Indonesia, Portugal and the United Nations were moving ahead positively, for the first time.

On 27 January it was announced that President Habibie would ask the Indonesian Parliament (MPR) to let East Timor become independent if the autonomy proposal were rejected. Two weeks later the Portuguese and Indonesian foreign ministers met in New York to draft a plan for holding the plebiscite, or popular consultation. On 5 May an agreement between Indonesia, Portugal and the UN on the plebiscite was signed in New York. It was to take the form of a consultation on whether or not the people of the territory accepted Indonesia's autonomy proposal. The option of independence was not in fact to be on the voting paper, but it was the clear alternative. President Habibie himself declared that if the Timorese did not accept Jakarta's autonomy offer, he would call on the Parliament to allow them to go their separate ways.

It was a tall order for the United Nations, but Kofi Annan moved quickly after the May agreement was signed to set up a UN mission to organise and conduct the 'popular consultation', as the Indonesians termed it. In line with the agreement UNAMET, the United Nations Assistance Mission for East Timor, was formally established by the Security Council (Resolution 1246) on 11 June 1999. Quite suddenly it was a time of unprecedented support by the international community for UN action. Australia's Howard government virtually abandoned the policy of accommodation that Canberra had been following for the previous twenty-five years, and was now a major supporter of the UN initiative. New Zealand had also radically shifted its policy. More importantly, in terms of influence in Jakarta, was the change in US policy on the issue. The cause for East Timorese self-determination had won the support the Clinton Administration, especially the support of Stanley Roth, the State Department's Assistant Secretary of State for East Asian affairs. Now that the issue was back on the international agenda the European Union, with vigorous prompting from Portugal and encouragement from countries like Ireland, had also come out in support of the issue. The long years of tireless work by legislators in North America, in Europe, Japan, and Australia, were at last bearing fruit.

UNAMET was placed under the able leadership of Ian Martin, a former secretary-general of Amnesty International. Despite the refreshing shift in international political attitudes, Martin was confronted with an awesome task. In a little over two months the UN mission had to register those eligible to vote, prepare the balloting arrangements and, without any real security capability of its own, ensure the kind of secure environment that would make the vote free and fair. Security was the issue of major concern to Kofi Annan, and special envoys like Yamsheed Marker, Francesc Vendrell and Tamrat Samuel. Militia violence had escalated in April with the TNI and militia killings now amounting to dozens of lives, including the widely reported massacres at the house of Manuel Carrascalão in Dili, and at the church complex in Liquiça. Faced with these disturbing incidents, and the reported involvement of ABRI troops, the UN negotiators again pressed for the mission to have a peacekeeping component, but this was strongly opposed by the Indonesian side, especially by General Wiranto who insisted that ABRI would provide effective security, and 'absolute impartiality' in relation to the ballot.

This was anything but satisfactory, and it presented a dilemma to the negotiators. The security aspect of the agreement was not really acceptable, but if they persisted with a demand for a peacekeeping presence, the plebiscite would be postponed or cancelled. This is what the TNI clearly wanted. If Habibie had bowed to international pressure, the TNI would not have accepted it, and just might have ousted him from office. Also, after the June elections for Indonesia's MPR, Golkar's strength in the parliament was decimated. The strongest party was now the PDI led by Megawati Sukarnoputri who was strongly opposed to the East Timorese referendum. Habibie seemed likely to lose office when the MPR met later in the year, and if Megawati were to succeed him this bold exercise in self-determination, probably the last chance for the East Timorese people, could well have been abandoned.

In short it was now or never. If the plebiscite had been cancelled, or even indefinitely postponed, a wave of violence would almost certainly have engulfed East Timor, as a bitterly disappointed people gave vent to their frustrations. It would have brought renewed suffering to a country that had already suffered so much in those past twenty-four years. As Ian Martin wrote later:

> It was inconceivable that the heaviest pressure that even a determined US government could have mobilised could have induced Habibie and Wiranto to accept international peacekeepers at this juncture: they could never have survived politically being responsible for such a decision. The announcement of the second option had already brought strong criticism in Jakarta, including from Habibie's likely rival for the Presidency, Megawati Sukarnoputri, and from retired and serving generals. When

the possibility of international peacekeepers was put to Habibie by Howard in their Bali meeting, it was instantly rebuffed and the discussion passed to the numbers of Civpol advisers.

There remains the question of whether a firmer stand by the UN and Portugal in the negotiations could have strengthened the security provisions. If so, it could probably only have been in the direction of the more explicit commitments which the UN was proposing, notably to disarm the militia. The inclusion of such commitments in the Agreements, instead of in the Secretary-General's memorandum, would have done little to increase the likelihood of their being respected on the ground in East Timor. The UN would still have faced the dilemma that lay ahead: whether to proceed or not to proceed in security conditions which clearly breached Indonesia's commitments under the Agreements.[15]

It was, therefore, a matter of seizing an opportunity that might never be repeated, as well as responding to the pleas of Timorese community leaders, so it was decided to go ahead. In the event, when Ian Martin arrived in Dili early in June 1999 he faced a formidable task, and precious little time to carry it out. Timorese expectations were at fever point on the one hand while on the other, the violent TNI led militia operation was stepping up its attempts to sabotage UNAMET's task. The mission was not particularly large, given the magnitude of the task before it. Ian Martin was assisted by fifteen political officers, 400 UN volunteers, 270 Civpol (unarmed, and with limited authority), some support staff, and 4000 staff recruited locally.

The UNAMET mission tried to bring the pro-independence and pro-integration leaders together in an effort to curb the violence. Although there were reconciliation meetings, which usually concluded with reconciliation noises, the violence went on unabated. It soon became clear that most of the Timorese leaders on both sides favoured such agreements, and it was TNI officers, probably led by General Zakky Anwar Makarim, who were urging the militia to keep up the momentum of the campaign of violence and intimidation. Zakky Anwar, a Kopassus expert in covert operations, who had headed the BIA, ABRI's main intelligence agency, had been in Dili at the time of the massacres in April. In May he was appointed 'security adviser' to the Indonesian Special Task Force for the East Timor Ballot (P3TT). Behind the scenes he was believed to be the chief coordinator of the militia operation, reporting directly to headquarters in Jakarta.

Although there were no further major massacres until the end of August, TNI militia activities were stepped up once UNAMET began its task. UN operations, in particular those outside Dili, were subjected to harassment, with seven UN workers being injured in a militia attack at Maliana on 29 June. Protests from Kofi Annan himself, and the supposed intervention of General Wiranto, made little difference, so the registration and the ballot dates were delayed. At first voting day was put back to 22 August, and then to 30 August. In the circumstances, the key task of voter registration did not commence until 16 July. In carrying out this function UNAMET officials continued to encounter intimidation and obstruction from the TNI and militia. In what was an extraordinary achievement, the registration was completed on 4 August, thanks to the tireless efforts of a dedicated staff most of whom worked long hours and seven days a week and to the determination and the enthusiasm of the Timorese themselves.

The UN mission sponsored several attempts to end the violence by appeals to Indonesian security chiefs, including General Wiranto, and by encouraging reconciliation meetings between pro-independence and pro-autonomy leaders. Several amiable gatherings took place with the involvement of João Tavares and Eurico Guterres, pro-independence leaders and Timor's bishops. Truces with undertakings to disarm were agreed to, but were never really implemented. Militia leaders continued to proclaim that a pro-independence vote would lead to bloodshed, while the militia units, according to intelligence material, and acting on instructions from TNI officers, continued their campaign of violence, especially in districts adjacent to the border, in particular Cova Lima, Bobonaro and Maliana. These militia activities were of course well away from the prying eyes of the international media which now had a presence in Dili. The violence caused thousands of Timorese to abandon their homes and flee to the comparative safety of the mountains where they were to depend on International Red Cross aid for their survival.

At some stage, probably in April, the TNI commanders evidently concluded that the vote would probably go against Indonesia. According to reports, apparently from Australian intelligence agencies, especially the SIGINT (communications intelligence) specialists, DSD, who closely monitored TNI communications in 1999, plans were drawn up for a last punishing military operation in the event of a vote against integration. Thus the plan for the massive *pembumihangusan*, or scorched-earth operation, was drawn up with the aim of leaving East Timor in ruins, and largely depopulated. It seems to have had two codenames, *Operasi Guntur*, and *Operasi Wiradharma*. One senior TNI officer told a militia leader that the aim of the Guntur operation was to create a wild wind of destruction that would sweep across the country. It would punish the East Timorese for what the TNI commanders considered an act of national humiliation, and so the scene was set for yet another bloody chapter in East Timor's cruel experience of Indonesian rule which ended in the same brutal way as it began twenty-four years earlier.

The last phase—the plebiscite and the TNI revenge
Militia provocation and intimidation continued right up to the day of the plebiscite, 30 August. The pro-autonomy voices became louder and more menacing with constant threats from TNI officers as well as militia leaders that a vote against autonomy would lead to bloodshed. This campaign caused considerable anxiety among UNAMET officials and observers who feared even greater violence. Organising the election had been a hasty affair, and without any help from the Indonesian security authorities there were fears that this

exercise in self-determination might founder. The result was quite astonishing. The voting proceeded peacefully and in an orderly fashion throughout the day, impressing the hundreds of foreign representatives, who included many parliamentarians and a large party of young Indonesian supporters of Timorese independence. During the polling hours there were very few incidents. The worst occurred at Gleno, in the Ermera area, where about 50 militia attacked the polling station, forcing the flight of more than 200 Timorese who were lined up at the booths. However the attackers withdrew after about half-an-hour and, to our astonishment, a short time later the queue had re-formed.[16] The Timorese response to the incident was a striking example of their determination in the face of intimidation. As Ian Martin has recorded, their courage and determination was largely responsible for the success of the ballot. The turnout spoke for itself; almost 98 per cent of those registered voted, surely close to a world record for a non-compulsory election.

A major concern for UNAMET officials was how to ensure that the ballot papers got to the Dili museum where the counting took place. There were some attempts by the militia to prevent cartons of votes from reaching Dili, but thanks to the courageous efforts of the UN police, the Civpol, all consignments managed to get through. Near Gleno the militia set up roadblocks and tried to stop the convoy from getting through, but their attempt failed. Its success in getting to Dili was made possible by the courageous stand of the predominantly Australian Civpol officers escorting the ballot papers. Trouble was also encountered at Maliana where a helicopter was used to ferry the ballots to Dili. It got away safely, but only just, after being fired on by militia and TNI troops.

Tensions started to explode after election day, causing Ian Martin to recall his teams to the comparative safety of the UNAMET compound in Dili. There was a wave of violence in the capital itself, much of it focused on the UNAMET compound, and any Timorese who had worked for the UN was gravely at risk. Anticipating the outcome, the pro-autonomy parties lodged fraud claims with the Electoral Commission, but these claims were spurious and were dismissed by the three-member Electoral Commission. The vote counting was undisturbed by the renewed violence, and was completed rather earlier than expected. In these tense circumstances Ian Martin wisely brought forward the date for the declaration of the polls. On the morning of 4 September the results were announced in Dili by Ian Martin and, on the same day, by Kofi Annan in distant New York.

While we had all expected the vote to go against the autonomy proposal, the final result surprised most UN officials and observers. A large majority (78.5%) of electors rejected the autonomy option. Twenty-four years after the Indonesian invasion of 1975, the vote was a stunning rejection of integration. While the Timorese and foreign observers celebrated the outcome, it was denounced as fraudulent by the pro-autonomy leaders, with demands that the border districts, Maliana, Bobonaro, Cova Lima and Ainaro be retained as part of Indonesia. However, the size of the vote, in the face of severe intimidation from the TNI and pro-autonomy leaders in the lead-up to the election, rendered such a claim preposterous.

It was not an unexpected outcome to the TNI commanders as their punishing response began within two hours of the announcement of the plebiscite result. Armed TNI and militia on motorcycles and trucks stormed in Dili, firing at random and setting fire to government buildings. The disorderly appearance of the assault was misleading. It was obviously a carefully planned and orchestrated operation. Before the end of the day Dili's leading hotel, the Mahkota (where the plebiscite result had been announced) was soon in flames, an early target for revenge. Within a few days the entire city was on fire, its houses and building having first been systematically ransacked by troops and militia with the loot being loaded onto barges and shipped to Indonesia, mainly to Flores. The deportations also proceeded in the same way. The Timorese were ordered to leave, mostly by TNI officers, with those who hesitated being threatened with weapons. Not all Timorese opted for the deportation. Some 200,000 fled inland, scrambling up the steep mountainsides immediately to Dili's south. It was not the first time in their recent history. In the aftermath of the bloody Indonesian assault on Dili on 7 December 1975 a large part of the population had sought refuge in East Timor's rugged mountains where the then large Falintil force offered them some protection from the invaders.

The TNI and the crimes against humanity

From intelligence sources, and from the Indonesian KPP HAM (Human Rights Investigation Committee) report, much is known about the TNI's commanding role in relation to events in East Timor from April to September. At most of the major killings TNI officers were present, in some cases playing a leading role. TNI troops openly assisted militia attackers. During the Liquiça attack, for example, they obligingly hurled tear gas grenades into the church. During the Suai massacre Kopassus Colonel Sediono stood outside the church in uniform, carrying an M16 and, according to witnesses, he was giving orders. As the attack then intensified it is inconceivable that, as the senior officer present, he was doing other than directing it. In major killings at Maliana Lieutenant Colonel Burhannudin Siagian also played a commanding role.

A study of the pattern of atrocities provides a further indictment of the military command as a whole. With some 17,000 troops in East Timor the TNI was in a position to halt the killings at any time, if it so desired. Yet not only did it fail to act against them; it aided them directly, helping organise their operations, especially in the border districts, using the pretext of a need to counter increased Falintil activity. At the time, however, as UN officials were able to observe, Falintil troops remained within their cantonments. A close study of the situation revealed that the TNI and militia operations were closely intertwined especially in the two months before the InterFET arrival, with the TNI exercising a command role, largely through the Kopassus officer Lieutenant Colonel Yayat Sudradjat.

It was during this latter period that the worst crimes against humanity were perpetrated, crimes that followed the pattern of reprisals during the previous twenty-four years since East Timor was first invaded by Indonesian troops. In the past the TNI had often used paramilitary groups to spearhead the attacks, and this technique was apparent during the wanton killing of hundreds of East Timorese in August and September 1999. The true figure for the total loss of life has not yet been fully established, and may never be known. However, on the basis of the information obtained from various sources, including discussions with Church officials, Timorese human rights activists, Civpol and InterFET officers, and from my own observations as a UN observer in the period around the plebiscite, the true death toll may well be greatly in excess of the 1000 people, unconvincingly concluded by the poorly administered UN Serious Crimes Unit. These killings were carried out systematically, deliberately directed against the opponents of integration with Indonesia. In the violence following the 1975 invasion church officials and property were respected. In 1999 nuns and priests were among those targeted, with killings in Lautem, Dili and Cova Lima. In some cases the bodies were mutilated. The violence was invariably one-sided with the victims being unarmed and unprotected by local law-enforcement authorities.

The major atrocities

Mass killings or executions have a special quality of horror about them, and for that reason the main focus in East Timor has tended to be on the horrific killings in Suai, Liquiça, Maliana, and other places. However numerous killings on a smaller scale, often involving individuals occurred elsewhere in the territory, attracting much less attention, including from UN investigators. These lesser-known killings and cases of assault on the person were nevertheless all part of the wave of brutalities instigated, if not carried out by the TNI, marking an inglorious end to an inglorious occupation. This pattern of violence reached most parts of East Timor, although there were great variations in intensity. A characteristic of the major atrocities is that the attacks were obviously organised and the killings systematic. The worst areas for these crimes in the month before the InterFET intervention were in the Covalima, Ainaro, and the Bobonaro–Maliana district. The violence intensified as it became clear that the vote was going to go against Indonesia. Even before the results of the plebiscite were announced attacks against Timorese UNAMET workers increased. The main wave of violence took place in September, however, when it accompanied the *pembumihangusan*.

To those of us who were able to witness some of the militia violence, its careful organisation was striking. Despite the wild flurry of shooting after the plebiscite results were announced, no UN official or observer was shot, and to have achieved that outcome called for tight discipline. Even the media escaped, except for Dutch citizen and *Financial Times* correspondent, Sander Thoenes, who was killed by TNI troops when the motorcycle on which he was a pillion passenger ran into a withdrawing territorial battalion. During this period, it was clear to observers that many, if not most, of the so-called militia were TNI troops, whose uniforms were scarcely concealed by their black Aitarak shirts. Many of them had been rushed in from Indonesian Timor to conduct the *pembumihangusan*, arriving on the day the results of the vote were announced. The destruction of 74 per cent of houses and buildings in East Timor, and the massive deportations that accompanied it, in the space of little more than two weeks, was an operation requiring skilful military organisation and transport logistics. There can be no doubt that the *pembumihangusan* was planned by TNI commanders, and closely directed by them.

There is evidence that the major massacres at Maliana and Oecussi and at Suai were carried out under direct military command. Thanks to a sluggish response on the part of UNTAET's Serious Crimes Unit it has been difficult to establish just how many Timorese were killed in the rampage between 4 September and the arrival of InterFET. My investigations produced a wide range of estimates from 37 to as many as 500 in Dili in this brief period.[17] In Liquiça a figure of more than 200 was mentioned for the April killing by leading local residents, although official figures suggest only about 50 died. The massacres deserve special attention because they required a degree of organisation and in most, if not all cases, there was a visible TNI participation with, at best, a total failure of the Polri to intervene to protect the citizens under attack, who were almost invariably unarmed.

Throughout most of 1999 the armed resistance forces, the Falintil, were inactive, in response to specific orders from their Commander, and were therefore not in a position to help protect their supporters. With some 18,000 TNI troops and perhaps 20,000 militia in East Timor the Falintil force of less than 2000 was, in any case, massively outnumbered. Any attempt to intervene also risked reprisals against the civilian population. This was demonstrated at Cailaco in the Maliana district when on 12 April, a Falintil-linked force killed Manuel Soares Gama and two TNI personnel, following the latters' alleged murder of six Timorese in Gama's house. The next day a force led by Lieutenant Colonel Siagian and João Tavares reportedly kidnapped, tortured, and then executed, six residents of Cailaco.

Liquiça

The Liquiça–Maubara district along the coast to the west of Dili was one of the first areas to experience militia violence. As early as 30 January, Mahidi militia were reported to have killed a civilian in the Liquiça district. It was also in Maubara that the Church became a target. BMP militia members surrounded the Carmelite Convent there on 16 March and threatened to kill anyone who tried to leave. On 5 April the same militia group, assisted by TNI troops and Mobile Brigade personnel, assaulted a pro-independence group in Maubara, killing two of them. They went on to Liquiça where they proceeded to burn the houses of known pro-independence supporters. They then surrounded the Liquiça Church where more than 1000 people were assembled. After some attempt at negotiation the compound was attacked and more than fifty killed,[18] with the bodies being disposed of with TNI help. Occurring as it did while the 5 May Agreement was being negotiated, the incident aroused a strong international reaction. However, General Wiranto dismissively informed journalists in Jakarta that both pro-integration and pro-independence groups had become 'emotional'. Interviews with Liquiça residents and a study of records held by Civpol and SCIU (Serious Crimes Investigations Unit) point to the TNI and Mobile Brigade personnel having played a leading role in the attack and in the disposal of the bodies.

Killings in the Dili area

The killing of Manuel Carrascalão's courageous teenage son Manuelito and at least 11 displaced Timorese from Liquiça, Alas and Turiscai, took place at the Carrascalão residence in Dili on 17 April 1999. Manuelito was murdered when he attempted to persuade the militia to stop their assault on the family home and to spare the lives of the refugees inside. This residence was also used as the secretariat of the Movement for the Reconciliation and Unity of the People of East Timor, of which Manuel Carrascalão was Chairman. Manuelito's companions and many refugees had sought refuge in the house as an escape from violence in their hometowns. The house was attacked by Aitarak and BMP militia following a rally that day by more than 5000 militia outside the Governor's office, which was presided over by Colonel Tono Suratnam, the Korem East Timor Military commander. The attack was particularly brutal, being on a house known to be a refuge for 143 Timorese from outside Dili.

Some killings were reported in the following months, but the presence of the UNAMET mission and a sizeable international media community seems to have deterred the militia from further massacres, that is until the destructive assault on the entire territory in September. However, as the Aitarak militia grew in size and aggressiveness, low-level violence began to increase, especially in August. On 5 September, the day following the release of the results of the plebiscite twenty-five people were reported to have been killed by Aitarak members at the Camara Ecclesiastica Diocese in Dili. On the following day some of the refugees in Bishop Belo's house were reported to have been murdered. Some East Timorese university students who had just returned from Java were also said to have been killed. Others, including a German priest and a civilian, were killed in the period before the arrival of the InterFET forces, but the full casualty list during this chaotic period is still not known. The claim that bodies were taken out to sea in barges and disposed of has not been proven, but nor can it be dismissed. I was in Dili at that time and was told by a Timorese that this form of disposal was taking place and I had witnessed two barges going out to a location roughly midway in the strait between Dili and Atauro.

The Oecussi massacre

While there were reports of murders and intimidation in the Oecussi enclave before August 1999 the main killings occurred on 8, 9, and 10 September. The killers included members of Battalion 745 of the TNI and a substantial number of militia. On Wednesday 8 September, a force of about 200 troops attacked the villages of Tumin, Kiobiselo, Nonkikan and Nibin, and killed about fourteen men. The next day at Imbate about seventy young men were selected, on the basis of their apparently educated appearance. These men were separated from the rest of the people gathered there, bound in pairs and marched to Passabe. At 1 a.m. on 10 September, following a pre-arranged signal, the slaughter of these young men was carried out, the victims being shot or hacked to death. According to the investigators, the main instigators of the massacre included the Police Chief of Passabe Gabriel Colo, Laurentino Soares, TNI soldiers and militia members. There may have been more killings, but the scene could not be investigated until after the arrival of InterFET forces on 2 October. This massacre was not brought before the Indonesian tribunal.

The Suai massacre

The Cova Lima district, or *kabupaten*, of which Suai is the administrative centre, was the location of the earliest militia killings carried out by the Mahidi in January, and the worst massacre at the end of this period, in early September 1999. The attack on the Ave Maria church in Suai took place on 6 September, in the aftermath of the declaration of the results of the plebiscite. TNI, Mobile Brigade troops and Militia, led by Kopassus Colonel Herman Sedono (also Sedyono), and Lieutenant Sugito, launched a vicious attack on several hundred refugees who had retreated to the church grounds following the looting and destruction of their houses.[19] It cost the lives of priests who tried to negotiate with the attacking troops. In all some 200 Timorese were reported to have been killed. After the assault several women survivors were taken to Covalima Kodim Headquarters and were sexually assaulted.

Maliana

The massacre at Maliana police station was the most serious incident in this area, but it was merely the culmination of the wave of violence that began in February. In that month militia groups launched attacks in Maliana, Atabai, and Cailaco. The Bobonaro–Maliana area militia groups[20] were numerous and were directly under the command of João Tavares, the militia *Panglima*. Their operations were inextricably linked with TNI operations, under the command of Lieutenant Colonel Burhanuddin Siagian. On 12 April six Timorese were kidnapped and murdered by Halilintar troops. This was followed by a Falintil revenge attack in which a Halilintar leader and two TNI soldiers were killed. On 13 April a force led by Siagian and Tavares allegedly kidnapped, tortured, and executed six Timorese randomly selected from Cailaco villagers in revenge for the Falintil killing. From mid-August the militia increased their activities. During this period several murders were committed and houses burnt. On the last day of the election campaign militia attacked Memo, killing three people and destroying twenty houses. On 2 September two UNAMET local staff were shot dead by a TNI sergeant. At the same time Lieutenant Colonel Burhanuddin Siagian is reported as having told UNAMET local staff that they would be killed after the election.[21] The Halilintar and Dadurus Merah Putih militias, backed by the TNI, began a campaign of destruction in Maliana on 4 September after the election result had been announced in Dili.

The main massacre occurred at the Maliana Police Station on 8 September when Dadurus Merah Putih militia, backed by TNI troops, attacked a large group of Timorese who were seeking refuge in the police station. According to InterFET investigators, more than seventy persons were killed, many of them in a brutal matter. One of these investigators described how the TNI were positioned around militia killers who had been given drugs, and their sharpshoopters picked off Timorese attempting to flee from the scene of the massacre.[22] The Maliana massacre and the role played by Lieutenant Colonel Burhanuddin Siagian have not been brought before the Indonesian human rights tribunal in Jakarta.

Lautem–Lospalos

The eastern districts of East Timor did not suffer the same level of violence, and several villages, among them Uatolari and Viqueque, almost escaped destruction by the TNI or their militia. Baucau suffered little damage, thanks to negotiations between Bishop Nascimento and the local TNI command post. Individual acts of violence including killing had, however, occurred earlier in the year. On 17 March 1999 Mariano Soares, a prominent citizen of Triloka village disappeared, and was believed to have been killed. A week later another Timorese was killed by TNI troops in the Baucau district. On 17 April members of Team Alpha killed a prominent independence supporter, Virgilio de Sousa, in his home in Bauro Village in Los Palos. In August, on the eve of the plebiscite Los Palos village chief, Verissimo Quintas, was brutally killed by local militia, following an attack on his house.

The darkest period for the Los Palos–Baucau area, the eastern zone of the province, occurred well after the plebiscite. On 12 September four Timorese were killed by TNI troops at the Los Palos Military subdistrict command, and on the same day five persons were said to have been killed at Baucau by Battalion 745 troops. The worst massacre in the area occurred on 25 September, five days after InterFET troops had landed at Dili. On the road between Los Palos and Baucau Team Alpha members killed and mutilated nine people, including nuns, deacons and an Indonesian journalist. The bodies were placed in the victim's vehicle which was then pushed into the Luro River. Team Alpha operated under the control of Kopassus officers and the local TNI commander. According to the

KPP HAM report a member of Kopassus, Lieutenant Sayful, was implicated in ordering this killing. In this instance, most of the Timorese killers were caught by InterFET forces and were eventually brought before the special court in Dili. The East Timor prosecutor issued a warrant for the arrest of Lieutenant Sayful, but the Indonesian authorities have so far refused to hand him over.

* * * *

There were also hundreds of cases of wounding, torture, sexual assault, and abduction. A Timorese human rights agency (Yayasan Hukum) reported these included 182 cases of gender-based human rights violations. The crimes that affected most Timorese were, however, the forced deportation of some 250,000 people to West Timor, most of whom were ordered to leave their homes. They were directed to leave (sometimes being told they would be shot it they refused) not by militia commanders, but by TNI officers. Their houses were subsequently ransacked and then, in all but a few cases, destroyed. These refugees were to become virtual prisoners in militia-controlled and poorly serviced camps in West Timor. Most Indonesian residents in Timor together with the families of militia and pro-autonomy leaders were not part of this deportation. They received instructions to leave East Timor some days before *Operasi Guntur* was launched.

Faced with rampaging militia and TNI, some 200,000 East Timorese abandoned their homes and fled to the mountains, as they had done in 1942 when the Japanese invaded, and after the Indonesian invasion of 1975. However, in the dry conditions of September 1999 (the middle of a six-month period when no rain falls north of Timor's high mountain ranges), they were soon at risk of starvation as well as facing harassment from TNI and militia patrols.

Thanks to the presence of a large international press contingent the new wave of violence received unprecedented international attention, at least until most of the media were forced to flee. Their vivid reports aroused a response that was to place the Indonesian government under unprecedented pressure to respect the outcome of the election and to allow international intervention. Australia, which has one of its largest military bases in the Darwin area, offered to provide a substantial part of a peace-enforcing operation, provided that it was authorised by the Security Council which, in turn, required a formal invitation from President Habibie. In spite of the decisive outcome of the plebiscite such an agreement was not immediately forthcoming. It was at first opposed by the military and a sizeable part of the Indonesian political establishment. Under the May 5 agreement, however, there was provision for Phases Two, and Three covering the transition to East Timor's new status, and the new wave of violence engulfing the country now made a decision on these phases urgent.

General Wiranto continued to insist that the TNI was capable of restoring order, a position he maintained until after a UN Security Council team which the

General accompanied arrived at the burning capital. Wiranto, along with other team members, was visibly shocked at the extent of the devastation. A strong consensus emerged that a UN peace-enforcing mission should intervene as soon as possible. The key issues were the composition of the mission, its leadership, and the all-important question of Indonesian acceptance. At first the Indonesians were strongly opposed to the intervention under Australian leadership, but President Habibie finally agreed, in the face of strong international pressures, including from all permanent members of the Security Council, as well as Japan, a long-time supporter of Indonesia's annexation of the former Portuguese colony.

The crucial pressure on the Habibie government came from an unexpected direction. As it happened, the mounting Timor crisis coincided with an APEC (Asia-Pacific Economic Cooperation) Heads of Government meeting in New Zealand on 9 September. Despite efforts by Indonesia and Malaysia to keep Timor off the agenda because of the non-economic character of the question, a special ministerial meeting was convened there. Indonesia was in a vulnerable position at that time, being one of the worst victims of the Asian economic crisis. Interestingly, both James Wolfensohn, President of the World Bank, and Michel Camdessus of the IMF (the International Monetary Fund), made a point of describing the Timor crisis as a matter 'of paramount concern'. Wolfensohn's letter to Habibie at the time was direct.

> For the international financial community to be able to continue its full support, it is critical that you act swiftly to restore order, and that your government carry through on its public commitment to honor the referendum outcome.

The decisive pressure probably came from President Clinton, the leader of a country with a long history of accommodating and even sheltering the Suharto regime from international criticism.[23] Following a meeting with Jose Ramos Horta in New Zealand the President conveyed the US position to Habibie in very firm language. He raised the threat of economic sanctions, and ended commercial arms sales to the TNI. In his press conference Clinton drove home his message in response to the violence. If it did not end Indonesia 'must invite' international help to restore security. After its mission had returned to Jakarta and had reported to New York on the grim scene in Dili, the UN Security Council held a six-hour meeting at which a majority of its members called on Indonesia to accept an international force. On 12 September, after a meeting with the Indonesian cabinet, President Habibie announced that he had called Kofi Annan and invited UN assistance to restore peace and security in East Timor, a decision, he said, without conditions.

In view of the urgent situation in East Timor the Security Council decided to authorise a multinational force, a 'coalition of the willing' to restore security and then hand over to a more traditional peacekeeping force under UN command. During this critical period Kofi Annan had been in regular contact with Prime Minister Howard whom he now invited to provide the main part of the force and the force commander. For that post Mr Howard chose Major General Peter

Cosgrove, and Thailand agreed to appoint a senior army officer as his deputy. On 19 September Major General Cosgrove, the deputy force commander and other senior officers, arrived in Dili, and informed the TNI commander, Major General Kiki Sjahnakri, that InterFET troops would start arriving on the following day. Thus, on 20 September 1999 a new dawn began for the people of East Timor.

* * * *

In the meantime the besieged UNAMET mission was in a hopeless position. Without any means of armed protection it was forced to withdraw its teams to the comparative safety of the UN compound in Dili. To the UN officials this was a painful decision for it meant leaving most of the hundreds who had worked for the UN mission elsewhere in the province to face the militia anger. Many were to lose their lives this way. However, UN staff were powerless to defend themselves, let alone the Timorese whose expectations they had raised. As the violence mounted, all UN staff and the few journalists who had not fled from Dili after the attack on the Mahkota retired to the UN compound at Balide where they were soon joined by more than 1000 desperate Timorese refugees. Many UNAMET staff were evacuated on 10 September, but eighty international staff who were distressed at the prospect of leaving the Timorese UN workers to the mercy of the militia remained behind.

The *pembumihungusan* resulted in the wanton destruction of some 74 per cent of the houses and buildings in East Timor. Government offices, military barracks, community centres, schools, most houses and shops, tertiary institutions, including the University of East Timor, the Polytechnical School at Hera and some churches, were gutted or badly damaged. All of these assaults were carried out with military precision. Whatever role the militia had played in past violence, this particular operation was under TNI command.

When Major General Cosgrove's InterFET force arrived in late September they were confronted with a degree of devastation few of them expected. Some organised destruction was still going on in a city almost deserted of its population. It was only after InterFET forces moved into Dili that the demoralised remnants of the population began trickling back. They were confronted with a near totally destroyed city where there were no services, no water, no electricity. The schools were in ruins with their books burnt. There was nothing left of the state infrastructure—no police, no courts, no postal service, no aid services. Those of us who surveyed this desolate scene called it 'Ground Zero'.

From InterFET to UNTAET—from colonial rule to UN mandate
The InterFET intervention under Major General Peter Cosgrove took place in stark contrast to the world body's response to the Indonesian military intervention in 1975. Then it was noted for its inaction. In September 1999, by contrast, the UN responded with commendable speed and commitment,

and authorised InterFET, arguably the most effective and most successful peacekeeping, or peace-enforcing, operation of its kind in the history of the United Nations. InterFET was mandated by Security Council Resolution 1264 on 15 September 1999. The main force was in fact already in Darwin. It comprised troops from more than twenty countries, and at full strength amounted to about 11,000 troops, 5000 of them from Australia. The force began to move into Dili on 20 September and it was to remain in Timor for five months, until February 2000. For the first weeks, that is, until 19 October 1999 when the Indonesia MPR rescinded the integration of East Timor, InterFET had the sensitive task of working alongside a much larger Indonesian force of over 15,000 whose troops were hostile to the international presence. In fact they continued with the destruction of buildings and the sabotaging of Dili's communications system. Major General Cosgrove had to deal with Major General Kiki Sjahnakri, a senior Kopassus officer who had earlier played a leading role in developing militia strategies. On the day of the ballot General Kiki Sjahnakri reportedly had met with General Zakky Anwar and Colonel Muis, and had helped plan the TNI and militia assault on Dili immediately following the declaration of the ballot.

The InterFET command handled its relations with the TNI with considerable skill and restraint, assisted by the presence of some Australian troops with a good knowledge of Bahasa Indonesia, including officers who had worked with the TNI on liaison missions. At first Cosgrove sought to establish and consolidate the security of the capital and its immediate environs. The Indonesian troops were in an angry mood, and at times behaved menacingly, pointing their weapons at the patrolling InterFET troops. The worst incident in the Dili area occurred a day after InterFET's arrival when troops of Battalion 745 which was at the time withdrawing from the eastern sector, murdered *Financial Times* journalist, Sanders Thoenes. This was followed by a tense encounter between this unit and InterFET forces. East Timor was still, formally speaking, Indonesian territory and there was a high degree of TNI resentment at this intrusion into the scene of the TNI's most painful humiliation. Had it not been for the courage and negotiating skills of Australian InterFET officers an armed clash could easily have occurred. It was a time when relations between Canberra and Jakarta were very brittle. Indonesian soldiers, smarting under the outcome of the plebiscite, tended to direct their chagrin at the Australians, who had been so accommodating in the past. Had not the InterFET commanders displayed great sensitivity and discipline in the face of this provocation, conflict could easily have broken out, risking an outright war between the two countries.

InterFET took some time to reach its maximum strength and was at first heavily outnumbered by the Indonesian forces. However, the TNI units began moving out, taking with them tonnes of looted equipment and personal belongings. Desperate appeals from the outlying districts reached InterFET headquarters, stressing the urgent need for InterFET forces to move as quickly as possible into all major centres. In the event General Cosgrove acted cautiously, to use his own words, 'ensuring that wherever InterFET troops went, they stayed'.

At a tripartite meeting on 28 September Indonesia agreed to concede *de facto* authority to the UN and three weeks later, on 20 October, the Indonesian Parliament (MPR) passed a decree annulling the 1976 incorporation of East Timor, thus bringing a formal end to almost twenty-four years of Indonesia rule and creating the necessary conditions for a UN mandate. The Secretary-General Kofi Annan moved quickly. On 25 October 1999, in UN Resolution 1272 the Security Council authorised a mandate for the setting up of the United Nations Transitional Administration in East Timor, which was to become the virtual government of the territory until indigenous self-rule began to take shape. The mission was also to provide governance and public administration, humanitarian assistance and emergency rehabilitation, and a peacekeeping component with a strength of just over 9000 troops, including military observers. In effect the United Nations took on its most comprehensive role—responsibility, not only for peacekeeping and rehabilitating a devastated nation, but also for nation-building, guiding East Timor to independent nationhood in the shortest possible time. To provide the necessary funding, an appeal for humanitarian assistance, led by the World Bank, was launched in Geneva a matter of days after UNTAET had been authorised by the Security Council.

In the meantime the UN civilian presence was maintained by the depleted and exhausted ranks of UNAMET. Soon after the final wave of violence began on 4 September, UN officials retreated to the UN compound at Balide where they were under constant threat from rampaging militia and where they were soon to be joined by more than 1000 desperate refugees. With food and water running short the compound was abandoned, the UNAMET staff and refugees being evacuated to Darwin. A brave group of twelve UN officials remained in the relative security of the fortress-like Australian consulate. After the arrival of InterFET a week later, this UNAMET group, headed by Ian Martin, formed a skeleton UN presence and eventually the nucleus of UNTAET, once the latter's existence was authorised by the Security Council. These officials included a number of experienced political and Civpol officers who were to occupy key positions in the new mission.

The landing of InterFET troops heralded the beginning of the end of Indonesia's long and harsh occupation of East Timor. Less than two weeks later the last party of Indonesian troops withdrew from East Timor, an historic occasion marked by a simple ceremony with a touch of irony. It was attended by, among others, Xanana Gusmão and Major General Kiki Sjahnakri, the Indonesian officer who had been responsible for his capture seven years earlier. It was the end of a sad chapter for both Timorese and Indonesians, one that had cost both dearly. In suffering and in destruction on the part of the East Timorese, and the abject failure of an attempted incorporation on the part of the Indonesian military.

Notes

1 See AI Index ASA 21/31/94.
2 For a detailed discussion of these moves, see Deliverance: Don Greenlees and Robert Garran (Allen & Unwin, Sydney 2002) pp 27-30
3 For a comprehensive of Habibie's shift on East Timor, see Greenlees & Garran, op.cit. Chapter 2
4 See Tomas Goncalves: Transcription of testimony.
5 Battalion 744 came under the command of Major Yunus Yosfiah, who had led the attacking force into Balibo
6 See 'Indonesia Confronts Unruly Past', article by Dan Murphy, in Christian Science Monitor, 20 Nov. 2000.
7 See Silent Witness, p 36, a report prepared by Professor Desmond Ball, Director of the Strategic and Defence Studies Centre, Australian National University, Canberra, 2000
8 See Peter Bartu: Op cit
9 See Peter Bartu Unpublished monograph on Militia activities in Maliana area. P 2.
10 Serka - Top Sergeant.
11 For more details on the militia structure and its operations, see 'Laporan Pelanggaran Hak Asasi Manusia', Januari - September 1999, Chapters IV and V (Yayasan Hukum, Hak Asasi dan Keadilan Timor Timur)
12 Based on interviews of militia who were present.
13 At that time, in the days of ABRI, Polri came under overall military command, and were generally subservient to Army commanders.
14 This shift is discussed at length in Greenlees and Garran. Op.cit ch.5.
15 Ian Martin: Unpublished report.
16 I accompanied the British Parliamentary Group as their guide.
17 James Dunn: Crimes against Humanity in East Timor, January to October 1999: Their Nature and Causes. (Reproduced in Masters of Terror - Canberra Papers on Strategy and Defence, No 145, ANU 2002.
18 According to my talks with Liquiça residents, the total killing around that event in fact amounted to more than 200!
19 See KPP HAM report - p.42, Masters of Terror.
20 Although Halilintar was the leading group, there were at least six other militia groups, including the notorious Dadurus Merah Putih, led by Natalino Monteiro.
21 Peter Bartu - Op cit. p.11.
22 Based on an interview of an Australian intelligence officer, who was among the first troops to reach Maliana.
23 See Report from Ian Martin.

Chapter Fourteen
UN mandate to independence

Once it became clear that Indonesia intended to accept the outcome of the plebiscite, the UN Secretary-General moved speedily to arrange East Timor's formal transition to a UN mandate. The green light came when the Habibie government indicated its acceptance at a tripartite meeting on 28 September 1999. On the same day UNAMET re-established its headquarters in Dili and began putting together a skeleton interim administration under Ian Martin. After 19 October when the Indonesian parliament had formally rescinded the 1976 incorporation, Kofi Annan acted quickly to set up UNTAET, the United Nations Transitional Administration in East Timor. It was established by Security Council Resolution 1272, which mandated the mission to provide an interim government with the full responsibilities that go with a national administration. Its peacekeeping force (PKF) had a strength of just over 9000 troops, including military observers. In effect the United Nations took on its most comprehensive role yet in relation to such a mission. It assumed responsibility, not only for peacekeeping and the rehabilitation of a devastated nation, but also for nation-building. UNTAET had the task of guiding East Timor to independent nationhood in the shortest possible time, a nation with durable democratic institutions and a commitment to the observance of international human rights. To provide the necessary funding, a World Bank led appeal for humanitarian assistance was launched in Geneva a matter of days after UNTAET had been authorised by the Security Council. Kofi Annan also moved to appoint the head of the UNTAET mission with this most challenging mandate— leading the devastated and impoverished territory of East Timor to the goal of independent nationhood. He chose Sergio Vieira de Mello, a youthful 51-year-old Brazilian who had already established an impressive record as a UN operational administrator, especially in the field of humanitarian affairs. In the 1990s, Vieira de Mello had held a number of senior positions, mostly in UNHCR (United Nations Commission on Human Rights) and other humanitarian affairs, in Cambodia, Rwanda, and in former Yugoslavia. For a period earlier in 1999 he was Kofi

Annan's senior representative in Kosovo. As it turned out he was an excellent choice for the position. His long experience in humanitarian affairs, in particular with refugees and dislocated peoples, was particularly appropriate to the situation in Timor. Vieira de Mello's most recent experience in the Balkans meant that he was familiar with the kind of devastation and demoralisation that greeted him on his arrival in Dili on 17 November. He also had a strong personal commitment to the advancement of human rights and, not least, he spoke Portuguese, the language strongly favoured by the East Timorese leaders.

The task ahead was not going to be easy, despite the flood of goodwill from Timor's grateful citizens. Starting from Ground Zero was going to be a formidable, if not unprecedented challenge for a UN mission. The administrative and physical infrastructures of the country were in ruins. In Dili the population was milling around, trying to patch up their damaged houses with some help from InterFET and aid agencies. The country was virtually without a national administrative system because most administrative positions in Timor had been held by Indonesians, who were no longer around. There was no police force or justice system and essential services were not functioning. There was no education system, the schools had been severely damaged, their books burnt, and nearly all of the teachers, most of them Indonesian, had fled the country. There were no shops and no postal service. The power and telephone services had been sabotaged, probably by the TNI, in its last weeks in Timor. These deficiencies were felt most strongly in Dili and other major towns. In the villages the traditional Timorese social structures provided a kind of order, but everywhere food was desperately short. The population was in fact surviving on international emergency assistance.

At that difficult time East Timor did have one important asset—impressive leaders. They included Xanana Gusmão, who had returned to Dili from Jakarta shortly after InterFET's arrival, bishops Belo and Nascimento, Jose Ramos Horta, Mario Carrascalão and Mari Alkitiri. At this early stage they provided a vital channel of communication between the InterFET and UNTAET leaderships on the one hand, and the people of the territory on the other. They counselled patience to their people, and directed the attention of an inexperienced administration to sectors of urgent need. CNRT came to be treated in a way similar to the UN mission's treatment of SWAPO in Namibia. Thus CNRT, whose ranks were bolstered by the return of Timorese political leaders from Portugal and Australia, was considered as 'the authentic representative' of the people of East Timor until the holding of election, with Xanana, Jose Ramos Horta and Bishop Belo being given special leadership status. Thus, from the outset Sergio Vieira de Mello wisely set out to develop a close relationship with the Timorese leaders, to consult them regularly and to win their confidence. It was an important measure, facilitating the resolution of disputes between UN officials, foreigners in general, and the Timorese.

Misunderstandings and other disputes were common for the first few months.

One serious problem was the status of the Falintil guerrillas, most of whom were encamped in the Aileu cantonment, a mountain town to the south of Dili. These courageous fighters had fought a lonely and desperate resistance against the TNI occupiers for more than two decades, and they now felt that they were being sidelined. They feared that they would be excluded from the emerging government by Fretilin leaders who had spent the occupation in exile, in relative comfort. At first the presence of armed Falintil fighters posed a problem for InterFET, whose mandate called for the disarming of all Timorese groups. Falintil commanders deeply resented the implication that they were in the same category as the militia. There were some minor incidents but General Cosgrove dealt with these problems with consummate skill and sensitivity. By the time InterFET left, relations between the Falintil leaders and the UN military commanders were good. The problem was eventually to be resolved when the East Timor Defence Force (ETDF) was established. It was not, however, until 1 February 2001 that the transition from the Falintil to the ETDF was formalised at a ceremony in Aileu with the respected Falintil Commander Taur Matan Ruak being appointed commander-in-chief of the ETDF with the rank of brigadier general. However, hundreds of former Falintil fighters who remained outside the new defence force remained resentful and discontented.

InterFET completed its task in February 2000 after an operation that was widely acclaimed as an outstanding success. It had provided an interim administration, urgent humanitarian assistance and, most important, it had won the hearts of the Timorese by driving away the hated TNI and their militia. In some ways, however, InterFET's role was easier, certainly less complicated than the role to be assumed by the PKF (peacekeeping force). The rules governing InterFET were different, and its operational period shorter. The PKF commanders faced more constraints, such as in the rules governing their engagement with hostile forces, and had the added responsibility of helping develop a national defence capability.

While the UN mission was at first warmly welcomed, many of the citizens of Dili and other major towns soon became impatient with what they saw as the sluggish pace of rehabilitation. Offices and accommodation had to be restored for use by the hundreds of officials and workers who poured into East Timor to service the mission and to promote its objectives. To local citizens, especially in Dili, it looked as if their own desperate housing needs were being given a lesser priority. Certainly, the initial flurry of building activity may have seemed impressive to visitors, but relatively little of it was of direct benefit to the Timorese. At least, that is the way it seemed to them. Much of the housing reconstruction was aimed at meeting the needs of the large international population. Also, a new bustling commercial activity was focused not on the Timorese, but on meeting the needs of UN workers and the growing foreign community of non-government organisations and consultants and the few carpet baggers who were out to make quick profits from East Timor's reconstruction.

Numerous restaurants opened in the first year and by the end of 2001 there were more than 140 of them but their prices were closer to those of New York or Sydney—well beyond the modest means of even the richer Timorese. Their patrons were UN staff, PKF personnel, business people and workers, mostly from Australia, some non-government organisations, and Dili's small but growing, diplomatic corps. Hotels were also being restored to service those in the international community who wanted to escape the confines of the *Olympia*, a floating hotel which accommodated hundreds of UN personnel in the first year of the UN interregnum. It was moored only one hundred metres from the shore, and in the evenings its bright lights and sounds of music and partying gaiety were taken in silently by the impoverished locals who gathered on the foreshore. While the *Olympia* was a practical way of providing secure accommodation in those first difficult months, it was unfortunately a constant reminder to the people of Dili that their long experience of being ruled by a privileged class was not yet over. The CNRT leaders were hostile to this accommodation intrusion, but they then proceeded to make a similar arrangement. At CNRT's initiative a floating hotel, offering high-class (and costly) accommodation was brought from Thailand, an arrangement that turned out to be even more elitist.

The dual economy was a sore point with the educated Timorese, but it was hardly a new experience. The people of Timor had lived under such conditions for centuries, including under Indonesian rule, and it aroused less hostility than might have been expected. What did cause concern was the slow pace of housing and school rehabilitation, and the fact that this new foreign intrusion was providing little employment, especially for the idle younger generation. As time passed a brooding resentment developed among the youth who came to the capital from elsewhere in the territory seeking work and excitement.

The first six months were particularly difficult for Sergio Vieira de Mello, or the SRSG (Special Representative of the Secretary-General, as the head of a UN mission is called). The positive international response to the plight of the East Timorese produced great expectations that it was quite impossible for UNTAET to live up to. While generous funding arrangements had been announced, special conditions and delivery timetables meant that getting access to these funds was not always easy. Some of it was earmarked for specific projects and was accessible only through tortuous UN bureaucratic channels.

By the middle of 2000 the foreign community had risen to more than 12,000 persons, from more than seventy countries. UNTAET was initially organised into three pillars. The biggest pillar was the PKF, which amounted to about 8000 personnel. At first it came under the command of Lieutenant General Jaime de los Santos from the Philippines with a very able Australian, Major General Mike Smith, as Deputy Force Commander. Los Santos was, however, recalled in July and replaced by a senior Thai commander, Lieutenant General Boonsrang Niumpradit. The PKF's role was critical in restoring stability and order, but its task was more or less straightforward, certainly easier than the situations in Somalia or in Cambodia. In East Timor there were no landmines, bridges and roads had not been damaged, and there were few weapons around, the militia and TNI having transported most of them to Indonesian Timor. Its most important responsibility was to round up militia elements, prevent militia border crossings, and maintain general security, especially in the border districts and in the Oecussi enclave. Apart from enforcing security, PKF units engaged in local reconstruction tasks, road repair, and the rehabilitation of essential services.

The second component was the Humanitarian Assistance and Emergency Rehabilitation pillar, headed by Akira Takahashi from Japan. Its aim was to coordinate the whole range of relief and humanitarian services. Its biggest task in the first months was emergency relief, especially food distribution, where its work was supported by non-government organisations. The most challenging pillar was designated governance and public administration, which was headed by an experienced former French Prefect, Jean-Christian Cady who also served as deputy to Sergio Vieira de Mello. This pillar had the task of restoring, or in reality, creating an administration at national and district levels, including establishing law enforcement agencies. It meant starting from scratch to create an entire system of government for an independent state. A Political Affairs division headed by the former US diplomat, Peter Galbraith, dealt with political matters and foreign affairs separately, and reported directly to the SRSG.

The UNTAET mission took some six months to build up to full strength. Assembling UN missions of this nature is a rather haphazard affair. Its personnel need to reflect the wide membership of the world body and the recruiting processes leave much to be desired. The quality of personnel varied greatly. The international diversity of UN missions may have romantic appeal, but in practice it creates difficulties. These missions are usually assembled hurriedly and not all the diverse nationalities sit down easily together. Selfish rivalries surface and can impair the functioning of the department concerned. The UNTAET mission was expected to be of short duration, and its officers were therefore on short-term appointments, which offered little scope for professional consolidation, affecting staff loyalties. Establishing the necessary teamwork spirit was at times an uphill task and often a matter of some frustration for the SRSG.

While the military seemed to function like a well-oiled machine[1] that was sometimes far from the case with UNTAET departments. Even at senior levels insurmountable differences surfaced. One notable example of this kind of discord was the testy relationship between Peter Galbraith, the Political Affairs Director and Mr. Paramaswaram, the Malaysian Chief of Staff, which did little to advance mission harmony. Yet the UNTAET mission was able to attract some impressive professional staff, many of whom worked seven days a week with great dedication. The Civpol component encountered serious problems. In the first six months they were far too few for the task of restoring law and order. At the end of February there were fewer than 500 Civpol, a fraction of the service's mandated strength of 1640. Many of its personnel were unsuited to conditions in East Timor. They, like many other UN personnel, were poorly briefed. Most knew little about the territory's tragic past, and some came from rather undemocratic environments to work for a mission which, from the outset, stressed upholding the high democratic standards set out in basic human rights conventions. The mission attracted many skilled and dedicated officials, but for others it was a well-paid temporary job.

One of the most difficult and least successful areas involved the courts and the prosecution. In the case of justice the problem was understandable, for there is no quick way to set up a justice system. In most countries such systems evolve over a long period of time. When UNTAET first arrived, East Timor had no judges or court officials. A number of magistrates were hastily trained, but because of their inexperience UNTAET officials at first often intervened. This affected both the confidence of the magistrates in their own ability, and the confidence of the local population in the court system. A Prosecutor-General's Office, under Moh Othman, an East African magistrate who had served in Rwanda, and a Serious Crimes Unit established in 2000 to focus on the crimes against humanity perpetrated in 1999, and on the serious crimes subsequently committed. While it had some excellent investigators and prosecutors this office suffered from poor management, its performance causing the SRSG considerably concern.

A number of low-ranking militia members were brought before the panel of judges with most being sentenced to lengthy prison terms for their part in crimes against humanity. The process was, however, far from satisfactory because those most responsible for these crimes were beyond the reach of the justice system. The real culprits were not the ordinary militia, but the TNI commanders and the leading militia leaders. Some of the latter were brought before Indonesian human rights tribunal that was eventually set up in Jakarta. So far, however, that tribunal has been a farce. Only a few TNI officers have been indicted, and those generals who planned and organised this exercise in state terrorism, generals like Zakky Anwar Makarim and Sjafrei Sjamsuddin, have so far escaped prosecution. Nearly all of the indicted TNI officers have been acquitted. This iniquitous outcome has presented the East Timor court with a dilemma, and has revived calls, including from human rights agencies in Indonesia and elsewhere, for the setting up of an international tribunal.

The problem is also complicating the commendable reconciliation progress so vigorously promoted by President Xanana Gusmão. While this process has been very successful in healing relationships between Timorese associated with the pro-autonomy movement, in particular with the militia, and the rest of the population, only part of the story has been dealt with. For a comprehensive and enduring resolution to the problem, the responsible TNI commanders—those who set up the militia and exhorted them to employ violence and intimidation— need to be identified and included in the process, by whatever means. Based on the Jakarta tribunal proceedings it seems that the Indonesian establishment is continuing to live with lies about their involvement in East Timor. As the Jakarta Tribunal's prosecutors have presented the case, in 1999, the TNI merely failed to prevent violence between the Timorese parties in dispute, a situation provoked by international interference. Therefore, the full exposure of this conspiracy is not only about justice for the individuals and communities affected by the atrocities: it is essential if a frank and enduring relationship between the Indonesian and East Timorese people is eventually to be achieved. The best way to bring out the truth would be for those who are believed to be responsible for crimes against humanity to be brought before an international tribunal.

Financing the UN mission and the rehabilitation of East Timor was a complicated process. The operations of the UNTAET mission were largely financed from UN headquarters in New York. In an arrangement managed by the World Bank, funds for the rehabilitation of East Timor began to be provided within weeks of the TNI's departure, by a consortium which included countries like Japan, Portugal, the United Kingdom, the United States, Canada and Australia. At its first meeting in November 1999 a basket of some USD550 million of international financial support was pledged. At subsequent annual meetings of the consortium similar pledges were forthcoming, following critical examinations of reports submitted by the UNTAET chief, Vieira de Mello.

UN specialised agencies, such as UNHCR (United Nations High Commissioner for Refugees), UNDP (United Nations Development Programme) and OCHA (United Nations Office for the Coordination of Humanitarian Affairs) were also established in Dili to deal with food assistance, health services and other aspects of humanitarian relief. Of special significance was the assistance provided by the IRC and non-government agencies like TimorAid and Médicins Sans Frontières (MSF), which moved in not long after InterFET's arrival, providing emergency relief to a population in desperate need. The presence of these diverse groups on occasion led to some rivalry and discord, but their contribution was of critical importance. Personnel from non-government organisations tended to be closer to the Timorese, sharing with them some resentment at the contrast between their modest living conditions, (some were merely paid living allowance) and the affluence of UN personnel, many of whom were also provided with UN vehicles.

In general however these were fairly minor problems. However, one problem that was still not fully resolved at the end of the UNTAET mission was arranging the return of the thousands of refugees in Indonesian Timor, most of whom were reportedly being held against their will by the militia. More than 20,000 managed to get back to East Timor in the last months of 1999, but from then on repatriation slowed. In the first year, militia violence and the TNI refusal to act against it, seriously hampered the work of the UNHCR delegation in Indonesian Timor, which was withdrawn after the murder of three of their staff at Atambua on 6 September 2000. The refugee crisis and a series of border incidents, resulting in the killing of two PKF personnel, led to a flurry of meetings between UNTAET and Indonesian officials. A visit from President Wahid in February 2000 promised a new chapter in relations with Indonesia, but the good intentions of the president were never translated into reality, and a year was to pass before the situation had improved, and almost two years before most of the refugees were at last able to return to East Timor. In October 2002, some 30,000 East Timorese remained in Indonesian Timor, many of whom may be resettled in other parts of Indonesia.

The first six months of the UNTAET mission were its most difficult. It began to attract criticism, especially from the Timorese political leaders. The rapid expansion of UNTAET operations and the surge of commercial activity had done little to reduce unemployment, which still stood at more than 75 per cent in mid-2000. This caused increasing unrest and a rapid growth in petty crime. However, there was nothing new about this situation in East Timor as unemployment had always been high under Indonesian rule. It was the better-off who were most critical, especially of the wide gap between the salaries of foreign UN personnel and the wages paid to the UN mission's Timorese staff. Ironically this resentment grew when Timorese began to assume senior positions in the administration. It was not uncommon for a Timorese head of a department to receive less than a tenth of the pay of his UN deputy, whose salary was based on determinations from New York. Also essential services, especially the Dili power supply, began to deteriorate, as increased demands were placed on them. One desperate measure to counter these demands was the drastic reduction in streetlighting. This had a distinct demoralising effect on the local population. While the postal service was restored in April, telephone communications, especially to towns and villages outside Dili, remained far from satisfactory with increasing dependence upon the mobile telephone service operated by Australia's Telstra.

In response to the unrest and the expectations of the Timorese leaders, Vieira de Mello introduced a radical program of 'Timorisation', one aimed at accelerating the progress towards full independence. As early as March 2000 a police training college was established in Dili and a few weeks later the Dili District Court began to function, serviced by a small number of magistrates, most of them the products of a short course organised by the United Nations. A civil service academy was also set up to train civil servants. The most far-reaching step was introduced in May 2000 when UNTAET announced its intention to bring the Timorese formally into the government in a partnership arrangement. In effect it offered the Timorese leadership a kind of apprenticeship to ministerial responsibility, and hands-on training for administrators. And so the Timorisation of the political and administrative institutions began. It was a particularly important step in the administration of the thirteen districts, some of which were being inefficiently managed by UN officials who had less experience and ability than the educated Timorese who were now returning from Portugal and Australia.

The most important first step was an agreement on 21 June 2000 between UNTAET and CNRT to broaden the membership of the National Consultative Council, which had been set up as an advisory forum. The new NCC would have a greatly expanded role, with thirty-three members, including one from each district and representatives from the church, women, and youth groups.

Within a month the NCC had set up a transitional cabinet of eight ministers, made up of four Timorese and four UNTAET representatives. This new venture in government was named the East Timor Transitional Authority (ETTA). It had its own budget, though a modest one. Xanana continued his role as the acknowledged leader of the East Timor nation, with the additional role of elected Speaker of the NCC. For Xanana this post was too close to the hurley-burley of politics for his liking and he later withdrew from it. Jose Ramos Horta became East Timor's *de facto* minister for foreign affairs.

Once the new phase got under way it was clear that independence was not far off. The prospect excited the Timorese political leaders but with elections proposed in the year ahead, it began to have a politically divisive effect on CNRT. There was at first less enthusiasm among the population at large; many feared it would lead to political disunity risking a return of the ghosts of 1975. There were also concerns about the country's security and about impoverished East Timor's capacity to survive as a nation. In that year, 2000, the militia forces in Indonesian Timor were still active, with their leaders occasionally coming out with bellicose threats to return and reclaim their lands. A number of small militia groups actually succeeded in crossing the border, in one case reaching the rugged mountainous centre of the territory. While these penetrations caused widespread alarm, it turned out that most of them were only interested in unobtrusively returning to their villages, bypassing the UN authorities—and possible war crimes accusations. However, the militia groups soon ran into trouble. In most cases their presence was quickly reported to PKF posts, and they often ran short of food, sometimes being forced to appeal to local villages to help them out. The problem eventually faded away, with most of the intruders returning to Indonesian Timor.

The border situation remained tense, however, with constant evidence that the militia were still undergoing military training on the western side, an activity that could sometimes be observed by the patrolling Australian Black Hawk helicopters. But despite UN fears there were few incidents. After the earlier militia clashes with PKF troops which cost the lives of two UN soldiers (one of them Private Manning from New Zealand), the most serious incident happened in Indonesian Timor at Atambua in September 2000 when three UNHCR workers were murdered by a militia-led group. These killings led to an angry reaction from the Security Council which passed a Resolution 1319 calling on the Indonesian government to 'take immediate steps' to disarm the militia, ensure the safety of the refugees and humanitarian workers, and prevent border incursions

From that time the security situation at the border improved, helped by the appointment of Major General da Costa as *panglima* of the Bali-based Udayana command. Da Costa, who had come from Indonesian Timor, set out to improve security in Indonesian Timor and to weaken the power of the militia leaders who had been behaving like war lords, preventing refugees in the camps they controlled from returning to East Timor. It was some months, however, before the refugees were able to get to East Timor in significant numbers. It also took time to weaken the authority of the militia. Some commanders, such as Eurico Gutteres and João Tavares, continued to retain control of sizeable units. Other militia leaders, notably Cancio de Carvalho, from Ainaro and Juanico da Costa from Baucau, began to negotiate their return, hoping to escape prosecution. These moves led to a series of contacts between UNTAET's chief of staff Paramaswaram and these leaders which were not particularly productive. More successful were the reconciliation meetings between East Timorese and militia leaders in which Xanana Gusmão played a leading part. In 2001 several of these leaders made brief visits to East Timor to assess the prospects of reintegration into their village communities, and some of them returned to engage in reconciliation confrontations with their communities.

The process of political change accelerated in 2001. In March Vieira de Mello announced that East Timor's first constituent assembly election would take place on 30 August, and civil registration began at once. In preparation for this advance towards self-government, in June CNRT was dissolved, and its constituent parties, plus some new ones, braced themselves for the country's first free election campaign. The election was held on 30 August, and was an outstanding success. The campaign was generally restrained, with little violence, and a big turnout went to the polls peacefully. As expected Fretilin emerged as the majority party, winning fifty-five seats (57.3 per cent of the vote) in the eighty-eight-member Constituent Assembly. Though a clear majority, it was not enough to allow Fretilin to impose its will in the ensuing drafting of the constitution. The ministerial arrangements were upgraded, with a twenty-four-member all-Timorese Council of Ministers being established to replace the transitional cabinet. In an early meeting the Constituent Assembly passed a resolution recommending that UNTAET hand over its authority to an elected Timorese government on 20 May 2002.

The main item on the political agenda of the Constituent Assembly was the formulating and adopting of a constitution for the new nation. Somehow the East Timorese worked their way through a process that would have taken much longer elsewhere. It was the outcome not only of Constituent Assembly debates, but also of extensive community consultation. The result, which was signed into force by the assembly on 22 March 2002, was a 170-article document, reflecting a mix of UN, Portuguese, Mozambican, and Australian, influences. The constitution strongly emphasised human rights protection, and provided for a separate president whose formal powers are titular in nature, and for a government elected by an eighty-eight-member National Assembly. With independence only weeks ahead, on 14 April 2002 East Timor held its first presidential elections. It was hardly a contest. Xanana was overwhelmingly the popular candidate, with Fretilin's first president, Xavier do Amaral, opposing him, in his own words 'for the sake of democracy'. It was a tame election campaign and, as expected, Xanana won decisively. At midnight on 19 May, witnessed by tens of thousands of Timorese, and hundreds of foreign dignitaries, UN staff, and non-government organisations, Alexandro Xanana Gusmão was appointed first president of the new Democratic Republic of East Timor in the presence of Kofi Annan, the United Nations Secretary-General. The East Timorese dream that had been dashed by the colony's annexation in 1975 had at last become a reality.

Conclusion

East Timor's formal independence has been a truly remarkable achievement, an outcome often dismissed as unrealistic less than ten years earlier. It was quite a triumph when judged against the scene of devastation that less than three years earlier confronted those of us who had returned to East Timor with InterFET. It was a bleak Ground Zero scene with its destroyed towns and villages, its missing people, and the demoralised survivors. The achievements in that short time have understandably been proclaimed as the UN's most successful mission of its kind. The outcome has been a personal success for Kofi Annan, who had devoted an extraordinary amount of time and effort to resolving the Timor problem in the five years since he came to office. On the ground it was also a personal triumph for Sergio Vieira de Mello who arrived in Dili at a time when the task ahead seemed like Mission Impossible. His tireless commitment, his determination, his patience, and deep sensitivity to the plight the rights and the dignity of the Timorese people, were key factors in this success story. In those two-and-a-half demanding years he had the task of leading a mission that was essentially, as I sometimes reminded him, the imperfect product of an imperfect world, and of striving to meet the expectations of an impatient Timorese leadership.

The outstanding heroes of the operation were the long-suffering East Timorese people themselves, as Vieira de Mello has acknowledged. They welcomed InterFET enthusiastically, and in the first difficult months of UNTAET they displayed extraordinary patience. At the outset there were expectations of violent clashes between the different *sucos* and later between members of rival political parties. Manifestations of such violence were few. There were demonstrations in Dili, often with good reason, but rarely was there any violence. One such incident occurred at the university in 2001, but it was partly the fault of the Civpol, one of whom discharged a pistol, a provocative and unnecessary act at a normal student demonstration. The worst political violence occurred in the eastern part of the island—in the Viqueque–Baucau area, but Xanana and other leaders quickly went to the scene and pacified the parties in a dispute that was less tribal than political. On the whole the Timorese behaviour at the three main elections was, by new nation standards, exemplary, the turnout in each case revealing a strong sense of community responsibility. It was a reminder that East Timor's cruel experiences with foreign intervention in the previous sixty years had had a unifying effect.

Inevitably there was widespread residual bitterness about events in the previous twenty-five years, including the brief civil conflict between UDT and Fretilin in August 1975. The process of reconciliation which became a centerpiece of Xanana's nation-building efforts, called for the fashioning of an enduring unity, one unthreatened by the ghosts of the past. The Reception, Reconciliation and Truth Commission is playing a central role in this regard, helping with the healing of wounds, and not only those created by militia actions. This process offers people who have suffered from the terrors and injustices of the past, to expose their grievances and, where possible, confront those responsible and achieve an enduring reconciliation, based on community understanding and compassion.

The process also involves exposure of Falintil's past misdeeds, which included unnecessary killing, torture, and suffering. The important missing piece from this reconciliation process, however, the role of the Indonesian military, the key players in the drama that engulfed East Timor for a quarter of a century, remains a serious obstacle to its resolution. Until the TNI admits its well-established guilt in the horrendous events of the past, and at least expresses some regret, reconciliation between the peoples of East Timor and Indonesia will be without substance.

Some Timorese leaders seem to want to forget the past, perhaps to bury a problem for which there is no apparent, or ready, solution. But that is concealing the cancer, rather than treating it. It is satisfactory neither to Indonesians nor to Timorese—or for that matter to the international community because to conceal, or distort, the ugly past is to allow criminals to be free to continue to pursue their brutal methods. To hide from the ugliness of a nation's past is for its citizens to hide from themselves, and risk diminishing the integrity of their nation. In the case of the major TNI atrocities in East Timor, the crimes were acts of state terrorism, actions that today are the focus of a worldwide campaign. What transpired in 1999 and for that matter throughout the Indonesian occupation, needs to be considered against this background. The full exposure of these crimes, and those who perpetrated them, is as much a matter of concern to the Indonesian people as it is to the Timorese, for their continued concealment presents a major obstacle to the advancement of Indonesia's democratic reforms. In the first instance, however, it is about justice for the victims and for their relatives. Reconciliation without justice misses the central point of the process. The pursuit of justice, in this matter, though a difficult issue to resolve, is essential to the achieving of the kind of relationship between Indonesia and East Timor that will ensure enduring peace and harmony.

The partnership arrangement between the Timorese and UNTAET that began in mid-2000 was generally successful, though it was not without problems. The ETTA ministers felt under-resourced, and in the circumstances their decision making was sometimes hesitant. Some UN staff did not work comfortably with the Timorese ministers, while the latter often became frustrated with tedious UN bureaucratic procedures. However, in general, the Timorese learnt quickly, and in some areas, especially in district administration, Timorese officials performed more effectively than UN staff, most of whom were out of their depth in an environment alien to them.

The development of East Timor's economy could not be counted as one of UNTAET great successes. The glittering hope for the future is the expected income from Timor Gap gas exploitation. Even if the proposed development goes ahead according to plan, that income will not be significant until nearer the end of the decade. Under UNTAET's tutelage perhaps the greatest success was in the field of agriculture. Rice and maize production levels returned to where they were in 1999. Coffee production has also increased substantially, though this advance was offset by the fall in prices on the world market. Attempts have been made to develop other industries such as fisheries, but the level of unemployment has remained dangerously high, posing a serious threat to security and political stability. Too little attention has been given to tourism which is potentially important to the new nation in more ways than one. East Timor is a beautiful country, with tropical seascapes and deep mountain valleys, and a people with a rich and rather diverse culture. As well as a valuable source of income, tourism is important to consolidating relations between the East Timorese and the people in many parts of the world who through the years have been deeply moved by their suffering and by their courage. Tourism offers a way of consolidating a relationship with the Timorese people, especially for Australians, who have always been their most committed supporters.

Two particularly important areas for the new nation are foreign relations and defence. Of these, foreign affairs is of more immediate importance, for East Timor can count on a PKF presence until it has established a stable relationship with Indonesia. A small defence force of battalion size was formally inaugurated in October 2002, but this force is essentially a deterrent. It would be no match for a major assault from Indonesia. The risk of that happening may have declined, but a new threat of terrorist penetration cannot be ignored, in the light of statements by Islamic extremists (including one by Bin Laden) denouncing President Habibie's surrender of East Timor in 1999. Infiltration by militia groups in December 2002, reportedly with low-level TNI backing, was a reminder of East Timor's continuing vulnerability to the covert activities of at least some elements of the TNI, and of Indonesia's continuing instability. As a result UN officials came under pressure to improve border protection, and to suspend the process of downsizing the PKF force. The UN's defence responsibility may well continue well beyond the period of two years envisaged at the time of independence.

The new Republic's foreign policy has understandably been focused on establishing a secure place in the international community, as well as ensuring a continuation of the international aid commitment which emerged with the setting up of UNTAET. East Timor had therefore formed a rather diverse network of relationships before formal independence. The most urgent challenge was to develop a stable working relationship with Indonesia, extinguishing that degree of smouldering resentment, particularly among the still powerful generals, at the humiliating loss of their 27th province. Xanana has devoted considerable effort to win over Indonesia rulers, for example, pleading with President Megawati to attend East Timor's independence ceremony in Dili. After considerable hesitation she put in an appearance, if only a brief one. In the case of Portugal a close relationship already existed. In many respects East Timor's closest relationship, at least for the present generation of leaders, is with their former colonial ruler. It is easy enough to understand. The Portuguese have always exerted a strong cultural impact on their colonial peoples, and they have made a strong commitment to helping East Timor through the difficult years ahead. Although the Portuguese had been East Timor's colonial rulers for several centuries, in the past two decades they had earned the affection of the people by their unflagging support for East Timor and their insistence that the people be accorded their right to self-determination. They steadfastly refused to allow the issue of East Timor to be removed from the UN agenda, somewhat to the chagrin of some of their EU partners. Despite its strong commitment, however, Portugal is a distant land with limits on the extent of the economic assistance it can offer the Timorese.

The relationship with Australia is of obvious importance, but East Timor's past experience shows that it is a link that should not be taken for granted. The history of Australian foreign policy reveals a pattern of ruthlessly opportunistic diplomatic manoevres that do nothing to encourage complacency. Australian official responses in 1974 and 1975 led to East Timor being all but abandoned to the Indonesian invaders, and Australia had been one of the few countries to extend *de jure* recognition to the annexation in 1979. After having first endorsed Indonesia's incorporation of East Timor the Howard government radically changed course in 1999 and Australians were to play a leading role in East Timor's rescue in 1999. Contentious issues, such as the Timor Gap treaty, and the renegotiation of maritime boundaries, may lead to serious differences. However, in any emergency the new nation can count on a helpful response from its large neighbour across the Arafura Sea, thanks to a strong public commitment to the welfare of its people, a commitment that has become a matter of national conscience. Most Australians are now aware of their government's shameful foreign policy failure in relation to East Timor in the past, when governments of this country accommodated the invasion of the territory and turned away from the catastrophic consequences. Any moves to return to such a policy would encounter vigorous political and public opposition.

Portugal, Australia and Indonesia are not the only major players in the development of the new nation. The EU, the United States and Japan are major sources of aid and, potentially, of investment. The Timorese leaders have also developed close relations with countries like China, South Korea, Ireland, and New Zealand, links that hold promise for the security and economic development of new state. East Timor's leaders have the stature and ability to play an active role in the United Nations, perhaps helping strengthen the world body at time when its leading creator is regarding it with some indifference. The UN system, and regional security cooperation arrangements are of considerable importance to small states. In East Timor's case it was the United Nations that nursed the battered territory into existence, and it can be expected to respond promptly to any threat to its protégé's security. East Timor has also become an active member of the Portuguese Community (the Communidade Portuguesa), whose collective influence is considerable. It is yet to join ASEAN, but has good prospects of doing so in the near future. Few small nations have basked in as much publicity and goodwill in their emergence to nationhood as has East Timor. The Timorese people's long struggle, and their determination to take charge of their own affairs have won them widespread admiration and offers of assistance which should enable the new nation to make steady progress in the first lean years of its independent existence. The achievements since 1999 have, however, done little to ease East Timor's poverty and to give the people confidence in their ability to develop a self-sustaining economy. Democracy has taken root, but its roots are still shallow and its capacity to endure depends heavily on the quality of East Timor's political leadership and their commitment to the democratic principles enshrined in the new constitution. Already the new government has encountered unrest and violence, manifestations of disillusionment at the gap between the optimistic rhetoric on the eve of independence, and the reality that the road ahead is not going to be easy.

For the international community it is not enough to applaud the emergence of the new nation and the success of the United Nations in making it possible. East Timor, as it is today, may represent a happy ending to a long tragic story, but it holds important lessons for our international system. The tragedy, which cost more than 200,000 Timorese lives, could have easily been avoided if the principles set out in the UN Charter had been observed by the principal parties in 1975. The catastrophe could have been averted if the major powers, who were well aware of what was transpiring, had rejected the Suharto regime's annexation of the colony. This human tragedy unfolded at a time when human rights protection had already gained prominence on the global agenda, yet very few of its advocates were disposed to one of the most serious violations of the time. East Timor's nightmare of occupation ended, it should not be forgotten, largely because of the Asian economic crisis, which precipitated the fall of the Suharto dictatorship, and not because of a change of heart on the part of those powers who 24 years earlier had readily accommodated the colony's annexation. Until the very end the Suharto regime continued to enjoy their support.

Note

1   See Mike Smith (Major General) *On Peacekeeping: the UN in East Timor.*

Glossary

Non-English Terms

administrador do concelho	regional administrator
ahi matan	clan, village units
alferes	junior lieutenant
apartidarisimo	standing apart from factional or party conflict
chef de suco	head of tribe
chef, or administrador, de posto	district officer
concelho	district, council or circumscription
criado	personal guide
dato	prince
deportado	Portuguese deportee
escola militar	military school
escudas	currency
Hansip	civil/village defence system
ikat	type of cloth or weave
integrasi	integration
jaco	islet
lading	slash and burn system of agriculture
lipa	Timorese traditional dress
liurai	petty king
lulik	sacred object
mestiço	mixed blood
nai, dato lulik	village sorcerer or priest
Nusatenggara group	West Timor
palapa	palm leaf or over-roofs
panglima	district commander
posto	sub-district
puosada	inn
povoaçao	settlement or hamlet
rai/reino	kingdom
retournado	Timorese returned to Portugal
suco	tribal group
tepo seliru	mutual understanding
Topasses	early Portuguese-Timorese descendants
tumengeng	villiage cheif
tupassi	interpreter
ultramar	overseas territories

Organisations

AAP	Australian Associated Press
ABRI	Angkatan Bersenjata Republik Indonesia (Armed Forces of the Republic of Indonesia)
Accão Nacional Popular	Portuguese political party under Salazar regime
ACFOA	Australian Council for Overseas Aid (NGO umbrella body)
Aditla	Associacão Democratica Integracao Timor-Leste Australia (Democratic Association for Integration of East Timor into Australia)
AID	Agency for International Development (US)
ALP	Australian Labor Party
Antara	official Indonesian press agency
ANU	Australian National University Australia
ANZUS	New Zealand and United States treaty
APMT	Associacão Popular Monarquia de Timor (Association of Popular Monarchists of Timor)
Apodeti	Associacão Popular Democratica Timorense (Timorese Popular Democratic Association, earlier, the Association for the Integration of Timor into Indonesia)
ASDT	Associacão Social Democrata Timorense (Timorese Association of Social Democrats, forerunner of Fretilin)
ASEAN	Association of South East Asian Nations
Asia Watch	New York-based human rights agency
ASIAT	Australian Society for Inter-Country Aid (Timor) (Australian NGO medical aid agency)
AWD	Action for World Development (Australian NGO)
Bakin	Indonesian intelligence coordinating body
Banco Nacional Ultramarino	Overseas National Bank, East Timor
BHP	Broken Hill Proprietary Company (Australian mining company)
Brawijaya	East Java Military Division
CAA	Community Aid Abroad (Australian aid NGO)
CCIR	US Congressional Committee on International Relations, June 1977
CIA	Central Intelligence agency (US)
CIET	Campaign for an Independent East Timor
CIIR	Catholic Institute for International Relations (US)
CNRM	Concelho Nacional da Resistancia Maubere (National Council of Maubere Resistance)

CP	Country Party (Australia)
CRS	Catholic Relief Service
CSIS	Indonesian Centre for Strategic and International Studies
Darul Islam	Javanese Islamic movement
DGS	Directorate-General of Security (successor to PIDE)
Diponegoro	Central Java division troops
DPRD	Dewan Perwakilan Rakyat Daerah (Indonesian Regional People's Representative Council)
DPRD-II	Dewan Perwakilan Rakyat Daerah (Indonesian Regional People's Representative Council Stage II)
DRET	Democratic Republic of East Timor
DSD	Defence Signals Division (Australia)
EC	European Community
EU	European Union
Falintil	Armed Forces for the National Liberation of East Timor
Frelimo	Mozambique liberation movement
Fretilin	Frente Revolucionaria de Timor-Leste Independente (Revolutionary Front for an Independent East Timor)
Hansip	Pertahanan Sipil (civil defence)
ICJ	International Commission of Jurists
ICRC	International Commission of the Red Cross
IGGI	Inter-Governmental Group on Indonesia (Western consortium for aid to Indonesia)
Junta of National Salvation	Portuguese provisional government after Lisbon coup
Kodam	Komando Daerah Militar
Kodam Nusatenggara	Udayana Military District Command
Kopasgat	Komando Pasukan Gerak Tjepat, Rapid Action Forces (air force, orange berets)
Kopassandha	Special Forces Command (army)
Kopkamtib	Indonesian Command for the Restoration of Security and Order
Korps Marinir (KKO)	marines (violet berets)
Kostrad	Indonesian Strategic Reserve Command
Kota	Klibur Oan Timur Aswain (Tetum, Sons of the Mountain Warriors)
Kowilhan II	Indonesian Regional Defence Command, Number 2
LCP	Liberal-Country Party (Australia)
MAC	Movimento Anti-Communist (Anti-Communist Movement)
MFA	Movimento das Forcas Armadas (Portuguese Armed Forces Movement)

MPLA	Angolan independence movement
NATO	North Atlantic Treaty Organisation
NCC	National Civic Council (Australian right-wing Catholic body)
NCO	non-commissioned officer
NGO	non-government organisation
Nossa Senhora de Fatima	Our Lady of Fatima Jesuit seminary at Dare
OPMT	Organizacão Popular da Mulher Timor (Popular Organisation of Timorese Women)
OPSUS	special operations group of ABRI
PAIGC	liberation movement in Guinea-Bissau
Palang Merah Indonesia	Indonesian Red Cross
Pangu Pati	Papua New Guinea political party
Partai Nasional Indonesia	Indonesian National Party
Partai Sosialis Indonesia	Indonesian Socialist Party
Partido Trabalhista	Timorese Labour Party
Pemerintah Pusat	Javanese central government
PGET	Provisional Government of East Timor
PIDE	Policia International e de Defesa do Estado (Portuguese political police)
PKI	Indonesian communist party
RAAF	Royal Australian Air Force
RMS	Republik Maluku Selatan (South Moluccas separatist movement)
RPKAD	Regimen Para Komando Angkatan Darat (Indonesian Army Commando Paratroop Regiment-red berets)
RSL	Returned Servicemen's League (Australia)
Sandi Yudha	Indonesian Commandos
Sao Bento	Portuguese National Assembly
SAPT	Sociedade Agricola Patria e Trabalho, (Portuguese enterprise, East Timor)
Siliwangi	West Java Military Division
SOTA	Sociedade Orientale do Transportes e Armazens (Portuguese enterprise, East Timor)
Tapol	agency for Indonesian human rights in London
TAT	Transportes Aereos de Timor (Portuguese airline in Timor)
TII	Tentara Islam Indonesia (Atjeh separatist movement, Sumatra)
UDT	União Democratica Timorense (Timorese Democratica Union)
UNCHR	United Nations Commission on Human Rights
UNGA	United Nations General Assembly
UNITEM	União Nacional de Estudantes Timor (National Union of Timorese Students)
WCC	World Council of Churches (Australia)

Agreements and campaigns

Estado Novo	Salazar's New State or Order
ganyang Malaysia	'Crush Malaysia' campaign
Gestapu	Attempted coup, Sept 1965
Harlan Merdeka	Indonesian National Day, 17 Aug
Konfrontasi campaign	Sukamo's campaign against Malaysia, 1962-65
Lisbon Convention	border agreement, 1893
Operasi Keamanan	Operation Security, 1981
Operasi Komodo	Indonesian covert military intelligence operation
Operasi Persatuan	Joint Operation, 1984
Operasi Seroja	Indonesian invasion of Dili, 7 Dec 1975
Operasi Tjendrawasih	Indonesian operation in West New Guinea
Orde Baru	New Order set up by Suharto regime
Organic Law of Portuguese Overseas Territories	1953
Pancasila	five principles of the Indonesian Republic
Permesta movement	Perdjuangan Semesta (Total struggles rebellion against Sukarno)
Sentenca Arbitral	border agreement, 1913
UDI	Unilateral Declaration of Independence
Wibawa VI/Jaya Nusa	Combined armed forces exercise, South Lampung, Feb 1975

Index